V. Good!

LOUISE YEOMAN is a curator of manuscripts at the National Library of Scotland and a Scots historian. She was born and brought up in Fife, attended school in Dunfermline, and studied British and Early Modern European History at St Andrews where she completed a PhD on the Covenanters in 1991. Since then she has worked in Scottish libraries and archives, specialising in 16th- and 17th-century history, but answering a wide range of enquiries on all kinds of topics.

She joined the National Library of Scotland in 1992, and began to play an active part in communicating information about Scottish history to the Library's users, as well as cataloguing the Library's Early Modern manuscripts. In 1997, she spent a year working for the BBC, writing and presenting the controversial popular history series *Stirring Times*. Her projects have included the Jacobite exhibition, 'A Nation Divided', and many radio and television appearances to answer demands for information on anything and everything from William Wallace to the alleged Geordie origins of 'Auld Lang Syne'. With the resources of the National Library of Scotland to hand, few Scottish historical queries have been beyond tackling!

A self-confessed historical magpie who finds nearly all aspects of the subject interesting, she was delighted to be asked by Luath Press to produce a Scottish book of reportage to mark the Millennium. *Reportage Scotland* is the result of a thorough pillaging of the Library's collections: writing up anything that took her fancy. She hopes that the book will also take the fancy of readers throughout Scotland and beyond.

First Edition 2000

The paper used in this book is recyclable. It is made from low-chlorine
pulps produced in a low-energy, low-emission manner
from renewable forests.

Printed and bound by
Omnia Books Ltd, Glasgow

Typeset in 10 point Sabon by
S. Fairgrieve, Edinburgh

Design by Tom Bee

Published in association with

www.nls.uk

Author text © National Library of Scotland

Reportage Scotland
History in the Making

LOUISE YEOMAN

Luath Press Limited

EDINBURGH

www.luath.co.uk

Notes on Scots transcription/translation – I have when transcribing rendered þ as 'th' and ȝ as 'y' and have expanded contractions. In translations I have altered sentence length and word order as well as translating vocabulary. The aim has been to provide an intelligible text for non-Scots readers.

Whilst every effort has been made to accurately transcribe the sources used, this book is not intended to be a definitive edition of the texts – this is particularly the case for the older English texts which have been extensively modernised. Those who wish to check exact readings of the sources are encouraged to consult the original texts, using the references given.

References to published sources – in each case where it is possible to supply it, the date of publication is given and the place of publication, except in the case of material supplied by Scottish or English historical clubs and societies where the name of the club and the date are supplied. Where it is impossible to supply this information, I have on occasion inserted a National Library of Scotland pressmark to assist with the identification of the item.

Note on manuscript references – manuscript transcriptions by the author are in every case from manuscripts held at the National Library of Scotland. The following prefixes are used:
Acc. – Accession
Dep. – Deposit
Adv. Ms. – Advocates' manuscript
Wod.Qu. – Wodrow Quarto – part of the Wodrow Collection, a sub-set of the Advocates' manuscripts
Wod.Lett.Qu – Wodrow Letters Quarto, as above.
MS. – National Library of Scotland catalogued manuscript
Blaikie – Blaikie collection of Jacobite prints. This collection belongs to the National Library of Scotland but is held at the Scottish National Portrait Gallery.
RB – Rare Books special collection at the National Library of Scotland.

[ ] – indicates glosses, notes and omissions from the text.
f., ff. – folio, indicating leaves of manuscripts.
r,v – recto and verso, indicates which side of a folio a text begins on.

Contents

Preface

A stranger to our culture picks up a newspaper (avoiding the sort that will devote ten pages to a football match or to a short-lived celebrity caught with some item of their morality astray). One of the first things to strike this stranger would be bewildering incongruity. Important, long-running new stories are mixed up with flash-in-the-pan trivia. Terrible accounts of individual or mass human suffering are interspersed with titillating anecdotes, humorous accounts of silly coincidences and the antics of self-promoting wanna-bes. The eye catches a photograph: is it the mass murderer being denounced in the headline to the left, or the wise Nobel Prize-winner being praised on the right? The attitude seems to be heap 'em high and sell 'em cheap. There seems no pattern, no sense. Newspapers (and TV news, where the juxtaposition of stories sometimes seems a joke in bad taste) unintentionally seem to evoke that honest but bewildered British historian of the sixth century, Gildas, who admitted that he had 'made a heap of all he knew' because though he knew it, he couldn't make sense of it.

Is this book a latter-day attempt to upstage Gildas? Well, I'd go some way down that path, but by no means the whole way. *Reportage Scotland* strongly evokes this sense of the chaos of 'as it happens' news gathering, of intense individual experience mingled with a story of some national event, of horror and humour both being newsworthy. The Gildas touch deliberately stresses the messiness of history and the difficulty of assessing reports. Some are factually accurate, but every writer (like every historian) has a spin (the trendy word for a perspective) that they put on events, intentionally or unintentionally, as they relate them. Some reports, like that of the aerial adventures of Father Damian, are inspired by malicious invention, others, like John Knox's account of the murder of Cardinal Beaton, mingle brilliant on-the-spot reporting with sly propaganda digs (the Cardinal was sleeping late because he had been 'at his accounts' with his mistress all night). Never be content to take reports at their face value: they are witnesses to be questioned.

But though there is this 'fresh-from-the-press-each-day' wild mixture of stories, some being concluded, some just breaking, some making their one and only appearance, in *Reportage Scotland* Dr

Yeoman is not content to stand aside as Gildas did, helpless before her sources. She has the long view denied the journalist, and has imposed a degree of order on the items included in the book. The overwhelming order is chronology – which is as it should be. Lives are lived in the sequence dictated by time, stories break in it. Central themes in Scottish history are touched on, sometimes several times, yet never dealt with comprehensively, for this is not intended as a history of Scotland. There is a sense of development – nation emerging, monarchy, fights for survival, union, social and economic change – but the balance between such themes, imposed with hindsight, and the confusion of the world of daily reportage is maintained. The climax is the opening of the new Scottish parliament. Dr Yeoman is, however, too good a historian to make this a 'Whig history' triumph of purpose and progress, leaving a smug air of 'and Scotland will live happily every after'. She samples reportage from (nearly) 2,000 years of time, but makes us aware that time – and therefore reportage – has not stopped just because it has reached that ever-moving feast, the present. We have a new parliament, but what we make of it (and what it tries to make of us) remains to be seen.

Reportage Scotland can be read from cover to cover, giving a splendid montage of snapshots of past happenings great and small. Or it can be treated like a sampler pack of miniature Scotch malts – a truly glorious one, running to over 150 brands. Run your eye over the pack. Take out one – perhaps its gaudy label caught your eye – sip it, savour it. Or just throw it back in a gulp. Then decide whether, good as it is, the miniature is enough. Or it is something you want to follow up, by visiting the National Library of Scotland or some other library to get hold of the source of the sample – or (lapsing back into the metaphor), nipping out to buy a full bottle. My prediction is that *Reportage Scotland* will make the owner of your off-licence a happy man. But a health-warning is necessary. History can become addictive.

David Stevenson
Emeritus Professor of Scottish History, St Andrews University

Introduction

THE PURPOSE OF THIS BOOK is to have a pleasurable journey through nearly 2,000 years of Scottish history, bringing events to life in the voices of people who were there. The book begins at the Roman invasion of AD 84, recorded by Tacitus in his life of Agricola, and ends at the opening of the new Scottish parliament. In between it covers anything from saints to suffragettes and presents material translated from French, Latin, Gaelic and Scots. Some material is transcribed from manuscripts in the collections of the National Library of Scotland and published for the first time. The texts (in one form or another) may be found in the National Library (although one or two have been accessed from websites).

Reports are taken from eye-witnesses and contemporary sources where possible. Occasionally (particularly in the early period) compromises have been made where original material is scarce. In these cases later sources drawing on earlier materials have also been included. Reports come in all degrees of contemporaneousness and reliability, so some attempt has been made to indicate when pieces were written, by whom, and roughly how reliable they are. Sometimes extremely unreliable reports of events have passed into folklore and these become worth examining in themselves. For example several people asked me to include Father Damian the 'bird-man' who allegedly jumped off the battlements of Stirling Castle around 1507, but the closest contemporary report of this was a scurrilous poem by William Dunbar, contradicted by more reliable information from other sources. Nonetheless I've included Father Damian for two reasons – firstly, the story is so well-known it is worth pointing out that it is probably fictitious; secondly, Dunbar's poem is so amusing. Poetry has also been used to record events in Gaelic-speaking Scotland as this was an important way of spreading news in a society which valued its oral culture. Newspapers have proved fruitful too, and parliamentary papers have also been drawn on for reports of living and working conditions.

The aim of these selections is not to produce a serious chronological history but to give a 'flavour' of events and the people who reported them. Some effort has been made to provide a little historical background for the pieces – a fraught job in the light of the sheer volume of new work being produced in all areas of Scottish history. The idea throughout has been to make the pieces comprehensible to a general reader with no specialist knowledge of Scottish history. With that in mind some new translations have been provided from old French (by Professor James Laidlaw of Edinburgh University) and from Latin (by Mr Julian Russell formerly of the National Library of Scotland) and from Gaelic (by Domhnall Uilleam Stiùbhart). Scots and Gaelic texts are reproduced both in translation and in the originals, where the original texts are accessible. This is because these are contemporary Scottish languages enjoyable to many modern readers. Translations of Scots text prior to the early part of the 17th century are by myself (see note on page iv). English prior to the early 17th century has been modernised in spelling. Archaic or obscure words have been glossed.

I am indebted to a great many colleagues in the National Library of Scotland for their assistance with this book. Betty Watson and Yvonne Carroll typed large parts of the text for me, and our bookfetching staff had the unenviable task of retrieving many of my sources. Thanks are also due to my immediate colleagues in the Manuscripts Division. Both Iain Maciver and Colm McLaughlin were especially helpful and contributed pieces for inclusion in the book. Colm drew my attention to George Ramage's World War 1 diary and allowed me to use some of his own work on it. Iain Brown made helpful suggestions on later 18th-century material, while Sally Harrower and Sheila Mackenzie helped obtain reproductions and gave advice on copyright. Kenneth Dunn, Olive Geddes and Linda Tindley offered general help and support, and Alex O'Hara, the manuscripts bookfetcher, was put to considerable trouble by my demands. In our Public Programmes Division, Jacqueline Cromarty oversaw the whole project, and Barbara Hegarty put great effort into obtaining permissions, while Kenneth Gibson and Fiona Morrison gave generous help in the last stages of the book. Christopher Taylor and Kevin Halliwell, both of the Collection Development Division, were generous with their advice and help, as were the staff of the Official Publications Unit, who helped me to find material in parliamentary papers, and the staff of our Reference Services Division, who gave general (and very patient) help with reference material. I should also like to thank Priscilla Bawcutt, Professor of English at Liverpool University, and the Association of Scottish Literary Studies, for permission to use Priscilla's excellent new edition of Dunbar's poetry.

Most of all, I should like to thank David Stevenson, Emeritus Professor of Scottish History at St Andrews, for casting an editorial eye over my first draft and providing many helpful suggestions.
Enjoy the book.

Louise Yeoman
April 2000

Saints, Battles and Sinners

'Scotland the What?' might be the best way of summing up the early stages of 'Scottish' history. After the Romans left, the area which was later to be called Scotland became a patchwork of peoples: Picts, Britons, Angles, and an increasing number of Gaels (confusingly, they were the people called Scots, although they were only one of the peoples in what is now modern-day Scotland). Later came the Norsemen and Normans. It was this diverse nation of different cultures, languages and faiths which gradually came under the MacAlpin dynasty of kings to claim a Scottish identity. That identity was centred on the royal dynasty at first, but it was later to be honed in the Wars of Independence until it came to transcend mere loyalty to a king. By that point, even without a king, a Scot could still feel Scottish.

Caledonians and Romans

Scotland AD 84: Gnaeus Julius Agricola, Roman governor of Britain, broke out north of the Forth to push deep into Caledonian territory. At an unknown location he encountered the forces of Calgacus, the name given to the leader of the local resistance force. Fifteen years later Agricola's son-in-law, the great Roman historian Tacitus, immortalised his campaign in his book The Agricola. *The battle, Mons Graupius, complete with Tacitus's imagined speeches of the commanders to their troops, became the first Scottish event to survive in written record.*

At the beginning of the next summer Agricola suffered a grievous personal loss in the death of a son who had been born a year before. He accepted this blow without either parading the fortitude of a stoic or giving way to passionate grief like a woman. The conduct of the war was one means he used to distract his mind from its sorrow. He sent his fleet ahead to plunder at various points and thus spread uncertainty and terror; then, with an army marching light, which he had reinforced with some of the bravest of the Britons who had proved their loyalty by long years of submission, he reached Mount Graupius, which he found occupied by the enemy. The Britons were, in fact, undaunted by the loss of the previous battle, and were ready for either revenge or enslavement. They had realized at last that the common danger must be warded off by united action, and had sent round embassies and drawn up treaties to rally the full force of all their states. Already more than 30,000 men could be seen, and still they came flocking to the colours – all the young men, and famous warriors whose 'old age was fresh and green', every man wearing the decorations he had earned. At that point one of the many leaders, a man of outstanding valour and nobility named Calgacus, addressed the close-packed multitude of men clamouring for battle. This is the substance of what he is reported to have said:

'When I consider the motives we have for fighting and the critical position we are in, I have a strong feeling that the united front you are showing today will mean the dawn of liberty for the whole of Britain. You have mustered to a man, and all of you are free. There are no lands behind us, and even on the sea we are menaced by the Roman fleet. The clash of battle – the hero's glory – has now actually become the safest refuge for a coward. Battles against Rome have been lost and won before; but hope was never abandoned, since we were always here in reserve. We, the choicest flower of Britain's manhood, were hidden away in her most secret places. Out of sight of subject shores, we kept even our eyes free from the defilement of tyranny. We, the most distant dwellers upon earth, the last of the free, have been shielded till today by our very remoteness and by the obscurity in which it has shrouded our name. Now, the farthest bounds of Britain lie open to our enemies; and what men know nothing about they always assume to be a valuable prize. But there are no more nations beyond us; nothing is there but waves and rocks, and the Romans, more deadly still than these – for in them is an arrogance which no submission or good behaviour can escape. Pillagers of the world, they have exhausted the land by their indiscriminate plunder, and now they ransack the sea. A rich enemy excites their cupidity; a poor one, their lust for power. East and West alike have failed to satisfy them. They are the only people on earth to whose covetousness both riches and poverty are equally tempting. To robbery, butchery, and rapine, they give the lying name of 'government'; they create a desolation and call it peace.

'Nature has ordained that every man should love his children and his other relatives above all else. They are now being torn from us by conscription to slave in other lands. Our wives and sisters, even if they are not raped by enemy soldiers, are seduced by men who are supposed to be our friends and guests. Our goods and money are consumed by taxation; our hands and limbs are crippled by building roads through forests and swamps under the lash of our oppressors. Creatures born to be slaves are sold once for all, and, what is more, get their keep from their owners. We Britons are sold into slavery anew every day; we have to pay the purchase-price ourselves and feed our masters into the bargain. In a private household the latest arrival is made the butt even of his fellow-slaves; so, in this establishment where all mankind have long been slaves, it is we, the cheap new acquisitions, who are marked out for destruction. For we have no fertile lands, no mines, no ports, which we might be spared to work in. Our courage, too, and our martial spirit are against us: masters do not like such qualities in their subjects. Even our remoteness and isolation, while they give us protection, are bound to make the Romans wonder what mischief we are up to. Since you cannot hope for mercy, therefore, take courage before it is too late to strive for what you hold most dear, whether it be life or honour. The Brigantes, with only a woman to lead them, burned a Roman colony and stormed a camp; and if success had not tempted them to relax their efforts, they might have cast off the yoke. We, who have never been forced to feel that yoke, shall be fighting to preserve our freedom, and not, like them, merely to avenge past injuries. Let us then show, at the very first clash of arms, what manner of men Caledonia has kept in reserve.

'Do you imagine that the Romans' bravery in war matches their dissoluteness in time of peace? No! It is our quarrels and disunion that have given them fame. The reputation of the Roman army is built up on the faults of its enemies. Look at it, a motley conglomeration of nations that will be shattered by defeat as surely as it is now held together by success. Or can you seriously think that those Gauls and Germans – and, to our bitter shame, many Britons too – are bound to Rome by genuine loyalty or affection? They may be lending their life-blood now to the foreign tyrant, but they were enemies of Rome for more years than they have been her slaves. Terror and intimidation are poor bonds of attachment: once break them, and where fear ends hatred will begin. All that can spur men on to victory is on our side. The enemy have no wives to fire their courage, no parents ready to taunt them if they run away. Most of them either have no fatherland they can remember, or belong to one other than Rome. See them, a scanty band, scared and bewildered, staring blankly at the unfamiliar sky, sea, and forests around them. The gods have given them, like so many prisoners bound hand and foot, into our hands. Be not afraid of the outward show that means nothing, the glitter of gold and silver that can neither avert nor inflict a wound. Even in the ranks of our enemies we shall find

willing hands to help us. The Britons will recognize our cause as
their own; the Gauls will remember their lost liberty; the rest of the
Germans will desert them as surely as the Usipi did recently. And
beyond this army that you see there is nothing to be frightened of –
only forts without garrisons, colonies of greybeards, towns sick and
distracted between rebel subjects and tyrant masters. Which will you
choose – to follow your leader into battle, or to submit to taxation,
labour in the mines, and all the other tribulations of slavery?
Whether you are to endure these for ever or take quick vengeance,
this field must decide. On, then, into action; and as you go, think of
those that went before you and of those that shall come after.'

This speech was received with enthusiasm, expressed, in barbarian
fashion, by singing and yelling and by discordant cries. Bodies of
troops began to move and arms flashed as the most adventurous ran
out in front, and all the time their battle-line was taking shape.
Agricola's soldiers were in such high spirits that they could scarcely
be kept within their defences. For all that, he felt it desirable to put
the final edge on their courage, and addressed them thus:

'This is the seventh year, comrades, since by loyal service – yours
and my own – you started to conquer Britain in the name of imperial
Rome's divinely guided greatness. In all these campaigns and battles,
which have called not only for courage in face of the enemy but for
toil and endurance in fighting, as it were, against Nature herself, I
have had no complaint to make of my men nor you of your general.
Thus we have advanced beyond the limits reached by previous
armies under my predecessors. The farthest boundary of this land,
which they knew only by report or rumour, we hold in our grasp
with arms and fortresses. We have both explored and conquered
Britain. Many a time on the march, as you trudged wearily over
marshes, mountains, and rivers, have I heard the bravest among you
exclaim: "When shall we meet the enemy? When will they come and
fight us?" They are coming now, for we have dug them out of their
hiding-places. The fair field for our valour that we desired is granted
to us. An easy path awaits us if we win, but if we lose the going will
be hard indeed. The long road that we have travelled, the forests we
have threaded our way through, the estuaries we have crossed – all
redound to our credit and honour as long as we keep our eyes to the
front. But if we turn tail, our success in surmounting these obstacles
will put us in the deadliest peril. We have not the exact knowledge
of the country that our enemy has, or his abundant supplies.
However, we have our hands, and swords in them, and these are all

that matter. For myself, I made up my mind long ago that neither an army nor a commander can avoid danger by running away. So – although an honourable death would be better than a disgraceful attempt to save our lives – our best chance of safety does in fact lie in doing our duty. And there would be glory, too, in dying – if die we must – here where the world and all created things come to an end.

'If you were confronted by strange nations and unfamiliar troops, I would quote the examples of other armies to encourage you. As things are, you need only recall your own battle-honours, only question your own eyes. These are the men who last year attacked a single legion like robbers in the night, and acknowledged defeat when they heard your battle-cry. These are the greatest runaways of all the Britons – which is the reason why they have survived so long. When we plunged into woods and gorges on the march, all the brave beasts used to charge straight at us, while the timid and slothful ones slunk away at the mere sound of our tread. It is the same now. The most courageous of the Britons have fallen long since; those who remain are just so many spiritless cowards. You have overtaken them at last, not because they have chosen to stand at bay, but because they are cornered. It is only their desperate plight and deadly fear that have paralysed their army where it stands, for you to win a great and brilliant victory over it. Have done with campaigning; crown fifty years with one glorious day, and prove to Rome that her soldiers were never to blame if wars have been allowed to drag on or the seeds of fresh rebellion sown.'

Even while Agricola was still speaking the troops showed intense eagerness, and the end of his speech was greeted with a wild burst of enthusiasm. Without delay they went off to arm themselves. The men were so thrilled that they were ready to rush straight into action; but Agricola marshalled them with care. The auxiliary infantry, 8,000 in number, formed a strong centre, while 3,000 cavalry were distributed on the flanks. The legions were stationed in front of the camp rampart: victory would be vastly more glorious if it cost no Roman blood, while if the auxiliaries should be repulsed the legions could come to their rescue. The British army was posted on higher ground in a manner calculated to impress and intimidate its enemy. Their front line was on the plain, but the other ranks seemed to mount up the sloping hillside in close-packed tiers. The flat space between the two armies was taken up by the noisy manoeuvring of the charioteers.

Agricola now saw that he was greatly outnumbered, and fearing that the enemy might fall simultaneously on his front and flanks, he opened out his ranks. The line now looked like being dangerously thin, and many urged him to bring up the legions. But he was always an optimist and resolute in the face of difficulties. He sent away his horse and took up his position on foot in front of the colours.

The fighting began with exchanges of missiles, and the Britons showed both steadiness and skill in parrying our spears with their huge swords or catching them on their little shields, while they themselves rained volleys on us. At last Agricola called upon four cohorts of Batavians and two of Tungrians to close and fight it out at the sword's point. These old soldiers had been well drilled in sword-fighting while the enemy were awkward at it, with their small shields and unwieldy swords, especially as the latter, having no points, were quite unsuitable for a cut-and-thrust struggle at close quarters. The Batavians, raining blow after blow, striking them with the bosses of their shields, and stabbing them in the face, felled the Britons posted on the plain and pushed on up the hillsides. This provoked the other cohorts to attack with vigour and kill the nearest of the enemy. Many Britons were left behind half dead or even unwounded, owing to the very speed of our victory. Our cavalry squadrons, meanwhile, had routed the war chariots, and now plunged into the infantry battle. Their first onslaught was terrifying, but the solid ranks of the enemy and the roughness of the ground soon brought them to a standstill and made the battle quite unlike a cavalry action. Our infantry had only a precarious foothold and were being jostled by the horses' flanks; and often a runaway chariot, or riderless horses careering about wildly in their terror, came plunging into the ranks from the side or in head-on collision.

The Britons on the hill-tops had so far taken no part in the action and had leisure to note with contempt the smallness of our numbers. They were now starting to descend gradually and envelop our victorious rear. But Agricola, who had expected just such a move, threw in their path four squadrons of cavalry which he was keeping in hand for emergencies and turned their spirited charge into a disorderly rout. The tactics of the Britons now recoiled on themselves. Our squadrons, obedient to orders, rode round from the front of the battle and fell upon the enemy in the rear. The open plain now presented a grim, awe-inspiring spectacle. Our horsemen kept pursuing them, wounding some, making prisoners of others, and then killing them as new enemies appeared. On the British side, each man now behaved according to his character. Whole groups, though they had weapons in their hands, fled before inferior numbers; elsewhere, unarmed men deliberately charged to face certain death.

Equipment, bodies, and mangled limbs lay all around on the bloodstained earth; and even the vanquished now and then recovered their fury and their courage. When they reached the woods, they rallied and profited by their local knowledge to ambush the first rash pursuers. Our men's over-confidence might even have led to serious disaster. But Agricola was everywhere at once. He ordered strong cohorts of light infantry to ring the woods like hunters. Where the thickets were denser, dismounted troopers went in to scour them; where they thinned out, the cavalry did the work. At length, when they saw our troops, re-formed and steady, renewing the pursuit, the Britons turned and ran. They no longer kept formation or looked to see where their comrades were, but scattering and deliberately keeping apart from each other they penetrated far into trackless wilds. The pursuit went on till night fell and our soldiers were tired of killing. Of the enemy some 10,000 fell; on our side, 360 men – among them Aulus Atticus, the prefect of a cohort, whose youthful impetuosity and mettlesome horse carried him deep into the ranks of the enemy.

For the victors it was a night of rejoicing over their triumph and their booty. The Britons dispersed, men and women wailing together, as they carried away their wounded or called to the survivors. Many left their homes and in their rage actually set fire to them, or chose hiding-places, only to abandon them at once. At one moment they would try to concert plans, then suddenly break off their conference. Sometimes the sight of their dear ones broke their hearts; more often it goaded them to fury; and we had proof that some of them laid violent hands on their wives and children in a kind of pity. The next day revealed the effects of our victory more fully. An awful silence reigned on every hand; the hills were deserted, houses smoking in the distance, and our scouts did not meet a soul. These were sent out in all directions and made sure that the enemy had fled at random and were not massing at any point. As the summer was almost over, it was impossible for operations to be extended over a wider area; so Agricola led his army into the territory of the Boresti. There he took hostages and ordered his admiral to sail round the north of Britain. A detachment of troops was assigned to him, and the terror of Rome had gone before him. Agricola himself, marching slowly in order to overawe the recently conquered tribes by the very deliberateness of his movements, placed his infantry and cavalry in winter-quarters. At about the same time the fleet, which aided by favourable weather had completed a remarkable voyage, reached Trucculensis Portus. It had started the voyage from that harbour, and after coasting along the adjacent shore of Britain had returned intact.

Tacitus, *The Agricola and the Germania,* trans. H. Mattingly, rev. S. A. Handford, Harmondsworth, 1970.

St Columba (d. 597)

Whilst Adomnán's Life of St Columba *is certainly not reportage (Adomnán, an abbot of Iona himself, was born after St Columba's death), it contains the only near contemporary accounts we have of the life of the great saint, apart from brief mentions in Irish Annals (given below). The* Life *is full of strange and moving tales, such as how Columba supposedly drove off a water beast in the River Ness. Adomnán does however give this account, which he tells us he had from an eye-witness, of a miracle which marked Columba's death, and for good measure here is the 'Nessie' story too – a terrible case of cruelty to monsters ...*

There was another vision seen in the same hour. One of those who had himself seen it, a soldier of Christ called Ernéne moccu Fir Roíde, when he was an old man, told the story to me, Adomnán, when I was a young man. This Ernéne was himself a holy monk and is buried in the burial ground of the monks of St Columba at Druim Tuamma, where he awaits with the saints the resurrection of the dead. This is the account which he told me, firmly attesting its reliability.

'On the night of St Columba's blessed and blissful passing from the world to the heavens, I and the men with me were hard at work, fishing in the fishful River Finn when all at once we saw the whole sky lit up. The miracle quite took us by surprise. When we looked eastwards, there seemed to be some sort of huge fiery pillar rising upwards in the middle of the night, which lit up the whole world like the summer sun at midday. When the column passed beyond the sky, darkness returned just as follows sunset. Those of us who were there together at that time looked on the brilliance of that praiseworthy column of light with huge astonishment. But later we learnt that many other fishermen, fishing in various places along the same river, saw a similar apparition, and they were seized with great fear.'

How a water beast was driven off by the power of
the blessed man's prayer

Once, on another occasion, when the blessed man stayed for
some days in the land of the Picts, he had to cross the River
Ness. When he reached its bank, he saw some of the local people
burying a poor fellow. They said they had seen a water beast snatch
him and maul him savagely as he was swimming not long before.
Although some men had put out in a little boat to rescue him, they
were too late, but, reaching out with hooks, they had hauled in his
wretched corpse. The blessed man, having been told all this,
astonished them by sending one of his companions to swim across
the river and sail back to him in a dinghy that was on the further
bank. At the command of the holy and praiseworthy man, Luigne
moccu Min obeyed without hesitation. He took off his clothes
except for a tunic and dived into the water. But the beast was lying
low on the riverbed, its appetite not so much sated as whetted for
prey. It could sense that the water above was stirred by the swimmer,
and suddenly swam up to the surface, rushing open-mouthed with a
great roar towards the man as he was swimming midstream. All the
bystanders, both the heathen and the brethren, froze in terror, but
the blessed man looking on raised his holy hand and made the sign
of the cross in the air, and invoking the name of God, he
commanded the fierce beast, saying:

'Go no further. Do not touch the man. Go back at once.'

At the sound of the saint's voice, the beast fled in terror so fast one
might have thought it was pulled back with ropes. But it had got so
close to Luigne swimming that there was no more than the length of
a pole between man and beast. The brethren were amazed to see that
the beast had gone and that their fellow-soldier Luigne returned to
them untouched and safe in the dinghy, and they glorified God in the
blessed man. Even the heathen natives who were present at the time
were so moved by the greatness of the miracle they had witnessed
that they too magnified the God of the Christians.

Adomnán, *Life of St Columba*, ed. Richard Sharpe, Harmondsworth, 1995.

Annals of Ulster

AD 574. The battle of Tola and Fortola, in the territory of the
Cruithne [Picts]. The death of Conall, son of Comgall, in the 16th
year of his reign, who granted the island of Ia [Iona] to Colum-Cille.
AD 575. The great Convention of Druim-Ceta [Druim Cett], at
which were Colum-Cille, and Aedh son of Ainmire.

AD 575. A spark of leprosy, and an unheard of abundance of nuts.

AD 597. The repose of Colum-Cille, on the 5th of the Ides of June, in the 76th year of his age.

Annals of Ulster, ed. W. M. Henessy, Dublin, 1867 (dates adjusted).

A Letter to the King of the Picts, AD 716

The image of the Picts as a war-like people has perhaps obscured their interest in matters spiritual. After their conversion to Christianity, their new religion began to show itself in their carved stones. However, under Nechtan Mac Derile they were not content simply to sit back and accept what they were taught from Iona. The Picts were aware that the Columban Church was out of step with Europe, or at least with their southern neighbours, on the matter of celebrating Easter and on some other matters. With calendar knowledge still on a shaky foundation, the calculation of the date of Easter was a difficult art, and the Picts wanted to have the most accurate and advanced knowledge possible. This, plus the diplomatic advantages of an alliance, led them to send to their Northumbrian neighbours for information. This account is from Bede, the historian and monk from Jarrow who wrote The Ecclesiastical History of the English People. *He was a monk under Abbot Ceolfrith and would probably have been present when the Pictish king's request for advice was received. As the Irish Annals show, Nechtan also expelled the Columban monks from Pictland, perhaps for political as well as spiritual reasons.*

At this time Nechtan, king of the Picts, who live in the northern parts of Britain, having been convinced by his assiduous study of ecclesiastical writings, renounced the error which he and his race had until then held about the observance of Easter, and led all his people to celebrate with him the catholic time of keeping the Lord's resurrection. In order to make the change more easily and with greater authority, he sought help from the English who, he knew, had long since based their religious practices on the example of the holy Roman and apostolic Church. So he sent messengers to the venerable Ceolfrith, abbot of the monastery of the apostles St Peter and St Paul, one part of which stands at the mouth of the river Wear and the other part near the river Tyne in a place called Jarrow. Ceolfrith ruled illustriously over this monastery after Benedict already mentioned. The king asked the abbot to send him information by letter to enable him to confute more convincingly those who presumed to celebrate Easter at the wrong time; also about the shape and method of tonsure by which it was fitting that clerics should be distinguished: notwithstanding this request he himself had no small measure of knowledge on these matters. He also asked for builders to be sent to build a church of stone in their country after the Roman fashion, promising that it should be dedicated in honour of the blessed chief of the apostles. He also said that he and all his people would always follow the customs of the holy Roman and apostolic Church, so far as they could learn them, remote though they were from the Roman people and from their language. Abbot Ceolfrith complied with his pious wishes and requests, sending the builders he asked for and also a letter couched in the following terms . . .

When this letter had been read in the presence of King Nechtan and many learned men and carefully translated into his own language by those who were able to understand it, it is said that he was greatly delighted by the exhortation; so he rose in the midst of the company of his assembled leaders, and knelt down, thanking God for having made him worthy to receive such a gift from England. 'Indeed,' he said, 'I knew before that this was the true observance of Easter, but I now understand the reasons for observing this date so much more clearly that I seem up to this to have known far too little about it in every respect. So I publicly declare and proclaim in the presence of you all, that I will for ever observe this time of Easter, together with all my people; and I decree that all clerics in my kingdom must accept this form of tonsure which we have heard to be so completely reasonable.' He at once enforced his word by royal authority also. The nineteen-year cycles for Easter were forthwith sent out by public order throughout all the Pictish kingdoms, to be copied, learned and acted upon, while the erroneous eighty-four-year cycles were everywhere obliterated. All ministers of the altar and monks received the tonsure in the form of a crown; and the reformed nation rejoiced to submit to the newly-found guidance of Peter, the most blessed chief of the apostles, and to be placed under his protection.

Bede, *Historia Ecclesiastica*, eds. B. Colgrave and R. A. B. Mynors, Oxford, 1991.

Annals of Ulster

AD 716. Expulsion of the community of Ia [Iona] across Dorsum Britanniæ [the spine of Britain] by King Nectan.

Annals of Ulster, ed. W. M. Henessy, Dublin, 1867.

Viking Raids – The Martyrdom of Blathmac

In AD *794 the Vikings sacked Iona for the first time. Whilst their
more peaceful compatriots settled all over Northern and Western
Scotland as farmers, traders and fishermen, some of them preferred
the ready profits and exciting lifestyle available from sea-borne
plundering of vulnerable targets such as monasteries. They returned
again and again to Iona, badly damaging though never quite
extinguishing the community founded by St Columba. Since
martyrdom at the hands of the heathen was considered to be the
most glorious death a monk could possibly die, not everyone in the
island community would flee the raids, despite the risk of death or
enslavement. One of the chief targets of the Norsemen was the shrine
of St Columba himself, or rather the precious gold, silver and jewels
which encased his remains. Needless to say, the monks preferred to
die rather than to reveal its whereabouts. In* AD *825 just such a raid
descended on the island. It produced a hero: the monk Blathmac,
who fearlessly defied the invaders and was killed by them. The news
of his death travelled from monastic community to monastic
community and so inspired his fellow monk, Walafrid Strabo [Strabo
– 'squinter'] (c.808-849), at the monastery of Reichenau, in modern-
day Germany, that he immortalised his death in Latin poetry. Here is
a prose translation of the story as told in the poetry of Strabo.*

An isle of the Picts, appears borne up by the wave-driven sea, Eo
[Iona] by name, where rests the body of Columba, the Lord's
saint. Blathmac sought out this island, wishing to endure Christ's
sacred wounds, for pagan hordes of Danes were accustomed to land
there, armed with wicked madness. But the Lord's saint Blathmac,
emptying his mind of vain fear, decided to put these lions to the test;
protected by the shield of faith and the helmet of salvation, he was
not afraid of the arms of wicked men. With the wise prophet, he
could have sung 'God is my helper, away with unworthy fear'. The
wars of nations had taught him to despise the Devil's servants, since
he had rightly overthrown that tyrant their Lord and alone had
overcome him in all his arms.

The time came when God's great mercy decided to unite his
servant with the shining bands above the stars and to confer a
certain crown upon the good victor. The hero's holy mind,
foreknowing events, realised by his heightened sense that the wolves
were approaching to tear the faithful sheep limb from limb. 'You my
comrades,' he said, 'search within yourselves whether you have

courage to endure with me pain and torment in Christ's name; whoever of you can await it, I ask you to arouse your manly feelings. But let those weak men whose inmost hearts tremble with fear flee quickly away, to avoid the impending dangers and to arm themselves in a better cause. The test of certain death stands close to us: let firm faith be vigilant, supported by hope in the future; let the careful safeguard of flight protect the less brave.' The company, stung by these words, decided upon what was possible; some rejoiced with calm mind to face the sacrilegious hands, and to submit their heads to violent swords. But others, whom confidence of mind did not yet persuade of this, chose flight by a footpath through places known to them.

Golden dawn, scattering dewy darkness, shone forth, and the brilliant sun glittered with beautiful orb, when this learned saint, celebrating the sacred offices of the mass, stood a spotless calf before the holy altar, a pleasing offering to God to be sacrificed by the threatening sword. The rest of the company lie still in tears and prayers commending to God the Thunderer their souls who are about to depart from the burden of the flesh. Behold the accursed raging host rush through the open buildings threatening cruel perils to the blessed men. After slaying the rest of the company with mad ferocity, they come to the holy father, to compel him to yield the precious metals in which the sacred bones of Saint Columba lie. But [the monks] had lifted the shrine from its abode and had placed it in the earth in a hollowed barrow under a thick layer of turf, already knowing of the wicked destruction to come. This plunder the Danes desired, but the holy man, though unarmed, stood firm. He had been trained to stand against the line of battle and to provoke the fight and he was not accustomed to yielding. There he spoke to the barbarian with words like these: 'I know nothing at all of the gold you look for, where it is placed in the ground or in which places it is hidden. If by Christ's permission it were granted to me to know, never would my mouth relate this to your ears. Draw your sword, barbarian, take the hilt and slay me now; dear God, I commend my humble self to your aid.' After this, the holy sacrifice was torn limb from limb, and since the fierce soldiers could not find out where the gold was, they began to seek for it by digging. And no wonder, for there always were and there re-appear again and again those who are stirred up by evil rage against all the servants of the Lord; so that what Christ's judgement has appointed for all, let all do this for Christ, although with deed unequal to his.

He [Blathmac], a witness, martyred for Christ's name, as the story records, rests in the same place and many signs of wonder are given there on behalf of his holy merits. There the Lord is reverently worshipped with worthy honour, together with the saints by whose merits I believe my sins to be loosed, whom on my knees I have praised. Christ denies nothing to those who have brought him their greatest riches, he who with his holy father and the holy spirit reigns throughout the centuries with eternal honour and is exalted without end.

Here end Strabo's verses on the life and death of Blathmac

Translated by J. Russell from Ernst Duemmler, *Poetae Latini Aevi Carolini*, ii, Berlin, 1884.

St Margaret – Tragedy in the Scots Royal Family

On 13 November 1093 the Scots royal family experienced a cataclysm. Malcolm Canmore, King of Scots, and his eldest son, Edward, were killed at the battle of Alnwick in Northumberland. Queen Margaret, his wife, was stricken with grief. Born in Hungary and descended from the English Saxon royal family, Margaret married Malcolm of Scotland in 1069. She developed an interesting reputation. Margaret could be best described as a royal saint-in-the-making, famous for her devotions and good deeds to the poor. The Queen was also a very determined woman with strong views about religion. She encouraged changes to bring the Scottish church more into the mainstream of European practice. Contemporary chroniclers noted the disaster which befel her husband and eldest son. Her confessor, Turgot, recorded her death which followed soon after.

Mael-Coluim, son of Donnchadh, archking of Scotland and Edward, his son, were killed by the Franks (namely, in Inber-Alda, in Saxonland). His queen, moreover, Margaret, died of grief therefore before the end of a novena [nine-day period of prayer].

Annals of Ulster, ii, ed. B. MacCarthy, Dublin, 1893.

The Anglo-Saxon Chronicle 1093

And then the Scots chose Malcolm's brother Dufenal [Donald Ban] as king and drove out all the English who had been with King Malcolm. When Duncan, King Malcolm's son, heard all this had happened in this way (he was at King William's court as his father had given him as a hostage to our king's father and so he had remained here), he came to the king, and did such homage as the king wished to have from him, and so with his consent went to Scotland with such support as he could get from Englishmen and Frenchmen, and deprived his kinsman Dufenal [Donald Ban] of the kingdom and was accepted as king. But some of the Scots assembled again and killed nearly all his force, and he himself escaped with a few men. Afterwards they came to an agreement, to the effect that he would never again bring Englishmen nor Frenchmen into the country.

The Anglo-Saxon Chronicle. A revised translation, eds D. Whitelock, D. C. Douglas, S. I. Tucker, London, 1961.

Symeon of Durham

And since none of his men remained to cover it with earth two of the natives placed the king's body in a cart, and buried it in Tynemouth.

Scottish Annals from English Chroniclers, AD 500 to 1286, ed. A. O. Anderson, London, 1908.

The Life of St Margaret

On the fourth day preceding her death, while the king was absent on an expedition, and at so great a distance that it was impossible for any messenger, however swift, to bring her tidings of what was happening to him, she became sadder than usual. Then she said to me, for I was seated near her, 'Perhaps on this very day such a heavy calamity may befall the realm of Scotland as has not been for many ages past.' When I heard these words I paid no great attention to them, but a few days afterwards a messenger arrived who told us that the king was slain on the very day on which the queen had spoken the words narrated. As if foreseeing the future, she has been most urgent with him not to go with the army, but it came to pass – how I know not – that he failed to follow her advice . . .

Her face was already covered with a deadly pallor, when she directed that I, and the other ministers of the sacred Altar along with me, should stand near her and commend her soul to Christ by our psalms. Moreover, she asked that a cross, called the Black Cross, which she always held in the greatest veneration, should be brought to her. There was some delay in opening the chest in which it was kept, during which the queen, sighing deeply, exclaimed, 'O unhappy

that we are! O guilty that we are! Shall we not be permitted once more
to look upon the Holy Cross!' When at last it was got out of the chest
and brought to her, she received it with reverence, and did her best to
embrace it and kiss it, and several times she signed herself with it.
Although every part of her body was now growing cold, still as long
as the warmth of life throbbed at her heart she continued steadfast in
prayer. She repeated the whole of the Fiftieth Psalm, and placing the
cross before her eyes, she held it there with both her hands . . .

It was at this point that her son [Edgar], who now, after his father,
holds in this realm the reins of government, having returned from
the army, entered the queen's bedroom . . .

The queen, who seemed to the bystanders to be rapt in an agony,
suddenly rallied and spoke to her son. She asked him about his
father and brother. He was unwilling to tell the truth, and fearing
that if she heard of their death she herself would immediately die, he
replied that they were well. But, with a deep sigh she exclaimed, 'I
know it, my boy, I know it. By this holy cross, by the bond of our
blood, I adjure you to tell me the truth.' Thus pressed, he told her
exactly all that had happened . . .

Feeling now that death was close at hand, she at once began the
prayer which is usually uttered by the priest before he receives the
Body and Blood of our Lord, saying, 'Lord Jesus Christ, who
according to the will of the Father, through the co-operation of the
Holy Ghost, hast by Thy death given life to the world, deliver me.'
As she was saying the words, 'Deliver me,' her soul was freed from
the chains of the body, and departed to Christ, the author of true
liberty; to Christ whom she had always loved, and by whom she was
made a partaker of the happiness of the saints, as she had followed
the example of their virtues. Her departure was so calm, so tranquil,
that we may conclude her soul passed at once to the land of eternal
rest and peace. It was remarkable that her face, which, when she was
dying had exhibited the usual pallor of death, became afterwards
suffused with fair and warm hues, so that it deemed as if she were
not dead but sleeping. Her corpse was shrouded as became a queen,
and was borne by us to the Church of the Holy Trinity [in Dun-
fermline], which she had built. There, as she herself had directed, we
committed it to the grave, opposite the altar and the venerable sign
of the Holy Cross which she had erected. And thus her body at
length rests in that place in which, when alive, she used to humble
herself with vigils, prayers, and tears.

Turgot, *Life of St Margaret*, ed. W. F. Leith, Edinburgh, 1896.

A Shrine Fit for a Saint

Devotion to Saint Margaret grew, and by 1250 King Alexander III
felt that she deserved to rest in more special surroundings befitting
a saint, but according to this account preserved in Scotichronicon,
Margaret had other ideas. The moral of the tale was that even if
she was a saint, a good woman did not want to be honoured above
her lord. Even in death she knew her place! So the bones of her
husband had to be moved too. An account of the miracles ascribed
to Margaret was discovered recently in the Spanish royal library in
Madrid: amongst other things she was famed for curing people
who had 'swallowed lizards': not, you would have thought, an
everyday occurrence in Dunfermline!

Next year, that is 1250, the king and the queen his mother along with the bishops and abbots and other magnates of the realm assembled at Dunfermline. There they raised the bones and earthly remains of the glorious Queen Margaret his great-great-great-grandmother from the stone sepulchre in which they had rested for many years, and with the utmost reverence raised them in a casket of fir wood entwined with gold and precious stones. When the grave had been opened up by digging, such an intense and sweet-smelling fragrance poured from it that men thought that the entire sanctuary had been sprinkled with the fragrance of spices and the scents of flowers in full bloom. And a miracle, sent by God, was forthcoming there and then. When that famous treasure had been placed in the outer church preparatory to re-burial in the choir beyond the high altar, a move intended as a mark of honour, it was raised without difficulty by the holy hands of the bishops and abbots, and was being carried in procession, with instruments playing and the choir singing harmoniously. They got as far as the chancel door just opposite the body of Margaret's husband, King Malcolm, which lay under an arched roof on the north side of the nave, when all at once the arms of the bearers became paralyzed, and because of the great weight they were no longer able to move the shrine which held the remains. Whether they liked it or not they were forced to halt and quickly lay their load on the ground. After some delay more helpers were added, perhaps stronger than the first, to help carry the shrine, but failed all the more feebly the more they tried to lift it. At last, as they were all marvelling one to another, and saying that they were not worthy to touch such a precious relic, they heard a voice coming from one of the bystanders, but as is believed divinely inspired, which loudly proclaimed that it was perhaps not God's will that the bones of the holy queen be translated before her husband's tomb had been opened, and his body raised and honoured in the same way. These words met with general approval, and following the advice which they conveyed, King Alexander, [Malcolm's great-] great-great-grandson, with companions chosen for this purpose, lifted up the casket containing the bones of the king along with that, now raised, which held the remains of the queen, without expending any effort or encountering any obstacle. They solemnly placed both coffins in tombs which had been decked out elegantly for that purpose, as the congregation sang and a choir of prelates followed in solemn procession, on 19 June. There God in his mercy has often worked all manner of miracles through [the merits of] that holy queen.

Walter Bower, *Scotichronicon*, v, eds S. Taylor, D. E. R. Watt, B. Scott, Aberdeen, 1990.

The Battle of the Standard, 1138

Margaret's son David I was another royal saint, but sanctity did not prevent him carrying on that other Scots royal tradition – invading England. Richard of Hexham, a contemporary English chronicler, gives this account of David's less-than-pious military adventuring. By Picts he probably means the Galwegians, who spoke Galloway Gaelic and who must have seemed exotic in the extreme to this English cleric.

And then that execrable army, more atrocious than the whole race of pagans, neither fearing God nor regarding man, spread desolation over the whole province, and murdered everywhere persons of both sexes, of every age and rank, and overthrew, plundered, and burned towns, churches, and houses. For the sick on their couches, women pregnant and in childbed, infants in the womb, innocents at the breast, or on the mother's knee, with the mothers themselves, decrepit old men and worn-out old women, and persons debilitated from whatever cause, wherever they met with them, they put to the edge of the sword, and transfixed with their spears; and by how much more horrible a death they could despatch them, so much the more did they rejoice . . .

That infamous army received accessions from the Normans, Germans, and English, from the Northumbrians and Cumbrians, from Teviotdale and Lothian, from the Picts, commonly called

Galwegians, and the Scots, and no one knew their number; for multitudes uncalled-for allied themselves with those above mentioned, either from love of plunder, or opportunity of revenge, or the mere desire of mischief with which that region was rife. Overrunning the province, and sparing none, they ravaged with sword and fire almost all Northumberland as far as the river Tyne, excepting the towns and the sea-coast which lies on the eastern side, but this they designed to devastate on their return . . .

[*The English army is mustered.*] While thus awaiting the approach of the Scots, the scouts whom they had sent forward to reconnoitre returned, bringing the information that the king with his army had already passed the river Tees and was ravaging their province in his wonted manner: They therefore hastened to resist them; and passing the village of Alverton [North Allerton], they arrived early in the morning at a plain distant from it about two miles. Some of them soon erected, in the centre of a frame, which they brought, the mast of a ship, to which they gave the name of the Standard . . .

Scarcely, then, had they put themselves in battle array, when tidings were brought that the king of Scotland was close at hand with his whole force, ready and eager for the contest. The greater part of the knights, then dismounting, became foot soldiers, a chosen body of whom, interspersed with archers, were arranged in the front rank. The others, with the exception of those who were to dispose and rally the forces, mustered with the barons in the centre, near and around the standard, and were enclosed by the rest of the host, who closed in on all sides. The troop of cavalry and the horses of the knights were stationed at a little distance, lest they should take fright at the shouting and uproar of the Scots. In like manner, on the enemy's side, the king and almost all his followers were on foot, their horses being kept at a distance. In front of the battle were the Picts; in the centre, the king with his knights and English; the rest of the barbarian host poured roaring around them.

As they advanced in this order to battle, the standard with its banners became visible at no great distance; and at once the hearts of the king and his followers were overpowered by extreme terror and consternation; yet, persisting in their wickedness, they pressed on to accomplish their bad ends. On the octaves of the Assumption of St Mary, being Monday, the eleventh of the kalends of September [22 August], between the first and third hours, the struggle of this battle was begun and finished. For numberless Picts being slain immediately on the first attack, the rest, throwing down their arms, disgracefully fled. The plain was strewed with corpses; very many were taken prisoners; the king and all the others took to flight; and at length, of that immense army all were either slain, captured, or scattered as sheep without a shepherd. They fled like persons bereft of reason, in a marvellous manner, into the adjoining district of their adversaries, increasing their distance from their own country, instead of retreating towards it. But wherever they were discovered, they were put to death like sheep for the slaughter; and thus, by the righteous judgement of God, those who had cruelly massacred multitudes, and left them unburied, and giving them neither their country's nor a foreign rite of burial, – left a prey to the dogs, the birds, and the wild beasts, – were either dismembered and torn to pieces, or decayed and putrefied in the open air. The king also, who, in the haughtiness of his mind and the power of his army, seemed a little before to reach with his head even to the stars of heaven, and threatened ruin to the whole or greatest part of England, now dishonoured and meanly attended, barely escaped with his life, in the utmost ignominy and dismay. The power of Divine vengeance was also most plainly exhibited in this, that the army of the vanquished was incalculably greater than that of the conquerors. No estimate could be formed of the number of the slain; for, as many affirm, of that army which came out of Scotland alone, it was computed by the survivors that more than ten thousand were missing; and in various localities of the Deirans, Bernicians, Northumbrians, and Cumbrians, many more perished after the fight than fell in the battle.

Richard of Hexham, 'The Acts of King Stephen and the Battle of the Standard', in *Church Historians of England*, ed. Joseph Stevenson, iv, pt. i, London, 1856.

The Stone of Scone and the Making of a King, 1249

On 13 July 1249, Alexander III had his formal inauguration as king. Despite this account he was not crowned. The account is preserved in the writings of Walter Bower, canon of Inchcolm. Writing 200 years later, he seems to have transferred some of the customs of his day back to the past. However, his account does have the main parts of the ceremony: the sitting on the stone, the acclamation of the people, the reciting of the genealogy, evidently in Gaelic. At this date Gaelic was beginning to be pushed out of use at the royal court – note how this account plays it down by implying that the seannachie [bard] had just popped up, as if from nowhere. Perhaps when Walter Bower incorporated the older material into his Scotichronicon, *he failed to understand the significance of the role of the 'Highland Scot'. Preserved by later chroniclers, the substance of this account gives the first detailed picture of the 'making' of a Scots monarch. Compare this with the account of a Norwegian ceremony witnessed by a Scot.*

How a certain highland Scot greeted the king as he sat upon the royal seat of stone

In accordance with the custom which had grown up in the kingdom from antiquity right up to that time, after the solemn ceremony of the king's coronation, the bishops with the earls brought the king to the cross which stands in the cemetery at the east end of the church. With due reverence they installed him there on the royal seat which had been bedecked with silk cloths embroidered with gold. So when the king was solemnly seated on this royal seat of stone, with his crown on his head and his sceptre in his hand, and clothed in royal purple, and at his feet the earls and other nobles were setting down their stools to listen to a sermon, there suddenly appeared a venerable, grey-haired figure, an elderly Scot. Though a wild highlander he was honourably attired after his own fashion, clad in a scarlet robe. Bending his knee in a scrupulously correct manner and inclining his head, he greeted the king in his mother tongue, saying courteously: 'God bless the king of Albany, Alexander mac Alexander, mac William, mac Henry, mac David.' And so reciting the genealogy of the kings of Scots he kept on to the end. In Latin [translated here into English] this is:

Hail Alexander, king of Scots, son of Alexander, son of William, son of Henry, son of David, son of Malcolm, son of Duncan, son of Bethoc, daughter of Malcolm, son of Kenneth, son of [Malcolm, son of Donald, son of Constantine, son of Kenneth, son of] Alpin, son of Eochaid [or Achay], son of Aed Find, son of Eochaid, son of Domnall Brecc, son of Eochaid Buide, son of Aedan, son of Gabran, son of Domangart, son of Fergus Mor, son of Erc, son of Eochaid Munremor, son of Engusafith, son of Fethelmech Aslingith, son of Enegussa Buchin, son of Fethelmech Romaich, son of Sencormach, son of Cruithlinch, son of Findachar, son of Akirkirre, son of Ecthach Andoch, son of Fiachrach Catmail, son of Ecddach Ried, son of Coner, son of Mogolama, son of Lugchag Etholach, son of Corbe Crangring, son of Daradiomore, son of Corbe Findmor, son of Coneremor, son of Ederskeol, son of Ewen, son of Eliela, son of Iair, son of Dethach, son of Sin, son of Rosin, son of Ther, son of

Rether, son of Rowem, son of Arindil, son of Mane, son of Fergus
the first king of the Scots in Albany.

Walter Bower, *Scotichronicon*, v, eds S. Taylor, D. E. R. Watt, B. Scott, Aberdeen,
1990.

A Scot abroad witnesses a coronation, 1261

The knight Missel, whom the king of Scotland had sent to king
Hacon, stood up over the choir, and wondered much at the
proceedings of the consecration; for it is not the custom in Scotland
to crown the kings. He was so struck at the ceremony that he
sobbed, before those who stood by told him what it all meant. And
when king Magnus was robed, and king Hacon, and those bishops
beside girded him with the coronation sword, then that Scottish
knight began to say, 'It was told me there were no knights dubbed
in this land; but never saw I any knight dubbed with equal honour,
when five of the noblest princes in this land gird him with the
coronation sword.' When king Magnus had to put on his royal
robes the archbishop led him out to his seat. After that they crowned
the queen.

'The Saga of Hacon', *Icelandic Sagas*, ed. G. W. Dasent, iv, London, 1894.

Battle on the Sands:
King Hacon Intervenes in Scotland, 1263

*These are the events leading up to and including the battle of
Largs in 1263. Modern historians consider the so-called 'battle' to
have been a series of minor skirmishes. Yet the Norse domination
of the Western seaboard did recede after this date. Perhaps the
failure of such a well fitted out invasion fleet indicated to them
that their days of domination were over. Three years later, in 1266,
the islands passed to the Scottish crown when their overlordship
was sold for the sum of 4000 marks plus 100 marks a year.
Hacon's Saga (written by Sturla Thordssen, just after Hacon's
death) gives an interesting picture of a time when the Western Isles
belonged to Norway.*

The summer before had come letters from the west from the
Southern [Western] Isles from the king there, and they made
much stir about that strife which the earl of Ross and Kjarnak
Machamal's son and other Scots had made in the Southern Isles
when they fared out into Skye, and burned farms and churches, and

slew a host of men and women. And they said this that the Scots had
taken small bairns and spitted them on their spear-points, and
shaken them till they fell down on their hands, and cast them dead
from off them. They repeated too, many big words of the king of
Scots, and said that he meant of a surety to lay under him all the
Southern Isles, if life were granted him. And when these tidings came
to King Hacon, they touched him with great care; he brought these
matters before his friends and councillors. But whatever any man
might say about it, king Hacon there and then let letters of summons
be sent round all Norway after Yule and called out the levies both
of men and stores as he thought the land could best bear it; he
summoned all the host to meet him early in the summer at Bergen.

[*The invasion fleet sailed, but, lying at anchor in Cumbrae Sound,
ships were driven ashore and attacked by the Scots.*]

When they saw that the main battle was drawing near, men begged
the king to get into a boat and row out to the ships to send them
much more force. The king offered to be on land with them, but
they would not bring him into such risk; and for that he put off in a
boat, and rowed out under the isle to his force. These were the
liegemen who were on land: Ogmund crow-dance, Erling Alf's son,
Andrew pot, Erlend the red, Andrew Nicholas' son, Thorlaug the
hot and Paul sour. There were near sixty men from the king's ship
and at their head was Andrew clubfoot. But by the reckoning of
most men there were in all eight or nine hundred of the Northmen
on land. Nigh two hundred men were up on the hillock with
Ogmund, but the other force stood down on the shingle. Then the
Scottish host began to draw near, and it was a very great host. It was
the reckoning of some men that they numbered five hundred
knights; but some called them something less. That force was very
well equipped, with mail-clad horses, and many Spanish steeds all
covered with armour. The Scots had a great host of footmen, but
that force was badly equipped as to weapons. They most of them
had bows and Irish bills. The Northmen who were on the hillock
dropped down towards the sea, so that the Scots should not hem
them in. Then Andrew Nicholas' son came up on the hill, and asked
Ogmund [crow-dance] if he did not think it wiser to go down to the
shingle to the force that was there; and that advice was taken.
Andrew bade his men to go down, but not to hurry like runaways.
Then the Scots came on fast, and pelted them with stones. Then a
great shower of weapons fell upon the Northmen. But they fell back

facing the enemy and shielded themselves. But when the Northmen came as far as the brow of the descent which went down from the hillock then each tried to be faster than the others. And when those who were down below on the shingle saw that, they thought that the Northmen wanted to flee. The Northmen ran to the boats, and in that way some of them put off from the land and came out to the ships. But most of the boats sunk, and then some men were lost. Many Northmen ran under the lee of the bark and some got up into her. When the Northmen came down from the hillock into the dell between it and the shingle, then most of them took to running. But some one called out to them to turn back. Then some men turned back, but still few. There fell one of the king's bodyguard Hacon of Stein. Then the Northmen still ran away. But when they got down on the shingle it was again called to them to turn back. Then again some of them turned back, but not many. That was south on the shingle beyond the long-ship which had drifted on shore. There two of the Northmen fell. Those who had turned back had then nothing left for it than to keep on the defensive, and so they fell back until they came north round the long-ship. Then they found there some force of the Northmen, and they all shared in the fight together. These were the leaders there – Ogmund crow-dance, Andrew Nicholas's son, Thorlaug the hot, and Paul sour. Then there was a hard battle, but still a very unequal one, for there must have been ten Scots to one Northman. There fell a young man of the Scots; his name was Perus; he was come of the best stocks, and was the son of a powerful knight, and rode more boldly than any other knight. There fell men on both sides, but more of the Scots . . .

When the day was wearing away the Northmen made an onslaught on the Scots up on the hillock and there fell on them most boldly. As is said in the Raven's Song:

The chosen barons of the king,
Chief justice of North-Mæren folk,
With war-songs hailed their sturdy foes,
What time the hill at Largs they scaled;

The valiant henchmen of the king,
Who keeps his throne in awful state,
Marched iron-hooded, cased in steel,
Against the foe in sword-stirred fray.
Brown brand bit the rebels sharply,
At the mail-moot on the hill;

Up the 'How' the red shields mounted,
Till their bearers reached the top,
Then the Scottish brand-gale cloudmen [shielded warriors]
Took to flight with terror stricken
Turned their heels those doughty soldiers
From the champions of the king.

Then the Scots fled away from the hillock as fast as each man
could to the fells. But when the Northmen saw that they went to the
boats and rowed out to the ships and got off with difficulty for the
storm.

'The Saga of Hacon', *Icelandic Sagas* iv, ed. G. W. Dasent, London, 1894.

Judgement Day – The Death of Alexander III

*Closer to the border than Carlisle, and only a few miles from
Scotland, Lanercost priory in Cumberland kept a chronicle which
is a rich source for Scottish affairs of the late 13th century. For
some reason the chronicler had no good opinion of Alexander III,
whose death he records in 1286. He depicts the king as indulging
in gluttony and mild blasphemy, then insisting under the worst
possible circumstances on setting off to see his bride Yoleta (thus
presumably also being motivated by lust). To later Scots the loss of
their king was seen as the dreadful accident which ushered in the
wars of independence. His tragic end was seen as the close of an
almost mythical golden age for Scotland. The chronicler seems to
indicate that it was all deserved because poor Yoleta was too
flighty to stay as a nun.*

When they had sat down to dinner, he [Alexander] sent a present
of fresh lampreys to a certain baron, bidding him by an
esquire to make the party merry, for he should know that this was
the Judgement Day. He [the baron], after returning thanks, face-
tiously replied to his lord: 'If this be the Judgement Day, we shall
soon rise with full bellies.'

The protracted feast having come to an end, he [Alexander] would
neither be deterred by stress of weather nor yield to the persuasion
of his nobles, but straightaway hurried along the road to Queensferry,
in order to visit his bride, that is to say Yoleta, daughter of the Comte
de Dru, whom shortly before he had brought from over the sea, to
his own sorrow and the perpetual injury of the whole province. For
she was then staying at Kinghorn. Many people declare that, before

her engagement beyond the sea, she had changed her dress in a convent of nuns, but that she had altered her mind with the levity of a woman's heart and through ambition for a kingdom.

When he arrived at the village near the crossing, the ferrymaster warned him of the danger, and advised him to go back; but when [the King] asked him in return whether he was afraid to die with him: 'By no means,' quoth he, 'it would be a great honour to share the fate of your father's son.' Thus he arrived at the burgh of Inverkeithing, in profound darkness, accompanied only by three esquires. The manager of his saltpans, a married man of that town, recognising him by his voice, called out: 'My lord, what are you doing here in such a storm and such darkness? Often have I tried to persuade you that your nocturnal rambles will bring you no good. Stay with us, and we will provide you with decent fare and all that you want till morning light.' 'No need for that,' said the other with a laugh, 'but provide me with a couple of bondmen, to go afoot as guides to the way.'

And it came to pass that when they had proceeded two miles, one and all lost all knowledge of the way, owing to the darkness; only the horses, by natural instinct, picked out the hard road. While they were thus separated from each other, the esquires took the right road; [but] he, at length (that I may make a long story short), fell from his horse, and bade farewell to his kingdom in the sleep of Sisara. To him Solomon's proverb applies: 'Wo unto him who, when he falls, has no man to raise him up.' He lies at Dunfermline alone in the south aisle, buried near the presbytery. Whence [comes it] that, while we may see the populace bewailing his sudden death as deeply as the desolation of the realm, those only who adhered to him most closely in life for his friendship and favours, wet not their cheeks with tears?

Chronicle of Lanercost, ed. Sir H. Maxwell, in Scottish Historical Review, vi, Glasgow, 1909.

And Finally . . .
Extreme Naughtiness in Inverkeithing, 1282

As well as reporting on affairs of state, the Lanercost Chronicler liked a good piece of scandal. This outrageous piece of clerical gossip was evidently thought to be well worth writing down (perhaps with a small measure of humbug – 'How unlike the home life of our own dear house!'). The recording of such a titillating

item could be justified as a moral tale because divine retribution
followed, in the shape of the violent death of Father John. What
would the tabloid press have made of it?

About this time, in Easter week, the parish priest of Inverkeithing, named John, revived the profane rites of Priapus, collecting young girls from the villages, and compelling them to dance in circles to [the honour of] Father Bacchus. When he had these females in a troop, out of sheer wantonness, he led the dance, carrying in front on a pole a representation of the human organs of reproduction, and singing and dancing himself like a mime, he viewed them all and stirred them to lust by filthy language. Those who held respectable matrimony in honour were scandalised by such a shameless performance, although they respected the parson because of the dignity of his rank. If anybody remonstrated kindly with him, he [the priest] became worse [than before], violently reviling him.

And [whereas] the iniquity of some men manifestly brings them to justice, [so] in the same year, when his parishioners assembled according to custom in the church at dawn in Penance Week, at the hour of discipline he would insist that certain persons should prick with goads [others] stripped for penance. The burgesses, resenting the indignity inflicted upon them, turned upon its author; who, while he as author was defending his nefarious work, fell the same night pierced by a knife, God thus awarding him what he deserved for his wickedness.

Chronicle of Lanercost, ed. Sir H. Maxwell, Glasgow, 1909.

Wars of Independence

Alexander III's death led to the prospect of Scotland's first ruling queen, but, alas, it was not to be. The little Queen Margaret, maid of Norway, died without setting foot on the mainland and the succession to the Scottish throne became uncertain. It was agreed by the rival claimants to acknowledge Edward I of England as overlord and to let him settle the matter. Edward chose John Balliol as king, not because Balliol was a weak man who would consequently end up in his pocket, but because by law Balliol actually had the best claim. Things soon went sour when Edward declared war on France and expected his Scots vassals to join in enthusiastically. John Balliol rebelled and invaded England. The English, not too surprisingly, were fairly outraged about this – they counter-attacked. Now read on.

1296 and All That

This is from the Lanercost Chronicler, in his role as war correspondent and army chaplain. Note the pro-English bias – what a difference those few miles over the border made. Even when Edward's troops were massacring the townsfolk, he was still a 'most clement prince'. Apparently he had been terribly provoked: the second paragraph does seem to indicate that the dreadful Scots secret weapon of 'mooning at the enemy' was being employed. No wonder he had to have them all killed!

Just as the Scripture uttered by God declareth that 'upon the evildoer shall fall his own device, nor shall he know whence it cometh upon him,' so that illustrious man Robert de Ros, the owner of much land, thinking to secure prosperity, broke faith and joined the King of England's enemies, betraying his secrets to them and promising them support. When this was found out, the king solemnly observed the thanks-giving services on Easter day at his castle of Wark, and tried to persuade the head men of Berwick to surrender, promising them safety in their persons, security for their possessions, reform of their laws and liberties, pardon for their offences, so that, had they considered their own safety, they would not have slighted the proffered grace. But they, on the contrary, being blinded by their sins, became more scornful, and, while he waited for three days, they gave no reply to so liberal an offer; so that when he came to them on the fourth day, addressing them personally in a friendly manner, they redoubled their insults.

For some of them, setting themselves on the heights, bared their breeches and reviled the king and his people; others fiercely attacked the fleet which lay in the harbour awaiting the king's orders and slew some of the sailors. Their women folk, also, bringing fire and straw, endeavoured to burn the ships. The stubbornness of these misguided people being thus manifest, the troops were brought into action, the pride of these traitors was humbled almost without the use of force and the city was occupied by the enemy. Much booty was seized, and no fewer than fifteen thousand of both sexes perished, some by the sword, others by fire, in the space of a day and a half, and the survivors, including even little children, were sent into perpetual exile. Nevertheless this most clement prince exhibited towards the dead that mercy which he had proffered to the living; for I myself beheld an immense number of men told off to bury the bodies of the fallen, all of whom, even those who began to work at the eleventh hour, were to receive as wages a penny a piece at the King's expense.

These events took place on the third of the kalends of April, being the Friday in Easter holy week, a penalty exacted by God corresponding to the crime.

Chronicle of Lanercost, ed. Sir H. Maxwell, Glasgow, 1909.

William Wallace Nearly Killed My Father

The catastrophic collapse of Scottish forces under King John Balliol left Scotland as an occupied land. Edward took Balliol prisoner and stripped him of his rank. English taxation and bureaucracy were set up in Scotland. But all was not lost. There were still Scots capable of resistance. William Wallace was amongst those prepared to take up where King John had left off. Sir Thomas Gray of Heaton in Northumberland was one of Wallace's first victims. Captured by the Scots in 1355, his son, also Sir Thomas, decided to write a history in which, amongst other things, he recorded his father's sometimes harrowing experiences.

At which time [1297] in the month of May William Wallace was chosen by the commons of Scotland as leader to raise war against the English, and he at the outset slew William de Hesilrig at Lanark, the King of England's Sheriff of Clydesdale. The said William Wallace came by night upon the said sheriff and surprised him, when Thomas de Gray, who was at that time in the suite of the said sheriff, was left stripped for dead in the mellay when the English were defending themselves. The said Thomas lay all night naked between two burning houses which the Scots had set on fire, whereof the heat kept life in him, until he was recognised at daybreak and carried off by William de Lundy, who caused him to be restored to health.

Sir Thomas Gray, *Scalacronica*, ed. Sir Herbert Maxwell, Glasgow, 1907.

Stirling Bridge

By 1297 there were not one but several rebellions in full swing. Robert Wishart, Bishop of Glasgow, James Stewart, Sir William Douglas, Robert Bruce, William Wallace and Andrew Murray all led uprisings. The Bishop and his friends were able to accomplish little, but Wallace and Murray were more successful. They managed to stay in arms, taking the war to the English who were advancing on Stirling. Against them came the English commander, the Earl of Warenne, and the most hated man in Scotland, Hugh de Cressingham – the king's Lord High Treasurer and the man responsible for extracting English taxes in Scotland and financing the English campaign.

De Cressingham, pompous, greedy, and a 'son of death' (and that's just what his own side said about him), was loathed by the Scots, which was a little unfair, as his accountant-like behaviour – demanding the cheapest possible military strategy regardless of its stupidity – was to cost the English the battle. William Wallace versus the accountant: the accountant lost. This narrative of the battle is by the contemporary Yorkshire Chronicler Walter de Guisborough, who ignores Wallace's role in the battle and concentrates instead on the heroic deeds of a certain Marmaduke de Tweng, who captured the bridge single-handed, if we are to believe his fellow Yorkshireman.

In the month of May in the same year, the perfidious nation of the Scots began to rebel in this way. The Earl of Warenne to whom our King [Edward 1] had entrusted the whole of the kingdom of Scotland on his behalf and in his name, giving as his reason the debasement of money, said that it was not sensible for him to stay there and he remained in England but in the North, and half-heartedly pursued the enemy who were living in exile, which was the source and origin of evil for us in the future. And the King's treasurer the lord Hugh de Cressingham, a solemn and lofty man, loved money exceedingly and failed to construct the stone wall which the lord the king himself had ordered to be constructed upon the new fortifications at Berwick; which turned out to be a scandal to our men as will be clear below. Now the King's justiciar, William Ormsby, prosecuting the King's command, began to send into exile all those without distinction of persons who had refused to make firm fealty to the King of England. There was also a certain brigand, William Wallace by name, who had been in exile many times. Since this man was wandering and fugitive, he assembled about himself all those who were living in exile, and became something of a chief to them, and they grew into a large people. To him also was joined the soldier James Douglas who in the capture of the castle of Berwick had given himself together with his men to the King, saving his life and limb, as has been said above. Although the King had restored him to everything he became forgetful of his goods, and a robber allied to a robber, pursued his liberator to death, at least in his subjects . . .

[*Sir William Douglas and the Bishop of Glasgow started an abortive rising. Warenne moved against them and both were soon handed over to him.*]

When that robber William Wallace had heard this [the imprisonment of the Bishop of Glasgow] he became angry in his mind and proceeded to the Bishop's house and drew to himself all his furniture, arms and horses, and the sons who were called by name of the bishop's nephews. And he was increased by an immense number of Scots to the point where the community of the realm began to follow him as their leader and prince. And entire households [retainers] of the nobles began to adhere to him and even though the nobles themselves were with our King [Edward I] in body, their hearts were a long way from him. Indeed our men having become so irritated, since they did not wish to put up with such things any longer, marched forward in arms to the town of Stirling where the Steward of Scotland and the Earl of Lennox and certain others of the nobles of Scotland came and asked our men to hold off for a short time in case they might be able to pacify their men and the people of the Scots in whatever way. Although this was granted to them, they came back, that is to say on the 11th of September, and replied precisely that they could not answer for them, promising however that they would come to the aid of our men the next day with forty armed horse.

*[The English army headed towards Stirling Bridge. Meanwhile, de
Cressingham was given the offer of reinforcements under Sir Henry
Percy.]*

. . . he [Sir Henry] received in the commands from the lord Hugh
de Cressingham the King's treasurer that he should send the same
people back with his thanks, saying that the army that they had
could be enough and that it was not useful to trouble them for
nothing or to consume the King's treasury more than was necessary.
He did this, and the people were mightily angered, wishing as if to
stone him, and so with various people reckoning various things,
some began shouting aloud that they should cross the bridge and
some on the contrary that they should not. Amongst them the King's
treasurer, a pompous man and a son of death, added, 'It is not fitting
my Lord Earl to prolong the matter further and to expend our King's
treasury in vain. But let us go up and pay our debt, rather than hold
ourselves back.' And so the Earl, moved by those words,
commanded that they should go up to the bridge and cross it. It was
astonishing to say, and terrible in its consequence, that such a large
number of individual men, though they knew the enemy was at
hand, should go up to a narrow bridge which a pair of horsemen
could scarcely and with difficulty cross at the same time. Since, as
some who had been in the same conflict were saying, if they had
crossed over from earliest morning until the eleventh hour, without
any interruption or hindrance, the last part of the army would have
remained in great part until then.

Nor was there a more appropriate place in the kingdom of
Scotland for shutting the English into the hands of the Scots, and the
many into the hands of the few. So there crossed over the King's and
the Earl's standard-bearers and amongst the first that most vigorous
soldier, the lord Marmaduke Tweng, and when the enemy had seen
that as many had come forth as they could overcome, as they
believed, they then came down from the mountain [high ground],
and sent the spearmen to occupy the foot of the bridge, such that
from then no passage or retreat remained open, but in turning back,
as also in making haste over the bridge, many were thrown headlong
and were drowned. And so as the Scots were descending from the
mountain, the lord Marmaduke said to his allies, 'Is it the time
brothers for us to ride at them?' And with them answering that it
was, they then spurred their horses and engaged together. And
whilst some of the Scots were falling together, the rest of the
horsemen, almost all, were turned to flight. Whilst those who were

fleeing followed after them, one of our men said to the lord
Marmaduke, 'My Lord, we have been cheated, for our men are not
pursuing and the King's and the Earl's standards are not present.'
Looking back to these things, they saw that many of our men, and
the King's and the Earl's standard-bearers had fallen to the ground,
and they said 'The way to the bridge is already cut off from us and
we have been cut off from our people. It is therefore better that we
put ourselves at risk of danger, in case we may cross over, than that
we should fall, as if for nothing, whilst penetrating into the enemy's
troops. Crossing through the middle of the Scots has already become
difficult – or rather – impossible for us.' In reply to this Marmaduke,
that most vigorous man, said, 'My dearest friends, may it certainly
never be said of me that I willingly drowned myself. And far be it
from you, but follow me, and I will make you a way through them
as far as the bridge.' And after goading his war-horse he then rushed
into the enemy, and submitting now these, now those to his sword,
he crossed over through the middle of them unharmed; and a great
way opened up to those who followed him. For he was powerful in
strength and of tall stature, and when he was fighting strenuously,
his own nephew, wounded and stunned but standing on his feet, his
horse having been killed, called out to him, 'My Lord, save me,' but
he said, 'Climb up behind me,' he said, 'I cannot, for my strength has
failed me.' Then his comrade, the same lord Marmaduke's shield-
bearer, got down from his own horse and made him mount and said
to his lord, 'I will follow you my Lord wherever you shall go' and
he followed him as far as the bridge and each of them was saved. So
with the bridge captured through the bravery of that vigorous
fighter, as many as stayed there fell to the number of about 100 men-
at-arms and about 5,000 foot-soldiers, amongst whom were 300
Welshmen, although they had deprived many of life. At length some
from amongst those who were left crossed the water by swimming.
Also one soldier from our men crossed the water with difficulty on
an armed horse.

On the same day amongst the Scottish spearmen fell the above-
named treasurer of the lord King, the lord Hugh de Cressingham,
rector of the church of Ruddeby, and chief judge at the assizes of
York. Although he was a prebendary of many churches and had the
cure of many souls, yet he never put on spiritual arms or the
chasuble, but helmet and cuirass, in which he fell. And he who had
previously terrified many by the sword of his tongue in many court
trials, was eventually slain by the sword of evil men. The Scots

stripped him of his skin and divided it amongst themselves in small parts, not indeed for relics but for insults, for he was a handsome and exceedingly fat man and they called him not the King's treasurer but the King's 'Treacherer' and this was truer than they believed. For he led many astray that day, but he too, who was smooth and slippery, exalted with pride and given over to avarice, was himself led astray.

At the first encounter of our men with the Scots, the Steward of Scotland and the Earl of Lennox, who previously had come in peace, when they saw that our men had fallen, immediately retreated to their own men who were lying hidden in the woods near the pows [slow-running streams feeding into the Forth]. Seeing the outcome of the abominable thing they came out in front of our men and killed many, particularly those who were running away in the same area, carrying off much plunder and leading away loaded waggons to the pows, for the waggons could not be easily be led away by those fleeing in lochs and marshes. Indeed our Earl, remaining throughout on this side of the bridge when the lord Marmaduke had returned with his men, ordered that the bridge be broken and burned, and entrusting the custody of the same castle of Stirling to the aforesaid lord Marmaduke, promised him faithfully with granted pledge that within the first ten weeks he would come to his help with a strong band of men; however he did not carry out what he had promised, and forgetting his own old age, he set out for Berwick with such haste, that the war-horse on which he had sat, which had been placed in the stable of the Friars Minor, nowhere tasted its fodder. From there he proceeded into southern parts to the King's son and left his fatherland entirely abandoned. This ruin was brought about on the third day before the Ides of September, namely the Wednesday in the year of grace above-stated.

Translated by J. Russell from *Chronicle of Walter of Guisborough*, ed. H. Rothwell, Camden Society, 1957.

Wallace's Execution

Wallace's success did not last. His co-commander Andrew Murray died, leaving Wallace alone as Guardian of the Kingdom to face a superior English force under Edward I himself at the battle of Falkirk in 1298. He lost. His credibility ruined, Wallace resigned the Guardianship, but did not give up the fight. He never surrendered to Edward and Edward always excepted him from any offers of clemency. Having served Scotland abroad by diplomacy in

France, Wallace returned to Scotland. On 3 August 1305 he was
betrayed to the English and captured. On 23 August he was
executed.

What follows comes from an 18th-century transcript of a medieval
manuscript from the Sir Robert Cotton collection, which was lost
in a fire in 1731. It is a contemporary record of Wallace's 'trial'
and sentence in London before an English court acting on behalf
of a king whose authority Wallace never recognised. It is a
translation from the original Latin.

William Wallace, a Scot, and born in Scotland, a prisoner for
sedition, homicides, plunderings, fire-raisings, and diverse
other felonies came and, after the same justices had read out how the
aforesaid lord the King had in hostile manner conquered the land of
Scotland over John Balliol, the prelates, the earls, the barons and
other enemies of his of the same land, in forfeiture of the same John,
and by the conquest of him had submitted and subjugated all the
Scots to right of ownership and his royal power as their King, he had
received in public the homages and pledges of the prelates, the earls,
the barons and very many others, and he had made his peace to be
proclaimed throughout the whole of the land of Scotland. He had
appointed and set up the Guardians of that land, appointing the
sheriffs, the provosts, the bailies and other ministers of his, in his
place, to maintain his peace and give justice to all whomsoever
according to the laws and customs of that land. The aforesaid
William Wallace, forgetful of his fealty and allegiance, raised up all
he could by felony and premeditated sedition against the same lord
the King, having united and joined to himself an immense number
of felons, and he feloniously invaded, and attacked the Guardians
and ministers of the same King, feloniously and against the same
lord the King's peace, insulted, wounded and killed William de
Heselrigg, sheriff of Lanark, who [   ] the appointments of the
said King in the regular meeting of the county court, and afterwards
in contempt of the same King without reason fought against the
same sheriff whom he had killed.

Thenceforth with the entire multitude of those who adhered in
arms to him and to his felony, he invaded the towns, the cities and
the castles of that land, and had his letters [orders] sent throughout
the whole of Scotland, as if they were the letters of the superior of
that land. He held and appointed parliaments and conventions after
all the Guardians and ministers of the aforesaid lord the King of the

land of Scotland had been evicted by William himself, and unwilling
to restrain himself to so much wickedness and sedition, decreed to
all the prelates, earls and barons of his land who adhered to his
party, that they were to subject themselves to the fealty and
dominion of the King of France, and they were to press for help
towards the destruction of the kingdom of England. Taking some
also from his accomplices with him he invaded the kingdom of
England, as in the counties of Northumberland, Cumberland and
Westmorland, and all whom he found there who were in the fealty
of the King of England, he feloniously put to death in various ways.

He feloniously and seditiously slaughtered religious men and
monks dedicated to God, and burnt and laid waste churches
constructed for the honour of God and the saints, together with the
bodies of the saints and other relics of them that had been
honourably collected therein; he spared no-one who spoke the
English language, but afflicted all, old men and youths, wives and
widows, children and babes in arms with a more grievous death
than could be considered. And so, every day and every hour, he
seditiously and feloniously persisted in contriving the death of the
same lord the King, and the destruction and the manifest weakening
of the crown and his royal majesty. And it is clear that after such
outrageous and horrible deeds, the aforesaid lord the King, together
with his great army, had invaded the land of Scotland and had
defeated the aforesaid William, who was bearing his standard
against him in mortal warfare, and other enemies of his, and had
granted his true peace to all from that land and had mercifully taken
the aforesaid William Wallace back into his peace, the said William
seditiously and feloniously, whole-heartedly and undauntedly
persevering in his above noted wickedness, disdained to submit
himself to the aforesaid lord King's peace and to come forth to it,
and so was publicly outlawed in the court of the same lord the King
as traitor, robber and felon, according to the laws and customs of
England and Scotland.

It is clearly both unjust and in disagreement with English laws and
it is held true that anyone thus outlawed and placed outside the laws
and not afterwards restored to his peace, is committed to the
forfeiture of his own status or accountability. It is considered that
the aforesaid William, for the open sedition which he had made to
the same lord the King by felonious contriving, by trying to bring
about his death, the destruction and weakening of the crown and of
his royal authority and by bringing his standard against his liege

lord in war to the death, should be taken away to the palace of Westminster as far as the Tower of London, and from the Tower as far as Allegate [Aldgate], and thus through the middle of the city as far as Elmes, and for the robberies, murders and felonies which he carried out in the kingdom of England and the land of Scotland he should be hanged there and afterwards drawn. And because he had been outlawed and not afterwards restored to the King's peace, he should be beheaded and decapitated.

And afterwards for the measureless wickedness which he did to God and to the most Holy Church by burning churches, vessels and shrines, in which the body of Christ and the bodies of the saints and relics of the same were wont to be placed together, the heart, liver, and lung and all the internal [parts] of the same William, by which such evil thoughts proceeded, should be dispatched to the fire and burned. And also because he had committed both murders and felonies, not only to the lord the King himself but to the entire people of England and Scotland, the body of that William should be cut up and divided and cut up into four quarters, and that the head thus cut off should be affixed upon London bridge in the sight of those crossing both by land and by water, and one quarter should be hung on the gibbet at Newcastle upon Tyne, another quarter at Berwick, a third quarter at Stirling, and a fourth quarter at St John's town [Perth] as a cause of fear and chastisement of all going past and looking upon these things &c.

Translated by J. Russell from *Documents Illustrative of Sir William Wallace, His Life and Times*, ed. Joseph Stevenson, Maitland Club, 1841.

The Comyn Murder

By 1306, Scotland was looking like a permanent addition to Edward's realms. Suddenly, that well-known trouble-maker Robert Bruce, Earl of Carrick, upset the king's peace. This time it was murder under trust at the high altar of a church. The man he murdered was John Comyn, a Scottish noble in good standing with Edward who had been one of the most powerful supporters of John Balliol. Comyn had supposedly informed the English king that Bruce was plotting against him. After the murder Bruce could not hope for a pardon from Edward. He felt he had no choice but to seize the throne himself.

Chronicler Walter Bower, writing over 100 years later, examined the written record. He was writing in a Scotland formed by the

exploits of the Bruce and his successors, and his report was
distinctly pro-Bruce. Bower probably blackens the Red Comyn's
reputation to make Bruce's action seem more justified.

As I have found it written, Sir Robert Bruce travelled with such
haste that he reached Lochmaben on the seventh day after
starting out from London. At Lochmaben he found his brother
Edward, who was greatly surprised at his arrival, as sudden as it was
secret. Robert told him how treacherously he had been accused
before the king of England, and how in the Lord's name he escaped
from his clutches.

On the same day before his arrival at Lochmaben, when the said
Robert was approaching the neighbourhood of the Borders, he met
a man on foot. Seeing him from a distance, he suspected both from
his gait and from his dress that he was a Scot. Seizing this man as he
turned away, he asked him where he was going to and where he was
coming from. When he gave one excuse after another for his sins,
Robert's own attendants on his orders investigated the secrets of this
messenger whom they had come across. Missive letters were at once
discovered with the seal of the said John the Red Comyn, addressed
to the king of England, concerning the secure confinement or
detention of Robert himself or his speedy execution in view of the
very serious and dangerous circumstances. These letters were
removed, the messenger beheaded, and God greatly praised for
guiding this journey.

At that time Sir John the Red Comyn was staying at Dumfries.
Bruce too hurried there to pay him back in a way that was fitting for
his offence. Robert came upon John in the choir of the friars of
Dumfries in front of the high altar. After an animated greeting and
an exchange of remarks for a time on lesser topics, the missive letters
of the same John were produced and the same John was attacked for
his betrayal and breach of faith. But soon the reply was given: 'You
lie!' A fatal blow was dealt in the same church on this slanderer; and
on being wounded by the said Sir Robert, John was carried behind
the altar by the friars. When this happened, Robert Bruce, like a
man beyond endurance and beside himself, made for his horses at
the entrance to the cemetery. His kinsman Sir James de Lindsay [and
Sir Roger] de Kirkpatrick ran up to help him as had been arranged
at Lochmaben; and as they attended Robert, faint and beside himself
as it were, they asked him how it had gone with him. 'Badly,' he said
'for I think I have killed John the Red Comyn.' 'Should so vital an
assumption be left in doubt?' said James de Lindsay. And Lindsay

himself, entering the vestry with Kirkpatrick, asked if Comyn might live. At once the reply came from Comyn himself: 'I can if I have a doctor.' A second wound was dealt [him] by these questioners, when the knight Sir Robert Comyn also fell wounded in the defence of his kinsman Sir John Comyn and along with him. And so on 10 February 1305 they were removed from this life, and Edward king of England, it is believed, was cheated of his desire both marvellously and wonderfully.

Walter Bower, *Scotichronicon*, vi, ed. D. E. R. Watt, Aberdeen, 1991.

The Bruce Women and the Coronation

After the Comyn murder, Bruce had himself crowned King of Scotland and went into open rebellion against the ailing Edward I. Some of his strongest and bravest supporters were women, such as Christiana, Lady of the Isles, who supplied him with galleys and troops, and the more famous Isabel, Countess of Buchan, who stole away from her pro-English husband in order to crown him. Isabel and the women of Bruce's family suffered terrible fates when they were captured by Edward's forces. He ordered the most active of the women to be confined in wooden cages on the tops of towers, exposed to the elements with only a little privy to which to retreat, yet their fate was better than that of the men who fell into his hands and whom he ordered to be hung, drawn and quartered.

Here is Walter of Guisborough's account of Bruce's coronation and what followed.

At the beginning of AD 1306, the aforesaid Robert de Bruce, on the day of the Annunciation to the Blessed Mary, had himself crowned as King of Scotland at Scone, in the presence and with the agreement of four bishops, five earls and the people of the land. And the wife of the Earl of Buchan, who was the daughter of the Earl of Fife, to whom by hereditary right it belonged to place the crown on the head of the new King, secretly withdrew from her lord, bringing her lord's war-horses which he had sent home, so that she might exercise that office. This angered her lord, who had stood forth in loyalty to the King of England, and since she had been captured in the same year, he wished to kill her, but the King forbade him and ordered her to be placed upon the wall [the top of a tower] of the castle of Berwick, secured in a wooden cage, so that she could be seen and recognised by those passing by. And she remained many days, thus enclosed and on a strict regimen. And the King sent two bishops, namely those of Glasgow and St Andrews in Scotland, together with the Abbot of Scone, since they had been captured the same year, into England to different castles and they remained closely confined until the death of the King. And so once he had heard and learnt of the coronation of the new King, the lord the King of England, on the feast of Pentecost, sent forward with an armed band, some of his soldiers, namely the Lord Henry de Percy, the Lord Aylmer de Valence and the Lord Robert Clifford to oppose the new King and hunt him down . . .

And the new King fled and they pursued him as far as the isle of Kintyre, and they besieged the castle of that place, believing that he had withdrawn into the same place, but he had gone away into the furthest isles of that region. And when the castle had been taken by storm, they found one of the new King's brothers, namely the Lord Neil de Bruce, with the new queen and many others. Taking them with them as far as Berwick in the presence there of the justices of the Lord, the King of England, who by the King's command had assembled in that place, the men were judicially condemned, hanged, drawn and beheaded. And because the new queen was a daughter of the Earl of Ulster, he at the beginning of the war waged by his son-in-law, the Lord Robert de Bruce (lest the lord the King of England should suspect him of any evil against him), sent his two sons to the King to be held fast at the King's good will to excuse himself because he had always shown himself loyal to him. Also on account of one word which she had said to her husband when at his coronation he was speaking to her and said, 'Rejoice now, my wife, because you have been made a Queen and I a King,' she is said to have replied to him, 'I am afraid my Lord that we have been made King and Queen, as boys are made in summer games.' Therefore for those two causes the King sent her with her household to stay at her manor of Brustewych and ordered her to be maintained with honour. [As to] the earl of Atholl, who had fled from that castle and after some interval had been captured, although the Queen of England and many nobles asked the King on his behalf for his life, especially because he was a near relative to the lord the King of England, the King ordered that he should be brought to London and hanged higher than the rest. And because he who had been a prominent blood relation was found to be a traitor, the King ordered him to be beheaded and burned after his hanging, which was done. As to Christopher Seton, who had married the new King's sister,

Mary [in fact Christian] by name, although he was English, when he was taken in the castle of Lochdore [Lochdoon Castle] and afterwards his wife and many others, the King ordered that he be taken to Dumfries, where he had killed a soldier, and there to be drawn, hanged and beheaded. His two brothers and others who all agreed to and were present at the death of the lord John Comyn had a similar sentence and this from the King's special command. However, the King placed Christopher's wife in the monastery of Thyxsel, in Lindesay [Sixhills, Lincolnshire], and he placed the new King's daughter in the monastery of Watthon [Watton, Yorkshire].

Translated by J. Russell, *Chronicle of Walter of Guisborough*, ed. H. Rothwell, Camden Society, 1957.

Barbour's Bruce – The Taking of Forfar Castle and the Herschip of Buchan

When John Barbour wrote his epic poem in the Scots language, 'The Bruce', the deeds of its hero were still within living memory. Barbour recorded the deeds of some of the more ordinary heroes, as well as just those of the king himself. This extract from his poem tells not only of Bruce's lightning civil-war campaign of 1307 against the Comyn lands in Buchan, but also of the brave exploit of Philip the Forester of Platen and his men, who took Forfar castle from the English.

Now ga we to the King agane,
   [go]   *[again]*
That of his victor wes richt fane,
         [was]   *[pleased]*
And gert his men burn all Bouchane
            [Buchan]
Fra end till end, and sparit nane;
[from]   *[spared]*
And heryit thame on sic maneir,
    [harried them on such manner]
That eftir that, weile fifty yheir,
  [after]   *[a good fifty years]*
Men menyt 'the heirschip of Bouchane.'
     [mourned the ravaging of Buchan]
The King than till his pes has tane
       [peace] *[taken]*
The north cuntre, that humylly
     [country]   *[humbly]*

Obeysit till his senyhory.
[gave obedience to his Lordship]
Swa that be north the Month war nane
[so]   *[none]*
That thai ne war his men ilkane.
         [that were not each one his man]]
His lordschip wox ay mair and mair.
                    [waxed more and more]
Toward Angus than couth he fair,
                    [knew]
And thoucht soyn to mak all fre
         [thought soon to make all free]
Apon north half the Scottis Se.
[upon]   *[sea]*
The castell of Forfer wes then
         [castle]
Stuffit all with Inglis men.
[filled with]
Bot Philip the Forster of Platan
                [forester]
Has of his frendis with him tane,
         [friends]   *[taken]*
And with ledderis all prevely
         [ladders]   *[secretly]*
To the castell he can him hy,
         [castle]   *[in haste]*
And clam out-our the wall of stane,
                         [stone]
And swagat has the castell tan,
[so]   *[taken]*
Throu falt of wach, with litill payn.
         [fault] *[watch]*
And syn all that he fand has slayn:
[then]   *[found]*
Syne yhald the castell to the King,
[then yielded]
That maid hym richt gud rewarding,
                [him right good]
And syne gert brek doune the wall,
         [then caused break down]
And fordid well and castell all.
         [did for]

J. Barbour, *The Bruce*, ed. W. M. Mackenzie, London, 1909.

Scaling Ladders

*The Scots re-took a whole succession of castles and towns, but at
Berwick in 1313 they failed. The Lanercost Chronicler explains the
military technology behind their otherwise successful campaign.*

Now oft-mentioned Robert [Bruce], seeing that thus he had the
whole March of England under tribute, applied all his thoughts
to getting possession of the town of Berwick, which was in the King
of England's hands. Coming unexpectedly to the castle on the night
of S. Nicholas, he laid ladders against the walls and began to scale
them; and had not a dog betrayed the approach of the Scots by loud
barking, it is believed that he would quickly have taken the castle
and, in consequence, the town

Now these ladders which they placed against the walls were of
wonderful construction, as I myself, who write these lines, beheld
with my own eyes. For the Scots had made two strong ropes as long
as the height of the wall, making a knot at one end of each cord.
They had made a wooden board also, about two feet and a half long
and half a foot broad, strong enough to carry a man, and in the two
extremities of the board they had made two holes, through which
the two ropes could be passed; then the cords, having been passed
through as far as the knots, they had made two other knots in the
ropes one foot and a half higher, and above these knots they placed
another log or board, and so on to the end of the ropes. They had
also made an iron hook, measuring at least one foot along one limb,
and this was to lie over the wall; but the other limb, being of the
same length, hung downwards towards the ground, having at its end
a round hole wherein the point of a lance could be inserted, and two
rings on the two sides wherein the said ropes could be knotted.

Having fitted them together in this manner, they took a strong
spear as long as the height of the wall, placing the point thereof in
the iron hole, and two men lifted the ropes and boards with that
spear and placed the iron hook (which was not a round one) over
the wall. Then they were able to climb up by those wooden steps just
as one usually climbs ordinary ladders, and the greater the weight of
the climber the more firmly the iron hook clung over the wall. But
lest the ropes should lie too close to the wall and hinder the ascent,
they had made fenders round every third step which thrust the ropes
off the wall. When, therefore, they had placed two ladders upon the
wall, the dog betrayed them as I have said, and they left the ladders
there, which our people next day hung upon a pillory to put them

to shame. And thus a dog saved the town on that occasion, just as
of old geese saved Rome by their gaggle . . .

Chronicle of Lanercost, ed. Sir H. Maxwell, Glasgow, 1909.

Bannockburn

*Having subdued his rivals the Comyns, Bruce started a steady war
of attrition against the English occupying forces. He took a
number of castles by stratagems, but Stirling Castle still held out
against him. His brother Edward besieged the castle and extracted
a promise of surrender from the garrison. Unless an English army
came in sight of the castle before midsummer's day 1314, the castle
would be his. The news was brought to Edward II. The Monk of
Malmesbury who wrote the* Vita Edwardi Secundi *takes up the
story. His narrative is anecdotal, concentrating on the deeds of
individual knights – for example, his disgust at the failure of the
English knights to save the Earl of Gloucester. By contrast the
Lanercost Chronicler and Sir Thomas Gray have accounts which
show more military understanding. This is how the English
chroniclers recorded Bannockburn.*

About the beginning of Lent messengers came to the king
[Edward II] with the news of the destruction of the Scottish
cities, the capture of the castles, and the breaching of the
surrounding walls. The constable of Stirling came, too, and pointed
out to the king how he had been compelled by necessity to enter
upon the truce. He persuaded the king to lead an army to Scotland,
to defend his castle and the country. When the king heard the news
he was very much grieved, and for the capture of his castles could
scarcely restrain his tears. He therefore summoned the earls and
barons to come to his aid and overcome the traitor who called
himself King [Bruce] . . .

When all the necessaries had been collected, the king and the other
magnates of the land with a great multitude of carts and baggage-
wagons set out for Scotland. On the sixth or seventh day before the
feast of St John the Baptist, our king with all his army left Berwick
and took his way towards Stirling. The cavalry numbered more than
two thousand, without counting a numerous crowd of infantry.
There were in that company quite sufficient to penetrate the whole
of Scotland, and some thought if the whole strength of Scotland had
been gathered together, they would not have stayed to face the king's
army. Indeed all who were present agreed that never in our time has

such an army gone forth from England. The multitude of wagons if they had been placed end to end, would have taken up a space of twenty leagues . . .

On Sunday, which was the vigil of St John's day, as they passed by a certain wood and were approaching Stirling Castle, the Scots were seen straggling under the trees as if in flight, and a certain knight, Henry de Boun [Bohun] pursued them with the Welsh to the entrance of the wood. For he had in mind that if he found Robert Bruce there he would either kill him or carry him off captive. But when he had come thither, Robert himself came suddenly out of his hiding-place in the wood, and the said Henry seeing that he could not resist the multitude of Scots, turned his horse with the intention of regaining his companions; but Robert opposed him and struck him on the head with an axe that he carried in his hand. His squire, trying to protect or rescue his lord, was overwhelmed by the Scots. This was the beginning of their troubles! . . .

[*The next day*]

The Earl of Gloucester counselled the king not to go forth to battle that day, but to rest on account of the feast, and let his army recuperate as much as possible. But the king spurned the earl's advice, and, growing very heated with him, charged him with treachery and deceit. 'Today,' said the earl, 'it will be clear that I am neither a traitor nor a liar,' and at once prepared himself for battle. Meanwhile Robert Bruce marshalled his men for battle and equipped his allies, gave them bread and wine, and cheered them as best he could; when he learned that the English line had occupied the field he led his whole army out from the wood. About forty thousand men he brought with him, and split them into three divisions; and not one of them was on horseback, but each was furnished with light armour, not easily penetrable by a sword. They had axes at their sides and carried lances in their hands. They advanced like a thick-set hedge, and such a phalanx could not easily be broken. When the situation was such that the two sides must meet, James Douglas, who commanded the first phalanx of the Scots, vigorously attacked the Earl of Gloucester's line. The earl withstood him manfully, once and again penetrated their wedge, and would have been victorious if he had had faithful companions. But look! At a sudden rush of Scots, the earl's horse is killed and the earl rolls to the ground. Lacking defenders, and borne down by the weight of his body-armour he could not easily arise, and of the five hundred cavalry whom he had led to battle at his own expense, he almost alone was killed. For when they saw their lord unhorsed, they stood astonished and brought him no aid. Accursed be the chivalry whose courage fails in the hour of greatest need!

Alas! Twenty armed knights could have saved the earl, but among some five hundred, there was not found one. May the Lord confound them! . . .

Giles de Argentine, a fighting soldier and very expert in the art of war, while in command of the king's rein, watched the fate of the earl, hurried up in eager anxiety to help him, but could not. Yet he did what he could, and fell together with the earl, thinking it more honourable to perish with so great a man than to escape death by flight; for those who fall in battle for their country are known to live in everlasting glory. On the same day Robert de Clifford, Payn Tibetot [Pain Tiptoft], William Marshal, famous, powerful, and active knights, were overcome by the Scots and died in the field.

When those who were with our king saw that the earl's line was broken and his men ready to run, they said that it would be dangerous to tarry longer and safer for the king to retreat. At these remarks the king quitted the field, and hastened towards the castle. Moreover when the royal standard was seen to depart, the whole army quickly dispersed. Two hundred knights and more, who had neither drawn their swords nor even struck a blow, were reduced to flight.

O famous race unconquered through the ages, why do you, who used to conquer knights, flee from mere footmen? At Berwick, Dunbar, and Falkirk you carried off the victory, and now you flee from the infantry of the Scots. But whatever others may say, the land of the Lord was not with you. Thus was Ben-hadad, a most powerful King of Syria, put to flight by the footmen of the princes of Samaria.

Vita Edwardi Secundi, ed. N. Denholm Young, London, 1957.

The Scots Prepare for Battle

The Lanercost Chronicler has the following . . .

On the morrow – an evil, miserable and calamitous day for the English – when both sides had made themselves ready for battle, the English archers were thrown forward before the line, and the Scottish archers engaged them, a few being killed and wounded on either side; but the King of England's archers quickly put the others to flight. Now when the two armies had approached very near each other, all the Scots fell on their knees to repeat *Pater noster*, commending themselves to God and seeking help from heaven; after which they advanced boldly against the English. They had so arranged their army that two columns went abreast in advance of the third, so that neither should be in advance of the other; and the third followed, in which was Robert. Of a truth, when both armies engaged each other, and the great horses of the English charged the pikes of the Scots, as it were into a dense forest, there arose a great and terrible crash of spears broken and of destriers wounded to the death; and so they remained without movement for a while. Now the English in the rear could not reach the Scots because the leading division was in the way, nor could they do anything to help themselves, wherefore there was nothing for it but to take to flight. This account I heard from a trustworthy person who was present as eye-witness . . .

[*The Bannockburn itself:*]

Another calamity which befel the English was that, whereas they had shortly before crossed a great ditch called Bannockburn, into which the tide flows, and now wanted to recross it in confusion, many nobles and others fell into it with their horses in the crush, while others escaped with much difficulty, and many were never able to extricate themselves from the ditch; thus Bannockburn was spoken about for many years in English throats.

Chronicle of Lanercost, ed. Sir H. Maxwell, Glasgow, 1909.

Sir Thomas Gray Senior in Trouble Again

Sir Thomas Gray must have wished that he had never heard of Scotland. Left for dead by Wallace in Lanarkshire, he recovered, only to come unstuck at Bannockburn while taking on the nephew of Bruce. Here is his son's account of his father's experiences at the battle.

While the said advanced guard were following this road, Robert Lord de Clifford and Henry de Beaumont, with three hundred men-at-arms, made a circuit upon the other side of the wood towards the castle, keeping the open ground. Thomas Randolph, Earl of Moray, Robert de Brus's nephew, who was leader of the Scottish advanced guard, hearing that his uncle had repulsed the advanced guard of the English on the other side of the wood, thought that he must have his share, and issuing from the wood with his division marched across the open ground towards the two afore-named lords.

Sir Henry de Beaumont called to his men: 'Let us wait a little; let them come on; give them room!'

'Sir,' said Sir Thomas Gray, 'I doubt that whatever you give them now, they will have all too soon.'

'Very well!' exclaimed the said Henry, 'If you are afraid, be off!'

'Sir,' answered the said Thomas, 'it is not from fear that I shall fly this day.' So saying, he spurred in between him [Beaumont] and Sir William Deyncourt, and charged into the thick of the enemy. William was killed, Thomas was taken prisoner, his horse being killed on the pikes, and he himself carried off with them [the Scots] on foot when they marched off, having utterly routed the squadron of the said two lords . . .

The Scots in the wood thought they had done well enough for the day, and were on the point of decamping in order to march during the night into the Lennox, a stronger country, when Sir Alexander de Seton, who was in the service of England and had come thither with the King, secretly left the English army, went to Robert de Brus in the wood, and said to him: 'Sir, this is the time if ever you intend to undertake to reconquer Scotland. The English have lost heart and are discouraged, and expect nothing but a sudden open attack.'

Then he described their condition, and pledged his head, on pain of being hanged and drawn, that if he [Bruce] would attack them on the morrow he would defeat them easily without [much] loss. At whose [Seton's] instigation they [The Scots] resolved to fight, and at sunrise on the morrow marched out of the wood in three divisions of infantry. They directed their course boldly upon the English army, which had been under arms all night, with their horses bitted. They [the English] mounted in great alarm, for they were not accustomed to dismount to fight on foot; whereas the Scots had taken a lesson from the Flemings, who before that had at Courtrai defeated on foot the power of France. The aforesaid Scots came in line of 'schiltroms' ['hedgehog-like' formations of spearmen], and attacked the English columns, which were jammed together and could not operate against them [the Scots], so direfully were their horses impaled on the pikes. The troops in the English rear fell back upon the ditch of Bannockburn, tumbling one over the other.

Sir Thomas Gray, *Scalacronica*, ed. Sir Herbert Maxwell, Glasgow, 1907.

Bruces in Ireland

*The war didn't stop after Bannockburn. The Bruces raided deep
into Northern England. Edward Bruce, the King's only surviving
brother, led an expeditionary force to Ireland, where he had
himself crowned king at Dundalk. The Book of Howth is an early
16th-century history, which drew on older sources for its account
of Scottish depredations.*

1315

The same year the said Scots, not contented with their own
territories, animated with too much pride, did invade the north
parts of Ireland. At Clondome did land fighting knights skilful in the
wars, that is to say, Lord Edward de Bruce, brother to Robert the
King of Scots, and with him the Earl of Morres, John de Ventythe,
John Steywarde, Sir John Campbell, Thomas Randoll, Fergus de
Andersane, John de Bossco, and John Bysset. A'Ultagh took their
part, and did repulse the Lord Thomas de Mandevelly and others,
faithful subjects.

From their own land the Scots did enter first into Ireland about
Augustine's day, and the Englishmen did meet them in the month of
May by Cragfergus, betwixt whom, by the Bande, the first field was
fought, where the Earl of Ulster was taken, and William de Burgo,
John Stantone, and many others was killed of the English side; and
the Scots wan the second field at Kellys in Mithe, where Roger
Mortymer with all his followers fled. The third conflict was at
Sketheres by Ardstoll, upon the morrow in the Conversion of St
Paul; the Englishmen fled, and the Scots had the over-hand. And the
said Edward de la Bruse, a little after the feast of Philip and James,
was crowned King of Ireland, and there took the Green Castle, and
put his ward there . . .

At Saint Peter's day the Scots came to Dundalke and burnt and
spoiled the town, and killed of the men of the town, and burned a
great part of Uryell, and came to Saint Mary's church in Arde, that
was full of men, women, and children, and burnt the church and all
that was in it . . .

Also shortly after there came news to Dublin that Robert Brusse,
King of Scotland, came into Ireland to aid his brother Edward Le
Bruce, and besieged the castle of Knockefergus, and destroyed St
Patrick's church of Doune and divers other abbeys, as well monks as
canons and friars . . .

1317

And after came a marvellous plague unto Ulster upon the Scots, which did prey and did much exceeding hurt in Ireland, and for a very vengeance did eat flesh in Lent without need. Therefore God sent a great plague upon them, which was that one did eat another; so that of 10 thousand there remained but a few, whereby may be understanded the wrath and displeasure of God. Also it was spoken for truth that certain of the said malefactors was so famished with hunger that they pulled out the dead bodies out of the earth, and did boil them and eat them, and the women for hunger did eat their children . . .

1318

. . . and the Englishmen, and John Mapas did enter in the foremost of the said battle, and the said John Mapas manfully did kill the said [Edward] Bruce very honorably, whose body was found dead, lying upon the said body of Bruce. And the Scots was slain to the number of 12 thousand, and very few more of them did escape.

The battle was fought between Done-Dalke and Fagharde; and the said Lord Bremyngham took Edward Bruce's head unto the King of England, for the which he was promised to him the earldom of Louthe, and had the barony de Atrie Dey given to him and to his heirs. And the said Edward his arms, quarters, and heart was sent to Dublin, and other men's quarters was sent to other places.

Calendar of the Carew Manuscripts . . . *Lambeth*, eds J. S. Brewer and W. Bullen, London, 1871.

Description of the Scots

The Bruces still had trouble getting the English regime to recognise their possession of the throne of Scotland. Right up until 1327, two years before his death, Robert Bruce was despatching invasion forces into the North of England. Finally even the belligerent young Edward III had to come to terms with him. The chronicler Jean Le Bel, who joined Edward's campaign to repel the Scots, reported on the Scots' methods.

The Scots are extremely courageous and hardy, and they are very enterprising soldiers. At this time they had very little fear of the English; I do not know if this is still the case. And when they invade the Kingdom of England, their army covers a distance of twenty or twenty-two leagues, whether by day or by night, a feat which would greatly astonish anyone unacquainted with their habits.

To be sure, when they set out on an invasion of England, they are all on horse-back with the exception of the rabble which follows them on foot: knights and squires mounted on good, stout saddle-horses and all their fellow countrymen on small ponies. They take no baggage-train with them on account of the difficult mountains which have to be crossed in these parts. Likewise they take no provision of bread or wine, for that is their custom when they are at war: they are of such sober habits that they can survive for a very long time on half-cooked meat without bread, and on good river water without wine. And so they have no need of cooking pots or pans for they cook their meat in the hide of the beast, even when it has been skinned. They know for certain that they will find cattle in great plenty in the country which is their destination, and so they carry no provisions beyond the large flat stone which each man carries between his saddle and his saddle-cloth, and the double bag of flour which is tied behind. When they have eaten so much of the badly-cooked meat that their stomachs feel weak and feeble, they throw the flat stone into the fire, mix a little flour with water once the stone is heated and make a little cake which resembles a 'beguine's wafer'[1] which they eat to soothe their stomachs. Thus it is no wonder that they cover a greater distance each day than others can, since they are all on horseback, apart from the rabble, and have no baggage-train or other gear with them, as you have heard. So equipped, they invaded the territory mentioned earlier, burned it and laid it waste, and there they found so many cattle that they did not know what to do with them. They numbered more than 3,000 men in armour, knights and squires, mounted on good stout horses and at least 20,000 men, experienced and courageous soldiers, armed with their choice of weapons and mounted on those little ponies. When they dismount they do not tether or groom their horses but let them loose to graze in meadowland or heathland. They had two very good captains for at that time King Robert of Scotland was old and was said to be suffering from epilepsy, and he had appointed as their captains the Earl of Moray, a very noble, worthy and valiant prince whose arms were *argent three cushions gules*, and Sir William Douglas who was considered to be the most courageous and enterprising captain in either country, and his arms were *azure a chief argent with three stars gules thereon*. These two lords were the most outstanding warriors in the whole of the kingdom of Scotland.

[1] The exact sense of *une ovlée de beguine*, the term used by Jehan le Bel, is not known. Since *ovlée* means a communion wafer, it may be that he intends a flat cake, possibly a bannock.

Translated by Professor J. Laidlaw from *Chronique de Jean le Bel*, eds Jules Viard and Eugen Deprez, Paris, 1905.

Bruce's Heart
....

It was from Le Bel that the famous later French chronicler Froissart took his story of James Douglas and the heart of Robert Bruce. Archdeacon Barbour tells the story too. To his version someone has added the words 'now passe thou foorth before as thou wast wont in field to be and I sall follow, or else dee'. This has led to the idea that the Douglas actually threw the heart into the battle. Here is Le Bel's more contemporary report. The heart was eventually buried at Melrose Abbey.

How Sir James Douglas left Scotland to undertake his mission

When spring came, the right time to set out for anyone who wishes to cross the high seas, and Sir James Douglas, that gentle knight, had made appropriate arrangements to carry out the commands given to him, he embarked in Scotland and sailed straight to Sluys in Flanders to enquire whether anyone there was making preparations to journey to the Holy Land of Jerusalem, so that he might travel in better company. He stayed at Sluys for a full twelve days before departing. At no time during those twelve days did he disembark but remained on board and kept great estate, to the sound of trumpets and drums, as if he were the King of Scotland himself. And he had in his company a knight-banneret and six others, some of the most valiant of his countrymen, and at least twenty handsome young squires, the most outstanding he could find in his country, together with the other members of his household. He had a great quantity of silver plate, pots, basins, bowls, goblets, bottles, basins, barrels and the like. Those who wished to go on board were entertained with two sorts of wine and two sorts of spices, provided they were persons of rank.

At last, when he had stayed there for a long time, he heard that the King of Spain was waging war on the King of Granada who was a Saracen, and he decided to go there to put his journey to better use; when he had done his duty there, he would cross the sea to do what was commanded of him. And so he left Sluys and went to Spain, landed at the port of Valencia the Great and went to see the King of Spain who was with the army he had raised to do battle with the King of Granada. The two kings were positioned very close to one another on the frontier between their two countries. A day after Sir

James Douglas arrived, the King of Spain advanced closer to his enemies. The King of Granada also advanced with the result that each king could see the other and all his banners, and they began to deploy their troops in opposing formation. Sir James stationed himself on one of the flanks, the better to do his duty and to display his strength in arms. When he saw all the troops lined up and saw the King's own troop move forward a short distance, he thought that battle was about to be joined. Preferring to be in the van rather in the rear, he spurred forward with all his followers, as far as the King of Granada's troop, thinking that the King of Spain and all his men were following, but he was seriously let down, for they did not advance that day. So Sir James and all his followers were surrounded by the enemy and not one of them escaped with his life. In what happened the Spanish were grievously at fault and their reputation suffered great damage.

Translated by Professor J. Laidlaw from *Chronique de Jean le Bel*, eds Jules Viard and Eugen Deprez, Paris, 1905.

A Cunning Plan

Bruce was succeeded by his young son David I. Scotland was soon struggling for its independence against the claims of Edward Balliol – the displaced heir of John – and the aggressive campaigns of Edward III, who was determined to blot out the humiliations of his father's reign. After the decisive battle of Halidon Hill in 1333 David was forced into exile, leaving a new generation of Scottish patriots to re-take the southern castles put by Balliol into English hands. In 1340 Sir William Douglas and his allies made a bold surprise attack on Edinburgh Castle. The English gains were rolled back but warfare was to be endemic between Scotland and England for at least the next 200 years.

So it was that Sir William Douglas devised a feate, and discovered his intencion to his companions, to the erle Patris, to Sir Robert Fresyell [Fraser], and to Alexander Ramsay; and all they agreed togider. Than they toke a ii.C. [200] of the wilde Scottes [Highlanders], and entered into the sea, and made provision of otes, mele, coles [oats, meal and coals], and wood; and so peaceably they arrived at a port, nere to the castell of Edenborowe. And in the night they armed them, and toke a 10 or 12 of their company, suche as they did trust best, and dide disguise them in poore torne cotes and hattes, like poore men of the contrey; and charged 12 small horses with sackes, some with otes, some with whete mele, and some with coles; and they dide set all their company in a busshment [in ambush] in an old distroyed abbey therby, nere to the fote of the hill. And wham the day began to appear, covertly armed as they were, they went up the hill with their marchandise. And whan they were in the midde way, Sir William Douglas and Sir Symode Frestll [Simon Fraser] disguised as they were, went a litell before, and came to the porter, and said 'Sir, in gret fere we have brought hither oates and whetemele; and if ye have any nede therof, we woll sell it to you fode chepe.' 'Mary', said the porter, 'and we have nede thereof; but it is so erly, that I darre nat awake the captaine nor his stuarde [steward]; but let them come in, and I shall opin the utter gate': and so they all entred into the gate of the bailes; Sir Willam Douglas sawe well how the porter had the keys in his handes of the great gate of the castell.

Than whan the firste gate was opinned, as ye have harde, their horses with cariages entred in; and the two that came last, laden with coles, they made them to fall downe on the grounsill of the gate, to the intent that the gate schulde nat be closed againe. And than they toke the porter, and slewe him so peaceably that he never spake worde. Than they toke the great keys, and opinned the castell gate; than Sir William Duglas blewe a horne, and did cast away their torne cotes, and layed all the other sackes overthwarte the gate, to the intent that it shulde nat be shutte againe. And whan they of the busshment [hidden force] harde the horne, in all hast they might they mounted the hill. Than the watchman of the castell, with noise of the horne, awoke, and sawe how the peple wer comming all armed to the castell warde. Than he blewe his horne, and cried, 'Treason, treason; sirs arise, and arme you shortly, for yonder be men of armes aprochinge to your fortresse.' Than every man arose, and armed them, and came to the gate; but Sir Willam Douglas and his 12 companions defended so the gate, that they coude nat close it; and so by great valiantnesse they kept thentre [the entry] opin, till their busshment [forces in hiding] came. They within defended the castell as well as they might, and hurt divers of them without; but Sir William and the Scottes did so moch that they conquered the fortresse, and all the Englisshmen within slaine, excepte the captaine and sixe other squires.

The Chronicle of Froissart, trans. Sir John Bourchier Lord Berners, ed. W. E. Hanley, London, 1901.

Stewart Scotland

David II was ultimately successful in fighting off the English and Balliol threats to his kingship, but he failed in one of the basic duties of a king – producing children. It was therefore the heirs of his sister Marjorie Bruce and her husband Walter the Stewart who inherited the throne, providing Scotland with its most famous dynasty: The Stewarts. Scottish medieval history has been characterised as turbulent and violent, when in fact, compared to other medieval kingdoms (especially to England which saw violent civil wars over a long period), it was on the whole well-governed and peaceful. As a result, wars and spectacular acts of violence attracted a great deal of attention from contemporary observers – and are duly mentioned here. It was also an age when Scotland experienced a boom in the arts: poetry, learning, and history writing, as well as music and architecture, flourished. Scots were proud of maintaining their separate identity from England in the Wars of Independence and this greatly influenced national identity and self-confidence.

This chapter follows the Stewarts and their descendants down to the fatal battle of Flodden.

'Contempt Cordiale' – Some Problems with the Auld Alliance

In 1371 David Bruce died and was succeeded by Robert Stewart – Robert II. Scotland had its first Stewart king. Border warfare continued and by now a pattern of alliance with France against the English was well in place. The fruits of this alliance were not always sweet. In 1380 a French contingent set foot in Scotland to help take forward the war against England. The results were somewhat embarrassing: so embarrassing that in 1746, in the wake of the Jacobite uprising, someone in London couldn't resist digging them up and producing a translation of this part of Froissart's Chronicles just to show what a rotten combination the French and the Scots made.

In the beginning of May, Sir John de Vien, Admiral of Fraunce, accompanied with a thousande speares of chosen knightes and esquiers, and five hundreth crosbowes, with harnesse to arme a thousande Scottes, landed in Scotland, and at the last arrived at

Edenbourgh, which is the chefest towne in Scotland. And assone as
the Erle Douglas, and the Erle Moret knewe of their coming, they
went to the haven, and met them, and received them right lovingly:
saying that they were right welcom into that countrie. And at that
time the king of Scottes was in the wilde Scottishe [the Highlands].
But it was shewed these knightes, that the King would be there
shortly, wherewith they were content, and so they were lodged
thereaboutes in the villages. For Edenbourgh though the King kept
therein his chiefe residence, yet it is not like Paris, nor yet like
Turney, nor Valenciens. For in al the towne there is not foure
thousand houses. Therefore these lordes and knightes were lodged
in villages about, as well as they might be in that countrie.

When knowledge came into the realme of Scotlande, that a greate
number of men of armes of Fraunce were come into their countrie:
some thereat did murmure and grudge, and sayde: Who the Devill
hath sente for them? What do they here? Cannot we mainteine our
warre with England without their helpe?

We shall do no good as long as they be with us, and so let them be
tolde, that they may returne againe. And say unto them, that we be
strong enough in Scotlande to mainteine our warre without them,
and therefore we will none of their companie, they understand not
us, nor we them. They will quickly rise and eate up all that ever we
have in this countrie. They will do us more despight and dammage,
then though the Englishemen fought with us. For if the Englishemen
brenne [burn] our houses, we care little therefore, for we may soone
make them againe cheape inough, for in three dayes we will make
them againe, if we may get foure or five stakes, and a few bowes to
cover them.

This was the communication of the Scottes at the comming of the
Frenche Men, for they set nothing by them, but hated and spake
shamefully, and vilanously of them, like to rude people without all
humanitie. And all thinges considered (sayth Froissart) it was too
great an armie of so many noble men to come into Scotland. For 20
or 30 knightes of Fraunce had bene better then all that number of a
thousand, and the cause is, that in Scotland ye shall find lightly no
man of honour or nobilitie, neyther that knoweth what belongeth to
a gentleman. They are like wilde and savage people, they covet to be
acquainted with no straunger, and they are full of envy at the
prosperous estate of others, and they are ever in feare to lose that
they have; for it is a poore countrie. And when the Englishemen
make any roade or voyage into the land, they are ever compelled to

have their victualles folowe them: for in Scotland they shall finde nothing. Neither is there in Scotland iron to shoe their horses, nor leather to make harnesse for their horse, as saddels, bridels, &c. But they have all these things readie made out of Flaundrys. And when that provision fayleth, then is there none to get in that countrie.

When the barons and knightes of Fraunce, who were wont to finde faire hosteryes, halles hanged, and goodly gastelles, and soft beddes to rest in, sawe themselves in that necessitie: They began to smile, and saide to the Lorde Admirall, Sir this is a pleasant journey, we never knewe what beggery was until now, and now we finde it true, our Old Fathers were wont to say: Go your way, and ye live long ye shall finde hard beddes.

The Admirall pacified them as well as he might, and saide: It behoveth us to suffer a little, and to speak fayre, for we be here in daunger, we have a great long way to go, and by England we can not returne, therefore let us quietly take in good worth that we finde . . .

Then divers knightes and squires had passage, and returned without either horse or harness, cursing the day that ever they came into Scotlande, saying that there were never men that had so hard a voyage, wishing that the French King had peace with Englande one year or two, and so both Kings together to go into Scotlande, utterly to destroy that realme forever, for they sayd they never sawe so evil people, nor so false, nor more soolfish people in feates of war.

A Parallel of Times and Events, London, 1746.

The Wolf of Badenoch

In 1390, Robert II was succeeded by the eldest of his three adult sons from his first marriage, John, Earl of Carrick. Considering that John was an unlucky name for a king of Scots (after John Balliol), he changed his name to Robert, and succeeded as Robert III. Auspicious name or not, he was to prove in some ways a 'lame duck' monarch. Disabled by the kick of a horse, he was twice pushed aside by his more vigorous brother Robert, Duke of Albany. At the same time his youngest brother, Lord Alexander Stewart, known as the 'Wolf of Badenoch', was successfully defending Stewart power in the Gaelic north where he had adapted himself successfully to local ways – much to the horror of essentially lowland lords and prelates who had staked claims there, only to find they had to recognise the power of Alexander and his Highland warriors.

The Moray chronicler who wrote this little note of memorable
events was no doubt a churchman, one of those who probably
suffered most from the depredations of the Wolf and his ilk. He
records not only the various outrages, such as the burning of Elgin
Cathedral, but also the strange episode of the clan fight on the
Inch of Perth between Clan Hay and the unidentified 'Clan
Qwhwle'. In his estimation the world is going to hell in a handcart
and Scotland is one great 'robbery'. It wasn't really all that bad,
except for short periods of civil disorder, but to a cleric in the
north with no band of armed men to defend him, it could be a
truly terrifying place.

Some memorable events

For a permanent remembrance of the event. It is to be known that
in the year 1390 of the Lord in the month of April, Robert
Stewart, King of Scotland, died at Dundonald and was buried at
Scone. To whom succeeded his elder son the earl of Carrick, called
Robert, crowned at Scone the Sunday following, on the vigil of the
Assumption of the Blessed Mary, and on the following day
Annabella his wife was crowned queen by Walter Trail, Bishop of St
Andrews.

In that year before the said coronation, the peoples of the lord
Alexander Stewart, son of the late king, at the end of the month of
May burnt the town of Forres and the choir of the church of St
Laurence and the manor of the Archdeacon below the town, and
during the month of June following, on the feast of the Blessed
Botulph, abbot, the same lord Alexander being present, they burnt
the entire town of Elgin and the church of St Giles therein, the
Maison Dieu [hospital] near Elgin, eighteen noble and beautiful
mansions of the canons and chaplains, and what is more bitterly to
be deplored, the noble and comely church of Moray, mirror of the
nation and adornment of the kingdom, together with all the books
and papers of the nation's goods preserved therein.

And after these things the same lord Alexander Stewart, by a
special commission of the lord Bishop Alexander Bur, was in the
presence of the lord the King, the Earl of Fife, the lords William
Keith, Malcolm Drummond, lord of Mar, and the lord Thomas
Erskine and many others, at Perth before the door of the Friars
Preachers and afterwards before the high altar, absolved by the Lord
Walter Trail, Bishop of St Andrews, from the sentence of
excommunication on condition that he gave satisfaction to the

church of Moray without delay and that he sent to the Pope for the obtaining of absolution, otherwise he would thereby incur again the previous sentence of excommunication.

It is to be remembered that in the year 1396 of the Lord on the 28th day of September at Perth in the presence of the lord Robert, King of Scotland and the nobles of the realm assembled there for this [purpose], because a firm peace could not be restored between the families Clan Hay and Clan Qwhwle [unidentified], but that murderings and plunderings were being committed hence and thence daily, thirty from each party, without armour of iron, but with bows, axes, swords and knives, came together by arrangement so that one part should kill and destroy the other, and they began the conflict and the entire party of Clan Hay submitted and died on the field except one, and from the other part ten survivors remained.

Also to be remembered, that in the year 1398 on the 28th day of the month of April, the aforesaid lord Robert King of Scotland, in the church of the monastery of St Michael of Scone created and raised the lord David his first-born son, then Earl of Carrick, to be Duke of Rothesay, and the lord Robert, brother of the same lord the King, then Earl of Fife, to be Duke of Albany, and he decorated them and clothed them with cloaks and furred caps solemnly and with other emblems suitable and accustomed to be handed over only to Dukes, during the solemnities of Mass, whilst the lord Walter Trail, Bishop of St Andrews at that time was solemnly celebrating Mass.

In those days there was not law in Scotland but whoever was more powerful oppressed the lesser and made the entire realm one robbery; homicides, plunderings and fire-raisings and therefore the other evils remained unpunished, and outlawed justice lived in exile beyond the boundaries of the kingdom.

Translated by J. Russell from *Registrum Moraviense*, ed. C. Innes, Bannatyne Club, 1837.

Scotland's First University

But Stewart Scotland was not all war and arson. It was a time of cultural flowering, and in 1414 Scotland received the papal privileges confirming the status of its first university: St Andrews. Teaching had started as early as 1410, but only when that vital papal piece of parchment arrived could the new institution truly call itself a university. Up to this point Scots had to go abroad, even for their first degrees. Often this had meant going to Oxford or Cambridge – difficult if Scotland and England were at war.

Scots still tended to go abroad for higher degrees but now at least they had caught up a little with their neighbours. England, for example, had two universities from the 13th century onwards.

Walter Bower, the Abbot of Inchcolm and writer of the Scoticronicon, *was one of the first graduates of St Andrews. Bower was very proud of his university education, which he felt made him a better historian. This is his account of the rejoicing at the receiving of the privileges.*

In the previous year (namely 1410) after Whitsunday an institution of higher learning of university standing made a start in the city of St Andrew of Kilrymont in Scotland when Henry de Wardlaw was the bishop of St Andrews and James Biset was the prior there. Master Laurence de Lindores (a great theologian and a man of respected life-style) was the first to begin lecturing there on the fourth book of the *Sentences*, Master Richard Cornell (a doctor of canon law and archdeacon of Lothian) on decrees, and Sir John Litstar (a licentiate in decrees and canon of St Andrews) [a man of great knowledge of the religious life and of distinguished life-style] in the same faculty in the mornings. Subsequently Master John Scheves official of St Andrews and Master William Stephenson (who was later bishop of Dunblane) lectured in the same faculty, and Master John Gill, Master William Fowlis and Master William Croyser in philosophy and logic.

They continued their lectures for two and a half years before the confirmation of the privileges [of the university]. At last in 1413 on 3 February (that is the morrow of the Purification of Our Lady, a Saturday, dominical letter F) the bearer of the privileges, Henry de Ogilvie MA, arrived in the city of St Andrews. On his happy arrival a peal of all the [bells of the] city's churches was sounded. The next day, that is the following Sunday, at the ninth hour there was a formal meeting of all the clergy in the refectory (which had been specially fitted up for the occasion) when the bulls of privileges were presented to the lord bishop as chancellor of this gracious university. When the bulls had been read out before everybody, the clergy and convent processed to the high altar singing the *Te Deum laudamus* in harmonious voice. When this had been sung and everyone was on bended knee, the bishop of Ross pronounced the versicle of the Holy Spirit and the collect *Deus qui corda*. They spent the rest of this day in boundless merry-making and kept large bonfires burning in the streets and open spaces of the city while drinking wine in celebration. It was decided moreover to hold a solemn procession on the following Tuesday so as to celebrate the feast of the arrival of the privileges along with the feast of the arrival of the relics. Who can easily give an account of the character of that procession, the sweet-sounding praise of the clergy, the rejoicings of the people, the pealing of bells, the sounds of organs? On that day the prior celebrated a high mass of the Holy Spirit, the bishop of Ross preached a sermon to the clergy, and the beadle counted four hundred clergy besides lesser clerks and young monks taking part in this procession for the glory of God and the praise and honour of the [new] university, together with an astonishing crowd of people.

Walter Bower, *Scotichronicon*, viii, ed. D. E. R. Watt, Aberdeen, 1987.

The Battle of Baugé

Scotland's cultural and military connections with France led to Scots interventions in the Hundred Years War, in which the French struggled to defend their independence against English claims to their crown. In 1421, the Scottish King James I was a prisoner of the English. Paris had been taken by Henry V of England. These were dark days for the forces of the auld alliance, when suddenly a brilliant Scots success in France brought a ray of hope for both sides. Walter Bower includes this account in his Scotichronicon.

In 1421 Henry V king of England and despoiler of France returned to England after the conquest of Normandy to gather a new army with the intention of subjecting all of France to his rule. His brother Sir Thomas duke of Clarence was left behind as his regent. In the hope of winning a great name for himself in the absence of the king of England his brother the duke assembled his troops to the number of 10,000 men, and after advancing to the castle of Baugé in Anjou he determined to besiege it. On hearing this the earl of Buchan wished to engage him in battle, and in the company of the earl of Wigtown and [a Frenchman] La Hire 'Bussak' and 6,000 men he approached the town of Le Lude which lies four miles from Baugé on Good Friday. His intention was to attend divine service and office there until Easter Monday out of reverence for the passion of Our Lord and the most central Christian communion service of the Eucharist. [Meanwhile both sides had agreed to a truce.] On hearing that the duke of Clarence had withdrawn from Baugé towards Beaufort, the said earl of Buchan settled down there around evening with his men for the night.

In the morning (that is on Easter Saturday) the duke of Clarence moved his army in an unexpected attempt to trick the Scots and to come upon them unprepared. [But their wicked plan was turned against them.] The earl of Buchan [had] feared the clever tricks of his enemies and sent Sir John Stewart knight lord of Darnley his kinsman with a Frenchman the sire de Fontaines and four hundred picked men to scout out the English. After suddenly coming upon the English force, the scouting party withdrew, and as they escaped this way and that the Scots [as a whole] became aware of the arrival of the English [and the retreat of their own men]. They were in a sleepy state at about 3 o'clock in the afternoon, but immediately roused themselves and flew to arms. At once the earl of Buchan despatched his kinsman Robert Stewart of Ralston, a man most active as a fighter, with thirty lightly-armed [archers] whose task was to seek out fords or a crossing of the deep stream at Baugé. As they approached a certain arched and narrow bridge (there being no other crossing), the duke of Clarence arrived with banner unfurled seeking to cross the bridge. The said Robert and his men stood their ground opposite him in manly fashion and obstructed his passage until about a hundred Scots belonging to the retinue of Master Hugh Kennedy who were lodged in a church nearby arrived and offered a major impediment to the passage of the English until, with the greatest difficulty and furious fighting and leaving their horses behind, the duke and his men gained a passage across the bridge on foot and sought the open country near Baugé. The earl of Buchan collected scarcely two hundred men as front-line troops by the sound of his trumpets and attacked him immediately. The duke of Clarence was wounded in the face by the lance of the lord of Swinton [who was the earl's sister's son and a grandson of the governor of Scotland] and met his end after being struck to the ground by the earl of Buchan's mace. Meanwhile the English rushed together in swarms from all directions; they joined the fight, were wounded, taken prisoner killed and put to flight well into the deep darkness of the night.

On the side of the Scots no more than twelve fell, and these from among the common soldiers; from among the French [gentlemen only] two fell, namely Charles le Bouteiller and the brother of the sire de Fontaines. On the English side the dead were Thomas duke of Clarence, the earl of Redesdale, the Lord Ros, Lord Grey of Condor, and others totalling 1617 men. Those captured were the earl of Somerset (taken by the Scot Laurence Vernon who was afterwards a knight), the earl of Huntingdon (taken by the Scottish

knight John Sibbald), Sir Thomas the brother of the said earl of
Somerset – the two were brothers of the Lady Joan [later] queen of
Scots – (taken by [   ]), the Lord Fitz Walter (taken by the Scot
Henry Cunningham) and many others.

On hearing a report of the battle of Baugé at Rome, Pope Martin
is said to have commented as follows: 'Truly the Scots are an
antidote to the English!' [as if to say that the poison of the English
infects those whom it touches, but the Scots lessen the swelling they
have caused]. Hence the saying:

Martin the fifth in office as supreme pontiff says:
'The Scots are well-known as an antidote to the English.'

Walter Bower, *Scotichronicon*, viii, ed. D. E. R. Watt, Aberdeen, 1987.

The Battle of the Herrings

*However, the Scots were not always so lucky. In 1429, the
Constable of Scotland, John Stuart of Darnley, took a leading part
in a Franco-Scottish attack on an English waggon convoy. It was
full of barrels of herrings: the Lent provisions of the English army
besieging Orleans. In command was the redoubtable warrior, Sir
John Falstof (later, apparently, given the William Shakespeare
treatment as Sir John Falstaff). Putting the wagons in a circle and
using them for defences, Falstof saved the day. The French failed
to follow up the determined assault made by the Scots. The
constable and many of his men were killed. This is chronicler John
de Waurin's account of the skirmish.*

The said Fastolf set out from the city of Paris at the beginning of
Lent; and he conducted his men and baggage in good order for
some days as far as a village called Rouvray-en-Beauce where he
lodged; and this village is situated between Jenville and Orleans.

And there came thither some French captains to fight him, who for
a good while before were well aware of his coming, such as Charles
duke of Bourbon, the two marshals of France, the constable of
Scotland and his son, the lord of La Tour, the lord of Chauvigny; the
lord of Graville, sir William d'Albret, the viscount of Thouars, the
bastard of Orleans, sir James de Chabannes, the lord of La Fayette,
Pothon de Saintrailles, La Hire, sir Théaulde de Valpergue and many
other noble men, who all together were from three to four thousand
combatants of good stuff. Of their coming the said English were
informed beforehand by some of their men who were in garrison
thereabouts in the fortresses holding their party, on account of

which news these English, like men full of confidence, put themselves in good order with great diligence, and with their waggons formed a large enclosure in the open fields in which they left two entrances open, and these all together they placed themselves in the manner following, that is to say, the archers guarding those entrances and the men-at-arms very near in the necessary places; and on one of the sides in the strongest place were the merchants, waggoners, pages, and other people with little power of defence, with the horses and mares.

In the way you have heard the English waited for their enemies for the space of full two hours, who came with great tumult and formed themselves in battle array before the said enclosure out of reach of the arrows; and it seemed to them, considering their noble quality and their great number, and that they had only to do with men gathered from many levies, of whom but from five to six hundred were English, natives of the country of England, that they could not escape from their hands, but would be very soon vanquished; nevertheless there were some wise persons who had great doubt lest the contrary should happen to them, especially because the intentions of the said French captains were not well accordant one with the other, for some, especially the Scots, wished to fight on foot, and others wished to remain on horseback.

There were made new knights, by the hand of the lord of La Fayette, Charles de Bourbon and some others; but meanwhile the said constable of Scotland, his son and his men dismounted and then very shortly they went to attack their enemies, some on foot and others on horseback, and were received by them very courageously; and their archers who were very well shielded by their waggons began to shoot very sharply, in such manner that at the onset they made their enemies fall back before them, fully two to three hundred horsemen who had come to fight at one of the entrances of the said enclosure. And there the said constable of Scotland, thinking he was well followed up by the French, was discomfited and slain on the spot, with him died his son and sir William d'Albret, the lord of Orval, the lord of Chasteau-Brun, the lord of Monpipel, sir John de Larget, the lord of Verduisant, the lord of Yvri, the lord of La Greve, sir Anthony de Prully, and full six score gentlemen, and others to the number of five hundred combatants or more, much the greater part of whom were Scots: the other captains seeing this departed thence and went away, flying in great confusion, so that one did not wait for another, and they returned to the places whence they had come.

And the English, filled with very great gladness on account of the fair victory that they had gained with so little loss, praised their Creator aloud, and then, after the dead were despoiled, they refreshed themselves and rested that night in the said village of Rouvray, and, on the next day departing thence sir John Fastolf and all his men, of whom he was supreme captain, took the road towards Orleans, and they and their waggons made such good progress that a few days after, exhibiting great joy, they arrived at the siege, where they were received with great gladness by their people, who, when they knew of their good fortune, heartily praised God for it, making a great noise with trumpets and clarions, and they were also very well refreshed by the victuals which they brought to them: and the said conflict from that day forward was commonly named the battle of the Herrings, and the reason for this name was because a great part of the waggons of the said English were loaded with herrings and other victuals for Lent. For this ill fortune of the French which had thus befallen, king Charles was very sad at heart, seeing that on all sides his affairs turned out contrary to his desire, and continued going on from bad to worse. This battle of the Herrings happened on the eve of Behourdis [the first Sunday in Lent] about three o'clock in the afternoon; and on the side of the English there died, of people of name, but one single man called Besautrau, a very handsome esquire and valiant man in arms, a nephew of sir Simon Morhier, provost of Paris; and there were made knights among the English, Le Gallois Damay lord of Orville, Gerard Rollin, and Louis de Lurieu, a Savoyard. And the said English might be about sixteen hundred combatants of good stuff besides the common people, and the French were six thousand men, all trained and expert in arms; many noble men also were made knights there with the duke of Bourbon, all of whose names I have not been able to learn, except those which follow, that is to say, the lord of Chasteau-Brun and Yvonet de Clichon; and there were no prisoners but one Scot. Thus then as you have heard sir John Fastolf master of the household of the regent arrived gloriously at the siege before Orleans with a great quantity of provisions and other things necessary for those who were at the said siege, the account of which we will leave until it be the time to return to it.

Jean de Waurin, *Collection of the Chronicles and Ancient Histories of Great Britain, now called England*, ed. E. L. C. P. Hardy, London, 1891.

Murder Most Foul
....

*In 1424, after 19 years of English captivity, James I returned to
Scotland. He had scores to settle over the regency of Scotland in
his absence. These involved beheading close members of his own
family. An energetic and determined monarch, he inevitably made
enemies. On the night of 20 February 1437, a group of disaffected
nobles crept into James's residence at the Blackfriars' monastery in
Perth with bloody revenge in mind. John Shirley, an English writer
and translator, gives this version of events which he seems to have
translated from a contemporary Latin account of the murder.*

The king that same time there standing in his night gown, all
unclothed save his shirt, his cap, his comb, his coverchief, his
furred pinsons [slippers], upon the form [bench] and the foot sheet;
so standing afore the chimney playing with the queen, and other
ladies and gentilwomen with her, cast off his night gown for to have
gone to bed. But he hearkened and hard great noise without and
great clattering of harness, and men armed, with great sight of
torches. Than he remembered him and imagined anone that it
should be [the] false traitorous knight, his deedy [deadly] enemy, sir
Robert Grame [Graham]; and suddenly the queen, with all the other
ladies and gentilwomen, ran to the chamber door and found it open;
and they would have shut it bot the lokes [locks] were so blundrid
[broken] that they neither could nor might shut it. The king prayed
them to keep the same door as well as they might and he would do
all his might to keep him to withstand the false malice of his
traitours and enemys, he supposing to have broken the farrementz
[fitments] of the chamber windows, but they were so square and
strongly sowdid [soldered] in the stones with molten lead that they
might not be burst for him, without more and stronger help. For
which cause he was ugly astonished and in his mind could think on
none other succour but start to the chimney and took the tongs of
iron that men righted the fire with in time of need, and under his feet
he mightily burst up a plank of the chamber floor and therwithall
covered him again, and entered adowne low beneath among the
ordure of the privy that was all of hard stone and none window nor
issue therupon, save a litill square hole even at the side of the
bothum [bottom] of the privay, that at the making therof old time
was left open to clense and ferme [firm] the said privy, by the which
the king might well [have] escaped, but he made to let stop it well 3
dayes afore hand [beforehand] with stone, because that when he

played there at the pawme, [palm – a ball-game] the balls that he played with oft ran in at that fowle hole, for there was ordained without a faire playing place for the king.

And so there [was] for the king nether resource nor remedy, but there he must abide, alas the while! The traitours without laid at the chamber doors and at the privy door also, with saws, with levers, and with axes, that at the last they break up all and entered, because the doors were not fast shut, with swords, axes, glaves, bills, and other terribill and ferefull weapons. Amongs the great press of the which tratours, there was a faire lady sore hurt in the back, and other gentilwemen hurt and sore wounded. With the which the ladies and all the wemen made a sorowfull skrye [scream], and ran away for the hideous fear of these boistous [violent] and merciless men of arms. The traitours furiously passed forth into the chambers and found the queen so dismayed and abashed of that horribill and fearfull gouvernance that she could neither speak nor withdraw her; and as she stood there so astonished as a creature that had lost her kindly reason, one of the traitours wounded her full villainously and would have slain her, had not one of sir Robert Grames sons, that thus spoke to him and said, 'What will ye do, for shame of your self! to the queen? She is bot a woman; let us go and fetch the king'. And then, not witing [knowing] well what she did or should do for that fearfull and terribill affray, fled in her kirtle, her mantle hanging about her; the other ladies in a corner of the chamber crying and weeping all distraught, made a piteous and lamentable noise with full heavy loking and chere [looks and countenance].

And there the traitours sought the king in all the chamber about, in the withdrawing chambers, in the litters, under the presses [cupboards], the forms [benches], the chairs, and all other places, but long they busily sought the king, but they could not find him, for they nether knew nor remembered the privy. The king, hearing of long time no noise nor stirring of the traitours, wende [believed] and deemed that they had all be gone, cryed to the wemen that they should come with sheets, and draw him up out of that uncleane place of the privy. The wemen at his calling came fast to the privy door that was not shut, and so they opened it with labour; and as they were about toward to help up the king, one of the ladies, called Elizabeth Douglas, fell into the privy to the king. Therwith one of the said traitours, called Robert [sic] Chamber, supposed verily sith [since] they could not find in none of all the said chambers the king, that he of necessity had hid him in the privy; and therefore he said

to his delawes [co-conspirators], 'Sirs,' quoth he, 'whereto stand we
thus idle, and lose our time, as for the cause that we be come for
hither? Come forth with me and I shall readily tell you where the
king is.' For the same Thomas Chamber [sic] had been before right
familiar with the king in all places, and therefore knew he well all
the privy corners of the chambers; and so he went forth straight to
the same privy where the king was, and perceived well an saw how
a plank of the floor was broken up, and lifted it up and with a torch
looked in, and saw the king there and a woman with him. Saying to
his fellows, 'Sirs, the spouse is found on wherefore we [have] been
come, and all this night have carolled here.' Therwithall, one of the
said tyrants and traitours, called sir John Hall, descended down to
the king, with a great knife in his hand; and the king, doubting him
sore of his life, caught him mightily by the shoulders and with full
great violence cast him under his feet, for the king was of his person
and stature a man right manly strong. And seeing [this], another of
that Hall's brethren that the king had the better of him, went down
into the privy also for to destroy the king; and anon as he was there
descended, the king caught him manly by the neck and cast him
above that other, and so he defouled them both under him that all a
long month after, men might see how strongly the king had held
them by the throats, and greatly the king struggled with them for to
have bereaved them [of] their knives, by the which labour his hands
were all forkute [cut]. But and the king had been in any wise armed
he might well have escaped their malice by the length of his fighting
with those 2 false traitours; for if the king might any while longer
have saved himself, his servants and much other people of the town
by some fortune should have had some knowledge thereof, and so
have come to his succour [and] help. But, alas the while, it will not
be! Fortune was to him adverse as in preserving of his life any
longer.

Therwithall that odious and false traitour, sir Robert Grame,
seeing the king laboured so sore with those two false traitours,
which he had cast under his feet, and that he wax [grew] faint and
weary, and that he was weaponless, the more pity was, descending
down also into the privy to the king, with an horribill and mortall
weapon in his hand. And then the king cried him mercy, 'Thou cruel
tyrant,' quoth Grame to him, 'thou hadest never mercy of lords
borne of thy blood, nor of none other gentilman that came in thy
danger, therefore no mercy shalt thou have here.' Thane said the
king, 'I beseech thee that, for the salvation of my soul, ye will let me

have a confessor.' Quoth the said Grame, 'Thou shalt never have other confessor but this same sword.' And therwithall he smote him through the body, and therwithall the good king fell down and lamentably with a piteous voice he cried him oft mercy, and behight [promised] to give him his kingdom and much other good to save his life. And then the said Grame, seeing his king and sovereign lord unfortuned with so much disease [distress], anguish, and sorrow, would have so lived and done him no more harm. The other traitors above, perceiving that, said onto the said sir Robert, 'We behote [promise] thee faithfully, but [that] if thou flee him or thou depart, thou shalt die for him on our hands soon doubtless;' and then the said sir Robert with the other two that descended first down fell upon that noble prince, and in full horribill and cruell wise they murdered him. Alas for sorrow, that so unmeasurably cruelty and vengeance should be done to that worthy prince, for it was reported by true persons that saw him dead, that he had sixteen deadly wounds in his breast, withouten many and other in diverse places of his body.

John Shirley, *Life and Death of King James I of Scotland*, ed. Joseph Stevenson, Maitland Club, 1837.

Thunderstruck

Chronicler Walter Bower was not only interested in history, but in all branches of knowledge, particularly as they fitted in with the 'Queen of the Sciences': theology. Here Bower uses a shocking but improving tale of impiety to talk about the nature of thunder as he understood it. The story seems to date to just before 1415 and illustrates how blasphemers could come to a sticky end.

The chance now arises of saying a little about thunder, because we have often made mention of it in our book, and because it is a subtle matter in its motion, yet according to the philosophers is nothing other than the result of the force of the winds drawing into the sky waters which are thickened into clouds. Enclosed in these the winds try to break out, and with a great crash dash the clouds to pieces and throw out a great flame. Thus the noise of the clouds and winds is thunder. The flame sent forth is lightning. This is so penetrative when it touches anything because it is much more precise than the flame we know and because it is driven by the great force of the winds from the north, whence it at times immediately knocks down and kills what it touches by the force of nature, and sometimes knocks down and burns up things by the incomprehensible will of God for reasons known only to himself, so that howsoever it happens, God's judgement is to be feared. On this it is said: 'Thick clouds came out of the radiance before him, hailstones and glowing coals. The Lord thundered from the heavens and the voice of the Most High spoke out'. And this was not unreasonable, as you know, since he wants us to respect him as our Lord; but what is written is true of many people: 'There is no fear of God before their eyes.'

What I add to this I have learnt from various trustworthy men, especially from the venerable man sir Richard Mongal, prior of the monastery at Dunfermline, a man undoubtedly devoted to the religious life, who piously with the permission of his superior [sir William de St Andrews the abbot] ended his life while on pilgrimage to Santiago de Compostela. For he said that he knew personally those women who one summer, when there was a great dearth of food in the kingdom, got together in a group of three or four from the town of Dunfermline to go down to the shore at Limekilns to gather seaweed, shell-fish and small fish. I do not recall whether it was when they were going or coming back, but it happened that following the gloom caused by a particular cloud which had become very thick above them, a great rainstorm, driven by a certain wind, suddenly descended which immediately soaked them right through to the skin. Then there was a crash of thunder and a flash of lightening appeared at which the poor wretched girls, as if besides themselves, protected themselves by devoutly making the sign of the cross and saying the *Benedicite*. One of them who was more forward, as if she despised all feeling of fear, mocked her companions and with a raised voice said: 'Cristis croice epon my ender endis', which is to say: 'The cross of Christ on my buttocks!' Scarcely has she said it when she was immediately thrown to the ground and by the violence of the lightening, as if by a hammer, dashed to pieces, and nothing of her body remained unburned except her genitals at the front and on the other side the entrance to her anus, which were visibly intact.

Walter Bower, *Scotichronicon*, iv, ed. D. E. R. Watt, Aberdeen, 1994.

The Tournament

On 3 July 1449 James II of Scotland married Mary of Gueldres,
niece of the Duke of Burgundy, a lady from one of the most
powerful and cultured courts in Europe. In celebration of such a
brilliant marriage, lavish festivities were held. One of the high
points was a tournament at Stirling between Scots, Burgundian
and Flemish knights. The Douglases, one of the most renowned
warrior families in Scotland, prepared to take on James and Simon
de Lalain, two very famous Flemish knights, and Hervé de
Meriadet, lord of Longueville (called Méliades below). The reporter
was the Burgundian chronicler, Mathieu d'Escouchy, castellan of
Péronne. He obviously had some problems understanding the Scots
names – the 'Lord of Haguet' was probably Sir John Ross of
Hawkhead, another prominent knight.

Very soon afterwards a trumpet sounded three times, and it was
commanded in the king's name that each of the opposing sides
should do its duty. At that the three Burgundian knights left their
tents, each of them most splendidly armed, clad in their coats of mail
and carrying the four weapons mentioned earlier. They began to
march purposefully towards their opponents who likewise came to
meet them with great noise and pomp. Thereupon those on the
Burgundian side, as they had previously agreed, threw their lances
high in the air behind them as they drew closer, and took their axes,
thinking to make better use of them than of their lances. When they
had done this, Sir James Douglas stepped in front of his companions
and strode forward proudly, intending to be the first to attack. Then
Hervey de Méliades, full of boldness and determination, came to
meet him. Méliades kept his visor up throughout this passage at
arms. He was struck on the arm by the first attack of the Scotsman's
lance, and his coat of mail was torn, but that caused him small hurt.
Very quickly he advanced towards his opponent and struck his
helmet with a savage blow from his axe, making him stagger, and
immediately afterwards struck a second blow which was so hard
and heavy that it brought him to the ground. Thereupon he used his
axe to strike Douglas's helmet several more times with such stout
blows that he thought that he had nothing more to fear from him
that day. Méliades, though of medium height, was nonetheless very
strong and had the reputation of being the most skilful soldier there
had been in the Duke of Burgundy's household for many a long year:
he was a man of great strength for his size, whether in combat or

other duties; moreover, he was courageous and had great experience of warfare.

When he saw himself rid of his opponent and thought that he had got the better of him, he looked towards his companions, who on their side were fighting valiantly and faced great odds, especially Messire Jacques de Lalain, for Sir John Douglas, whom he had challenged, was a very doughty and valiant knight. Douglas had attacked him strongly, causing him such difficulties that, of the three weapons he had left after throwing down his lance, he had lost two, his axe and his dagger. He had only his sword left, with which he was defending himself, and was in great danger because his adversary was pressing him very hard.

On the other side Messire Simon de Lalain and the Lord of Haguet were joined in fierce combat and Messire Simon was beginning to gain the upper hand. Thereupon Méliades, seeing the situation, and knowing that the rules of the combat allowed him to do so, went to the aid of his companions. But, when he was half way there, he took care to look round and saw that his opponent had got to his feet and was coming back to the attack. He turned to face him, as he had done previously, and brought him to the ground once more with a heavy blow of his axe, and with his fist aimed several blows at his behind.

In fact it was open to him to hit Douglas in the body with the axe from below, but his noble spirit would not allow that. Then, as he had done before, Méliades began to march towards his companions to come to their aid. But, when he was very close, and, as it appeared, wished to join the fight, the king threw down his staff. Immediately all the combatants were held and made to stop by the guards to whom that task was assigned. However, after Méliades was in the hands of these guards, his opponent who had got up for a second time, came up and tried to strike him in the face, which caused the king great displeasure. Furthermore, during these passages at arms, two of the servants of Sir James Douglas, when they saw him brought to the ground, jumped over the lists to come to his aid. But the king and the members of his Council shouted orders that they should be captured. When they heard that, they fled, making their escape as best they could.

Translated by Professor J. Laidlaw from Mathieu de Escouchy, 'Chroniques de Mathieu de Coussy', in *Collection des chroniques nationales françaises . . . avec notes et éclaircissements, par J. A. Buchon*, vols 35-36, Paris, 1826-27.

Murder Most Royal

We have already met the Sir James Douglas who carried Bruce's heart to Spain. The Douglases became one of the most important noble families in Scotland, so important that sometimes the monarchy felt threatened by them. Sometime prior to June 1452, William, 8th Earl of Douglas made a bond with the Earls of Crawford and Ross to secure Douglas interests in the north. This was a matter of disquiet and distaste to James II, the king 'that had the fyer mark in his face'. He called a special meeting with Douglas, inviting him to supper in Stirling Castle to discuss breaking off his agreement with the other earls. The author of 'Ane schort memoriale of the scottis corniklis for addicion', perhaps a monk of Paisley Abbey, has this contemporary record of events.

That same year Erll william of douglas wes slane in the castell of
That same year William Earl of Douglas was slain in Stirling Castle by

striuling be king James the second that had the fyre mark in his face.
King James the second who had the fiery mark on his face.

The forsaid king James send owt of Stirling with William Lawder' of
King James sent from Stirling with William Lauder of

Haltoun a speciale assouerans and respite under his preve sele and
Haltoun a special assurance and safe conduct under his privy seal,

subscriut with his awne hand and all the lordis that war with the king
signed with his own hand. All the Lords that were with the King

that time gaf bodely aithis to kepe that respite & assouerance and
at that time gave personal oaths to keep the safe-conduct and each

subscriuit ilk man with thair awne hand and all the lordis that war'
man signed in his own hand. All of them were bound by it that

with the king that time war' oblist supposs the king wald brek the
supposing the King should break the safe conduct, they should use all

band forsaid that thai suld let it at their powere. This beand done the
their powers to resist. This being done,

forsaid willam of lawder of haltoun passit to the forsaid erll william
William of Lauder of Haltoun went to William

of douglas and brocht him to striuling to the king on the monunday
Earl of Douglas and brought him to Stirling to the King on the Monday

befor' fastrennis evyn that was the xxj day of februare and this samyn
before Shrove Tuesday (the 21st of February). That day he went to the

monunday he passit to the castell and spak with the king that tuke
castle and spoke with the King, who got on well with him, to all

richt wele with him be apperans and callit him on the morne to the
appearances, and invited him the next day to dinner

dynere & to the supper and he come and dynit and sowpit and thai
and supper. He came and dined and drank. However it was said that

said their was a band betuix the said erll of dowglass and the erll of
there was a bond signed [against the king] between the Earl of Douglas

ross & the erll of craufurd and efter supper' at sevyne houris the king
and the Earl of Ross and the Earl of Crawford. After supper, at seven

then beand in the Inner' chalmer & the said erll he chargit him to
o'clock, when the King was in the inner chamber with the Earl, he charged

breke the forsaid band he said he mycht nocht nor wald not. Than the
him to break that bond. The Earl said he could not. Then the

king said falss tratour sen yow will nocht I sall and stert sodanly till
King said 'False traitor since you will not, I shall!' and attacked him

him with ane knyf and straik him in at the colere and down in the
suddenly with a knife and struck him in at the collar and down in the

body and thai sayd that patrik gray straik him nixt the king with ane
body. It is said that Patrick Gray struck him after the King with a

poll ax on the hed and strak out his harnes and syne the gentillis that
poleaxe on the head and struck out his brains and then the gentlemen who

war' with the king gaf thaim ilkane a straik or twa with knyffis and
were with the King each gave him a stroke or two with knives. These

thire ar' the names that war' with the king that strake him for he had
are the names of those who were with the King that struck the Earl, for he

xxvj woundis In the first sir alex boyd the lord dernelie sir androw
had 26 wounds. In the first Sir Alexander Boyd, the Lord Darnley, Sir

stewart sir william of gremston sir symond of glendonane and the
Andrew Stewart, Sir William of Grimston, Sir Simon of Glendonan and

lord gray
the Lord Gray

The Asloan Manuscript, ed. W. A. Craigie, Scottish Text Society, 1923.

Further Royal Catastrophe

The Stewarts continued their family habit of violent death.

The yere of god 1460 the thrid sonday of August king James the
The year of God 1460 the third Sunday of August King James the

secund with ane great ost was at the siege of Roxburgh and unhappely
second with a great host was at the siege of Roxburgh and unhappily

was slane with ane gun the quhilk brak in the fyring for the quhilk
was slain with a gun, which broke in the firing for the which

was there great dolour throu all Scotland and nevertheless all the
there was great sorrow though all Scotland. Despite this the

lordis that war thar remanit still with the ost and on the Fryday efter
Lords that were there remained with the army and on the Friday after,

richt wysly and manfully wan the forsaid castell and tynt nocht a man
right wisely and manfully they won the forsaid castle and lost not a man

in the winning of it.
in the winning of it.

The Asloan Manuscript, ed. W. A. Craigie, Scottish Text Society, 1923.

James III

*James III was no luckier. His struggles with his nobles led to his
death in mysterious circumstances after the battle of Sauchieburn
in 1488. Adam Abell, an observantine Friar at Jedburgh, born
perhaps around 1475, recorded the events in his chronicle* The
Roit or Quheill of Tyme *[The Circle or Wheel of Time].*

Scots king 104 wes James 3 sone of forsaid James. He wes ane
The 104th Scots king was James III, son of the forsaid James. He was a

dewot man bot he wes gretumlie gewin to carnale plesence, by his
devout man but greatly given to carnal pleasure, despite the advice of his

halie quene and privat counsall of sympill [common] men be the whilk
holy queen. He also took private advice from common men. On this

counsall he destroeit his awne breder [brother] maist necessair to him.
advice he destroyed his own brother who was most necessary to him,

For the herll [earl] of Mar wes slane be counsall of ane trucur [a
for the Earl of Mar was killed on the advice of a rogue called

commoner] callit cochren [Cochrane] and alexander the duke of
Cochrane and Alexander the Duke of

albany wes banest diverss tymes the yere of God 1480 or thare about.
Albany was banished several times in 1480 or thereabout.

The forsaid duke brot the inglis men in Scotland with duke of
This Duke brought the English men into Scotland with the Duke of

glossistir [Gloucester] . . .
Gloucester.

Efter that the yere of god 1480 wes the raid of lawdir [Lauder]
After that in 1480 there was the raid of Lauder where

quhar the king wes tane be the lordis and put in the castell of
the king was taken by the Lords and put in the castle of

edinburgh als cochren [Cochrane] and the laif of his priwat counsall
Edinburgh and Cochrane and the rest of his Privy Council

wes tane and iustifit to be hangit. Suyn [soon] eftir the duke brot the
were taken and condemned to be hanged. Soon after the Duke brought

inglis men to edinburgh and deliverit the king bot the lordis
the English men to Edinburgh and delivered the king but the Lords

conjurators fled in argile. Notwithstanding, soyn eftir the king tuke
conspirators fled into Argyll. Notwithstanding, soon after the King

thame to grace and suyn eftir the duke wes flemyt [exiled] agane to
forgave them and soon after the Duke was banished again to

ingland.
England.

The yere of God 1486 the forsaid duk and the herll [earl] of
In 1486 the Duke and the Earl of

dowgless [Douglas] with the inglis men straik batell on the magdalene
Douglas with the English men gave battle on Mary Magdalen's

day quhare thai wer wincust [vanquished] be the lordis of the west
Day when they were vanquished by the Lords of the west

bordor and mony inglis men wes slane. The erll [Earl] of dougless
border and many Englishmen were killed. The Earl of Douglas

[Douglas] wes tane. The duke wes lattin awa and passit agane to
was taken. The Duke was allowed to escape and went again to

ingland quhare he wes accusit be the king of ingland for the slauchtir
England where he was accused by the King of England for the deaths

of the inglis men. Bot be the help of Johne liddaill, Sir James of
of the English troops but by the help of John Liddell, Sir James

liddallis son, quietlie he stail out of ingland and come in Scotland to
Liddell's son, he secretly stole out of England and came into Scotland to

his broder [brother]. Suyn eftir be dewiouss counsall he wes tane and
his brother. Soon after by devious advice he was taken and

put in the castell of edinburgh. Bot first he slew the lard of
put in Edinburgh Castle, but first he killed his jailer, the laird of

Manerstone his kepar and syne be lynnyng clathis [probably sheets]
Manderston and then by linen cloths

he passit awa downe at ane windo and salit to France and wes
he escaped down at a window and sailed to France and was

graciuslie thare be the king resaifit and mareit ane gret lady of
graciously received there by the King and married a great lady, an heiress,

heretage this duks moder [mother] bot eftirwert unhappelie in iusting
the mother of the present Duke, but afterwards he was unluckily killed in

he wes slane. Than the forsaid Lordis conjurators (his breder slain)
a jousting accident. Then the forsaid Lords conspirators (his brother

thai conspirit agains the king and gaif him batell beside striwiling
killed) conspired against the King and gave battle to him beside Stirling

[Stirling] and thare wes he slane. He wes confessit before with maister
and there he was killed. He made his confession beforehand to master

Johne Yrland [Ireland] proffessor of theologe. He wes berist [buried]
John Ireland, professor of Theology. He was buried

in cambuskynneth [Cambuskenneth] the 29 yere of his ring [reign] of
in Cambus-kenneth in the 29th year of his

God 1489.
reign 1489.

Adam Abell, *The Roit or Quheill of Tyme*, MS. 1746, ff.109r-110r.

The Marriage of the Thistle and the Rose

Under James IV, relations between Scotland and England seemed to take a happier turn with his glorious marriage to Margaret Tudor, daughter of Henry VII and sister of Henry VIII. It was this marriage into the English royal family which was to lead eventually to the Scots succession to the throne of the Tudors in 1603. Few would have forseen this in 1503. John Young, Somerset herald, was a young English official who accompanied the Princess Margaret on her journey to Edinburgh. He took a careful note of all the festivities he witnessed, in a narrative showing the precise concern for ceremonial detail to be expected of a herald. Since this was essentially a report confirming that the English princess was well treated, James IV gets rather pushed into the background at his own marriage.

The king was conveyed to the queens chamber, where she met him at her great chamber door, right honourably accompanied. At the meeting he and she made great reverences the one to the other, his head being bare, and they kissed together, and in likewise kissed the ladies, and others also. And he in especial welcomed the earl of Surrey very heartily.

Then the queen and he went aside and commoned together by long space. She held good manner, and he [was] bare headed during the time, and many courtesies passed. Incontinent [at once] was the bord [table] set and served. They washed their hands in humble reverences, and after, set them down together, where many good devices were rehearsed . . .

The town of Edinbourgh was in many places hanged with tappissery [tapestry], the houses and windows were full of lords, ladies, gentlewomen, and gentlemen, and in the streets war so great multitude, of people without number, that it was a fair thing to see.

The which people war very glad of the coming of the said queen: and in the churches of the said town bells rang for mirth.

The same day the king supped in his chamber, accompanied of many of the part of the said queen within her own. And after that, the king went to see her, and he danced some bass dances. This done, the king took his leave, and bade her good night joyously, and after the same to ychon [each one] also.

The 8th day of the said month every man appointed himself richly, for the honour of the noble marriage. Between 8 and 9 of the clock everychon [everyone] was ready, nobly apparelled; and the ladies above said came richly arrayed, sum in gowns of cloth of gold, the others of crimson velvet and black. Others of satin and of tinsel, of damask, and of camlet of many colours, hoods, chains and collars upon their necks, accompanied of their gentlewomen arrayed honestly their guise, for to hold company to the said queen . . .

A little after, the queen was by the said lords and company brought from her chamber to the church crowned with a very riche crown of gold garnished with pierrery [jewellery] and pearls. She was led on the right hand by the archbishop of York, and on the left hand by the earl of Surrey. Her train was born by the countess of Surrey, a gentleman usher helping her. The said queen was nobly accompanied with her ladies arrayed that is to wit, the said countess of Surrey arrayed in a rich robe, of cloth of gold; the two ladies Nevill, the lady Lille, the lady Stanneley, and the lady Guilleford, in riche apparel; and all the others following had rich collars and chains upon their necks; and good jewels. It was ordered by the said earl of Surrey, that two of the greatest ladies of England going together should take with them two of the greatest ladies of Scotland, and so all four to go together in a row; and so sewingly always two of the best ladies and gentlewomen of England and two of Scotland to go together as before, where they had room so to do: and thus they did daily.

Thus the said queen was conveyed to the said church, and placed near to the font; Mistresse Denton, her mistresse, being always near her; and all her noble company standing in order on the left side of the church. Incontinent [straight away] cam the right reverend father in god my lord the archbishop of Glasgow, accompanied with the prelates, all in pontificals, and other notable folks of the church.

Then the king was brought by a very fair company, consisting of his said brother and of the lords above said, his steward, chamberlain, the constable, and the marischall, with all their staffs of their offices, and other nobles, knights, squires, and gentlemen, richly and honestly arrayed and with good chains. The lord of Hamilton bore his sword before him. His officers of arms were in their coats, and all his nobles stood in order on the right side of the church.

Then the king coming near to the queen, made reverence and she to him very humbly. The king was in a gown of white damask, figured with gold and lined with sarsenet. He had on a jacket with sleeves of crimson satin, the lists [borders] of black velvett, under that same a doublet of cloth of gold, and a pair of scarlet hose. His shirt broided [embroidered] with thread of gold, his bonnet black, with a riche balay [ruby], and his sword about him.

The queen was arrayed in a rich robe, like himself, bordered of crimson velvet, and lined of the self. She had a very riche collar of gold, of pierrery and pearls, round her neck, and the crown upon her head; her hair hanging. Between the said crown and the hairs was a very riche coif hanging down behind the whole length of the body.

Then the noble marriage was performed by the said archbishop of Glasgow; and the archbishop of York, in presence of all, read the bulls of our holy father the Pope of Rome, consenting thereto . . .

At dinner the queen was served before king, with all the honour that might be done, the officers of arms, and the sergeants at arms, proceeding before the meal. On that day sir John Willars was sewar [attendant at the meal], sir Davie Owen carver, and sir Edward Stanneley cupbearer; and with her dined the said archbishop of Glasgow. The chamber in which she dined was richly dressed, and the cloth of estate where she sat, was of clothe of gold very rich.

At the first course, she was served of a wild boars head gilt, within a fair platter, then with a fair piece of brain, and in the third place with a gambon, which were followed by diverse other dishes, to the number of 12, of many sorts, in fair and rich vessel.

Collectanea de Rebus Anglicanis, iv, ed. John Leland, London, 1809.

Flodden

....

In 1513 the glittering Renaissance reign of James IV came to an
abrupt end in a war against his English brother-in-law Henry VIII.
James had the most modern Swiss tactics and an impressive
contingent of artillery but, in the event, both were badly
misapplied. The result was the slaughter of Flodden and the death
of James. This is a contemporary English account, apparently by a
Northumbrian. Curiously, however, it contains no mention of
James's fate. The original communication seems to have been
dispatched before his death was certain. The letters of Thomas
Ruthal, bishop of Durham, reveal his end. He fell near his banner,
struck by an arrow and gashed by a halberd. The corpse was taken
to Berwick.

And as soon as the Scots perceived my said Lords to be within the
danger of their ordenance, they shot sharply their guns which
were very great, and in like manner our party recountered them,
with their ordenance, and notwithstanding that other our artillery
for war could do no good nor advantage to our army because they
were continually going and advancing up toward the said hills and
mountains, yet by the help of God, our guns did so break and
constrain the Scottish great army, that some part of them wer
enforced to come down the said hills toward our army. And my
Lord Hawarde [Howard] conceiving the great power of the Scots,
sent to my said [Lord] of Surrey, his father, and required him to
advance his rerewarde [rearguard] and to join his right wing with his
left wing, for the Scots were of that might that the vawarde
[vanguard] was not of power nor able to encounter them. My said
lords of Surrey perfectly understanding this with all speed and
diligence lustily came forward and joined him to the vawarde, as
afore was required by my said Lord Hawarde, and was glad for
necessity to make of two battalles [divisions] one good battell to
adventure of the said four batelles.

And for so much as the Scots did keep them several in four batelles
therefore my Lord of Surrey and my Lorde Hawarde suddenly were
constrained and enforced to divide their army in other four batelles,
and else it was thought it should have been to their great danger and
jeopardy.

So it was that the Lord Chamberlain of Scotland, being Captain of
the first bataill of the Scots, fiercely did set upon Mr Edmonde
Hawarde Captaine of th'uttermoste parte of the field at the west

side, and between them was so cruel battle that many of our party
Chesshiremen and other did flee, and the said Master Edmonde in
manner left alone without succour, and his standard and bearer of
the same beaten and hewed in pieces, and himself thrice stricken
down to the ground; howbeit like a courageous and an hardy young
lusty gentleman he recovered again and fought hand to hand with
one Sir Davy Home, and slew him with his own hand, and thus the
said Maister Edmonde was in great peril and danger till that the
lorde Darce like a good and a hardy knight relieved and come unto
him for his succour.

The second batell came upon my Lord Hawarde. The third batell
wherein was the King of Scots and most part of the noblemen of his
realm came fiercely upon my said Lord of Surrey, which two
battelles by the help of Almighty God were after a great conflict
venquesshed [vanquished], overcome, beaten down and put to
flight, and few of them escaped with their lives. Sir Edward Stanley
being at the uttermost part of the said rerewarde [rear guard] on the
East part, seeing the fourth batelles ready to relieve the said King of
Scots batell, courageously and like a lusty and hardy knight, did set
upon the same and overcame, and put to flight all the Scots in the
said batell. And thus by the grace succour and help of Almighty God
victory was given to the realm of England, and all the Scottish
ordenance won and brought to Ettell and Berwick in surety.

Over and above the said persons, there are slain of the Scots
viewed by my lorde Darce, the number of 11 or 12 thousand men
and of Englishmen slain and taken prisoners upon 1200. Divers
prisoners are taken of the Scots, but no notable person, only Sir
William Scott knight councillor of the said king of Scots, and as is
said a gentleman well learned, also Sir John Forman knight brother
to the Bishop of Murrey, which Bishop as is reported, was and is
most principal procurer of this war; and an other called Sir John of
Coolchome; many other Scottish prisoners could and might have
been taken but they were so vengeable and cruel in their fighting
that when Englishmen had the better of them they would not save
them, though it so were that diverse Scots offered great sums of
money for their lives.

It is to be noted that the field began between 4 and 5 after noon,
and continued within night, if it had fortuned to have been further
afore night many more Scots had been slain, and taken prisoners.
Loving be to allmighty God all the noble men of England, that were
upon the said field both Lord and knight are safe from any hurt and

none of them wanting, save only M. Harry Gray [and] Sir Humfrey Lisle booth prisoners in Scotland Sir John Gower of Yorkeshire and Sir John Boothe of Lancashire both wanting and as yet not found.

In this battle the Scots had many great advantages that is to wit, the high hills and mountains, a great wind with them, and sudden rain, all contrary to our bows and archers. It is not to be doubted, but the Scots fought manly, and were determined either to win the field or to die, they were also as well appointed as was possible at all points with arms and harness, so that few of them were slain with arrows, how be it the bills did beat and how them down with some pain and danger to Englishmen.

The said Scots were so plainly determined to abide battle and not to flee, that they put from them their horses and also put of their boots and shoes, and fought in the vamps of their hoses [their stocking soles], every man for the most parte with a keen and a sharp spear of 5 yards long, and a target afore him. And when their spears failed and were spent, then they fought with great and sharp swords, making little or no noise without that for the most part, any of them would desire to be saved.

The field where the Scots did lodge, was not to be reproved but rather to be commended greatly, for there was many, and a great number of goodly tents and much good stuff in the same, and in the said field was plenty of wine, beer, ale, beef, mutton, salt fish, cheese and other victuals necessary and convenient for such a great army Albeit our army doubting that the said victuals had been poisoned for their destruction, would not save but utterly them destroyed.

'A contemporary account of the battle of Floddon 9th September 1513 from a manuscript in the possession of David Laing', ed. D. Laing, *Proceedings of the Society of Antiquaries*, Edinburgh, 1867.

Father Damian and the Birds

A favourite of the cosmopolitan James IV was John Damian, Abbot of Tungland, a would-be alchemist and general shyster who was always full of outlandish (and expensive) schemes. It was reported by later historians that Damian had offered to fly to France on an embassy and had actually jumped off Stirling Castle clad with a pair of wings. Despite this, there seems to be no contemporary evidence for the story of Damian's attempt at executive class flying. The culprit for popularising, if not inventing, the whole tale, was court poet William Dunbar who found his heart filled with envy and his pen inspired to verse. Not content with savaging

Damian's alleged skills in physic, Dunbar conjured up a scene worthy of Hitchcock, in which the outraged birds of Scotland queued up to assault the impostor. Of course, this isn't exactly reportage – but with a poet of Dunbar's stature, who cares? The extract from the poem is taken from Priscilla Bawcutt's new edition for the Association of Scottish Literary Studies.

A Ballat of the Abbot Tungland

. . .

In Scotland than, the narrest way
He come, his cunning till assay;
To sum man thair it was no play,
    The preving of his sciens.
In pottingry he wrocht grit pyne,
He murdreist in to medecyne.
The low was of a grit engyne,
    And generit was of gyans.

In leichecraft he was homecyd.
He wald haif, for a nicht to byd,
A haiknay and the hurt manis hyd,
    So meikle he was of myance.
His yrnis was rude as ony rawchtir.
Quhair he leit blude it was no lawchtir,
Full mony instrumentis for slawchtir
    Was in his gardevyance.

He cowth gif cure for laxatyve,
To gar a wicht horss want his lyve.
Quha evir assay wald, man or wyve,
    Thair hippis yeid hiddy giddy.
His practikis nevir war put to preif.
But suddane deid, or grit mischeif.
He had purgatioun to mak a theif
    To dee withowt a widdy.

Vnto no mes pressit this prelat,
For sound of sacring bell nor skellat.
As blaksmyth bruikit was his pallatt,
    For battering at the study.
Thocht he come hame a new maid channoun,
He had dispensit with matynnis channoun.
On him come nowther stole nor fannoun,
    For smowking of the smydy.

Me thocht seir fassonis he assailyeit,
To mak the quintessance, and failyeit,
And quhen he saw that nocht availyeit
    A fedrem on he tuke,
And schupe in Turky for to fle.
And quhen that he did mont on he,
All fowll ferleit quhat he sowld be,
    That evir did on him luke.

Sum held he had bene Dedalus,
Sum the Menatair marvelus,
Sum Martis blaksmyth Wlcanus,
    And sum Saturnus kuke.
And evir the tuschettis at him tuggit,
The rukis him rent, the ravynis him druggit,
The hudit crawis his hair furth ruggit,
    The hevin he micht not bruke.

The False Friar of Tungland

(a paraphrase with apologies to Dunbar)

He came to Scotland by the shortest route to try his skills –
no joke for the unfortunates he tried them on,
for in pharmacy, he was literally a pain.
He murdered with his brand of medicine.
The trickster was of such subtle genius,
that he must have been born of giants.

In physic, he was homicide.
His rate for one night's visit was a horse
and his patients hide (if possible), so huge were his fees.
Despite which, his blood-letting kit was rough as a plank, and no laughing matter when he employed it,
for the man's black-bag was chock-full of instruments of slaughter.

His cure for the runs could make a cart horse drop dead.
Whoever tried it, of either sex, went like the clappers.
The man's theories were never put to the test
without sudden death or other harm ensuing.
No need for hanging, when Father Damian's
purgatives could kill a thief without a halter.

For a priest, he wasn't exactly keen on mass.
Its consecration bell meant nothing to him - too busy with his alchemical works - black as a smith from the forge.
Though he came to Scotland a newly-ordained canon,
the canonical hours soon went out the window.
The man couldn't put on a vestment for reeking of the smiddy.

The reason for all these strange goings-on was his failed attempt to make the alchemical 'quintessence'
When he saw that that wasn't going to work, he had the bright idea of doing himself up in feathers to fly to Turkey.
When he took to the air, all the birds of Scotland that saw him wondered what on earth he could be.

Some thought he was Daedalus,
some the marvelous Minotaur,
some the God of War's blacksmith Vulcanus,
and some thought him Saturn's cook.

And ever the peewits tugged at him
The rooks rent him, the ravens dragged him.
The hoodies tore his hair out
That he might not stay up in heaven.

The myttane, and Sanct Martynis fowle
Wend he had bene the hornit howle,
Thay set avpone him with a yowle,
        And gaif him dynt for dynt.
The golk, the gormaw, and the gled
Beft him with buffettis quhill he bled,
The sparhalk to the spring him sped.
        Als fers as fyre of flynt.

The tarsall gaif him tug for tug,
A stanchell hang in ilka lug,
The pyot furth his pennis did rug,
        The stork straik ay but stynt.
The bissart, bissy but rebuik,
Scho was so cleverus of hir clvik,
His bawis he micht not langer bruik
        Scho held thame at ane hint.

Thik was the clud of kayis and crawis,
Of marleyonis, mittanis, and of mawis,
That bikkrit at his berd with blawis,
        In battell him abowt.
Thay nybbillit him with noyis and cry,
The rerd of thame raiss to the sky,
And evir he cryit on Fortoun, 'Fy!'
        His lyfe was in to dowt.

The ia him skrippit with a skryke
And skornit him, as it was lyk.
The egill strong at him did stryke
        And rawcht him mony a rowt.
For feir vncunnandly he cawkit,
Quhill all his pennis war drownd and drawkit.
He maid a hundreth nolt all hawkit
        Beneth him with spowt.

He schewre his feddreme that was schene,
And slippit owt of it full clene,
And in a myre, vp to the ene
        Amang the glar did glyd.
The fowlis all at the fedrem dang,
As at a monster thame amang,
Quhill all the pennis of it owtsprang
        In till the air full wyde.

And he lay at the plunge evirmair,
Sa lang as any ravin did rair.
The crawis him socht with cryis of cair
        In every schaw besyde.
Had he reveild bene to the rwikis,
Thay had him revin all with thair clwikis.
Thre dayis in dub amang the dukis
        He did with dirt him hyde.

The air was dirkit with the fowlis,
That come with yawmeris and with yowlis,
With skryking, skrymming and with scowlis,
        To tak him in the tyde.
I walknit with the noyis and schowte,
So hiddowis beir wes me abowte.
Sensyne I curs that cankerit rowte
        Quhair evir I go or ryde.

The Poems of William Dunbar, ed. P. Bawcutt,
Glasgow, 1998.

The hawk and the hen-harrier
reckoned he was a horned owl
and attacked him, screeching,
with blow upon blow.
The cuckoo, the cormorant and the kite
struck him more dunts while he bled.
The sparrow hawk, fierce as sparks from a flint,
hastened to battle.

The peregrine gave him tug for tug.
A kestrel hung in both his lugs.
The magpie pulled the pinions out his wings.
The stork struck him non-stop.
The buzzard busied herself beyond reproach.
 She was so smart with her talons,
that his balls were in extreme danger from her
clutches.

A thick cloud of jackdaws, crows
and merlins and others
bickered at his beard with blows,
nibbling him with noisy cries.
The racket fairly reached the sky.
And ever he cried 'Fortune! Fy!'
 – his life in doubt.

The jay shrieked in mockery.
The mighty eagle struck at him strongly
with many a hard knock.
For fear, his bowels loosened,
besmearing his feathers
and daubing a hundred head of cattle
beneath him with the results.

He totally shed his beautiful plumage,
plummeting into a bog
up to his eyeballs in glaur.
The birds still struck at the monster's feathers,
until they all shot out into the air.

Meanwhile, their victim cowered in the marsh
while the ravens roared
and the crows, cawing,
scanned the neighbourhood.
If the rooks had found him
they would have torn him to bits.
Three days in the puddles amongst the ducks
he lurked.

The air was darkened
with yowling, shrieking, scolding birds
on search-and-destroy missions.
I wakened with the noise and shout,
so hideous to hear round about,
ever since I curse that angry crowd
Wherever I go or ride.

L. Yeoman

Towards the Reformation

In early 16th-century Scotland religious upheaval did not seem too likely. The old church, despite its problems, remained fairly popular. True, there were signs of corruption – royal bastards were given preferment in the church both in James V's reign and in his father's. Money was skimmed off from the kirk to fill the bottomless hole of royal finances. A new sect of heretics – Lutherans – had appeared and they were persecuted by the authorities. Yet the Scottish church was still associated with a vibrant culture of religious devotion, art and music which appealed to many people. There was more talk of improvement and reform, than of violently sweeping away the old religion and its arts. The reform movement that sprang up in neighbouring England initially horrified and repelled most Scots.

On the political front, Scotland stressed its French ties. James V took two French brides in succession, the short-lived Princess Magdalene and her successor Marie de Guise. James's untimely death in 1542 left Scotland with an infant queen – Mary. The lack of an adult monarch made Scotland vulnerable to foreign intervention both by England and by France. At the same time, support for first Lutheranism and then Calvinism grew – complicating an already unstable situation, and eventually leading to the outbreaks of iconoclasm which stripped Scotland's churches bare.

The Old and the New

Adam Abell, the chronicler, was nostalgic for the good old days. Here he gives a picture of the ideal Scottish abbot who would have adorned the monasteries of the Auld Kirk. In the course of his long life, Abell not only witnessed the old church at its best, but also lived to hear of the upheavals of the Reformation and the stunning news of a new world ripe for spiritual conquest. Here are two more excerpts from his 'Wheel of Time'.

1500 . . . the abbot of halie rudhouss callit robert bellentyne left his
1500 The Abbot of Holyroodhouse, Robert Bellenden, left his

office and dignite and entrit in the ordur of chartors monks
position and entered the order of the Carthusians for the

[Carthusians] for heill of his saule and lufe of god. Thot [though] he
well-being of his soul and the love of God. Yet previously he

wes myrror before till oder [other] abbats of Scotland in pece and
was the mirror to other abbots in Scotland, by means of his peaceful

exemplair life. He wes born in saut prestone [Prestonpans] quhar
and exemplary life. He was born in Prestonpans

[where] I wes born and his sister mareit my gudschirrs [grandfather's]
where I was born and his sister married my great uncle.

broder. I sall schaw not of Inordinad [inordinate] effectioun to him
I shall not show excessive affection to him, but write the truth.

bot werite. [Th]at I knaw quhen [when] I wes at burd [boarding] in
I know that when I was boarded as a child

barnhage [childhood] with a chanon [canon] of the forsaid abbay. He
with a canon of Holyrood, he gave in alms to the poor

gaif ilk friday to the pure [poor] folks in almswss [alms] four bolls of
every Friday, 4 measures of wheat in baked bread

quheit [wheat] in bakin breid and gife that steddit not the multitude
and if that was not enough for the multitude

at [that] come he gart gife silv[er] [money] almswss [alms] to the laif
he would give money in alms to the rest.

[rest]. He biggit [built] the brig of leith. The quhit [white] kirk of
He built the bridge of Leith, the White Kirk of

lowdian [lothian] and mony oder briggs in the West land. He biggit
Lothian and many other bridges in the west. He built

the stepill in the kirk yard and brocht hame the bellis of it and cust
the steeple in the kirk yard and brought back [probably from Flanders]

ane oder gret bell in the toder [other] stepill hingand. He feft the
the bells for it and cast another great bell hanging in the other steeple.

almwshouss of sanct leonardis. He thekit [roofed] the kirk all with
He endowed the alms houses of St Leonards. He roofed the kirk with

leid he brot hame the funt [font] of brass and pillars of brass about the
lead. He brought home the brass font and pillars of brass for the

altaris. He brocht hame all the capis of ony priss, mony stands of
altar. He brought home all the capes, of any price, many suits of

claith of gold and finalie a sort of kapis all of quhit [white] silk for all
cloth of gold and finally a sort of vestment all of white silk for the

the chanonis to wss [use] in the fests of our lady. He gart mak the gret
canons to use at the feasts of our lady. He caused make the great

and precius eucharist and ferttur in silver and gold, mony crocis and
and precious monstrance and shrine in silver and gold, many crosses and

otheris sancts reliks. many od[er] notabill turnis he did eftir and
other saints' relics. He did many other notable deeds before and after

before [th]at I wes in that place. In his exemplair life abbats now
I was there. Modern abbots could learn from his example. He came daily

ma[y] tak documents. He cam dailie to lady mess, pryme mess quhen
      to mass for Our Lady, The office of Prime, when he

he held cheptur and hie mess and eynsaing [evensong] quhen he wes
      held his chapter, Highmass and evensong, when he was not

not stoppit be hes erands. In principall fests [feasts] he did the office
      prevented by business. In important feasts, he officiated in the

in the queir and oft tyme come to mateinis. He lauborit all wais to
      body of the kirk and often came to matins. He worked hard to encourage

causs obseruance [observance] to be kepis bot maisterfull subdis
      observance, but rebellious underlings constantly

[subjects] ay resistit to him and wexit [vexed] him. He yeid [went] ay
      resisted and vexed him. He always went about

in the place awder in caip ouder kirtill or fut mantill with abbot hind.
      the abbey in either cape or kirtle or foot mantle with Abbott Hind.

In his hall wes not admittit bards na fenyeit fulis bot ane certane of
      In his hall he admitted neither bards nor pretended fools but a certain

pure [puir] barinis [bairns] callit his saulis and ane of thame wes his
      number of poor bairns, called his souls, and one of them was his .

playfule.
      play-fool

He was never fund ydill [idle] bot ay in honest exercition. He wes
      He was never found idle but always in honest exercise. He was a

ane cunning man and a gret poeyn. Of him in sport yronice [ironic]
      learned man and a good poet. Lord Lyle once spoke ironically

spak the lord lile to the king sayand 'schir this abbat bellentyne of
      to the king, saying 'Sir, this Abbot Bellenden is not

halie rudhouss is not for wss [us] courteowrs he builds briggis, repalis
      for us courtiers. He builds bridges, repairs

halie kirks reknand hes is before said etc. Than said he concludent put
      holy churches etc.' (as mentioned before) 'Then' said he 'Let us

down this abbot and get ane [th]at will play ane hundret merks at ane
      get rid of this Abbot and get one that will put a hundred marks on one

cast of the diss [dice]. That is ane man for wss [us]. Sic abbats hes
      cast of the dice. That is the man for us'. Such Abbots as

robert bellentyne ar now far to seik.
      Robert Bellenden are now hard to find.

MS. 1746, f.112.

1532 – News of the New World Reaches Jedburgh

Just as the Reformation was gathering pace, the Catholic world seemed to be at its height, gaining rather than losing ground in the Spanish conquests in the New World. Here is Abell's attempt to take in the enormity of these developments and the extent of the Catholic missionary work in the New Spain. It paints an overly-rosy picture of Spanish conquest, and shows in what form the news began to trickle into Scotland.

Heir come word with our ministers fra the generall cheptur [General
Our delegates who attended the General Chapter of our Order brought
Chapter] of the new spanye [Spain] or hirketan [Yucatan] at we call
news of the New Spain or Yucatan that we call the Newfound Isle
the new fund yle [island] in gret ynd [Ind] in afrik. Broder martin of
in Great Indie in Africa. Brother Martin of Valencia [Juan Martino
Walence [Valencia] wrait to mathi Wincent [Mathew Vincent],
de Boil of Valencia wrote with the news to Matthias Vincent
comisser generall. This martin wes custos custodiens secti evangelii in
Commissary General. He (Martin) was
this forsaid land and he send and said 'We [th]at are in the extreme
the superior in this land and he wrote and said 'We are
part of the warld in gret ynd in gret asy quhare be our breder Minors
at the extreme part of the world in Great Indie in Great Asia, where
of observance your subdits [subjects] first the halie ewangell is prechit
the holy gospel is preached by your subjects, the Observantine Friars
and the seid of it wes sawin quhilk hes accresit and multiplieit I sa[y]
and the seed of it was sown, which has increased and multiplied. I
to yor faderhede [fatherhood] that be our breder in ynd ar baptist ma
say to you, Father, that by our brethren in the Indies are baptised
na [more nor] 10 hundreth thousand of foresaid ind. Ilk ane of the 12
more than 10 hundred thousand of the Indians. Each one of the 12
breder at wes send with me be maist reverent fader francis of angellis
brethren that were sent with me by the Most Reverend father
(than Minister generall, now cardinall of the halie cruss) ma than a
Francis of Angels (then Minister General, now Cardinal of the Holy
hundred thousand hes baptist and thai all bot I hes lerit [learned] the
Cross) has baptised more than a hundred thousand people and all of

leds [tongues] of the land diverss and prechis to thame and instrukkis
them except myself have learned the various local languages and

the multitude of pepill and amang thame are mony barins [bairns]
preach to them and instruct the multitude of people, and among

nobilis sonns at geves to ws [us] gret hoip of profectioun [profession].
them are many children, noblemen's sons, who give us great hope of

Thai ar instrukkit be our breder in life and gude maneris and are
profession. They are instructed by our brethren in life and good

nwrist [nourished] spiritualie in our placis quhilks places ar biggit to
manners and are spiritually nourished in our houses, of which there

the nowmer of 20 and ma ar multiplian dalie, bigand be the yndis
are now 20 built and the number increases daily. They are built by

[indians] and herd [hard] beside ilk place is an oder [other] houss
the Indians and close by each place there is another house built for

biggit for the instruktioun of the forsaid barins with librell, dortur
the instruction of children with library, dormitory, refectory and

fratur and chapell. Thir barins ar werra [very] meik and obtemperand
chapel. The bairns are very meek and obliging to the brethren and

to the breder and lufis the breder bettir na thare carnall faders.. Thai
love the brethren better than their natural fathers. They are chaste

ar chest and faithfull to the breder. Thai ar ingenuoss in pictur. Thai
and faithful to the brethren. They are ingenuous in expression. They

preche to thare fader and moders when thai ar weill instrukkit in
preach to their fathers and mothers when they are well instructed in

christin doctrin . . .
Christian doctrine' . . .

Mulierum Commendatio [in commendation of women] Wemen
Mulierum Commendatio [in commendation of women] Women

thare schenis [shines] with ontrowable honeste and womenlie scham
there shine with unbelievable honesty and womanly modesty.

[shame], confessionis thare and principale of wemen all full of purite
Confessions there and principally those of women are full of purity

without palliatioun, the body of christ with abundance of teris thai
without attempts at excuses. They devoutly receive the body of

dewotlie [devoutly] resawis [receives]. Religioss men principalie
Christ with abundance of tears. Religious men and especially

breder minors thai had in gret rewerence because thai spiratualie first
brother minors they hold in great reverence because they spiritually

generit thame to god [converted them]. Thai obey to tham and taks
first begot them [converted them]. They obey them and take

penance thankfullie and all doctrin concernand the faith. All this yere
  penance thankfully and all doctrine concerning the faith. This last year,
bigane the bischep of tymistitan [Tenochtitlan] of our ordur and the
  the Bishop of Tenochtitlan of our order and the
breder with him in that sam forsaid land send a pistill [epistle = letter]
  brethren with him in that land sent a letter
to the generall cheptur haldin in tholoss [Toulouse] the yere of christ
  to the General Chapter held in Toulouse, in
1532, schawand mekill before saids and ekand [th]at 500 tempillis of
  1532, showing the above and even that 500 temples of
falss goddis thare ar distroeit and ma than 20, 000 figuris [images] of
  false gods there were destroyed and more than 20,000 figures of
evill sprets [spirits] at thai anormit [adored] ar brokin and birnt
  evil spirits that they adored are broken and burnt
[burnt] and in thar placis kirks and ymage [image] of the cruss [cross]
  and in their places kirks and images of the cross
ar put up and ar honorit be ynds [indians] men and wemen. As it
  are put up and are honoured by Indian men and women. As is
[th]at is horrible to heir before in the said cete [city] of tymistitan thare
  horrible to hear, they previously in the city of Tenochtitlan
wes offerit to thare falss godds ilk yere ma than 20 thousand harts of
  offered to the false gods more than 20,000 hearts of
thare slane barins and young Wirgins [virgins] in sacrifice bot now
  their slain bairns and young virgins in sacrifice, but now
thai harts not to ydolis [idols] bot to almychty god ar offerit in honor
  they give their hearts, not to idols but to Almighty God, in honour
and dewotion not deid bot in lewand [living] lufe and glore to god be
  and devotion, not dead but in living love and glory to God by
doctrin and halie exempill of our breder minors. This dewot [devout]
  doctrine and holy example of our Brothers Minor. This devout
pepill multipleis in fastin, disciplin and orison with teris and sichin
  people multiplies in fasting, discipline and prayers with tears and sighing.
[sighing]. Mony of their barins can weill reid and writ, sing and pnynt
  Many of their bairns can read and write well and sing and do penance as
oft thai confess thaim. And with maist dewotion resaifis the body of
  often as they confess and with the most devotion receives the body of
christ. Special devotion thai have to the Glorious Virgin.
  christ. They have a special devotion to the Glorious Virgin.

MS. 1746, ff.118v-19r. All transcriptions of Abell in this book are by L. Yeoman.

Other transcriptions can be found in 'The final folios of Adam Abell's "Roit or quheill of tyme": an Observantine friar's reflections on the 1520s and 30s' by Alasdair M. Stewart in *Stewart Style : essays on the court of James V*, edited by J. Hadley Williams, East Linton, 1996. Norman MacDougall's *James III*, Edinburgh, 1982 and 'Adam Abell, Martin of Valencia . . . or Jedburgh, Mexico, Yucatan and Fez in 1532' also by Alasdair M. Stewart in *Bulletin of the Scottish Institute of Missionary Studies*, Aberdeen, 1972.

'It Came Wi' a Lass'

James V, father of Mary Queen of Scots, presided over a court at which Scottish poetry and drama flourished. Writers such as David Lindsay and George Buchanan owed their advancement to the king. Despite being a devout Catholic, James did not scruple to enrich himself at the expense of his church, using the spectre of the English break with Rome to encourage the church to pander to him. His private life, with its succession of mistresses, was not exactly in line with church teaching either. On the other hand he passed severe statutes against heresy and several Lutherans, including the talented young courtier and preacher Patrick Hamilton, were burnt at the stake in his reign. As noted above, he pursued a pro-French foreign policy through his marriages and diplomacy.

None of this was to the taste of John Knox, a young man growing up in James's reign. Knox's commitment to Protestantism led him to see James, his widow Marie de Guise and their daughter Mary as calamities for Scotland. James died not long after another military disaster for Scotland – the lost battle of Solway Moss in 1542. Here, in his History *Knox records James's death and the birth of Mary Queen of Scots. Knox's version of James's last words passed into tradition as 'It came wi' a lass, it'll pass wi a lass' – a reference to the Stewart claim to the throne inherited from Marjorie Bruce all those years ago.*

Cuming to the Hallyards [he] was humainlie ressavit of the Ladie
   Coming to the Hallyards the King was kindly received by Lady
of Grange, ane antient and godlie Matrene (the Laird at his cuming
   Grange, a godly old matron (the Laird was absent at the time).
was absent). In his Cumpany was only with him William Kirkaldie,
   In his company was only William Kirkcaldy, now
now Laird of Grange, and sum uther that waytit upoun his Chalmer.
   Laird of Grange, and some others from his bedchamber.

The Ladie at Supper, persaving him pensive, begane to comfort him,
At supper the Lady, seeing him pensive, began to comfort him

and willed him to take the Ward of God in gud Parte. My Portioun
and willed him to take the Word of God in good part. My portion

of this Warld, said he, is schorte, for I will not be with you 15 Dayis.
of this world, said he, is short, for I will not be with you 15 days.

His Servand repaired unto him asking, Quhair he wald have
His servant came and asked him where he wanted

Provision maid for his Yuill, quhilk than aprochit? He answerit,
preparations to be made for Yule, which was approaching. He answered

with at disdainfull Smirk, I cannot tell, chuse ye the Plaice; but this
with a disdainful smirk. I cannot tell, you choose the place, but this

I can tell you, or Yulle-Day ye will be Maisterless, and the Realme
I can tell you, by Yule you will be Masterless, and the realm

without a King. Becaus of his Displesur, no Man durst mak
without a king. Because of his temper, no man dared

Contradictioun unto him. Sa efter he had visitit the Castell of
contradict him. So after he had visited the Castle of Carnie,

Carney, perteining to the Erle of Craufurde, quhair the said Erle's
belonging to the Earl of Crawford, where the said Earl's daughter

Dochter was, ane of his Huiris, he returnit to Falkland, and tuk Bed.
was one of his mistresses, he returned to Falkland and took to bed.

And albeit thair apearit unto him na Signs of Deyth, yit he
And although no signs of death appeared on him, yet he

constantlie affirmit, Befair sick a Day I sal be deid. In this mein
constantly affirmed 'Before such a day I shall be dead.' In the mean-

Tyme was the Quein, upoun the Point of hir Deliverie in Linlythgow,
time the Queen was about to give birth in Linlithgow,

quha was deliverit the aucht Day of December, in the Yeir of God
and was delivered of a daughter on the 8th December,

1542 Yeiris, of Marie that then wes borne, and now dois reigne for
1542, of Mary who was born then and now reigns as a

a Plague to this Realme, as the Progres of hir haill Lyif had to this
plague to this realm, as the progress of her entire life to this day

Day declars. The Certaintie that a Dochter was borne unto him,
declares. The certainty that a daughter was born to him,

cuming to his Eris, he turnit frome sick as spak with him, and said,
coming to the ears of the King, he turned from such as spoke to him and

The Devil ga with it, it will end as it begane; it come frome a
said 'The Devil goe with it, it will end as it began, it came from a woman

Woman, and it will end in a Woman. Efter that he spak not mony

and it will end in a woman.' After that he spoke not many words which

Wordis that war sensibill.

were intelligible.

John Knox, *Historie of the Reformatioun of Scotland*, Edinburgh, 1732.

Diplomatic Manoeuvres:
A First Glimpse of Mary Queen of Scots

Ralph Sadler was Henry VIII's ambassador to Scotland in 1543, the year after the birth of the new young Queen. Mary was only three months old but already a Queen and an important marriage prospect for Edward, Prince of Wales, only a child himself. Much of the extract concerns Marie de Guise's subtle diplomatic efforts to impress the English, and cast their current ally Regent Arran 'the governour' in a suitably bad light. She calculated that the sight of her robust infant would favourably impress her visitor and improve Scotland's bargaining power in diplomacy with Sadler's master, but she had no intentions of carrying through a match with Protestant England. A devout Catholic and a Frenchwoman, her main aim was to frustrate Henry and to keep young Mary safely out of his hands, but she had to at least appear to play along with her more powerful neighbours for the time being.

To the King's Majesty, 23 March 1543

Please it your royal majesty to understand, that yesterday I had access to the queen-dowager of Scotland, to whom I delivered your majesty's letters, with your highness's hearty commendations, and declared also my credence unto her, according to mine instructions. I found her most willing and conformable in appearance to your majesty's purpose, for the marriage of her daughter to my lord prince's grace; and also, that your majesty should have her delivered forthwith into your hands and custody, which she confesseth to be for her chief surety, and wisheth with all her heart that it were so. She accounteth herself most bound to your majesty, that it hath pleased the same to determine such honour and advancement to her said daughter. And discoursing with her thereof, the rather to settle her in that part, she said, 'The world might justly note her to be the most unnatural and unwise woman that lived, if she should not heartily desire and rejoice of the same; for greater honour and benefit could not be offered unto her, nor she knoweth not throughout the world such a marriage could be found so proper, so beneficial, and so honourable, as this is;' saying, 'that she cannot otherwise think but it is the work and ordinance of God, for the conjunction and union of both those realms in one; for she hath had none before but sons [one living, from her first marriage in France and two princes who died in infancy prior to the birth of Mary, from her marriage to James v], and now it is her chance to bring forth a daughter, for the best purpose she trusteth.'

And when she had thus declared her affection in that behalf, with assurance that she would be advised by your majesty in all things, and would walk plainly on a right sort with your majesty, as she said it became her not to dissemble with so noble a prince; and so bade me advertise your majesty. 'That the governour [the Regent Arran], whatsoever pretence or fair weather he made unto your majesty, minded nothing less, than that her daughter should marry into England, and so had himself told her, with this much more, that, for to please your majesty, they would offer unto the same, that there should be a contract made of the marriage, but they would have the custody of the child till she should be of lawful age; by which time, God might dispose his pleasure of your majesty, being already well grown in years; and then they would handle it so, as that contract should serve to no purpose. This', she said, 'the governour told her himself, and this was the secret thing that she desired for to have one of your trusty servants to come to her, to the intent she might, by the same, advertise your majesty thereof, because she durst not commit the same neither to French nor Scot.' But here she made great instance unto me, 'That this might be most secret; for else being in their hands here, as she is straitly looked unto, insomuch that she hath none about her of her own servants, nor one that she may trust, it might be to her great danger.' And, to verify the same, she saith, 'That the governor and council have determined in their parliament, that your majesty shall not have the child delivered into your hands, for sundry considerations alledged amongst them. One was, that, because she is queen of the realm, it were not meet to have her out of the same, by whose authority and name the governour should use his office, and all things executed for the common wealth of this realm. Another is, that, if she were delivered unto England, she should never die; but if God should call her, they would ever be sure in England to have another to succeed her [ie. if she died in England they would easily find a replacement]. And, again, if God should dispose his pleasure of my lord prince's grace, the child being in England, might be married there to some other, contrary to the weal and good of this realm; so that if they should deliver her out of their hands, your majesty, howsoever the game should go, would dispose the inheritance and crown of this realm at your pleasure:' with many other considerations, as she saith, she gat information. She saith, 'Assuredly the governour mindeth to marry her daughter to his son; wherefore,' she saith, 'if your majesty stand not fast upon that point, to have her delivered into your hands, the marriage will never take effect.' And here, she said, 'The cardinal, if he were at liberty, might do much good in the same.' I told her, I thought the cardinal would rather do hurt, for he had no affection towards England. She said, 'He was a wise man, and could better consider the benefit of the realm than all the rest.' And ever in her discourse she inculked [insisted], 'That your majesty should see, they would not deliver the child, nor yet pledges for performance of the marriage.' She told me, 'That she was sure the governour would now, knowing that I had been with her, come shortly to see her, the rather to know what had passed betwixt her and me. And,' quoth she, 'when he cometh, I shall (as my custom is) make as though I were not well willing to this marriage; and then', quoth she, 'as he is but a simple man, he will tell me his whole intent in that part; and if I should not do so,' quoth she, 'he would keep himself the more covert and close, and tell me nothing. And what I shall farther perceive by him, how is disposed in the matter, now upon your coming, if I can find any mean,' quoth she, 'to speak with you, or send to you, ye shall have knowledge of it.' I told her, that knowing the least part of her mind in that behalf, I would make some errand again to see her; which she also desired. And then she told me, 'That the governour shewed her, that your majesty had written unto him, how there had been a [marriage] contract betwixt the earl of Lennox and her.' Whereunto she answered, 'That the contrary thereof was true; and that now, since she had been a king's wife, her heart was too high to look any lower.' I told her, I was sure your majesty had written no such matter to the governour; 'but,' quoth I, 'I remember that such a saying was, that your grace should marry with the earl of Lennox.' 'By my truth,' quoth she, 'it is utterly untrue; for I never minded it. And so,' quoth she, 'it was a saying, that my father should come here with an army, which likewise is untrue. It may be,' quoth she, 'that the earl of Lennox came hither, with what power I cannot tell; but sure I am,' quoth she, 'my father is in Champagne, to prepare the French king's army there against the emperour, as a Frenchman told her, that arrived here lately by sea.' After we had discoursed a good while of those things, (in which talk she asked me, 'How it stood between your majesty and the French king? And wished, that there should ensue no war nor dissention betwixt you:' wherein I told her, that I knew not but all was well) I descended to that part of mine instructions, touching the strange demeanour of her servant whom she lately sent unto your majesty, and declared the same unto her in such sort as is contained in my said instructions. She besought your majesty 'to conceive no suspicion of her for sending her said servant in such manner into France; whom,' she saith, 'she commanded to tell your highness of his journey, and humbly to supply unto your majesty for his passport, both to go and return by your majesty; alledging, she was right sorry your majesty should have any cause of suspicion, whereof she protested there was no cause.' I told her, your majesty had information of her virtue, wisdom, and experience, to be such, as your highness could not therefore suspect her, but rather doubted not she would apply to that which should be to her honour, and the most surety and benefit of her daughter; which, if she weighed well, she might perceive did chiefly rest in your majesty, and without the same might be in great danger. She confessed the same, and wished to God that she were in your majesty's hands; 'for,' quoth she, 'it hath been seldom seen, that the heir of a realm should be in the custody of him that claimeth the succession of the same, as the governour is now established by parliament the second person of this realm, and, if her daughter fail, looketh to be king of the same. And,' quoth she, 'he said, that the child was not like to live; but you shall see,' quoth she, 'whether he saith true or not;' and therewith she caused me to go with her to the chamber where the child was, and shewed her unto me, and also caused the nurse to unwrap her out of her clothes, that I might see her naked. I assure your majesty, it is as goodly a child as I have seen of her age, and as like to live, with the grace of God.

State Papers and Letters of Sir Ralph Sadler, ed. A. Clifford, Edinburgh, 1809.

Burning Wishart

Young, charismatic and convinced, George Wishart was one of the new breed of Lutheran heretics who were appearing in Scotland. The teacher and friend of John Knox, he was captured preaching the new Protestant faith. The Catholic establishment felt bound to proceed against him to the full rigour of the law, lest he spread his opinions to others. The chief of the Scottish Church, Cardinal David Beaton, took a personal interest in bringing him to trial. Wishart had been preaching in Beaton's diocese. The case was

*conducted before him, in 1546, in Beaton's own city of St
Andrews. Wishart was condemned to death and burned at the
stake, a sentence for which the infant Protestant party in Scotland
never forgave Beaton. The story is told by Scots chronicler Robert
Lindsay of Pitscottie, a contemporary Fife gentleman and a
colourful writer of Scots prose. Lindsay would have known friends
or neighbours who were present, however there are elements of
pious myth-making in his account.*

The said Mr George condemnit in this matter and maner to the deid
The said Mr George, condemned in this matter to death,

was brocht out of the abbay kirk and haid agane to the castell to the
was brought out of the Abbey Kirk and taken again to the castle to the

captans challmer in the sie tour quhair he remanit all the night at his
Captain's chamber in the sea tower where he remained all the night at his

contemplatioun and prayer quhill on the morne the bischopeis send
contemplation and prayer till the morning, and the Bishops sent

the freiris into him to mak his confessioun schawand to him that he
the friars into him to take his confession, showing to him that he

behovit to suffer. ...
was ordained to be executed . . .

Inmediatlie heirefter . . . thar was tuo tormentouris send to Mr
Immediately hereafter . . . there were two tormentors sent to Mr

George Wischart, the on haueand ane cott of bucrum, the wther
George Wishart, the one having a coat of buckram, the other,

certane pokis of pulder and quhene they had putt the cott wpoun the
some bags of gunpowder and when they had put the coat upon the

said Mr George, the wther pat the pulder round about him in his
said Mr George the other put the powder round about him in his

sleiffis and in his body and bucklit it fast thairinto witht cordis. Syne
sleeves and in his body and tied it tightly to him with cords. Then

he brocht him fourtht to the captane to his wtter challmer thair quhair
they brought him forth to the Captain to his outer chamber there, where

he remanit ane quhill, quhill the fyre was prepairit and the skaffald
he stayed a while, while the stake was prepared and the scaffold

was maid and syne the artaillye chargit and laid ower the wall and
made and then the artillery was loaded and aimed over the wall and

cuschouns laid on the wallis prepairit for the bischopis to sitt wpoun
cushions laid on the walls for the Bishops to sit upon

and also all the gentillmen and men of weir war chargit to pase
and also all the gentlemen and men of war were told

to thair airmor, that is to say, tak speir and harnes to stand about the
to arm, that is to say, take spear and armour to stand about the

skaffald and fyre quhair the said Mr George sould suffer, and also the
scaffold and stake where the said Mr George should suffer and also the

gouneris to stand be thair artaillye for dreid of bak heir . . .
gunners stand by their artillery in case of attack from behind.

Be this the offiecers and tormentaris was chargit to proceid all
By this the officers and tormentors were ordered to proceed

fordwart. Then the trumpatis blew and the offiecearis and tormentaris
forward. Then the trumpets blew and the officers and tormentors

brocht fourtht this poore innocent man to the fyre quhilk was buldit
brought forth this poor innocent man to the fire which was built

and prepairit befor the castell yeitt, on the wast syde fornent the wast
and prepared before the castle gate on the west side in front of the west

blok house quhair the bischopis might ly on the wallis and sie the
block house where the bishops might lie on the walls and see the

sacriefice. And quhene Mr George was put on the skaffald and bund
sacrifice. And when Mr George was put on the scaffold [stake] and bound

to it witht irone chennyieis he desyrit licence to mak his spetiall
to it with iron chains, he desired permission to make his particular

prayeris to allmightie god for support of his kirk quhilk was in danger
prayers to Almighty God for support of his kirk, which was in danger

of wollfis that was lyk to devoir the samin, nochtwithstanding godis
of wolves which were likely to devour it, despite this, God's

promise was ane sicker targe to all thame that wald belief thairin, and
promise was a sure shield to all those who would believe in it and at

at lenth wald confound the enemeis quhene he thocht tyme. At the last
length would confound the enemies when he thought it time. At the last

quhene Mr George had maid ane end of his prayeris and wriesouns to
when Mr George had made an end of his prayers and orisons to

allmightie god and had randerit his spreit in the handis of the Lord,
Almighty God and had rendered his spirit into the hands of the Lord,

then they laid fyre into him and gaif him the first blast of pulder
then they kindled the fire and gave him the first blast of the powder

quhilk was werie terribill and odieous to sie, for thair raise so great
which was very terrible and odious to see, for there rose so great

ane bobe of wind out of the sie and so great ane clude of raine out of
a gust of wind out of the sea and so great a cloud of rain out of

the heavnis that quhene the wind and weit mett to gither it had sic
the heavens, that when the wind and wet met together, it had such

noyis and sound that all men was affrayit that saw or hard, it had sic
noise and sound that all men were afraid that saw or heard it, it had such
force and strength that it blew doune the stane wallis and the men that
force and strength that it blew down the stone walls and the men that
sat thairin to the number of ij^c persouns, quhilk fell on the bischopis
sat on them to the number of 200 persons, which fell on the Bishop's
yaird abone the wall thairof quhilk so money of thame fell thairin that
yard above the wall thereof from which so many of them fell, that
ane of thame was drowinitt immediatlie and so thair was sacriefice
one of them was drowned immediately and so there was sacrifice both
botht of fyre and watter. Then the captane of the castell exortit Mr
of fire and water. Then the Captain of the Castle exhorted Mr
George Wischart to remember on god and ask forgivenes of his sinns.
George to remember on God and ask forgiveness of his sins.
He ansuerit againe stoutlie howbeit the fyre had perturbit him, and
He answered again stoutly, howbeit the fire had peturbed him and
said 'Captane, god forgif yone man that lyis so glorieous on the wall,
said 'Captain, God forgive that man that lies so gloriously on the wall,
and within few dayis he sall ly allis schamfullie as he lyis glorieous
within a few days he shall lie as shamefully as he lies gloriously
now'. Witht that they put the tow and lute him speik no more bot
now.' With that they pulled the rope and let him speak no more, but
buldit the great fyre round about him; and quhene he was brunt all fre
built the great fire around him and when he was all burnt from
the waist doune, they bad him remember on god and mak ane signe
the waist down they asked him to remember on God and make a sign
thairof. To that taikin he bend into the fyre ane fute of height, quhilk
thereof. To that token he bent into the fire, a foot in height, which was
was great reioyssing to thame that faworit godis worde; bot the
matter of great rejoicing to those who favoured God's word, but the
bischopis and preistis dischargit all men wnder the paine of curssing
Bishops and priests forbade all men under pain of excommunication
to pray for him because they said he was ane heretick he aught nocht
to pray for him, for they said he was a heretic and ought not
to be prayit for.
to be prayed for.

Robert Lindsay of Pitscottie, *The Historie and Cronicles of Scotland from* the *Slauchter of King James I to Ane Thousande Fyve Hundreith Thrie Scoir Fyfteen Yeir . . .*, ed. A. J. G. Mackay, Scottish Text Society, 3 vols, 1899-1911.

The Murder of the Cardinal

Revenge for Wishart's death came swiftly. Norman and John Leslie, William Kirkcaldy of Grange and some other members of the local Fife gentry were part of the pro-Protestant pro-English party who would have liked to have seen Mary married to Henry VIII's son, Prince Edward. They embarked on an English-backed enterprise to assassinate the pro-French cardinal. This undertaking led to the occupation of St Andrews castle and later to a desperate resistance against the French forces of Marie de Guise sent to dislodge them. One of those who joined the defenders of the castle was John Knox, an action which would lead to his capture and sentence to several years hard labour on the French galleys. In his time in St Andrews he had the opportunity to talk first hand to Beaton's murderers when the deed was still fresh in their minds. The result is a harrowing narrative of violence told in a gloating tone. Knox drags the name of the dead cardinal through the mud with sexual innuendo and aspersions of greed. Certainly Beaton was no saint and he had just presided over the gruesome execution of Wishart, but the self-righteousness of his murderers still seems chilling even today.

Mony purpoises war devysit, how that wickit man mycht have bein
Many plots were devised for getting rid of that wicked man, but they all

taikin away; bot all faillit, till Fryday the 28th of Maii, anno 1546,
failed until Friday 28th May 1546,

quhen the foirsaid Normand [Leslie] came at nycht to St Androis,
when Norman Leslie came to St Andrews

William Kirckaldie of Grainge youngar was in the toun befoir,
at night. William Kirkcaldy of Grange younger was already in the town,

awaytting upoun the purpois. Last came Johne Leslie forsaid, who
ready and waiting for the plot. John Leslie came last, as he

was moist [most] suspected: quhat conclusion they tuik that nicht it
was the most suspect of them. What decision they reached that night

was not knawin, bot by the ischew [issue] that followed. Bot airlie
was not known, but by what followed. Early

upoun the Settorday in the morning, the 29th of Maii, war thay in
upon the Saturday morning, the 29th of May, they came together in

sundrie cumpanies in the Abbay Kirkyaird, not far distant frome the
companies in the Abbey kirk yard, not far from the castle.

Castell: first, the yettis [gates] being oppin and the draw-brig lattin
    The gates of the castle were open and the draw-bridge

down for receaving of lyme and stanis, and uther things necessarie for
    down to allow lime, stones and building materials in,

building, for Babilon [the cardinal's new block-house] was almost
    for Babylon [the Cardinal's new block house] was almost

finisched. First we say, assayit William Kircaldie of Grange younger,
    finished. First William Kirkcaldy of Grange and

and with him sex [six] personis, and getting entres, held purpois with
    six persons with him tried, and getting in asked the

the porter, gif my Lord Cardinall was wakin? Who answered, No: and
    porter whether my lord cardinal was awake? The porter answered no,

so it was indeid, for he had bein bussie at his accomptis with Mestres
    and so it was indeed, for he had been 'busy' at his 'accounts' that night

Marioun Ogilby that nicht, who was espyit to departe from him by
    with Mrs Marion Ogilvy, who had been seen sneaking out via the

the privie posterne that morning; and therefoir quietnes, efter the
    privy postern that morning and therefore according to the dictates of

reullis of physick and a morne sleip was requisite for my Lord. Quhille
    medicine he needed a good sleep in the morning. While William

the said William and the Porter talked, and his servandis maid thame
    Kirkcaldy and the porter talked, and his servants pretended to be

to luik the wark and the warkmen, aproched Normond Leslie with his
    looking at the work and the workmen, Norman Leslie and his

cumpanie; and because they war no grit number, thay easilie gat
    company came up, and because there were not many of them, they easily

entres. Thay addres thame to the middis of the clois, and immediatelie
    got in. They took up the middle of the close when suddenly

came Johne Leslie sumquhat rudelie, and foure personis with him: the
    John Leslie and another four of the company came in somewhat roughly.

porter fearing, wald have drawn the brig, bot the said Johne being
    The porter, being afraid would have drawn up the bridge, but John

enterit thairone, stayit and lap in: and quhill the porter maid him for
    Leslie being on it, stayed on it and leapt in and while the porter tried to

defence, his heid was brockin, the keyis was taikin frome him, and he
    defend himself, his head was broken, the keys taken from him and he was

castin in the fowsie [ditch], and so the plaice was seisit. The warkmen,
    thrown in the ditch and so the castle was taken. The workmen

to the number of mo than ane hundreth, ran of the wallis, and war
    to the number of more than a hundred ran off the walls and were

without hourt put furthe at the wickit yet [wicket gate]. The first thing
put out of the wicket gate unharmed. The very first thing that was

that evir was done Williame Kirkcaldie tuk the gaird of the privie
done was for William Kirkcaldy to guard the privy

posterne, fearing that the fox sould have eschaipit. Than go the rest to
postern, fearing that the fox should have escaped. Then the rest went to

the gentilmenis chalmeris, and without violence done to ony man,
the gentlemen's chambers and without any violence done

thay put mo than fyiftie personis to the yet: the number that
they put more than fifty people out of the gate. The number which dared

interprysit and did this war but sextein personis. The Cardinall
and did this were but 16 persons. The cardinal awakened

wacknit with the schoutis, askit frome his window, quhat meanit that
by the shouts, asked from the window, what the noise meant?

noyis? It was answerit that Normond Leslie had taikin his castell:
It was answered that Norman Leslie had taken his castle,

which understaude, he ran to the postern; bot perceaving the passage
understanding this, he ran to the postern, but realising that the exit

to be keipit without he returnit quicklie to his chalmer, and tuk his
was guarded outside, he returned to his chamber, and took his

two handit sword, and garth [the] chalmerchyild cast kistis and uther
two-handed sword and ordered the chamber boy to put chests and other

impedimentis to the dure [door]. In this mein tyme came Johne Leslie
barriers against the door. In the meantime John Leslie came to it

unto it, and biddis opin. The Cardinall asking who callis? He answerit
and asked them to open it. The cardinal asked 'Who calls?' He answered

my name is Leslie. He redemands, is that Normond? The other sayis
'My name is Leslie'. The cardinal asked again 'Is that Norman?' The other

nay, my name is Johne. I will have Normond sayis the Cardinall, for
replied 'No, my name is John.' 'I will have Norman' replied the cardinal

he is my friend. Content your self with suche as ar heir, for uther sall
'for he is my friend.' 'Content your self with such as are here, for you

ye get nane. Thair war with the said Johne, James Melvell, a man
won't get any others.' There were the said John, James Melville, a man

familiarlie acquainted with the said Mr George Wischeart, and Petir
who knew George Wishart well, and Peter

Carmichell, a stout gentilman. In the mein tyme, whyll they force at
Carmichael, a courageous gentleman. In the meantime whilst they forced

the dure, the Cardinall hyddis a box of gold under coills that war layd
the door, the cardinal hid a box of gold under coals in a secret corner of

in a secret corner. At lenth he asketh Will ye save my lyif? The said

the room. At length he asked 'Will you save my life?' John Leslie answered

Johne answerit It may be that we will. Nay sayis the Cardinall Sweir

'It may be that we will.' 'No' said the Cardinal 'Swear

unto me by Godis Woundis, and I sall oppin unto yow. Than answerit

to me by God's Wounds and I shall open the door to you.' Then John

the said John, It that was said is unsaid; and so he cryit Fire, fire for

Leslie answered 'It that was said was unsaid' and so he called 'fire, fire'

the dure was verie stark and so was brought ane chimlay full of

for the door was very strong and so a grate full of burning coals was

burning coallis, quhilk perceavit the Cardinall or his chalmer-chyld (it

brought to him, on perceiving this the cardinal or the chamber boy (it is

is uncertain) oppinit the dure, and the Cardinall sat doun in a chayre

uncertain which) opened the door and the Cardinal sat down in a chair

and cryit I ame a preist, I ame a priest, ye will not slay me. The said

and cried out ' I am a priest, I am a priest, you will not slay me.'

Johne Leslie, according to his former vowis [to avenge Wishart], straik

John Leslie, according to his former vows [to avenge Wishart] struck

him anis or twyis, and so did the said Petir. Bot James Melvell, a man

him once or twice and so did the said Peter, but James Melville, a man

of nature moist gentill and most modest, perceaving thame bayth in

of a most gentle and modest nature, seeing that they were both enraged,

cholere, withdrew thame and said the wark and judgement of god,

pulled them back and said 'The work and judgement of God

althocht it be secreit yit aucht to be done with gritter gravitie. And

although it is hidden, yet it ought to be done with greater gravity.' And

presenting unto him the point of the sword said 'Repent of thyne

presenting to the cardinal the point of the sword said 'Repent of your

former wickit lyif, but especiallie of the schedding of the bluid of that

former wicked life, but especially of the shedding of the blood of that

notable instrument of God, Mr George Wiseheart whiche albeit the

notable instrument of God, Mr George Wishart, which although

flame of fyre consumit befoir men, yit cryis it a vengeance upoun

consumed by the flame of fire before men, yet it cries a vengeance upon

the[e] and we from God ar sent to revenge it. For heir befoir my god,

you and we from god are sent to revenge it. For here before my God, I

I protest, that neither haitrent of thy persone, the love of thy ryches,

protest that neither hatred of your person, the love of your riches,

nor the feir of anie trouble thow could have done to me in particular,

nor the fear of any trouble you could have done to me in particular,

muisit or movethe me to straik the[e]; bot onlie because thow hes bein,
inspires or moves me to strike you, but only that you have been and

and remainis ane obstinate enemie to Chryist Jesus and his holie
remain an obstinate enemy to Christ Jesus and his holy gospel.'

evangell.' And so he straik him twys or thryis throw with a stoge
And so he struck him twice or thrice through with a stabbing sword,

sword: and so he fell, nevir a word hard out of his mouthe bot I ame
and so he fell, never a word heard out of his mouth but 'I am a

a priest. I ame a Preist. Fy, fy all is gone.
priest, I am a priest. Fy, fy, all is gone.'

Whill they war thus occupyed with the Cardinal, the fray ryissis in
While they were busy with the cardinal, a stir rose in

the toun; the proveist assembles the commonalitie, and cumis to the
the town, the provost assembled the ordinary people and came to the

fouseis syde, crying Quhat have ye done with my Lord Cardinal? Let
ditch-side crying 'What have you done with my lord cardinal.' They

us sie my Lord Cardinall. Thay that war within answerit gentillye,
that were within answered gently

'The best it war to yow to returne to your awin houses; for that man
'The best thing for you would be to return to your own houses, for that

you call the Cardinall hes receaved his reward, and in his awin
man you call the cardinal has received his reward and in his own

persone wil trouble the warld na mair. Bot then mor inragitlie they
person will trouble the world no more.' But then more enragedly they

cryit We sall nevir departe till that we sie him. And so was he brocht
cried 'We shall never depart until we see him.' And so he was brought to

to the Eist Blokhouse Heid and schawin deid over the wall to the
the east blockhouse head and shown dead over the wall to the

faythles multitude, which would not beleve befoir that it saw. And so
faithless multitude, which would never believe until they saw. And so

they departit, without requiem aeternam & requiescat in pace sung
they departed without requiem mass being sung for his soul. Now

for his saull. Now because the wedder [weather] was hotte, for it was
because the weather was hot, for it was May, as you have heard, and his

in Maii, as ye have hard and his funerallis culd not suddantlie be
funeral could not suddenly be prepared,

prepaired, it was thocht best (to keip him frome stinking) to give him
it was thought best (to keep him from stinking) to give him

grit salt yneuche, a cope of leid, and a nuck in the bottome of the Sey-
enough salt, a winding sheet of lead and a corner in the bottom of the sea

tour, a plaice quhair mony of God's children had bein imprisonit
    tower, a place where many of God's children had been imprisoned
befoir to await quhat exequies his brethren and bischopis wald
    before to await what funeral ceremonies his brethren and bishops would
prepair for him. These thingis we wrytte merrille, bot we would that
    prepare for him. These things we write with gladness, but we would wish
the reidar sould observe God's just judgementis, and how that he can
    that the reader should observe God's just judgements and how he can take
deprehend the wardlie wyis in their awin wisdome, mak their tabill to
    the worldly wise in their own wisdom, make their table to
be a snair to trappe thair awin feit, and thair awin presuppoisit streth
    be a snare to trap their own feet and their own pre-supposed strength
to be thair awin destructioun. These ar the warkis of our God,
    to be their own destruction. These are the works of our God,
whereby he wald admonisch the tirrants of this earthe, that in the end
    whereby we would admonish the tyrants of this earth, that in the end he
he will be revengit of thair crueltie, quhat strenth soevir they mak in
    will revenge their cruelty, whatsoever strength they make to
the contrair . . .
    the contrary . . .
    The deith of this forsaid tirrant [tyrant] was dolourous to the
    The death of this tyrant was sorrowful to the
preistis, dolourous to the Governour, and moist dolourous to the
    priests, sorrowful to the regent and most sorrowful to the
Quein Dowager: for in him perisched faythfulness to France, and
    queen dowager, for in him perished faithfulness to France and
comfort to all gentilwemen and especiallie to wantoun wedowis: his
    comfort to all gentlewomen and especially to wanton widows: his
deith muist be revengit.
    death had to be revenged.

John Knox, *Historie of the Reformatioun of Scotland*, Edinburgh, 1732.

Pinkie

The death of the cardinal came at a time when foreign invasions were a constant threat. The English now wanted something more than the dowager queen's smooth words – they wanted custody of little Mary herself. The result was another in the series of invasions known to later history as 'the Rough Wooing' and the catastrophic Scots defeat at the battle of Pinkiecleuch, on 10 September 1547. William Patten, a Londoner (as he proudly styles himself on the

title page of his work), came up with the invasion force and saw
for himself the dreadful carnage left in the wake of the successful
English assault. To the Scottish Catholic church, the English
invaders were heretics, and a good turn-out of church men and
their vassals was a feature of the Scottish side. Alas, the Kirk
militant had little success. The battle was a disaster, with casualties
greater than at Flodden. Mary had to be spirited to safety at the
island priory of Inchmahome whilst arrangements were made to
evacuate her to France.

Soon after this notable strewing of their footmen's weapons, began
a pitiful sight of the dead corpses lying dispersed abroad, some
their legs off, some but houghed, and left lying half-dead, some
thrust quite through the body, others the arms cut off, diverse their
necks half a sunder, many their heads cloven, of sundry the brains
pasht out, some others again their heads quite off, with other many
kinds of killing. After that and further in chase, all for the most part
killed either in the head or in the neck, for our horsemen could not
well reach the lower with their swords. And thus with blood and
slaughter of the enemy, this chase was continued five miles in length
westward from the place of their standing, which was in the fallow
fields of Inveresk until Edinburgh Park and well nigh to the gates of
the town itself and unto Leith, and in breadth nigh 4 miles, from the
Firth sands up toward Dalkeith southward. In all which space, the
dead bodies lay as thick as a man may note cattle grazing in a full
replenished pasture. The river ran all red with blood, so that in the
same chase were counted, as well by some of our men that
somewhat diligently did mark it as by some of them taken prisoners,
that very much did lament it, to have been slain above 14 thousand.
In all this compass of ground what with weapons, arms, hands, legs,
heads, blood and dead bodies, their flight might have been easily
tracked to every of their three refuges. And for the smallness of our
number and shortness of the time (which was scant five hours, from
one to well nigh six) the mortality was so great, as it was thought,
the like aforetime not to have been seen. Indeed it was the better
maintained with their own swords that lay each where scattered by
the way, whereof our men, as they had broke one still took up
another; there was store enough, and they laid it on freely, that right
many among them at this business broke three or four ere they
returned homeward to the army. I may well perchance confess, that
herein we used some sharpness (although not as much as we might)
and little courtesy, and yet I can safely avow, all done by us, as

rather by sundry respects driven and compelled, then either of cruelty or delight in slaughter. And like someway to the diligent master that sharply sometime (when warning will not serve) doth beat his scholar, not hardly for hate of child, or his own delight in beating, but for love he would have him amend his faults or negligence and beats him once surely because he would need to beat him no more. One cause of the correction we used, I may well count to be their tyrannous vow they made (which we certainly heard of) that whensoever they fought and overcame, they would slay so many, and spare so few, a sure proof of whereof they plainly had showed at our onset before, where they killed all, and saved not a man.

Another respect was to revenge their great and cruel tyranny shown at Panyarhough [the battle of Ancrum Moor, 1545 – a Scottish victory] where they slew the Lord Evers [Sir Ralph Eure] and cruelly killed as many else of our men as came in their hands . . . Another thing and not the meanest matter was that their armour amongst them so little differed, and their apparel so base and beggarly, wherein the Lurdein [rascal] was in a manner all one with the Lord, and the loun [commoner] with the laird: all clad alike in jacks covered with white leather, doublets of the same or of fustian and most commonly all white hose. Not one with either chain, brooch, ring or garment of silk that I could see, unless chains of latten drawn four of five times along the thighs of their hose and doublet sleeves for cutting; and of that sort I saw many. This vileness of port [appearance], was the cause that so many of their great men and gentlemen were killed and so few saved. The outward show, the semblance and sign whereby a stranger might discern a villein from a gentleman was not among them to be seen. As for words and goodly proffer of great ransoms, [they] were as common and rife in the mouths of the one as of the other. And therefore hereby it came to pass that after, at the examination and counting of the prisoners we found taken about above twenty of their villeins to one of their gentlemen: whom no man need to doubt, we had rather have spared, then the villeins, if we could have known any difference between them in taking. And yet notwith-standing all these our just causes and quarrels to kill them, we showed more grace and took more to mercy then the case on our side, for the cause aforesaid did well deserve or require . . . for the prisoners accounted by the Marshal's book were numbered to above 1500. Touching the slaughter, sure we killed nothing so many as (if we had minded cruelty so much) for the time and opportunity right well we might, for my Lord's grace, of his wonted mercy, much moved with the pity of this

sight, and rather glad of victory, than desirous of cruelty, soon after
(by guess) five of the clock stayed his standard of his horsemen at the
furthest part of their camp westward and caused the trumpets to blow
a retreat. Whereat Sir Ralph Sadler treasurer (whose great diligence at
the time and ready forwardness in the chiefest of the fray before did
worthily merit no small commendation) caused all the footmen to stay
and then with much travail and great pain, made them to be brought
into some order again. It was a thing yet not easily to be done, by
reason they all as then somewhat busily applied their market to the
spoil of the Scottish camp, wherein were found good provision of
white bread, ale, oatcakes, oatmeal, mutton, butter in pots, cheese and
in diverse tents good wine also; good store to say truth, of good
victual for the manner of the country. And in some tents among them
(as I heard say) were also found of silver plate a dish or two, 2 or 3
goblets and 3 or 4 chalices, the which the finders (I know not with
what reverence but with some devotion hardly) plucked out of the
cold clouts and thrust into their warm bosoms . . .

It was a wonder to see, but that (as they say) many hands make
light work, how soon the dead bodies were stripped out of their
garments stark naked, even from as far as the chase went until the
place of our onset; whereby the personages of our enemies might by
the way easily be viewed and considered; the which for tallness of
stature, cleanness of skin, bigness of bone with due proportion of all
parts, I for my part advisedly noted to be such, as but that I saw that
it was so, I would not have believed sure so many of that sort to
have been in all their country. Among them lay there many priests
and kirkmen, as they call them, of whom it was bruited amongst us,
that there was a whole band of 3 or 4 thousand, but we were after
informed, it was not altogether so . . .

Among these [the Scots] weapons and beside several other
banners, standards and pennons, a banner of white sarcenet was
found under which it was said these kirkmen came, whereupon was
painted a woman with her hair about her shoulders, kneeling before
a crucifix, and on her right hand a church; after that written a long
upon a banner in great roman letters *afflictae sponsae ne obliviscaris*
[Do not forget your afflicted spouse]; which words declared that
they would have this woman to signify the church, Christ's spouse
and thus in humble wise making her petition unto Christ her
husband that he would not now forget her, his spouse, being
scourged and persecuted, meaning at this time by us. It was said it
was the Abbot of Dunfermline's banner; but whether it was his or
the Bishop of Dunkeld's, the governor's brothers [brothers of the

Regent Arran] (who I understand were both in the field) and what
the number of kirkmen was, I could not certainly learn: but I was
sure it was some devout papist's device, that not only be like would
not endeavor to do ought for atonement and peacemaking between
us, but all contrariwise brought forth his standard stoutly to fight in
field himself against us; pretexting this his great ungodliness thus
bent toward the maintenance of a naughty quarrel with colour of
religion to come in aid of Christ's church. Which church to say
truth, coming thus to battle full appointed with weapon and
guarded with such sort of deacons to fight; however in painting he
had set her out, a man might well think in that in condition he had
rather framed a cursed quean [hussy] that would pluck her husband
by the pate except she had her will, than like a meek spouse that
went about humbly by submission and prayer to desire her
husband's help for redress of things amiss.

William Patten, 'The Expedicion into Scotlande', printed in *Fragments of Scottish
History*, ed. Sir J. G. Dalyell, Edinburgh, 1798.

How Inchcolm was Captured from the English

*After the disaster of Pinkie, Marie de Guise became Regent of
Scotland, but she was faced with a large and victorious English
army encamped in the heart of her country. Now the only hope for
the two Marys was help from France. It came in the shape of André
de Montalembert, sieur d'Essé, who landed with 6,000 troops at
Leith on 16 June 1548. His friend, Jean de Beaugué, records how
d'Essé cleared the strategic island of Inchcolm, in the Forth
estuary, of the English invaders. Being written by a Frenchman, the
account is, of course, not very flattering to Les Anglais!*

All our soldiers landed with much difficulty, meeting great
resistance. But when the fighting began on the island and
Monsieur de Dessé and his men joined battle, the enemy took fright
on seeing their general struck down and killed before their eyes, that
same general who had not long before caused the death of
Desboryes. Their fright was such that they put up no more resistance
but retreated in disorder to the tip of the island where they were all
captured like sheep. I do not wish to recall the fear the English had
in the face of death. 'For I consider that other men's fear, being
something so unworthy of a soldier, should not be set before the eyes
of young men who make profession of valour and virtue.' I can say
that, with the loss of only two men, we captured Inchcolm from the

English who numbered more than 800 seasoned, experienced
soldiers, while we had less than 700 to give them battle. We found
there a good quantity of medium and heavy artillery, stocks of food
and munitions, and all sorts of tools and materials to fortify the
island, together with a large transport ship, loaded with malmsey,
cross-bolts, silk and woollen cloth, and other items required to
garrison and fortify a place of great strategic importance. In this
connection I must say that, of all the nations in the world, the
English are those who take the greatest care in provisioning the forts
which they capture, but they are also bad at holding them. Monsieur
de Dessé refused to take a share of the booty captured on the island,
saying to those who endeavoured to make him change his mind that
he would never take for himself the things which should belong to
the soldiers as a reward for their deeds of valour. 'I myself,' he said
'have never wished to return to France enriched with anything other
than glory.' Truly these words were spoken by a generous heart
which sought honour alone as reward for its valour.

Jean de Beaugué, *Histoire de la guerre d'Ecosse, pendant les campagnes 1548 et
1549*, ed. Joseph Bain, Maitland Club, 1830.

Mary's Wedding

*Mary, aged five, was sent off to the French court on 29 July 1548.
On Sunday 24 April 1558, aged fifteen, her dream marriage to the
Dauphin of France finally took place (given the shifting diplomacy
of her new father-in-law Henri II of France, it had never been a
foregone conclusion). This account of the wedding was apparently
written by a Scots student in Paris, and it survives only as a
fragment recovered from the binding of a work by David Lindsay
the poet. As at most traditional Scottish weddings, a 'poor oot' –
coins being thrown to crowds in the street – was in order.*

[They scattered] gold and silver amang the pepill
      They scattered gold and silver amongst the people

on every side of the scaffald within the kirke. Whar
      on every side of the platform within the kirk. Where

with *qui potest capere capiat* was sik yalping and
      with 'who could seize, let him seize it' there was

yeoling, sik calling and crying as, as the like (I
      such yelping and yowling, such calling and crying,

think) was never hard. Ther gentillmen tint [lost]
      as the like, I think, was never heard. There

their clokis, gentilwemen ther fartingales,
gentlemen lost their cloaks, ladies their

merchantmen ther gownes, maisters in art ther
farthingales, merchants their gowns, masters of

hudis, studentis ther cornet cappis, and religious
arts their hoods, students their cornered caps and

men had ther scapilliries violently riven fra ther
clerics had their scapularies violently torn from

shulders. Whar also amang the rest was a stout
their shoulders. Amongst the rest was a stout young

yong baire futed freir of Sainct Francis ordir, the
bare-footed Franciscan friar, who got more of the

whilk freir gat mair of the cast money than four of
'poor-oot' than four of his companions. Being

his cumpanions. The whilk beand demandid
challenged what he was doing handling money

wharfor he did handill money contrary to his
contrary to his vows of poverty, he answered

profession: he answerid, hola my freindis hola,
'Hola, my friends, Hola! Content yourselves, for if

content your selves, for gife [if] Sanct Francis him
St Francis himself was present here this day, who

self war heir present this day whilk was the chief of
was the chief of our order, he would put out his

our profession, he wald put to his hand, as I have
hand as I have done and my companions in

done, and my com[pan]ions, in handling and
handling and keeping this alms money (thereby

keping this [almis] m[on]ey (therby mening na
meaning that he was not being greedy)

cuvetou[snes]) to the laude of God, and honour of
to the praise of God and honour of this most godly

[this] maist godly and triumphant marriage . . .
and triumphant marriage . . .

[To see the merchantmen in ther] doublettis,
To see the merchants in their doublets without their

gounles, maisters in art hudles, and studentis with
gowns, the masters of arts hoodless, and students

many uthers caples, it was a merie sport for him
with many others capless, it was a merry sport for

that tint nathing. And thane to heir thare
him who lost nothing. And then to hear their

lamentation, it was na les sport. Some saing, I have
lamentation, it was no less sport, some saying 'I

tint my cloke wurth ten crownes and gat but a
have lost my cloak worth ten crowns and got only a

teston. Ane uther sais, alace my gowne was
teston (about a shilling). Another says alas my gown was

pluckide fra my bak wurth six crownes, and gat but
plucked from my back worth six crowns and I got but 5 sous

5 sous. The third sais my purs is gane and 50
(roughly pennies). The third says my purse is gone and 50

crownes in it and gat nathinge. I have gotine quod
crowns in it and I got nothing. I have gotten,

ane uther a cuppill of gud crownes of the sonne and
said another a couple of good crowns of the sun and

tint nathinge. Wharfor I heringe and seing this gud
lost nothing. Wherefore, I hearing and seeing these good

fellowes having sike gret tinsell [loss] for gredines
fellows having such great loss for greediness

in getting of few pecis of monie, and specialy him
in getting a few pieces of money, and particularly him

that tint his purs and 50 crownes in it and gat
who lost his purse and 50 crowns in it and got

nathing: I was forced, not alanerly to say with the
nothing. I was forced, not alone, to say with the

poet Virgil Quid non mortalia pectora cogis, auri
poet Virgil 'Accursed greed for gold, what dost thou not drive

sacra fames
hearts of men to do?'. Aeneid III, 55.

The Marriage of Mary Queen of Scots to the Dauphin: a Scottish Printed Fragment,
ed. Douglas Hamer, The Bibliographical Society, London, 1932.

The St Giles Riot

Though John Knox is not exactly famous as a satirist, his gift for mocking, bitterly satirical narratives was one of the most powerful weapons in his armoury. Here he describes the riot of 1558, when the Edinburgh Protestants decided to take direct action against the city's St Giles Day procession. This was meant to be a display of strength by the city's Catholic majority, but the shock troops of the Reformation were determined to 'rain on their parade', to use an American phrase. Knox's militant and unrepentantly bigoted views can seem shocking to modern ears, but they were precisely what delighted his original readership. Tolerance was considered a dangerous weakness on both sides of the Reformation/Counter-Reformation divide, and the most strident authors were often the most highly cherished. However, it is possible to enjoy Knox's pungent Scots without necessarily sharing his views.

A nd in Edinburghe was that grit idoll, callit Sanct Geill, first
    And in Edinburgh was that great idol called St Giles, first

drowned in the Northe Loche, and, efter brunt whiche raysit no
    drowned in the Nor loch and afterwards burnt which raised no

small trubill in the town . . .
    small trouble in the town . . .

But yit culd the bischopis in no sorte be quiet; for Sanct Geill's day
    But yet could the Bishops in no sort be quiet; for St Giles day was

approching, they gave chairge to the proveist, baillies, and counsaill of
    approaching. So they gave the order to the Provost, bailies and council of

Edinburgh, eyther to get agane the auld Sanct Geill, or ells upoun thair
    Edinburgh, either to get again the old St Giles or else at their own

expens to mak a new image. The counsaill answered, that to them the
    expense to make a new image. The council answered that the order

chairge appeired verie injust, for they understude that God, in some
    appeared very unjust to them for they understood that God in some places

places had commandit idolls and images to be destroyit; bot quhair he
    had commanded idols and images [of saints] to be destroyed but where he

had commandit images to be set up they had not red; and desyrit the
    had commanded images to be set up, they had not read and desired the

bischope to find a warrant for his comandment. Quhairat the bischope
    Bishop to find a precedent for his command. At this the Bishop was

offendit admonisched thame under pane of cursing, which they
    offended, and admonished them under pain of excommunication. They

preventit by a formall appellatioun, appeilling frome him, as from a
prevented this by a formal appeal, appealing from him, as a partial and

partiall and corrupt juge, unto the pape's holines; and so gritter thingis
corrupt judge, to the Pope's holiness, but greater things

schortlie following, that passit in oblivioun: yit wald not the preastis
shortly following, that was forgotten. Yet the priests

and frearis ceis to have that grit solempnitie and manifest
and friars insisted on having that great solemnity and manifest

abhominatioun, whiche they accustomablie had upoun Sanct Geill's
abomination, which they traditionally had upon St Giles' Day, to wit

day, to wit, they wald have that idoll borne, and tharefoir was all
they would have that idol borne [in procession] and therefore preparation

preparatioun deuly maid. A marmorset idoll was borrowed from the
was duly made. A marmoset [monkey] idol was borrowed from the

Gray Frearis, (a silver piece of James Carmichell was laid in pledge) it
Greyfriars (a silver piece of James Carmichael's was given in pledge). It

was fast fixed with irone nailles upoun a barrow called thair fertour.
was securely fixed with iron nails upon a barrow called their shrine.

Thare assembled preastis, frearis, chanonis, and rottin papistes, with
There assembled preists, friars, canons and rotten papists with

tabournes and trumpetis, baneris and bagge pypes: and who was thare
tabours and trumpets, banners and bag-pipes; and who was there

to leid the ring, but the Quein Regent herself, with all hir schavelings,
to lead the festivities but the Queen Regent herself with all her clergy

for honour of that feast. West about goes it, and cumis doun the hie
for honour of that feast. West about it went, and came down the

streat, and doun to the comone crose. The Quein Regent dyned that
high street and down to the common cross. The Queen Regent dined that

day in Sandie Carpytynis hous betwix the bowis, and so quhen the
day in Sandy Carpenter's house between the Bows and so when the

idolle returned back agane, sche left it, and past in to her denner. The
idol returned back again, she left it and went into her dinner. The

heartes of the brethrein war wonderouslie inflamed, and seing sick
hearts of the brethren were greatly excited and seeing such

abhominatioun so manifestlie manteined, war decreed to be revenged.
abomination so manifestly supported, they decided to be revenged.

They war devyded in severall cumpanies, quhairof not ane knew of
They were divided into several companies of which, none knew of the

ane uther. Thare war some temporissaris that day, amonges quhome
others. There were some compromisers that day, amongst whom

David Forress, called the Generall, was ane, who fearing the chance to
David Forres, called 'The General' was one, who fearing the deed to

be done as it fell, laboured to stay the brethrein; but that could not be;
be done as it fell out, tried to stop the brethren, but that could not be done,

for immediatelie efter that the Quein was entered in the lugeing, some
for immediately after the Queen entered in her lodging, some of those

of those that war of the interpryis drew ney to the idoll, as willing to
that were in on the enterprise, drew near to the idol, as if willing to help to

help to bear him, and getting the ferteour upoun thair schuldeours,
carry him, and getting the shrine upon their shoulders,

began to schuder, thinking that thareby the idoll sould have fallin; but
began to shake it, thinking that the idol should have fallen,

that was provyded and prevented by the irone nailles, as we have said;
but that was provided for and prevented by the iron nails, as we have said,

and so begane ane to cry, down with the idoll, doun with it, and so,
and so one began to cry 'Down with the idol, down with it' and so

without delay, it was pulled down. Sum bragis maid the preistis
without delay, it was pulled down. The patrons of the priests made some

patrounis at the first; bot when they saw the febilnes of thair god, for
boasts at first, until they saw the weakness of their God, for

one tuke him be the heallis, and dadding him heid to the calsay, left
one took him by the heels and smacking his head on the pavement, left

dagoun without heid or handis, and said, fy upoun the thow young
Dagon without head or hands and said 'Fy upon thee, thou young

Sanct Geill, thy father wald have taryed four suche. This considderit,
St Giles! Thy father could have taken four such!' This considered we say,

we say, the preistis and freiris fled faster then they did at Pinkie
the priests and friars fled faster than they did at the battle of Pinkie.

cleuche. Thair micht have bein sein so suddane a fray as seldome hes
There might have been witnessed such a scuffle as seldom has been seen

bein sein amongis that sorte of men within this realme; for down gois
amongst that sort of men within this country, for down go

the crocis, of gois the surplyses, round capis, cornet with the crownis.
the crosses, off go the surplices, round caps, cornets with crowns.

The Gray Freirs gaiped, the Blak Freirs blew, and the prestis panted
The Greyfriars gaped, the Blackfriars blew and the priests panted

and fled, and happie was he that first gat the hous; for suche ane
and fled and happy was he that first made it indoors, for such a sudden

suddane fray came nevir amongist the generatioun of antichrist
fray never before came amongst the generation of Antichrist

within this realme befoir. By chance thair lay upoun a stair a merrie
in this realm. By chance, there was upon a stair a merry Englishman,

inglische man; and seing the discomfitour to be without blude, thoicht
and seeing the upset to be without bloodshed, he thought

he wald adde sum merrines to the matter: and so cryed he over the
he would add some humour to the matter and so he yelled over the

stair, and said, Fy upoun yow hooressones, quhy have ye brockin
stair and said 'Fy upon you whoresons! Why have you broken

ordour, down the streate ye passit in array, and with grit mirthe:
ranks? Down the street you passed in pomp and with great mirth!

Quhy fly ye villanes now without ordour? Turne and stryke everie ane
Why fly you villains now without order? Turn and strike every one

a straik for the honour of his god; Fy cowartis fy, ye fall nevir be
a blow for the honour of his God! Fy cowards! Fy! You shall never be

juged worthie of your wages agane. Bot exhortatiounis war then
judged worthy of your wages again!' But exhortations were then

unproffitable: for efter that Bell had brockin his neck, thair was na
unprofitable, for after Bael had broken his neck, there was no

comforte to his confusit armie.
comfort for his confused army.

John Knox, *Historie of the Reformatioun of Scotland*, Edinburgh, 1732.

Mary's Scotland

Of all Scottish monarchs, Mary Queen of Scots is perhaps the most controversial. The subject of books, films, plays, painting and poetry, no other character from Scots history seems to exercise such a hold over the imagination – not only of Scots but of people all over the world. Elizabeth I herself referred to Mary as 'the daughter of debate', and ever since, historians have been squabbling as to whether Mary's misfortunes were tragic bad luck, or the result of her own stupidity or wickedness. Strictly speaking Mary's reign ended with her forced abdication at Loch Leven and with the accession of her little son James in 1567; however this chapter covers Scotland from Mary's return (to Scotland from France) to her death.

Mary's Return

Welcome to Edinburgh! Home of fountains running with wine and er . . . anti-catholic speeches by children. Not quite what Mary Queen of Scots was expecting to find from her loyal subjects. On 5 December 1560, François, the young King of France, had died, leaving Mary a widow, and she soon saw that the best of her few options was to go back and govern her native land. She arrived at Leith on Tuesday 19 August 1561, returning to a country which had undergone a pro-protestant religious revolution in the meantime. The Reformation was not consolidated in Scotland and the nation was deeply divided. Despite this, Mary was received in the capital with joy and great ceremony.

The 'Diurnal of Occurrents', a 16th-century chronicle of Scottish events, contains what seems to be a contemporary description of the festivities. It's notable that the children of Edinburgh were given the religiously controversial parts of the display. One child gave Mary Protestant translations of the Bible and the Psalms, which in the words of Catholic courtier Lord Herries 'were scarce savourie to her', and it was the 'bairns in the cairt' with the Queen's present who gave her a speech about getting rid of the mass before singing a psalm at her. Under the circumstances Mary could hardly give them a good clip round the ear.

Upoun the secund day of September lxi [1561] the quenes grace
Upon the second day of September 1561 the queen's grace

maid hir entres in the burgh of Edinburgh on this maner. Hir hienes
made her entry to the burgh of Edinburgh in this manner. Her highness
depairtit of Halyrudhous, and raid be the lang gait on the north syid
left Holyroodhouse and rode by the long street on the North side
of the said burgh, unto the tyme scho come to the castell, quheir wes
of the burgh, until she came to the castle, where a gate was
ane yet maid to hir, at the quhilk scho accumpaniit with the maist
made for her. There she was accompanied by the most
pairt of the nobilitie of Scotland except my lord Duke
part of the nobility of Scotland except for the Duke and
[Chateauherault] and his sone, come in and raid up the castell bank
his son [the Hamiltons]. They rode up the castle bank and
to the castell, and dynit thairin; and quhen sho had dynit at tuelf
dined in the castle and at noon, after she had dined, her
houris, hir hienes come furth of the said castell towart the said burgh,
highness came out of the castle towards the burgh. At her
at quhilk depairting the artailyerie schot vehementlie. And thairefter,
departure the artillery shot loudly. After that as she
quhen sho was rydand down the castellhill, thair met hir hienes ane
was riding down the castle hill, an
convoy of the young mene of the said burgh, to the nomber of fyftie,
escort of about fifty of the young men of the burgh met her highness.
or thairby, thair bodeis and theis coverit with yeallow taffateis, thair
Their bodies and thighs were covered with yellow taffeta. Their arms
armes and leggs fra the kne doun bair, cullorit with blak in the maner
and legs from the knee down were bare, coloured black as though they
of Moris, upon thair heidis blak hattis, and on their faces blak
were moors. They had black hats upon their heads and black masks on their
visouris, in their mowthis rings, garnesit with intellable precious
faces, in their mouths were rings decorated with innumerable precious
staneis, about thair neckkis, leggis and armes infynit of chenis of gold;
stones. About their necks, arms and legs were uncountable chains of gold.
togidder with saxtene of the maist honest men of the toun, cled in
Together with 16 of the most notable men of the town, clad in
velvot gownis and velvot bonettis, berand and gangand about the paill
velvet gowns and bonnets, they bore and accompanied the canopy of cloth
under the quhilk her hienes raid; quhilk paill wes of fyne purpour
under which her highness rode. The canopy was of fine purple

velvet lynit with reid taffateis, freinyiet with gold and silk; and efter
velvet lined with red taffeta, fringed with gold and silk. Behind them
thame wes ane cart with certane bairnes, togidder with ane coffer
was a cart with some children, together with a coffer in which was the
quhairin wes the copboard and propyne quhilk suld be propynit to hir
cupboard [a special piece of furniture for displaying plate] and the gift
hienes; and quhen hir grace come fordwart to the butter trone of the
which was to be presented to her highness [costly plate]. Then the queen
said burgh, the nobilitie and convoy foirsaid precedand, at the quhilk
came on to the Butter Tron [a public weighing machine and by extension the
butter trone thair was ane port made of tymber, in maist honourable
marketplace in which one stood] of Edinburgh, preceded by the nobility
maner, cullorit with fyne cullouris, hungin with syndrie armes; upoun
and her escort. At the tron was a gate made of timber, in the most stately
the quhilk port thair wes ane cloud opynnand with four levis, in the
fashion, coloured with fine colours, hanging with various heraldic devices
quhilk wes put ane bony barne. And quhen the quenes hienes was
and over the gate was a cloud which opened in four pieces, in the cloud
cumand throw the said port, the said cloude opynnit, and the barne
was a pretty child. When the queen's highness was coming through the
discendit doun as it had bene ane angell, and deliverit to hir hienes the
gate, the cloud opened and the child descended as if it had been an angel
keyis of the toun, togidder with ane bybill and ane psalme buik,
and delivered to her highness the keys of the town, together with a bible
coverit with fyne purpourit velvot; and efter the said barne had
and psalm book, covered with fine purple velvet. After the child had made
spoken some small speitches, he deliverit alsua to hir hienes thre
some small speeches, he delivered three documents to her highness, the
writingis, the tennour thairof is uncertane. That being done, the barne
nature of which is uncertain. When that was done the child went
ascendit on the cloud and the said cloude stekit; and therefter the
up on the cloud and the cloud closed. After that the queen came down to
quenis grace come doun to the tolbooth, at the quhilk was [   ]
the Tolbooth, at which was a [   ]
upoun two skassattis, ane abone and ane under that; upon the under
upon two scaffolds, one above and one under it, on the bottom one was
was situat ane fair wirgin, callit Fortoune, under the quhilk was thrie
a fair maiden representing Fortune, beneath whom were three fair

fair virgynnis, all cled in maist precious attyrement, callit [   ] justice

maidens all clothed in the most precious garments called [   ] justice and

and policie. And efter ane litill speitche maid thair, the quenis grace

policy. And after a little speech made there, the queen's grace came to the

come to the croce, quhair thair was standand four fair virgynnis, cled

burgh cross, where four fair maidens clothed in the most heavenly

in maist hevenlie clething, and fra the quhilk croce the wyne ran out

clothing were standing. From the cross wine poured out abundantly at the

at the spouttis in greit abundance; thair wes the noyis of pepill casting

spouts, there could be heard the noise of people throwing down the

the glassis with wyne. This being done, our soveràne ladie come to the

glasses with wine. This being done, our sovereign lady came to the

salt trone, quhair thair wes sum spekaris; and efter ane litill speitche,

Salt Tron, where there were some speakers and after a little speech,

thai brunt upoun the skasset maid at the said trone, the maner of ane

they burnt the representation of a sacrifice upon the scaffold made at that

sacrifice; and swa that being done, sho depairtit to the nether bow,

tron. That being done, she left for the Nether Bow

quhair thair wes ane uther skasset maid, havand ane dragoun in the

where there was another scaffold made with a dragon in it

samyn, with some speiches; and efter the dragoun wes brynt, and the

and more speeches. After the dragon was burnt, the

quenis grace hard ane psalme song, hir hienes past to hir abbay of

queen heard a psalm sung. Her highness then went to the abbey of

Halyrudhouse with the said convoy and nobilities; and thair the

Holyroodhouse with her escort and the nobles. There the

barins quhilk wes in the cairt with the propyne maid some speitche

children in the cart with the gift made a speech about

concernyng the putting away of the mess and thairefter sang ane

abolishing the mass and after that sang a

psalme; this being done, the cart come to Edinburgh, and the said

psalm. This being done the cart came to Edinburgh and the notable

honest men remaynit in hir utter chalmer, and desyred hir grace to

men of the burgh remained in her outer chamber and desired her grace to

ressave the said copebord, quhilk wes double ourgilt; the price wes

receive the cupboard which was double gilded and worth

2,000 merkis; quha ressavit the samyne, and thankit thame thairof.

2,000 marks. She received it and thanked them and so the notables

And sua the honest men and convoy come to Edinburgh.

and the escort returned to Edinburgh.

A Diurnal of Remarkable Occurrents that have passed within the Country of
Scotland since the death of King James the Fourth, ed. T. Thomson, Bannatyne
Club, 1833.

A Night to Remember

*At first Mary's reign seemed to justify the rejoicing. She made
admirable efforts to be even-handed in her treatment of Scotland's
two principal faiths and, despite her French upbringing, she
adopted a conciliatory tone with England. For almost four years
Mary's reign was fairly stable. There was one expedition against
the troublesome (militantly Catholic) Earl of Huntly, but apart
from that peace reigned – at a time when Europe was being torn
apart by religious war. Mary, working under the advice of her
illegitimate half-brother the Earl of Moray, seemed to be doing a
good job. In 1565, she had married the handsome Henry, Lord
Darnley, tall, blond and dim, but crucially close in blood to the
English throne. The outsmarted Elizabeth I was furious, Moray
equally so – he led an abortive rebellion which ended in his
banishment.*

*But who cared? Mary was soon pregnant. A fairytale conclusion?
Unfortunately not. Darnley was not just the upper-class twit
people took him for, but a malign, spoilt, adulterous, drunken thug
who was easily manipulated by others. He was soon taken for a
ride by the hard-men of Scotland's native aristocracy. They played
on his jealousy of Mary's preference for more civilised company.
Their intended victim was supposedly her secretary and musician
David Riccio, their real aim was probably to scare nearly six-
month pregnant Mary into a miscarriage and to snatch power,
allowing Moray and his banished friends to return. Mary outwitted
them, but she would never forgive and never forget. Here is her
own account of Riccio's murder in her letter to the Archbishop of
Glasgow, James Beaton, her ambassador in Paris.*

Upon the 9th day of March instant we being, at even about seven
hours, in our cabinet at our supper, sociated with our sister the
countess of Argyle, our brother the commendator of Halyrudhouse,
laird of Creich, Arthur Erskin [these are two of Mary's bastard half-
siblings by her father James v], and certain others our domestick
servitors, in quiet maner, especially by reason of our evill disposition

[poor health], being counsell'd to sustean ourselves with flesh [meat – the supper party took place in Lent], having also then past almost to the end of seven moneths in our birth [pregnancy]; the King our husband came to us in our cabinet, placed him beside us at our supper. The earl of Morton and lord Lindsay, with their assistars, bodin in warlick maner [armed in warlike manner], to the number of eightscore persons or thereby, kept and occupied the whole entry of our palace of Halyrudhouse, so that as they believed it was not possible to any person to escape forth of the same. In that mean time the lord Ruthven, bodin [armed] in like manner, with his complices, took entry perforce in our cabinet, and there seeing our secretary David Riccio among others our servants, declared he had to speak with him. In this instant, we required the King our husband, if he knew any thing of that intreprise? Who denied the samyne [same]. Also we commanded the lord Ruthven, under the pain of treason, to avoid him forth of our presence; declaring we should exhibite the said David before the Lords of Parlament, to be punisht, if any sorte he had offended. Notwithstanding the said lord Ruthven perforce invadit [attacked] him in our presence (he then for refuge took safeguard, having retired him behind our back) and with his complices cast down our table upon ourself, put violent hands in him, struck him over our shoulders with whinzeards [whingers – swords], one part of them standing before our face with bended daggs [aimed pistols], most cruelly took him forth of our cabinet, and at the entry of our chamber give him fifty six strokes with whinzeards and swords. In doing whereof, we were not only struck with great dreadour, but also by sundrie considerations was most justly induced to take extream fear of our life. After this deed immediately the said lord Ruthven coming again in our presence, declared how they and their complices foresaid were highly offended with our proceedings and tyranny, which was not to them tolerable; how we was abused by the said David, whom they had actually put to death, namely in taking his counsell for maintenance of the ancient religion [Catholicism], debarring of the lords which were fugitive, and entertaining of amity with foreign princes and nations with whom we were confederate; putting also upon council the lords Bothwell and Huntly, who were traitors, and with whom he associated himself. That the lords banist in England were the morne to resort towards us, and would take plain part with them in our contrary; and that the king was willing to remit them their offences. We all this time took no less care of ourselves, than for our council and nobility, maintenars of our authority, being with us in our palace for the time; to wit, the earls of Huntly, Bothwell, Athole, lords Fleming and Levingston, sir James Balfour, and certain others our familiar servitors: against whom the interprise was conspired as well as for David; and namely to have hanged the said sir James in cords. Yet, by the providence of God, the earls of Huntly and Bothwell escaped forth of their chambers in our palace at a back-window by some cords; wherein thir [these] conspirators took some fear, and thought themselves greatly disappointed in ther interprize. The earl of Athole and sir James Balfour by some other means, with the lords Fleming and Levingston, obtained deliverance of their invasion. The provost and town of Edinburgh having understood this tumult in our palace, caused ring their common bell, came to us in great number, and desired to have seen our presence, intercomoned [communicated] with us, and to have known our welfare: to whom we was not permitted to give answer, being extreamly bosted [threatened] by thir lords, who in our face declared, if we desired to have spoken them, they should cut us in collops [slices of meat], and cast us over the walls. So this community being commanded by our husband, retired them to quietness.

All that night we were detained in captivity within our chamber, not permitting us to have intercomoned scarcely with our servant-women, nor domestick servitors. Upon the morn hereafter proclaimation was made in our husband's name, by our advice, commanding all prelates and other lords conveened to Parlement, to retire themselves of our burgh of Edinburgh. That haill day we was keeped in that firmance [captivity], our familiar servitors and guard being debarred from our service, and we watched by the committars of thir crimes; to whom a part of the community of Edinburgh, to the number of fourscore persons, assisted.

Alexandre Labanoff, *Lettres, Instructions et Mémoires de Marie Stuart*, London, 1852 .

A Diplomatic Incident

Despite the horror of the murder of Riccio in her presence and the rigours of escape on horseback, Mary did not lose her baby. On 19 June 1566, the baby prince who would all too soon become James VI of Scotland was born in Edinburgh Castle. Mary rejoiced, but her relationship with the father of her child deteriorated. Darnley was firmly out of favour after the Riccio murder and his anti-social

behaviour had, if anything, worsened. He was all but left out when
Mary prepared the dazzling festivities of James's baptism at
Stirling: Scotland's first Renaissance pageant. This was an
international event: the Queen of England, the King of France and
the Duke of Savoy were to be godparents by proxy of the little
boy. Their ambassadors attended bearing magnificent gifts, such as
a golden font, two stones in weight, from Elizabeth.

There were fireworks and masques, banqueting and music. It was
to be a showcase of Mary's success and prestige as monarch of
Scotland. Her impresario, the Frenchman Bastian Pages, was doing
his best to make an impression on the foreign guests.
Unfortunately, his device of 'satyrs', mythological creatures half-
man, half-goat, was taken all too personally by the English
contingent when they waggled their tails in their direction. This
was thought to be an allusion to the old medieval racist slur that
the English had tails – 'tailed dogs!' as their enemies used to cry.
An international incident was in the offing, but luckily for Mary,
one of her most seasoned diplomats, Sir James Melville of Halhill,
helped to nip the trouble in the bud. Here is his account of the
incident in his Memoirs. Note that the English ambassadors could
see plainly that all was not right in Mary's marriage . . .

And when all the rest of the ambassadours wer com, they envyed
And when the rest of the ambassadors came, they were envious to see
to se the Englis men mair frendly and famylierly used than they; for
the English treated in a more friendly and familiar way than they were,
then sche had mair ado with England than with France, and the
for then she [Mary] had more to do with England than with France, and
Frenche erle that was sent was na courteour, bot a semple man; and
the French earl who was sent was no courtier, but a politically-naive
Mons de Morat the Duc of Scavoyes his ambassadour, being farr aff,
man. Monsieur de Morat, the Duke of Savoy's ambassador, travelling
cam efter the baptesme. During ther being in Stirling, ther wes daily
from a distance, came after the baptism. During their stay in Stirling,
banketing, dancing, and triumphe; and at the principall banket ther
there was daily banqueting, dancing and triumph; and at the principal
fell our ane gret eylest and gruge amang the Englis men; for a
banquet, there fell out a great offence and grudge amongst the English.
Frenchman callit Bastien devysed a number of men formed lyk
A Frenchman called Bastian, devised a number of men dressed up like

sattyres, with lang tailes and whippis in ther handis, runnyng befoir
satyrs with long tails and whips in their hands, running in front of the

the meit, quhilk wes brocht throw the gret hall upon ane trym
food, which was brought through the great hall upon an ingenious

engyn, marching as apperit it alain, with musiciens clothed lyk
contrivance, proceeding, as it seemed, by itself, with musicians dressed

maidins, playing upon all sortis of instrumentis and singing of
as maidens, playing on all sorts of instruments and singing

musick. Bot the sattiers wer not content only to red rown, bot pat
music. But the satyrs were not content just to run round, but put

ther handis behind them to ther tailes, quhilkis they waggit with
their hands behind them to their tails, which they wagged with

there handis, in sic sort as the Englismen suppoinit it had bene
their hands in such a way, that the English supposing it had been

devysed and donc in derision of them, daftly apprehending that
made up to ridicule them, stupidly jumped to conclusions

quhilk they suld not seam to have understand. For Mester Hattoun,
which they should not have understood in that manner. For Mr Hatton,

Mester Ligniche, and the maist part of the gentilmen desyred to
Mr Ligniche and the most part of the gentlemen desired to

sowp before the Quen and gret banket, that they mycht se the better
eat in front of the Queen and the main table, that they might

the haill ordour and cerimonies of the triumphe; bot sa schone as
have a view of the whole order and ceremonies of the pageant, but as

they saw the sattires waging ther tailes or romples, they all set down
soon as they saw the satyrs wagging their tails or rumps, they all sat

upon the bair flure behind the bak of the burd, that they suld not see
down on the bare floor behind the back of the table, that they should not

them selves scornit, as they thocht. Mester Hattoun said unto me, gif
see themselves insulted, as they thought. Mr Hatton said to me if it

it wer not in the Quenis presens and hall, he suld put a dagger to the
were not in the Queen's presence and hall, he would put a dagger in

hart of that Frenche knaif Bastien, whom he allegit did it for dispyt,
the heart of that French knave Bastian, whom he alleged did it for spite,

that the Quen maid mair of them then of the Frenchemen. I excused
because the Queen made more of them than of the French. I excused

the matter the best I mycht, bot the rumour was sa gret behind the
the matter as well as might, but the rumour was so great behind the

Quenis bak wher hir Maieste sat, and my L of Bedford, that they
Queen's back, where her Majesty sat and the Earl of Bedford, that they
hard and turnit about ther faces to wit what the matter menit. I
heard and turned round their faces to see what was going on. I
schew them how that it was for the sattiers; sa that the Quen and
showed them how it was because of the satyrs, so that the Queen and
my L of Bedford had baith anough ado to get them satiffied. It fell
Earl of Bedford had both enough to do to satisfy them. It fell out
out unhappely at sic a tym, and the Englis gentill men committed a
unluckily at such a time and the English gentlemen committed a
gret errour to seam till understand it as done against them; bot my
great error to seem to understand it as done against them, but the
L of Bedford was discret, and interpret all thingis to the best.
Earl of Bedford was discreet and interpreted everything in the best light.
My L of Bedford was rewardit was a riche chaingye of dyamontis,
The Earl of Bedford was rewarded with a rich chain of diamonds,
worth twa thowsand crownis; Mester Caro with a chaingye of perle,
worth 2,000 crowns. Mr Caro with a chain of pearls
and a ring with a fair dyamont; Mester Hattoun had a chain with
and a ring with a fair diamond; Mr Hatton had a chain with
hir Maiesteis picture and a ring; Meister Lignynce and fywe [five]
her Majesty's picture and a ring. Mr Lignynce and five
uther of qualite had all chaines. I wes commandit with many uthers
others of quality all had chains. I was commanded with many others
to convoy them to the bound rod, and parted all very weill content
to accompany them to the border, and parted all very well content
and satisfied with the Quenis Maieste, bot lamented that they saw
and satisfied with the Queen's Majesty, but lamented that they saw
sa litle accompt maid of the King; and my Lord of Bedford desyred
so little account made of the King; and the Earl of Bedford desired
me to request hir Maieste, to interteny him as sche had done at the
me to request her Majesty to entertain him as she had done at the
beginning, for hir awen honnour and advancement of hir affaires;
beginning, for her own honour and the furthering of her affairs
quhilk I forget not to do at all occasions.
which I forgot not to do on all occasions.

James Melville of Halhill, *Memoirs of His Own Life*, ed. T. Thomson, Bannatyne
Club, 1827.

Another Night to Remember

On 9 February 1567, an explosion shattered the quiet of Edinburgh. The house at Kirk o' Field where Mary's estranged husband slept had been blown up. Darnley himself had somehow spotted his danger and managed to escape from a window – too late. Persons unknown caught him in the garden beneath and strangled him. The man the Queen had become so anxious to rid herself of was finally dead – but at whose hand? The truth was that almost every member of the Scots nobility, excepting Darnley's own father, had a motive, but the finger was soon pointed at ladies' man, and man of action, the Earl of Bothwell. Whether he was guilty or not (there had probably been a general conspiracy of several of the Scots lords) he seemed to be getting too close to the Queen. It was an ideal opportunity for those involved to kill two birds with one stone: having dispatched Darnley, they could now get rid of Bothwell too, by pinning the whole affair on him. But instead of abandoning the accused man, Mary made a vital political error: she stood by Bothwell, thus seeming to implicate herself in the murder. To make matters even worse, she later married him. The results would, in the end, prove nearly as catastrophic for Mary as they had been for Darnley. Here is her response in her own words. Mary's picture of events suggests that she thought the plot was aimed at her life too.

Maist reverend fader in God, and traist counselor, we greit ye weill.
Most Reverend father in God, and trusty councillor, we greet you well. We
We have recevit this morning your letteris of the 27 Januar by your
have received this morning your letters of the 27 January by your servant
servand Robert Dury, containing in ane part sic advertisement as we
Robert Dury, containing in one part such news as we find in reality to be
find by effect over true, albeit the succes has not altogether been sic as
all too true, however the success of that mischievous deed has not been
the authoris of that mischievous fact had preconcevit in thair mind,
altogether such as the authors of it had preconceived in their mind, and
and had put it in executioun, gif God in his mercy had not preservit
had put in execution. God in his mercy has preserved us, and kept
us, and reservit us, as we traist, to the end that we may tak a rigorous
us, as we trust, to the purpose that we may take a rigorous vengeance on
vengeance of that mischievous deid, quhilk or it sould remain
that mischievous deed, which rather than that it should remain

unpunischit, we had rather loss life and all. The mater is horrible and

unpunished, we had rather lose life and all. The matter is horrible and so

sa strange, as we believe the like was never hard of in ony country.

strange, as we believe the like was never heard of in any country. This last

This night past being the 9th february, a litle after twa houris after

night the 9th February, a little after two hours after midnight, the house in

midnight, the house quhairin the King was logit was in ane instant

which the King was lodged was in an instant blown in the air, whilst he

blawin in the air, he lyand sleipand in his bed, with sic a vehemencie,

was lying sleeping in his bed, with such force, that of the whole

that of the haill loging, wallis and other, thare is nathing remanit, na,

lodging, walls and other, there is nothing remaining, no, not a stone above

not a stane above another, bot all other carreit far away, or dung in

another, but all other carried far away, or dung in dross [smashed to

dross to the very grund-stane. It mon be done be force of powder, and

smithereens] to the very ground-stone. It must have been done by force of

apperis to have been a myne. Be quhom it has been done, or in quhat

gunpowder, and appears to have been a mine. By whom it has been done,

maner, it apperis not as yit. We doubt not bot according to the

or in what manner, it is not yet known. We doubt not but according to

diligence oure Counsal hes begun alreddie to use, the certainty of all

the efforts our Council have already begun to make, the facts

salbe usit schortly; and the same being discoverit, quhilk we watt God

shall be known shortly; and that being discovered, which we believe God

will never suffer to ly hid, we hope to punisch the same with sic rigor

will never suffer to lie hidden, we hope to punish the same with such

as sall serve for exemple of this crueltie to all ages tocum. Allvayes

rigour as shall serve for example of this cruelty to all ages to come. At any

quha ever have taken this wicked interprys in hand, we assure our self

rate whoever has taken this wicked enterprise in hand, we believe

it wes dressit alsweill for us as for the King; for we lay the maist part

it was intended for us as well as for the King; for we lay the most part

of all the last oulk in that same loging, and wes thair accompanyit

of all the last week in that same lodging, and were there attended by

with the maist part of the lordis that are in this town that same night

the most part of the lords that were in town that same night at

at midnight, and of very chance taryit not all night, be reason of sum

midnight, and only by chance did not stay the night, by reason of some

mask in the abbaye; bot we believe it wes not chance, bot God that
       masque in the abbey [of Holyrood]; but we believe it was not chance, but
put it in our hede.
       God that put it in our head.

  We depeschit this berair upon the sudden, and thairfor wraitis to
       We dispatched this bearer immediately, and therefore write to you
yow the mair schortlie. The rest of your letter we sall answer at
       briefly. The rest of your letter we shall answer at more leisure within
mair lasor within four or five dayis by your aine servand. And sua
       four or five days by your own servant. And so for the present commits you
for the present committis yow to allmightie God.
       to Almighty God.
At Edinburgh, the 11 day of februar 1566-7.
       At Edinburgh, the 11 day of February 1566-7.
Marie R.
       Marie R.

Alexandre Labanoff, *Lettres, Instructions et Mémoires de Marie Stuart*, London, 1852.

The Escape from Lochleven

*Mary's marriage to Bothwell led to a successful rebellion against
her. She was taken captive and was imprisoned in the island
fortress of Lochleven. The victorious party, the Regent Moray and
his comrades, tried to discredit both Mary and her erstwhile
husband (who had fled to the continent), but the matter was far
from over. On 2 May 1568, she escaped, threatening all their
plans. Scotland was in uproar. The matter was international news.
One of Mary's rescuers was John Beaton, brother of the
Archbishop of Glasgow, her ambassador in Paris. He was sent on a
mission to Paris to seek aid for Mary from the French King. Whilst
he was there, he reported the details of her escape to the Venetian
ambassador, Giovanni Correr. But no sooner had the loyal Beaton
arrived in Paris than reports of Mary's defeat at the battle of
Langside began to trickle through too. This is how Correr reported
the intelligence to his masters in Venice.*

A gentleman came from Scotland with confirmation of the
Queen's flight, which took place thus.

  The Queen of Scotland was advised by Lord Seton (*Sciatun*), her
most confidential Catholic friend, and a very brave gentleman, by
means of a lad of the house who never returned, that he on an
appointed day would be with about fifty horsemen at the lake of

Lochleven, where the Queen was held a prisoner. Seton remained with forty horsemen in the mountains at a short distance, so as not to be discovered by the occupants of the castle in the lake, and the other ten, approaching nearer, entered a village, pretending to be travellers; and one of these men went to the edge of the lake itself, and prostrating himself on the ground, so as not to be seen, waited, according to the order given, until the Queen should come forth, as arranged.

Guard was continually kept at the castle gate day and night, except during supper, at which time the gate was locked with a key, every one going to supper, and the key was always placed on the table where the Governor took his meals, and before him. The Governor is the uterine brother of the Earl of Moray, Regent of Scotland, the Queen's illegitimate brother and her mortal enemy. The Queen, having attempted to descend from a window unsuccessfully, contrived that a page of the Governor's, whom she had persuaded to this effect, when carrying a dish, in the evening of the 2nd of May, to the table of his master with a napkin before him, should place the napkin on the key, and in removing the napkin take up the key with it, and carry it away unperceived by anyone. Having done so, the page then went directly to the Queen, and told her all was ready; and she, having in the meanwhile been attired by the elder of the two maids who waited upon her, took with her by the hand the younger maid, a girl ten years old, and with the page went quietly to the door, and he having opened it, the Queen went out with him and the younger girl (*et con la putta*), and locked the gate outside with the same key, without which it could not be opened from within. They then got into a little boat which was kept for the service of the castle, and displaying a white veil of the Queen's with a red tassel, she made the concerted signal to those who awaited her, that she was approaching. On seeing this, the person stretched on the ground on the bank of the lake arose, and by another signal summoned the horsemen from the village, amongst whom a principal person was he [John Beaton] who is now come to give account of these facts to these Majesties, and who is the brother of the Scottish Ambassador here [James Beaton, Bishop of Glasgow]. The horsemen from the mountains being also informed came immediately to the lake, and received the Queen with infinite joy, and having placed her on horseback with the page and the girl, they conveyed her to the sea coast, at a distance of five miles from thence, because to proceed by land to the place which had been designated appeared manifestly too dangerous. All having embarked, the Queen was conducted to Niddry (*Nidre*) a place belonging to Lord Seton, and from thence to Hamilton, a castle of the Duke of Châtellerault, where his brother, the Archbishop of St Andrew's, with other principal personages of those parts, acknowledged her as Queen.

Hamilton is a favourable basis for military operations, and four leagues distant from Dumbarton, which is a seaport and a very strong fortress, but the Queen will not proceed thither because she feels quite safe in Hamilton, for the Archbishop of St Andrew's has command over all the adjacent country, and she can thus more easily receive at Hamilton, the friends who may come to her assistance than in the fortress of Dumbarton, whither, however, she might proceed at any time in case of necessity.

All Scotland is in motion, some declaring for the Queen, and some against her and for the Earl of Murray.

She sends this gentleman to ask the King of France, for her present need, for a thousand harquebusiers [troops armed with arquebuses, an early fire-arm], but should she wish to recover Edinburgh and other fortresses occupied by the rebels, she would require to be assisted by a greater number. She has also written a letter to the Cardinal of Lorraine which should move every hard heart to have compassion upon her; the first lines express that she begs pardon of God, and of the world, for the past errors of her youth, which she promises to amend for the future; then she acknowledges her release solely from His Divine Majesty, and returns Him most humble thanks for having given her so much strength in these her afflictions; and she declares that she has never swerved in the least from her firm purpose to live and die a Catholic, as she now intends to do more than ever.

With regard to her flight it is judged here, by those who know the site, and how strictly she was guarded, that her escape was most miraculous, most especially having been contrived by two lads, under ten years of age, who could not be presupposed to have the requisite judgment and secrecy.

To the greater satisfaction with the result may be added, that the inmates of Lochleven castle perceived the flight; but being shut up within it, and thus made prisoners, they had to take patience, and to witness the Queen's escape, while they remained at the windows of the castle.

But now, if the current report be true, the Queen of Scotland, following the course of her fickle fortune, gives news of her troops having been routed near Glasgow; all her chief adherents being killed, or made prisoners, and the Captain (sic) of Domberdran

(*Dumilrenan*) [possibly a mistake for Dumbarton] having fled to England by sea. We are now awaiting information, as the Scotch here support themselves with the hope that all may not be true, assigning reasons for their doubts.

The English Ambassador [Sir Henry Norris], before he knew this last fact, went to his most Christian Majesty, and told him he had heard that there was a project to succour the Queen of Scotland, which in his opinion would be superfluous, because his Queen would not fail to favour and assist her with what was needed. These words were instantly repeated to the Queen [of France], who told the Ambassador that this was precisely the time to have compassion on the Queen of Scotland and to favour her, after having taken refuge in England.

The Ambassador seemed not to know the last news, but affirmed that his Queen would certainly do as anticipated.

Her Majesty [of France] has dispatched a gentlemen [sic] to know in what condition the Queen of Scotland is, and whether she is in Scotland or in England.

Paris, 26th May 1568.

Calendar of State Papers Venetian 1558-90, vii, ed. R. Brown and C. Bentinck, London, 1890.

Defeat and Flight

The rumours of defeat turned out to be all too true. Mary had indeed failed in her attempt to regain her Kingdom, and strangest of all, she had sought refuge in England – Scotland's ancient enemy which had taken prisoner and ransomed more than one reigning Scottish sovereign. Not only that, but England was mostly Protestant, and Mary was a Catholic claimant to its throne. She was a natural rallying point for Catholics and others disaffected to her cousin, the Queen of England. Whatever appearances she made to the contrary, Elizabeth could hardly have been pleased to see her. Here is Giovanni Correr's next letter, confirming his previous report.

The news of the defeat of the troops of the Queen of Scotland was true. She had assembled about eight thousand men, who had flocked to her from divers parts, and for greater security she wished to shut herself up in Dumbarton, which is a very strong castle, but she could not get there without crossing the Clyde, over which there is but one bridge near Glasgow, and that was already occupied by the enemy. It was therefore determined to cross the river where it flows into the sea, a number of boats being sent to the spot for that purpose. The Regent, aware of this, went in pursuit with four thousand men; whereupon the Queen appointed as her Lieutenant-General the Earl of Argyll, who had just joined her, and who is her brother-in-law through his wife, Queen Mary's natural sister, and he with six thousand men gave Moray battle.

The contest lasted for three-quarters of an hour, when the Queen's troops were worsted, but only one hundred and fifty of her followers were killed, for the Regent exerted himself extremely to prevent his troops shedding blood. The prisoners exceeded three hundred, including many noblemen, amongst whom, moreover, is that Lord Seton who was the chief instrument and leader in effecting the Queen's escape. Finding herself defeated, the Queen set out for England, accompanied by a son of the Duke of Châtellerault, by Lord Fleming, by the Earl of Maxwell, and some twenty-five other attendants, and she travelled a distance of one hundred and twenty-five miles without any rest. She stopped at a place called Workington, which is four miles within the English border. She did not discover herself, but was recognised by a Scotchman, who informed the warden of the castle, and the latter went immediately to receive her, with great marks of respect, and posted guards on all sides to prevent pursuit by the enemy.

When the Queen of England heard this news she appeared much pleased, and immediately dispatched to Carlisle, where the Queen of Scotland now is, her Lord Chamberlain (sic) and the Governor of the place [Lord Scrope, Warden of the Marches], with clothes of silk and jewels for her wear, and in London a palace is being prepared for her with great pomp. Queen Elizabeth promises to give her all aid for the recovery of her kingdom, and has written to this effect to their Majesties here, who have besought her warmly thus to do; but it is said that she will not allow Queen Mary to come to France, as was believed to be her intention, but will detain her in England until she sees the result, it appearing that there is already some talk of an adjustment.

The same Scottish gentleman, John Beaton, who brought the news of Queen Mary's escape, in which he indeed took part, has come to me in her name, to say that all her valuables, and especially her jewels, are in the hands of the enemy, who got possession of them when they imprisoned her. She is now apprehensive of their being sent for sale abroad, and possibly to Venice, which is one of the chief and wealthiest marts in the world; and he therefore requested me to co-operate with him in assisting her by writing to your Serenity, in order that should any jewels reach our city and be recognised, from their extreme beauty and quality, or through any other circumstance, the Signory may be pleased to have them detained until the Queen can send the necessary proofs. This I readily promised him to do, assuring him at the same time, that out of the love ever borne by your Serenity towards his Queen, you would willingly comply with the present request or any other that could possibly be of service to her.

Paris, 6th June 1568.

Calendar of State Papers Venetian 1558-90, vii, ed. R. Brown and C. Bentinck, London, 1890.

The Half-Roasted Abbot

Elizabeth's good graces did not last and Mary soon found herself a prisoner. In the meanwhile Scotland experienced a vicious civil war and a succession of Regents, two of whom were assassinated by rival factions. In such an atmosphere, disorder could flourish. The following is a complaint to the Privy Council, in 1571, recorded in the Memorials of Richard Bannatyne – the famous case of the half-roasted abbot. The abbot in question was really a commendator – a man who was given the title and the lands of a pre-Reformation cleric without having to have any ecclesiastical ties himself.

Walter Scott used the unfortunate abbot as inspiration for a scene in Ivanhoe, *explaining in a note to his novel the historical roots of the episode. A sensational case of violence like this fitted in nicely with the general 19th-century idea that before the Union of 1707 Scots were barbarous, violent and backwards and not fit for polite society. Particularly amusing in this respect is the detail which shows that 16th-century Scottish nobility evidently knew what a serviette was for – gagging recalcitrant prisoners.*

Unto your grace and lordis of secret counsall, humblie meanis and
   Unto your Grace and Lords of Privy Council,
schawis your servitor, Mr Alane Stewart, commendater of
   Mr Alan Stewart, commendator of
Croseraguell; that whair, upon the 29 day of August lastbypast, I
   Crossraguel humbly declares and shows that upon the 29th day of August
beand within the woud of Croseraguell, doand my leasome errandis
   last year I was in the wood of Crossraguel on my lawful errands
and busines, beleivand no harme nor invasione to have bene done to
   and business, expecting no harm or attack to come upon

me be ony persone or persones: Nochttheles Gilbert erle of Cassilis,
me by any person or persons. Nonetheless, Gilbert, earl of Cassilis and

Thomas maister of Cassilis, with thair complices, to the number of
Thomas, the heir, with their accomplices, to the number of

16 persones or thairby, come to me and perswadit me, be thair
16 persons or thereabouts, came to me and persuaded me by their flattery

flatterie and deceitfull wordis, to pas with thame to his castle and
and deceitful words to pass with them to his castle and

place of Dunure; being always myndit, gif I had made refuisall to
place of Dunure, always thinking, if I had refused to go

pass with thame, to haue taken me perforce. And he puttand me
with them, they would have taken me by force. And he putting me

within the same, that I shuld be in suire firmance, commandit sex of
in the castle, so that I should be securely imprisoned, commanded six of

his servandis to wait upoun me, sa that I eschewit not; wha tuike fra
his servants to take charge of me, so that I did not know who took from

me my hors with all my weaponis, and than depairtit quhill the first
me my horse with all my weapons. He then left until the first

day of September thaireftir, that he come agane and requyrit me to
day of September, when he came back and required me to

subscryv to him ane few chartore brocht with him, maid in
sign a charter in his favour, which he had brought with him, on

parchment, of the whole landis perteining to the said abbacie,
parchment. This, he alleged, was of the whole lands pertaining to the abbey

togidder with 19 and 5 zeir takis of the fruitis, teyndis, and dewties
together with 19 and 5 year tacks of the fruits, teinds and duties

thairof, as he alledgit, of the whole kirkis and personages perteining
of the entire kirks and parsonages belonging to it.

thairto; whairof I neuer having red a word of, ansuerit, 'It was a
I had never read a word of it, and I answered 'It was an

thing vnreasonabill, and that I could na wayis doe, in respect the
unreasonable thing which I could not do, in respect that it was all

same long of befoir was alreadie disponit to the kyndlie tennentis
long ago parcelled out to kindly tenants and possessors of tenancies,

and possessouris thairof, and to James Stewart of Cardonall; and
and to James Stewart of Cardonell, and

thairfoir, the samen being furth of my handis, I could nawayis grant
therefore, being out of my hands I could not grant

his vnreasonabill desyre.'
his unreasonable desire'.

What then, after long boasting and minassing of me, caused me to
After long threatening and menacing me, he had me

be caried be Johne Kennedie, his baxter, John Mccleire, his cuike,
taken by John Kennedy, his baker, John Mccleir, his cook,

Alexander Richard, his pantryman, Alexander Eccles, and sir
Alexander Richard, his pantry man, Alexander Eccles and Sir

William Tode, to ane hous callit the Blake Voute of Dunvre; whair
William Tod to a house called the Black Vout of Dunure, where

the tormenteris denudit me of all my cloathis, perforce, except only
these torturers stripped me of my clothes by force, except for

my sarke and doublate, and then band baith my handis at the
my shirt and doublet and then bound both my hands at the

shaklebones with ane corde, as he did baith my feit, and band my
wrists with a cord and both my feet. Then they bound my

soilles betuix an irone chymlay and a fyre; and beand bound thairto,
soles between an iron chimney and a fire so I could not

could nawayis steir nor move, but had almost inlaikit throuch my
stir or move at all, until I nearly died through my

cruell burning. And seing na uther apeirance to me, but ather to
cruel burning. Seeing no other option for me, but to either

condiscend to his desyre, or ellis to continow in that torment quhill
give in to his desire or else continue in that torment until I died,

I died, tuke me to the longest life, and said, I wald obey his desyre,
I acted to save my life and said I would obey him

albeit it was sore against my will; and, for to be releivit of my said
against my will. To be relieved of the

paine, subscryvit the foirnamet chairtore and takis, quhilk I neuer
pain, I signed the above mentioned charter and tacks, which I had never

yit red, nor knew what thairin was conteaned. Which beand done,
read and did not know what was contained in them. Which being done,

the said erle causit the said tormentaris of me sweir, upoun ane
the Earl made my torturers swear upon a Bible,

byble, never to reveill ane word of this my unmercifull handling to
never to reveal a word of my cruel treatment by them to

ony persone or persones.
any person or persons.

Yit, he not beand satisseid with thir proceidings, come againe
  But not satisfied with these proceedings, he came again on the
upoun the 7 day of the foirsaid moneth, bringand with him the
  7th of the same month, bringing with him the
foirsaid chairtore and take, which he compellit me to subscrive, and
  foresaid charter and tack which he compelled me to sign and
requyred me to ratifie and approve the same befoir notar and
  required me to ratify and approve before a notary and
witnessis; which alluterlie I refuised. And therefoire he, as of befoir,
  witnesses, which I totally refused. And so he once more
band me and pat me to the same maner of tormenting; and I said,
  bound me and put me to the same torture and I said,
nochtwithstanding, he sould first get my life or euer I agreit to his
  despite this, that he should take my life, before I ever agreed to his
desyre: And being in so grit paine, as I truste neuer man was in, with
  desire. And being in such great pain as I hope no man ever felt in
his lyfe, whair I cryed, 'Fye upoun yow! Will ye ding whingaris in
  his life, I cried 'Shame upon you! Will you run swords through
me, and put me of this world! Or ellis put a barrell of powder undir
  me and put me out of this world! Or else put a barrel of gunpowder under
me, rather nor to be damaned in this unmercifull maner!' The said
  me, rather than treat me in this unmerciful manner!' The Earl
erle hearing me cry, bad his servant, Alexander Ritchart, put ane
  hearing me shout, bade his servant Alexander Richard put a
serviat in my throat; which he obeyed. The same being performed at
  serviette in my mouth which he obeyed. This was done at
xj [11] houris in the nicht. Wha than seing that I was in danger of
  11 pm at night. The Earl seeing that I was in danger of
my life, my fleshe consumed and brunt to the bones, and that I wald
  my life, my flesh consumed and burnt to the bones and that I would
nocht condiscend to thair purpose, I was releivit of that paine;
  not give in to their purpose, relieved me of that pain,
whairthrow, I will neuer be so able nor weill in my lyftyme.
  through which I will never be so able or well in my lifetime.
Sic ane crweltie neuer being hard of befoir, done to ony frie
  Such cruelty was never heard of before, to be done to any free
persone that had not committed offence. And gif your grace and
  person who had not committed an offence, and if your Grace and

lordschipis takis nocht guid order heiranent, for punishment of the
            your lordships to not take care to punish it the
same, it will giue occasiounes to otheris proud persounes,
            same will give encouragement to other proud persons,
contemners of the kingis grace authoritie, to brek guid ordour, and
            despisers of the King's Grace's authority to break the law and
truble the commoun weill of the cuntrie.
            trouble the commonwealth of this country.

Richard Bannatyne's *Memoriales* 1569-73, ed. Robert Pitcairn, Bannatyne Club,
1836.

Mary's Execution

*Despite the attempts of her supporters to seize power in Scotland
and to help her, Mary remained a prisoner in England and a focus
for Catholic plots against Elizabeth. The last straw came in 1586,
when she was found to have given her consent to the Babington
Plot – a plot to assassinate Elizabeth and to rescue Mary and place
her on the English throne. Elizabeth's spy-master Walsingham had
set up everything so that Mary in effect signed her own death
warrant when she replied to the plotters, approving of their
scheme. She was tried and executed at Fotheringay Castle on the
morning of 8 February 1587. Here is a contemporary English
account of her death.*

A report of the manner of execution of the Scottish Queen
performed the eighth day of February anno 1586 [1587 by
modern dating] in the great hall within the castle of Fotheringham
with relation of speeches uttered and actions happening in the said
execution from the delivery of the said Scottish Queen unto Mr
Thomas Andrewes, Esq., Sheriff of the country of Northampton
unto the end of the same execution.

First, the said Scottish Queen, being carried by two of Sir Amias
Pawlett's gentlemen and the Sheriff going before her, came most
willingly out of her chamber into an entry next the hall; at which
place the Earl of Shrewsbury and the Earl of Kent, commissioners
for the execution, with the two governors of her person and divers
knights and gentlemen, did meet her; where they found one of the
Scottish Queen's servants, named Melvin, kneeling on his knees;
who uttered these words with tears to the Queen of Scots, his
mistress, 'Madam, it will be the sorrowfullest message that ever I
carried when I shall report that my Queen and dear mistress is dead.'

Then the Queen of Scots shedding tears, answered him, 'You ought to rejoice and not to weep for that the end of Mary Stuart's troubles is now done. Thou knowest, Melvin, that all this world is but vanity and full of troubles and sorrows. Carry this message from me and tell my friends that I died a true woman to my religion, and like a true Scottish woman and a true French woman; but God forgive them that have long desired my end. And He that is the true Judge of all secret thoughts knoweth my mind, how it hath ever been my desire to have Scotland and England united together. And commend me to my son, and tell him that I have not done any thing that may prejudice his kingdom of Scotland. And so, good Melvin, farewell.' And kissing him she bade him pray for her.

Then she turned her unto the Lords and told them that she had certain requests to make unto them. One was for a sum of money (which she said Sir Amias Pawlett knew of) to be paid to one Curle, her servant. Next, that all her poor servants might enjoy that quietly which by her will and testament she had given unto them. And lastly, that they might be all well entreated and sent home safely and honestly into their own country. 'And this I do conjure you, my Lords, to do.' Answer was made by Sir Amias Pawlett. 'I do well remember the money your grace speaketh of, and your grace needeth not to make any doubt of the not performance of your request, for I do surely think they shall be granted.' 'I have (said she) one other request to make unto you, my Lords, that you will suffer my poor servants to be present about me at my death, that they may report when they come into their countries how I died a true woman unto my religion.' Then the Earl of Kent, one of the commissioners, answered, 'Madam, that cannot well be granted, for that it is feared lest some of them would with speeches both trouble and grieve your grace and disquiet the company; of which already we have had some experience, or seek to wipe their napkins in some of your blood, which were not convenient.'

'My Lord (said the Queens of Scots), I will give my word and promise for them that they shall not do any such thing as your Lordship hath named. Alas, poor souls, it would do them good to bid me farewell, and I hope your mistress, being a maiden Queen, in regard of womanhood will suffer me to have some of my own people about me at my death; and I know she hath not given you so straight a commission but that you may grant me more than this if I were a far meaner woman than I am.' And then feigning to be grieved, with some tears uttered these words: 'You know that I am cousin to your Queen and descended from the blood of Henry the viith., a married Queen of France and the anointed Queen of Scotland.' Whereupon after some consultation they granted that she might have some of her servants according to her grace's request, and therefore desired her to make choice of half a dozen of her men and women. Who presently said that of her men she would have Melvin, her apothecary, her surgeon, and one other old man besides; and of her women those two that did use to lie in her chamber. After this she, being supported by Sir Amias's two gentlemen aforesaid and Melvin, carrying her train, and also accompanied with Lords, knights, and gentlemen aforenamed, the Sheriff going before her, she passed out of the entry into the hall with her countenance careless, importing therby rather mirth than mournfull chere, and so she willingly stepped up to the scaffold which was prepared for her in the hall, being two foot high and twelve foot broad with rails round about, hanged and covered with black, with a low stool, long cushion and block, covered with black also. Then having the stool brought her, she sat down, by her, on her right hand the Earl of Shrewsbury and the Earl of Kent, and on the left hand stood the Sheriff, before her the two executioners; round the rails stood knights, gentlemen, and others.

Then silence being made the Queen's Majestie's commission for the execution of the said Queen of Scots was opened by Mr Beal, clerk of the council, and these words pronounced by the assembly, 'God save the Queen', during the reading of which commission the Queen of Scots was silent, listening unto it with as small regard as if it had not concerned her at all; and with as cheerfull countenance as if it had been a pardon from her majesty for her life; using as much strangeness in word and deed as if she had never known any of the assembly or had been ignorant of the English language.

Then Mr Doctor Fletcher, Dean of Peterborough, standing directly before her without the rails, bending his body with great reverence, began to utter this exhortation following: 'Madam, the Queen's most excellent Majesty', etc; and uttering these words three or four times she told him, 'Mr Dean, I am settled in the ancient Catholic Roman religion, and mind to spend my blood in defence of it.'

Then Mr Dean sayd, 'Madam, change your opinion and repent you of your former wickedness, and set your faith only in Jesus Christ, by Him to be saved.'

The she answered again, 'Mr Dean, trouble not yourself any more, for I am settled and resolved in this my religion, and am purposed herein to die.'

Then the Earl of Shrewsbury and the Earl of Kent, perceiving her so obstinate, told her that since she would not hear the exhortation begun by Mr Dean, 'We will pray for your grace that if it standeth with God's will you may have your heart lightened even at the last hour with the true knowledge of God, and so die therein.'

Then she answered, 'If ye will pray for me, my Lords, I will thank you, but to join in prayer with you I will not, for that you and I are not of one religion'.

Then the Lords called for Mr Dean, who kneeling on the scaffold stairs began his prayer, 'O most gracious God and merciful Father', etc., all the assembly, saving the Queen of Scots and her servants, saying after him: during the saying of which prayer the Queen of Scots, sitting upon a stool, having about her neck an Agnus Dei, in her hand a crucifix, at her girdle a pair of Beads with a golden Cross at the end of them, a Latin book in her hand, began with tears and loud voice to pray in Latin, and in the midst of her prayers she slided off from the stool and kneeling said divers Latin prayers. And after the end of Mr Dean's prayer she kneeling prayed to this effect in English; for Christ, His afflicted Church, and for an end of their troubles, for her son and for the Queen's Majesty, that she might prosper and serve God aright. She confessed that she hoped to be saved by and in the blood of Christ, at the foot of whose crucifix she would shed her blood.

Then said the Earl of Kent, 'Madam settle Christ Jesus in your heart and leave those trumperies.' Then she, little regarding or nothing at all his honor's good counsel, went forward with her prayers; desiring that God would avert His wrath from this Island, and that He would give her grace and forgiveness of her sins. These with other prayers she made in English, saying she forgave her enemies with all her heart that had long sought her blood, and desired God to convert them to the truth; and in the end of prayer she desired all Saints to make intercession for her to Jesus Christ, and so kissed the crucifix, and crossing of herself, said these words, 'Even as Thy arms, O Jesus, were spread here upon the cross, so receive me into Thy arms of mercy and forgive me all my sins.'

Her prayer ended, the executioners kneeling desired her grace to forgive them her death. Who answered, 'I forgive you with all my heart, for now I hope you shall make an end of all my troubles.' Then they with her two women helping of her up, began to disrobe her of her apparell. Then she laying her Crucifix upon the stool, one of the executioners took from her neck the Agnus Dei, which she laying hands of it gave it to one of her women and told the executioner that they should be answered in money for it. Then she suffered them with her two women to disrobe her of her apparell, of her chain, of her pomander beads, and all other her apparell most willingly; and with joy rather than with sorrow helped to make unready herself, putting on a pair of sleeves with her own hands which they had pulled off, and that with some haste, as if she had longed to be gone.

All this while they were pulling off her apparell she never changed her countenance, but with smiling chere she uttered these words that she had never such grooms to make her unready, and she never put off her clothes before such a company.

Then she being stripped of all her apparell saving her petticoat and kertell her two women beholding her made great lamentation and crying and crossed themselves prayed in Latin. Then she turning herself to them embracing them, said these words in French, 'Ne criez vous, j'ay promis pour vous'; and so crossing and kissing them, bade them pray for her, and rejoice and not mourn, for that now they should see an end of all their mistress's troubles.

Then she with a smiling countenance, turning to her men-servants, as Melvin and the rest standing upon a bench nigh the scaffold, who sometimes weeping, sometimes crying out, and loudly and continually crossing themselves, prayed in Latin, crossing them with her hand, bade them farewell, and wishing them to pray for her even until the last hour.

This done one of her women, having a Corpus Christi cloth lapt up the corner ways, kissing it, put it over the Queen of Scot's face and pinned it fast to the caul of her head. Then the two women departed from her, and she kneeling down upon a cushion most resolutely and without any token or fear of death, she spake aloud this Psalm in Latin, 'In te Domine confido, non confundat in eternum' [the ending of the Te Deum, 'I trust in thee Lord, I shall never be counfounded'], etc. Then groping for the block she laid down her head, putting her chin on the block with both her hands, which holding there still had been cut off had they been not espied. Then lying upon the block most quietly, and stretched out her arms and legs, cryed, 'In manus tuas, Domine', etc., three or four times.

Then she lying very still on the block, one of the executioners holding of her slightly with one of his hands, she endured two strokes of the other executioner with an axe, she making very small noise or none at all, and not stirring any part of her from the place where she lay; and so the executioners cut off her head saving one little gristle, which being cut asunder he lifted up her head to the view of all the assembly and bade God save the Queen. Then her dressing of lawn falling off from her head it appeared as grey as one of threescore and ten years old, and polled very short, her face in a moment being so much altered from the form she had when she was alive as few could remember her by her dead face. Her lips stirred up and down almost a quarter of an hour after her head was cutt off. Then Mr Dean said with a loud voice, 'So perish all the Queen's enemies', and afterwards the Earl of Kent came to the dead body, and standing over it with a loud voice said, 'Such be the end of all the Queen's and the Gospel's enemies.'

Then one of the executioners pulling off her garters espied her little dog, which was crept under her clothes, which could not be gotten forth but by force. It afterwards would not depart from the dead corpse, but came and laid between her head and her shoulders, which being imbrued with her blood was carried away and washed, as all things else were, that had any blood, was either burned or clean washed, and the executioners sent away with money for their fees; not having any one thing that belonged unto her. And so every man being commanded out of the hall except the Sheriff and his men she was carried by them up into a great chamber lying ready for the surgeons to embalm her.

Hon. Mrs Maxwell Scott, *The Tragedy of Fotheringay*, Edinburgh, 1905.

Jamie Saxt's Scotland

*Put on the throne in Mary's place in 1567 when he was only a year
old, James never saw Mary again. He was brought up by
governesses and strict tutors such as George Buchanan, who beat
the Latin language into him. Despite this he grew up to be an
astute king with a genuine intellectual talent. His most affectionate
relationships would always be with men, but nevertheless he made
a sensible marriage which produced three children who survived to
adulthood. Despite his mother's execution by Elizabeth, James's
Protestant upbringing and Tudor blood made him the obvious
candidate to succeed her on the English throne. So in 1603 he
inherited the throne of England and had himself declared the first
King of Great Britain – but his reign was not without dangers.*

Enemy on the Doorstep

*In 1588 Spain was a Catholic super-power whose possessions
stretched from South America to the Phillipines. She was also
famous for her inquisition which vigourously persecuted heretics.
The fear of Spain invading Protestant Scotland as a 'soft' route into
England reached fever-pitch in 1588 when the news reached Scots
that the Spanish Armada had set sail.*

*James Melville, minister of Anstruther and Kilrenny in Fife, was
asleep in bed one morning when the news came that there was a
ship-full of Spaniards in Anstruther harbour. They came not to put
the East Neuk to the sword, but to ask for help. These were the
shipwrecked survivors of El Gran Grifon – wrecked off Fair Isle as
it tried to make its way back round the top of the British Isles.
Rescued by a Shetland laird the survivors were ferried down to
Fife, before moving on to Edinburgh and thence home. Admiral
Juan Gomez de Medina was grateful for the kindly reception his
men received and returned the hospitality to a crew from
Anstruther at a later date. Here is James Melville's account of the
Spaniards' arrival from his diary.*

That wintar the King was occupied in commenting of the
That winter the King was occupied in writing commentaries on the
Apocalypse, and in setting out of sermontes thairupon against the
Apocalypse and writing sermons from it against the Catholics and
Papists and Spainyarts: And yit, by a piece of grait owersight, the
Spaniards. And yet by great official negligence the Catholics were

Papists pracetised never mair bisselie in this land, and maid graitter
never more active in Scotland and never made greater preparations

preparation for receaving of the Spainyarts nor that yeir. For a lang
for receiving Spanish forces than in that year. For a long time the

tyme the newes of a Spanishe navie and armie haid bein blasit
rumours of a Spanish navy and army had been circulating. About

abrode; and about the Lambes tyde of the 1588, this Yland haid fund
Lammas 1588, this island found the fearful truth of those rumours.

a feirfull effect thairof, to the utter subversion bathe of Kirk and
This would have been to the total subversion of church and state, if

Polecie, giff God haid nocht wounderfullie watched ower the sam,
God had not wonderfully watched over us and mightily fought and

and mightelie fauchten and defeat that armie be his souldiours, the
defeated that armada by his soldiers, the elements [the storms which

elements, quhilk he maid all four maist fercelie to afflict tham till
broke up the Spanish fleet], all four of which he made to fiercely

almost utter consumption. Terrible was the feir, persing war the
afflict them to almost total devastation. There was terrible fear,

pretchings, ernest, zealus, and fervent war the prayers, sounding war
heart-piercing preaching, earnest, zealous and fervent prayers, loud

the siches and sobbes, and abounding was the teares at that Fast and
sighs and sobs, and many tears at that year's fast and General

Generall Assemblie keipit at Edinbruche, when the newes war credible
Assembly, held at Edinburgh, when the news was believably reported,

tauld, sum tymes of thair landing at Dumbar, sum tymes at St Androis,
sometimes of their landing at Dunbar, sometimes at St Andrews

and in Tay, and now and then at Aberdein and Cromertie first: And
and in Tay, and sometimes that they had landed in Aberdeen and Cromarty

in verie deid, as we knew certeanlie soone efter, the Lord of Armies,
first. And indeed, as we knew certainly afterwards, the Lord of Armies

wha ryddes upon the winges of the wounds, the Keipar of his awin
who rides upon the wings of the winds, the Keeper of his own

Israell, was in the mean tyme convoying that monstruus navie about
Israel, was in the mean time moving that monstrous navy about

our costes, and directing thair haulkes and galiates to the ylands,
our coasts, and directing their hulks and galleons to the islands,

rokkes, and saundes, wharupon he haid destinat thair wrak and
rocks and sands, where he had destined their wreck and

destruction. For within twa or thrie monethe thairefter, earlie in the
destruction. For within two or three months after, early in the

morning, be brak of day, ane of our bailyies cam to my bedsyde,
morning, by break of day, one of our bailies came to my bedside

saying, (but nocht with fray,) 'I haiff to tell yow newes, Sir. Ther is
saying (but not with fear) 'I have news to tell you, Sir. A ship full of

arryvit within our herbrie this morning a schipe full of Spainyarts, bot
armed Spaniards has arrived in our harbour this morning, but

nocht to giff mercie bot to ask!' And sa schawes me that the
not to give mercy but to ask!' And so he showed me that the

Commanders haid landit, and he haid commandit tham to thair
Commanders had landed, and he had ordered them to their

schipe againe till the Magistrates of the town laid advysit, and the
ship again, until the magistrates of the town had conferred. The

Spainyarts haid humblie obeyit: Therfor desyrit me to ryse and heir
Spaniards had humbly obeyed. He asked me to rise and hear

thair petition with tham. Upe I got with diligence, and assembling the
their petition with them. I got up immediately and assembling the

honest men of the town, cam to the Tolbuthe; and efter consultation
honest men of the town, came to the Tolbooth. After consulting

taken to heir tham, and what answer to mak, ther presentes us a verie
about hearing them and what answer to make, there came to us a very

reverend man of big stature, and grave and stout countenance, grey-
imposing man of a big build and grave and courageous countenance, grey-

heared, and verie humble lyk wha, efter mikle and verie law
haired and seemingly very humble, who after much and very abased

courtessie, bowing down with his face neir the ground, and twitching
politeness, bowing down with his face near the ground and touching

my scho with his hand, began his harang in the Spanise toung, wharof
my shoe with his hand, began a speech in the Spanish tongue.

I understud the substance; and being about to answer in Latine, he
I understood the substance, and was about to answer in Latin, when

haiffing onlie a young man with him to be his interpreter, began
the young man with him as his interpreter started to

and tauld ower againe to us in guid Einglis. The sum was, that King
repeat it to us in good English. The gist was that King

Philipe, his maister, haid riget out a navie and armie to land in
Philip, his master, had rigged out a navy and army to land in

Eingland for just causes to be advengit of manie intolerable wrangs
England for their just causes to be avenged of many intolerable wrongs

quhilk he haid receavit of that nation; but God for ther sinnes haid
done to them by that nation; but God for their sins had

bein against thame, and be storme of wather haid dryven the navie by
been against them, and by storm of weather had driven the navy past

the cost of England, and him with a certean of Capteanes, being the
the coast of England. He with some of the captains (he was the

Generall of twentie hulks, upon an yll of Scotland, called the Fear Yll,
admiral of twenty hulks) had been driven by the weather onto a Scottish

wher they maid schipewrak, and whar sa monie as haid eschapit the
island called Fair Isle. There they were shipwrecked and those of them

merciles sies and rokes, haid mair nor sax or sevin ouks suffred grait
who had escaped the merciless sea and rocks, had for more than 6 or 7

hunger and cauld, till conducing that bark out of Orkney, they war
weeks suffered great hunger and cold, until hiring a ship from the

com hither as to thair speciall frinds and confederats to kiss the King's
Orkneys, they came here: to their special friends and allies, to kiss the

Majestie's hands of Scotland, (and thairwith bekkit even to the yeard,)
hand of the King of Scotland (and with that he bowed to the ground)

and to find releiff and comfort thairby to him selff, these gentilmen
and to find relief and comfort to himself these gentlemen,

Capteanes, and the poore souldarts, whase condition was for the
the captains and the poor soldiers whose condition was for the

present maist miserable and pitifull.
present most miserable and pitiful.

I answerit this mikle, in soum: That whowbeit nather our frindschipe,
I answered this much, that we could not be great friends to them,

quhilk could nocht be grait, seing ther King and they war frinds to the
seeing that their King and they were friends to the greatest enemy

graitest enemie of Chryst, the Pape of Rome, and our King and we
of Christ, the Pope of Rome, and our King and we defied him [the Pope].

defyed him, nor yit thair cause against our nibours and speciall frinds
Their cause against our neighbours and special allies of England could not

of England could procure anie benefit at our hands for thair releiff and
win them any favour at our hands for their relief and comfort. Nevertheless,

confort; nevertheles, they sould knaw be experience, that we war men,
they should know by experience, that we were men and moved

and sa moved be human compassione, and Christiannes of better
by human compassion and by Christianity of a better sort than their

religion nor they, quhilk sould kythe, in fruicts and effect, plan contrar
religion, which should show itself in fruits and effect to be the opposite of

to thars. For wheras our peiple resorting amangs tham in peacable
theirs. For despite the fact that our people visiting amongst them in peaceful

and lawfull effeares of merchandise, war violentlie takin and cast in
and lawful business affairs were taken by force and thrown into prison,

prisone, thair guids and gear confiscat, and thair bodies committed to
their goods and belongings confiscated and their bodies committed to the

the crewall flaming fyre for the cause of Relligion, they sould find na
cruel flaming fire of the stake for the cause of religion, they should find no-

thing amangs us bot Christian pitie and warks of mercie and almes,
thing amongst us but Christian pity and works of mercy and alms,
leaving to God to work in thair harts concerning Relligion as it
leaving it to God to move their hearts concerning religion, as it
pleased him. This being trewlie reported again to him be his
pleased him. This being accurately reported to him by his
trunshman, with grait reverence he gaiff thankes, and said he could
interpreter, with great reverence he gave thanks and said he could
nocht mak answer for thair Kirk and the lawes and ordour thairof,
not answer for their Kirk and its laws and discipline, only
onlie for him selff, that ther war divers Scotsmen wha knew him, and
for himself. There were various Scotsmen who knew him and to whom
to whome he haid schawin courtesie and favour at Calles, and as he
he had shown courtesy and favour at Calais and as he supposed, some
supposit, sum of this sam town of Anstruther. Sa schew him that the
had been from this same town of Anstruther. So [we] showed him that
Bailyies granted him licence with the Capteanes, to go to thair ludging
the bailies granted him permission with the captains to
for thair refreshment, but to nane of thair men to land, till the ower-
refresh themselves [ashore], but to none of their men to land, until
lord of the town war advertised, and understand the King's Majestie's
the laird of the town was notified, and understood the King's mind
mynd anent thame. Thus with grait courtessie he departed.
concerning them. Thus with great courtesy, he departed.

That night, the Lard being advertised, cam, and on the morn,
That night, the Laird [of Anstruther] being notified, came and next
accompanied with a guid nomber of the gentilmen of the countrey
morning, accompanied by a good number of the gentlemen of the country
round about, gaiff the said Generall and the Capteanes presence, and
round about, he gave audience to the General and captains and after the
efter the sam speitches, in effect, as befor, receavit tham in his hous,
same speeches, in effect, as before, received them in his house
and interteined tham humeanlie, and sufferit the souldiours to
and entertained them humanely and allowed the soldiers to come ashore
com a-land, and ly all togidder, to the number of threttin score, for
and stay all together to the number of 260. For the most part they
the maist part young berdles men, sillie, trauchled, and houngered, to
were young, beardless men, simple, care-worn and hungry, to the whom
the quhilk a day or twa, keall, pattage, and fische was giffen; for my
a day or two's worth of kale, porridge and fish were given; for my
advyse was conforme to the prophet Elizeus his to the King of Israel,
advice was the same as the prophet Elizeus's to the King of Israel

in Samaria. 'Giff tham bread and water,' &c. The names of the
in Samaria: 'Give them bread and water' etc. The names of the

commanders war Jan Gomes de Medina, Generall of twentie houlkes,
commanders were Juan Gomez de Medina, admiral of twenty hulks,

Captain Patricio, Captain de Legoretto, Captain de Luffera, Captain
Captain Patricio, Captain de Leggoretto, Captain de Luffera, Captain

Mauritio, and Seingour Serrano.
Mauritio and Senor Serrano.

Bot verelie all the whyll my hart melted within me for desyre of
But indeed, the whole time my heart melted within me for desire of

thankfulnes to God, when I rememberit the prydfull and crewall
thankfulness to God when I remembered the normally proud and cruel

naturall of they peiple, and whow they wald haiff usit us in ceas they
temper of those people and how they would have treated us if they

haid landit with thair forces amangs us; and saw the wounderfull
had landed with their forces. I saw the wonderful

wark of God's mercie and justice in making us sie tham, the cheiff
work of God's mercy and justice in allowing us to see the chief

commanders of tham to mak sic dewgard and curtessie to pure simen,
commanders of them make such greeting and courtesy to poor seamen,

and thair souldarts so abjectlie to beg almes at our dures and in our
and their soldiers begging alms so abjectly at our doors and in our

streites.
streets.

In the mean tyme, they knew nocht of the wrak of the rest, but
In the meantime, they did not know of the wreck of the rest, but

supposed that the rest of the armie was saifflie returned, till a day I gat
thought that the rest of the army was safely returned, until one day I got

in St Androis in print the wrak of the Galliates in particular, with the
in St Andrews a printed pamphlet on the wreck of the Galleons, in

names of the principall men, and whow they war usit in Yrland and
particular, with the names of the important men [on them] and how they

our Hilands, in Walles, and uther partes of Eingland; the wuhilk when
were treated in Ireland and our Highlands, in Wales and other parts of

I recordit to Jan Gomes, be particular and speciall names, O then he
England, which I communicated to Juan Gomez, mentioning specific

cryed out for greiff, bursted and grat. This Jan Gomes schew grait
names, O then he cried out for grief, and burst into tears. Juan Gomez

kyndnes to a schipe of our town, quhilk he fund arrested at Calles at
showed great kindness to a ship of our town which he found arrested at

his ham-coming, red to court for hir, and maid grait rus of Scotland
Calais at his return. He went to court for her and made great praise of

to his King, tuk the honest men to his hous, and inquyrit for the Lard
        Scotland to his King. He took the good men to his house and asked after
of Anstruther, for the Minister, and his host, and send hame manie
        the Laird of Anstruther, for the minister and his host, and sent home many
commendationes. Bot we thanked God with our hartes, that we haid
        kind regards. But we thanked God with our hearts that we had
sein tham amangs us in that forme.
        seen them amongst us in that manner.

James Melvill's Diary and Autobiography, ed. R. Pitcairn, Wodrow Society, 1842.

Dr Fian's Love Magic

*Spanish invaders were not the only enemy. There were of course,
the minions of the Devil to be considered: the witches. In 1590, it
was brought to James's attention that some witches had been
apprehended. They confessed to trying to destroy James by magic
as he returned from his Danish honeymoon with his new Queen,
Anne of Denmark. Those accused were supposed to have raised
storms to sink the newly-weds' ship. James interrogated the
offenders himself and they produced the strangest stories of
witches' sabbaths in North Berwick and thereabouts.*

*Here is an account of the confession of Dr Fian, alias
Cunningham, the village schoolmaster in Tranent. It is taken from
'Newes from Scotland', a sensational pamphlet attributed to James
Carmichael, the minister of nearby Haddington and published in
London in 1591. Fian was accused not only of the attempt on
James's life, but also of using magic for other ends. His love magic
allegedly had unpredictable results.*

Hee confessed, that by his witchcraft hee did bewitch a gentleman
        He confessed that he bewitched a gentleman
dwelling neare to the Saltpans, where the said Doctor kept schoole,
        living near Prestonpans (where Fian was a schoolmaster)
onely for beeing enamoured of a gentlewoman whome hee loved
        because he was in love with a lady also loved by Fian.
himselfe; by meanes of which his sorcery, witchcraft and divelish
        By sorcery, witchcraft and devilish practises he caused
practises, hee caused the saide gentleman, that once in xxiiii [24]
        the gentleman, for one hour out of every twenty four,
howers [hours] hee fell into a lunacie and madnes, and so continued
        to fall into a fit of madness.

one whole hower [hour] together: And for the veritie of the same, hee
He proved this by having the gentleman brought

caused the gentleman to bee brought before the Kinges Majestie,
before the King on 23 December

which was uppon the xxiiii day of December last, and beeing in his
and in the king's chamber the victim

Majesties chamber, suddenly hee gave a great scritch [screech], and
suddenly gave a loud scream and

fell into madnesse, sometime bending himself, and sometime capring
fell into lunacy for a whole hour, sometimes

[capering] so directly up, that his heade did touch the seeling
throwing himself about so that his head almost touched the ceiling,

[ceiling] of the chamber, to the great admiration of his Majestie and
to the great wonder of the king and the others who were present.

others then present; so that all the gentlemen in the chamber were
All the king's bedchamber gentlemen together were not capable of

not able to holde him, untill they called in more helpe, who together
holding the victim down until they called for more help and

bound him hand and foot; and suffering the saide gentleman to lie
bound him hand and foot and forced the victim

still untill his furie [insanity] were past, he within an hower [hour]
to lie still until his insanity left him.

came againe to himselfe; when, being demaunded [asked] by the
Within an hour he came to, and when asked by

Kinges Majestie, 'what he saw or did all that while', answered, that
the king 'what he saw or did all that time' he answered

'he had been in a sounde sleepe'.
that he had been in a sound sleep.

The said Doctor did also confesse, that hee had used meanes
The Doctor also confessed that he had used

sundry times to obtaine his purpose and wicked intent of the same
various ways on a number of occasions to persuade

gentlewoman; and seeing himselfe disappointed of his intention, he
the lady in question to let him have his wicked

determined, by all wayes hee might, to obtaine the same; trusting by
way with her and seeing that he was getting

conjuring, witchcraft and sorcerie, to obtaine it, in this manner. It
nowhere he decided to use magic. The lady

happened this gentlewoman, being unmarried, had a brother, who
was unmarried and had a brother who

went to schoole with the saide Doctor; and calling the saide scholler
was one of the Doctor's pupils. He called the

[pupil] to him, demaunded 'if he did lie with his sister' [sharing a
pupil to him and asked 'if he and his sister

bed was common], who answered 'he did': By meanes whereof, hee
shared a bed?' The boy answered that 'he did.'

thought to obtaine his purpose; and therefore secretly promised, to
Fian, seeing a way to obtain his desire, promised to

teach him without stripes [beating], so he woulde obtaine for him
teach the boy without beatings, if he would fetch him

three hairs of the sisters privities, at such time as hee should spie best
three of his sister's pubic hairs when he had the

occasion for it; which the youth promised faithfully to performe,
opportunity. The boy promised faithfully to perform

and vowed speedily to put it in practise, taking a peece of conjured
this and took a piece of magically-charmed paper

paper of his maister, to lap [wrap] them in, when he had gotten
from his master to wrap them in when he had obtained

them; and thereupon the boy practised nightly to obtaine his
them. The boy then tried nightly to get the hairs,

maisters purpose, especially when his sister was asleep. But God,
especially when his sister was asleep. But God

who knoweth the secrets of all harts, and revealeth all wicked and
who knows the secrets of all hearts and who reveals all wicked and

ungodly practises, would not suffer the intents of this divelish
ungodly practices would not allow the Devilish

Doctor to come to that purpose which he supposed it woulde; and
Doctor to succeed in his intentions, as he supposed he would,

therefore, to declare that he was heavily offended with his wicked
and therefore to show how offended he was with the

intent, did so work by the gentlewomans owne meanes, that in the
Doctor's wicked intentions, he worked through the lady

ende the same was discovered and brought to light; for shee being
herself to bring the fact to light. One night when she was

one night a sleepe, and her brother in bed with her, sodainly cried
asleep with her brother in bed she suddenly cried

out to her mother, declaring that her brother woulde not suffer her
out to her mother, declaring that her brother would not let her

to sleepe; whereupon her mother having a quicke capacitie [being
sleep. Her mother being very quick to work things out,

quick to work things out], did vehemently suspect Doctor Fians
was deeply suspicious of Dr Fian's

intention, by reson she was a witch of her self; and therefore,
intentions, because she herself was a witch. She therefore got up

presently arose, and was very inquisitive of the boy to understand
immediately and quizzed the boy carefully to understand what his

his intent; and the better to know the same, did beate him with
intention was, and the better to find out she gave him a good beating,

sundrie stripes, wherby hee discovered the truth unto her.
until he told her the truth.

The mother, therefore, beeing well practised in witchcraft, did thinke
The mother being adept in witchcraft decided

it most convenient to meete with the Doctor in his owne art; and
to give the doctor a dose of his own medicine, and

thereupon took the paper from the boy, wherein hee should have put
took the paper from the boy, that he was supposed to have put

the same haires, and went to a yong heyfer [heifer] which never had
the hairs in and went to a young heifer which had never

borne calfe, nor gone unto the bull, and with a paire of sheeres
given birth to a calf or been put to the bull and with a pair of shears

[shears] clipped off three haires from the udder of the cow, and
she clipped off three hairs from the udder of the cow

wrapt them in the same paper, which shee again delivered to the boy;
and wrapped them in the same paper which she gave back to the boy,

then willing him to give the same to his saide maister, which hee
telling him to give the paper to his master, which he

immediately did. The schoole maister, so soone as he had received
did as soon as possible.

them, thinking them indeede to be the maid's haires, went straight
The school master as soon as he had received them,

and wrought his arte upon them: But the Doctor had no sooner
believing them to be the young lady's hairs, went and straight away

doone his intent to them, but presently the heyfer [heifer] cow,
cast his magic upon them. He had no sooner done

whose haires they were indeede, came unto the door of the church
what he intended to them, but immediately the heifer cow,

wherein the schoole maister was, into the which the heyfer went,
whose hairs they really were, came to the door of the church where

and made towards the schoole maister, leaping and dauncing upon
he was and went inside. She made towards the schoolmaster leaping

him, and following him forth of the church, and to what place
and dancing about him and following him out of church

soever he went; to the great admiration of all the townes men of
wherever he went, to the great wonder of everybody in

Saltpans, and many other who did beholde the same. The report
Prestonpans and everyone else who saw it. The incident

whereof made all men imagine he did worke it by the Devill, without
made everyone think that he did it by the work of the Devil, without

whome it coulde never have been so sufficiently effected; and
whom it could never have been done, and

thereupon, the name of the saide Doctor Fian (who was but a yoong
because of this Dr Fian (who was only a

[young] man) began to growe common among the people of
young man) gained a reputation amongst the people of

Scotland, that hee was secretly nominated for a notable conjurer.
Scotland as a notorious conjurer.

All which, although in the beginning he denied, and woulde not
He denied all of this to begin with and would not

confesse, yet having felt the paine of the bootes [a Scottish
confess, yet having been tortured with the boots (an

instrument of torture, which involved driving wedges of wood into
instrument of torture which involved crushing the legs with wedges of

the legs] . . . he confessed all the aforesaid to be most true, without
wood) . . . he confessed all this to be true, without

producing any witnesses to justifie the same; and therupon, before
producing any witnesses to back up his story and

the Kings Majesty, hee subscribed the sayd confessions with his
to this effect he signed his confession with his own hand before the king,

owne hande; which for truth remaineth upon record in Scotland.
which fact remains on record in Scotland.

After the depositions and examinations of the sayd Doctor Fian
After the depositions and examinations of Dr Fian

alias Cuningham was taken, as alreadie is declared, with his own
alias Cunningham were taken, as has already been declared, with his

hand willingly set thereunto, hee was by the maister of the prison
own signature put to them voluntarily, he was put in jail
committed to ward, and appointed to a chamber by himselfe; where,
by the master of the prison and given a cell to himself, where
foresaking his wicked wayes, acknowledging his most ungodly lyfe,
forsaking his wicked ways and acknowledging his most ungodly life
shewing that he had too much folowed the allurements and
he admitted that he had followed the allures and
enticements of Sathan, and fondly practifed his conclusions, by
enticements of Satan too much and enthusiastically practiced the
conjuring, witchcraft, inchantment, sorcerie, and such like, hee
Devil's work by conjuring, witchcraft, enchantment sorcery and such
renounced the Devill and all his wicked workes, vowed to leade the
like. He renounced the Devil and all his wicked works and vowed to
lyfe of a Christian, and seemed newly converted towards God.
lead the life of a Christian – seeming newly converted to God.

Robert Pitcairn, *Criminal Trials in Scotland from 1488 to 1596*, Edinburgh, 1833.

Away with the Fairies

Fian, a schoolmaster, was a very atypical witch suspect. Much more commonly prosecuted were poor women who had dabbled in the healing (or cursing) arts. Here is a slightly earlier case from James's reign. In 1588, a suspected witch, Alison Peirson, was dragged before the justice court and charged with consulting with the fairies and with healing the Archbishop of St Andrews by supernatural means. To her prosecutors, her fairy-belief was a sign of dealings with the Devil. Either tortured or sleep-deprived to obtain her confession, Alison produced a rambling account of the supernatural. The verdict of the jury against her is given below.

VERDICT. The said Alesoune, being put to the knawledge of ane
VERDICT. The said Alison being tried by a jury of the
Assyis of the personis aboune writtin, wes conuict be thair
persons written above was convicted by their
delyuerance, of the using of Sorcerie and Witchcraft, with the
verdict of using sorcery and witchcraft, and
Inuocatioun of the spreitis of the Dewill; speciallie, in the visioune and
invoking the spirits of the Devil. Especially this was in the vision and

forme of ane Mr William Simpsoune, hir cousing and moderbrotheris-
shape of Mr William Simson, her cousin and maternal uncle's

sone, quha sche affermit wes ane grit scoller and doctor of medicin,
son, whom she affirmed was a great scholar and doctor of medicine

that haillit hir of hir diseis in Lowtheane, within the toun of
who in Lothian, in the town of Edinburgh, healed her of her disease,

Edinburghe, quhair scho reparit to him, being twell yeiris of aige; and
when she visited him, aged twelve. She came and went there

thair cuming and ganging be the space of sewin yeiris, quhen scho wes
for the space of seven years, when she was helped with her sickness,

helpit of hir seiknes, quhilk scho had quhan hir poistee and power wes
which she had when her ability and power was taken

tane fra hir hand and fute; continewing thairby in familiaritie with
from her hand and foot. She continued to be in touch with

him, be the space foirsaid; dealing with charmes, and abusing of the
him, over that time, dealing with charms and deluding the

commoun people thairwith, be the said airt of Witchcraft, thir diuers
ordinary people with them, by the said art of witchcraft, for some

yeiris bypast.
years past.

(2) ITEM, for hanting and repairing with the gude nychtbouris and
(2) ITEM, for associating with and visiting the good neighbours [fairies]

Quene of Elfame, thir diuers yeiris bypast, as scho had confest be hir
and the Queen of Fairy these years past as she had

depositiounis, declaring that she could not say reddilie how lang she
confessed in her depositions. She declared that she could not easily

was with thame; and that scho had mony guid freindis in that court
say how long she was with them. She had many good friends at that

quhilk wes of, hir awin blude quha had gude acquentance of the
court who were of her own blood and who had good relations

Quene of Elphane, quhilk mycht haif helpit hir: bot scho wes quhyles
with the Queen of Fairy, who might have helped her, but she was

weill and quhyles ewill, and ane quhyle with thame and ane vthir
sometimes well and sometimes very ill, sometimes with them, other

quhyle away; and that scho wald be in hir bed haill and feir, and wald
times away. She would be in her bed, healthy and fine, and would

nocht wit quhair scho wald be or the morne: And that scho saw nocht
not know where she would be before morning. She had not seen the

the Quene thir sewin yeir: And that scho had mony guid freindis in
Queen for seven years. She had many good friends at

that court, bot wer all away now: And that scho wes sewin yeir ewill
that court but they were all away now: and that for seven years she

handlit in the Court of Elfane and had kynd freindis thair, bot had na
had been badly treated at the court of Fairy and had kind friends there but
will to visseit thame eftir the end: And that itt wes thay guide
had no will to visit them after the end. It was these good
nychtbouris that haillit hir under God: And that scho wes cuming and
neighbours that healed her under God: and that she had been coming
gangand to Sanct Androus in hailling of folkis, thir saxtene yeiris
and going to St Andrews, healing people these sixteen years
bypast.
past.

(3) ITEM, convict of the said airt of Wichecraft, in sa far, as be hir
(3) ITEM, convicted of the said art of witchcraft, in so far as by her
depositioune scho confest that the said Mr Williame Sympsoun, quha
deposition she confessed that the said Mr William Simson, who
wes hir guidschire-sone, borne in Striviling, his fader wes the Kingis
was her grandfather's son born in Stirling (where his father was the King's
smyth, lernit hir craft, quha wes tane away fra his fader be ane mann
smith), he had taught her that craft. He was taken away from his father
of Egypt, ane gyant, being bot ane barne, quha had him away to
by an Egyptian [a gypsy], a giant, being at the time only a child. The gypsy
Egypt with him quhair he remanit to the space of tuell yeiris or he
took him away to Egypt with him where he stayed for 12 years before he
come hame agane; and his fader deit his fader deit in the meane tyme
came home again. His father died in the meantime
for opining of ane preist-buik and luking uponne it: And that the said
from opening a priest's book and looking at it. The said
Mr Willame haillit hir, sone eftir his hame cuming.
Mr William healed her soon after he came home.

(4) ITEM, that scho being in Grange-mure, with the folkis that past
(4) ITEM, she was in Grangemuir, with the people who went to the
to the Mure, scho lay doun seik alane; and thair come ane man to hir,
muir, and she lay down alone, sick. Then a man came to her, clad in
cled in grene clathis, quha said to hir, 'Gif scho wald be faithfull, he
green clothes, who said to her 'If she would be faithful, he would do
wald do hir guid'; and that scho seing him, cryit for help, bot nane
her good'. She seeing him, cried for help, but nobody heard her, and
hard hir; and thane, scho chargeit him, 'In Godis name and the low he
then she charged him 'In God's name and the law he
leuit one', that if he come in Godis name and for the weill of hir saull,
lived on' that if he came in God's name and for the good of her soul,
he sould tell: Bot he gaid away thane, and apperit to hir att ane uther
he should tell her. But he went away then and appeared to her at another

tyme, ane lustie mane, with mony mene and wemen with him: And
time with a handsome man, with many men and women with him.

that scho sanit hir and prayit, and past with thame fordir nor scho
Then she blessed herself and prayed and went with them further than she

could tell; and saw with thame pypeing and mirrynes and gude scheir,
could tell, and saw with them piping and merryness and good cheer

and wes careit to Lowtheane, and saw wyne punchounis with tassis
and was carried to Lothian, and saw wine casks and cups

with thame: And quhene scho tellis of thir thingis, declarit, scho wes
with them. When she tells these things, she declares that she was

sairlie tormentit with thame: And that scho gatt ane sair straik, the
painfully tormented by them, and that she got a painful blow

fyrst tyme scho gaid with thame, fra ane of theme, quhilk tuke all the
first time she went with them from one of them. It took all the

poistie of hir car syde fra hir, the mark quhairof wes blae and ewill
power of her left side from her. The mark of it was blue and ugly.

faurrit; quhilk mark scho felt nocht, and that hir syd wes far war.
She didn't feel the mark, and her side was far worse

(5) ITEM, that scho saw the guid nychtbouris make thair sawis, with
(5) ITEM, that she saw the good neighbours make their salves with

panis and fyris; and that thay gadderit thair herbis, before the sone
pans and fires. They gathered their herbs before sun-

rysing, as scho did: And that thay come verry feirfull sumtymes, and
rise as she did. Sometimes they came in very terrible guises and

fleit hir verry sair, and scho cryit quhene thay come: And that thay
scared her very much and she cried out when they came. Sometimes they

come quhyles anis in the aucht dayes, and quhene scho tauld last of it,
come once in eight days. When she last told of it,

thay come to hir and boistit hir, saying, scho sould be war handlit nor
they came to her and threatened her, saying she should be worse treated

of befoir; and that thaireftir thay tuke the haill poistie of hir syde, in
than before and after that they took the whole power of her side in

sic soirt, that scho lay tuentie oulkis thaireftir: And that oft tymes thay
such a way that she lay sick for 20 weeks after that. Often they would

wald cum and sitt besyde hir, and promesit that scho sould newir
come and sit beside her and promise that she should never be poor,

want, gif scho wald be faithfull and keip promeis; bot, gif scho wald
if she would be faithful and keep promise, but if she would

speik and tell of thame and thair doingis, thay sould martir hir: And
confess and tell about them and their deeds they would martyr her.

that Mr Williame Sympsoun is with thame, quha haillit hir and teichit
Mr William Simson is with them, who healed her and taught

hir all thingis, and speikis and wairnis hir of thair cuming and saulfis
her all things and he speaks and warns her of their coming and saves

hir; and that he was ane young man nocht sax yeiris eldar nor hirselff;
her. He is a young man, not six years older than herself, and

and that scho wald feir quhene scho saw him and that he will appeir
she is afraid when she sees him and that he appears to her only, before

to hir selff allane before the Court cum; and that he before tauld hir
the Court comes. He told her before how he was carried away with

how he wes careit away with thame out of middil-eird: And quhene
them out of middle-earth. When we hear the whirl-wind blow in the

we heir the quhirll-wind blaw in the sey, thay wilbe commounelie with
sea, they will commonly be with it, or coming soon after. Then Mr

itt, or cumand sone thaireftir; than Mr Williame will cum before and
William comes beforehand and tells her, and bids her be watchful and

tell hir, and bid hir keip hir and sane hir, that scho be nocht tane away
bless herself, so she will not be taken away with them again, for a teind

with thame agane; for the teynd of thame gais ewerie yeir to hell.
of them goes every year to hell [every year they give a sacrifice to hell].

(6) ITEM, of hir confessioune maid, That the said Mr Williame tauld
(6) ITEM, of her confession that the said Mr William told her of

hir of ewerie seiknes, and quhat herbis scho sould tak to haill thame,
every sickness and what herbs she should take to heal them and how

and how scho sould use thame; and gewis hir his directioune att all
she should use them; and that he gives her his direction at all times. In

tymes: And in speciall, scho said, that he tauld hir, that the Bischop of
particular she said that he told her that the bishop of St Andrews had

Sanct Androus had mony seiknessis, as the trimbling fewer, the palp,
many sicknesses, such as the trembling fever, palpitations, a weak

the rippillis and the flexus; and baid hir mak ane saw and rub it on his
back, and the flux, and told her to make a salve and rub it on his

cheikis, his craig, his breist, stommak and sydis: And siclyke, gaif her
cheeks, his head, his breast, stomach and sides; and suchlike. He gave

directiounis to use the yow mylk, or waidraue with the herbis, claret
her directions to use ewe milk, or woodruff with herbs, or claret

wyne; and with sume uther thingis scho gaif him ane sottin fowll; and
with some other things. She gave him a marinated chicken; and she made

that scho maid ane quart att anis, quhilk he drank att twa drachtis,
a quart [of medicine] at once, which he drank in two draughts, at two

twa sindrie dyetis. Convicta et combusta.
separate meals. Convicted and burnt.

Robert Pitcairn, *Criminal Trials in Scotland from 1488 to 1596*, Edinburgh, 1833.

The Subtlety of Love

James's Danish marriage was not only the source of witch trials – it also produced one of the most charming love stories of Scottish history. Margaret Vinstarr, one of Anne's ladies in waiting, fell in love with the young Scots laird of Logy. Alas! Her lover soon fell victim to the chaos produced by Francis Earl of Bothwell (a worthy successor to Mary's troublemaker of that title). James believed that Bothwell, his rake-hell cousin, was trying to murder him, both by witchcraft and by more direct means. When the young laird of Logy was found to be associating with such a royal bête noir his life was soon in danger, but James had reckoned without the gallant lady-in-waiting. The 'love interest' of this story inspired the chronicler of the Historie of King James the Sext *to record it.*

I n this close tyme, it fortunit that a gentilman callit Weymis of Logy,
In the mean time, it happened that a gentleman called Weymss of

being also in credence at court, was delatit as a traffekker with
Logy, being in favour at court, was accused of having dealings with

Frances Erle Bothuell; and he being examinat before king and
Francis Earl of Bothwell. Being examined before King and council, he

counsall, confessit his accusatioun to be of veritie; that sundrie tymes
confessed that his accusation was true. He had at various times

he had spoken with him, expreslie aganis the King's inhibitioun
spoken with him, expressly against the King's proclamation to the

proclamit in the contrare; whilk confession he subscryvit with his
contrary. He signed a confession to that effect. And because the

hand: And because the event of this mater had sik a succes, it sall also
consequence of the matter had such a result, it shall also be praised by

be praysit be my pen, as a worthie turne, proceiding from honest,
my pen, as a worthy turn, proceeding from honest chaste love and

chest love and charitie, whilk sould on na wayis be obscurit from the
charity, which, as a good example, should not in any way be hidden

posteritie for the gude example: and tharefore I have thoght gude to
from posterity, and therefore I think it good

insert the same for a perpetuall memorie.
to insert it for perpetual memory.

Queyne Anne, oure noble Princess, was servit with dyvers
Queen Anne, our noble princess, was served by various

gentilwemen of hir awin cuntrie, and naymelie, with ane callit
women of her own nationality, and in particular by one called

Maistres Margaret Twynstoun, to whome this gentilman, Weymes
Margaret Vinstarr, for whom this gentleman, Weymss

of Logye, bure great honest affectioun, tending to the godlie band of
of Logy, had deep, well-intentioned affection, tending towards

marriage; the whilk was honestlie requytit be the said gentilwoman,
marriage. This was genuinely returned by the lady,

yea evin in his greatest mister. For howsone she understude the said
even in his greatest misfortune. As soon as she realised that

gentilman to be in distres, and apperantlie be his confessioun, to be
he was in distress, and apparently by his confession to be sentenced to

puneist to the death; and she having privelege to ly in the Queynis
death, she (who had the privilege to sleep in the Queen's

chalmer, that same verie night of his accusatioun, whare the King
chamber), that very same night of his accusation, when the King

was also reposing that same nycht, she came furth of the dur
was also sleeping there, stealthily crept out of the chamber door,

prevelie, bayth the prencis being then at quyet rest, and past to the
whilst their majesties were asleep, and went to the

chalmer whare the said gentilman was put in custodie, to certayne
chamber where the gentleman was kept in custody. She went to some of

of the garde, and commandit thayme that immediatlie he sould be
the guard and commanded them that he should immediately be

broght to the King and Queyne; whareunto thay geving sure
brought to the King and Queen, which they believing implicitly,

credence, obeyit. But howsone she was cum bak to the chalmer dur,
obeyed. But as soon as she came back to the chamber door,

she desyrit the watches to stay, till he sould cum forth agayne; and
she told the guard to wait outside, until Logy should come back out again.

so she closit the dur, and convoyit the gentilman to a windo, whare
She closed the door, and took the gentleman to the window, where

she ministrat a lang corde unto him to convoy himself doun upon,
she produced a long cord for him, to let himself down

and sa be hir gude cheritable help he happelie escapit be the subteltie
on, and so by her good charitable help, he escaped by the subtlety

of loove.
of love.

Historie of King James the Sext, ed. D. Laing, Bannatyne Club, 1825.

Bad Bairns and Jailbreaks

*James's motto was 'Blessed are the peacemakers', perhaps inspired
by the unruly characters his Scottish kingdom produced from time to
time. Here are a few examples of late 16th-century news items
which Robert Birrel, burgess of Edinburgh, noted down in his diary:*

*some murderous grammar school boys and an audacious attempted
break-out from Edinburgh's Tolbooth prison.*

1595. The 15 of September, Johne Macmorrane slaine be the shott
of ane pistole out of the schooll. This Johne Macmorrane being baillie
for the tyme, the bairns [children] of the said gramar schooll came to
the tounes counsell conforme to thair yeirlie custome, to seek the
priviledge [of a half holiday], quha [who] wes refusit; upone the
quhilk [which], ther wes ane number of schollaris, being gentelmens
bairns, made ane mutinie, and came in the night and tooke the
schooll, and provydit thameselfis with meit, drink, and hagbutis
[guns], pistolet [pistols], and sword: they ranforcit [reinforced] the
dores [doors] of the said schooll, sua that refusit to let in their master
nor nae uthir man, without they wer grantit ther privilege, conforme
to their wontit [accustomed] use. The Provost and baillies and
counsell heiring tell of the same, they ordeinit John Macmorrane
baillie, to goe to the gramar schooll and take some order therwith.
The said Johne, with certein officers, went to the schooll, and requestit
the schollaris to opin the doreis [doors]: thai refusit. The said baillie
and officers tooke ane geast [joist] and rane at the back dore with the
geast. Ane schollar bad him desist from dinging up [breaking down]
the dore, utherways, he vowit to God, he wald shute [shoot] ane pair
of bulletis throw hes heid. The said baillie thinking he durst [dared]
not shute, he, with his assisters, ran still with the geast at the said dore.
Ther came ane schollar callit William Sinclair, sone to William Sinclair
chansler of Catnes [chancellor of Caithness], and with ane pistolet
shott out at ane window, and shott the said baillie throw the heid, sua
that he diet [died]. Presentlie the haill tounesmen ran to the schooll,
and tuik the said bairns and put thame in the tolbuith [tolbooth –
town prison]: bot the haill [whole] bairns wer letten frie without hurte
done to thame for the same, within ane short time thairafter

1600. The 2 Apryll, being the Sabbathe day, Robert Achmutie,
barber, slew James Wauchope at the combat [duelling] in St
Leonard's Hill, and, upone the 23, the said Robert [was] put in ward
in the tolbuith of Edinburgh: and in the meinetyme of hes being in
ward [imprisoned], he hang ane cloke [a cloak] without the window
of the ironehous [jail], and anuther within the window there, and
saying that he wer seik [sick], and might not sie the light: he had
aquafortis [nitric acid] continuallie seithing at the irone window,
quhill at the last the irone window wes eiten [eaten] throw; sua [so],
upone a morneing, he caused hes prentes [apprentice] boy attend
quhen [when] the toune gaird [guard] should have dissolvit [fallen

out], at quhilk [which] tyme the boy waitit on and gaif [gave] hes Master ane token that the said gaird wer gone, be the schaw or waiff [wave] of hes hand-curche [handkerchief]. The said Robert: hung out an tow [rope], whereon he thought to have comeit doune; the said gaird spyit the waiff of the handcurche, and sua the said Robert: wes disappoyntit of hes intentione and devys [device]; and sua, on the 10 day, he wes beheidit at the crosse upone ane scaffolt [scaffold].

'Robert Birrell's Diary' printed in *Fragments of Scottish History*, ed. Sir J. G. Dalyell, Edinburgh, 1798.

Union

James is most famous for being the monarch who united the crowns of England and Scotland on the death of Elizabeth I in 1603. Here is how a family of Edinburgh burgesses recorded this great event in the chronicle of notable events which they kept in their family. The grandson of the originator of the chronicle, David Johnston, gifted it to Thomas, Lord Fairfax in 1655. Note that the Edinburgh businessmen didn't see the Union as being all to their advantage.

Upon the foirsaid 24 of March betuix 8 and 9 howris in the
Upon the 24th of March between 8 and 9 hours in the morning the
morneing the Lordis of the prive cownsell of England being
Lords of the Privy Council of England were convened and
convened and understanding, as said is, caused procleim at the
understanding what had happened, ordered a proclamation to be
yetis [gates] of hir lait majesteis cowrt and schaw to the haill
made at the gates of her late Majesty's court, informing the whole
peopill thair assembled that hir majestie was dead and that the
people assembled there that her Majesty was dead and that the
successive richt of the croun and awthoritie of hir dominionns
right of succession to the crown and authority of her dominions
apperteaned only to James King of Scotland, so the said proclamation,
pertained only to James King of Scotland. So the proclamation
so soon as could be possible, was publisched till all his majestes
was published as soon as possible to all his Majesty's subjects.
subjects, now justlie intitled King of England, Scotland, France and
He was now justly entitled King of England, Scotland France and
Ireland, Defender of the Faith and at tuo houris efternoon the
Ireland, Defender of the Faith and at two hours in the
same was proclamed at the gilt cruss at Chaipsyd in London
afternoon this was proclaimed at the gilt cross of Cheapside in London

quhair thair was grit numbers of pepill, baith kirkmen, gentilmen
where there were great numbers of people, both clergy, gentlemen

and laicks convened admyring that the matter could be [*Sir*
and ordinary folk convened wondering what the matter could be.

Robert Cecil read the proclamation] . . . and hering the content
[The proclamation was read by Sir Robert Cecil] *Hearing the content*

thereof and being very glaid thairat thai all cryed in one consent
of it and being very glad at it, they all cried with one consent 'God save

'God Save King James!'. The word 'king' was a very strange word till
King James!'. The word King was a very strange word to them having

them, haifing now wanted a king the spaice of 50 yeiris compleit
now been without a king for 50 whole years since

since the day of Edward the sax quho died in anno 1553.
the time of Edward VI who died in 1553.

Upon the Satterday following Sir Robert Cary (brother till Sir Johne
Upon the Saturday following, unknown to the Lords of the English

Cary, governor of Berwick) unknawn to the Lords of the English
Council, Sir Robert Cary (brother to Sir John Cary, governor of Berwick)

cownsell haifing gotin intelligence thairof be the seang of the
arrived at Holyroodhouse. He had got intelligence [of the Queen's death]

quenis gentilwemen out of the window quhair of ane she lay,
by seeing one of the Queen's ladies in waiting, out of the window where

arryved at Holyroodhouse and haifing hurt his coller bain be the way
she lay. Having hurt his collar bone on the way [due to rushing to be first

schew to his majestie of the quenis death and of his new inheritance
with the news] he told his Majesty of the Queen's death and of his new

quho was not a litill glad at it and baith then and efterward
inheritance, who was not a little glad of it and both then and afterward

rewarded him honorably for his pains.
rewarded him honourably for his pains.

[*The official English delegation turned up soon after and asked James
to accept the Crown. He did so gladly.*]

Upon Mononday the 28 of March, his majestie sent John Bothwell
Upon Monday the 28 of March, his Majesty sent John Bothwell,

Lord of Holyroodhouse to the town of Berwick to tak possession
Lord of Holyroodhouse, to the town of Berwick to take possession

thairof for his use quho being reallie possessed of the keys and staff
of it for his use. Being actually given the keys and staff

thairof and the oth of allegance being taken, he cheirfully in the
of the town and the oath of allegiance being taken, he cheerfully in the

King's name rendereth the forsaid staff and keyis thairof to the
King's name rendered the staff and keys to the mayor

Major and governor thairof, shawing to them that his Majesteyis
and governor of the town, telling them that his Majesty's good

goode plasur was thai sould enjoy all thair ancient privileges
pleasure was that they should enjoy all their ancient privileges, charters

charteris and libertyis and not only they bot also all otheris his
and liberties and not only them but also all his other good and loving

goode and looving subjectis schawing and continewing in the
subjects who shared similar obedience and who continued to be obedient.

lyk obedience and the said Lord returned again to his Majestie in
Continuing in obedience the said Lord returned again to his Majesty in

Holyroodhouse.
Holyroodhouse.

At this tym grit was the confluence baith of noblemen and other
At this time there was great confluence of both noblemen and other

peopill in Edinburgh alsweall of English as of Scotismen to see the
people in Edinburgh both English and Scots. To see the

rejoysing thair, it was wonderfull. Bot the wysser sort of Scots men
rejoicing there was wonderful. But the wiser sort of Scots

said as efter it is turned to pas that King James getting England,
men said (as after turned out with King James getting England),

Scotland wald baith tyn their King and their court and in tym of
Scotland would lose both her king and court and in time of

thair grit afflictionnis or oppressions be over many staitsmen as
great affliction or oppression would have too many politicians as

kinges, [and] thei wald haif far till go to worschip or till
kings and thus would have far to go to pay court [to the real king]

seik relieif or redres.
or to seek relief or redress.

'Johnstons' History', Adv. Ms. 35.4.2, ii, ff.640r-v.

Mad Cows and Two-Headed Bairns in Leith

*The Johnstons were not the only Edinburgh people to keep a
private record of events. Another Edinburgh chronicler was very
fond of foreign news, business news and what might be termed
'News of the Weird'.*

*Here are some of the more unusual occurrences which took place
in James's Scotland: mad cows, babies with two heads, and whales
stranded in the Forth. To a 17th-century writer, these were not just*

sensational events, they were signs from God of his displeasure
with national behaviour and politics: portents of troubles to come.

1612

In the moneth of March 1612 thair fell furth sundrie uncouth and
In the month of March 1612 there happened sundry uncouth and

prodigious thinges sic as ane quha baith murdreist his father
prodigious things, such as someone near Glasgow who

and mother besyd Glasgow and ky quha brocht furth quicke
murdered his father and mother; and cows which gave birth to

dog quhelps in steid of calfis to the nowmer of fourtine or therby
live puppies instead of calves to the number of fourteen or thereabouts

at ane tyme and ane uther kow efter scho had calfit tuik sic ane
at one time. Another cow after she had calved lowed non-stop,

lowing that scho gaid stark mad sua that the awner wes compellit
so she went stark mad, so that the owner had to

to caus slay hir and thairefter thair wes ane deid barne fund in
kill her and thereafter a dead baby was found in her

hir wombe with sundrie uther uncouth and prodigious thinges not
womb. There were also various other strange and prodigious things never

hurd of before in this cuntrey.
heard of before in this country.

1620

About this same tyme thair wes ane woman in Leith, the belman and
About this time there was a woman in Leith, the wife of the church

kepar of the kirkis wyfe, that wes delyver[it] of ane bairne quhilk
beadle, who was delivered of a child

wes ane monster having tua heidis and thre armes baith the heidis
which was a monster having two heads and three arms. Both the

brething lyfe and uttering ane small vaik voce mourning. The ane
heads were breathing and crying in a small weak voice. The one

heid left murning sum few hours befoir the uther and than the
head stopped crying a few hours before the other and the

uther left greting lykwyis and sua deit within xxiiii hours eftir
other stopped crying likewise and so died within 24 hours after

the birth. The lyke had not bene sene nor knawin in this cuntry
the birth. The same had not been seen or known in this country

for many yeirs of befoir and it wes thocht be all men that hurd if it
for many years previously and was thought by all men who heard of it

to be ane ominis and prodigius thing quhilk never falls out bot befoir
to be an ominous and prodigious thing which never happens but before

sum grite alteratioun or trubill.
some great change or trouble.

1626

Upoun Sonday the nynt of July 1626 in the middis of the day thair
Upon Sunday 9th July 1626 in the middle of the day a whale

come in at the Blackstanes, ane mile be eist Leith, ane quhaill scho
came in at the Blackstones, one mile east of Leith. She

wes bot ane young ane yit monstruis for scho wes of threttie thre
was only a young one, but monstrous, for she was 33

futtis of lenth or thairby and very thik and gross of body sua that all
feet in length or thereabouts and very thick and fat of body. All the

the pepill in Edinburgh and Leith and rund about that culd have the
people of Edinburgh and Leith and round about that could have the

occasioun, alsweill men as wemen, repairit to the place quhair the
opportunity, men as well as women, went to the place where the

quhaill wes to sie hir and upoun the Mononday thairefter be the
whale was to see her. Upon the Monday thereafter by the

appointment of sic as had richt scho wes cuttit in peces and maid saill
order of those that had the right, she was cut into pieces and

of hir to thair use. And lyk wyis at this same tyme thair come in four
sold for their profit. And likewise at the same time there came in four

or fyve quhaillis in sundrie uther partis of the cost of the same
or five whales in various other parts of the coast of the same

bignes to the grit admiratioun of all the pepill every ane declairing that
size, to the great wonder of all the people, everyone declaring that

it wes ominus and prodigius betakening grite evillis to cum.
it was ominous and prodigious, betokening great evils to come.

'Edinburgh Chronicler', Wod.Qu.IX. ff.64r,136r, 233v-4r.

Covenanters and Anti-Covenanters

Scots national pride has always been as prickly as its emblematic thistle. In the 17th century it rested on two things: pride in the antiquity of the Scots monarchy – now inaccessible to ordinary Scots since the court moved to London in 1603 – and pride in the Scots Reformation, according to its adherents one of the purest in Europe. When successive kings, beginning with James VI and I, took a 'Monarch knows best' approach to Scottish religion, it caused riots. James's interference in church ceremonial upset a vocal minority. Charles I's interference in Scottish affairs upset not only the unco' guid but also most of the Scottish nobility. When he tried to suppress opposition in his ancient kingdom, he started a chain reaction which set off rebellions in all his three kingdoms. The repercussions of these movements were still being felt in the reigns of his sons Charles II and James II and VII, but it all started to go badly wrong over reform of worship.

The Stoneyfield Sabbath Day

Any attempt to change forms of worship which had become traditional was likely to prove controversial, but Charles I, distant and convinced of his right to impose what he saw as improvements, showed no sign of realising that he was venturing into a minefield. The changes proposed were particularly offensive to most Scots as they seemed designed to bring their worship into line with English practices, which offended national pride. Far worse, they were seen as Roman Catholic or 'papist' in tendency and by contemporary Scottish standards there could be nothing more shocking than that.

Groups of disgruntled Scots decided that it was time to give Charles a lesson to remember. 'The Stoneyfeild Saboth Day' is an account of the riot in Edinburgh when the Dean of St Giles tried to use the hated book. The women of Edinburgh were to the fore in the fray, and even if it wasn't the mythical Jenny Geddes who chucked the stool, her real-life sisters gave a good account of themselves.

A breiff descriptioun of the tumult which fell upone the Lordis day the 23 of Julii 1637, throw the occatioun of a blak popish superstitious service booke, which was then wickedlie introduced, and violentlie urged upone our Mother churches of Edinburghe.

In the old church of St Geillis, thair wes graitt malcontentment and a wonderfull confused tumult many mouthes wer thair oppined to the bischopes publict disgrace. Fals Anti-christiane wolf, beastlie bellygod, and craftie foxe, wer the best epithets and tytles of dignitie whiche wer given him. The Dean Mr James Hanna wes michtelie upbraided. Sum cryed he is one of a witches breeding and the devill's gette [offspring], no wholsume watter can cum furthe from suche a polluted funtane [fountain]. Utheris cryed 'ill hanged theiff, if at that tyme when thow wentest to court thow haidest bene weill hanged as thow wes ill hanged, thow haidest not bene heir to be a pest to God's church this day'. On did cast a stoole at him intending to have given him a tickit of rememberance, but jowking [ducking] became his saifgaird at that tyme . . . a voluntarie [volunteer] who came officious-lie to say amen wes put in no small danger of his lyfe. His gown wes rent, his service booke takin frome him, and his body pitifullie beattin and brused so that he cryed often for mercie and vowed nevir efterward to give his concurrence to such clagged [besmeared, polluted] devotioun. The bischope in the mane tyme thocht to have removed him selff peaceablie to sume houss bot no s[o]oner wes he sein upone the streetis when the confused multitud rusched violentlie in upone him and enragedlie persewed efter him with rayling and clodding [mud throwing], and if thar hand could have bein als active as thair myndis were willing, they had doubtles demolisched the great butt which they aymed at. A certane woman cryed 'Fy, if I could gett the thropple [throat] out of him!' and when one replyed that tho she obteind hir desyre, yit thair mycht perchance cum one muche worss in his rowme [place], scho ansuered 'Efter Cardinall Betoun wes sticked [stabbed], we haid never another Cardinall sen syne. And if that fals judas (meaning the Bischope) wer now stabt and cutt of[f] his place wold be thocht so prodigious and ominous that scairce any ma durst hasard or undertak to be his successor'. I can not heir omitt that worthie reproofe of a trewlie religeous Matrone, for when scho persaved one of Ismallis [Ishmael's] mocking dochteris, to deryde hir for hir fervent expressiones in the behalff of hir heavenlie master, scho thus schairplie rebuked hir with ane elevated voyce saying 'Woe be thes that laughis when Sion murnis [mourns]'. No les worthie of observatioun is that renouned Cristian valyancie [valour] of ane other godly woman at this same seasone: for when scho hard a young man behind hir sounding furth amen to that new composed church comedie (God's service or worschipe it deserves not to be called) which then wes impudentlie acted in publict sicht of the congregatioun, scho quicklie turnd hir about and efter scho haid warmed both his cheikis with the weght of hir handis, scho thus schott against him the thunderbolt of hir zeale 'Fals theiff (said scho) is thair no other pairt of the churche to sing mess in but thow most sing it at my lug?'. The young man being dasched at such a suddant rencounter, gave place to silence.

'The Stoneyfeild Saboth Day,' Adv. Ms. 33.2.32, pp.47-8.

The National Covenant

The King was not for turning. Charles not only refused to withdraw the hated service book, he demanded that his privy council punish the organisers of the riot. He did not understand that control of Scotland was slipping from his grasp. The protest movement gathered pace and excitement. It now decided to band together and to openly defy the King – but how? Edinburgh lawyer Archibald Johnston of Wariston helped to draw up the document which nailed the dissidents' colours to the mast: The National Covenant. Swearing it was more than a political statement: for many it was a religious experience. It welded thousands of Scots together, ready to live or die to defend what they believed in. Here are Wariston's accounts of the swearing of the Covenant in Edinburgh and Currie kirk.

Upon Wedensday, 28 Februar [1638], that glorious mariage day of the Kingdome with God, I was al foranoone with the Commissioners of the barons, quho [who] after long reasoning upon Perth Articles [James VI's innovations in the church] did al appreive [approve] except the Laird of Ethie; so the burroues [burghs]. The noblemen haiving apoynted the body of the gentrie to meit at tuo [two] hours in the Grayfrear Kirk to hear bot copyes of it read and to aunsuear [answer] objections, I propons [proposes] and resolves to haive the principal ready in parchment in al hazards, that, in cais [case] of approbation, it might be presently subscryved [signed]. I mett al the gentlemen in one troupe going up the cassie [street] to the Kirk. I resolved to read and did read the parchment itselth publikly, quhilk, after som feu [few] doubts of som, was approvin; and, after ane divine prayer most fit for the tyme and present purpose maid be Mr. Al. Henderson, The Covenant was subscryved first by the noblemen and barons al that night til 8 at night.

On Foorsday [Thursday] morning I had wryting in the night foor [four] principal copyes in parchment; at nyn [nine] hours it was subscryved be al the ministerie; at tuo [two] hours be the burroues [burghs].

On Frayday, [Friday] in the College Kirk, after ane sensible exhortation be Mr. H. Rollok, taiken from 4 v. 3 c. Jer., and Samson's mothers aunsuer to Manoah, and ane pithie prayer forcing the [thee] to tears, thou read it publikly befor the people of Edr. [Edinburgh], quho [who] presently fell to the subscryving of it al that day and the morrou [morrow] . . .

On Sunday, the 18 day of Merch, 1638, after motion [emotion] in your familie prayer ye went to Rothau [Rothes], heard Mr. J. Hamilton follou [follow] out his text verry sensibly. Ye went with sense to the second taible [at communion] of the morning service; got motion and tears at the taible; ryde presently away with your familie and Riccarton, conferring on the sermons til we came to Currie, quhair Mr. Jhon [John] Chairtres minister was reading the 28 and 29 of Deuteronomy, quhilk he pressed in his exhortation. He preatched on 17 Genes. 1 v., 'I am thy alsufficient God; walk thou befor me, and be perfyte [perfect].' After sermon, being a solemne fast day apoynted for subscription of the Covenant, he read it al over again as he had doone the Sunday of befoir; he syne [then] explained to the people al the pairts of it. Thairafter, to schau [show] his warrand for seiking [seeking], and thairs for giving, ane oath at the renovation of the Covenant, he pressed the 10 ch. Nehemiah. v. 28 and 29, 'Al the rest of the people, thair wyves [wives], sons, and daughters, every on haiving knowledge and understanding; they claive [adhered] to thair brethren, the nobles, and entred into a curse, and unto ane oath to walk in Gods lau [law]'; and the 2 Chronicles. ch. 15 v. 12, 'And they entred into a covenant to seek the Lord God of thair faythers with al thair heart and al thair saule; that quhosoever [whosoever] would not seek the Lord God of Izrael sould be put to death, whither great or small, man or woman. And they suare [swore] unto the Lord with a loud voyce, with schouting, trumpets, and cornets. And al Judah rejoyced at the oath: for they had suorne [sworn] with al thair heart, and sought him with thair whol desyre; and he was found of them; and the Lord gaive them rest round about'; quhairof applied verry weal every word. Yet in al this tyme thair was no motion [emotion] nor tears in any of the congregation; bot immediately thairafter at his lifting up of his hand, and his desyring the congregation to stand up and lift up thair hands and sueare [swear] unto the aeternal God, and at thair standing up and lifting up thair hands, in the tuinkling [twinkling] of ane eye thair fell sutch ane extraordinarie influence of Gods Sprit upon the whol [whole] congregation, melting thair frozen hearts, waltering [watering] thair dry cheeks, chainging thair verry countenances, as it was a wonder to seie [see] so visible, sensible, momentaneal [momentous] a chainge upon al, man and woman, lasse and ladde, pastor and people, that Mr. Jhon, being suffocat almost with his auin [own] tears, and astonisched at the motion of the whol people, sat doune in the pulpit in ane amazement, bot presently rose againe quhen [when] he sau [saw] al the people falling doune on thair knees to mourne and pray, and he and thay for ane quarter of ane houre prayed verry sensibly with many sobs, tears, promises, and voues [vows] to be thankful and fruitful in tym-coming. Honor and prayse be to the naime of the aeternal God, quho only can work wonders and maiks us daylie seie wonders, as this a pryme remarquable [prime remarkable] one quherby [whereby] he testifyed from the heavens this work to be his auin [own] work, his real reentrie [re-entry] in the Covenant with his people, his acceptance of thair offer, his reservation of ane work of mercie for the congregations of this land, albeit personal plauges [plagues] schal [shall] light upon particular persons. 'Lord, let me never forget that I was ane spectator and actor in it; bot proove thankful and fruitful in it,' as the Lord maid thy heart and the hearts of thy familie sensible in the mean tyme, and had maid the instruct thy tenents and servants befor hand for it . . .

Edinburgh April 1 – Thairafter he [Henry Rollock, minister of Edinburgh] desyred the nobles, and al the people, stand up unto the Lord; and first desyred the noblemen, Montrois [Montrose], Boyd, Laudin [Loudon], Balmerino, to hold up thair hands and suear be the naime of the living God, and desyred al the people to hold up thairs in the lyk maner; at the quhilk instant of rysing up, and then of holding up thair hands, thair rayse sik a yelloch [such a yell], sik aboundance of tears, sik a heavenly harmony of sighs and sobbes, universally through al the corners of the churche, as the lyk was never seien [seen] nor heard of. The Sprit [spirit] of the lord so filled the sanctuary, warmed the affections, melted the hearts, dissolved the eyes of al the people, men and women, poore and noble; as for ane long tyme they stood stil up with thair hands up unto the Lord, til Mr. Hery after he recovered himselth, scairse [scarce] aible to speak, after ane schort exhortation to thankfulnes and fruitfulnes, closed al up in ane heavenly prayer and prayse, and gart sing the 74 Ps. fra [the] 18 v. Thou was mooved unto many tears in his first exhortation and prayer befor sermon; and in al the tyme of the solemnity both of the exhortations, prayers, lifting up of hands, and the praysing, thy heart was lyk to burst; thou got aboundance of tears and sobbes, blisse the Lord for they particular motion; bot, above al expression, blisse his naime for that glorious work of his immediat presence, and unexpressable influence of his Sprit upon the whol congregation, testifying from heaven that he directed the work, did nou blisse it, and wald croune [crown] it with some great mercies to the quhilk he is, by this livly, pouerful, spritual maner of reneuing [renewing] his covenant, praepairing this poor nation, albeit our persons sould suffer. We heard that, in the Grayfrier Kirk, it pleased the Lord both foranoone and afternoone at the suearing [swearing] of the Covenant thair, by the lyk motion, to schau [show] the lyk presence of his Sprit. The Lord maik us never forget his presence in it, bot rayther maik us tell it to our posteritie, and maik us walk worthy of it, and within the compasse of this Covenant, as Mr. H. R. concluded in his prayer, 'Give to us, O Lord, quhat thou asks and requyrs of us; and then ask quhat thou wil.' O Edinburgh, O Edinburgh, never forget this first day of Apryle, the gloriousest day that ever thou injoyed; blissed, ten thousand tymes blissed, be the naime of the aeternal God.

Diary of Sir Archibald Johnston, Lord Wariston 1637-1639, ed. G. M. Paul, Scottish History Society, 1911.

The Church Militant

But not the whole of Scotland was signing the Covenant with tears of inexpressible spiritual joy. Up in the North East, Catholic and Episcopalian Scots were far from impressed by all this seemingly traitorous presbyterian zeal. Both sides began to arm and the deteriorating situation soon became unsafe for women and children as the more lawless elements sought to take advantage of the impending troubles.

Luckily for the Dowager Countess of Aboyne, she had her trusty Catholic mission priest, Father Gilbert Blackhall, to turn to – a man equal to any situation. This is how the chivalrous Father Gilbert protected his charges. Ironically his main problem came not from marauding bands of Covenanters, but from his own side!

Nather was it without a raisonable [reasonable] cause that my ladye used to cal me the captaine [Captain] of her castel, which would have bein very evil keeped without me; for, when I did enter in her service, ther was but only two pistolets in al the house, and they belonged to Allexander Davidson, a man who keeped ever a pair of pistolets, but never in al his lyf did fire one; so they served to him only for parade, as he avouched to me. Al her servants had swordes of their

owne, but theise armes al alon are too short to defend houses. It is true
that her owne personne was a more then sufficient guard for her
house and household, in tym of peace; but, when the country became
troubled, and divided in factions of Covenanters and Anty-
Covenanters, every one had nede [need] of armes, both offensive and
defensive. For then every on[e], for the most part, thought wel
purchassed what they could ravish [take] from another; and they who
had nothing of their owne to loose, were, or at least fained [pretended]
themselves to be, of a contrary faction to those who had meanes, but
wanted force aneugh to defend them; which I forsieing [forseeing] and
knowing the necessity and greed of our Heilanders (who carye [carry]
no respect to ather [either] sex or quality of personnes whom they
may oppresse, when justice hath no power to punish malefactors), did
make provision of armes, to defend the person, house, and tenantes of
my ladye; to wit, eight double muskeats [muskets], with bal and
poudre [powder] and matche conforme [with ammunition to match],
and as many light gunnes, with snape workes [snaphance firing
mechanisms]; with a long smal fowling gun, and a very wyde
carrabinne, capable of nynne or tenne pistolet balles at a charg[e],
which I used to hing [hang] at my shoulder when I rode through the
country. So we had eighteen peaces of fire work [fire arms], forby four
pistolets that I had, and two that Alexander Davidson had, in al four
and twentie, and an hundreth pounds of powder, wherof I receaved
fyftie with the muskeats, and I bought as much with the other gunnes,
with balles conforme . . . *[First of all, Blakhall repelled some un-
desirables from Badenoch, who claimed that the Marquis of Huntly
has billeted them on his lady, but this was only the beginning of his
troubles.]*

After that the Badenogh men were gone home to their owne
country, with their armes, the clanne Cameron, vassels of my Lord
Marquis of Huntley, did come from Loquhaber [Lochaber], a wyld
[wild] kind of people, to mak their pray in the lawlande [prey on
lowlanders], betwixt fourtie and fyftie men. They did come to
Aboyne, thinking to mak their fortune their, knowing that ther was no
lord their to resist them, but only a ladye, a most desolat and deulful
[doleful] widow. They were within the court, and readie to come in at
the house gette [gate] befor we knew of their coming. I sent the porter
to bid them go to the outer gate, and their mak their demandes. They
did so, lyk simple fooles, when they might have bein maisters of the
house for their was not a man within the gates, but only the porter
and I. We amused [diverted] them, saying, my lady was impeshed

[busy] hearing the comptes [accounts] of her domestick officers, and, therfor, we could not speak to her so soone, which they did believe, and wa[i]ted long. In the mean tym, the serving men came in, and, when I sie [saw] a sufficient number, I went to the gate in that same manner as I had gone to the Badenogh men, and tould them that my ladye would not show herself to them, nor accustome them to come seeking moneyes from her. (They were, indeed, something more civil than the Badenogh men, for they asked not to loge in my ladyes house, but only to sie herself, and get moneyes from her); but if they would be contented of meat and drink for a passad [a dole-out to a traveller], she would bestow that willingly upon them. They went from the gate, gromeling [grumbling], and stayed at the Peit Hil. We thought they had been waiting for a passad of meat and drink, but that was not the cause of their staying; for, when it was sent out to them, their captain forbid any of them to touch any thing therof, and went away menacing, and bidde the servante who brought it to them tel my ladye that the morrow she should hear of their newes; which they performed, for that same night they did go to the house of Allexander Finlay, who keeped a taverne, and made him kill mouton, and al the poultrie that he had, and made good cheer that night; and the morrow, in place of paying him for their suppers, they did plunder his house, taking away al that could be usseful for them; and went from him to Malcolme Dorward his house at the Milne of Bounty, thinking to get my ladyes moneyes ther, because he was her chamerlanne [chamberlain].

How soone they left Allexander Finlay, he came to the place, betwixt seaven and eight houres, and told me how they had treated him that night, and that they were gone from him to the Milne of Bounty, and were plundring the house of Malcolme Dorward. I was yet in my bed when he tould me, but did rise and cloath myself speedily, and go to my ladye, and tould her, and said, Madame, I wil go against them, with so many as I can find heir in your house. She said, it wil be better to stay until my tenants be conveined, and then go their commander; for what can you be able to doe with so few against so many. Wil you, Madame, said I, that I bring them to you prisonniers, and then you wil know what I can doe? No, said she, for God's sake do not bring them heir, for then I must enterteane [keep] them; but put them out of my land, if you can. What can I not doe, Madame, said I, for your service? I shal ather put them out of your land, or lye myself upon the place; for I shal never return to your housse, if I do not put them away. For then I thought that I had as

great strenth and courage as any other man could have, and my hart
could not endure to lette her be wronged or oppressed. So we
marched, with a dowsen [dozen] of gunnes, eight pistolets, and my
bigge carabein. Before we went out at the gate, I tould them what
order I desired to be kept, which was this: we must seik by al meanes
to surprise them in the house plundring; and to doe it we must march
as the Heilanders doe, every one after another, without any wordis
among us. And when we have entered the courte, Alexander
Davidson, and George Stuart, his nephew, have each of them two
pistolets, they shall go to the window next the gate, and, houlding
their pistolets in at the window, look in themselves, and remark wel
the countenance and actions of the Heilanders, and, if they sie any
man mak to a weapon, shoote him dead; for al consists in the keiping
of the dore and windowes. For if they can be maisters of them to gette
their gunnes out at the windows, with a full sight of us, they will kil
us, without any domage to themselves; or, if they get free passage out
at the dore, they may come out and beat us, for they are three for
every one of us. And I ordeaned my owne man, Thome Blackhal, and
George Cosky, to the other window. Thome had my wyde carabin, ful
of pistolet balles, which would have made great slaughter among
them, so thick together as they were, and Cosky two pistolets. Then I
commanded the twelfe [twelve] gunners to keepe the dore, six on
every syde, with order to shoote but one at once, since the dore could
not give way to more but one to come out at once; and that he who
is next to the dore, on the right hand, shoot first, and go to the last
rank and charge againe, and if he misse so as the man come forward,
the next ranck shoote at him, and go behinde and charge againe.

I prayed them to keep wel this order, and asseured them of the
victory by doing so. Then we marched every one after another, and
not one word among us. When we were very near the house, their
sentinel perceaved that we were not Heilanders (whether he had
been sleping, or by our marching had thought us Heilanders, I know
not), but having discovered us, he did runne to the house, and we
after him, so nere that he had not leasour to shut the gate of the
courte behinde him. Al the vantage that he had before us was to
winne the house, and shut that dore behinde him, which chanced
wel for both parties; for if we could have entred the housse with
him, we should have killed everye one another, for we were in great
furie to be revenged of them, and they could do no lesse than defend
themselves, selling their lyffes at the dearest rate that they could, as
men in dispaire should doe. They would have had a great avantage
upon us, for they, being in a dark housse, would have sein us wel,

and we, coming in from the snow, would have bein blinde for some space of tyme, in the which they might have done us great skaith before we could have done them any, not sieing them. But God provyded better for us.

How soon we were in the courte, I said, with a loud voice, Every one to his poste; which was done in the twinckling of an eye. Then I went to the dore, thinking to brack it up with my foote, but it was a thick double dore, and the lock very strong. Whilst I was at the dore, one of them did come to boult it, and I, hearing him at it, did shoot a pistolet at him. He said afterwarde that the balles did passe through the haire of his head; whither he said true or not, I know not. I did go from the dore to the windowes, and back again, still encouraging them, and praying them at the windowes to hould their eyes stil upon our ennemyes, and to kille such as would lay their handes to a weaponne; and to theise at the dore to heave their gunnes ever ready to discharge at such as would mean to come foorth without my leave. And I stil threatened to burne the house, and them al into it, if they would not render themselves at my discretion, which they were loath to doe, until they sie the light of bottes of strae that I had kendled to throw upon the thatch of the housse, although I did not intend to do it, nor burne our friends with our foes. But if Malcolme Dorward, and his wyf and servants, and his sonne, George Dorward, and Jhon Cordoner, al whom the Heilanders had lying in bonds by them, had bein out, I would not have made any scruple to have brunt the housse and al the Heilanders within it, to give a terrour to others who would be so broutal as to oppress ladyes who never wronged them.

They sieing the light of the burning stray coming in at the windows, and the keepers of the windowes bidding them render themselves [surrender] befor they be brunt, they called for quarters. I tould them they should not gette other quarters but my discretion, unto which, if they would submit themselves faithfully, they would find the better quarters, if not, be at their hazarde.

Gilbert Blackhall, *A Breiffe Narration of the Services Done to Three Noble Ladyes*, Spalding Club, 1844.

Civil War

As Britain descended into civil war, a new leader emerged for the Covenanters. In the Lowlands he was Earl (later Marquis) of Argyll, in the Highlands, however, he was MacCailein Mòr: the great chief of Clan Campbell. He brought to the covenanting cause an acute mind and a following of thousands of fighting men. He

*also brought with him the grudges held against his people by other
clans of the Western Gaedhealtachd, pushed aside by the successful
Campbells. As Argyll rose, James Graham, Earl (later Marquis) of
Montrose found himself squeezed out of the covenanting hierarchy.
When the Covenanters made common cause with the king's
enemies in England, Montrose switched sides and supported the
king. Nobody very much cared – until the young man had an
amazing stroke of luck.*

*Roaming the Highlands of Scotland trying to raise forces for his
master, Montrose chanced on a company of clan warriors: the battle-
hardened men of Alasdair MacColla, fresh from the bloody civil
wars of Ireland. They had crossed the sea to take revenge on the
Campbells who had some years previously forced them out of their
Scottish lands. Montrose had nothing to do but to put himself at the
helm of MacColla's forces – giving royalist respectability to clan
warfare. In 1644, he led his new army on the covenanting garrison
of Aberdeen. Little did he know what he was letting loose.*

*John Spalding, who wrote this account of what followed, was a
royalist like Montrose: but he was also an Aberdonian, and to him
the covenanting army was 'our' army, because it defended the
town. The royalists who attacked it were therefore 'the enemy,'
though Spalding shows his divided loyalties by avoiding
denouncing Montrose and heaping blame instead on his Irish
troops.*

Upone Frydday the 13th of September [1644], about ellevin houris,
oure army beginis to marche out of the toun. Liuetennand
Montroiss wreittis ane letter to the provest and balleis of Abirdein,
sendis ane drummer to touk ane parle [call a parley], and ane
commissioner to deliver the letter, quhilk [which] boor [bore] ane
command and charge to rander [surrender] the toune to him
lieutenant to his Majestie and in the Kingis name, quhairby [whereby]
he micht receave peciabill entress [peaceable entry] to use his Majesteis
proclamationis and sic orderis as he thoucht fitting, promesing
assureans [assurance] that no moir [more] harme nor preiudice should
be done to the toun, bot to take thair intertynnement [lodging] for that
nicht; utherwayis [otherwise] if thay wold disobey, that then he desyrit
them to remove old aigit [aged] men, wemen and children out of the
get [gate], and to stand to thair awin [own] perrell [peril].
    This letter was deliverit to the provest. He convenis his counsall at
the Bowbrig in Alexander Fyndlateris houss, quhair the Lord Burlly,

Lieutennand Arnot, Mr James Baird, and sum otheris wes [were]. Thay causit the commissioner and drummer drink hardlie, sendis ane ansuer; and be the way the drummer wes unhappellie slayne. Montroiss fand thair ansuer wes to stand out, and defend thame selffis to the uttermost. And, fynding his drummer, aganes [against] the law of nationis, most inhumanelie slayne, he grew mad, and becam furious and impatient, oure army being upone thair merche [march] (when he wes slayne) about ellevin houris, towardis the boundis of Justice Millis. At the recept [receipt] of the quhilk [which] answer the lieutennand cumis quiklie merchand [marching] fra the tua myll [two mile] cross to meit us, chargeing his men to kill and pardon none.

Oure cannon begins the play. Oure trouperis persewis hardlie [pursue hard]. The enemy schootis thair cannon also, and defendis stoutlie with muskiteires [musketeers]. The fight contynewis [continues] hotlie dureing the space of tuo houris. At last we tak the flight. Oure trouperis upone horsbak wan saiflie away, except Schir Williame Forbes of Craigiwar and Johne Forbes of Lairgy war takin prissoneris. Thair wes littill slauchter in the fight, bot horribill wes the slauchter in the flight fleing bak to the toune, whiche wes our toune's menis distruction; whairas if they had fled and not cum neir the toune thay micht haue bein in better securitie: bot being commandit be Patrik Leslie provest to tak the toune thay war undone, yit himself and the pryme convenanteris [covenanting leaders] being on horsbak wan saiflie them selffis away [escaped]. The lieutennand followis the chaiss [chase] in to Abirdein, his men hewing and cutting doun all maner of man thay could overtak within the toune, upone the streites, or in thair houssis, and round about the toune, as oure men wes fleing with brode suordis [broad swords] but [without] mercy or remeid. Thir cruell Irishis, seing a man weill cled [well clad], wold first tyr [strip] him and saif [save] the clothis [clothes] onspoyllit [unspoilt], syne [then] kill the man. We lost thrie piece of cannon with muche goode armour, besydis the plundering of oure toune houssis, merchand buithis [merchant shops], and all, whiche wes pitifull to sie. The Lord Burly, Mr Alexander Joffray [Joffray] and his sones, Mr Robert Farquhar, Walter Cochrum, Mr James Baird, aduocat in Edinburgh, and diverss utheris covenanteris, wan upone horss saif away [escaped on horseback]. Alwayes Montroiss follouis [follows] the cheass [chase] in to Abirdene, leaving the bodie of his army standing cloiss [nearby] unbrokin whill [until] his returne, except such Irishis as faucht [fought] the field. He had promesit to them the plundering of the toun for thair good service. Alwaies [any way] the lieutennand stayit not, bot returnit bak fra Abirdene to the camp this samen

Frydday at nicht, leaving the Irishis killing, robbing, and plundering of this toune at thair plesour. And nothing hard bot pitifull howling, crying, weiping, murning, throw all the streittis.

This, thir Irishis contynewit Frydday, Setterday, Sonday, Mononday. Sum wemen thay preissit to defloir [rape], and uther sum thay took perforce to serve thame in the camp. It is lamentabill to heir how thir Irishis who had gottin the spoyll [spoil] of the toune did abuse the samen [same]. The men that they killit thay wold not suffer to be bureit [buried], bot tirrit [stripped] thame of thair clothis, syne left thair naikit bodeis lying aboue the ground. The wyf [wife] durst [dared] not cry nor weip at her husbandis slaughter befoir hir eyes, nor the mother for the sone, nor dochter for the father; whiche if thay war hard [heard], then thay war presentlie slayne also.

As thir savage Irishis ar at this wark, the lieutennand gave ordoris [orders] to the bodie of the army, upone Setterday, the 14th of September, to marche (except sic Irishis as wes plundering the toun and killing oure men, whiche went not with thame) forduardis [forward] to Kintor, Innervrie, and Gareoche.

John Spalding, *Memorialls Of The Trubles in Scotland and in England A.D. 1624-1645*, Spalding Club, 1851.

Clan Donald Strikes Back

Alasdair MacColla's men had not come to Scotland to slaughter the innocent townsfolk of Aberdeen, but to devastate Argyll, revenging themselves on Clan Campbell for the loss of their clan's lands. Late in 1644, Montrose wished to hole up in winter quarters, but MacColla's men insisted on going on the march. Crossing the almost impenetrable passes into Argyll in the depths of winter, they fell upon the men, women and children of the Campbells: plundering, burning and massacring. As they left Argyll, a Campbell army of vengeance came up behind them. Taking routes which would be difficult at the best of times, Montrose and MacColla doubled back, descending upon the Campbell forces at the battle of Inverlochy in February 1645, and routing them.

Gaelic poet Iain Luim (John MacDonald, the Keppoch bard) could not conceal his glee at how the mighty were fallen. He took MacColla the Gael as his hero and not Montrose.

The Battle of Inverlochy

Hi rim ho ro, ho ro leatha,
Hi rim ho ro, ho ro leatha,
Hi rim ho ro, ho ro leatha,
Clan Donald won the day.

Have you heard of the heroic countermarch made by the army that was at Kilcumin? Far has gone the fame of their play – they drove their enemies before them.

Early on Sunday morning I climbed the brae above the castle of Inverlochy. I saw the army arraying for battle, and victory on the field was with Clan Donald.

When you were ascending the spur of Culachy I perceived in you the enthusiasm your bravery inspired; although my country was in flames what has happened is compensation.

Although the earldom of Brae Lochaber should remain for these seven years in its present condition without sowing or harrowing or cultivation, good is the interest from which we are paid.

I declare to you, Laird of Lawers, although loudly you boast in your sword, many a young warrior of your father's kin is lying at Inverlochy.

Many a warrior with cuirass and cavalry saddle, as good as ever was in your clan, was not allowed to escape dry-shod, but had to learn to swim at Nevis Estuary.

Many a warrior with helmet and bow and slender straight musket lay stretched at Inverlochy, and the darling of the women of Kintyre was among them.

The most pleasing news every time it was announced about the wry-mouth Campbells, was that every company of them as they came along had their heads battered with sword blows.

On the day when they thought success would be theirs, heroes were pursuing them on frozen ground; many a great sallow-skinned sloucher lay on the surface of Ach an Todhair.

Whoever should climb Tom na h-Aire (would find there) many a freshly hacked paw badly pickled, and the film of death on their lifeless eyes from the slashing they had from sword-blades.

You engaged in a hot foray round Lochy, smiting them on the noses. Numerous are the blue-fluted well-balanced swords that were wielded in the hands of Clan Donald.

When the great work of blood-letting came to a height at the time of unsheathing slender swords, the claws of the Campbells lay on the ground with sinews severed.

Numerous are the naked unclothed bodies which lie stretched on Cnoc an Fhraoich, right from the battlefield on which the heroes were urged onwards to the far end of Leitir Blàr a' Chaorainn.

I could tell another tale with veracity, as accurately as a learned clerk can write it, that those heroes exerted themselves to the uttermost, and routed their enemies.

John of Moidart of the bright sails, who would sail the seas on a dark day, you were not found guilty of breaking your tryst; it pleases me that you have Barbreck in your power.

That was no ill-guided expedition that Alasdair made to Scotland, plundering, burning and killing, and by him the Cock of Strathbogie [Huntly] was laid low.

That poor fowl which lost its comeliness in England, in Scotland and in Ireland, a feather is he from the corner of the wing: I am displeased that he has surrendered.

Alasdair of the sharp cleaving blades, you promised yesterday to destroy them; you directed the rout past the castle, an excellent plan for keeping in touch with them.

Alasdair of the sharp venomous blades, had you had the heroes of Mull, those of them who escaped you would have induced to stay, when the dulse-eating rabble was in retreat.

Alasdair, son of handsome Coll, expert at breaking castle asunder, you routed the sallow-skinned Lowlanders, and if they had drunk kail you knocked it out of them.

Were you familiar with the Goirtean Odhar? Well was it manured, not by the dung of sheep or goats, but by the blood of Campbells after it had congealed.

Perdition take you if I feel pity for your plight, as I listen to the distress of your children, lamenting the company which was in the battlefield, the wailing of the women of Argyll.

Latha Inbhir Lòchaidh

Hì rim hó ro, hó ro leatha,
Hì rim hó ro, hó ro leatha,

Hì rim hó ro, hó ro leatha,
Chaidh an latha le Clann Dòmhnaill.

'N cuala sibhse 'n tionndadh duineil
Thug an camp bha 'n Cille Chuimein?
'S fada chaidh ainm air an iomairt,
Thug iad ás an nàimhdean iomain.

Dhìrich mi moch madainn Dòmhnaich
Gu bràigh caisteil Inbhir Lòchaidh;
Chunnaic mi 'n t-arm dol an òrdugh,
'S bha buaidh a' bhlàir le Clann Dòmhnaill.

Dìreadh a-mach glùn Chùil Eachaidh,
Dh'aithnich mi oirbh sùrd bhur tapaidh;
Ged bha mo dhùthaich 'na lasair,
'S éirig air a' chùis mar thachair.

Ged bhitheadh iarlachd a' Bhràghad
An seachd bliadhna seo mar tha e,
Gun chur gun chliathadh gun àiteach,
'S math an riadh o bheil sinn pàighte.

Air do làimh-sa, Thighearna Labhair,
Ge mór do bhòsd ás do chlaidheamh,
'S iomadh òglach chinne t'athar
Tha'n Inbhir Lòchaidh 'na laighe.

'S iomadh fear gòrsaid is pillein
Cho math 's a bha beò de d' chinneach
Nach d'fhaod a bhòtainn thoirt tioram,
Ach fòghlam snàmh air Bun Nibheis.

'S iomadh fear aid agus pìce
Agus cuilbheire chaoil dhìrich
Bha 'n Inbhir Lòchaidh 'na shìneadh,
'S bha luaidh nam ban á Cinn-tìr' ann.

Sgeul a b'aite 'nuair a thigeadh
Air Caimbeulaich nam beul slidgneach;
H-uile dream dhiubh mar a thigeadh
Le bualadh lann 'n ceann 'gam bristeadh.

'N là a shaoil iad a dhol leotha
'S ann bha laoich 'gan ruith air reodhadh:
'S iomadh slaodanach mór odhar
A bh'air aodann Ach' an Todhair.

Ge b'e dhìreadh Tom na h-Aire,
'S iomadh spòg ùr bh'air dhroch shailleadh,
Neul marbh air an sùil gun anam
An déidh an sgiùrsadh le lannan.

Thug sibh toiteal teth mu Lòchaidh,
Bhith 'gam bualadh mu na srònaibh:
'S lìonmhor claidheamh claisghorm còmhnard
Bha bualadh 'n lamhan Chlann Dòmhnaill.

'Nuair chruinnich mòr dhragh na falachd,
'N àm rùsgadh na greidlean tana,
Bha iongnan Dhuibhneach ri talamh
An déidh an lùithean a ghearradh.

'S lìonmhor corp nochdte gun aodach
'Nan sìneadh air Chnoc an Fhraoiche
O'n bhlàr an greasta na saoidhean
Gu ceann Leitir Blàr a' Chaorainn.

Dh'innsinn sgeul eile le fìrinn,
Cho math 's nì cléireach a sgrìobhadh,
Chaidh na laoich ud gu'n dìcheall,
'S chuir iad maoim air luchd am mìoruin.

Iain Mhùideartaich nan seòl soilleir,
Sheòladh an cuan ri là doilleir,
Ort cha d'fhuaradh bristeadh coinne:
'S ait leam Barra-breac fo d' chomas.

Cha b'e siud an siubhal cearbach
A thug Alasdair do Albainn,
Creachadh losgadh agus marbhadh,
'S leagadh leis Coileach Shrath Bhalgaidh.

An t-eun dona chaill a cheutaidh,
An Sasann 'n Albainn 's an Éirinn,

Ite e á cùrr na sgéithe:
Gur misde leam on a ghéill e.

Alasdair nan geurlann sgaiteach,
Gheall thu 'n dé a bhith cur ás daibh;
'Chuir thu 'n ratreut seach an caisteal,
Seòladh glé mhath air an leantainn.

Alasdair nan geurlann guineach,
Nam biodh agad àrmainn Mhuile,
Thug thu air na dh'fhalbh dhiubh fuireach,
'S ratreut air pràbar an duilisg.

Alasdair mhic Cholla ghasda,
Làmh dheas a sgoltadh nan caisteal,
Chuir thu 'n ruaig air Ghallaibh glasa,
'S ma dh'òl iad càl chuir thu asd' e.

'M b'aithne dhuibh-se'n Goirtean Odhar?
'S math a bha e air a thodhar:
Chan innear chaorach no ghobhar,
Ach fuil Dhuibhneach an déidh reodhadh.

Sgrios oirbh mas truagh leam bhur càramh,
'G éisdeachd anshocair bhur pàisdean,
Caoidh a' phannail bh'anns an àraich,
Donnalaich bhan Earra-Ghàidheal.

Orain Iain Luim, *Songs of John MacDonald, Bard of Keppoch*, ed. A. M.
Mackenzie, Scottish Academic Press for the Scottish Gaelic Texts Society, 1964.

The End of Montrose

*Montrose and MacColla went on to win battle after battle, leaving
Scotland open before them. After a final victory at Kilsyth the true
weaknesses of Montrose as a politician became apparent. He could
devastate Scotland, but he could not write a political settlement in
blood. Even most of his fellow royalists would not join his regime.
Undaunted, Montrose decided to invade England with his few
remaining troops. Alasdair had left him to pursue his own clan
agenda, and meanwhile the covenanting professional army was on its
way home from England under General David Leslie. At Phillip-
haugh, they devastated his forces and massacred his camp followers.*

It was a blow from which Montrose never recovered. He was still

*full of schemes to restore the royalist cause in Scotland, but they
never came off. His last futile attempt to conquer came unstuck at
the Battle of Carbisdale in 1650. He was captured soon
afterwards. In the hands of the Covenanters, there was no hope of
clemency for him. It was all over. They took Montrose to
Edinburgh and to his death.*

*James Fraser, minister of Wardlaw, later compiled this account of
Montrose's last journey, which reflects the reverence for a royalist
hero which grew in the years after his death. While Fraser
preserves many details taken from eye-witnesses, myth is taking
over from recollection – the copiously weeping executioner appears
to be a pious embellishment to events.*

Thus conducted through the country, and near Inverness, uppon
the rode under Moortoun, where he desired to alight, and calld
[called] for a draught of water, being then in the first crise [crisis] of
a high fever, and here the crowd from the town came forth to gase
[gaze], the two ministers [Mr William Fraser and] Mr John Annand
wait here uppon to comfort him, the latter of which the Marques
was well acquaint with. At the end of the bridge, stepping forward,
an old woman, Margret Nin George, exclaimed and brauled
[brawled], saying, Montross, looke above, view these ruinous
houses of mine quhich [which] yow occasioned to be burnt down
quhen [when] yow besieged Invernesse. Yet he never altered his
countenance, but with a majesty and state beseeming him, keept a
countenance high.   At the cross, a table covered, the magistrates
treat him with wines, which he would not tast [taste] till allayed
with water: the statly prisoners, his officers, stood under a forestare
[fore stair], and drunk heartely. I remarked Colonell Hurry, a
robust, tall, statly fellow, with a long cut in his cheek. All the way
through the streets he never lowed his aspect [lowered his gaze]. The
provost, Duncan Forbes, takeing leave of him at the towns end, said,
My Lord, I am sorry for your circumstance. He replied, I am sory
for being the object of your pitty. The Marques was convoyed that
night to Castle Stuart, where he lodged.
    From Castle Stuart the Marquess is convoyed through Murray, and
be the way some loyall gentlemen wait upon his Excellency, most
awouedly [avowedly] and with grieved hearts, such as the Laird of
Culbin Kinard. Old Provost Tulloch in Narden, Tannachy Tulloch,
Captain Thomas Mackenzy Pluscaden, the Laird of Gockstoun, and
old Mr Thomas Foulerton, his acquaintance at colledge. He was

overjoyed to see those about him, and were his guard forward to
Forres, where the Marques was treated; and thence, afternoon,
convoyed to Elgin city. Where all those loyall gentlemen waited on him,
and diverted him all the time. With allowance of the Generall, in the
morning Mr Allexander Symmer, parson of Duffus, waited on him at
Elgin, being colledge acquaintance with the Marques, 4 yeares his
condisciple at St Andrewes. This cheered him wonderfully, as the
parson often told me, and thence convoyed him all the way to the River
of Spey, and a croud [crowd] of Loyalists flockt about him
unchallanged. Crossing Spey, they lodged all night at Keith, and next
day, May 10, being the Saboth, the Marquess heard sermon there, a
tent being set up in the fields for him, in which he lay, and the minister,
Master William Kinendmond, altering his ordinary [his normal text],
and chused for his theam [theme] and text the words of Samuel the
prophet to Agag, the King of the Amalakits, coming before him
delecatly [delicately]: And Samuel said, As thy sword hath made
women childless, so shall thy mother be childless among women, etc.
This unnatural, merciless man so rated, reviled, and reflected uppon
the Marquess in such an invective, virulent, malicious manner, that
some of the hearers who were even of the swaying side condemned
him. Montross, patiently heareing him a long time, and insisting still,
he said, Rail on, Rasoke; and so turnd his back to him in the tent; but
all honest men hated Kinendmond for this ever after. Montross desired
to stay in the field all night, lying upon straw in the tent till morning.

Moonday after, they march through the Mearnes south. By the
way the Marquess came to his father in laws house, the Earle of
Southask, where he visited two of his own children; but neither at
meeting or at parting could any change of his former countenance,
or the least expression heard, which was not suitable to the
greatness of his spirit and the fame of his former actions, worth, and
vallour. *In transitu* his Excellency stayed one night at Dundee, and
its memorable that, though this towne suffered more losse by his
army than any else in the kingdom, yet were they so farr from
insulting over him that the whole town expressed a great deal of
sorrow for his condition, and furnished him with cloathes and all
other things suitable to his place, birth, and person. At Lieth [Leith]
he was receaved by the magistrates of Edinburgh, and thence
convoyed up to the city by the water gate of the Abby, and with him
all the prisoners of qualety [quality] on foot, about 40 persons; but
according to the sentence of the Parlement the Marquess himselfe
had the favour to be mounted on a cart horse. Having ended this

part of his journay with as much state as in tryumphs is accustomed
to be, he was met at the end off the Canongate under the Netherbow
by some other officers, and the executioner hangman in a liverey
coat, into whose hands he was delivered. There was framed for him
a high seat in fashion of a chariot, uppon each side of which were
holes, and throwgh these a cord being drawn crossing his breast,
and arms bound, his [person?] fast down in that mock chaire. The
executioner then tooke of the Marques's hat, and put on him his
own bonnet, and this chariot being drawn with 4 horses, mounted
of the first, and solemnly drive along towards the tolebooth
[tolbooth]. By this conduct was confirmed and fullfilled Thomas
Rithmers prophesys, never understood till now:

Visa la fin
On an ouler tree green
Shall by many be seen, etc.

Visa la fin, looke to the end, is Montross or Grahm's [Graham's]
motto; and this cart was made of green owler, alder timber which
happened to be brought in, newly cut, to the marcat place, and there
sold.

The vast croud of people who assembled to gase [gaze] uppon this
noble peer, who before wished to see this spectacle, and wisht him all
vengence and misfortun, could not now refrain teares, wringing their
hands, began to be shaken with the first sheue [show] of his tragedy.
Then, being incarcerat in the tolebooth, so closly shut up that non of
his dearest friends were suffered to come nigh him, being now in the
mercy of his implacable foes, not satisfied with his calamities, reviled
him with all possible spite, objecting to him his former condition and
present misery, pronouncing heavy judgements against him, and,
being asked whey they could not otherwayes be satisfied but by so
ignominously handling of him, replyed that they knew no other way
to humble him and bring him home to God.

The Committy apointed be the Parliament to draw up a sentence
against him did it in these words: that he should be hanged on a
gibbet at the Cross of Edinburgh untill he dyed, his history and
declaration being tied about his neck, and so hang 3 houres in
publick view of all the people, after which he sould be beheaded and
quartered, his head set upon the prison house of Edinburgh, his legs
over the gates of Sterling and Glasgow, his arms at Pierth and
Aberdeen, the trunk of his body to be burried in the Gallow Moore,
under the common gallows.

The Parliament sent some of their members and ministers to examin him, but he disdaind, refusing to give them answeir any till he knew and was satisfied uppon quhat [what] tearmes they stood with the King, his royall master. They told the King and they were agreed; then saith the Marquess I desire to be at rest, for I am weary with a long journay, and the complement yow put uppon me is somquhat [somewhat] tedious, and I desire to be rid of yow, for I set no great value uppon your converse. Yow punies [pygmies], yow thought ye had affronted me the day before by carrying me in a cart, but yow are much mistaken, for I judged it the most honorable and joifull [joyful] cavilcade that ever I made, God having all the most comfortably manifested his presence to me, and furnisht me to overlook the reproaches of men, and behold him for whose cause I suffered. And so yow may be gone; I have enugh [enough] of yow . . .

[He was tried before parliament.]

The Chancelour [Chancellor] desired the sentence to be read, which he heard with a setled and unmoved countenance, and desireing to be further heard, was presently stopt by the Chancelour who commanded he should be presently convoyed back to prison, where he was no sooner come but the ministers assaulted him afresh, aggravating the terrour of the sentence, therby to fright him. He acknowledged himselfe much beholding to the Parliament for the honour they had put uppon him, saying he tooke it for a greater grandur [grandeur] to have his head stand uppon the prison gate for his quarrel then to have his pictur set up in the Kings bedchamber; and, lest his loyalty should be forgotten, they had highly honored him in designing lasting monuments to 4 of the cheefest cities of this realm to beare up his memoriall to all posterity, wishing he had flesh enugh to have sent a piece of the same to every city in Christendome, to witness his loyalty to his King and country.

That night none of his friends were suffered to come neare him, but a rude guard still in the chamber with him, so that he had neither time nor place for his privat devotions but in their heareing: cruel barbarity. The fatall day being come designed to put a period to all his troubles, there was erected in the midle of the marcat place, tuixt the Cross and Tron, a large 4 square scaffold breasthigh, in the midest of which was planted a gibbet of 30 feet height. He was convoyed out be the baliefe out of the gaile [jail], cloathed in a scarlet cloake richly shammaded [ornamented] with golden lace. He stept along the streets with so great state, and there appeared in his countenance so much beuty, majesty, and gravity, as amazed the beholders; and many of his enemies did acknouledg him to be the bravest subject in the world, and in him a gallantry that braced all the croud [crowd], more becoming a monarch than a mean peer; and in this posture he stept up to the scaffold, quher, all his friends all wellwillers being debarred from coming neare, they cause a young boy to sit uppon the scaffold, by him designed for that purpose, who wrot his last speech in brachography [shorthand] . . .

The ministers, because he was under the sentence of excommunication, would not pray for him, and even on the scaffold were very bitter against him. Being desired to pray apart, he said, I have already poured out my soul before the Lord, who knowes my heart, and into whose hand I have committed my spirit, and he hath been pleased to return to me a full assurance of peace in Jesus Christ my Redeemer; and therefore, if yow will not join with me in prayer, my reiterating it again will be but scandalous to you and me. So, closing his eyes and holding up his hands, he stood a good space with his inward, devout ejaculations, being perceived to be mightily moved all the while. When he had done he called for the executioner, and gave him 4 pieces of gold, who, weeping, tooke his booke and declaratioun and other printed papers which he had published in his life, and being all tied in a string, hanged them together about his neck; when he said, I hug this more than my badge of being Knight of the Garter which his Sacred Majesty was pleased to make me; nay, more my honour than a chain of gold. Then, his arms being tied, he asked the officers if they had any more dishonour as they conceived it to put uppon him, he was readdy to receive and accept of the same; and so, with an undaunted currage [courage] and gravity, in spite of all their affronts, uncivil and barbarous usage, he went up to the top of that prodigious gibbet, where, having freely pardoned the executioner, desired him that at the uplifting of his hand he should tumble him over, which was accordingly done by the weeping hangman, who, with his most honest teares seemed to revile the cruelty of his countrymen, which may serve for a test of the rebellius and diabolicall spirit of that malicious consistory. After 3 houres he was taken down and had his head cut off, which was fixed on the iron pin, west end of the toleboth; his quarters sent to be placed and set up in the several cities; and the rest of his mortall parts burried under the gallows.

James Fraser, *Chronicles of the Frasers, the Wardlaw Manuscript,* ed. William Mackay, Scottish History Society, 1905.

Disaster at Dunbar – The Fate of the Prisoners of War

*Montrose, as a royalist, was an understandable enemy for the
Covenanters, but Oliver Cromwell might seem like a strange foe
for godly Calvinists. How did the Covenanters come to be at war
with the great English puritan? Were they not on the same side?
They were (give or take some disagreement over church
government), until he and his comrades executed the king.
Remember that the two main sources of Scottish national pride in
the 17th century were the monarchy and the Scots brand of
Protestant religion. Scots might have waged war on the king
(without actually declaring it), but to them his person was sacred.
When the English decided to execute Charles I, who, for all his
many faults, had been born in Dunfermline and was still
technically a Scot, there was trouble. His son Charles II was
instantly proclaimed king in Scotland and Cromwell felt himself
left with no option but to invade.*

*He did so successfully. Never had there been so much infighting
amongst Scots. The religious bigots at the top who saw this war as
amounting to a presbyterian 'jihad' started to purge the army on
the grounds that only the godly were good enough to fight
Cromwell's army of puritan 'saints'. The godly started to dominate
the army councils too. War by religious committee – the outlook
was not good. On 3 September 1650 Cromwell took his bickering
enemies apart. Thousands of Scots perished, either on the field of
Dunbar or afterwards as prisoners, or were transported to the
colonies or pressed into English service. This account relates the
fate of hundreds of these men.*

A Letter From Sir Arthur Hesilrige, To the Honorable Committee
Of The Councel Of State For Irish and Scotish Affairs at White
Hall, Concerning the Scots Prisoners

Gentlemen,

I Received your Letter dated the Twenty sixth of October, in that
you desire me, That Two thousand three hundred of the Scotch
Prisoners now at Durham or elswhere, able and fit for Foot Service,
be selected, and marched thence to Chester and Liverpool, to be
shipped for the South and West of Ireland, and that I should take
special care not to send any Highlanders.

I am necessitated upon the receipt of this, to give you a full

accompt concerning the Prisoners: After the Battel at Dunbar in
Scotland, my Lord General writ to me, That there was about Nine
thousand Prisoners, and that of them he had set at liberty all those
that were wounded, and, as he thought, disabled for future Service,
and their Number was, as Mr Downing writ, Five thousand one
hundred; the rest the General sent towards Newcastle, conducted to
Berwick by Major Hobson, and from Berwick to Newcastle by some
Foot out of that Garison, and the Troop of Horse; when they came
to Morpeth, the Prisoners being put into a large walled Garden, they
eat up raw Cabages, Leaves and Roots, so many, as the very seed
and the labor, at Four pence a day, was valued by sufficient men at
Nine pounds; which Cabage, as I conceive, they having fasted, as
they themselves said, near eight days, poysoned their Bodies; for as
they were coming from thence to Newcastle, some dyed by the way-
side, and when they came to Newcastle, I put them into the greatest
Church in the Town, and the next morning when I sent them to
Durham, about Sevenscore were sick, and not able to march, and
three dyed that night, and some fell down in their march from
Newcastle to Durham, and dyed; and when they came to Durham,
I having sent my Lieutenant Colonel and my Major, with a strong
Guard both of Horse and Foot, and they being there told into the
great Cathedral Church, they could not count them to more then
Three thousand; although Colonel Fenwick writ to me, That there
were about Three thousand five hundred, but I believe they were not
told at Berwick and most of those that were lost, it was in Scotland,
for I heard, That the Officers that marched with them to Berwick,
were necessitated to kill about Thirty, fearing the loss of them all,
for they fell down in great Numbers, and said, They were not able
to march; and they brought them far in the night, so that doubtless
many ran away. When I sent them first to Durham, I writ to the
Major, and desired him to take care, that they wanted not any thing
that was fit for Prisoners, and what he should disburse for them, I
would repay it. I also sent them a daily supply of bread from
Newcastle, and an allowance equal to what had been given to
former Prisoners: But their Bodies being infected, the Flux encreased
amongst them. I sent many Officers to look to them, & appointed
that those that were sick should be removed out the cathedral
Church into the Bishops Castle, which belongs to Mistris Blakiston,
and provided Cooks, and they had Pottage made with Oatmeal, and
Beef and Cabages, a full Quart at a Meal for every Prisoner: They
had also coals daily brought to them; as many as made about a

hundred Fires both day and night, and Straw to lie upon; and I appointed the Marshal to see all these things orderly done, and he was allowed Eight men to help him to divide the coals, and their Meat, Bread and Pottage equally; They were so unruly, sluttish and nasty, that it is not to be believed; they acted rather like Beasts then Men, so that the Marshal was allowed Forty men to cleanse and sweep them every day: But those men were of the lustiest Prisoners, that had some small thing given them extraordinary: And these provisions were for those that were in health; and for those that were sick, and in the Castle, they had very good Mutton Broth, and sometimes Veal Broth, and Beef and Mutton boild together, and old Women appointed to look to them in the several Rooms: There was also a Physitian which let them Blood, and dressed such as were wounded, and gave the sick Physick and I dare confidently say, There was never the like care taken for any such Number of prisoners that ever were in England. Notwithstanding all this, many of them dyed, and few of any other Disease but the Flux; some were killed by themselves, for they were exceeding cruel one towards another. If a man was perceived to have any Money, it was two to one but he was killed before morning, and Robbed; and if any had good clothes, he that wanted, if he was able, would strangle him, and put on his clothes: And the Disease of the Flux still encreasing amongst them, I was then forced, for their preservation, if possible it might be, to send to all the next Towns to Durham, within four ot five miles, to command them to bring in their Milk, for that was conceived to be the best Remedy for stopping of their Flux, and I promised them what Rates they usually sold it for at the Markets, which was accordingly performed by about Threescore Towns and places, and Twenty of the next Towns to Durham continue still to send daily in their Milk, which is boiled, some with Water, and some with Bean flower, the Physitians holding it exceeding good for recovery of their health.

Gentlemen, You cannot but think strange this long preamble, and to wonder what the matter will be; in short its this, Of the Three thousand prisoners that my Officers told into the Cathedral Church at Durham, Three hundred from thence, and Fifty from Newcastle of the Sevenscore left behinde, were delivered to Major Clerk by order from the Councel, and there are about Five hundred sick in the Castle, and about Six hundred yet in health in the Cathedral, the most of which are in probability Highlanders, they being hardier then the rest, and other means to distinguish them we have not, and about Sixteen hundred are dead and buried, and Officers about Sixty, that are at the Marshals in Newcastle. My Lord General having released the rest of the Officers, and the Councel having given me power to take out what I thought fit, I have granted to several well-affected persons that have Salt-works at Sheels, and want Servants, Forty, and they have engaged to keep them to work at their salt-pans; and I have taken out more about Twelve Weavers, to begin a Trade of Linnen cloth like unto the Scotch-cloth, and about Forty Laborers. I cannot give you on this sudden a more exact Accompt of the prisoners, neither can any Accompt hold true long, because they still dye daily, and doubtless so they will, so long as any remain in Prison. And for those that are well, if Major Clerk could have believed that they had been able to have marched on foot, he would have marched them by Land; for we perceive that divers that are seemingly healthy, and have not all been sick, suddenly dye, and we cannot give any reason of it, onely we apprehend they are all infected, and that the strength of some holds it out till it seize upon their very hearts. Now you fully understand the condition and the number of the Prisoners, what you please to direct, I shall observe, and intend not to proceed further upon this Letter, until I have your Answer upon what I have now written. I am,

Gentlemen,
Your affectionate Servant,
Art: Hesilrige
Octob, 31, 1650

A Letter From Sir Arthur Hesilrige, To the Honorable Committee Of The Councel Of State For Irish and Scotish Affairs at White Hall, Concerning the Scots Prisoners, London, 1650.

Royalist Revenge

All this godliness and consequent war and destruction was too much for the not exactly sober citizens of Linlithgow. According to outraged covenanting chronicler James Kirkton, they celebrated the first anniversary of the restoration of Charles II in 1661 with an outrageous drunken knees-up.

Upon the first 29th of May, 1661, the town of Lithgow [Linlithgow], Robert Mill being chief author, and Mr James Ramsey (who afterward ascended the height of the pitifull bishoprick of Dumblane) being minister, after they hade filled their streets with bonfires very throng, and made their crosse run wine, added also this ridiculous pageant: They framed ane arch upon four pillars, and upon one side the picture of ane old hagge with the Covenant in her hand, and this inscription above: A GLORIOUS REFORMATION. On the other side of the arch was a whigge [radical Covenanter] with the Remonstrance in his hand, with this inscription, NO ASSOCIATION WITH MALIGNANTS. On the other side was the Committee of Estates, with this inscription, ANE ACT FOR DELIVERING UP THE KING. On the fourth side was the Commission of the Kirk, with this inscription, THE ACT OF THE WEST KIRK. On the top of the arch stood the Devil, with this inscription, STAND TO THE CAUSE. In the midst of the arch was a litany:

> From Covenants with uplifted hands,
> From Remonstrators with associate bands,
> From such Committees as govern'd this nation,
> From Church Commissioners and their protestation,
>   Good Lord deliver us.

They hade also the picture of Rebellion in religious habit, with the book Lex Rex [by Covenanter Samuel Rutherford] in one hand, and the cause of God's wrath [a book by Johnston of Wariston] in the other, and this in midst of rocks, and reels, and kirk stools, logs of wood, and spurs, and covenants, acts of assembly, protestations, with this inscription, REBELLION IS THE MOTHER OF WITCHCRAFT. Then after the minister hade sanctified the debauch with a goodly prayer, and while they were drinking the king's health, they put fire to the whole frame, which quickly turned it to ashes. Lastly, in place of this there appeared a table supported by four Angels with a sonnet to the king's praise, and so with drunkenness enough they concluded the day. This was not required by any law, but they would outrun the law. All these men some twelve years before hade renewed the covenant with uplifted hands, but single perjury could not satisfie them, except they boasted in their sin with a triumph.

James Kirkton, *Secret and True History of the Church of Scotland*, ed. C. K. Sharpe, Edinburgh 1817.

Digging Up Montrose

Mercurius Caledonius *was Scotland's first regular newspaper, edited by Thomas Sydserf. This was the hot news in its first edition*

in 1661. Montrose, now that his side had won, was reburied in a
state funeral.

This day, in obedience to the Order of Parliament, this City was
allarmed with Drums and nine Trumpets, to go in their best
Equipment and Arms for transporting the Dis-membered Bodies of
his Excellency the Lord Marquesse of Montrose, and that renowned
Gentleman Sir William Hay of Dalgety, murthered both for their
prowes and transcending Loyalty to King and Country, whose
Bodies to their Glory and their enemies shame, had been
ignominiously thrust in the earth, under the publike Gibbet half a
mile from Town. That of the Lord Marquesse was indeed intended
for ignominy to his high Name, but that of the other ambitiously
covet by himself as the greatest honour he could have, when being
incapable to serve his Majesty longer, to engrave nigh his great
Patron, which doubtlesse proceeded from a faith typical of a more
glorious one. The Ceremony was thus performed: The Lord
Marquesse of Montrose, with his friends of the name of Graham,
the whole Nobility and Gentry, with Provest, Baillies and Council,
together with four Companies of the Trained Bands of the City, went
to the place, where having chanced dirctly (however possibly
persons might have been present able to demonstrate) On the same
Trunk, as evidently appeared by the Coffin, which had been
formerly broke a purpose by some of his friends in that place nigh
his Chest, whence they stole his heart, embalmed it in the costliest
manner, and so reserves it: as also by the Trunk it self found without
the skull, and limbs distracted in the four chief Towns of the Nation;
but these through the industry and respect of friends carried to the
Martyre, are soon to welcome the rest. That other of Sir William
Hay of Delgety, was as surely pluckt forth, lying next to that of his
Excellency. The Noble Lord Marquesse and his friends took care
that these ruins were decently wrapt in the finest linnen; so did
likewise the friends of the other, and so incoffined suitable to their
respectful dignities.

The trunck of his Excellency thus Coffined, was covered with a
large and rich black Velvet Cloath, taken up and from thence carried
by the Noble Earls of Marre, Athol, Linlithgow, Seaford, Hartfield
and others of these Honourable Families: The Lord Marquesse
himself, his brother Lord Robert, and Sir John Calquhoun Nephew
to the deceased Lord Marquesse, supporting the head of the Coffin,
and all under a very large Pale (or Canopy) supported by the Noble
Viscount of Stormond, and Lords Stranaver, Fleeming, Drum-

lanerick, Ramsay, Matherty and Rollock. Being accompanied with a Body of Horse of Nobility and Gentry, to the number of 200, rallied in decent Order by the Viscount of Kenmure, they came to the place where the Head stood, under which they set the Coffin of the Trunk on a Scaffold made for that purpose till the Lord Naper the Barons of Morphy Inchbrakie, Urchell and Gorthy, and severall other Noble Gentlemen placed on a Scaffold next to the Head (and that on the top of the Towns Tolbooth six Story high) with sound of Trumpet, discharge of many Canon from the Castle, and the honest peoples loud and joyful acclamation, all was joyned and crowned with the Crown of a Marquesse, conveyed with all Honour befitting such an action to the Abbay Church of Holy-roodhouse, a place of Buriall frequent to our Kings, there to continue in State, untill the Noble Lord his Son be ready for the more magnificent Solemnization of his Funerals.

All our Solemnities, both that of the High Commissioners reception, that of Riding the Parliament, and this great Honour done to the memory of the Grand Exemplar of Loyalty his Excellency the Marquesse of Montrose was accompanied with infinite Acclamations of the People: Great Volleys of shot by the City Companies, and thundering of Canon from the Castle: It's many years since those sparks of Loyalty has been smothered by the ashes of Tyranny: It's true, though a considerable part of our Nation were the first that transgressed upon their duty, yet they never reached the length of a boundlesse disobedience, for they no sooner discovered the depth of the Treason wherein their rebellious Confederates in England would have ensnared them, but they presently faced about to their Allegiance, and it is well known to the world, that since the year 1648, there was never a people enterprised such honourable and probable wayes to redeem former Escapes than we did; and though it was the pleasure of Providence to disappoint our designes, yet we never grudged neither at our Imprisonments, the losse of the dearest of our blood, nor devastation of our Fortunes; And which is our grand comfort, we have attained so much knowledge as never again to be juggled out of our reason, under the notion of specious pretences: for the drowsiest Clown of our most Northern Islands can with content smile at the cheats of Liberty, and the Good old Cause. And therefore the Blasphemers, Rumpers, and other Antimonarchicall Vermin in England must cast about some where else then for companions in Scotland.

Mercurius Caledonius, Monday, 7 January, 1661.

Judas Be Taken!

*But whilst royalist heroes were being fêted, religious intolerance
took a new turn. The popular presbyterianism which had taken
hold in many parts of Scotland was to be rooted out. Despite the
excesses of the most extreme fanatics, many covenanting ministers
were devoted and professional men, seeking to better the religious
instruction of their flocks. Many ministers would not accept
bishops in the church, as they believed that the bible explicitly
decreed that they, like Christ's disciples, should all be equal and
that there should be no hierachy in the kirk. Bishops also had a
bad reputation amongst Scots presbyterians for being essentially
politicians who served an earthly master first and foremost. When
the government pushed for recognition of the bishops, a third of
Scotland's clergy walked out, taking most of their people with
them.*

*These were the people usually remembered as 'The Covenanters'.
Many of these dissidents carried out a peaceful strategy of
conscientious resistance to the government, despite heavy
persecution, but a tiny handful of them believed in armed struggle.
It was these rebels, the 'freedom fighters' or 'terrorists', depending
on your point of view, who carried out many of the most
notorious acts of resistance to episcopacy. Here is part of the
account of the murder of the Archbishop of St Andrews, James
Sharp, written by James Russell, one of the men who took part in
the killing. Originally a zealous Covenanter, Sharp switched sides
at the Restoration, ditching presbyterianism for the archibishopric.
This gave him his unsavoury reputation amongst his old comrades
as a 'Judas'. He was one of the most energetic persecutors of
dissent. In 1679 dissent of the armed and dangerous sort caught
up with him.*

[*When Russell and his fellow covenanters caught sight of the
archbishop's coach a debate ensued*] . . . But [David Hackston of]
Rathillet answered, that the Lord was his witness he was willing to
venture all he had for the interest of Christ, yet he durst [dared] not
lead them on to that action, there being a known prejudice betwixt
the bishop and him, which would mar the glory of the action, for it
would be imputed to his particular revenge, and that God was his
witness he did nothing on that account; but he would not hinder
them from what God had called them to, and that he should not

leave them; which John Balfour hearing, said, Gentlemen, follow me: whereupon all the 9 rode what they could to Magusmuir, the hills at the nearest, and Andrew Henderson riding afore, being best mounted, and saw them when he was on the top of the hill, and all the rest came up and rode very hard, for the coach was driving hard; and being come near Magus, George Fleman and James Russell riding into the town and James asked at the goodman if that was the bishop's coach? He fearing, did not tell, but one of his servants, a woman, came running to him and said it was the bishop's coach, and she seemed to be overjoyed; and James riding towards the coach, to be sure, seeing the bishop looking out at the door, cast away his cloak and cried, Judas be taken! The bishop cried to the coachman to drive; he firing at him, crying to the rest to come up, and the rest throwing away their cloaks except Rathillet . . . fired into the coach driving very fast about half a mile, in which time they fired several shots in at all parts of the coach, and Alexander Henderson seeing one Wallace having a cock'd carrabine going to fire, gript him in the neck, and threw him down and pulled it out of his hand. Andrew Henderson outran the coach, and stroke the horse in the face with his sword; and James Russell coming to the postiling [postillion], commanded him to stand, which he refusing, he stroke him on the face and cut down the side of his shine, and striking at the horse next brake his sword, and gripping the ringeses [reins] of the foremost horse in the farthest side: George Fleman fir'd a pistol in at the north side of the coach beneath his left arm, and saw his daughter dight of the furage [brush off the wadding from the cartridge]; and riding forward, gripping the horses' bridles in the nearest side and held them still, George Balfour fired likewise, and James Russell got George Fleman's sword and lighted of his horse, and ran to the coach door, and desired the bishop to come forth, Judas. He answered, he never wronged man: James declared before the Lord that it was no particular interest, nor yet for any wrong that he had done to him, but because he had betrayed the church as Judas, and had wrung his hands, these 18 or 19 years in the blood of the saints, but especially at Pentland; and Mr Guthrie and Mr Mitchell and James Learmonth; and they were sent by God to execute his vengeance on him this day, and desired him to repent and come forth; and John Balfour on horseback said, Sir, God is our witness that it is not for any wrong thou hast done to me, nor yet for any fear of what thou could do to me, but because thou hast been a murderer of many a poor soul in the kirk of Scotland, and a betrayer of the church, and an open enemy and persecutor of Jesus Christ and his members, whose blood thou hast shed like water on the earth, and therefore thou shalt die! and fired a pistol; and James Russell desired him again to come forth and make him for death, judgement, and eternity; and the bishop said, Save my life, and I will save all yours. James answered, that he knew that it was not in his power either to save or to kill us, for there was no saving of his life, for the blood that he had shed was crying to heaven for vengeance on him, and thrust his shabel [sabre] at him. John Balfour desired him again to come forth, and he answered, I will come to you, for I know you are a gentleman and will save my life; but I am gone already, and what needs more? And another told him of keeping up of a pardon granted by the king for 9 persons at Pentland, and then at the back side of the coach thrust a sword at him, threatening him to go forth; whereupon he went forth, and falling upon his knees, said, For God's sake, save my life; his daughter falling on her knees, begging his life also. But they told him that he should die, and desired him to repent and make for death. Alexander Henderson said, seeing there has been lives taken for you already, and if ours be taken it shall not be for nought; he rising of his knees went forward, and John Balfour stroke him on the face, and Andrew Henderson stroke him on the hand and cut it, and John Balfour rode him down; whereupon he, lying upon his face as if he had been dead, and James Russell hearing his daughter say to Wallace that there was life in him yet, in the time James was disarming the rest of the bishop's men, went presently to him and cast of his hat, for it would not cut at first, and hacked his head in pieces.

Having thus done, his daughter came to him and cursed him, and called him a bloody murderer; and James answered they were not murderers, for they were sent to execute God's vengeance on him; and presently went to the coach, and finding a pair of pistols, took them, and then took out a trunk and brake it up, and finding nothing but women's furniture, and asked what should be done with it; and it was answered, that they would have nothing but papers and arms; and Andrew Henderson lighted, and took a little box and brake it up, and finding some papers, which he took; and opening a cloak-bag they found moe papers and a Bible full of porterers [portraits], with a little purse hung in it, a copper dollar, two pistol ball, two turners, two stamps, some coloured thread, and some yellow coloured thing like to pairings of nails, which would not burn, which they took. At this time James Russell was taking the rest of his men's arms, and Wallace, as he would have resisted, came roundly forward, and James Russell smote him on the cheek with his shabel and riped all their pockets, and got some papers and a knife and fork, which he took; and crying to the rest to see that the bishop be dead, William Danziel lighted, and went and thrust his sword into his belly, and the dirt came out; turning him over, ript his pockets, and found a whinger [sword] and knifes conform, with some papers, which he took. James Russell desired his servants to take up their priest now. All this time Andrew Guilon pleaded for his life. John Balfour threatening him to be quiet, he came to Rathillet, who was standing at a distance with his cloak about his mouth all the time on horseback, and desired him to come and cause save his life, who answered, as he meddled not with them nor desired them to take his life, so he durst not plead for him nor forbid them.

Appendix to James Kirkton, *Secret and True History of The Church Of Scotland*, ed. C. K. Sharpe, Edinburgh, 1817.

The Cameronians

After the murder of Sharp, the tiny band of desperadoes involved fled to the west of Scotland where they found support for an uprising, which failed at the battle of Bothwell Bridge. Yet still they continued to resist. Soon they obtained the most famous recruit to their cause, a young firebrand of a preacher, Richard Cameron, from Falkland in Fife. Hackston of Rathillet, who was present at the murder of Sharp, was captured in a skirmish at Airdsmoss and wrote this account of it. It was in this battle that the charismatic but fierce Cameron was killed. His death gave his followers the name by which they are best-known to Scottish history – the Cameronians.

We getting notice of a party out seeking us, sent two, on Wednesday night late, to know their motion, and lay on a moor-side all night, and Thursday, about ten hours, we went to take some meat, and sent out other two, and desired them to consult with the first two, who had not come to us, but were lying down to sleep, who all four returned and told us, it was unnecessary to send any for intelligence, they having secured it. Whereupon, after we had gotten some meat, we came to a piece of grass, and lay down, and presently we were all alarmed that they were upon us, and so making ready, we saw them coming fast on, and that about three or four hours in the afternoon, and each one resolving to fight, I rode off to seek a

strength for our advantage, and being desired by a country man to
go into such a place for the best strength, I went, and they followed;
but coming to it, I found we could go no further, and so turning and
drawing up quickly, eight horse on the right hand with R. D. and
fifteen on the left with me, being no more, the foot not being forty,
and many of them ill armed, in the midst, I asked all if they were
willing to fight, who all said yes, especially J. G. The enemy
advanced fast, whom I took to be above an hundred and twelve,
well armed and horsed, who sending first about twenty dragoons on
foot, to take the wind of us, which we seeing, sent a part on foot to
meet them, and the rest of us advanced fast on the enemy, being a
strong body of horse coming hard on us, whereupon, when we were
joined, our horse fired first, and wounded and killed some of them,
both horse and foot. Our horse advanced to their faces, and we fired
on each other; I being formost, after receiving their fire, and finding
the horse behind me broken, I then rode in amongst them, and went
out at a side without any wrong or wound. I was pursued by
severals, with whom I fought a good space; sometimes they
following me, and sometimes I following them. At length my horse
bogged, and the foremost of theirs, which was David Ramsay, one
of my acquaintance; we both being on foot, fought it with small
swords without advantage of one another; but a length closing, I
was stricken down with three on horseback behind me, and received
three sore wounds on the head, and so falling he saved my life,
which I submitted to. They search me, and carried me to their rear,
and laid me down, where I bled much, where were brought severals
of their men sore wounded. They gave us all testimony of brave
resolute men. What more of our men were killed I did not see, nor
know, but as they told me after the field was theirs. I was brought
towards Douglas. They used me civilly, and brought me drink out of
an house by the way. At Douglas, Janet Clellan was kind to me, and
brought a surgeon to me, who did but little to my wounds, only
stanched the blood. Next morning I was brought to Lanark, and
brought before Dalziel, lord Ross, and some others, who asked
many questions at me: but I not satisfying them with answers,
Dalziel did threaten to roast me; and carrying me to the tolbooth,
caused bind me most barbarously, and cast me down, where I lay till
Saturday morning, without any, except soldiers, admitted to speak
to me, or look my wounds, or give me any ease whatsomever. And
next morning they brought me and John Pollock, and other two of
us, near two miles on foot, I being without shoes, where that party,
which had broken us at first, received us. They were commanded by

Earlshall. We were horsed, civilly used by them on the way, and
brought to Edinburgh, about four in the afternoon, and carried
about the north side of the town, to the foot of the Canongate,
where the town magistrates were who received us; and setting me on
an horse with my face backward, and the other three bound on a
goad of iron, and Mr Cameron's head carried on an halbert before
me, and another head in a sack, which I knew not, on a lad's back;
and so we were carried up the street to the parliament-closs, where
I was taken down, and the rest loosed.

Robert Wodrow, *History of the Suffering of the Church of Scotland*, iii, Glasgow,
1828.

The Holyrood Riot

*In 1685, Charles II died and his brother James II and VII became
King of Scotland, Ireland and England. This initiated what came to
be known to Cameronians as 'The Killing Times' when they could
be shot on the spot for failing to take the necessary oaths of
loyalty. But it wasn't for cruelty to radical Covenanters that James's
peoples rose up against him, but for his kindness to Catholics and
for being a Catholic himself. Religious tolerance was on the whole
considered to be a vice, not a virtue, in 17th-century Britain (and
for that matter most of Europe). James thought that the best way
to push his own religion was to decree that it and other faiths must
be tolerated and then to favour Catholicism as much as possible.*

*Public opinion was outraged. The old religion was still tarred in
the Protestant mind with memories of heretic-burning, French
domination and Spanish threat. Large-scale persecution of
Protestants in neighbouring France scared James's subjects – was
this what living under a Catholic monarch could lead to? The
King's policy of toleration was too radical a step, too soon. When a
son and heir who could potentially carry on James's policies was
born, there was uproar. William of Orange was invited to invade.
James was effectively deposed. On 10 December 1688, James was
not even out of the country when the Scottish mob rose up,
determined to cleanse Edinburgh of the Jesuit 'threat'. Alexander
Adamson, then a divinity student, was one of the rioters.*

The nixt morning be 10 the toun counsel sat and about 11 in the
forenoon emitted a proclamation: discharging tumults and
requiring maisters of families to keep their children and servants

within doors, but it was no sooner read than it was torn: the officers and drummers being severly beat in several places of the citty. They were forced to return to their maisters to tell how they were treated. All continowed quiet till twilight when the mob began to gather. The first appearance they made was about the Cougatte [Cowgate] head from thence going to the Grasse Mercatte [Grassmarket] where they provided themselves with staves and torches. They come up the West Bow and enter a drummers house in the Castel Hill [Castlehill] whence they took two drums, on[e] of which they broke before they passed the whyhous [weigh house?] so doun the street they come beating with their drum, till past the Nether Bow and in the Canongate head they made a stope, seing the guaird [guard] drawing out att the Canongate tolbooth and sent one to enquire what the matter was. The Captain replyed it was to put respect upon them. They answeared they would have non[e] of his respect and required he might call in his guairds immediately. When he did so on they march till they com to the Cana. cross [Canongate Cross] where they stop again and took down the Earl of Perth's pictor which they caried down with them to the Aby [Abbey] where they mett Captain Wallace advanced with 2 fills [files] of Musketeers as far as the strand without the Aby gatte [Abbey Gate]. Here they stopt and required entry into the court and being refused they beat their drum and advised to run in upon him, which as soon as he heard the cry of, he ordered thes[e] he had with him to fire upon them which did abundance of mischief, for several were killed upon the spotte and many wounded, the most pairt whereof shortly after dyed of their wounds to the number of 36 or 38 and verry few recovered.

After the first fire was over, tho some were killed and many wounded, the rest first made a fierce asalt [assault] upon that party and forced them off the street with great fury, in so much as befor they could enter the Aby gatte, two of them were beat doun and killed outright. When the party was entered, finding they could pursue them no further the gattes being shutt against them they returned a little and ordered some of their number to carry up the wounded to the citty as also to require assistance, the rest lodging themselves within close heads till assistance should come to them. Capt Wallace and his men mein tyme contineued still firing up the street from this tyme which was about nine at night till eleven. Thes[e] who came to the citty caried in some of the hands and arms that were shott off the lads to Patrick Steel's, a vintner, where several Gentilmen were drinking, which were laid before them, shewing how the poor lads had been treated be the souldiers. Att which they were so enraged that they rose and went into the toun counsel (which was then sitting) and required the train bands to be raised but gatt no incuradgement however the Capt. Med. without the counsel's order caused the drumms to be beat. Thes[e] gentlemen in the mean time got a Coram [quorum] of the Privie Counsel conveined who presently sent doun 2 Lyon Heralds in their coatts requiring Capt. Wallace to deliver up the Aby in the Counsel's name, which he refusing they ordoured the toun gaird to goe doun against them folowed by the train bands. Att their dounconing, Wallace fired once or twice upon them as they did upon him with little execution upon either side. Att last the leager of the toun gaird with the third of their men came in by a back entry and were upon them ere they were awarr upon which they all cast doun their arms and run. The lads having nottice broke into the court and killed all they gott their hands upon but by reason of the darknesse of the night, the most of them made their esceap throw the K[ing's] park it was reported that 14 of the soldiers were killed. The lads having gott the Aby, they presently fall a pulling doun the cheapels burning the timber work in the closse. They went up to their seats and bringing forth their liberary, they burnt their books without distinctione but for a long time could not learn where their images were, but att last being informed by a certain persone that they were hid in ane oven and an old presse sett before the mouth of it, thither they goe and finding them they bring them forth one by one and by companies carie them in triumph throw the citty, one or two of their number crying continualie what they carried. The last that came was the babe in the cradle, of which they cryed without intermission 'This is the holiest thing off all' and having finished their processione throw all the publick streets of the citty they returned to the Aby closse, where they burne them all, yea, the silver lamps and candles-stickes were thrown into the fire this continowed till about 2 in the morning when all went to rest . . .

What is contained in the first two colum[n]s is what I was eye witnesse to, but being dangerously wounded I was forced to goe off with the wound before the Aby was taken, so what follows I had by information but I think my information was tollerable good, being the wholl tyme upon the place. This is a peice of history in my oppinion worthy to be transmitted to posteritie for the hand of god may evidently be seen in it and its effects are obvious to this day. I bear the marks of it upon the hollow of my thigh.

Alexander Adamson, 'The Holyrood Riot', Wod.Qu.XXXVI, f.241v.

Revolution, Riot and Parliament

In the aftermath of James II and VII's fall from power, a Convention of the Scottish Estates assembled in Edinburgh. This was the ad hoc equivalent of the Scottish parliament. In their Claim of Right they declared James deposed and forfeited. The Scottish Crown (with strict conditions) was offered instead to William and his wife Mary. This was the beginning of a period of rapid change for Scotland which saw disasters like Darien and Glencoe, upheavals like the 1689, 1715 and 1719 Jacobite attempts to restore the Stuarts, and one of the most significant turning points in Scotland's history apart from 1314 and 1603 – the Union of the Parliaments of 1707.

Killiecrankie

To men such as John Graham, Viscount Dundee (formerly plain Graham of Claverhouse – the 'Bluidy Clavers' of the Covenanters), James's deposition was an outrage. Dundee took to the hills, managing to raise some of the clans, but otherwise finding little support. A government army under General Hugh Mackay, who was a Highlander himself, marched against him, but at Killiecrankie in 1689 it all went wrong, for both sides. Mackay was defeated, but Dundee was killed. Here is part of Mackay's own account of the battle.

The ennemys being upon their ground much about the same time with us, seemed to extend their order beyond our right wing; which the General observing made his line move to the right by the flank, least their design might be to flank, get betwixt him and pass, which would be a very advantagious post for them, whereby they could cut all communication betwixt us and Perth, from whence we expected six troops of horse and dragoons more, as well as a further supply of provisions, and where they could, by the favour of the Athole men, subsist, and have convenience to joyn as many horse and foot as Dundee's credit in the counties of Angus and Perth could procure in a considerable number, without that we could hinder them but by making a motion which readily might furnish them occasion to attack us with a seen advantage: which motion brought the ennemy, whatever his design might have been, to a stand, and so we lookt upon one another for a least two hours.

The General not willing to attack, for the reasons already alledged, and the Highlanders apparently out of irresolution, which he apprehended to be of design to expect the night, wherein they might happily hope to frighten our men by a sudden motion doun the hill with a loud shout, after their manner, very likely to put new men unaccustomed with an ennemy in a fright and disorder, tho' they could be kept more allert and ready then he could hope for during the whole night; neither durst he venture to pass the river in their presence and so near them, both by reason of the hazard, the souldiers, ordinarily taking such a motion for a subject of apprehension, and the imputation which he had to expect, if he were beat in retiring. He resolved then to stand it out, tho' with great impatience, to see the ennemy come to a resolution, either of attacking or retiring, whereof they had more choice than he; and to provoke them, he ordered the firing of three little leather field-pieces, which he caused carry on horse-back with their carriages, which proved of little use, because the carriages being made too high to be more conveniently carried, broke with the third firing.

The ennemy having a full view of our forces, by reason of the height they possess above us, discerned presently the General, which drew their shot into all places where he stood or walked, whereby severals of our men were wounded before the engagement; and to have the so much nearer aim, they possess themselves of some houses upon the ascent of the height whereon they stood, which the General not willing to suffer, least the ennemy should be emboldned thereby, ordered his brother, commanding his own regiment, before whose front the houses were, to detach a captain with some fire-locks to dislodge them; judging withall that that skirmish might draw on a general engagement, which he earnestly longed for before the night approached. The captain chased the ennemy's detachment of their body with the loss of some of their number; but shortly thereafter, and about half an hour before sunset, they began to move down the hill.

The General had already commanded the officers, commanding battalions, to begin their firing at the distance of 100 paces by platoons, to discourage the approaching Highlanders meeting with continual fire: That part of their forces which stood opposite to Hastings, who had the right of all, before the Generals, Levins and Kenmore's regiments, came down briskly together with their horse, and notwithstanding of a brisk fire, particularly from the General's own battalion, whereby many of the chief gentlemen of the name of Macdonald, who attacked it, were killed, pushed their point, after they had fired their light pieces at some distance, which made little or no execution, with sword in hand, tho' in great confusion, which is their usuall way: Which when the General observed, he called to

the Lord Belhaven to march up with the first troop of horse,
ordering him to flank to the left hand the ennemy, the fire being then
past on all hands, and coming to handy strokes if our men had
stood, appointing the second troop to do the same to the right; but
scarcely had Belhaven got them without the front of the line, where
they had orders to wheel for the flank, tho' their very appearance
made the ennemy turn away from the place where they saw the
horse coming up, but contrary to orders, they began to pass, not
knowing whereat, and presently turned about, as did also Kenmore's
and the half of Levin's battalion.

The General observing the horse come to a stand, and firing in
confusion, and the foot beginning to fall away from him, thinking
happily that the horse would be picked to follow his example, and
in all cases to disengage himself out of the croud of Highlanders
which came doun just upon the place where he was calling to the
officers of the horse to follow him, spurr'd his horse through the
ennemy, (where no body nevertheless followed him, but one of his
servants, whose horse was shot in passing), where he judged, but the
way they made for him, tho' alone, that if he had had but fiftie
resolute horse, such as Colchester's, he had certainly, by all human
appearance recovered all, notwithstanding the foot was just plying
over all, tho' sooner upon the left, which was not attacked at all,
than to the right, because the right of the ennemy had not budged
from their ground when their left was engaged. Balfour's regiment
did not fire a shot, and but the half of Ramsays made some little fire.
Lieutenant Colonel Lawder was posted advantageously upon the left
of all, on a little hill wreathed with trees, with his party of 200 of the
choice of our army, but did as little as the rest of that hand, whether
by his or his men's fault is not well known, for the General would
never make search into the failings of that business, because they were
a little too generally committed; resolution and presence of mind in
battle being certainly a singular mercy of God, he denyeth and giveth
it when and to whom he will, for there are seasons and occasions, that
he most firm and stout-hearted do quake and shake for fear: As
Solomon saith, 'The wicked flee when none pursueth, but the
righteous is bold as a Lyon'; and tho' all sincere christians be not
resolute, it is because it is not their vocation, for I dare be bold to
affirm that no truly sincere christian, trusting in God for strenth and
support, going about his lawfull calling, shall be forsaken of him,
whether military, civil, or ecclesiastick; not that sure victory shall
always attend good men, or that they shall always escape with their

lives, for experience doth teach the contrary, but that God, upon whom they cast their burdens and care, shall so care for them, that they shall be preserved from shame and confusion, and that they have his promises by whom are the issues against death and innumerable means inconceivable to us, to redress the disorders of our affairs, to support their hope and mind in the greatest of difficulties: As the General confest, that immediately upon this defeat, and as he was marching of the field, he could not cast his thoughts upon any present means to redress his breach, but recommended earnestly unto God to direct his judgement and mind to fall upon such methods as the success should manifest him to be the chief Author thereof, wherein he hath also been heard, as the pursuit of this relation shall demonstrate. But to return to our purpose. Having passed through the croud of the attacking Highlanders, he turned about to see how matters stood, and found that all his left had given way, and got down the hill which was behind our line, ranged a little above the brow thereof, so that in the twinkling of an eye in a manner, our men, as well as the ennemy, were out of sight, being got doun pall mall to the river where our baggage stood.

At which sad spectacle it may be easily judged how he was surprized, to see at first view himself alone upon the field, but looking further to the right he espyed a small hep [heap] of red coats, whither galloping, he found it to be a part of the Earle of Levin's regiment, with himself, his Lieutenant Colonel, Major, and most of his officers upon their head, whom the General praised for their stedfastness; but seeing the men in confusion, there being some few of other regiments got among them, prayed the Earle with his officers to see to get them speedily in condition to receive the ennemy, whom he minutely expected, while he galloped further to a part of Hastings, which the Colonel was marching up to their first ground, which he affirmed to have lost in pursuit of the ennemy, who, thinking to fall in his flank, he wheeled with his picks to the right upon them, whereby they leaving him, repaired to the rest of their forces, which they saw among the baggage at the river-side, the plundering whereof gave time to many of our runnaways to get off, and having joined Hastings with the rest of Levins, he dispatched a nephew of his, captain of his regiment, seeing him on horseback, (tho he had eight wounds with broad swords upon his body) after his runnaways to exhort all officers, whom he could meet with, to keep up their men, and labour to bring them back to joyn him, in which case he assured them of advantage.

Mean time seeing the officers could bring their men into no order, and looking every minute for the ennemy's appearing, he visited a garden which was behind, of a design to put them in there in expectation of succour, but presently changed his purpose, considering, if succour failed, as readily would fall out, there was not hope of escaping out of the ennemy's hands by defending an inclosure so far from new relief.

While he was in those irresolutions, in expectation of his nephews return, he brought at last news that all was gone clear away out of all reach, and that such as he had spoke to, noticed him not; mean time he espyed numbers of men as it were forming themselves along the edge of the wood which was on Balfour's left, and where Lawder had been posted with 200 men, and because he had not as yet been particularly informed of the behaviour of that wing, and it being already after sun-set, he was doubtful whether those men might not be some of his own men, who had retired to the wood upon the Highlanders descent; so, exhorting the officers to labour to get their men in a condition to make at least one discharge if they were attacked, galloped up to the wood to view those men nearer, which having discovered to be ennemy's, he stepped back softly to his men, and bid them have special care to march off very softly, whereby happily the ennemy judging they were resolved to receive them briskly, would have respect for them and let them retire quietly, the obscurity hindring them of a full view of our number, but that if they should offer to run, they should be sure to have the Highlanders among them; so, leading them softly down the hill he past the river, where he halted a little to get over all his men, and to observe whether the ennemy would approach the river after him. A little before his retreat the Lord Belhaven with the Earle of Annandales Lieutenant and Cornet and some four or five horsemen came up to us, which served for scouts to discover during the retreat.

The ennemy lost on the field six for our one, the fire to our right having been continued and brisk, whereby not only Dundee, with several gentlemen of quality of the countys of Angus and Perth, but also many of the best gentlemen among the Highlanders, particularly of the Macdonalds of the Isles and Glengarie were killed, coming down the hill upon Hastings, the General, and Levin's regiments, which made the best fire and all the execution.

Memoirs of the War Carried on in Scotland and Ireland by Major General Mackay, Bannatyne Club, 1833.

'Alace!' 'Woe is me!' 'Quarters for Jesus!'

Donnchadh nam Pìos (Duncan MacRae of Inverinate) was the
compiler of a manuscript of Gaelic poetry which contains an
account of Killiecrankie from the opposite side. As an Episcopalian
and a loyal supporter of the royal dynasty, MacRae was a Jacobite.
This poem in his collection carries a forthright denunciation of the
Revolution and the Scottish convention parliament. It laments the
death of Clavers (Viscount Dundee) and others on the Jacobite side
who fell. Its imagery of the battle is particularly vivid, immediate
and shocking, suggesting that the poem was written by someone
who was present.

A greeting, put into poetic metre, for the Gaelic nobles who were at Killiecrankie

1
A hundred greetings to the nobles
Who wrought the great deed
On the day of Killiecrankie
Where there were guns aplenty;
The saying is an old one:
'No great victory without danger';
And it came to pass then:
Their grit won them glory.

2
The news of what befell them that day
Reached even Ireland;
It won glamour and wonder
For hundreds of Gaels;
And not scant was the sadness
The Hollanders suffered:
What happened to their host,
How Mackay there was routed.

3
The Clan Donald nobles
Were there with their warbands;
MacLean and his brave lads,
Sir Ewen and the Camerons,
Advancing on the hated foe
With gentle Clavers their leader.

It was two against three there
But he didn't hold back –

4
Against Mackay, cunningly
In order of batallions,
With thousands of swords,
His banners raised up high.
Anyone seeing the terrible sight,
It was time for him to pray;
A shower of lead bullets
And the thunder of the cannons.

5
Many the gentle lad
Who fell to the ground,
Of the nobles of Clan Donald,
Clan Cameron, Clan Ranald;
But those who survived the lead
Charged with their swords,
To compel a retreat
With effort, with force.

6
No mercy was given
To the odious rebels;
They tore them apart
With shield blows and swords blows.
But they made a retreat
In a rush to the river
And hundreds were left there
Prostrate in the melée.

7
Plentiful then
Were the wounded corpses, moving,
Heads, hats and wigs,
Men earless and voiceless.
No-one heard but was shouting:
'Alace!', 'Woe is me!'
'Quarters for Jesus'
Was always their English.

8
Round the river
Was a terrible sight:
Thousands spread out
Who still haven't risen;
Some without hands,
Mouths bawling at the heavens;
[And if the day had lasted,
Death was waiting for those who escaped your sword]

9
Good health to the heroes
Who fought the tough fight;
There hasn't been like them
Since the day of Inverlochy.
The Mull men did well
And every man of Clan Donald.
And they'd have done still more
Had the villain remained.

10
It wasn't your wish
That he ran away from you,
But through the blackness of night
And horses' élan.
A pity he wasn't on the plain
Where his heroes dried up;
He wouldn't beat Clavers
Without Herr William [of Orange] beside him.

11
And if Clavers hadn't fallen
Then there were wonders.
It set back and defeated
The return of King James.
Another trifle just now,
A cause of reproach for you:
Friends, you can't see past
The folk who destroy him.

12

Many's the able hand
Between Ireland and Britain
Who'd fight for James,
Who'd rise before long
But for fear of their troopers,
Their servants and horses,
[They'd grow sparse themselves
If they'd desert their homes].

13

Had I a bellows
And a good portion of tools,
I'd fight him myself
As much as I was able;
But since this isn't easy
Because of every wrong I see,
My prayer's with James
That you turn from this fashion.

14

And chiefs of the tribes
Who are used to deceiving -
If you want smooth sailing
Stop at once the injustice,
The heavy sighs of the widows,
The empty children:
They'll take a tax from you
Unless you stop your imposture.
[*line missing in MS*]

15

Don't you know the sort
Who took orders from William,
Who exiled King James
From his grandsire's estate?
Was there ever heard such an evil
So craftily contrived
Than what they forced upon us:
That cold-hearted Hollander?

16
Never was heard
Worse lies than theirs,
How they declared
In their first manifesto
The death of King Charles, his brother,
And that earl of Essex,
That Britain's heir was replaced
By the son of a blacksmith.

[a reference to the anti-Jacobite claim that James's heir was a
common child smuggled into the Queen's chambers in a bed-
warming pan]

17
Many more things
They loudly declared to him
To hoodwink the army
And split from him the clergy.
He put their accusations to debate
In a fair parliament,
But since they couldn't get bribes,
They sent James into exile.

18
It was a peculiar excuse
In that villainous parliament:
They turned him out of his place
And he fled from their anger.
William and Mary took
His place with their faction:
God of the Graces knows
Their nature and habits.

19
It's been long since it was heard
That the blood tie was so cold;
What they then showed
With great hatred and spite:
Chased out by a sister's son
So closely related;
Among the odious Turks
Was never the like.

20
Though their faith is a pretence
They'd forswear the Bible;
Doubtless Achitophel
Has something in Mary;
When they turned their back on family
And honest Charity
And they loathesomely broke
The commandment Christ gave them.

21
The God who laid mercy upon us,
Love, truth and obedience;
It's not difficult for him
To send the couple back.
But, as happened to David,
When his beautiful son hounded him,
King James will come to his own
Despite the hypocrisy of presbytery.

22
And though your host would arise
For him because of [?their houses]
The smith's son you left
Will come to his forge with a fight.
Every warrior who left him
He'll give a hot and fierce roasting,
He'll nail heads to forts
And to the top of the steeples.

23
But my thoughts make me anxious
About all of these happenings,
Britain badly hurt,
And blood bruised in Ireland,
That the bone will be broken
Between Mary and James,
That the Frenchman will have the marrow
Unless moderation
Prevails with you both.

24
God who ordered the monarchs
To keep peace with all,
Since it's you who have power
More so than the others,
Put an end with your prowess
To this struggle completely,
Punish the robbers of James
And drown William's rebels.

25
But you who journey from us
To the nobles of honour
Who were at Killiecrankie
And those who fought with them,
I'm happy how they struck
That attack upon them,
Don't hide how you heard it
And take from me a hundred greetings.

Soraidh a chaidh a chur am meadarachd dàin, dh'ionnsaigh nan uailsean Gaidhealach a bha ann an là Raoin Ruaraidh

Ceud soraidh do na h-uailsean
Leis na bhuaileadh an crunnart,
Ann an latha Raoin Ruaraidh
An robh fuathas mór ghunnan;
Gur fad o'n là chualas:
'Cha bhi buaidh mhór gun chunnart;
Bha 'bhuil anns an uair sin;
Choisinn cruadal duibh h-onoir.

Chuaidh an sgeula do dh' Éire
Mar dh' éirich an là ud,
Choisinn cliù agus ceutadh
Do cheudaibh de Ghaidheil;
Cha bu lugh' a' chuid bhrònan
'San Òlaind ri àireamh,
Mar thàrladh do'n mhór-shluagh,
'S mar dh' fhògradh Mac Aoidh ann.

Bha maithean Chloinn Dòmhnaill,
Le 'n còmhlain 'san àm seo;
Mac Gill-eathain is òigfhir,
Sir Eóbhan 's Clann Chamshroin.
Dol an coinne an fhuathais,
Cleubhar suairce mar cheannard;
Gun e dithis mu'n triùir ann,
Cha do dhiùlt e 'n adbhansadh,

Air Mhac Aoidh, 's e gu seòlta
Ann an òrdugh bhataillean,
Le mhìltibh de shlòghraidh
'S a shróiltean ri crannaibh;
Ge b'e chitheadh am fuathas,
B'e siud uair dha gu achain;
Fras pheilearan luaidhe,
Le mòr fhuaim nan canan.

'S iomadh òganach suairce
Thuit 'san uair ud gu talamh,
De dh' uailsean Chloinn Dòmhnaill,
Chloinn Chamshroin, 's Shìol Ailein;
Ach na theàirneadh bho'n luaidhe,
Thug iad ruathar le 'n lannaibh,
Thoirt am mach an ratreuta
Le ceart éiginn 's le aindeoin.

Cha do nòsadh leo aodann
Thoirt do reubaltaibh grathail,
Ach an tabhairt bho chéile
Le beum-sgéith agus claidheamh;
Ach gun ghabh iad ratreuta
Le réis chum na h-abhna;
'S gu'n d' fhàgadh leo ceudan
'San t-streup ud 'nan laighe.

Bu lìonmhor 'san uair ud
Corp a' gluasad, 's e leònte,
Cinn, aid agus gruagan,
Fir gun chluasan, gun chòmhradh;
Cha chluinnt' ann dh' éigh
Ach: 'Alace!' agus 'Woe is me!'
'Quarters for Jesus'

Bu bheurla dhaibh 'n còmhnaidh.

Mu thimcheall na h-abhna –
Bu ghrathail a léirsinn –
An robh mìltibh 'nan laighe,
Tha ann fathast gun éigheachd;
Bha cuid diubh gun làmhan,
Beòil ri flaitheas ag éigheachd;
'S na'm maireadh an latha,
Na dh' fhàg nur claidheamh, gu'm b'eug dhaibh.

Gu'm bu slàn do na curaidhean
Leis na chuireadh an dòrainn,
Nach cualas an coimeas
Bho là cur Inbhir-lòchaidh;
'S math a fuaras fir Mhuile
'S gach duine Chloinn Dòmhnaill;
'S gu'n dèarnadh siad tuilleadh
Nam fuireadh an rògair.

Cha b'ann le ur dùrachd
Thàir e uathaibh mar th' aca;
Ach le dùbhraileachd oidhche
Agus mìoraileachd eachaibh;
Truagh mach robh e 'san réidhlean
An deubhadh a ghaisgeach,
Ach nach beireadh e Cleubhar
Gun Uilleam Herre 'na thaice.

'S mur bitheadh bàs Cleubhair,
Bu tréitheach mar thachair;
Chuir siod moill' agus éis-mhor
Air Rìgh Seumas thiochd dhachaidh;
Rud beag eile ta 'g éirigh
'S a géile ta 'g éirigh
'S ag éigheachd ur maslaidh:
A chàirdean cha léir dhuibh
Seach an treubh tha cur ás da.

Gur iomadh làmh thréitheach
Eadar Éire agus Breatann
A chathadh le Seumas
'S a dh' éireadh an ceartuair,

Mur bhi eagal an treudan,
An céilean 's an capull:
Gu'n tearcteadh leibh péin iad
Na'n tréigteadh leo 'n dachaidh.

Na mhealadh mise builg-séididh
Is tréin mhath de'n acfhainn,
Mur cathainn-sa féin leis
Cho fad 'sa dh' fhaodadh mo phearsa
Ach bho 's beart so nach réidh dhomh,
Thaobh gach eucoir thaim faicsinn,
Bidh mo ghuidheadh le Seumas,
Ach gu'n tréig sibh am fasan-s'.

'S a cheannaibh nan treubhan
D' am beusan am mealladh-s',
Madh àill leibh cùis réidh leibh,
Casgaibh 'n eucoir-s' gu h-ath-luath
'S trom ostnadh nam banntrach,
'S gu'n trog iad so càin diubh
Mur ceannsaich sibh 'r mealladh.
[line missing in MS]

Nach eòl duibh an seòrsa
Ghlac òrdugh bho Uilleam,
Chuir Rìgh Seumas air fògar
Bho chòirean a sheanar;
An cualas riamh dò-bheart
Bu shèolt air a h-iomairt
Na mar tharainn iad oirnne
Am Fòlandach fionnfhuar?

Ni mò chualas breugan
Bu tréine na bh' aca,
Mar chuir iad an céill duinn
'Nan ceud manifesto,
Murt a bhràthar, Righ Seurlas,
'S an t-Iarla sin Essex,
'S Mac Gobha na ceàrdaich
Bhi 'n àit oighre Bhreatainn.

Gur iomadh ni bhàrr seo
Chuir iad àirdmhor an céill da;

Ach gu'n mhealladh leo 'n armailt,
'S gu'n thearb iad a' chléir bhuaidh;
Leig e 'n umhail gu'n dearbhadh
Ann am Parliament reusont';
Ach bho nach faighteadh leo cnòdach
'Sann a dh'fhògradh leo Seumas.

Bha 'n leisgeul sin àraid
'Sa Parliament euc'raich;
'S gu'n d' éigh iad as àit' e,
'S gu'n theàrn e bho 'n eugbhoil.
Ghlac Uilleam is Màiri
An t-àite le reusan:
Tha fios aig Dia nan gràsan
An nàdur 's am beusan.

Gur fad o'n la chualas
Gu'm b' fhuarail a' chleamhnas,
Na dhearbh iad 'san uair-sa
Le fuath mhór is gamhlas,
Mac a pheathar d' a fhuadach,
'S e fuaighte ris seabhrach;
Measg Thurcachaibh truaillidh
Cha d' fhuaradh riamh 'shamhladh.

Ged tha 'n creideamh mar sgàil ac',
Is tur dh' àicheadh iad Bìoball;
Fuair Achitophel àite
Ann am Màiri cheart rìreadh;
Dar a thréigeadh leo càirdeas
Agus Càritas dìreach,
'S a bhrist iad gu gràineil
Air an àithn' a thug Crìosd daibh.

An Dia chòirich bàidh dhuinn,
Ùmhladh, gràdh agus fìrinn,
Ni'm bheil e mar chàs air
A' chàraid-s' a philltinn;
Ach réir 's mar thachair a Dhàibhidh,
'S a mhac àlainn d' a shìor-ruith,
Thig Rìgh Seumas gu àite
Dh' aindeoin cràbhadh Phresbìtri.

'S ged dh' éireadh ur feachd-sa
Dhàsan thaobh ìosda,
Thig Mac a' Ghobhainn a dh' fhàg sibh
Gu cheàrdaich le caonnaig;
Bheir e garadh teth gàbhaidh
Do gach àrmann a dhìobair e;
Ni e tàirngneadh cheann air dùin
'S air bharraibh nan stìobal.

Ach 's mòr m' imnidh 's mo smuaintinn
Thaobh gach cùis a ta 'g éirigh,
Gu'm bi Breatunn deth ciùrrte
'S fuil bhrùit ann an Éire;
Gu'm bi bristneadh a' chnàimh
Eadar Màiri is Seumas;
'S gu'm bi 'n smior aig an Fhrangach
Mu'n ceannsaich sibh a chéile.

Dhé dh' òrduich na rìghean
Chumail sìth ris gach duine,
Bho is tusan is brìoghmhoir
Na gach tì dhiubh diod uile,
Caisg féin le do mhìorailt,
An t-srì-sa gu h-uile;
Ceartaich robairean Sheumais;
Bàth reubaltan Uilleim.

Ach fhir a shiùbhlas air chuairt bhuainn
Dh' ionnsaigh uailsean na h-onoir,
Bh' ann latha Raoin Ruaraidh,
Gachar fhuaradh leo cothrom,
Gur ait leam mar bhuail iad-s'
An ruathar orra:
Na ceil thusa mar chuala,
'S beir bhuamsa ceud soraidh.

Translated by D. U. Stiùbhart from *Dorach laoidhean do sgriobhadh le Donnchadh Mac Rath 1688*, ed. C. Macfarlane, Dundee, 1923.

The Massacre of Glencoe

Without a charismatic leader, Jacobite resistance in Scotland died down. The government, however, was determined to make an example of any Highland clans who stood out against them. It was decreed that all clan chiefs must take the oath of allegiance to William and Mary by New Year 1692. Delayed by a snowstorm and by having found the wrong government official to take his oath, the chief of Clan MacIan (a sept of the MacDonalds) missed the crucial date. Little did he know that a deadly example was to be made of his clan. Here are two reports of the massacre. The first was written the day after the event by the Governor of Fort William, whose second in command, Campbell of Glenlyon, carried out the massacre. The second is a popular account circulated in 1695 at a time when demands to punish the culprits were being heard in the Scottish Parliament.

Fort William 14th February
1692

My Lord,
This is to give your Lordship an account that the house off Invergary was surrendered to my order on Thursday last, at which tyme I sent an officer and a partie to take possession off Island Donan, which a strict and positive order from Major Generall Buchan to those who keepe it, to surrender it to my order which I beleeve is done ere this (if the horrid storme on Fryday night did not retard him). I have alsoe ruined Glencoe. Old Glencoe and Achtriaton (the two Cheifes off the two familyes off the Clanean in Glencoe) being killed with 36 more, the rest by reason off an extraordinary storme escaped, but their goods are a prey to the souldiers and their houses to the fire, who may get other broken men to joyne them and be very troublesome to the countrey, off which (not to give your Lordship too great trouble) I have written more fully to the Commander in Chief and aboute a proclamation which will be necessary to be issued out against them. They come from all partes to submit to the King's mercy, and take the oath of allegiance and soe (according to my orders) save their lifes. I hope this example off justice and severity upon Glencoe will be enough.
The next will be to thinke of a civill jurisdiction which will be most likely to compleat the settlement off which I have given formerly several memorandums to the councell and the secretaryes.

This is what is requisite at present from him who covets the honor
of your Lordship's commands and is
   My Lord,
   Your Lordship's most humble and obedient servant
   [John Hill]
'Yester papers', MS. 7014, f.13.

Gallienus Redivivus or Murther Will Out

The soldiers being disposed five or three in a House, according to
the number of the Family they were to assassinate, had their
orders given them secretly. They had been all receiv'd as Friends by
those poor People, who intending no Evil themselves, little suspected
that their Guests were designed to be their Murtherers. At 5 a Clock
in the Morning they began their bloody Work, surprised and
butchered 38 persons, who had kindly received them under their
Roofs. Mac-ian himself was murthered, and is much bemoan'd; he
was a stately well-favoured Man, and of good Courage and Sense:
As also the Laird Archintrikin, a Gentleman of more than ordinary
Judgment and Understanding, who had submitted to the
Government, and had Collonel Hill's Protection in his Pocket, which
he had got three Months before. I cannot without horror represent
how that a Boy about Eight Years of Age was murthered; he seeing
what was done to others in the House with him, in a terrible Fright
run of the House, and espying Capt Campbell, grasped him about
the Legs, crying for Mercy, and offering to be his Servant all his Life.
I am inform'd Capt Campbell inclined to spare him, but one
Drummond; an Officer, barbarously run his Dagger through him,
whereof he died immediately. The rehearsal of several Particulars
and Circumstances of this tragical Story, makes it appear most
doleful; as that Mac-ian was kill'd as he was drawing on his
Breeches, standing before his Bed and giving orders to his Servants
for the good Entertainment of those who murthered him; while he
was speaking the words, he was shot through the Head, and fell
dead in his Ladies Arms, who thro' the grief of this, and other bad
Usages she met with, died the next day. It is not to be omitted, that
most of those poor People were kill'd when they were asleep, and
none was allowed to pray to God for Mercy. Providence ordered it
so, that that Night was most boisterous; so as a Party of 400 Men,
who should have come to the other end of the Glen, and begun the
lie Work there at the same hour, (intending that the poor Inhabitants

should be enclosed, and none of them escape) could not march that length, until it was Nine a Clock, and this afforded to many any opportunity of escaping, and none were kill'd but those in whose Houses *Campbell of Glenlyon's* Men were Quartered, otherwise all the Male under 70 Years of Age, to the number of 200, had been cut off, for that was the order; and it might have easily been executed, especially considering that the Inhabitants had no Arms at that time; for upon the first hearing that the Soldiers were coming to the *Glen*, they had conveyed them all out of the way: For tho' they rely'd on the Promises which were made them for their Safety; yet they thought it not improbable that they might be disarm'd. I know not whether to impute it to difficulty of distinguishing the difference of a few Years, or to the Fury of the Soldiers, who being once glutted with Blood, stand at nothing, that even from above Seventy Years of Age were destroyed. They set all the Houses on Fire, drove off all the Cattle to the Garison of *Inverlochy, viz.* 900 Cows, 200 Horses, and a great many Sheep and Goats, and there they were divided among the Officers. An how dismal may you imagine the Case of the poor Women and Children was then! It was lamentable, past expression; their Husbands and Fathers, and nearest Relations were forced to flee for their Lives; they themselves almost stript, and nothing left them, and their Houses being burnt, and not one House nearer than six Miles, and to get thither they were to pass over Mountains, and Wreaths of Snow, in a vehement Storm, wherein the greatest part of them perished through Hunger and Cold. It fills me with horror to think of poor stript Children, and Women, some with Child, and some giving Suck, wrestling against a Storm in Mountains, and heaps of Snow, and at length to be overcome, and give over, and fall down, and die miserably.

You see in *Hamilton's* Order to *Duncanson*, there's a special Caution, *that the old Fox, nor none, of his Cubs should escape*; and in *Duncanson's* Order to Capt *Campbell of Glenlyon, that the old Fox, nor more of his Sons escape*; but notwithstanding all this wicked Caution, it pleased God that the two young Gentlemen, *Mac-ian's* Sons escaped: for it happened that the younger of these Gentlemen trusted little to the fair Promises of *Campbell*, and had a more watchful Eye over him than his Father or Brother, who suffered themselves by his reiterated Oaths to be deluded into a Belief of his Integrity: He having a strong Impression on his Spirit, that some mischievous Design was hidden under *Campbell's* specious Pretences, it made him after the rest were in Bed, remain in a retired Corner, where he had an advantageous prospect into their Guard. About midnight perceiving several Soldiers to enter it, this encreased his Jealousie; so he went and communicated his Fears to his Brother, who could not for a long time be persuaded there was any bad Design against them, and asserted, that what he had seen was not a doubling of their Guards in order to any ill design, but that being in a strange place, and at a distance from the Garrison, they were to send out Sentinels far from the Guard, and because of the Extremity of the Weather relieved them often, and that the Men he saw could be no more but these. Yet he persisting to say, that they were not so secure, but that it was fit to acquaint their Father with what he had seen, he prevailed with his Brother to rise, and go with him to his Father, who lay in a room contiguous to that they were in. Though what the younger Son alledged made no great Impression on his Father, yet he allowed his Sons to try what they could discover. They well knowing all skulking places there, went and hid themselves near to a Sentinel's Post, where instead of one they discovered eight or ten Men; this made them more inquisitive, so they crept as near as they could without being discovered, so near that they could hear one say to his Fellows, *that he liked not this Work, and that had he known of it he would have been very unwilling to have come there; but that non, except their Commanders, knew of it till within a quarter of an hour.* The Soldier added, that he was willing to fight against the Men of the Glen, but it was base to murder them: But to all this was answered, *All the blame be on such as gave the Orders; we are free, being bound to obey our officers.* Upon hearing of these words the young Gentlemen retired as quickly and quietly as they could towards the House, to inform their Father of what they had heard; but as they came nigh to it they perceived it surrounded, and heard Guns discharged, and the People shrieking; whereupon, being unarm'd, and totally unable to rescue their Father, they preserved their own Lives in hopes yet to serve their King and Country, and see Justice done upon those Hell-hounds, treacherous Murtherers, the Shame of their Country and Disgrace of Mankind.

I must not forget to tell you, that there were two of these Officers who had given their Paroll of Honour to *Mac-ian*, who refused to be concerned in that brutal Tragedy, for which they were sent Prisoners to *Glascow*, where if they remain not still, I am sure they were some Weeks ago.

Thus, Sir, in obedience to your Commands I have sent you such account as I could get of that monstrous and most inhuman

Massacre of the Laird of *Glenco*, and others of this Clan. You desire some Proofs of the Truth of the Story; for you say there are many in *England* who cannot believe such a thing could be done, and publick Justice not executed upon the Ruffians: For they take it for granted, that no such Order could be given by the Government; and you say they will never believe it without a downright Demonstration. Sir, As to the Government; I will not meddle with it, or whether these Officers who murdered Glenco, had such Orders as they pretended from the Government; the Government knows that best, and how to vindicate their own Honour, and punish the Murtherers who pretended their Authority, and still stand upon it. But as to the Matter of Fact of the Murther of *Glenco*, you may depend upon it, as certain and undeniable: It would be thought as strange a thing in *Scotland* for any man to doubt of it, as of the Death of my Lord *Dundee*, or with you that the Duke of *Monmouth* lost his Head. But to Put you out of all doubt, you will e'er long have my Lord *Argyle's* Regiment with you in *London*, and there you may speak with *Glenlyon* himself, with *Drummond* and the rest of the Actors in that dismal Tragedy; and on my Life, there is never a one of them will deny it to you; for they know that it is notoriously known all over *Scotland*, and it is an admiration to us that there should be any one in *England* who makes the least doubt of it. Nay, *Glenlyon* is so far from denying it, that he brags of it, and justifies the Action publickly: He said in the Royal Coffee-house in *Edinburgh*, that he would do it again; nay, that he would stab any Man in *Scotland* or in *England*, without asking the cause, if the King gave him orders, and that it was every good Subject's duty so to do; and I am credibly informed, that *Glenlyon* and the rest of them have address'd them selves to the Council for a Reward for their good Service, in destroying *Glenco* pursuant to their Orders.

There is enough of this mournful subject: If what I have said satisfie you not, you may have what Proof, and in what manner ye please to ask it.

Gallienus Redivivus Or Murther Will Out, Edinburgh, 1695.

Darien

By the late 17th century Scotland had begun to breed a new type of dangerous character: the economic guru. William Paterson was one of the first of these: a founder of the Bank of England, an evangelist for foreign trading schemes and the architect of the Darien disaster. Paterson's get-rich-quick schemes included a

Scottish trading colony on the isthmus of Panama. Patriotic investors queued up to subscribe to his company. The problem was that when the first expedition sailed in July 1698 they soon found out that Darien was a malarial swamp on land owned by the Spanish. Also there was nobody to trade with there, apart from a few not very commercially-minded native peoples. After terrible suffering and near starvation the colony was abandoned. Five months later the second colonising expedition from Scotland heaved into view. Alas for the bravery of the men and women of both expeditions, there was no way of making a success of the venture. Even more sadly, King William commanded the English colonies not to assist the Scots in any way. This order only made the resulting humanitarian disaster worse.

One of the ministers on the second expedition was Alexander Shields, who managed to write to his colleague at home, Robert Wyllie. As a radical ex-Cameronian minister of the strictest sort, Shields found his fellow adventurers to be less-than-wholesome company, and he was not slow to denounce them. Only a handful of the colonists ever made it back to Scotland. Shields was not one of them. He died in Jamaica in 1700.

From on board the 'Rising Sun' in Caledonia Bay, December 25th 1699

Our passage hither was very prosperous for the weather, but in other respects tedious and miserable. Our company very uncomfortable, consisting for the generality, especially the officers and volunteers of the warst of mankind, if yow had scummed the Land and raked to the borders of hell for them, men of lewd practises and venting the wickednesse of principles: for these things God was provoked to smite us very signally and severely with a contagious sickness which went through the the most part and cutt off by death about sixty of us on our ship and near a hundred on the rest of the fleet, the most since our departure from Montserrat. I cannot with this send you a particular list of the dead because I have not gathered them yet but the most lamented by the better part of us were Mr Alexander Dalgleish, minister, the Laird of Dunlop, Capt. Wallace engineer, and several others of the best sort. The means contributing to the encrease of this sickness and mortality were our too great crowds in every ship, straitening and stiffling one another, our chests of medicines ignorantly or knavishly filled and as ill-dispensed by our chirurgeons [surgeons], our water in wooden bound casks very unsavoury and unclean, our beef much of it rotten, many things redundant which were useless and many things needful wanting. It is a wonder of mercy that so many of us escaped and that at length we arrived at our part in safety tho in great sorrow three weeks agone by November 30. We had heard at Montserrat the colony was deserted but did not believe, tho some of us feared it all along. Arriving at this bay, we found the nest was flown. The ground that was cleared was all grown up again with Mangroves. The little fortification standing waste their batteries and huts all burnt doun (which some said was done by a Frenchman, others by an Englishman) and nothing of shipping there but two little sloups from New England and New York . . . They told us the Colony had deserted the 20th of June last for sickness (having destroyed themselves by working excessively on the fortifications) and for fear of want of provisions, that the St Andrew with her men was gone to Jamaica and the Unicorn and Caledonia to New York . . .

Upon this sad emergent our council sat and called for advice all the Captains together. Some proposed the ministers should be called and that it wer fitt to begin with prayer. This motion was not intertained. They had long debates about sustaining the commissions of some councellors . . . The Question being put considering all difficulties: our provisions much diminished, not to hold out long, our wanting tools either for fortifying or planting axes, saws, mattocks etc. or whether we should settle or not it carried nemine contradicente [unanimously]: Resettle.

'Shields' Letters', Wod.Qu.XXX, ff.252-3.

The Road to Union

After William's death there was no improvement for Scotland. His successor Queen Anne was even more unsympathetic to problems north of the Border. She had no surviving children, and the uncertainty of the succession seemed to present the Scottish Parliament with an opportunity to flex its muscles. It insisted that the succession to her would not be ratified until Scottish trading grievances were redressed. Panicking, the English Government decided that the only way to get over this problem was to opt for a union between the two parliaments. There was popular uproar in the streets of Edinburgh. George Lockhart of Carnwath, a staunch

anti-unionist, recorded the disturbances in his Memoirs
Concerning the Affairs of Scotland. *Here is the scene in 1706, in
the run-up to union.*

During this Time, the Nation's Aversion to the Union increas'd;
the Parliament-Close, and the Outer-Parliament House, were
crowded every Day when the Parliament was met, with an infinite
Number of People, all exclaiming against the Union, and speaking
very free Language concerning the Promoters of it. The
Commissioner [the Marquis of Queensberry], as he pass'd along the
Street, was cursed and reviled to his Face, and the D——of H——n
[Duke of Hamilton – the leader of the opposition] huzza'd and
convey'd every Night, with a great Number of Apprentices and
younger Sort of People, from the Parliament House to the Abbey,
exhorting him to stand by the Country and assuring him of his being
supported. And upon the Twenty Third of *October* above Three or
Four Hundred of them being thus employ'd, did, as soon as they left
his Grace, hasten in a Body to the House of Sir *Pat Johnston* (their
late darling Provost, one of the Commissioners of the Treaty, a great
Promoter of the Union, in Parliament, where he sat as one of the
Representatives of the Town of *Edinburgh*) threw Stones at his
Windows, broke open his Doors, and search'd his House for him,
but he having narrowly made his Escape, prevented his being torn in
a Thousand Pieces. From thence the Mob, which was encreas'd to a
great Number, went thro' the Streets, threatening Destruction to all
the Promoters of the Union, and continued for four or five Hours in
this Temper; till about three next Morning, a strong Detachment of
the Foot Guards was sent to secure the Gate call'd the *Netherbow
Port*, and keep Guard in the Parliament Close. Tis not to be
express'd how great the Consternation was that seiz'd the Courtiers
on the Occasion: Formerly they did, or pretended not to believe the
Disposition of the People against the Union; but now they were
throughly convinc'd of it, and terribly afraid of their Lives. This
Passage making it evident that the Union was crammed down
Scotland's Throat. For not only were the Inclinations of the Elder
and Wiser known by the Actions of the Rasher and Younger, but
even the very Soldiers as they march'd to seize the Port, were
overheard saying to one another, 'tis hard we should oppose those
that are standing up for the Country, 'tis what we can't help just
now, but what we won't continue at. The Mob being once
dispatch'd, Guards of regular Forces were plac'd in the Parliament
Close, *Weight-House* and *Netherbow-Port*, and the whole Army,

body Horse and Foot, was drawn together near *Edinburgh*, and continu'd so all the Session of Parliament: Nay the Commissioner (as if he had been led to the Gallows) made his Parade every Day after this, from the Parliament House to the Cross, (where his Coaches waited for him, no Coaches, no Person, that was not a Member of Parliament, being suffer'd to enter the Parliament Close towards the Evening, of such Days as the Parliament was sitting) thro' two Lanes of Musqueteers, and went from thence to the Abbey, the Horse Guards surrounding his Coach, and if it was dark, for the greater Security, a Part of the Foot Guards likewise. This Mob was attended with bad Consequences to the Country Party; for falling out before the Nation was equally inform'd of the State of Affairs, and equally inflam'd with Resentment, it was the easier dispatch'd and discourag'd others from making any Attempts for the Future, and gave Occasion to the Courtiers here, to represent to the Ministry of *England* not to be alarmed, for it consisted of a Parcel of rascally Boys, no others being concern'd in it, tho' the Chief of the Country Party had encourag'd and hir'd them out; besides, the Placing of these Guards overaw'd many, both in and out of the House.

Tho' it was plain to all unbyass'd People, that this Mob had its Rise very accidentally, yet the Government was not fond of any such Amusements, and therefore the next Day after it happen'd, the Privy Council met and ordained these Guards to be continu'd, and emitted a Proclamation against Tumultuous Meetings, wherein they commanded all Persons to retire off the Streets when ever the Drum should beat and give Warning, order'd the Guards to fire upon such as would not obey, and granted an Indemnity to such as should on that Occasion, kill any of the Leidges.

George Lockhart of Carnwath, *Memoirs Concerning The Affairs of Scotland from Queen Anne's Accession to the Throne to the Commencement of the Union of the Two Kingdoms of Scotland and England in May 1707*, Edinburgh, 1714.

Storming the Castle – An Amateur Attempt

Here are some more entertaining memoirs, this time from John Master of Sinclair. The Union was especially unpopular with the Jacobites. The new British Parliament had sorted out the succession question in favour of the distant, but Protestant, House of Hanover. With the death of Queen Anne, the last Stuart monarch, in 1715, the Jacobites under the Earl of Mar decided to try to overturn the new Hanoverian Succession. This piece of amateur subversion, the attempted storming of Edinburgh Castle, was not exactly their finest hour. A contemporary newsletter also reports the event, along with the intimation that more serious attempts at rebellion were under way.

It was before this, that the surpriseing the Castle of Edinburgh had failed. I can't be positive who laid the scheme; but it was projected after the Queen's death, and gone into by some younge people about Edinburgh, who had screwd themselves into the belief that the King was then to land, at which time they were readie to put it in execution. But the hopes of that being over, through impatience to shew their diligence, they communicated it to a great many of their friends; and, as it is usuall, everie new plotter was racking his brain how to improve the first scheme, to have a share of the honour in case ane opportunitie offered, and thereby the measures of the whole project were more and more disconcerted. And thus they continued untill the beginning of August 1715, that the intention of Lord Mar's goeing to the Highlands was publicklie known; and then those who had been all alonge the principall contrivers of that affair thought there was no time to be lost in comeing to a finall resolution about the proper methods, and even in putting them to the tryell, applied themselves to my Lord Mar, who encouraged it; because, whatever the event might be, it dipt so manie who must be oblidged to refuge to him. My Lord Drummond, who, amongst the many good qualities he has inherited of his familie, has that of imagining nothing can be well done except he has the management of it, would undertake the direction of all; and, for that effect, made choice of a little broken merchant, Charles Forbes, a man according to his own heart, who was to be principall engineer and conductor of that affair. Thomas Arthur, who had formerlie been ane officer in the Castle had, six months before, gained a serjeant, and brib'd a sojer of the garrisone; the serjeant, when he'd have the guard, was to place that sojer sentrie at a post on the Castle wall, which they had agreed on. The sentrie was to have a clew of small cordes in his pocket, one end of which he was to throw down to those who were to surprise the Castle, who were to tye it to a grapling iron, fastned at the end of the scaladeing ladders, which he was to pull up and fix in the head of the wall or parapet. They proposed to doe the work with fourscore or nintie men, whereof fortie were to be Highlandmen, who were sent to toun by my Lord Drummond about the time appointed, all by different roads, with orders to obey one

Drummond of Bouhadie. Fiftie younge apprentices, advocates'
servants, writers, and some servants to those in the Government,
were let into the secret, to make up the number to be imploy'd in the
attack. At last, the serjeant letting them know the night he could
serve them, and the time, the West Kirk, a place under the Castle
wall, was agreed on to be the place of rendevous, preciselie at nine
of the clock at night, where they were to come armed with pistells
and suords. They all mett at the place and hour appointed. Things
having thus far succeeded to their wish, they, and it must be own'd
reasonablie, having brought it so great a length, reckoned
themselves sure of their stroak; but the principall thing was still
wanting. They had imploy'd a fellow in the Caltone to make the
ladders, which Mr Arthur and his brother, Doctor Arthur, were to
mount the first, because they knew the Castle best; and had brought
the greatest part of the ladders, with the grapling iron, alonge with
them to the West Kirk at the hour appointed; and Charles Forbes
had taken it upon him to bring the rest of the ladders preciselie at
the same hour, but instead of that, stay'd till after ten in the citie,
drinkeing to good news from the Castle, while the others were
waiteing impatientlie at the West Kirk; for they had designed to
begin the attack at ten, which being past, and receaveing no neus of
Forbes or their ladders, not knowing what to doe, and afraid the
sentrie would loose patience, or be relieved, scrambled up the rock,
and posted themselves at the foot of the wall, with a resolution, in
all events, to stay there as longe as they could. And thus they
continued till eleven of the clock, when, being out of all patience,
and the sentrie telling he was to be relieved at twelve, they made him
pull up the grapling irone, in order to try if the ladders they had
could doe; but, as they suspected, they found them above a fathome
too short; and in this situation did they continue untill half an hour
after eleven, when the sentrie perceaveing the rounds comeing
about, called down to them, 'God damn you all! you have ruined
both yourselves and me! Here comes the round I have been telling
you of this hour, I can serve you no longer.' And with that threw
down the grapling iron, fired his piece, and called out 'Enemie;'
upon which everie man shifted for himself, the round fireing over
the wall after them. And at this time, when the fireing from the wall
hapned, Mr Forbes, the ingeneer, had onlie advanced to the back of
Bareford's Parks, on the north side of the North Loch, with the rest
of the ladders, and could not been up in time before that sentrie was
to be reliev'd.

My Lord Justice-Clerk, having got a hint of the designe, was the occasion of that round's goeing about, having given the Gouvernour the alarme, and at same time, with difficultie, got twelve men of the Burgers' Guard from the Magistrats of the toun, to goe without the walls, under the command of ane officer, who saw no bodie but two boys, who said, they came there by chance, whome he took prisoners, together with ane old man, who had fallen from the rock. But all agree, that had the ladders come in time, the Justice-Clerk's advertisement had come too late; and blamed my Lord Drummond for the choise of his ingeneer. It was, I may say, miraculous, that so many keept the secret, or rather, that the Gouvernment was not sooner informed by some indirect way or other; for they were so far from carrieing on their affairs privately, that a gentleman, who was not concerned, told me that he was in a house that evening where eighteen of them were drinking, and heard the hostess say, they were poudering their hair to goe to the attack of the Castle.

John Master of Sinclair, *Memoirs Of The Insurrection In Scotland, 1715*, ed. Walter Scott, Abbotsford Club, 1858.

An Edinburgh Newsletter

Edinburgh Sept 10

Sir,

On the 8th about 10 at night the justice clerk was informed by a secret hand, that the Jacobites wer that night between the hours of 11 and 12 to put in execution a desinge they had deeply laid of taking the castle by surprise. Some of the centinells [sentinels] wer bribed and all things in a readyness his Lordship sent to acquaint Col. Steuart with the information. This to be sure put our friend Lindsay on his mettall in taking all measures to frustrate that attempt which was after this manner. Lindsay ordered the sentinels who stood nixt the place where the affair was to be execute, to be sure to fire his peice upon the first alarume. This fellow, who unknown to Lindsay was upon the plott, finding the secret was discovered, resolved to be honest and do as directed and at the time appointed which was some few minutes after Lindsay had spoken to him, seeing one Thomson his fellow sentinel let doun the rope, to which the grapling hook was to be fixed by those without, by those who had scaling ladders along with them, very fitt for their purpose and hearing the whispers of those without, fired his peice. Upon which they run away and lost their ladders and arms about the foot of the castle. While this was doing the justice clerk sent for Messrs.

Aikman, Drummond and one or two more and desired them to apply to the Provost for part of the city guard to. After some difficulty they got ane order from his Lordship for a sergeant and 12 men, with this small number they went round the castle to see what was a doing. Before they came the scoundrels wer all gone, houbeit they picked up four stragglers, one Capt Mclain and three writer [solicitor] lads whom they brought into the toun gaird. They wer examined yesterday, but wer not ingenous. Three castle soldiers wer concerned, two of which have made clean breasts and discovered the whole plott and that they wer corrupted by Thomas Archer, Ensign of the castle under the earl of Levin lately out.

This day we are informed that the marquis of Huntly is to joyn the Highland camp as soon as possible. In Angus they are nou openly rendevouzing their men. By this time we expect all the honest people have fled from that country and will arrive this night or tomorrow.

'Newsletter', Wod.Lett.Qu.X, ff.19r&v.

Rob Roy and the 1715

On 6 September 1715, John Erskine, Earl of Mar, raised the standard of the Old Pretender, James VIII and III, at Braemar. By the 16th he had seized Perth, but the arch-courtier turned out to be no match as a general for the energetic Duke of Argyll. All Mar's efforts were thwarted at the Battle of Sheriffmuir, where his irresolution threw away his vastly superior advantage in manpower. However the rebellion was not yet over. James landed in Scotland that December at Peterhead, and meanwhile Rob Roy MacGregor, failed cattle-dealer, outlaw and free-booter, was taking the opportunity to terrorise Fife. Here are two letters to Alexander Archer, candlemaker in Hamilton, from another candle-maker in Leslie, where they were fighting off Rob Roy's men.

Dear brother, – I received yours this evening, but I find you have been quite mistaken about our condition. You date our freedom and liberty from the rebels long before its commencement; and for proof, take the following account of what passed here these last ten days: – Upon the 4th instant, Rob Roy, with one hundred and fifty men, came to Falkland, and took possession of the Palace for a garrison, from which they came through the country side, and rob and plunder, taking clothes and victuals, and every thing that makes for them, none to oppose them till this day eight days. The 6th instant there come thirty-two Highlandmen (I had almost said devils) to

Leslie. We saw them at Formand Hills, and resolved to resist, and so man, wife, and child drew out. The men went to the east end of the town, and met them in the green, with drawn swords in their hands, and we asked them what they were for? They said they wanted clothes and money. We answered, they should get neither of them here, at which they stormed and swore terribly; and we told them, if they were come for mischief they should have their full of it, at which there were some blows; but they seeing us so bold, began to fear that we should fall upon them, and so they asked liberty to march through the town, and got not so much as the kiss of a caup [cup], and they were so afraid, that they did not return, but went down over the Hawk Hill, and east to the minister's land, and there they fait [turned] about, and fired ten shot in upon the people that were looking to them; but, glory to God, without doing the least hurt. And so they went off to the Formand Hills, and plundered all they could carry or drive, and threatened dreadfully they should be avenged on Leslie, and burn it.

We sent off two expresses, one to Dunfermline to Rothes, and one to Burntisland. My Lord ordered two hundred and fifty of Dutch and Switzers from Burntisland for our relief. The sabbath proved stormy, so that neither they nor the enemy could come at us; but on Monday morning the King's [George I's] forces came most seasonably. Rob Roy was on his way to us on the head of a hundred men, and when they heard of our help they returned. Upon Tuesday the forces were for marching back to Burntisland, and so we were in worse case than before; but we almost forced them to leave fifty Switzers with us, which they did. And the [next] day Rothes came with one troop of horse, and two hundred foot, and turned back [those] of Burntisland, so that when we began to think ourselves safe they staid [but two] nights and two days. But upon sight we are cast down. Then comes an order to my Lord to march back to Dunfermline with his men, which he did yesterday morning. It was a sorrowful parting. He left seventy men with us, and called in the fencible men round about us for our help, which they do [give] very readily. We have four hundred men this night beside the town. All above was written on the 13th. On the 14th there is a garrison of the King's forces placed at Burleigh. Upon the 16th several parishes here were warned to go there, among which I was one, where a hundred volunteers engaged to assist that garrison. Upon the 18th I was obliged to go to Burleigh again with candles for the use of that garrison, and did wade to the boot tops for the most part of the way among snow, and was in hazard of my life, and the man that was with me, by a terrible tempest that arose on us by the way.

The rebels have placed a garrison in Balvaird, one in Naughton, one in Samford, and this day one in Balgonie, about which take the following melancholy account. This garrison of Leslie thought to have prevented them, and this morning they early detached twelve Switzers, twenty-five Kirkcaldy men, and when they came to Markinch there are a hundred and fifty rebels in the town, which they knew nothing of till they are in among them, who presently surrounded them, and took them all prisoners, and carried them to Balgonie with them. Several Kirkaldy men are wounded, one of whom is mortally wounded, and two Switzers dying in their wounds at Balgonie. Betty Key has a son among the wounded. It's thought they will all be carried to Perth to-morrow. It's said there are many of the rebels wounded; but we know not what number. So if speedy relief come not, this country will be full of garrisons of rebels, and so will be the seat of war, so that our circumstances are not so good as you think. If we could get fled I would remove all my family from this, but the storm is so great that it is not possible, and we are in constant expectation of the enemy. All friends are in ordinary health, and desire the sympathy of all friends with you at the throne of grace. I rest your affectionate brother, G.

L[eslie], Jan. 20, 1716.

Dear brother, – Just now I had yours of the 3d instant, and having presently an occasion I have given you this short answer. Know, then, that since my last we were in continual fear till the 30th of January, upon which day we got the doleful news of burning, and we having always been threat with the same fate we looked for no less, and our fear was no greater than there was cause for. Rob Roy had a commission to burn Leslie and all betwixt it and Perth. We having intelligence of it got all to arms. The Swiss and Dutch being all gone, we had a mind to stand for our defence, and so all the men in the town, and several of the country that came in for our assistance, stood in arms that whole night. But so it was that the time of our extremity was God's opportunity, for about two o'clock in the morning we had the good news that Roy and all his men were fled to Dundee, and his flying was after this manner. About twelve o'clock at night he had all his men save a few drawn out before the Palace of Falkland in arms to come to Leslie for its ruin, and just when he is coming off there come two expresses to him that the King's army was approaching Perth, upon which he changed his resolution, and presently went of for Dundee, as did all the garrisons of rebels in Fife, so that I suppose in twenty-four hours there was not a Highlandman left in Fife. And ever since we have been in peace and quiet; and all the King's garrisons in Fife are given up save Burntisland.

And to let you see how uneasy this country has been under these rebels, I shall give you but one instance. Those in Falkland continued there about a month, and for ordinary they were but about one hundred and fifty at most. In that time they eat and destroyed three thousand sheep in Falkland and the adjacent parishes next to it. But we, in this place, have much to remark of the preventing mercy of God. Our case was looked upon as most desperate by all since this rebellion began, and yet we of all the places in Fife, by-east Dunfermline, have been the easiest. Our ministers are now returned to their charges, and once more we have the Gospel in purity and plenty. O for grace to improve it!

I have nothing to write about the rebels' flight; for I suppose you will have the account as soon as we. Only we hear there are many of them dispersed, and some have got into the castle of Dunottar, and there are nine pieces of cannon gone from Perth, by Argyle's order to that place. I must leave particulars about the rebels' conduct here till meeting, for I design to see you if once my tallow were made up. My trade for ordinary is as good in June and July as it has been these two months past. I am surprised to hear of your cotton; it's strange how any man could send it out so. I have not got mine yet; but it is like it will come to me after the same manner. All friends are in ordinary health. My wife and I give our respects to you and your wife, and to your brother. We expect he will be setting his face homeward now. I rest your affectionate brother, G.

L [Leslie], Feb. 9, 1716.

The Correspondence of the Rev. Robert Wodrow, ii, ed. T. M'Crie, Wodrow Society, 1843.

More Spanish Invasion

Most people have heard of the Spanish Armada, but few have heard of the other failed Spanish invasion attempt which concerned Scotland. In 1719 the Old Pretender obtained a small Spanish invasion force, which, commanded by the Earl Marischal and the Marquis of Tullibardine, intended to take Inverness. However, on reaching the Western mainland the force was surprised near the pass of Glenshiel on 1 April 1719 by the forces of General Wightman. The Highlanders who had joined the

attempt ran for it. The Spanish, no doubt having had quite enough
of their Scottish holiday, surrendered. Here is how it was reported
in the Edinburgh Evening Courant.

POSTSCRIPT to the Edr. Evening-Courant No. 84

Giving an Account of the Particulars of the Engagement on the 10th of June, sent by Major General Wightman, dated from Glensheels the 11th of June 1719.

About four in the afternoon, I came up within a mile of the rebels camp, at a place called Glensheels, such a strong pass that is hardly to be paralelled; I took about an hour to view their situation, and without loss of a moment made my disposition. About five I begun the attack, which lasted about three hours and an half continual fire and hazardous dispute; but at last providence was on our side, and we beat them from all corners, over all their mountains and rocks.

I've sent your Lordship a true list of our kill'd and wounded. Afor the enemy, 'tis impossible to give any account of them, more than the late Lord Seaforth and George Murray are wounded, the first in the arm, the other, in the leg. We lay on our arms last night to bring off our wounded, and this morning arrived at this place, where I no sooner came, than I had a letter of capitulation from the commander of the Spaniards, who were allowed as prisoners at discretion, and at about two in the afternoon they surrendered with all their arms and ammunition, which was some relief to us, who had wasted near all we had in the action. The Spanish colonel gives account, that Seaforth and all the rest are shifted for themselves and he believes will get off as soon as possible; and I cannot hear of any considerable body of the highlanders together. The Numbers of the highlanders that were engaged were 1640, besides the Spaniards who defended the pass, and 500 on the Hills, in hopes to have catch't our baggage, but by good fortune have preserved all.

Our numbers, your Lordship knows, was only three regiments of foot, four companies of Amerong's and a hundred and fifty dragoons, out of which were left at Inverness an hundred foot and thirty dragoons, so that we had not above 840, (excluding what men were left to secure the baggage,) which was not near half the number of the rebells we engaged. It will be almost impossible to perswade the world, horses were brought to this place, and to have few or any out of order.

Towards the end of the action I observed some Spaniards left in the pass to defend it, which obstructed our finishing the affair, and obliged me to dismount 30 dragoons, which with about 40 foot, was all we had as a reserve; with which numbers I attackt them, and carried it in 10 minutes. They were better at climbing the rocks than we at their retreat, so that we have few or any prisoners except a Spanish captain and their physician.

For my part, I leave my caracter to all the gentlemen whom I have had the honour to command on this expedition.

The Disposition of his Majesty's Forces commanded by Major General Wightman, when they attackt the Rebels, June 10th 1719, who were commanded by the late Lords Seaforth, Tullibardine, Marishal, &c.

All the Grenadeers on the right, commanded by Major Milbourne, being about 140 to begin the attack; the Regiment of Montague by Colonel Laurence, that of Harrison by Colonel Harrison, to sustain the Grenadeers, and that of Hussele's, and four companies of Amerong's to sustain the two afore-mentioned English, right wing commanded by Colonel Clayton, (who acted as Brigadeer) and were to gain the tops of the mountains, and attack the left of the rebels, who were drawn up on a half circle. Fifty of Lord Strathgnaver's country, under the command of Lieutenant Mackay, a half-pay officer, on the flank of his wing.

The Dragoons under the command of Major Robinson, kept the road that led to the pass with four cohorns in their front; the regiment of Clayton under the command of Colonel Reading on the left, and on his flank 100 of the Monro's, commanded by Monro of Culcairne, to attack the right wing of the rebels.

'Postscript to the Edinburgh Evening-Courant No.84', MS. 488, f.3.

The Porteous Mob

On 14 April 1736, the Scottish poet Allan Ramsay got more than he bargained for when he attended an Edinburgh execution. Hangings in those times were as much a spectator pastime as a football match, and a large, somewhat sympathetic crowd had turned out to watch the event. The condemned man, Edinburgh merchant Andrew Wilson, had robbed the custom house of Pittenweem. This, plus his gallant efforts to help a friend escape, made him something of a local hero. In the wake of the Union, excise duties and taxes in Scotland had increased vastly, and sometimes actually in contradiction to the terms of the Union

treaty. Smugglers and enemies of the excisemen were regarded as
patriots. The captain of the Edinburgh Town Guard, John
Porteous, fired into the hostile crowd at the execution and left
several people dead. Ramsay had a lucky escape.

This is only the first part of the story. Porteous was tried for his
actions, condemned, pardoned and then lynched by the Edinburgh
mob – resulting in a huge fine on the city.

Atrue and faithfull account of the Hobleshaw [riot] that
happened in Edinburgh, Wednesday, the 14th of Aprile 1736 at
the hanging of Wilson, housebreaker.

On the Sunday preceeding viz the 11th, the two condemn'd
criminalls Wilson and Robertson were taken as usual by four sogers
[soldiers] out of prison to hear their last sermon and were but a few
minutes in their station in the Kirk when Wilson who was a very
strong fellow took Robertson by the head band of his breeks and
threw him out of the seat, held a soger fast in each hand and one of
them with his teeth, while Robertson got over and throw the pews,
push'd o'er the elder and plate at the door, made his escape throw
the Parliament Close down the back staire, got out of the Poteraw
[Potterrow] Port before it was shut, the mob making way and
assisting him, got friends, money and a swift horse and fairly got off
nae mair to be heard of or seen. This made them take a closer care
of Wilson who had the best character of them all (til his foly made
him seek reprisals at his own hand), which had gaind him so much
pity as to raise a report that a great mob would rise on his execution
day to relieve him, which noise put our Magistrates on their guard
and maybe made some of them unco flayd [unusually afraid] as was
evidenced by their inviting in 150 of the Regement that lys [lies] in
Cannongate, who were all drawn up in the Lawn Market, while the
criminal was conducted to the tree by Captain Porteous and a strong
party of the City Guard. All was hush, Psalms sung, prayers put up
for a long hour and upwards and the man hang'd with all decency
& quietnes. After he was cut down and the guard drawing up to go
off, some unlucky boys threw a stone or two at the hangman, which
is very common, on which the brutal Porteous (who it seems had
ordered his party to load their guns with ball) let drive first himself
amongst the inocent mob and commanded his men to folow his
example which quickly cleansed the street but left three men, a boy
and a woman dead upon the spot, besides several others wounded,
some of whom are dead since. After this first fire he took it in his

head when half up the Bow to order annother voly & kill'd a taylor in a window three storys high, a young gentleman & a son of Mr Matheson the minister's and several more were dangerously wounded and all this from no more provocation than what I told you before, the throwing of a stone or two that hurt no body. Believe this to be true, for I was ane eye witness and within a yard or two of being shot as I sat with some gentlemen in a stabler's window oposite to the Galows. After this the crazy brute march'd with his ragamuffins to the Guard, as if he had done nothing worth noticing but was not long there till the hue and cry rose from them that had lost friends & servants, demanding justice. He was taken before the Councill, where there were aboundance of witnesses to fix the guilt upon him. The uproar of a mob encreased with the loudest din that ever was heard and would have torn him, Council and Guard all in pices [pieces], if the Magistrates had not sent him to the Tolbooth by a strong party and told them he should be tried for his life, which gave them some sattisfaction and sent them quietly home. I could have acted more discreetly had I been in Porteous's place.

More Culloden Papers, ed. D. Warrand, Inverness, 1927.

The '45 and After

On 23 July 1745, Prince Charles Edward Stuart, son of the Old Pretender, set foot on Scottish soil. He had come without the men, the money, or the guns thought necessary to stage a successful invasion. Even the staunchest of Jacobite chiefs wanted him to go back home to France, but Charles was determined, and it was already too late. Hanoverian spies had wind of his landing. The chiefs, such as Cameron of Locheil, felt that they had no option but to come out in rebellion to protect the Prince. The standard was raised, the Jacobite army was on the march, and, to everyone's surprise, by 17 September they had reached Edinburgh. Only the army of General Sir John Cope stood between them and control of Scotland.

Prestonpans

Having landed his forces at Dunbar, Cope came up towards Tranent, near Edinburgh. The Jacobite army under Lord George Murray advanced to meet him. On the night of 20 September there was a tense stand off. During the night the Jacobite forces were given intelligence of a track through a nearby marsh which could bring them upon Cope with a good chance of surprise. At first light next morning, battle was joined. Cope's forces, hardly out of their beds, were cut to pieces in less than fifteen minutes – hence the famous song 'Hey Johnny Cope are ye wauken yet?' The Prince's private secretary Andrew Lumisden witnessed the battle.

The Highlanders, pulling off their bonnets and looking up to heaven, made a short prayer, and ran forward. In advancing Lord George Murray observed that by the turn of the morass [marsh], there was a great interval between his left and the ditch of the before mentioned inclosure: he therefore ordered the Camerons to incline that way, in order to take it up, to prevent being flanked by the enemy's dragoons. By this movement there became a considerable interval in the center, which the second line was ordered to fill up.

We were now discovered by the enemy, who played their artillery furiously upon our left; yet only one private man was killed, and one officer wounded. The Highlanders ran on with such eagerness that they immediately seized the cannon. The Dragoons on right and left made a very regular fire, which was followed by close platoons of all their infantry, which our men received with great intrepidity. But what by the Huzzahs of the Highlanders, and their fire, which was very brisk, the Dragoons were immediately thrown into disorder, which occasioned some confusion among their foot. The Highlanders threw down their muskets, drew their swords, and carried all before them like a torrent: so that in seven or eight minutes both horse and foot were totally routed, and driven from the field of battle. The Prince during the action was on foot on the second line. He was with great difficulty prevailed on not to attack with the first line inasmuch that the officers refused to march if he insisted on it. As soon as the victory declared for him, he mounted his horse and put a stop to the slaughter, calling out – 'make prisoners: spare them, spare them, they are my father's subjects'. When General Cope saw how things were going, and that he could not rally his forces, he, with about 350 Dragoons, and some volunteer officers, gained Carberry Hill, by a road that led to it from Preston and as we had not time, nor horse to pursue, got away undisturbed to Lauder and from thence to Berwick. As our second line had no occasion to engage, it may with justice be said that 1,400 highlanders, unsupported by horse or canon routed a regular army of 2,000 foot and 700 dragoons defended by a fine train of artillery, and obtained a most compleat victory. Such is the impetuosity of a highland attack.

'Account of the Battle of Prestonpans by Andrew Lumisden, Private Secretary to the Prince', MS. 279, pp. 13-15.

Occupied Edinburgh

The Jacobites could occupy towns and win battles, but they could not take Edinburgh Castle. They simply did not have the artillery to reduce it. The Prince took up residence at Holyrood Palace, whilst his forces tried ineffectively to blockade the Castle. The citizens of Edinburgh were caught in the middle. Here are some extracts from the letters of Francis Kennedy of Dalquharran to Thomas Kennedy, his brother, the Lord Advocate, with details of everyday life during such trying circumstances.

5th October 1745

We are here in a state of war, for the castle is in a manner besieged by the Highlanders who expect, as I am told, to oblige it to surrender by hindering any provisions to be carried up to them and the castle for these four days past have been fyring all round them upon every place where they suspected or saw the

Highlanders – I don't hear that many are killed on either side, but the castle has burnt and beat down houses about Livingston's yards, the West Port and Grassmarket and the Castlehill towards the North Loch as far down as James' Court and this siege is like to be carried on till the castle surrenders, so you may judge what kind of situation the inhabitants both of town and subburbs are in and how unadvisable it is for you to think of coming to town till things are on a more peaceable footing. I don't hear but the greatest care is taken to hinder the Highlanders from committing any disorders, and the inhabitants of the town seem to dread nothing so much as their leaving Edinburgh: since they have no magistrates to keep the peace and order of the town when they are gone, they say there are some dissentions amongst the officers of the castle about the vigorous orders that came to destroy the town, some few executing them and others preferring to quit their commissions rather than do so cruel an action, of which last number is General Guest, tho he persists as strongly as any to defend it to the last extremity, but you will have a more particular account of what is doing from A–s who is going about to hear what is doing which I canot do, he will send you the newspapers which don't come out as regularly as usual . . .

Postscript

I am told that the Prince is so hardy and vigilant that he is even like to kill the most robust Highlander, he lies every night in a tent no better than the poorest soldier, goes frequently thro his camps to see that the men have their necessaries rightly provided for them, in order to give an example to his officers which they are not so ready to follow, as their interest, now they have gone so far should oblige them to.

Abbeyhill, 8th September [October] 1745

When I wrote my dearest brother on Saturday last, the town of Edinburgh was in the utmost consternation from the castle firing down the town and burning some houses, but as the blockade is removed people seem a little eased of their terror and enjoy some more quiet than they did last week, however the castle still fyres about West Port and Grassmarket and wherever they spye any Highlanders so that the innocent inhabitants very often suffer in going to places within view of the castle, where there may happen at the same time to be Highlanders, which makes me think that it would not be very advisable for you to be at Fontbridge till the Highlanders are quite gone from this and when that may be nobody that I see can pretend to tell, most people of fashion that are not engaged with the Prince are out of town and everybody within reach of the castle have left their houses, tho since this last proclamation it's thought they will return to them when the Highland army is gone.

Friday October 11th 1745

I told you in my former letters how improper and even dangerous it was for you to come to town while the castle was blockaded, they have retired the blockade and given over, I am told, any thoughts of taking the castle since it endangered so much the inhabitants of the town, and are come to a resolution on both sides not to fyre but at them that attack them, so that things are in a more peaceable way than they were last week and people think that the army will remove from this as soon as all their body of Highlanders and others are come here, but how feasible and safe the town and subburbs will be after they are gone is a question I don't yet hear is resolved, so that I believe it will be best to suspend your journey till you hear the army has gone and know what footing people are upon in this place as to preserving the peace and order of the town.

Saturday 19th October 1745

Things here seem to be in the greatest quietness and its now talked for certain that the Prince with his army will march from this the beginning of next week they say they are all in high spirits and very confident of success, there is another ship (the size of the one that brought the French Minister) come to a port near Montrose with more money and arms and some officers, they expect to enter England with a body of men superior to any that can be brought against them, and that Lord Marshall is to land in England with a very great army from France, this force together with the commotions in London and other parts of England makes some people think that the dispute will be decided without much bloodshed, tho others dread the contrary, however vast numbers of people of all ranks every day flock to the Abbey and the number of the Prince's friends have increased beyond most people's imagination, I pray God conduct all in the way that may be most for the good of our country, I have not yet heard how the town of Edinburgh is to be governed after the army leaves it, but as it is not expected that they will leave any force behind sufficient to guard it against the attempts of the garrison of the castle to regain it. It will probably be left to govern itself.

'Letters of Francis Kennedy of Dalquharran to Thomas Kennedy, the Lord Advocate his Brother', MS. 1704, ff.33-43.

Banking under a White Flag

*It wasn't just dodging the bullets from the Castle that was a
nuisance. John Campbell, cashier of the Royal Bank, had a
different set of problems. His banknotes promised 'to pay the
bearer on demand' the face value in gold and silver coin, and now
the Jacobites were demanding precisely that. They had notes to the
value of £3,164 which they needed cashed to help pay for the
Jacobite army. They threatened to take action to get the sum from
the estates and effects of the directors of the bank if they did not
pay up. Unfortunately, all the money was safely locked up in the
castle which they were busily besieging. What was a banker to do?
They may have been the King's rebels, but business was business.
Campbell's diary tells what happened: the Jacobites got their cash
in a deal presided over by the Hanoverian generals commanding
the castle. There was, it seems, general agreement that financial
transactions should not be interrupted by a mere war.*

Saturday, 14 September 1745.

On news of the Highland army's approach, all the effects of the
Bank were packt up, and partly transported to the Castle this
night, per memorandum apart.

Tuesday, 1 October 1745.

Had a verbal message from Provost Coutts now at Allanbank, per
his friend, Mr Coutts, about Bank affairs. Between 6 and 7 o clock
at night a protest was then taken against me, as Cashier of the Royal
Bank, by John Murray of Broughton Esq. as Secretary to the Prince,
for payment of £857 Royal Bank Notes (which he exhibited), in the
current coin of the kingdom, and on failyure therof within 48 hours,
that the estates and effects of the directors and managers should be
distress'd for the same. I answer'd that by reason of the commotion
in the countrey, the effects of the Bank were lately carried up to the
Castle, for the security of all concern'd, for as the directors acted, in
a manner, as factors for their constituents, the proprietors, it was
judg'd reasonable, and what every body in their circumstances had
done, to secure the effects of the Company, that none might be
sufferers in the issue: and matters were in that situation at present
that there was no access to the Castle at any rate, for that Mr. Jo.
Hamilton and Mr. John Philp, two of the directors, had essayed to
get in on Saturday last with the accomptant and tellers and myself
in order to do business, but that access was refused, tho' they

continued at the gate for about an hour. Duply'd [duply – a reply to a reply] by Mr Murray that he would in name of the Prince grant a pass and protection for going to the gate, and that he hoped the Governor would give admittance. But whether he did or not, if the payment was not made, the order should be put in execution, after elapse of the time limited; and thereupon took instruments in the hands of William M'Kewan, notary publick, in presence of Mr. Peter Smith, brother to deceast David Smith of Methven, and [   ] Purves, Writer to the Signet; and thereafter a schedule of the protest was sent to me by Mr. M'Kewan the notar, but not sign'd. Immediately on Mr. Murray's taking the above protest I waited upon Mr. Jo. Hamilton and Mr. Philp, the only two directors in town, at Mrs Clerks, vintner, there shewed them the schedule, and what I have before here marked down, and after reasoning theron agreed to try to get into the Castle to morrow, and ordered Mr. Shairp, the only other director about the town, to be summond for that purpose, to meet with them at my house by 9 in the morning, that this affair might be further concerted, and if possible money might be got out for answering the demand. And to prepare the way to the gate, a pass and protection was to be obtain'd from the Prince, or from Mr. Murray, as Secretary, for the directors and officers of the Bank to go that length to try if the Governor would give admittance. Mean time that a letter be prepared to be sent to General Guest for notification, to be first transmitted to Mr. Murray for his perusall to prevent all mistakes, and another to the absent directors to acquaint them with this event, that the directors present might be justified at the hands of their constituents.

Wednesday, 2d October.
. . . Dispatched James Lyon, porter, to the Castle with my letter to General Guest, under safeguard from Lochiel per white flagg. Had a letter from St. Germans, which I answered, thanking him for his kind invitation to me to go to his house to shun the calamity threatned against the City of Edinburgh from the Castle. Sent Lady Dunstaffnage by her boy 20 shillings in silver, and thank'd her for her kind invitation to stay at her house during these troubles. While at dinner at Mrs. Clerks about 3 o clock afternoon, Mr. Peter Smith, brother to Methven, calld me to another room and notified to me as Cashier that the Prince had a further demand of current specie from the Royal Bank for the sum of £2307 sterling of their notes, which he as Attorney for his highness required payment of within 48

hours, under the penaltys containd in Mr. Murray of Broughtons former protest of yesterdays date, and exhibited the Bank notes, in presence of W. Mackewan, notary publick, before these witness [   ] Writer to the Signet, and [   ]. This further demand I immediately notified to the directors present in the next room, viz⸱. Messrs. Hamilton, Shairp, Philp, Hathorn, and Forbes. After reasoning some time theron, they agreed to comply with this demand, as well as the former, if access could be got to the Castle. Some time after this, James Lyon, the porter, returned, and brought back the letter for General Guest open, his excellency having read the same, but did not incline to give a written answer, not having a lawyer to advise with, but added that if the directors had come in a private manner, they might dispose of their own as they wou'd. After talking over this matter a little Mr. Peter Smith calld me again, and presented a pass to the Castle for the three ordinary directors and my self, which pass was only to last and continue to this night at 10 o clock. I expostulated with him upon the impossibility of the thing, but he said that all excuses was in vain, for that a gentleman, who understood the business of banking, was with the Prince, when the pass was agranting, who said that there was no difficulty in the thing, for that all the gold and silver must be in baggs of certain sums, and therefore that it was an easy matter, and required no great time to execute this affair, and so the Prince was positive to grant no longer indulgence. Hereupon Mr. Smith left me and I return'd to the directors and reported what past, and being now towards evening, they found the measure proposd by the pass impracticable, so adjourned to my house to drink coffee, and further to deliberate of the affair. Bespoke a pott of coffee at Muirhead's. The directors talk'd over this exigency fully, and then resolv'd that a letter should be written by me to Mr. Murray of Broughton, desiring that the pass should be renewd for to morrow, when they would try to get access to the Castle and bring down the cash, and that the new pass should comprehend not only the three ordinary directors containd in the former, vizt. Messrs. Hamilton, Shairp, and Philp and my self, but likewise William Mitchell, accomptant, and Alexander Innes, teller. Accordingly I wrote a letter in these terms, which was read to and approvd of by the meeting, and being copied over fair by David Baillie (who had formerly transcribed the other letters to General Guest and Mr. Murray of Broughton in the forenoon), the same was sign'd by me, as the other letters were, in presence of and by appointment of the meeting. On this the directors dismiss'd, and twas resolv'd that the three ordinary directors, accomptant, and A. Innes, teller, should meet at my house tomorrow between 8 and 9 in the morning. But before the meeting was over, A. Innes, teller, was calld upon, to know if his brother, George, was in the Castle, who told he was not, on which he was dispatched to his house, to know if he had lodg'd the keys of the Castle vault, where the Bank repositories were lodg'd, with his wife, and if he had, to bring them, which accordingly he delivrd to me in a seald parcell, which I opened in presence of the directors, and then kept the keys, George Innes having gone in to the countrey some days agoe, as his wife told his brother. Mr David Baillie got the charge of delivering the letter to Mr. Murray of Broughton, after sealing, but after all search for him, he could not be found in town or abbey, on which Mr. Baillie and I concerted that I should call for Lochiel in Mrs. Clerks, and tell him of the case, who brought me Mr. Smith, who, with others, were in company with him, and in Lochiel's presence I deliverd the letter to Mr. Smith, who took burden to get and send me the answer this night. I then parted with these two gentlemen, all this discourse with them having past in the passage to Mrs. Clerks great room, and afterwards I went to John's Coffeehouse, where David Baillie waited me, to whom I told all that past, and then came home between 7 and 8 oclock.

Thursday, 3d October 1745.
About 7 this morning I wrote a letter to General Guest in the Castle acquainting him that Messrs. Jo. Hamilton, Alexander Shairp, and John Philip, directors of the Royal Bank, William Mitchel, accomptant, A. Innes, teller, and my self, as cashier, intended to go up to the Castle upon Bank business, therfore that he would please to give the proper orders to the Captain of the Guard to give us admittance upon our displaying a white flagg. This letter I sent up with James Lyon, porter, who us'd likewise a white napkin for his signall, and he reported we should be admitted. About 8 o clock the five gentlemen above nam'd met at my house, and after breakfast we proceeded on our expedition. This side of the Weigh house I calld for the Captain of the Highland guard (one Mr Cameron) to whom I shewd our pass, and after his reading the same, he calld for one of his men to go through all the centinells [sentinels] posted between that and the Reservoir to give them due notice, and after waiting about a quarter of an hour, the Captain desired us to proceed, for that all was safe before us. He kept the pass in his

Custody to be deliverd to the next captain when he was relieved off guard. I then hoisted my white flag and ushered the rest of the gentlemen, saluting the centinells with it as we past, and as we approached the Castle gate wav'd it often. At last the centinells there calld to us to come forward, and on our arrival at the bridge, telling who we were, 'twas lett down; the Captain received us in between the bridge and the gate, where he compard our names with my letter to General Guest which he had in his hand. On our arrival at General Guest's lodgings (which is the Governors new house) the directors and I went in, told him our errand in general was to get into the Royal Bank depositories to do some business, and General Preston having come in at that instant, he was likewise told the same. After some short conversation we left the two Generalls, and proceeded to the place where all the Bank things are lodg'd, and executed the affairs we came about, according to particular memorandums and minutes therof apart. During our continuance in the Castle which was from about 9 till near three o clock, there was closs firing from thence upon the Gardner's house at Livingston's yeards, occupied by R. Taylor, the shoemaker, at the head of a party of volunteers for the prince, to stop the communication thereabouts with the Castle, and one Watson, a soldier, was so couragious as to go down over the Castle wall upon a rope, fire upon the Gardners house, kill some of the volunteers there, carried off a firelock or two from them, sett the house in fire, return'd with these firelocks by his rope into the Castle, where he was received with loud huzzas for his valour. On his return the garrison was preparing for a sally, but as the men were a drawing up we got liberty from General Guest to go out again, and Captain Robert Mirry escorted us to the gate, where I again rais'd my white flagg, and with my friends return'd to town in safety, landed at my house from whence we adjournd to dine at Mrs. Clerks, vintner. No sooner were we sett down in Mrs. Clerks than we were inform'd that upon the sally from the Castle, Taylor and some of his men were taken and carried thither prisoners, leaving others dead on the spott, their house being sett on fire, the rest of the party having made their escape. Before I went to dinner I waited upon John Murray of Broughton, Esq., and told him I was come from the directors to acquaint him that they were ready to exchange current coin for their notes, in terms and in consequence of the two several demands made upon the Bank by way of protests and certification, on which he appointed six o clock at night to receive the money at my house, which I reported to the directors in

Mrs. Clerks. After dinner I came down to make all ready and to keep the appointment, having packd up the gold in baggs to the net amount of the demands, being £3,164. About 7 oclock in place of Mr. Murrays coming himself, he sent one Mr Andrew Lumisdean (son to Wm. Lumisdean, writer, in Edinburgh), his depute secretary, who had with him the Bank notes. I told him the money was ready on the table, but that I hop'd he had the two protests duely discharg'd. He told me he had not, that they were of no moment, as they were never extended. On this we sent for Wm. M'Kewan, the notary, who acknowledged they were not drawn up, but tho' they were 'twas to Mr. Murray and not to me he was to deliver them; nor would Mr. Lumisdean promise to get them discharg'd, not knowing Mr. Murray's mind on that head. Being difficulted in this particular, and having no directors at hand to advise with, it was agreed, and Mr. M'Kewan promis'd faithfully to make out the protests against to morrow's morning to be deliverd to Mr. Murray, in case he should think proper to deliver them to the Bank. Hereupon I calld up A. Innes, teller, to compt over the Notes, and that being done, the gold was likewise told over, first by Mr. Innes, then by Mr. Mackewan, and last of all by Mr. Lumisdean, who put it up in several baggs, and these again in one large bag seald, which he caus'd carry up to his chair, and so we parted about eleven oclock at night, having drunk one bottle of wine during our business. Thereafter I lodged notes in their proper place in Bank. The net sum paid was 3076lb., Mr. Lumsdean having disposed of £88 of the notes some other way. The Castle continued firing on the Highland guards at the Weigh house. When in the Castle today I deliverd two letters to General Guest, the charge of which I had from John M'Farlane, Writer to the Signet.

'Leaves From The Diary of John Campbell, An Edinburgh Banker In 1745', *Miscellany of the Scottish History Society*, ed. Henry Paton, Scottish History Society, 1893.

What's the Betting?

Nobody knew how the rebellion would turn out, but Justice Clerk Lord Milton and his Hanoverian friends were willing to put their alcohol where their mouths were – or something like that. They placed bets to be paid up in bottles of rum, spirits and claret as to what the Jacobite army would do next. Perhaps not strictly reportage, but definitely a snapshot of the times, this was Lord Milton's betting paper.

Mr Fotheringham says the rebels shall not go into England, but the Lord Justice Clerk says they will go into England – two bottles of rum [marked paid].

That the Lord Elchies says that the rebel army shall not return to Edinburgh without a battle but Mr Fletcher says they will, ditto

That Lord Belhaven says that the first battle with the rebels will be in Scotland, but Mr Grant says no, ditto

The above is certified by George Cheyne.

Berwick 8th November 1745

That Lord Elchies says the rebels will not re-cross the Forth without a battle, that Mr Webster says no – half a gallon of arrack to be drunk at Edinburgh Gallon scots [measure].

That Lord Home says the rebel army shall march into England but Mr Fotheringham says no – 6 bottles claret.

Eodem Die certified by GC.

Lord Elchies says the rebels now in England will not attack the town of Glasgow if they do he forfeits 2 bottles of rum in punch.

Mr Cross says ditto for the rebels in the north under the same forfeiture.

Both wagers at Edinburgh 23rd November 1745 certified by GC.

Edinburgh 23rd November 1745

Lord Dunmore says Lady Pile will not be in Edinburgh on or before the 9th of June next, Mr Cross says she will ditto above – 2 bottles rum in punch.

1745 23rd November, Mr Andrew MacDougall says Lady Walass was not at the Abbey visiting the Tartan Prince my Lord Justice Clerk says she was – 2 bottles of rum in punch certified GC.

That Mr Grant says there shall be a battle betwixt our army and the rebels on or before the 20th December next that the Reverend Mr Webster says no – 2 bottles of wine.

That the Reverend Mr Webster says the bridge at Warrington will not be broken down or defended but Mr John Graham says yes – 2 bottles of rum on the side of Mr Webster to one on the side of Mr Graham.

That Major Cawfield says the Highland army will not penetrate 20 miles into Wales but Mr Stewart says yes – 2 bottles of rum.

That Messieurs Cheape and Caffield say the rebels will not march within 100 miles of London that Mr Forest and Lord Justice Clerk say yes – 4 bottles of rum.

That Lord Belhaven says they will be in Yorkshire before they be in Wales, but Mr James Grant says no – 2 bottles of rum.

That Lord Dromore says that 1,000 of the rebels now in England shall not return to the Highlands. That Mr Forrest says yes – 2 bottles of rum.

That Mr Grosset says the Duke of Cumberland shall be in Carlisle on and before 12 o'clock on Wednesday night being 25th of December that Messieurs Cranston and Fletcher say no – 4 bottles of rum

'The Lord Justice Clerk's betting paper on the Rebellion', MS. 17526, f.33.

Derby – Black Friday
....

The Jacobite army marched into England, but as they came nearer and nearer to their goal in London, Lord George Murray, the Jacobite general, had doubts. Wade and Cumberland were closing in on them. The French help and English support which the Prince had promised had not materialised. Murray could see nothing but certain death for his army if it continued. Putting the lives of his men first, he told the Prince to turn back. John Daniel, a soldier in the Prince's army, recorded his forebodings and disappointment.

On the first of December we departed from Macclesfield, in order to march to Leek; where we staid all night, and marched the next day for Derby. All that morning it was rumored amongst us, that we should have an engagement as the enemy's army was said to be lying about five or six miles from us at Newcastle and Stone in Staffordshire. So we marched in the best order we could to receive them: and about eleven o'clock, having espied a party at some distance on the mountains, we drew up in order of battle, and stood so for some time, and would have fought them: but perceiving it was a false alarm, we continued on our route to Derby, where we arrived somewhat late and fatigued. But two days' repose sufficiently refreshed us.

Derby is a large and handsome town. The heads of it were much terrified at our entrance, many of them having made large subscriptions to Government; and therefore had quitted their houses with the utmost precipitation. It fell to my lot to be quartered in one of them, vizt., one Mr Chambers. Coming in with my billet, I asked if I could lodge there. The Steward immediately replied that I could

– adding 'And any thing we can do for you, shall be done: only pity
us in our situation, which is most deplorable.' At this wondering
much what he meant, I told him to be of good courage – that neither
I nor any of us were come to hurt him or any one. Having thus
abated the horrid notion they had of us, which was only capable of
being conceived too hard for expression, being so very strange; he
conducted me to the Housekeeper, who was also in tears. She was
somewhat seized with horror at the sight, though my countenance
was none of the roughest: but soon collected herself and made the
same answer with the utmost feminine tenderness, putting
themselves and the whole house under my mercy. I truly was much
surprised, for anything of this kind was quite new to me: however,
after pulling off my riding-coat and boots she conducted me into a
fine room; where, at entering, I perceived a number of jewels and
watches lying confusedly up and down, and many things else in the
utmost confusion. I demanded, to whom they belonged, and what
was the reason of their being so carelessly laid up. The housekeeper
then began to tell me the whole affair – 'Sir,' said she, 'Mr
Chambers, the master of this house, no enemy to you, has retired
with his lady and family into the country.' 'Why so?' said I. 'Not
conscious,' replied she, 'of any thing particular against you, but out
of fear of what the Highlanders might do against him.' She then
begged, that I would have compassion on them, and be their
protector; which, after some short discourse, I promised, telling
them, that what was consistent with reason, and a countryman, they
should always find in me. I then ordered all the things that lay so
confusedly thrown about, to be locked up, assuring them, that
nothing should be touched or broke open, unless with authority. So
for two days I ruled master there, and, I hope they will generously
acknowledge, much to their content and satisfaction in that
situation of affairs – having preserved the Young Lady's jewels from
the hand of rapine, and hindered the house from being damaged.

A rumor was here spread amongst us, that Cumberland, Will and
Ligonier [government generals] intended to give us battle; which I
believe would have happened, if we had marched a day or two more
towards London. Every one prepared himself to act in the best
manner the valiant Soldier. But the Prince's Council judged it more
proper to retire back into Scotland without risking a battle, and
there to await the arrival of foreign Succors. How far they acted
amiss or well in this, I know not: but a great alteration was
afterwards seen amongst us. The brave Prince at that out of a

generous ardour and Love to his country, wished he had been twenty feet under ground! But, notwithstanding all this, a march back was agreed upon, after we had halted two days at Derby. Here I cannot pass by an accident that happened somewhat ominous – though I am none of the most credulous – but thence we may date our first misfortune. Great numbers of People and Ladies (who had come from afar to see the Prince), crowding into his room, overturned a table, which in falling overturned and broke the Royal Standard – soon after our return was agreed upon – so I leave the reader to judge and make his reflexions on this. It would seem certain at least that Providence miraculously concurs, while such and such things are carried on. Thus, when Moses held up his hands, Joshua prevailed; but when through weariness he in the least relaxed the Israelites had the worst of it. So perhaps it was, that our enterprise was not vigorously enough pursued; and remarkable it certainly was, that the Royal Standard should be broken immediately after our return was resolved upon.

Origins of the 'Forty-Five, ed. W. B. Blaikie, Scottish History Society, 1916.

Falkirk

The government forces finally caught up with the rebels at Falkirk on 17 January 1746, where the Jacobites won a surprise victory under difficult conditions, but they lacked the generalship and the resources to follow it up. The performance on the government side was equally lamentable. Despite the popular image, it was not true that all Highlanders were fighting with Charlie. There were English men and Lowland Scots who were Jacobites and Highlanders who were staunch Hanoverians. The rising crossed geographical and ethnic lines. Gaelic poet Duncan Ban Macintyre had the misfortune to be with the Argyll militia on the Government side – faced with a fearsome Highland charge from the opposition. Macintyre decided that the only sensible thing to do was to run away. He also had the wit and humour to immortalise this not so glorious performance in his Gaelic poem, Oran do Bhlàr na h-Eaglaise Brice.

A Song on the Battle of Falkirk

Once while we, the Whiggish army,
Were down on the Scottish Lowlands,
Chanced the Rebels to come on us,
Folk whose company liked we little;

When they put the retreat on us,
And pursued us to make slaughter,
If we had not used our feet well
Ne'er again had we fired musket.

Happily we did go forward
That we might Prince Charles encounter,
We thought, to get the better of him,
We had but to go and seek it;
When they smote upon each other
High we'd leap as we retreated,
And we rushed across the river,
To our neck's height in the water.

When we put on our equipment
That we might repulse the Rebels,
We ne'er believed, until we yielded,
That ourselves 'twas should be routed;
Just as sheep rush down a glen-side,
When the sheepdog's set upon them,
Thus it was the folk were scattered
On the side which we belonged to.

And when the foe had come and shown us
That to meet them was no pleasure,
Twas the Lowland troop that lost most,
Death and slaughter they received;
We did flee from unknown country
When a third of us had fallen,
Ne'er again shall I go forward
To the Whiggish King's assistance.

Shod and bridled were the horses,
In troops well-girthed, thonged, and skittish,
And the men were armed and well-trained,
Specially prepared for battle;
When Clan Donald happened on them,
They engaged them on the hillside,
And many a man lay hacked and wounded
On the meadow after falling.

Terror in the rout did strike us,

When the host broke down the hill-slope,
There was Prince Charles with his Frenchmen
Full of eagerness to catch us;
Not a word's command did we get
Telling us to strike our foemen,
But leave to scatter everywhere,
And some of us have not yet got it . . .

Argyll's gentry folk collected
A mighty army of Militia,
And they went to meet Prince Charlie,
Hoping that his camp they'd ruin;
Many a man there was in that place
Who, unlike me, was not saved,
Though I left my broadsword lying
On the battlefield of Falkirk.

Oran do Bhlàr na h-Eaglaise Brice

Latha dhuinn air machair Alba
Na bha dh'armailt aig a'Chuigse,
Thachair iad oirnne na Reubail,
'S bu neo-éibhinn leinn a'chuideachd;
'N uair a chuir iad an ratreut oirnn,
'S iad 'nar déidh a los ar murtadh,
Is mur dèanamaid feum le'r casan
Cha tug sinne srad le'r musgan.

'S a' dol an coinneamh a' Phrionnsa
Gum bu shunndach a bha sinne,
Shaoil sinn gum faigheamaid cùis deth,
'S nach robh dhuinn ach dol 'ga shireadh;
'Nuair a bhuail iad air a chéile
'S àrd a leumamaid a' tilleadh,
'S ghabh sinn a-mach air an abhainn
'S dol g'ar n-amhaich anns an linne.

An àm do dhaoinibh dol 'nan éideadh
Los na Reubalaich a thilleadh,
Cha do shaoil sinn, gus na ghéill sinn,
Gur sinn féin a bhithte 'g iomain;
Mar gun rachadh cù ri caoraibh,

'S iad 'nan ruith air aodainn glinne,
'S ann mar sin a ghabh iad sgaoileadh
Air an taobh air an robh sinne.

'S an uair thàinig càch 's a dhearbh iad
Gum bu shearbh dhuinn dol 'nan cuideachd,
'S e 'n trup Gallda 'g an robh 'chall sin,
Fhuair iad am marbhadh 's am murtadh;
'S ann a theich sinn as na cianaibh
An déidh trian againn a thuiteam,
'S cha téid mi tuilleadh gu dìlinn
Chuideachadh le Rìgh na Cuigse.

Bha na h-eich gu cruidheach, srianach,
Giortach, iallach, fiamhach, trupach,
'S bha na fir gu h-armach fòghlaimt',
Air an sònrachadh gu murtadh;
'Nuair a thachair riuth Clann Dòmhnaill,
Chum iad còmhdail air an uchdan,
'S lìonmhor spòltaich a bha leònta
Air an lòn an déidh an tuiteim.

Dh'éirich fuathas anns an ruaig dhuinn
'Nuair a dh'aom an sluagh le leathad,
Bha Prionns' Teàrlach le 'chuid Frangach
'S iad an geall air teachd 'nar rathad.
Cha d'fhuair sinn focal comanndaidh
A dh'iarraidh ar nàimhdean a sgathadh,
Ach comas sgaoilidh feadh an t-saoghail,
'S cuid againn gun 'fhaotainn fhathast.

[stanzas omitted]

Chruinnich uaislean Earra-Ghàidheal
Armailt làidir de mhilìsidh,
'S chaidh iad mu choinneamh Phrionns' Teàrlach,
'S dùil aca r'a champ a bhristeadh;
'S iomadh fear a bh'anns an àit' ud
Nach robh sàbhailt' mar bha mise,
Ged tha mo chlaideamh air 'fhàgail
Ann am Blàr na h-Eaglais' Brice.

Highland Songs of the 'Forty-Five, ed. J. L. Campbell, Scottish Academic Press for
the Scottish Gaelic Texts Society, 1933.

Culloden

....

*By now the Jacobites were on the defensive. As a last throw of the
dice, Lord George Murray tried to mount a surprise night attack
on the enemy while they were celebrating the Duke of
Cumberland's birthday, but his forces were too hungry and weary
to carry out the attack. They straggled back to Drummossie Muir,
only to find that the government army was now bringing the fight
to them. It was a battle which should never have happened. Facing
into wind and rain, the disorganised army suddenly found itself
under a hail of superior firepower. The Highland charge was
ragged. There was never even a chance of breaking the enemy lines.
John Daniel, whom we last met at Derby, continues the story.*

I shall now proceed to give account in what manner we were ranged
in battle-array. The brave McDonalds, who till then had led the
van, and behaved at all times with great courage and bravery, were
now displaced, and made to give way, at the pleasure of Lord
George Murray, to the Athol men, whom he commanded. The rest
of the front line was composed of Highlanders: the second, of
Lowlanders and French, with four pieces of cannon at each wing:
and in the rear was the Prince attended by all the horse, and some
foot. In this manner were we drawn up – four thousand men to fight
eleven thousand. The enemy being by this time in full view, we
began to huzza and bravado them in their march upon us, who were
extended from right to left in battle-array, it being upon a common.
But, notwithstanding all our repeated shouts, we could not induce
them to return one: on the contrary, they continued proceeding, like
a deep sullen river; while the Prince's army might be compared to a
streamlet running among stones, whose noise sufficiently shewed its
shallowness. The Prince, the Duke of Perth, the Earl of Kilmarnock,
Lord Ogilvy, and several other Highland and Lowland Chiefs, rode
from rank to rank, animating and encouraging the soldiers by well-
adapted harangues.

The battle being now begun, the whole fury of the enemy's
artillery seemed to be directed against us in the rear; as if they had
noticed where the Prince was. By the first cannon shot his servant,
scarcely thirty yards behind him, was killed; which made some
about the Prince desire, that he would be pleased to retire a little off:
but this he refused to do, till seeing the imminent danger from the
number of balls that fell about him, he was by the earnest entreaties
of his friends forced to retire a little, attended only by Lord

Balmerino's corps. Frequent looks and turns the Prince made, to see
how his men behaved: but alas! Our hopes were very slender, from
the continual fire of musketry that was kept up upon them from
right to left. We had not proceeded far, when I was ordered back,
lest the sight of my standard going off, might induce others to
follow. In returning, various thoughts passed my soul, and filled by
turns my breast with grief for quitting my dear Prince, now hopes of
victory, then fear of losing – the miserable situation the poor
loyalists would again be reduced to – and what we had to expect if
we left the field alive: these thoughts, I say, strangely wrought upon
me, till, coming to the place I was on before, and seeing it covered
with the dead bodies of many of the Hussars who at the time of our
leaving had occupied it, I pressed on, resolving to kill or be killed.
Some few accompanied my standard, but soon left it. At this time,
many of ours from right to left were giving way and soon the battle
appeared to be irretrievably lost. The enemy, after we had almost
passed the two ranks, flanking and galling us with their continual
fire, forced us at last back, broke our first line, and attacked the
second, where the French troops were stationed. I happened then to
be there, and after receiving a slight grazing ball on my left arm, met
with Lord John Drummond, who, seeing me, desired I would come
off with him, telling me all was over and shewing me his regiment,
just by him, surrounded. Being quickly joined by about forty more
horse, we left the field of battle in a body, though pursued and fired
upon for some time. When we arrived at the foot of the hills, some
of us took one way, and some another: I, however, with about six
more, continued with Lord John Drummond; and it was with some
difficulty we passed the rapid torrents and frozen roads, till one
o'Clock that night, when we came to a little village at the foot of a
great mountain, which we had just crossed. Here we alighted, and
some went to one house and some to another. None of these cottages
having the conveniences to take in our horses, who wanted
refreshment as well as we, many of them perished at the doors. I
happened to be in one of the most miserable huts I had ever met
with during my whole life; the people were starving to death with
hunger. However, having laid myself down on the floor to rest
myself after having been almost thirty hours on horse-back; the
people came crying about me and speaking a language I did not
understand, which made my case still more unpleasant. But by good
luck, a soldier soon after came in, who could speak both to them
and me, and brought with him some meal, which was very

acceptable, as I was almost starving with hunger. Of this meal we made at that time a very agreeable dish, by mixing it very thick with cold water, for we could get no warm: and so betwixt eating and drinking we refreshed ourselves, till four o'Clock in the morning; when Lord John Drummond and the rest of us began our march, we knew not whither, through places it would be in vain to describe; for we saw neither house, barn, tree, or beast nor any beaten road, being commonly mid-leg deep in snow, till five o'Clock that afternoon; when we found ourselves near a village called *Privana a Badanich* [Ruthven Barracks], the barracks of which, as I mentioned before, the Prince had destroyed. Being now, to our surprize, almost upon it, we consulted amongst ourselves how we might best get intelligence from it; for, as it lay on the road from Inverness twenty-four miles we apprehended the enemy might be there. But fortunately a soldier coming out told us, that the village was occupied by the Prince's men. This intelligence gave us great pleasure; and having accordingly entered the place, we found a great many of the Prince's adherents, the chief of whom was Lord George Murray and the Duke of Perth; but we heard no news where the poor Prince was. At first we had great hopes of rallying again: but they soon vanished, orders coming for every one to make the best of his way he could. So some went one way, some another: those who had French Commissions surrendered; and their example was followed by my Colonel, Lord Balmerino, tho' he had none. Many went for the mountains, all being uncertain what to do or whither to go.

Origins of the 'Forty-Five, ed. W. B. Blaikie, Scottish History Society, 1916.

Aftermath

....

Most casualties in pre-modern battles took place in the rout as the victorious army pursued the defeated. Captain John Maclean was killed at Culloden. His diary was taken from his body and continued by another hand. Ensign John Fraser escaped, but only just, and following the kind of cruel treatment which was standard on the European battlefields of that time. The saddest thing about the stories of the aftermath of Culloden is that there was nothing much exceptional about them at all.

In this battle the greatest barbarities was committed that ever was heard to be done by either Christians, Turks or Pagans. I mean by our enemies who gave no quarters killed our men that was wounded in cold blood and continued so doing for three or four days or any others they could catch.

'Capt. John Maclean's Diary', Acc. 11241.

An Account of the Signal Escape of John Fraser

John Fraser, Ensign in the Master of *Lovat's* Regiment, was shot through the Thigh by a Musket Bullet, at the Battle of *Culloden*, and was taken Prisoner after the Battle, at a little Distance from the Field, and carried to the House of *Culloden*, where a Multitude of other wounded Prisoners lay under strong Guards. There he, and the other miserable Gentlemen (for most of them were Gentlemen) lay with their Wounds undressed, for two Days, in great Torture. Upon the third Day he was carried out of *Culloden* House, and with other eighteen of his Fellow Prisoners slung into Carts, which they imagined were to carry them to *Inverness* to be dress'd of their Wounds: They were soon undeceived; the Carts stopt at a Park Dyke at Some Distance from the House, there they were dragged out of the Carts: The Soldiers who guarded them, under Command of three Officers, carried the Prisoners close to the Wall or Park-Dyke, along which they ranged them upon their Knees, and bid them prepare for Death. The Soldiers immediately drew up opposite to them – It is dreadful to proceed! They levell'd their Guns; they fired among them! Mr *Fraser* fell with the rest and did not doubt but he was shot. But as those Gentlemen, who proceeded thus deliberately in cool Blood, had their Orders to do nothing by Halves, a Party of them went along and examined the Slaughter, and knocked out the Brains of such as were not quite dead; and observing Signs of Life in Mr *Fraser*, one of them with the Butt of his Gun, struck him on the Face, dashed out one of his Eyes, and beat down his Nose, flat and shattered, to his Cheek, and left him for dead. The Slaughter thus finished, the Soldiers left the Field. In this miserable Situation, Lord B–d riding out that Way with his Servant, espied some Life in Mr *Fraser*, who by that Time had crawled to a little Distance from his dead Friends, and calling our [sic] to him asked what he was. *Fraser* told him he was an Officer in the Master of *Lovat's* Corps. Lord B–d offered him Money, saying he had been acquainted with the Master of *Lovat*, his Colonel. Mr *Fraser* said he had no Use for Money, but begged him for God's Sake to cause his Servant to carry him to a certain Mill and Cott-House where he said he would be concealed and taken care of. This young Lord had the Humanity to do so, and in this Place Mr *Fraser* lay concealed, and by God's Providence recovered of his Wounds, and is now a living Witness of as unparallell'd a Story, in all its Circumstances, as can be met with in the History of any Age.

Mr *Fraser* is well known, and his Veracity attested by all the *Inverness* People.

An Account of the Signal Escape of John Fraser, n.p. n.d. (Blaikie 13/18)

Search and Plunder

After the retreat of the Jacobite army and during the hunt for the Prince, crimes were committed in parts of the Highlands by government forces who had little regard for the local population. Rape, casual killing and thorough looting were common complaints. Some of the worst perpetrators of this kind of act were naval officers, who were able to descend on even the most remote islands, plundering and destroying. Many accounts of such cruelties were collected by Bishop Robert Forbes who gathered them together in his work, The Lyon in Mourning.

The extent of government cruelty in the wake of the '45 is often exaggerated. Many comparable or worse things happened in the Montrose wars of the 17th century or in inter-clan warfare, but whatever bench-mark it is judged against, the people caught up in these reprisals still suffered. These were the experiences of the folk of Canna. The following extract is unusual in recording incidents which took place just before Culloden, as well as afterwards.

Upon the 3d of April 1746, Lieutennant Thomas Brown, an Irish gentleman with a command of 80 men, did sail with a tender from the *Baltimore* man of war by Captain Fergusons order, which layed then at the harbour of Lochnadaal at Sky, at whose end Lord Loudon had a camp then, came to the haven of Canna, and after sending for James M'Donald, bailie of the Island, and uncle to Glenaladal, told him he was sent by Captains Ferguson and Dove for some fresh beef and mutton, vizt., 20 fat cows and so many wedders. The gentleman asking his orders was answered he woud show him noe commission of that kind, but if he would not present his demands without further controul [do what he was told at once] he would take them *brevi manu* [by force]. He had 60 armed men at his heels; the flower of the Islanders was with the Prince; soe that the bailie judged it safer both for himself and inhabitants to grant his request, and consequently sent off to the meadows for the above number of cattle, and took them up in proportion to the number of the tenements the Isle consisted of. But being wind-bound for 4 days in Canna harbour, behold! They complained to the said bailie the beef of the cattle slaughter'd stunk, and that the country should give them the same number over again. The bailie reckoned this both unjust and cruel, and that it was enough for the poor inhabitants to gratify him of what they received already. Upon which the officer was petted [peeved] and said with a rage he knew where and by whom he would be served. He meant [the laird of] Laaig's cattle, whom he heard was in the Prince's army. So he hurls away his 60 armed men, gathers all the cattle of the Isle into a particular creek, shot 60 of the best dead, threw the old beef overboard and would not allow the poor distressed owners to finger a gobbet of it, no, not a single tripe of the first or former. 40 of the last cattle belonged to Laaig, 20 to the tennants.

Captain Duff and Captain Ferguson aboard the *Commodore* came again a little, or about the 15 of April, harrass'd all the Isle, and at a certain night when they became fully acquaint through all the country, they (I mean all the young luxurious men among them) combined to make ane attack upon all the girls and young women in all the Isle married or otherwise. But a certain marine who had some grains of Christian principles about him advertised the whole, and was obliged to climb and hide themselves in grottos and in the hollow of hideous precipices that were somewhat unaccessable, which rescued them from the unhumanity of those libidinous hounds. A certain company of them came to execute their sensuality into a certain family, Evan More MacIsaac, his house, from which fled two girls, the landlord's daughters. Their mother who was fifty years old, worn with sickness and within a month of her time, stayed at home as dreading noe danger of that sort. But they missing their aim and getting none of the females within a houseroof but that poor creature, they setts a strong guard with drawn swords upon the door of her house, fettered her husband in order to quench their concupiscence on his spouse. Providence favourd the creature so far that she wonn out through the guard, and the darkness of the night concurrd to make her rescue. For they got out in pursuit of her in a great hurry, and 12 of them was at her heels, when she meeting and sinking down into the very depth of a quaggmire, they leaps over her believing she was still before them. The poor woman contented herself to continue there all the night, till she understood they were all back to their ships. But then she was so much afflicted with the rigour of the cold, and she being bigg with child, turned ill, aborted

and died next night. The rest continued their sculking in a starving
condition till the men of war sail'd off. After the battle of Culloden
was hard fought, Captain Dove and Captain Fergusone went to
Canna successively and committed several branches of cruelty upon
the poor people, wanting them to inform them of the Prince or any
of his officers. After General Campbell turned back from the search
of his Royal Highness from the Western Coast, he calls at Canna,
and hurls away the honest bailie prisoner into his ship without
allowing him to speak for himself, or as much time as to shift
himself or take leave of his wife. At this stretch he was brought the
length of Horseshoe in the shire of Argile, from Horseshoe was
brought back to Canna. Then he believed he would be liberate, but
instead thereof they caus'd 40 of his cows to be slaughtered, would
not permit him as much liberty as goe ashore to take leave of his
wife or children, or to bring his cloaths with him, but brought him
prisoner to London where he continued upwards of 12 month,
notwithstanding of Loudon's protection in his pocket.

Robert Forbes, *The Lyon in Mourning*, iii, ed. H. Paton, Scottish History Society,
1896.

'Betty Burk'

*After Culloden, the Prince became a hunted man with a heavy
price on his head. Even so, he still found assistance. He had with
him his two faithful Irish officers Felix O'Neil and John
O'Sullivan, but for all their loyalty they were of little use to him in
terms of local knowledge. Having escaped as far as the little island
of Benbecula, to Clanranald's lands, Charles found that his host
had a helper for him. Neil MacEachan Macdonald, an experienced
secret agent in the French service, was waiting specifically to assist
Charles in his escape. The famous Flora Macdonald was Neil's
cousin, and it was no accident that led to her encounter with the
prince. In his own lively and sometimes comic narrative,
MacEachan, talking of himself in the third person, explains how it
happened. His manuscript breaks off, however, before the ending
of the story. Charles's escape to France on the* Du Teillay, *and his
subsequent descent into a miserable alcoholic old age, are well-
known.*

The scheme was this: to send his [Macdonald of Kingsburgh's]
stepdaughter, Miss Florence MacDonald, to Sleet, to live with
her mother 'till the enemy was out of Wist [Uist]. The prince at the

same time was ordered to dress in woman's close [clothes], that he might pass for her servant-maid, and Neil was appointed to take care of both. The scheme pleased the prince mightely, and he seemed very impatient to see it put in execution.

But to return to the top of the hill, the prince with Neil and Mr. O'Neil remained there the whole day. About sunset the prince told Neil that he entrusted himself in his hands, and that his life and safety depended upon him, Neil answered that the charge was more than what his life was worth; but yet, with God's assistance that he would find means to preserve him from all danger till every thing was got ready to leave the country. After this they took a refreshment of bread-and-cheese, and set out towards the north end of the country, every body carrying his own share of the baggage, the prince carried his own few shirts, O'Neill carried his own linnen, and Neil carried the provision, his own gun and sword, and the prince's fusee and one of his holsters, while the other hung upon his own belt. As they were going on, the prince clapt Neil's shoulder, often telling him if ever it was their good fortune to get free of their present troubles, he would make him live easie all his days for the fatigue of that night. Neil was informed some days before, that Miss Flora lived with her brother in a glen near Locheynort, where they had all their cattle a grazing at that time, and which happened to be very near the rod [road] they were to pass that night.

When the prince was informed of it, he would needs go to see her, and tell her of the message he had from her stepfather. When they were near the little house where she was asleep, for her brother was not at home, Neil left the prince and O'Neil at a distance off, 'till he went in and wakened her; she got scarcely on the half of her close [clothes], when the prince, with his baggage upon his back, was at the door, and saluted her very kindly; after which she brought to him a part of the best cheer she had, among the rest was a large bowl full of creme, of which he took two or three hearty go-downs, and his fellow-travellers swallowed the rest.

He discovered to her her stepfather's proposal, and ask't whether she was willing to run the risque. She joyfully accepted of the offer without the least hesitation, and that no time might be lost, she was ordered immediately away to Benbicula to consult with her stepfather and the Lady Clanranald, to get every thing in readiness as soon as possible, and to send them word back again next day how all was going on with them. Having taken leave of Miss Flora, they pursued their journey, and about sunrise they arrived upon the side

of a hill three miles from Corrodale, where they sate down under a
rock in order to take some rest . . .

It is almost inexpressible what torment the prince suffered under
that unhappy rock which had neither height nor bredth to cover him
from the rain which poured down upon him so thick as if all the
windows of heaven had broke open, and, to compleat his tortures,
there lay such a swarm of mitches [midges] upon his face and hands
as would have made any other but himself fall into despair, which,
notwithstanding his incomparable patience, made him utter such
hideous cries and complaints as would have rent the rocks with
compassion.

Neil, who stood all this time aside him, could be of no more
service to him than to let run to the ground the rain which stagnated
in the lurks of the plaid wherein he lay wrapt. In this miserable
condition he continued for about three hours, till their faithful
scoote [scout] came for the last time, and told them they might
return to the house, for that the militia was gone; Neil helped him
to his feet, and they marched away to the house, where the good
derrymaid [dairy maid] took care to make a roozing [rousing] fire
for their coming. He was no sooner entered but Neil stripped him of
all his clothes from top to toe, and hung ropes round the house to
dry them on; he sate down in his shirt at the fireside as merry and
hearty as if he was in the best room at Whitehall.

After he had warmed himself, he desired Neil to ask the wife if she
had any eatables. She said that she had nothing except a chapin of
milk she kept for her bairns, which Neil desired her to warm in a
pot, and when it was hot to froth it up with the machine made for
that purpose. When all was ready, the wife placed the pot before the
prince and Neil, and gave them two horn spoons as coarse as ever
was made use of, the prince ask't Neil what it was, who told it was
fresh creme, he not doubting but it was really so, and at the same
time believing it to be solid, pushed his hand to the very wrist in the
scalded milk, which made him draw back his hand in the greatest
hurry, all full of wrath, and dropt his spoon in the pot. Neil had all
the difficulty imaginable to keep his gravity, to hear him curse the
wife and her pot a hundred times, calling her a vile witch for (says
he) she contrived it a purpose that we might burn ourselves. Neil,
seeing him altogether out of humour, in order to pacify him, told he
would take a stick and labour her to an inch of her life with it, and
immediately ran to an oar of the boat that was lying before him to
knock out her brains. The prince, believing him to be serious,

begged of him not to touch her, for, if he came to do her any hurt, she would certainly run off and bring a party upon them . . .

The company being gone, the prince, script of his own cloaths, was dressed by Miss Flora in his new attire, but could not keep his hands from adjusting his head dress, which he cursed a thousand times. There they lay till the evening, waiting impatiently for the night to set off. Here they were alarmed by five wherries [boats], the same, as they supposed, that landed the Campbells the night before in Benbicula, supposing, by taking this precaution, to keep the prince from making his escape. But their fears were soon over; for the wherries sailed by to the southward without ever stopping. After sunset they got into their boat, which was managed by the following persons – Rory McDonald, John McDonald, John McMurich, Duncan Campbell, and Rory McDonald of Glengary family; the prince passed for Miss McDonald's maid, and Neil McDonald in the quality of a servant.

The weather proving calm in the beginning of the night, they rowed away at a good rate; but, about twelve, there blew a gale of westerly wind, which eased the Rowers not little, but at the same time there came on such thick mist as robbed them of the sight of all lands; great was the debate among the boatmen upon this occasion, some asserted that they lost their course, while others maintained the contrary, till their dispute end'd at last to cease rowing till day would decide their error. In the morning, the weather being quite clear, they rowed along the coast of Sky, but the wind, shifting about to the north, blew at nine o'clock so strong in their teeth, that for an hour and a half it was impossible to discern whether they made any way or not.

The prince, who, all this time, was not in the least discouraged, encouraged them to row still better, saying that he would relieve him that was most fatigued. The poor men, almost ready to breathe out their last, at length made the point of Watersay on the north corner of the Isle of Sky, where, having got into a cliff in a rock, they rested themselves for an hour, and at the same time revived their drooping spirits with a plentiful repast of bread and butter, while the water that fell from the top of the rock furnished them drink.

This gave them fresh vigour for to undertake the remaining part of their labour, the weather being quite calm again, they rowed round the point close by the land. They had not gone far on the other side, when they spyed two centrys [sentries] upon shore, one of whom approached nearer, and ordered them to put to, but they rowed the faster; which he observing, advanced as far as the sea would permitt him, bad them put to, a second time in a more threatning manner, and seeing them like not to obey, he cocked his piece, which he thought to fire upon them, but, as Providence ordered it, she misgave, and so he was disappointed. The other who look'd on all this time, made to heels to a neighbouring village, about a cannon shot off, to acquaint their officer (if there was any) of what had happened.

The boatmen, justly judging what he was going about, made them now row for dear blood. They very soon saw the event of their conjectures, for a body of about fifteen men, full armed, marched straight from the village to the rock, where their centry was post'd, and if they had the presence of mind to launch out one of their boats (of which they had two close by them) we must have been inevitably taken.

The prince by this time was sensible of his error in not allowing the men at parting from Uist to have any arms in the boat, which if they had had, were fully resolved to fight it out to the last man, notwithstanding the inequality of numbers. The enemy seeing it quite out of their power to execute their design in coming thither, as we got fairly out of their reach, took a walk along the shore, without giving the prince or crew any uneasiness, further than to gaze at them till they landed in Kilbride in Troterniss within a cannon shot of Sir Alexander Mcdonald's house, twelve miles from the place where we saw the enemy.

In the neighbourhood of this place was another party of the Sky[e] militia, who was post'd there to examine all boats that came from the isles, as they were pretty well assured that the prince was there at that time. Miss and Neil having kept the prince in the boat as well as they could, went to the house, leaving strict orders with the boatmen not to stir from it till they came back, or some word from them, and in case their curiosity led any body thither, who might perhaps take the liberty to ask who was the person kept in the boat, to answer Miss McDonald's maid, and to curse her for a lazy jade, what was she good for, since she did not attend her Mrs.

About an hour before sunset they set off for Kingsborough, where they were to be that night. Miss Flora, who staid for dinner at Mungstot, that she might not be suspected by Lieut. MacLeod, followed a horseback at some distance, and was mightily diverted to hear several of the country people with whom she fell in upon the road, as they returned from the meeting house at Mungstot, it being

Sunday, make their remarks upon the behaviour of Betty Burk, her maid, which name the prince borrowed when he left the Isle of Wist.

Neil, who walked a little behind the prince, and Kingsborough, hearing the subject the fellows were upon, went slower till they came up and joined him, but they, notwithstanding, continued to speak with the same freedom as before, of the impudence and assurance of Miss Burk, who was not ashamed to walk and keep company with Kingsborough, and was no less vexed than surprised how he took so much notice of her, when he never minded her mistress, who was so near at hand. Betty, very easie of what would be said of her, went on always at such a rate, that she very often got a piece before her fellow travellers, which gave occasion to some of the fellows to cry out, 'Curse the wretch do you observe, sir (meaning Neil), what terrible steps she takes, how manly she walks, how carelessly she carries her dress', and a hundred such like expressions, which they repeated over and over again.

But what they most took notice of all was, when Kingsborough and his companion was come to a rivulet about knee deep, which crossed the high rod [road], to see Burk take up her petty coats so high when she entred the water. The poor fellows were quite confounded at this last sight, which made them rail out against Burk, calling her all the names in the world, and ask't of Neil if he was acquainted with her. Neil told them that he knew nothing about her further than to hear she was an Irish girl who met with Miss MacDonald in Wist, and uppon a report of her being a famous spinister [spinner] of lint, engaged her for her mother's use.

The honest people soon after departed with Neil and Miss Flora, and made for their different homes full of astonish –

[*Manuscript ends abruptly.*]

Origins of the 'Forty-Five, ed. W. B. Blaikie, Scottish History Society, 1916.

Enlightenment and Empire

After a shaky start marked by Jacobite risings, malt tax riots and grumblings against the Union, Scots began to benefit more from their status as North Britons. Traditionally they had enhanced their prospects by emigration and in many ways the opportunities of the new British Empire suited them perfectly. As settlers, administrators, military men and later missionaries, Scots played a disproportionate part in this enterprise. At home Scotland was experiencing a cultural flowering known as the Enlightenment. Literature, architecture, science and philosophy were the talk of the town in Edinburgh, Glasgow, Aberdeen and beyond. The literacy and education encouraged by presbyterianism now became tools for scepticism in the hands of the elite. In some cases, skills for debate honed by previous generations on a diet of bible study, religious confessions and catechisms, now applied themselves to the rights of man and revolutions in France and America. It was an exciting time economically and intellectually.

Kidnapped!

Ever since the 17th century, one of Scotland's main exports had been people. Gradually its direction changed, from the traditional exodus into Eastern Europe, to the English, now British, colonies in the Americas. Access to British colonies meant embroilment in Britain's international squabbles – such as repeated wars with the French. In 1754 one such conflict proved disastrous for Aboyne man Peter Williamson. Kidnapped as a small boy from Aberdeen and sold into slavery in America, he gained his freedom as a farmer on the frontiers of Pennsylvania. Fate, however, had more problems in store for him. The local Native Americans had thrown in their lot with Britain's French enemies. The unfortunate Scot was kidnapped again and later forced to join them on scalping missions. Here is his account of his capture. He later returned safely to Scotland and compiled the first Edinburgh postal directory.

Terrible and shocking to human nature were the barbarities daily committed by the savages, and are not to be parallelled in all the volumes of history! Scarce did a day pass but some unhappy family or other fell victim to *French chicanery*, and savage cruelty. Terrible indeed it proved to me, as well as to many others; I that was now happy in an easy state of life, blessed with an affectionate and tender wife, who was possessed of all amiable qualities, to enable me to go through this world with that peace and serenity of mind, which every Christian wishes to possess, became on a sudden one of the most unhappy and deplorable of mankind; scarce can I sustain the shock which for ever recoils on me, at thinking on the last time of seeing that good woman. The fatal 2d of *October* 1754, she that day went from home to visit some of her relations; as I staid up later than usual, expecting her return, none being in the house besides myself, how great was my surprize, terror and affright, when, about eleven o'clock at night, I heard the dismal war-cry, or war-whoop of the savages, which they make on such occasions, and may be expressed *Woach, woach, ha, ha, hach woach*, and to my inexpressible grief, soon found my house was attacked by them; I flew to the chamber-window, and perceived them to be twelve in number. They making several attempts to come in, I asked them what they wanted? They gave me no answer, but continued beating, and trying to get the door open. Judge then the condition I must be in, knowing the cruelty and merciless disposition of those savages should I fall into their hands. To escape which dreadful misfortune, having my gun loaded in my hand, I threatened them with death, if they should not desist. But how vain and fruitless are the efforts of one man against the united force of so many! And of such merciless, undaunted and blood thirsty monsters as I had here to deal with. One of them that could speak a little *English*, threatened me in return, 'That if I did 'not come out, they would burn me alive in the 'house;' telling me farther what I unhappily perceived, 'That they were no friends to the '*English*, but if I would come out and surrender 'myself prisoner, they would not kill me.' My terror and distraction at hearing this is not to be expressed by words, nor easily imagined by any person, unless in the same condition. Little could I depend on the promises of such creatures; and yet, if I did not, inevitable death, by being burnt alive, must be my lot. Distracted as I was in such deplorable circumstances, I chose to rely on the uncertainty of their fallacious promises, rather than meet with certain death by rejecting them; and accordingly went out of my house with my gun in my hand, not knowing what I did or that I had it. Immediately on my approach they rushed on me like so many tygers, and instantly disarmed me. Having me thus in their power, the merciless villains bound me to a tree near the door: they then went into the house and plundered and destroyed every thing there was in it, carrying off what moveables they could; the rest, together with the house, which they set fire to, was consumed before my eyes. The Barbarians not satisfied with this, set fire to my barn, stable, and out-houses, wherein were about 200 bushels of wheat, six cows, four horses and five sheep, which underwent the same fate, being all intirely consumed to ashes. During the conflagration to describe the thoughts, the fears, and misery that I felt, is utterly impossible, as it is even now to mention what I feel at the rememberance thereof.

Having thus finished the execrable business about which they came, one of the monsters came to me with a *Tomahawk* in his hand, threatening me with the worst of deaths, if I would not willingly go with them, and be contented with their way of living. This I seemingly agreed to, promising to do every thing for them that lay in my power; trusting to Providence for the time when I might be delivered out of their hands. Upon this they untied me, and gave me a great load to carry on my back, under which I travelled all that night with them, full of the most terrible apprehensions, and oppressed with the greatest anxiety of mind, lest my unhappy wife should likewise have fallen a prey to these cruel monsters. At day-break, my infernal masters ordered me to lay down my load, when tying my hands again round a tree with a small cord, they forced the blood out of my fingers ends. They then kindled a fire near the tree whereto I was bound, which filled me with the most dreadful agonies, concluding I was going to be made a sacrifice to their barbarity.

This narrative, O reader! may seem dry and tedious to you: My miseries and misfortunes, great as they have been, may be considered only as what others have daily met with for years past; yet, on reflection, you can't help indulging me in the recital of them: For to the unfortunate and distressed, recounting our miseries is, in some sort, an alleviation of them.

The Life of Peter Williamson, Edinburgh, 1762.

The Bloody Tragedy of Douglas

Scotland's literary and intellectual renaissance sometimes fell into sharp conflicts with the strict religious inheritance of the 17th century. Play-going was still a Scottish shibboleth – the mark of the ungodly, wasting their time on vain frivolity instead of spending it on bible-reading, prayer and business. It was bad enough for the great unwashed to divert themselves by going to the theatre, but for ministers to write a play and to attend it was unthinkable – the whole moral fabric of Scotland would collapse. John Home, minister of Athelstaneford, was determined to prove the moral majority wrong. His great ambition was to have one of his plays staged, and since he could not get it done in London he was determined to do it at home. Egged on by his friends, his tragedy Douglas *was produced on 14 December 1756. His friend and fellow minister Alexander Carlyle, another leading Enlightenment figure, plucked up his courage and attended a later performance. Needless to say, the Kirk was enraged.*

It was in the end of this Year 1756 that Douglas was first acted at Edinr. [Edinburgh], Mr Home had been unsuccessful in London the year before, but he had been introduc'd to the Duke of Argyle, and was well with Sir Gilbert Elliot, Mr Oswald of Dunnikier, and had the Favour of Friendship of Lord Milton here and all his Family; and it was at Last agreed among them That since Garrick [in London] could not yet be . . . with to get Douglas acted, that it should be brought on here, for if it succeeded on the Edinr. Theatre, Then Garrick could Resist no Longer.

The Play had unbounded Success for a Great Many Nights in Edinr. and was attended by all the Literati, and most of the Judges, who except one or two had not been in use to attend the Theatre. The Town in Gen. was in an uproar of Exultation, That a Scotchman had written a Tragedy of the First Rate, and that its Merit was first Submitted to their Judgment. There were a few Opposers however among those who pretended to Taste and Literature, who Endeavour'd to Cry Down the Performance in Libellous Pamphlets and Ballads, (for they Durst not attempt to oppose it in the Theatre itself), and were openly Countenanc'd by Robert Dundas of Arniston, at that time Lord Advocate, and all his Minions or Expectants. The High Flying Set, were unanimous against it, as they thought it a Sin for a Clergyman to write any Play, Let it be ever so Moral in its Tendency. Several Ballads and Pamphlets were publish'd on our side in answer to the Scurrili[ti]es against us, one of which was written by Adam Ferguson, and another by myself. Ferguson was Mild and Temperate, and besides other arguments Supported the Lawfullness and Use of Dramatick Writers, from the example of Scripture, which he Exhibited in the Story of Joseph and his Brethren, as having truly the Effect of a Dramatick Composition. This was much read among the Grave and Soberminded, and Converted Some, and Confirm'd Many in their Belief of the Usefullness of the Stage. Mine was of such

a Different Nature, That many people read it at First as Intended to
Ridicule the Performance, and bring it into Contempt. For it was
Entitled, An Argument to Prove, that the Tragedy of Douglas, Ought
to be Publickly Burnt by the Hands of the Hangman. The Zeal and
Violence of the Presbytery of Edinr., who had made Enactments, and
Declarations to be read in the Pulpit provok'd me to Write this
Pamphlet, which in the Ironical Manner of Swift, Contain'd a Severe
Satire on all our Opponents. This was so well Conceal'd however,
That the Pamphlet being publish'd when I was at Dumfries about the
End of January visiting Provost Bell who was on his Deathbed, some
Copies arriv'd there by the Carrier, which being open'd and Read by
my Sister and Aunt when I was abroad, they conceiv'd it to be Serious,
and that the Tragedy would be quite Undone, till Mr Stewart the
Controller of the Customs, who was a Man of Sense and Reading,
came in, who soon undecievd them, and convincd them that Douglas
was Triumphant, This Pamphlet had a Great Effect, by Elating our
Friends, and perhaps more in exasperating our Enemies. Which was
by no Means Soften'd by Ld Elibank and David Hume &c. Running
about and Crying it up as the first performance the World had seen
for half a Century.

What I really Valued myself most upon how[eve]r was half a sheet
which I pen'd very suddenly. Diggs rode out one forenoon to me
Saying, That he had come by Mr Home's Desire to Inform me, that
all the Town had seen the Play, and that it could run no Longer,
unless some Contrivance was fallen upon to make the Lower Orders
of Tradesmen and apprentices come to the Playhouse. After Hearing
several ways of raising the Curiosity of the Lower Orders, I Desir'd
him to take a walk for half an Hour, and Look at the View from
Inveresk Church Yard, which he Did; and in the mean time, I Drew
up what I Entitled, A full and True History of the Bloody Tragedy
of Douglas, as it is now to be seen acting at the Theatre in the
Cannongate. This was cried about the Streets Next Day, and fill'd
the House for 2 nights more.

I had attended the Playhouse not on the 1st or 2d but on the 3d
night of the Performance, being well aware that all the Fanaticks,
and some other Enemies, would be on the Watch, and make all the
Advantage they possibly could against me. But 6 or 7 Friends of the
Authors, Clergymen from the Merse, having attended, who
Reproachd me for my Cowardice, and above all the Author himself,
and some Female Friends of his, having Heated me by their
upbraidings, I went on the 3d night, and having taken Charge of the

Ladies, I drew on myself all the Clamour of Tongues, and Violence of Prosecution which I afterwards underwent. Every thing relating to this is pretty Correctly Narated in the Scotch Mage. [magazine] for the Year 1757. I believe I have already mention'd that Dr. Pat. Cuming having become Jealous of Wm. Robertson and John Home and myself on acct. of our Intimacy with Ld Milton, and Observing his Active Zeal about the Tragedy of Douglas, took into his Head that he could blow us up, and Destroy our Popularity, and Consequently Disgust Ld Milton with us. Very Warmly with all the Friends he could Get to follow him, particularly Hyndman his second, [he] Join'd with Webster and his Party, in Doing every thing they could to Depretiate the Tragedy of Douglas, and Disgrace all its Partisans. With this View besides the Act of the Presbytery of Edinr. which was Read in all the Churches, and that of the Presby. of Glasgow who follow'd them, [they] had Decoy'd Mr Thos. Whyte Minister of Liberton, who had attended the Play, Honest by a Quiet Man, to Submit to a Six Weeks Suspension for his having attended the Tragedy of Douglas, which he had Confest he had done. This they Contriv'd as an Example for prosecuting me, and at least of getting a Similar Sentence pronounc'd against me by the Presbytery of Dalkeith. On Returning from Dumfries in the 2d Week of Feby. [1757] I was surpris'd to find not only the amazing Hue and Cry that had been Rais'd against Douglas but all the Train that had been laid against me, and a summons to attend the Presbytery to answer for my Conduct on the 1st Day of March.

Alexander Carlyle, *Anecdotes and Characters of the Times*, ed. James Kinsley, Oxford, 1973.

The Siege of Quebec

Back to Scotland's useful human exports: after the shock of the 1745 Jacobite uprising, the British army became convinced that Highlanders might make excellent troops on the government side. Soldiering was a prestigious occupation in the Gaedhealtachd. With the land often stretched to feed its people, taking the king's shilling was one way of keeping body and soul together, at least temporarily. A career in the army was just as attractive to the younger sons of impoverished lairds as it was to their tenants. Donald Cameron of the Fassiefern family was one of those who paid for his commission and went abroad with his regiment to try his luck. He arrived in America in time to be present at the decisive siege of Quebec under General Wolfe, who famously died there in

the moment of victory. Donald Cameron had more practical things
on his mind, however: a neighbouring Highlander from back home
had died and there was a valuable gold watch to be considered.
Here is his account of the battle and of the precarious financial
situation of a young Highland officer in Canada.

My Dear Brother,

This is my first letter to you since I left Greenock and the reason
is because I had nothing to say till now. We arrived at Virginia
the twentieth of June 1758 after a long and tedious pasage and from
Virginia we were ordered for York, and from York up the river to
Albany, where we parted with Captain Campbell's componay
[company], then we were ordered down that same river to York
again and from York to Luisbrough [Louisburgh] up the river Sant
Lawrence to the sage [siege] of Quebeck. We arrived in camp before
Quebeck September the 3 and we came time enowch to see
everything that was done and one of the most glorious battles that
ever was fought in America, General Wolf Comander in Chief of our
army ordored us all up the river above the town; for the town lies
on the side of a hill and close to the river and on the 13 we landed
on the other side and that with little or no loss. After we landed we
got our men drawn up on the top of the hill in the order of battle.
General Montcalum [Montcalm] as soon as he heard of our landing
ordored all his troops, that wer encamped at Bewport to march and
drive us off, and he himself cam[e] along with them, but great was
his surprise when he saw us drawn up in the order of battle and
ready to receive him, upon which he drew up his men and began the
attack. He gave us three full fires befor we returned the complement
but our second fire brok[e] the enemy and put [them] in the greatest
confusion imagenable. They advanced within baynoet [bayonet]
length of us before they gave way, we pursued them up the very
walls. The army in general behaved themselves with extraordinary
spirit but without partiality our regiment did there part attacking
with their broad swords and pursuing them into the very city. You
may consider what pleasure we took in pursuing those rascalls, a
great deal more than a few writer [solicitor] lads would take about
[devouring] a dozen of rolls and a quart of ale. But for our comfor[t]
an[d] after this glorious victory we have got Quebeck for our winter
quarters and I asure you I would look as well to be on the top of
Benevas [Ben Nevis], but I wish the foluing [following] news was as
good as the former. The very day that I arrived here, which was the
3 of September, Dungalon dyd [died]. I came time enouch to see him

interd [buried] and that was all. Hew Cameron who is now Capt[ain] took care of all his things and saw everything rouped [sold] but his silver hilted sword and good wa[t]ch and ring. I have his ring at present till such time as Glendesary [Glendessary – another local gentleman] calls for it but I hope I will get [it] [back] from Glendesary, which if I do I will send it home to you. I suppose Glendesary himself goes home this winter, which if he does you can see him yourself and perhaps get the gold wa[t]ch for Glendesery has one of his own. I have also got a very pretty fusi [fusil = musket] mounted with silver, which if I had an opportunity I would send home to you. I took it off the field of battle. There is a great deal of promotion now in our regiment. Ronald Macdonald Cappock [Keppoch] has got a company and so has Hugh Cameron and Glengarays brother is Captain Lieutenant and I am now of Capt. Cameron's componay, for the officers are put into different componys. I am very sorry that I am obleged to trouble my father with that bill of 40 pound but I assure you, dear Ewen, that I was obleged to do it, or if I had not done it I would be obleged to sell out rather than to be put under stopages at 18d per diem [18 pence per day] when my whole pay is but 36 for we don't get arrears in this country and if my father will be so indulgent as to say I assure you it will be the last of the kind that ever I will truble him with and I believe after the first year is over that I can lay by a little money and I assure you although I take 6 years to make up the sum to my father that I will do it. [scored out: for things are so very dear hear that it would at most take up a subaltern's pay to...] I have no more to truble you with but I am

My Dear Ewen
your very affectionat
brother Donald Cameron
Quebek
October the 30 1759.
PS. Capt Cameron desires to be rememberd

'Cameron of Fassiefern', Acc. 11157/41.

Death and David Hume

Two of the most famous late 18th-century Scots were James Boswell and David Hume. Convivial, but neurotic, Boswell was the biographer, friend and admirer of Samuel Johnston, compiler of the first English Dictionary and arbiter of literary taste down

south. David Hume was the philosopher who dared to expose the
fatal flaws in some of the most popular and generally accepted
arguments for the existence of God. He rubbished the argument
that the study of nature showed that it must have an intelligent
creator. He attacked belief in miracles. To his disappointment, his
most biting treatises seemed to make little impact on the society
around him – but his ideas had an impact on someone. Poor
Boswell suffered from DOUBT, which he was always trying to
assuage. The atheism of one of the most brilliant minds in Scotland
was a horror to him. Here is Boswell's own account of his
interview with Hume on the latter's death bed in 1776.

An Account of my Last Interview with David Hume, Esq.

Partly recorded in my Journal, partly enlarged from my memory,
3 March 1777

On Sunday forenoon the 7 of July 1776, being too late for
church, I went to see Mr David Hume, who was returned from
London and Bath, just adying. I found him alone, in a reclining
posture in his drawing-room. He was lean, ghastly, and quite of an
earthy appearance. He was dressed in a suit of grey cloth with white
metal buttons, and a kind of scratch wig. He was quite different
from the plump figure which he used to present. He had before him
Dr. Campbell's *Philosophy of Rhetoric*. He seemed to be placid and
even cheerful. He said he was just approaching to his end. I think
these were his words. I know not how I contrived to get the subject
of immortality introduced. He said he never had entertained any
belief in religion since he began to read Locke and Clarke. I asked
him if he was not religious when he was young. He said he was, and
he used to read *The Whole Duty of Man*; that he made an abstract
from the catalogue of vices at the end of it, and examined himself by
this, leaving out murder and theft and such vices as he had no
chance of committing, having no inclination to commit them. This,
he said, was strange work; for instance, to try if, notwithstanding his
excelling his schoolfellows, he had no pride or vanity. He smiled in
ridicule of this as absurd and contrary to fixed principles and
necessary consequences, not adverting that religious discipline does
not mean to extinguish, but to moderate, the passions; and certainly
an excess of pride or vanity is dangerous and generally hurtful. He
then said flatly that the morality of every religion was bad, and, I
really thought, was not jocular when he said that when he heard a

man was religious, he concluded he was a rascal, though he had known some instances of very good men being religious. This was just an extravagant reverse of the common remark as to infidels.

I had a strong curiosity to be satisfied if he persisted in disbelieving a future state even when he had death before his eyes. I was persuaded from what he now said, and from his manner of saying it, that he did persist. I asked him if it was not possible that there might be a future state. He answered it was possible that a piece of coal put upon the fire would not burn; and he added that it was a most unreasonable fancy that we should exist for ever. That immorality, if it were at all, must be general; that a great proportion of the human race has hardly any intellectual qualities; that a great proportion dies in infancy before being possessed of reason; yet all these must be immortal; that a porter who gets drunk by ten o'clock with gin must be immortal; that the trash of every age must be preserved, and that new universes must be created to contain such infinite numbers. This appeared to me an unphilosophical objection, and I said, 'Mr. Hume, you know spirit does not take up space'.

I may illustrate what he last said by mentioning that in a former conversation with me on this subject he used pretty much the same mode of reasoning, and urged that Wilkes and his mob must be immortal. One night last May as I was coming up King Street, Westminster, I met Wilkes, who carried me into Parliament Street to see a curious procession pass: the funeral of a lamplighter attended by some hundreds of his fraternity with torches. Wilkes, who either is, or affects to be, an infidel, was rattling away, 'I think there's an end of that fellow. I think he won't rise again.' I very calmly said to him, 'You bring into my mind the strongest argument that ever I heard against a future state'; and then told him David Hume's objection that Wilkes and his mob must be immortal. It seemed to make a proper impression, for he grinned abashment, as a Negro grows whiter when he blushes. But to return to my last interview with Mr Hume.

I asked him if the thought of annihilation never gave him any uneasiness. He said not the least; no more than the thought that he had not been, as Lucretius observes. 'Well,' said I, 'Mr Hume, I hope to triumph over you when I meet you in a future state; and remember you are not to pretend that you was joking with all this infidelity.' 'No, no,' said he. 'But I shall have been so long there before you come that it will be nothing new.' In this style of good humour and levity did I conduct the conversation. Perhaps it was wrong on so awful a subject. But as nobody was present, I thought it could have no bad effect. I however felt a degree of horror, mixed with a sort of wild, strange, hurrying recollection of my excellent mother's pious instructions, of Dr. Johnson's noble lessons, and of my religious sentiments and affections during the course of my life. I was like a man in sudden danger eagerly seeking his defensive arms; and I could not but be assailed by momentary doubts while I had actually before me a man of such strong abilities and extensive inquiry dying in the persuasion of being annihilated. But I maintained my faith. I told him that I believed the Christian religion as I believed history. Said he: 'You do not believe it as you believe the Revolution'. 'Yes,' said I; 'but the difference is that I am not so much interested in the truth of the Revolution; otherwise I should have anxious doubts concerning it. A man who is in love has doubts of the affection of his mistress, without cause.' I mentioned Soame Jenyns's little book in defence of Christianity, which was just published but which I had not yet read. Mr. Hume said, 'I am told there is nothing of his usual spirit in it.'

He had once said to me, on a forenoon while the sun was shining bright, that he did not wish to be immortal. This was a most wonderful thought. The reason he gave was that he was very well in this state of being, and that the chances were very much against his being so well in another state; and he would rather not be more than be worse. I answered that it was reasonable to hope he would be better; that there would be a progressive improvement. I tried him at this interview with that topic, saying that a future state was surely a pleasing idea. He said no, for that it was always seen through a gloomy medium; there was always a Phlegethon or a hell. 'But,' said I, 'would it not be agreeable to have hopes of seeing our friends again?' and I mentioned three men lately deceased, for whom I knew he had a high value: Ambassador Keith, Lord Alemoor, and Baron Mure. He owned it would be agreeable, but added that none of them entertained such a notion. I believe he said, such a foolish, or such an absurd, notion; for he was indecently and impolitely positive in incredulity. 'Yes,' said I, 'Lord Alemoor was a believer.' David acknowledged that he had some belief.

I somehow or other brought Dr. Johnson's name into our conversation. I had often heard him speak of that great man in a very illiberal manner. He said upon this occasion, 'Johnson should be pleased with my *History*.' Nettled by Hume's frequent attacks upon my revered friend in former conversations, I told him now that

Dr. Johnson did not allow him much credit; for he said, 'Sir, the fellow is a Tory by chance.' I am sorry that I mentioned this at such a time. I was off my guard; for the truth is that Mr. Hume's pleasantry was such that there was no solemnity in the scene; and death for the time did not seem dismal. It surprised me to find him talking of different matters with a tranquility of mind and a clearness of head which few men possess at any time. Two particulars I remember: Smith's *Wealth of Nations*, which he commended much, and Monboddo's *Origin of Language*, which he treated contemptuously. I said, 'If I were you, I should regret annihilation. Had I written such an admirable history, I should be sorry to leave it.' He said, 'I shall leave that history, of which you are pleased to speak so favourably, as perfect as I can.' He said, too, that all the great abilities with which men had ever been endowed were relative to this world. He said he became a greater friend to the Stuart family as he advanced in studying for his history; and he hoped he had vindicated the two first of them so effectually that they would never again be attacked.

Mr. Lauder, his surgeon, came in for a little, and Mr. Mure, the Baron's son, for another small interval. He was, as far as I could judge, quite easy with both. He said he had no pain, but was wasting away. I left him with impressions which disturbed me for some time.

(ADDITIONS FROM MEMORY 22 JANUARY 1778.) Speaking of his singular notion that men of religion were generally bad men, he said, 'One of the men' (or 'The man' – I am not sure which) 'of the greatest honour that I ever knew is my Lord Marischal, who is a downright atheist. I remember I once hinted something as if I believed in the being of a God, and he would not speak to me for a week.' He said this with his usual grunting pleasantry, with that thick breath which fatness had rendered habitual to him, and that simile of simplicity which his good humour constantly produced.

When he spoke against Monboddo, I told him that Monboddo said to me that he believed the abusive criticism upon his book in *The Edinburgh Magazine and Review* was written by Mr. Hume's direction. David seemed irritated, and said, 'Does the *scoundrel*' (I am sure either *that* or '*rascal*') 'say so?' He then told me that he had observed to one of the Faculty of Advocates that Monboddo was wrong in his observation that [   ] and gave as a proof the line in Milton. When the review came out, he found this very remark in it, and said to that advocate, 'Oho! I have discovered you' – reminding him of the circumstance.

It was amazing to find him so keen in such a state. I must add one other circumstance which is material, as it shows that he perhaps was not without some hope of a future state, and that his spirits were supported by a consciousness (or at least a notion) that his conduct had been virtuous. He said, 'If there were a future state, Mr. Boswell, I think I could give as good an account of my life as most people.'

Boswell in Extremes 1776-8, eds. C. McC. Weis and F. Pottle, London, 1971.

John Paul Jones

'The Father of the American Navy', as he was known, was born plain John Paul, son of a gardener in Kirkbean, Kircudbrightshire. He became involved first in the slave trade and then in smuggling, before he inherited an estate in Virginia. In the American Revolution, Scots in the New World found themselves forced to take sides. Some, such as Flora Macdonald, whose family had emigrated, chose to back King George and to support the loyalist cause (a very ironic decision in her case). Others, such as John Paul, backed the rebels and the cause of independence.

Under the assumed name of Jones, he was given a commission in the continental navy. By June 1777 he was in command of the Ranger, a new frigate with which he sailed the Atlantic, to carry on the war against British trade. Cruising British waters soon brought him back to his old boyhood haunts. He led raids on Whitehaven Harbour and St Mary's Isle in Kirkcudbrightshire. The Caledonian Mercury *reported the results.*

Kirkcudbright, April 23, twelve o'clock noon.

This morning, about ten o'clock, an American privateer, thought to be about 20 guns, appeared in this bay, and have plundered the house of St Mary Isle, the seat of the Earl of Selkirk, within a mile of Kirkcudbright, of all the silver-plate, &c. We expect a visit from them on the return of the tide, as they still hover in our bay. We are not in a state of defence, nor do we believe any thing effectual can be done, unless some of the King's ships had notice of them. If you had any troops, we should be much the better of them; but I suppose all our injury will be over before you can assist us. Give notice to any person you think in danger. The vessel is three masted, or ship rigged, I am, Sir,

Your most obedient humble servant,
JOHN MURDOCH.

Extract of a letter from Dumfries, April 24.

As you will be anxious to hear of the rumours of yesterday, which may have reached you from this place, I will shortly give you an account of them. – Yesterday afternoon, an express arrived from Kirkcudbright, with accounts, that an American privateer of 20 guns had landed near the Isle (St Mary's); and that a party from her had plundered Lord Selkirk's house. Two or three hours after, came another express from Carlisle, desiring the instant forwarding of expresses with packets, which were sent, to Glasgow and Port Patrick. The letter from Carlisle contained no more than that an express had arrived at Carlisle from Whitehaven, intimating that the *French had landed.* Mrs Wood, Lady of the late Governor of the Isle of Man, at present residing here, had gone two or three days ago, on a visit to Lady Selkirk, and returned here last night. She informs that they were all well, and in good spirits; and says, that yesterday morning, between ten and eleven, a servant brought word that a pressgang had landed near the house. This the party from the privateer had given out, in order, as was supposed, to get out of the way all the servants and others who might oppose them. Presently between 30 and 40 armed men came up, all of whom planted themselves round the house, except three, who entered, each with two horse pistols at his side; and with bayonets fixed, they demanded to see the Lady of the house; and upon her appearing, told her, with a mixture of rudeness and civility, who they were, and that all the plate must be delivered to them. Lady Selkirk behaved with great composure and presence of mind. She soon directed her plate to be delivered, with which, without doing any other damage, or asking for watches, jewels, or any thing else, (which is odd); the gentleman made off. Something, however, had been said about their returning; and the Kirkcudbright people were in expectation of a visit last night. There is reason to think that there were some people among them acquainted with persons and places, and in particular one fellow, supposed to have been once a waiter at an inn in Kirkcudbright. The leader of the party, who was not the Captain of the vessel, told, that their intention was to seize Lord Selkirk, who is now in London; that two other privateers were at hand; and that they had been at Whitehaven, where they had burnt some small vessels, but did not get done what they intended. When the affair was ended Lady S. with her family and visitors, left the house. Her Ladyship remained last night at Carlingwork, in order to be near information.

Extract of a letter from Dumfries, April 23.

A gentleman who left Whitehaven this morning, informs, that a privateer, of about 260 tons burden, landed two boats crews of 20 men at Whitehaven, about half past one this morning, and called at Nicol Alison's, the first public-house, standing alone on the quay; struck a light, and guarded the house, that there should be no information; went to the battery, and spiked the guns; then proceeded with combustibles they brought in the boats, to the ships in all parts of the harbour, in number at present about 100. One man of the crew happily deserted, and gave the earliest intimation to the town, who, upon oath, declares, that there are other two armed ships in the Channel; and the commission of the Captains is, to do all the damage possible, both by sea and land; that the Captain of said vessel is John –, late in Scotland; that they came from France, (Nantz, if I remember right) and consist of Americans, French, Irish, and British; that, to his knowledge, they had sunk three vessels in the Channel a few days past, and sent one to France; that the crew of said vessel consists of 150 men. The said crew that landed, carried away four lads that were guarding their ships. The town was not fully alarmed till five in the morning. About that time the two boats left the harbour, and made for their ships. The guns were prepared to bear upon her by six o'clock; but she was by that time lying two miles off, and they could do her no injury. When three guns were fired, she changed her course, and steered toward the Scots shore. About half past ten, she was out of sight, steering, as was apprehended, to the Kirkcudbright shore. Expresses were sent to London, Liverpool, &c. and a cutter was dispatched towards Ireland, to give information to the frigates lying in the Belfast loch, and other ports in the Channel. During their fray at Whitehaven, they set fire to eight ships; but two of them only suffered materially, and the loss is computed to about 600 L. [£600]

Caledonian Mercury, 25 April 1778.

Enlightenment Edinburgh

Edinburgh was changing in many ways – for instance, the building of the beautiful New Town, the founding of learned societies, and the anglicisation of its manners. At the same time the city's more commercially orientated rival, Glasgow, was also home to Enlightenment figures of the first magnitude, such as the economist Adam Smith mentioned below. Henry Mackenzie, the Scots novelist and author of The Man of Feeling *was an Edinburgh man. Here he tries to convey the magnitude of the changes to William Carmichael, ambassador to Spain of the newly fledged American republic. The recent American Revolution led to discussion of the most radical ideas in some circles but not in Mackenzie's.*

His letter hinted at these political stirs but he refused to get involved in such debates – perhaps he regarded them as either beneath the notice of intellectuals or simply as dangerous matters. Despite the fact that he was writing in 1781 when Britain was still at war with the US, he wrote to Carmichael as a friend and countryman, rather than to an enemy diplomat.

Scotland in the language of MacDuff 'stands as it did', yet its manners are somewhat alter'd in the progress of Refinement and that dissipated sort of state to which the whole of our country I am sorry to be obliged to say has been verging this some time past. Edinburgh as the Capital of Scotland has felt the influence of this in a more immediate and strong degree and the communication with London is now so constant that the manners of the one town are a transcript (a little later only in progress and a little fainter in the copy) of the other. On the external of Edinburgh there is a wonderfull change since you last saw it. The New Town built on the ground to the North Side of the North Loch which we used to walk over under the name of Barefoots Parks, Mutrees Hill etc. is covered with regular and splendid buildings; the luxury of living increased in every department is in none so much augmented as in the article of houses. Where you remember our judges and people of the first rank lodged, now you would find shopkeepers and tradesmen.

I cannot just say so much for the improvement of our Scottish literature. The brilliant era seems rather to be past, tho the talent of writing as well as the idea of publication is now become infinitely more universal that it was 20 or 30 years ago. But we have lost D[avid] Hume and his namesake Kames; Dr Robertson I rather incline to think has now (having got the Congesta Cibaria) dedicated the rest of his life to ease and will not write. Fergusson has given the world lately an important work, a history of the rise and fall of the Roman Republic. Of this there are different opinions but the most prevalent is rather not so high as the former character of the author would have led people to form. He has treated the subject rather in a narrative than in a reflective way and has been sparing of the general and philosophic views of the subject which is a great distinction between modern history since the time of Montesquie and the ancients. His stile in this work is very different from that of his former being studiously simple and unadorn'd even sometimes to a degree of coarse incorrectness, instead of the pompous rich and sometimes I think bombastic periods of his essay on the History of Civil society. Dr Blair has at last published his lectures on Rhetoric and Belles Lettres, which I think very good, both in point of criticism and taste, tho perhaps not so original and deep as the metaphysical enquiring turn of this age might have required. This book, however has not had a success equal to the expectations of the booksellers or nearly as great as his sermons had, which run thro' 9 or 10 editions. Dr [Adam] Smith whom I reckon the first of our writers both in point of genius and information is now revising both his theory of moral sentiments and his Essay on the Wealth of Nations in the new editions of both which (to be published in the spring) there will be considerable alteration and improvements. He has lying by him several essays, some finish'd but the greater part I believe not yet quite completed, on subjects of criticism and Belles Lettres which when he chuses to give them to the world will I am confident no wise derogate from his former reputation as an author.

After the mention of such great names, it were presumption to talk of myself, were it not that I know your friendship will make you interested in the subject. There was published in the year 1779 and 1780, a performance of a kind quite novel here, a periodical work after the manner of the Spectator of which I had the conduct, entitled the Mirror which the public have since its publication in the form of volumes stamped with an approbation beyond my most sanguine expectation, as it has already gone thro' 5 editions. Edinburgh was a theatre rather narrow for a publication of this kind; but it was of a kind from which I derived considerable amusement as the editor and in which I had such assistants as render'd it a work peculiarly agreeable to me. This work, as sometimes peculiarly relating to the manners of a country which I know you retain a warm remembrance, I wish to send you a copy of, if I could contrive the means how a copy can go transmitted to you and I will give orders to Mr Cadell my bookseller for the purpose; or if you have any correspondent at London by whose channel you could get it, I will desire him to deliver one to him for you.

An event in the literary history of Scotland, of which you will like to be acquainted and of which perhaps Mr Liston may have already informed you is the late establishment of the Royal Society at

Edinburgh which includes 2 branches a physical for subjects of Chemestry, natural history etc. and a literary for those of criticism philology and Belles Lettres. It includes all the celebrated names of this country in both departments and several illustrious ones of other nations as non resident members of whom your great [Benjamin] Franklin is one. The meetings hitherto except the last have only been for the purpose of adjusting the form and regulations of the society. One or two essays have been read; the society means to give an annual volume of such of those as are thought best fitted for publication. How they may succeed in this I know not; mean time it brings together the literary men of this country and gives something of an additional energy to the enquirys of the learn'd and ingenious.

But the voice of the muses is at present drown'd in the debates of politics and the clamour of party. The extraordinary occurrences in our parliament must be the subject of speculation in every part of Europe. I will say no more of them than what any good citizen may safely say that the conjuncture is of a nice kind for the constitution, the great leading points of which it is perhaps dangerous to probe too nearly – and when they come into discussion betwixt contending parties, there is great hazard that either the one or the other gains too much for the safety of the people.

'Henry Mackenzie to William Carmichael 1781', MS. 646, ff.3-4.

Thomas Muir

Scots radical Thomas Muir was a great supporter of both the American and French Revolutions and a proponent of far-reaching parliamentary reform in Great Britain. Born in Glasgow, he studied to become an advocate – not the Scots profession most readily linked with radicalism, but Muir was a man of a different stamp from most of his fellows at the Edinburgh bar. He was active in spreading the London Society of the Friends of the People to Scotland. This was a pressure group for parliamentary reform, but in the wake of the beginnings of the French Revolution, any demands for reform were enough to cause government hysteria. Muir read an address from the United Irishmen – another radical group – which led the government to accuse him of sedition. To make matters worse, he then set off on a fraternal visit to France, on behalf of the Friends of the People, to plead against the execution of Louis XVI. He arrived too late to make any difference and instead busied himself in making political and intellectual contacts in France. He was outlawed in Edinburgh and returned home to be tried on sedition charges.

The result was a highly politicised trial in which Muir was found
guilty of distributing and recommending Thomas Paine's radical
work The Rights of Man. *He was sentenced to fourteen years*
transportation to Botany Bay, a penal colony from which he had a
remarkable but arduous escape (which he did not long survive).
Here is the account from the Gazette Nationale – *the primary*
newspaper of the French Revolution – of his escape and his arrival
in France in 1797.

The celebrated Scot Thomas Muir, escaped from a thousand
dangers is on the point of arriving in Paris. His transportation
belongs to the history of revolutions; his courage in the face of
adversity must serve as an example to the converts of philosophy
and the happy issue of all his misfortunes must encourage all the
martyrs of liberty.

The Scots have never forgotten their ancient independence, the
massacre of their ancestors, the tragic death of their last Queen, the
expulsion of the Stuarts from the throne of Great Britain: these
memories, the consciousness of their want, the shocking contrast of
English luxury, perhaps finally the example of our revolution, were
the causes of the revolutionary movements which appeared in
Scotland in 1792, in which Thomas Muir played one of the premier
roles.

The secret committees which had been formed throughout the
whole of Scotland unmasked themselves all at once. They sent
delegates to Edinburgh who met together in a national convention
with the avowed goal of obtaining parliamentary reform. Thomas
Muir, enlightened thinker and impassioned orator was a member of
this convention and left his mark on it. The British government
deeply alarmed by the sudden meeting of this assembly, at once
dispersed it. Many members were arrested and brought to trial in
1794, some of them, amongst others one named Jackson, were
condemned to death; Thomas Muir and three others were deported
to Botany Bay.

The uprising in Scotland gave great hopes to our revolutionary
government; the hopes evaporated; but the republicans of France,
who saw in the Edinburgh convention only the friends of liberty,
interested themselves deeply in their fate. When the old committee
of public safety learnt of the deportation of Muir and many of his
companions, it sent out several frigates to rescue them, but they did
not succeed and these unfortunates were left on the desolate shore
of New Holland [Australia] Botany Bay: the vast tomb where the

British government indiscriminately heaps together the most vile scoundrels and brave thinkers against whom it has taken umbrage.

It was there that Thomas Muir, treated as a criminal for having wanted the liberty of his native land, was to end his days, but one often says and I repeat with a sort of devout credulity: a benevolent spirit watches over the friends of man and the destiny of free peoples. Such a guardian angel took an interest in our unfortunate philanthropist, an American boat landed in this place of despair. Thomas Muir was received on board and conducted to the North West coast of America, but there he met new dangers, an English warship left Botany Bay several days before the American, and anchored in the same waters. Muir was in danger of being discovered and recaptured. To escape his persecutors once more, he resolved to traverse the continent of America: a terrifying enterprise, for which he needed the courage of a hero and the resignation of a sage. Happily the Captain of a Spanish schooner which he found in the harbour of Nootka gave him passage to Saint Blas, at the mouth of the gulf of California. As soon as he arrived Muir wrote to the viceroy of Mexico asking for hospitality in the name of the Republic of France, friends of the King of Spain. His request was favourably accepted and he was permitted to cross Mexican territory. He arrived next at Havana. The governor of this colony, without giving reasons, treated the stranger as a prisoner of war. Captive for four months, Muir suffered the most horrible treatment. Such are the most part of the petty despots who govern the colonies of great powers, they demonstrate their authority on defenceless individuals and think that the arbitrary power they exercise makes them equal to their masters. Finally, Thomas Muir was put on board a frigate to be taken to Spain, but this wasn't the end of his misfortunes. When the frigate was about to enter Cadiz it was attacked by part of Jervis's squadron who were blockading the port. The English had been informed that Thomas Muir was on board this ship and they wanted to put an end to the escape of this famous republican. This made them very eager for combat. The Spaniards defended themselves bravely. Muir saw the captivity awaiting him and preferred death. He armed himself, he fought, he hurled himself into the midst of danger. He had the courage of despair. He was wounded in the face and fell bathed in his own blood. The frigate was forced to surrender to the English. Muir became the principal object of their search. The English were told that he had been killed in combat and thrown in the sea. He lay for six days in their custody without being recognised – due to the disfigurement of his wound. Finally persuaded that he was no more, the English returned him to shore with the other prisoners.

Transported to the hospital at Cadiz, Muir was recognised by a Frenchman. The consul of the republic hurried at once to see him and to offer him his condolences, help and testimony of his high regard.

Muir addressed to the Directory the tale of his adventures and solemnly declared that he adopted the Republic of France as his native land. He received a very favourable response from the government, which was all that he could desire. Since then he has considered himself our fellow-citizen, free in the universe. He waits only for his recovery to come to France.

David.

Translated by L. Yeoman from *Gazette Nationale ou le Moniteur Universel*, No 72, 2 December 1797

Paris 6th December
Thomas Muir arrived at Paris. The ministry of foreign affairs, at which he presented himself, received him with the regard due to his great character, the services which he rendered to liberty and the sufferings which he endured in defending this sacred cause.

Translated by L. Yeoman from *Gazette Nationale ou le Moniteur Universel*, No 77, 7 December 1797

Storm of Seringapatam

The Darien scheme had foundered, not only on its own inherent implausibility but also on the hostility of the deeply jealous East India Company. With the Union, times had changed. Scots could now find their way to the highest echelons of this formerly English bastion. Under the patronage of Henry Dundas, President of the Board of Control, more and more Scots sought their fortunes in India. As the Company, with the aid of both British regulars and its own private army, extended its territories and fought off the French, it also encountered serious local resistance. The most determined resistance came from Tipu Sultan of Mysore. Many Scots were involved in the final storming of his fortress, including Sir David Baird who was amongst the first to discover the body of the Sultan – a moment immortalised by Sir David Wilkie in his famous painting of the scene. Baird had been a prisoner in Tipu's dungeons for several years – making the moment especially sweet.

*This letter, however, is from an ordinary soldier in the 73rd
Highland foot regiment, Thomas Beveridge, who took part in the
action.*

Camp near Seringapatam, 12th June 1799

My Dear Mother,

I wrote you from Poonamalie on the 14th October last informing
you that there was a report of our taking the field against Tippoo –
The 73rd Regiment accordingly marched from Poonamalie on the
29th of December and arrived at the ground where the grand army
was to assemble on the 5th January. We marched for the enemy's
capital (Seringapatam) early in February and encamped opposite the
west side of that place on the 5th of April, when we in the night of
the same day began our attack on the enemy and on the 4th May the
garrison was stormed between the hours of one and two o'clock in
the afternoon.

About three o'clock in the morning of the 4th May the troops who
composed the assault, consisting of his Majesty's 12th, 33rd, 73rd
and 74th regiments, the flank companies of the Scotch Brigade and
Regiment de Meuron and a few battalions of Sepoys marched from
their lines to the works erected against Seringapatam, from which
our camp was distant about two miles. We remained in the trenches
till about one o'clock when orders were given to commence the
assault. We immediately rushed out of the entrenchments and
advanced about 400 yards to the breach, exposed to a most heavy
and continued discharge of fire arms and rockets of every
denomination, which killed and wounded a considerable number,
especially in crossing the river which runs round Seringapatam, the
bottom of which is composed of huge rocks which rendered the
passage very tedious and difficult. In some places the water did not
reach to our knees, and in others many were obliged to swim over,
by which means their ammunition was completely destroyed, so that
the bayonet was the only defence after getting up the breach which
was soon cleared of the enemy. After getting into the fort, one half
of the troops was ordered to scour the walls to the right and the
other those to the left, which was completely effected in about an
hour. After and during this time we had the good luck to supply
ourselves with ammunition belonging to Tippoo's troops, which we
found in great abundance.

Tippoo's body was found in the course of the afternoon in a
gateway amongst a vast number of his own people who were killed
in endeavouring to make their escape from the garrison. His two

sons who were hostages with Marquis Cornwallis were taken that evening and next morning the greater part of his army surrendered – the whole have since come in and all is now quiet.

Tippoo had a considerable body of French troops in his service who also gave themselves up and have since been sent off to Madras [as] prisoners of war, a number of deserters from our army during the former war and since gave themselves up, several of them are hanged.

The treasure found in Seringapatam in money and jewels is immense, but I believe very little of it will fall to the share of the lower ranks of the army. Be that as it may, we have totally destroyed a formidable and inveterate enemy and entirely disappointed the hopes of the French of deriving any assistance from this quarter in their attacks on the English settlement in India. I have been very well, considering the bad water, provisions and fatigue that we were exposed to during a long and tedious march and thanks be to God I did not receive the least hurt during the storm or siege. We expect to remain in this part of India for some months until the country is divided between the Nizam and the company.

Many men in the army made a great deal of money by plundering after the storm was over but instead of gaining anything, I have lost the only pair of shoes I had at the top of the breach . . .

Remember me to all friends and acquaintances and wishing that the Almighty may protect you . . . the earnest prayer of.

your affectionate son
Thomas Beveridge

'Thomas Beveridge's letter', Acc. 9250.

Food Riots in Glasgow

Meanwhile the shift from a predominantly agricultural economy to an urban and industrial one was bringing increased hardship for those forced off the land and into the factories. At the same time as Scotland's cities grew, their populations had to be fed. Despite recent improvements in agriculture, Scotland was still vulnerable to food scarcity which could lead to prices being driven up out of the reach of the pockets of the urban poor. In 1800, the result of one of these periods of shortage led to food riots in Glasgow. The following proclamation was issued.

LORD PROVOST AND MAGISTRATES OF THE CITY OF GLASGOW

A PROCLAMATION

WHEREAS, on Saturday the 15th. instant, a Mob of RIOTOUS and DISORDERLY PERSONS did, in an illegal and unwarrantable manner, assemble on the Streets of the said City, and (under the illegal pretext of searching for MEAL, POTATOES, and other ARTICLES of PROVISIONS, falsely alledged by them to be concealed) did commit many acts of outrage and depredation on the Property and Persons of the peacable Inhabitants; AND WHEREAS, it is the duty of every Inhabitant of this City to promote peace and good order, both in his Family and in the Community, and to prevent such disgraceful proceedings, as those before alluded to, whereby the misguided multitude run a risk of bringing upon themselves the calamities of famine, by intimidating Farmers and Dealers from supplying the City with Meal and other Articles of Provision.

The LORD PROVOST and MAGISTRATES Do therefore hereby intimate, their determined resolution to use every legal means in their power (by the most exemplary punishment of offenders) to prevent and suppress all TUMULTS and RIOTS within the City; And all Persons are strictly prohibited from assembling in crowds in the Streets and Lanes of the City, in the evenings and night time, as they shall answer at their highest peril; And Parents, Heads of Families and Masters, are enjoined to keep their Children, Apprentices and Servants, within doors after it is dark, as they will be considered accountable for their conduct, and liable for the consequences that may ensue.

During the Scarcity with which it has pleased God at present to visit Britain, and the other Countries of Europe, cheap Provisions cannot be expected; dearth, therefore, to a certain degree must be submitted to, with resignation to the Will of Heaven. All that human foresight can do, is to take measures to procure such Supplies of Provisions as will preclude the risk of absolute want. The Magistrates, in conjunction with the other respectable and opulent Inhabitants, are doing every thing in their power to avert that evil, and they have every reason to believe, that their endeavours will be crowned with success, unless they be counteracted by the folly and wickedness of a deluded rabble.

Finally, The Lord Provost and Magistrates do hereby declare, their determined resolution to support, protect, and encourage all Persons who shall contribute to the Supply of provisions necessary for the consumption of the City, and they do most earnestly entreat the Farmers and dealers in Corn, to bring their Grain to Market as speedily as they possibly can.

GIVEN AT GLASGOW, THIS 17TH DAY OF FEBRUARY, EIGHTEEN HUNDRED YEARS.

GOD SAVE THE KING.

'Proclamation, 17 February 1800', MS. 5390, f.307.

The Glasgow Courier *carried these reports.*

On Saturday last, a mob of disorderly persons, under pretence of searching for meal, &c alledged to be concealed in various part of the City, excited a considerable degree of alarm, but by the timely and spirited exertions of the Magistrates, they were soon dispersed, several persons apprehended, and order and tranquillity restored. *See proclamation.* The Magistrates, we understand, are at present busily employed in a precognition.

Glasgow Courier, 18 February 1800.

For the last three days the Magistrates have continued to take a precognition against the persons accused as accessory to the riot which took place here last Saturday evening, on account of provisions. Several persons suspected to be guilty, have been apprehended and imprisoned; and warrants have been issued for apprehending others on the same charge. The most speedy measures will be adopted for bringing those accused to a legal trial.

It gives us pleasure to observe, that two other vessels have arrived in the Clyde with oats; that oatmeal has fallen twopence per peck in Edinburgh market; and that the price of oats fell five shillings per boll in Haddington market on Friday last.

Yesterday, eggs were sold in our market at eight-pence per dozen; they were lately so high as fourteen-pence.

Amidst the present distress, the mind feels consolation in witnessing the various means adopted to relieve the necessitous. On this occasion, we cannot forbear noticing the benevolent intentions of the Directors of the Sacred Music Institution, by their appointing a Public Meeting for the behoof of the poor. The promoters of this laudable scheme, we trust will meet with every encouragement and support.

Glasgow Courier, 20 February 1800.

The Splendour and the Squalour: Early 19th-Century Scotland

There could be no greater contrast between the romantic, imaginary Scotland of Walter Scott's novels and the harsh conditions of many Scots of the time: working in the mills, in the subsistence economy of the Highlands or scraping a living in the great cities. The industrial and agricultural revolutions had improved living standards for many, yet as in all societies there were sharp contrasts: between the romantic and the industrial, royal visits and factory life, the diversions of the better-off and the vulnerability of the poor. Industrial Scotland became more troublesome with radical uprisings such as the 'Radical War' and clamours for reform. In the Highlands, voluntary emigration, forced eviction and, later, famine made serious inroads into Gaelic society and culture.

Clearances

The famous Sutherland clearances took place in the early years of the 19th century. Tenants (not very profitable) were evicted in favour of sheep runs (profitable). This was nothing new. The phenomenon of clearing had started well before then and continued throughout the first half of the 19th century. When Harriet Beecher Stowe, the well-meaning heroine of America's anti-slavery movement, came to visit Scotland in 1853, she took in the Sutherland estates on her tour. Her Uncle Tom's Cabin *was a best-seller in America, which helped to raise awareness of the plight of the Southern slaves. Her* Sunny Memories of Foreign Lands *was, unfortunately, a testimony to her naivety and gullibility in the face of Scotland's aristocracy.* Gloomy Memories of the Highlands *was Donald Macleod's outraged response. Macleod actually witnessed the events which Beecher Stowe was told about.*

MY DEAR C.:–

As to those ridiculous stories about the Duchess of Sutherland, which have found their way into many of the prints in America, one has only to be here, moving in society, to see how excessively absurd they are.

All my way through Scotland, and through England, I was associating, from day to day with people of every religious denomination, and every rank of life. I have been with dissenters and with churchmen; with the national Presbyterian church and the free Presbyterian; with Quakers and Baptists.

In all these circles I have heard the great and noble of the land freely spoken of and canvassed, and if there had been the least show of a foundation for any such accusations, I certainly should have heard it recognized in some manner. If in no other, such warm friends as I have heard speak would have alluded to the subject in the way of defence; but I have actually never heard any allusion of any sort, as if there was anything to be explained or accounted for.

As I have before intimated, the Howard family, to which the Duchess belongs, is one which has always been on the side of popular rights and popular reform. Lord Carlisle, her brother, has been a leader of the people, particularly during the time of the corn-law reformation, and she has been known to take a wide and generous interest in all these subjects. Everywhere that I have moved through Scotland and England I have heard her kindness of heart, her affability of manner, and her attention to the feelings of others spoken of as marked characteristics.

Imagine, then, what people must think when they find in respectable American prints the absurd story of her turning her tenants out into the snow, and ordering the cottages to be set on fire over their heads because they would not go.

One anecdote of the former Duke of Sutherland will show the spirit which has influenced the family in their management of the estate. In 1817, when there was much suffering on account of bad seasons, the Duke of Sutherland sent down his chief agent to look into the condition of the people, who desired the ministers of the parishes to send in their lists of the poor. To his surprise it was found that there were located on the estate a number of people who had settled there without leave. They amounted to four hundred and eight families, or two thousand persons; and though they had no legal title to remain where they were, no hesitation was shown in supplying them with food in the same manner with those who were tenants, on the sole condition that on the first opportunity they should take cottages on the sea-shore, and become industrious people. It was the constant object of the Duke to keep the rents of his poorer tenants at a nominal amount.

What led me more particularly to inquire into these facts was, that I received by mail, while in London, an account containing some of these stories, which had been industriously circulated in America. There were dreadful accounts of cruelties practised in the process of inducing the tenants to change their places of residence. The following is a specimen of these stories:-

'I was present at the pulling down and burning of the house of William Chisholm, Badinloskin, in which was lying his wife's mother, an old, bed-ridden woman of near one hundred years of age, none of the family being present. I informed the persons about to set fire to the house of this circumstance, and prevailed on them to wait till Mr. Sellar came. On his arrival I told him of the poor old woman being in a condition unfit for removal. He replied, 'The old witch! She has lived too long; let her burn.' Fire was immediately set to the house, and the blankets in which she was carried were in flames before she could be got out. She was placed in a little shed, and it was with great difficulty they were prevented from firing that also. The old woman's daughter arrived while the house was on fire, and assisted the neighbours in removing her mother out of the flames and smoke, presenting a picture of horror which I shall never forget, but cannot attempt to describe. She died within five days.'

With regard to this story, Mr. Loch, the agent, says, 'I must notice the only thing like a fact stated in the newspaper extract which you sent to me, wherein Mr. Sellar is accused of acts of cruelty towards some of the people. This Mr. Sellar tested, by bringing an action against the then sheriff substitute of the county. He obtained a verdict for heavy damages. The sheriff, by whom the slander was propagated, left the county. Both are since dead'.

Having, through Lord Shaftesbury's kindness, received the benefit of Mr. Loch's corrections to this statement, I am permitted to make a little further extract from his reply. He says, –

'In addition to what I was able to say in my former paper, I can now state that the Duke of Sutherland has received from one of the most determined opposers of the measure, who travelled to the north of Scotland as editor of a newspaper, a letter regretting all he had written on the subject, being convinced that he was entirely misinformed. As you take so much interest in the subject, I will conclude by saying that nothing could exceed the prosperity of the county during the past year; their stock, sheep, and other things sold at high prices; their crops of grain and turnips were never so good, and the potatoes were free from all disease: rents have been paid better than was ever known. As an instance of the improved habits of the farmers, no house is now built for them that they do not require a hot-bath and water-closets.'

From this long epitome you can gather the following results; first, if the system were a bad one, the Duchess of Sutherland had nothing to do with it, since it was first introduced in 1806, the same year her grace was born; and the accusation against Mr. Sellar dated in 1811, when her grace was five or six years old. The Sutherland arrangements were completed in 1819, and her grace was not married to the duke till 1823, so that, had the arrangement been the worst in the world, it is nothing to the purpose so far as she is concerned.

As to whether the arrangement is a bad one, the facts which have been stated speak for themselves. To my view it is an almost sublime instance of the benevolent employment of superior wealth and power in shortening the struggles of advancing civilization, and elevating in a few years a whole community to a point of education and material prosperity, which unassisted, they might never have obtained.

Harriet Beecher Stowe, *Sunny Memories of Foreign Lands*, London, 1854.

Here is part of Donald MacLeod's reply.

Letter IV.

In the month of March, 1814, a great number of the inhabitants of the parishes of Farr and Kildonan were summoned to give up their farms at the May term following, and, in order to ensure and hasten their removal with their cattle, in a few days after, the greatest part of the heath pasture was set to and burnt, by order of Mr. Sellar, the factor, who had taken these lands for himself. It is necessary to explain the effects of this proceeding. In the spring, especially when fodder is scarce, as was the case in the above year, the Highland cattle depend almost solely on the heather. As soon, too, as the grass begins to sprout about the roots of the bushes, the animals get a good bite, and are thus kept in tolerable condition. Deprived of this resource by the burning, the cattle were generally left without food, and this being the period of temporary peace, during Buonaparte's residence in Elba, there was little demand for good cattle, much less for these poor starving animals, who roamed about over their burnt pasture till a great part of them were lost, or sold for a mere trifle. The arable parts of the land were cropped by the outgoing tenants, as is customary, but the fences being mostly destroyed by the burning, the cattle of the incoming tenant were continually trespassing throughout the summer and harvest, and those who remained to look after the crop had no shelter; even watching being disallowed, and the people were hunted by the new herdsmen and their dogs from watching their own corn! As the spring had been severe, so the harvest was wet, cold, and disastrous for the poor people, who, under every difficulty, were endeavouring to secure the residue of their crops. The barns, kilns, and mills, except a few necessary to the new tenant, had, as well as the houses, been burnt or otherwise destroyed and no shelter left, except on the other side of the river, now overflowing its banks from the continual rains; so that, after all their labour and privations, the people lost nearly the whole of their crop, as they had already lost their cattle, and were thus entirely ruined.

But I must now go back to the May term and attempt to give some account of the ejection of the inhabitants; for to give anything like an adequate description I am not capable. If I were, the horrors of it would exceed belief.

The houses had been all built, not by the landlord as in the low country, but by the tenants or by their ancestors, and, consequently, were their property by right, if not by law. They were timbered chiefly with bog fir, which makes excellent roofing but is very inflammable: by immemorial usage this species of timber was considered the property of the tenant on whose lands it was found. To the upland timber, for which the laird or the factor had to be asked, the laird might lay some claim, but not so to the other sort, and in every house there was generally a part of both.

In former removals the tenants had been allowed to carry away this timber to erect houses on their new allotments, but now a more summary mode was adopted, by setting fire to the houses! The able-bodied men were by this time away after their cattle or otherwise engaged at a distance, so that the immediate sufferers by the general house-burning that now commenced were the aged and infirm, and the women and children. As the lands were now in the hands of the factor himself, and were to be occupied as sheep-farms, and as the people made no resistance, they expected at least some indulgence, in the way of permission to occupy their houses and other buildings till they could gradually remove, and meanwhile look after their growing crops. Their consternation, was, therefore, the greater when, immediately after the May term day, and about two months after they had received summonses of removal, a commencement was made to pull down and set fire to the houses over their heads! The old people, women, and others, then began to try to preserve the timber which they were entitled to consider as their own. But the devastators proceeded with the greatest celerity, demolishing all before them, and when they had overthrown the houses in a large tract of country, they ultimately set fire to the wreck. So that timber, furniture, and every other article that could not be instantly removed, was consumed by fire, or otherwise utterly destroyed.

These proceedings were carried on with the greatest rapidity as well as with most reckless cruelty. The cries of the victims, the confusion, the despair and horror painted on the countenances of the one party, and the exulting ferocity of the other, beggar all description. In these scenes Mr. Sellar was present, and apparently, (as was sworn by several witnesses at his subsequent trial), ordering and directing the whole. Many deaths ensued from alarm, from fatigue, and cold; the people being instantly deprived of shelter, and left to the mercy of the elements. Some old men took to the woods and precipices, wandering about in a state approaching to, or of absolute insanity, and several of them, in this situation, lived only a few days. Pregnant women were taken with premature labour, and several children did not long survive their sufferings. To these scenes I was an eye-witness, and am ready to substantiate the truth of my statements, not only by my own testimony, but by that of many others who were present at the time.

In such a scene of general devastation it is almost useless to particularize the cases of individuals – the suffering was great and universal. I shall, however, just notice a very few of the extreme cases which occur to my recollection, to most of which I was an eye-witness. John M'Kay's wife, Ravigill, in attempting to pull down her house, in the absence of her husband, to preserve the timber, fell through the roof. She was, in consequence, taken with premature labour, and in that state, was exposed to the open air and the view of the by-standers. Donald Munro, Garvott, lying in a fever, was turned out of his house and exposed to the elements. Donald Macbeath, an infirm and bed-ridden old man, had the house unroofed over him, and was, in that state, exposed to wind and rain till death put a period to his sufferings. I was present at the pulling down and burning of the house of William Chisholm, Badinloskin, in which was lying his wife's mother, an old bed-ridden woman of near 100 years of age, none of the family being present. I informed the persons about to set fire to the house of this circumstance, and prevailed on them to wait till Mr. Sellar came. On his arrival I told him of the poor old woman being in a condition unfit for removal. He replied, 'Damn her, the old witch, she has lived too long; let her burn.' Fire was immediately set to the house, and the blankets in which she was carried were in flames before she could be got out. She was placed in a little shed, and it was with great difficulty they were prevented from firing it also. The old woman's daughter arrived while the house was on fire, and assisted the neighbours in removing her mother out of the flames and smoke, presenting a picture of horror which I shall never forget, but cannot attempt to describe. She died within five days.

I could multiply instances to a great extent, but must leave to the reader to conceive the state of the inhabitants during this scene of general devastation, to which few parallels occur in the history of this or any other civilized country. Many a life was lost or shortened, and many a strong constitution ruined;– the comfort and social happiness of all destroyed; and their prospects in life, then of the most dismal kind, have, generally speaking, been unhappily realized.

Mr. Sellar was, in the year 1816, tried on an indictment for a part of these proceedings, before the circuit court of Justiciary at Inverness.

Letter V

. . . Can you, or any other believe, that a poor sinner like Donald M'Leod would be allowed for so many years to escape with impunity, had he been circulating and publishing calumnious absurd falsehoods against such personages as the House of Sutherland. No, I tell you, if money could secure my punishment, without establishing their own shame and guilt, that it would be considered well spent long ere now – they would eat me in penny pies if they could get me cooked for them.

I agree with you that the Duchess of Sutherland is a beautiful accomplished lady, who would shudder at the idea of taking a faggot or a burning torch in her hand, to set fire to the cottages of her tenants, and so would her predecessor, the first Duchess of Sutherland, her good mother; likewise would the late and present Dukes of Sutherland, at least I am willing to believe that they would. Yet it was done in their name, under their authority, to their knowledge, and with their sanction. The Dukes and Duchesses of Sutherland, and those of their depopulating order, had not, nor has any call to defile their pure hands in milder work than to burn people's houses; no, no, they had, and have plenty of willing tools at their beck to perform their dirty work. Whatever amount of humanity and purity of heart the late or the present duke and duchess may possess or be ascribed to them, we know the class of men from whom they selected their commissioners, factors and underlings. I knew every one of these wicked servants who ruled the Sutherland estate for the last fifty years, and I am justified in saying that the most skillful phrenologist and physiognomist that ever existed could not discern one spark of humanity in the whole of them, from Mr. Loch down to Donald Sgrios, or in other words, damnable Donald, the name by which he was known. The most part of those vile executors of the atrocities I have been describing are now dead, and to be feared but not lamented. But it seems the chief were left to give you all the information you required about British slavery and oppression. I have read from speeches delivered by Mr. Loch at public dinners among his own party, 'that he would never be satisfied until the Gaelic language and the Gaelic people would be extirpated root and branch from the Sutherland estate; yes, from the highlands of Scotland. He published a book, where he stated as a positive fact, that when he got the management of the Sutherland estate, that he found 408 families on the estate who never heard the name of Jesus,' – whereas I could make an oath that there were not at that time, and for ages prior to it, above two families within the limits of the county who did not worship that name, and holy Being every morning and evening. I know there are hundreds in the Canadas who will bear me out in this assertion. I was at the pulling down and burning of the house of William Chisholm, I got my hands burnt taking out the poor old woman from amidst the flames of her once comfortable though humble dwelling, and more horrifying and lamentable scene could scarcely be witnessed. I may say the skeleton of once a tall, robust, high cheek boned respectable woman, who had seen better days, who could neither hear, see, nor speak, without a tooth in her mouth, her cheek skin meeting in the centre, her eyes sunk out of sight in their sockets, her mouth wide open, her nose standing upright among smoke and flames, uttering piercing moans of distress and agony, in articulations from which could be only understood, oh, *Dhia, Dhia, tein, tein* – oh God, God, fire, fire. When she came to the pure air her bosom heaved to a most extraordinary degree, accompanied by a deep hollow sound from the lungs, comparable to the sound of thunder at a distance. When laid down upon the bare, soft, moss floor of the roofless shed, I will never forget the foam of perspiration which emitted and covered the pallid death-looking countenance. This was a scene, Madam, worthy of an artist's pencil, and of a conspicuous place on the stages of tragedy. Yet you call this a specimen of the ridiculous stories which found their way into respectable prints, because Mr. Loch, the chief actor, told you that Sellar, the head executive, brought an action against the sheriff and obtained a verdict for heavy damages. What a subterfuge; but it will now answer the purpose, *'the bed is too short to stretch yourself, and the covering too narrow and short to cover you.'* If you took your information and evidence upon which you founded your Uncle Tom's cabin from such discreditable sources, (as I said before), who can believe the one-tenth of your novel? I cannot. I have at my hand here the grand-child of the murdered old woman, who recollects well of the circumstance. I have not far from me a respectable man, an elder in the Free Church, who was examined as a witness at Sellar's trial, at the spring assizes of Inverness, 1816, which you will find narrated in letters four and five of my work. I think, Madam, had you the opportunity of seeing the scenes which I, and hundreds more, have seen, and see the ferocious appearance of the infamous gang, who constituted the burning party, covered over face and hands with soot and ashes of the burning houses, cemented by torch grease and their own sweat, kept continually drunk or half drunk, while at work; and to observe the hellish amusements some of them would get up for themselves and for an additional pleasure to their leaders. The people's houses were generally built upon declivities, and in many cases not far from pretty steep precipices, they preserved their meal in tight made boxes, or chests, as they were called; when this fiendish party found any quantity of meal, they would carry it between them to the brink, and dispatch it down the precipice amidst shrieks and yells; this was considered grand sport to see the box breaking to atoms and the meal mixed with the air. When they would set fire to a house, they would watch any of the domestic animals making their escape from the flames, such as dogs, cats, hens or any poultry, these were caught and thrown back to the flames; grand sport for demons in human form. I assure you the Dukes and Duchesses of Sutherland had no need to try their hand in burning houses while James Loch, William Young, Patrick Sellar, Francis Suther, John Horseburgh, Captain Kenneth McKay, and Angus Leslie were alive, nor while George Loch, George Gunn, and Robt. Horseburgh, &c., is alive. Mr. Sellar (as I said before) was brought to trial for culpable homicide and fire-raising; and those dog, cat, and hen murderers who acted under him and took act and part with him were the exculpatory witnesses, who saved his neck from a sudden jerk, or himself from teasing oakum in the hulks for many years.

Donald Macleod, *Gloomy Memories of the Highlands*, Toronto, 1857.

Sir Walter Scott and the Honours of Scotland

Of all Scots who have formed their countrymen and women's perceptions of Scottish history, Sir Walter Scott was one of the most important. His romantic view of the Scottish past helped to lead to the 'discovery' of Scotland as a popular tourist destination. Perhaps the greatest gift which he possessed was the uncanny ability to fasten onto emblematic events in Scotland's past, such as the Jacobite risings or the Porteous riots, and to convey them to his audience in ways which gripped and fascinated them. It was a talent which succeeded not only with the reader in the street but also with royalty. George IV, the former Prince Regent, was so impressed by Scott that he gave him permission to carry out one of his most cherished projects – to open the chest in the little strong room in Edinburgh Castle where the Scottish Regalia had been stowed away after the Union of 1707. By promoting such a striking Scots image, Sir Walter helped to reassure his countrymen and women of their importance within the Union and of their distinctiveness as a nation at the very time when they were becoming more and more subsumed in the common purpose of the Empire.

The regalia themselves – the 'Honours of Scotland' – were among the most potent symbols of Scottish nationhood. They were a vital part of the panoply of the old Scottish Parliament, where the sceptre was used for touching acts in token of royal assent and where the crown sat in state on its cushion in front of the throne. During Cromwell's occupation of Scotland in the 1650s, the Honours were one of his most sought after targets, but due to the heroism of minister's wife Christian Grainger, they were spirited away out of Dunottar castle. Scott here tells the story not only of his own discovery, but of the previous adventures of the jewels.

Edinburgh, 4th Feb. 1818

My dear Croker, – I have the pleasure to assure you the Regalia of Scotland were this day found in perfect preservation. The Sword of State and Sceptre showed marks of hard usage at some former period; but in all respects agree with the description in Thomson's work. I will send you a complete account of the opening tomorrow, as the official account will take some time to draw up. In the meantime, I hope you will remain as obstinate in your belief as St. Thomas, because then you will come down to satisfy yourself. I know nobody entitled to earlier information, save one, to whom you can perhaps find the means of communicating the result of our researches. The post is just going off. Ever yours truly,

Walter Scott

Edinburgh, 7th February 1818

My dear Croker, – I promised I would add something to my report of yesterday, and yet I find I have but little to say. The extreme solemnity of opening sealed doors of oak and iron, and finally breaking open a chest which had been shut since 7th March 1707, about a hundred and eleven years, gave a sort of interest to our researches, which I can hardly express to you, and it would be very difficult to describe the intense eagerness with which we watched the rising of the lid of the chest, and the progress of the workmen in breaking it open, which was neither an easy nor a speedy task. It sounded very hollow when they worked on it with their tools, and I began to lean to your faction of the Little Faiths. However, I never could assign any probable or feasible reason for withdrawing these memorials of ancient independence; and my doubts rather arose from the conviction that many absurd things are done in public as well as in private life, merely out of a hasty impression of passion or resentment. For it was evident the removal of the Regalia might have greatly irritated people's minds here, and offered a fair pretext of breaking the Union, which for thirty years was the predominant wish of the Scottish nation.

The discovery of the Regalia has interested people's minds much more strongly than I expected, and is certainly calculated to make a pleasant and favourable impression upon them in respect to the kingly part of the constitution. It would be of the utmost consequence that they should be occasionally shown to them, under proper regulations, and for a small fee. The Sword of State is a most beautiful piece of workmanship, a present from Pope Julius II to James IV. The scabbard is richly decorated with filigree work of silver, double gilded, representing oak leaves and acorns, executed in a taste worthy that classical age in which the arts revived. A draughtsman has been employed to make sketches of these articles, in order to be laid before his Royal Highness [the Prince Regent]. The fate of these Regalia, which his Royal Highness's goodness has thus restored to light and honour, has on one or two occasions been singular enough. They were, in 1652, lodged in the Castle of Dunnottar, the seat of the Earl Marischal, by whom, according to his ancient privilege, they were kept. The castle was defended by

George Ogilvie of Barra, who, apprehensive of the progress which the English made in reducing the strong places in Scotland, became anxious for the safety of these valuable memorials. The ingenuity of his lady had them conveyed out of the castle in a bag on a woman's back, among some *hards*, as they are called, of lint. They were carried to the Kirk of Kinneff, and intrusted to the care of the clergyman named Grainger and his wife, and buried under the pulpit. The Castle of Dunnottar, though very strong and faithfully defended, was at length under necessity of surrendering, being the last strong place in Britain on which the royal flag floated in those calamitous times. Ogilvie and his lady were threatened with the utmost extremities by the Republican General Morgan, unless they should produce the Regalia. The governor stuck to it that he knew nothing of them, as in fact they had been carried away without his knowledge. The Lady maintained she had given them to John Keith, second son of the Earl Marischal, by whom, she said, they had been carried to France. They suffered a long imprisonment, and much ill usage. On the Restoration, the old Countess Marischal, founding upon the story Mrs. Ogilvie had told to screen her husband, obtained for her own son, John Keith, the Earldom of Kintore, and the post of Knight Marischal, with £400 a-year, as if he had been in truth the preserver of the Regalia. It soon proved that this reward had been too hastily given, for Ogilvie of Barra produced the Regalia, the honest clergyman refusing to deliver them to any one but those from whom he received them. Ogilvie was made a Knight Baronet, however, and got a new charter of the lands, acknowledging the good service. Thus it happened oddly enough, that Keith, who was abroad during the transaction, and had nothing to do with it, got the earldom, pension, &c., Ogilvie only inferior honours, and the poor clergyman nothing whatever, or, as we say, *the hare's foot to lick*. As for Ogilvie's lady, she died before the Restoration, her health being ruined by the hardships she endured from the Cromwellian satellites. She was a Douglas, with all the high spirit of that proud family. On her deathbed, and not till then, she told her husband where the honours were concealed, charging him to suffer death rather than betray them. Popular tradition says, not very probably, that Grainger and his wife were *booted* (that is, tortured with the engine called the boots). I think that the Knight Marischal's office rested in the Kintore family until 1715, when it was resumed on account of the bearded Earl's accession to the Insurrection of that year. He escaped well, for they might have taken

his estate and his earldom. I must save post, however, and conclude
abruptly. Yours ever,

  Walter Scott

Letters of Sir Walter Scott, ed. H. J. C Grierson, London, 1933.

New Lanark

*Robert Southey was Poet Laureate in 1819 when he joined civil
engineer Thomas Telford on a tour to Scotland. One of the places
of interest on their itinerary was New Lanark and a meeting with
its utopian co-owner – Robert Owen. New Lanark was a water-
powered cotton spinning factory but it was also meant to be a
model village, where the workers and their families were cared for
in their physical and moral needs. Owen was unusual in
demanding only 10³/₄ hours work per day from his employees, and
for refusing to employ children under ten in his mills. Left to
himself, he would not have employed children under twelve, but to
protect the interests of his business partners he felt obliged to
compromise over this. Owen was a definite exception in these
respects – in other mills children could be expected to work for 14
hours a day or more.*

Tuesday, September 28th. After breakfast we walked to New
Lanark which is about a mile from the town . . . I had written
to Owen from Inverary; and he expected us, he said to stay with him
a week, or at the very least three days; it was not without difficulty
that we persevered in our purpose of proceeding the same evening
to Douglas mill.

  He led us through the works with great courtesy, and made as full
an exhibition as time allowed. It is needless to say anything more of
the Mills than that they are perfect in their kind, according to the
present state of mechanical science, and that they appeared to be
under admirable management; they are thoroughly clean, and so
carefully ventilated, that there was no unpleasant smell in any of the
apartments. Everything required for the machinery is made upon the
spot, and the expence of wear and tear is estimated at £8000
annually. There are stores also from which the people are supplied
with all the necessaries of life. They have a credit there to the
amount of sixteen shillings a week each, but may deal elsewhere if
they chuse. The expences of what he calls the moral part of the
establishment, he stated at £700 a year. But a large building is just

completed with ball and concert and lecture rooms. All for the 'formation of character'; and this must have required a considerable sum, which I should think must surely be set down to Owen's private account, rather than to the cost of the concern.

In the course of going through these buildings, he took us into an apartment where one of his plans, upon a scale larger than any of the Swiss models was spread on the floor. And with a long wand in his hand he explained the plan, while Willy and Francis stood by, with wondering and longing eyes, regarding it as a plaything, and hoping they might be allowed to amuse themselves with it. Meantime the word had been given: we were conducted into one of the dancing rooms; half a dozen fine boys, about nine or ten years old, led the way. Playing on fifes, some 200 children, from four years of age until ten, entered the room and arranged themselves on three sides of it. A man whose official situation I did not comprehend gave the word, which either because of the tone or the dialect I did not understand; and they turned to the right or left, faced about, fell forwards and backwards and stamped at command, performing maneouvres the object of which was not very clear with perfect regularity. I remembered what T. Vardon told me of the cows in Holland. When the cattle are housed, the Dutch in the spirit of cleanliness, prevent them from dirting their tails by tying them up (to the no small discomfort of the cows) at a certain elevation, to a cross string which extends the whole length of the stalls: and the consequence is that when any one cow wags her tail all the others must wag theirs also. So I could not but think that these puppet-like motions might, with a little ingenuity have been produced by the great water wheel, which is the primum mobile of the whole Cotton-Mills. A certain number of the children were then drawn out and sung to the pipe of a music master. They afterwards danced to the piping of the six little pipers. There was too much of all this, but the children seemed to like it. When the exhibition was over, they filed off into the adjoining schoolrooms.

I was far better pleased with a large room in which all the children of the establishment who are old enough not to require the constant care of their mothers, and too young for instruction of any kind, were brought together while their parents were at work, and left to amuse themselves, with no more superintendence than is necessary for preventing them from hurting themselves. They made a glorious noise, worth all the concerts of New Lanark, and of London, to boot. It was really delightful to see how the little creatures crowded about Owen to make their bows and their curtesies, looking up and smiling in his face; and the genuine benignity and pleasure with which he noticed them, laying his hand on the head of one, shaking hands with another, and bestowing kind looks and kind words upon all.

Owen in reality deceives himself. He is part-owner and sole director of a large establishment, differing more in accidents than in essence from a plantation: the persons on it are white, and are at liberty by law to quit his service, but while they remain in it they are as much under his absolute management as so many Negro slaves. His humour, his vanity, his kindliness of nature (all these have their share) lead him to make these human machines as he calls them (and too literally he believes them to be) as happy as he can, and to make a display of their happiness. And jumps at once to the monstrous conclusion that because he can do this with 2,210 persons, who are totally dependent on him – all mankind might be governed with the same facility.

Robert Southey, *Journal of a Tour in Scotland in 1819*, ed. C. H. Herford, London, 1929.

The Radical War

In 1819 economic depression revived the radical cause. 'Union Societies', based on the ideas of English radical Joseph Brayshaw, helped to provide a framework for secret meetings to plot the overthrow of the government. In the aftermath of the Peterloo massacre in England – in which a peaceful demonstration for reform was put down by a bloody cavalry charge – Scottish radicals began to contemplate violence. On April Fool's Day 1820 three weavers from Parkhead in Glasgow produced the Address to the Inhabitants of Great Britain and Ireland *which urged a general strike against the government to gain rights for the working classes. Sixty thousand Glasgow workers downed tools and a general insurrection was planned, but failed to take place.*

Despite the failure of the revolution to materialise, some small groups of radicals still decided to take action. At Strathaven one hundred radicals took the village and started to march on Glasgow. In Glasgow another much smaller group met on Glasgow Green and decided to march on Carron iron works and take some cannon. It was the latter group who encountered a cavalry force at Bonnymuir. Eighteen were taken prisoner,

*including the two leaders, Andrew Hardie and John Baird. The
leader of the Strathaven men, James Wilson, was also later
captured. All three were executed. The incidents passed into
tradition as the 'Radical War'.*

*Below are two contemporary accounts of skirmishes between
radicals and government volunteers.*

Battle of Bonnymuir

A n Account of the Battle which took place at Bonnymuir, on
Wednesday the 5th April, 1820, betwixt about 50 of the
Radicals and a party of the Military; with the names of the 15
Radical prisoners. – Also, the names of those Killed and Wounded
at Greenock, on Saturday last. [*Placed at the end of the account of
the skirmish in Greenock.*]

Kilsyth, 5th April 1820

This morning a gentleman residing in this parish belonging to the
Falkirk troop of Yeomanry Cavalry; left home to join his troop at
Falkirk, and had proceeded a short way from his own house, when
he came up with between 25 to 30 Radicals, all armed with pikes,
muskets, and pistols, who stopped him and requested him to give up
his arms, which he refused to do, and showed them a disposition to
resist. They told him (at the same time presenting at him several
pistols) that resistance would be vain, as they would kill him on the
spot. He, however, got off retaining his arms and meeting with an
Orderly from Kilsyth going with dispatches to Stirling, informed
him it would be improper to proceed. They accordingly both
returned to Kilsyth and reported, when the Commanding-Officer
there ordered ten men and a serjeant from the 10th Hussars and as
many of the Yeomanry Cavalry, to escort the Orderly and the other
Gentleman on their several roads, and to endeavour to fall in with
these armed Radicals if possible. The Radicals, in the interval, had
been joined by a number more, who proceeded along the Canal
Bank towards Bonny-muir, having taken several fowling-pieces and
a pitch-fork from farmhouses in the neighbourhood of Bonnybridge.
  The Cavalry, on their arrival at Loanhead, being informed of their
proceedings, immediately went to Bonnymuir in search of the
Radicals, and, on coming up with them, they showed a disposition
to fight rather than fly; having taken their position behind an old
dyke, they allowed the Cavalry to come within thirty yards of them,
when they fired a volley; the Cavalry instantly charged, firing a few

shots when going over the dyke; the Radicals received the charge with their pikes, and made all the resistance in their power, but they soon found themselves in a bad situation, and throwing away their arms, endeavoured to escape, when the Cavalry secured nineteen prisoners; three of whom are wounded, two remained on the field so badly wounded as not to be able to be carried to Stirling Castle, where the prisoners are lodged. Eight or ten of those who escaped are said to be wounded, and have not been able to go from the place where the affair happened. The whole number of the Radicals did not exceed forty or fifty. None of the Cavalry are severely wounded; two are slightly in the hand; and one horse severely wounded in three different places (since dead) and a number of horses slightly.

It is reported that the whole of the prisoners belong to Glasgow, except one of the name of Baird, said to be their leader, who lately resided at Condorrat. It is said that the whole had been drilling in the Calton Green of Glasgow this morning, that they left that place about four o'clock, and went over the country in a straggling way till they arrived at Bonnymuir, where they expected to be joined by a number from all parts of the country during the evening and tomorrow.

Names of the Prisoners

John Baird,	Andrew Hardie,
Thomas M'Culloch,	John Barr,
William Smith,	Benjamin Moir,
Allan Murchy,	Alexander Latimer,
Alexander Johnston,	Andrew White,
David Thomson,	James Wright,
Thomas Pink,	Robert Gray.
James Cleland,	

Saturday morning, about three o'clock, the prisoners were put on board a Steam Boat at Stirling, under the charge of a Macer of Justiciary, and a party of the 4th Veterans. They were landed at Newhaven, where six carriages were waiting for them to be conveyed to the Jail.

An Account of the Skirmish, which took place at Greenock on Saturday last; betwixt the Port Glasgow Volunteers (escorting five Radical prisoners from Paisley) and the inhabitants; when Nine of the latter were Killed, and 15 dangerously Wounded.

Port-Glasgow, Monday, 10th April, 1820.

In consequence of the daring and rebellious movements of the Radicals at Glasgow, Paisley, and the adjoining districts on Saturday week, an express arrived here on Sunday, ordering the Volunteers on duty, when they turned out with the greatest alacrity and went to Paisley on Monday, where their presence was of the most essential service. Circumstances, however, having rendered their stay there any longer unnecessary, they received orders to march home on Saturday morning, and to escort five prisoners, apprehended for seditious practices, to Greenock Jail. They arrived here about half-past four o'clock, and their loyal townsmen, proud of the services they had rendered, received them with acclamations.

As they had received strict orders to take particular care of their prisoners, in order to prevent any attempt at escape, and it had been observed here, during the whole of the week, that a considerable number of idle people from the disturbed districts were passing through the town, towards Greenock, it was deemed prudent to send the whole corps on with the prisoners in place of a detachment, and the eminent danger in which they were afterwards involved, which produced the lamentable catastrophe which followed, showed the propriety of this area sure. On the march to Greenock, they received intimation to be on their guard against a surprise, as there were evident indications of intended insult, if not injury to the corps. This intelligence placed the Officers in no pleasant situation.

Crowds of men and boys met them before they had gone a mile from this, and increased considerably on their route. On entering Cartsdyke with drums and fifes, (which greatly increased the mob), they were astonished to observe all the shops shut; and here, voices began to bawl from the crowd to the prisoners. 'Cheer up, you will soon be relieved from your situation;' and after passing the first bridge, a large stone struck one of the sentinels in the cart with them. From this time the crowd increased rapidly till they reached the Goal [jail]; when one company went inside the Goal Yard with the prisoners, and the other remained outside the gate.

At this time a number of men on a pile of deals in a joiner's yard to the westward of the Goal, and a crowd on the height of the Reservoir to the east, began to assail the company, stationed inside the gate with vollies of stones, when several of the corps were severely injured, and, as the lives of all were in danger, two or three shots were fired over the heads of the party to the west, who made off. The prisoners being now lodged in Goal, the corps, according to the orders of their Commanding-Officer, Captain Dunlop, began to retire, in order to return home, and were accompanied to the Square adjoining by Mr. Denniston, the Chief Magistrate. The mob by this time had became so excessive that the Volunteers had not room to form as they wished, but immediately began their march out of the town in close order, and here a scene of tumult commenced which most unfortunately terminated in the loss of many lives. The mob instantly began to shower vollies of stones on the Volunteers, many of whom were severely wounded, notwithstanding the Magistrate, and several Gentlemen on the spot, at the moment, were using every effort to protect them. The corps seeing their lives in such danger, now began to fire occasional shots in the air, in order, if possible, to intimidate the assailants, till they reached the Rue End, the east outlet of the town; but as the ferocity of the mob seemed to increase, and they even attempted to wrest some of the arms from them, some shots were fired low, and here one or two people fell. Notwithstanding this awful circumstance the mob continued to hang on the flanks and rear of the corps with the utmost fury, till they reached the open main road at the east end of Cartsdyke (a mile from the Square) adding thereby a number more to the melancholy list of the killed and wounded, when they found it prudent to desist. There were Nine killed and Fifteen most severely wounded.

In the evening the mob again collected and began an attack on the Goal which they forced, and relieved the Radicals, but not any of the other prisoners. They then tore down the iron railings in front of some of the houses for weapons; and an immense number armed in this way, as also with swords and guns, preceded by a piper, set off to attack this place. Apprised of this by express from Greenock, the Volunteers, and the most respectable population were under arms for the night. Cannon [was] got in readiness – the bridge leading from Greenock barricaded, having a powerful detachment in rear communicating with the main body stationed in town, and a strong patrole in incessant motion through every street and avenue in the place. The mob after reaching Mr. Gemmill's gate returned, having learnt the preparations here. In the course of the night a troop of Hussars arrived at Greenock, and in the morning a party of Riflemen from Glasgow, but the town has since remained quiet.

Printed for John Muir, Glasgow

Names of the Killed and Wounded at Greenock

Names	Age	Wounds	
Adam Glephane,	48	Under the groin	Dead
Archibald Drummond,	20	Shot dead through chest	Dead
James Kerr,	17	Through the belly	Dead
John McWhinnie,	65	Through shoulder and chest	Dead
Hugh Paterson,	14	Through leg	Leg amputated
John Patrick,	30	Through the thigh	Doing well
David McBride,	14	Through the cheek and jaw	Doing well
A McKinnon	17	Through chest and arm	Doubtful
Catherine Turner	65	Through the leg.	Leg amputated

The above in the Infirmary

John Boyce,	33	Through the belly	Dead
George Tillery,	25	Through the thigh	Doing well
Robert Spence,	11	Slightly in the foot	Slightly
William Lindsay,	15	Shot dead on the spot	Dead
James McGilp,	8	Ball in right thigh	
Gilbert McArthur,	18	Through the left thigh	Flesh wound
John Turner,	22	Through the calf of the leg	Flesh wound
Peter Cameron,	14	Through the right leg	Flesh wound
John Gunn,	24	Through calf of left leg	

Battle Of Bonnymuir and An Account of the Skirmish, which took place at Greenock on Saturday last; betwixt the Port Glasgow Volunteers (escorting five Radical prisoners from Paisley) and the inhabitants; when Nine of the latter were Killed, and 15 dangerously Wounded, Radical tracts RB.m.145 (3) - (4), Glasgow, 1820.

George IV's Visit

Radicals being cut down by cavalry – this was not the kind of picture which Sir Walter Scott, publicist for Scotland, had in mind to show his sovereign when George made his exceptional trip North of the Border. Scotland had not seen a reigning monarch since the days of Charles II. A royal visit was a splendid novelty of the first order. Heralds, uniforms, banquets, a 'Gathering of the Clans' for the King's benefit, with acres and acres of tartan – it was as though the Edinburgh Military Tattoo had been invented a hundred years before its time.

This was an outbreak of what modern historians have labelled
'Highlandism'. At the very point at which actual Gaelic culture
was being destroyed by market pressures, clearances and
emigration, dressing up in tartan and wearing the kilt had become
all the rage with the middle and upper classes. The phenomenon
had its roots in the late 18th century with the suppression of
Jacobitism, the recruitment of Highland regiments and a change in
taste which classified Highland landscapes as sublime and
picturesque. Adopting Highland dress gave Lowland Scots a way
of distinguishing themselves from their neighbours in England at a
time when the country had never been more anglicised. Ironically
it also led to the increasingly urbanised Lowlands adopting the
dress and trappings of a rural people whom they had formerly
despised. Walter Scott's novels and the royal visit played an
important part in cultivating this image. The King was thrilled by
all the colourful pageantry and Scotland was, at last, fashionable!

At an early hour on Thursday the 22d of August, the city presented
a scene of extraordinary bustle, in consequence of the
arrangements which had been agreed upon for his Majesty's
procession to the Castle. The weather was peculiarly unpropitious.
The sky was overcast with heavy clouds, which, descending in
drizzling and unintermitting showers, threatened the postponement of
the royal pageant. Notwithstanding the state of the weather, immense
crowds flocked in from the surrounding country to witness a spectacle
so interesting to the feelings of Scotsmen; and, in addition to the hum
of the constantly accumulating multitude who occupied its streets, the
city was enlivened by the appearance of the different trades, marching
in array, and with their banners displayed, to the sound of martial
music. The view of the High Street, towards mid-day, was animated
in the extreme, as the different public bodies, headed by their officers,
with their insignia of office, proceeded, in seemingly interminable
lines, to occupy the stations assigned to them. The windows of the
High Street, as far as the eye could reach, and the different balconies,
all covered with green, red or scarlet cloth, were thronged to excess;
and the motionless anxiety of those who occupied them, contrasted
with the lively bustle that prevailed on the streets, had a most
imposing effect.

About one o'clock the different public bodies, incorporations, and
trades, had taken up the ground assigned to them, reaching from the
precincts of the Abbey to the Castle-hill: they were in lines two deep,

and in many places three. To a man they were well dressed; and had crosses on their breasts, with heather or thistles in their hats, and most of them white rods in their hands. We cannot pass over the society of gardeners without remark: it was numerous beyond all former precedent, and exhibited an unusual display of appropriate emblems, garlands, and fruits. Among these a plume, composed of the flowers of the brightest varieties of the hollyhock, and tastefully arranged so as to form the triple feather, so long the crest of his Majesty while Prince of Wales, attracted much attention. In the Canongate, the society of glass-blowers was particularly conspicuous. The officer at their head wore a glass hat, with a glass sword and target; and each member carried a long glass rod . . .

We also observed Sir Walter Scott, dressed in the Windsor uniform, walking up the centre of the street along with two other gentlemen, and, as he advanced, casting a glance of lofty enthusiasm upon the marshalled bands of hardy burghers, whose military appearance must have been associated, in his mind, with awful but proud recollections. A number of those assembled did homage to the genius of the worthy Baronet, by loudly cheering him . . .

The procession was most impressive; it was splendid without being gaudy; and while the variety of the different costumes was admirably calculated for effect, the judicious intermixture of the clans, with their tartan habiliments, and of the troops, formed a happy relief to the official splendour which marked other parts of the pageant. The dresses which attracted the greatest attention by their brilliancy and richness were those of Sir Alexander Keith, Knight Marischal; the Earl of Kinnoull, Lord Lyon King at Arms; and the Duke of Hamilton, who carried the crown.

The Knight Marischal was mounted on a black Arabian horse, richly caparisoned. His dress was a white satin cloak, over a richly embroidered doublet of white and gold, with a white plume in his hat. On each side of him walked a Henchman, habited in rose-coloured satin, slashed with white; their under-clothes white, with white silk stockings, and white roses in their shoes.

The Lord Lyon was superbly mounted on an Arabian horse. He wore a long and superb mantle of crimson velvet, lined throughout with white silk; a green velvet surcoat, edged with a broad band of gold; white pantaloons, with a gold stripe; on his head a crown of gold, with a cap of crimson velvet, and a border of ermine; and in his hand he held his baton of office of green enamel, flowered with golden thistles; he wore also his collar and badge. His splendid appearance attracted general attention. He was attended by two grooms, one on each side, who wore white surtouts, with red collar and cuffs, and red caps . . .

Marchmont Herald, on reaching the Castle-gate, announced to the Governor of the Castle the approach of his Majesty. He, with the trumpeters who preceded him, followed by the whole of the rest of the procession in front of the King's carriages, then turned to the right, and proceeded behind the scaffolding on the north side of the Castle-hill, until the front of the column reached the eastern extremity of the scaffolding, when it halted, the whole forming up close, so as not to impede the approach of the King's carriage to the Castle-gate.

When the King arrived at the barrier-gate, he alighted from his carriage on a raised platform, covered with crimson cloth, where the Lord High Constable and Lord Cathcart were stationed to receive him. The keys of the Castle were then tendered to his Majesty, by Lieutenant-General Sir Alexander Hope, the Lieutenant-Governor, accompanied by Major-General Sir Thomas Bradford, Commander of the Forces, besides a numerous body of officers belonging to the garrison. His Majesty having returned the keys, walked with a firm step along the drawbridge, till coming to the inner-gate, he stepped into another carriage, which stood waiting, the grenadier company of the 66th regiment forming his guard of honour. The carriage was surrounded by the principal nobility and gentry, the Lord High Constable walking alone by the King's right hand. The procession moved slowly through the winding passages of the Castle, till it came to the half-moon battery, where were erected two platforms, raised one upon the other, with a stair leading up to them. The under platform and stair were covered with grey cloth; the handrail of the stair and upper platform with scarlet cloth. The King ascended the upper platform, and presented himself to the view of his admiring subjects. At this moment a royal salute was fired from the guns on the ramparts, the bands played 'God save the King', and the soldiers on the different batteries presented arms. The King remained on this elevated situation a considerable time, cheered by the amazing multitude who occupied the Castle-hill. One of his attendants expressed an apprehension, that the King would get wet. 'O, never mind,' replied his Majesty, with great animation, 'I must cheer the people;' and taking off his hat, he waved it repeatedly, and gave three cheers, which were heard at some distance. The people, whose enthusiasm was now wound up to the highest pitch, again made the air resound with their loudest acclamations. The thick fog that brooded over the landscape deprived his Majesty of the full enjoyment of a prospect unequalled, perhaps, in variety and magnificence. But the same circumstances cast an air of sublimity over the wide expanse; and the broken outlines of crags, and cliffs, and stupendous buildings, peered out from amidst the incumbent gloom with a wild and most romantic effect. The King surveyed this singular prospect with the most marked interest; and, turning to his attendants, exclaimed, 'This is wonderful! – what a sight!'

Robert Mudie, *Historical Account of His Majesty's Visit to Scotland*, Edinburgh, 1822.

In the Dundee Mills

The Dundee textile mills were as far away from the pomp of a royal visit as it was possible to get. James Myles was one of those child labourers for which the 19th century is so famous. His slender wages were desperately needed by his family after the catastrophe of his father's arrest and transportation for manslaughter. His family had no option but to move to the town and to send the boy to work in the mills. At this stage, in 1824, bills restricting child labour were a thing of the future. Employers worked men, women and children for as much as they could get out of them. It was the Victorians who began to introduce legislation to curb this kind of cruelty and exploitation. In Myles's autobiography, he recorded the harsher conditions of the earlier era.

It was on a Tuesday morning in the month of 'Lady June' that I first entered a spinning mill. The whole circumstances were strange to me. The dust, the din, the work, the hissing and roaring of one person to another, the obscene language uttered, even by the youngest, and the imperious commands harshly given by those 'dressed in a little brief authority,' struck my young country heart with awe and astonishment. At that time the twelve hours' factory act had not come into operation, and spinning mills were in their glory as huge instruments of demoralization and slavery. Mercenary manufacturers, to enable them to beat more upright employers in the markets, kept their machinery and hands active fifteen, and, in many case, seventeen hours a-day, and, when tender children fell asleep under the prolonged infliction of 'work! work! work,' overseers roused them with the rod, or thongs of thick leather burned at the points. The lash of the slave driver was never more unsparingly used in Carolina on the unfortunate slaves than the canes and 'whangs' of mill foremen were then used on helpless factory boys. When I went to a spinning mill I was about seven years of age. I had to get out of bed every morning at five o'clock, commence work at half-past five, drop at nine for breakfast, begin again at half-past nine, work until two, which was the dinner hour, start again at half-past two, and continue until half-past seven at night. Such were the nominal hours; but in reality there were no regular hours, masters and managers did with us as they liked. The clocks at the factories were often put forward in the morning and back at night, and instead of being instruments for the measurement of time, they were used as cloaks for cheatery and oppression. Though this was known amongst the hands, all were afraid to speak, and a workman then was afraid to carry a watch, as it was no uncommon event to dismiss any one who presumed to know too much about the science of horology. In country mills, a more horrific despotism reigned than in Dundee. There, masters frequently bound the young by a regular contract, which gave them a more complete control over their labour and liberties than taking them from week to week. In one establishment in the vicinity of Dundee, the proprietor, a coarse-minded man, who by accident had vaulted out of his natural element into the position of a 'vulgar rich' man, practised the contract system, and had bothies where he lodged all his male and female workers. They were allowed to cook, sleep, and live in any dog and cat manner they pleased, no moral superintendence whatever being exercised over them. His mill was kept going 17 and frequently 19 hours per day. To accomplish this all meal hours were almost dispensed with, and women were employed to boil potatoes and carry them in baskets to the different flats; and the children had to swallow a potato hastily in the interval of putting up 'ends.' On dinners cooked and eaten as I have described, they had to subsist till half-past nine, and frequently ten at night. When they returned to their bothies, brose, as it is a dish that can be quickly made, constituted their suppers, for they had no time to wait the preparation of a different meal. They then tumbled into bed; but balmy sleep had scarcely closed their urchin eyelids, and steeped their infant souls in blessed forgetfulness, when the thumping of the watchmen's staff on the door would rouse them from repose, and the words, 'Get up; its four o'clock,' reminded them they were factory children, the unprotected victims of monotonous slavery. At this mill, and indeed all mills, boys and girls were often found sleeping in stairs and private places, and they have been seen walking about the flats in a deep sleep, with cans of 'sliver' in their hands. When found in this state, they were caned or kicked according to the mood of their superiors. One poor boy, who is still alive, and who, by force of mind, great persistency and rectitude, rose to be a mercantile clerk in Dundee, and now fills a responsible situation on one of the principal railways in England, was for some time in this factory. One day he was carrying an armful of bobbins from one flat to another. When ascending the stair, he sat down to rest himself, as his legs were sore and swollen by incessant standing. In a few moments he was fast asleep. Whilst enjoying this stolen repose, the master happened to pass. Without the least warning he gave him a violent slap on the side of the head, which stunned and stupified him. In a half-sleeping state of stupefaction he ran to the roving frame, which he sometimes attended, and five minutes had barely elapsed when his left hand got entangled with the machinery, and two of his fingers were crushed to a jelly, and had to be immediately amputated. His unfeeling taskmaster gave him no recompense – in fact never asked after him; he was left to starve or die, as Providence might direct. The reader will no doubt imagine that boys working 18 and 19 hours a-day would have nearly double wages to boys at the present time, who only work ten. I can only speak from experience, and what has come under the range of my own knowledge on this point. When I went to the mill, I was paid with 1s 6d per week, and my nominal hours, as already remarked, were 13 hours per day. When the Twelve Hours' Act was in operation, boys had from 3s up to 4s per week; and now since the Ten Hours' Act came into force, their wages vary from 3s 8d up to 4s 3d. In short, as far as I can learn, their wages are as good under the Ten Hours' Act as they were under the Twelve Hours' Act. Of course the Act precludes such young boys as I was from working; yet, considering the hours I was confined, and the wages I was paid with, the contrast is highly favourable to the humanity and wisdom of those good men who procured protection to factory children, and said to competition and capital, 'Hitherto shalt thou come but no farther.'

James Myles, *Chapters in the Life of a Dundee Factory Boy*, Dundee, 1850.

The Great Fire of Edinburgh

*This is a vivid first-hand account of the aftermath of the fires
which raged down the High Street of Edinburgh in the winter of
1824. The witness was Hugh Miller, later to become the greatest
Scottish journalist of his age and a noted geologist, who was at the
time a young journeyman stonemason near Edinburgh.*

The great fires of Parliament Close and the High Street were
events of this winter. A countryman, who had left town when
the spire of the Tron Church was blazing like a torch, and the large
group of buildings nearly opposite the Cross were enveloped in
flame from ground-floor to roof-tree, passed our work-shed, a little
after two o'clock, and, telling us what he had seen, remarked that,
if the conflagration went on as it was doing, we would have, as our
next season's employment, the Old Town of Edinburgh to rebuild.
And as the evening closed over our labours, we went into town in a
body, to see the fires that promised to do so much for us. The spire
had burnt out and we could but catch between us and the darkened
sky, the square abrupt outline of the masonry a-top which had
supported the wooden broach, whence, only a few hours before,
Fergusson's bell had descended in a molten shower. The flames too,
in the upper group of buildings, were restricted to the lower stories,
and glared fitfully on the tall forms and bright swords of the
dragoons, drawn from the neighbouring barracks, as they rode up
and down the middle space, or gleamed athwart on the street on
groups of wretched-looking women or ruffian men, who seemed to
be scanning with greedy eyes the still unremoved heaps of household
goods rescued from the burning tenements. The first figure that
caught my eye was a singularly ludicrous one. Removed from the
burning mass but by a thickness of a wall, there was a barber's shop
brilliantly lighted with gas, the uncurtained window of which
permitted the spectators outside to see whatever was going on in the
interior. The barber was busily at work as if he were a hundred miles
from the scene of danger, though the engines at the time were
playing against the outside of his gable wall; and the immediate
subject under his hands, as my eyes rested on him was an immensely
fat old fellow, on whose round bald forehead and ruddy cheeks the
perspiration occasioned by the oven like heat of the place, was
standing out in huge drops, and whose vast mouth widely opened to
accommodate the man of the razor, gave to his countenance such an
expression as I have sometimes seen in grotesque Gothic heads of

that age of art in which the ecclesiastical architect began to make
sport of his religion. The next object that presented itself was,
however, of a more sobering description. A poor working man,
laden with his favourite piece of furniture, a glass fronted press or
cupboard, which he had succeeded in rescuing from his burning
dwelling, was emerging from one of the lanes, followed by his wife,
when striking his foot on some obstacle in the way, or staggering
from the too great weight of the load, he tottered against a
projecting corner, and the glazed door was driven in with a crash.
There was hopeless misery in the wailing cry of his wife – 'Oh ruin,
ruin, it's lost too!' Nor was his own despairing response less sad –
'Ay, ay puir lassie, it's a' at an end noo.' Curious as it may seem, the
wild excitement of the scene had at first rather exhilarated than
depressed my spirits; but the incident with the glass cupboard served
to awaken the proper feeling and as I came into contact with the
misery of the catastrophe, and marked the groups of shivering
houseless creatures that watched beside the broken fragments of
their stuff, I saw what a dire calamity a great fire really is. Nearly
two hundred families were already at this time cast homeless into
the streets.

Hugh Miller, *My Schools and Schoolmasters*, Edinburgh, 1852.

Resurrection Men

*When science meets the slums, the results are not always happy. In
1828, Edinburgh University had one of the most renowned
medical schools in Europe. It was lacking only one thing: bodies, a
steady supply of the dead variety. Even among the most stricken
sections of Edinburgh's poor, no inducement would persuade most
people to sell a relation's body for medical research, or to donate
their own. Dissection had been reserved in Scotland as a
punishment, suitable for the body of a hanged man. Nobody
wanted it to happen to them or to anyone they knew. However, in
any big city, there are always those desperate enough to be bought,
even to steal the bodies of the dead. Two such men were William
Burke and William Hare – only they went one step further. Rather
than howking about in graveyards, dodging the watch which was
often put on a grave by relatives, they decided to kill to order, in a
grisly series of killings which became known as the West Port
murders.*

When caught, Hare turned king's evidence, exposing his partner

*William Burke and his wife Helen M'Dougal to the full force of
the law. The case was sensational. All of the Edinburgh papers
covered it heavily. Here, from the coverage of the* Edinburgh
Evening Courant, *is the evidence of Ann Black, a near neighbour
of Burke's, concerning the last of the killings, that of Margery
Campbell, which led to Burke's arrest.*

HIGH COURT OF JUSTICIARY

TRIAL OF BURKE, AND M'DOUGAL, HIS WIFE

Yesterday the Court proceeded to the trial of W. Burke and Helen
M'Dougal, indicted for murder. No trial that has taken place for
a number of years past has excited such an unusual and intense
interest; all the doors and passages to the Court were accordingly
besieged at an early hour, even before daylight: and it was with the
greatest difficulty, and by the utmost exertions of a large body of
police that admission could be procured for those who were
connected with the proceedings. At nine o'clock the court-room was
completely filled by members of the Faculty and by the jury. Lord
Macdonald and another noble Lord were seated on the bench. A few
minutes before 10 o'clock, the prisoners were brought to the bar.
Burke is of a short and rather stout figure, and was dressed in a
shabby blue surtout. There is nothing in his physiognomy, except
perhaps a dark lowering of the brow, to indicate any peculiar
harshness or cruelty of disposition. His features outwardly appeared
to be firm and determined; yet in his haggard and wandering eye,
there was at times a deep expression of trouble, as he unconsciously
surveyed the preparations which were going forward. The female
prisoner appeared to be more disturbed; every now and then her
breast heaved with a deep drawn sigh, and her looks were
desponding. She was dressed in a dark gown, checked apron, cotton
shawl, and a much worn brown silk bonnet.

[*Witnesses were called.*]

Ann Black, or Connaway, lived in Wester Portsburgh. Her house
consisted of one room. In entering her house they went down a few
steps and through a passage. The door to her house was the first you
come to, and a little farther in there is a door on the same side – but
led first into another passage, at the end of which there is another

door that leads to a room – a room inclosed by two doors. Burke, the prisoner, occupied that inner room in October. The other prisoner, M'Dougal, lived with Burke. There was a house on the opposite of the first passage, occupied by a Mr Law. — Had seen Hare and his wife coming about Burke. During that week of October a man named Grey and his wife lived a few days in Burke's house. On Friday the 31st October (Hallowe'en), about mid-day, witness saw Burke pass along the passage, going inward, with a woman following him. She was a stranger, whom witness had never before seen. Mrs Law was sitting with witness. In the afternoon, about three o'clock, witness went into Burke's house, and found the woman who she had seen go in with Burke, sitting at the fire supping porridge and milk. She had her head tied up in a handkerchief, and no gown; they said they had been washing. Was not sure of her having on any thing but a shift and the handkerchief. Witness said to M'Dougal, 'I see you have got a stranger?' and she replied, they had got a friend of her husband's, a Highland woman. Had no farther conversation at that time, and saw nothing to induce her to suppose that the woman was drunk . . . Some time after dark M'Dougal came and asked witness to take care of her door till she returned. As there was no person in the house, witness's husband, who was sitting at the fire, said he thought there was somebody gone into Burke's. She in consequence took a light, and went in, when she saw no one there but the woman, who came towards the door, being then the worse of drink. She said that she was going to St Mary's Wynd to meet a boy who had promised to bring her word from her son; and asked the name of the land of houses, that she might find her way back, for she had no money to pay for a bed. Witness told her not to go away, for should not get her way back; and she did not go. She told witness that Burke, whose name she called Docherty, had promised her a bed and her supper. She came into witness's house, and had good deal of conversation with witness's husband. She said, as Docherty had promised her a bed and supper, she was to stay for a fortnight. She was the worse of liquor; and insisted on calling Burke Docherty, for she said that was the name he called himself to her. She remained in the house for about an hour, and while there, prisoner (M'Dougal) and Mr and Mrs Hare came in; Mrs Hare had a bottle, and Hare insisted on drinking; they all tasted, and witness's husband gave them a dram. The stranger partook of it, and so did M'Dougal. They were merry. Hare, Campbell, and M'Dougal were dancing. The woman was quite well; she had hurt her foot, but otherwise she was in good health. Mrs Campbell remained in the house a long time, refusing to go until Burke came home; he had been out the most of the night. Witness insisted on her going out, but she would not, until Burke went in; and on witness observing Burke passing to his own house, between ten and eleven, she informed Mrs Campbell, who rose and followed him into his house. Witness slept none from the disturbance in Burke's house, which commenced after Mrs Campbell went in. The disturbance was as if Burke and Hare were fighting. Witness got up between three and four, to make her husband's breakfast, but again went to bed, and rose about eight o'clock. The first thing she then heard was Hare calling for Mrs Law, who did not answer him. A little while after, a girl, whose name she understood to be Paterson, came and asked for her husband; it turned out that it was Burke she wanted. Witness directed the girl into Burke's. M'Dougal came into witness's house, and William (Burke) wanted to speak to her. She went in accordingly, and found there M'Dougal, Burke, Mrs Law, and young Broggan. Burke had a bottle of spirits in his hand. He filled out a glass, and then dashed out the spirits upon a bed. Witness asked him, why he wasted the spirits? and he replied, he wanted to get more. Witness asked M'Dougal, what had become of the old woman? and she replied, that Burke and her had been too friendly together, and she had kicked her out of the house, asking, at the same time, 'Did you hear it?' Burke asked, if witness had heard the dispute between him and Hare? And she said no; he added, it was just a fit of drink, and they were friends enough now. They were all quiet before she got up to make her husband's breakfast, and she heard no more till after eight o'clock. Burke's wife sung a song while witness was in the house. Observed a bundle of straw at the bottom of the bed; it has lain there most of the summer. Witness left Burke's house a little after ten. Was there again in the afternoon; was asked in by Mrs Gray. Burke, Broggan, and M'Dougal were there. At a later hour, near eight o'clock, went in again with Gray's wife, to see what she had told her of; she saw nothing but was so frightened that she came out without seeing anything; the straw was turned. Before hearing of what took her in to see, Mrs M'Dougal said Gray's wife had stolen things, and wished witness to look after her door because it would not lock. Did not see Burke till far on in the night, till it was reported that he had murdered a woman. Mrs Burke laughed very loud, and he said he defied all Scotland, for he had done nothing he

cared about, she said no one breathing could impeach them with any
thing that was indifferent. Burke said he would go and see the man
who said he had done amiss – and when he went to the passage the
police apprehended him.

Edinburgh Evening Courant, 25 December 1828.

Reform!

....

*This witness to one of the great popular demonstrations for
political reform in Scotland, the great Glasgow procession of
September 1831, was Henry, later Lord Cockburn, then one of the
leaders of the Whig party in Scotland, and the drafter of the Act
that did lead to a dramatic extension of the political nation,
though the franchise still remained restricted to the propertied
classes. Cockburn was an accomplished diarist and excellent
observer, but though he was a cautious reformer he was also a
member of the social and political establishment, and his account
makes it clear that, while he accepted that profound change was
coming, he was more than half-fearful of this novel demonstration
of people power. Note the continuing fear, still very strong in the
governing classes, and articulated here by Cockburn, of the
influence of revolutionary and republican ideas from France. Yet
these were much milder manifestations than had been seen in the
'Radical War'.*

2d October 1831 . . . on the 8th [September] saw one of the great
Glasgow processions . . . It was a magnificent and gratifying yet
fearful spectacle. All the villages within many miles were in motion
early in the morning, all pouring with devices and music into the
Green. I went to a window in the Court-house about eleven, and
saw the platform erected for the managers, and all round it an ocean
of heads and banners. I afterwards took pains . . . to ascertain the
facts, and I don't believe that there were, including spectators, fewer
that 100,000 persons on that field . . . Indeed it is one of the pleasing
or (as it may happen) alarming features of these modern movements,
that the people completely understand how much their force is
increased by being orderly. All their plans were previously explained
to the authorities, and whatever was objected to was changed. The
procession took above two hours to pass, walking four abreast.
Those engaged were about 12,000. They were divided into crafts,
parishes, towns, mills, or otherwise, variously and irregularly, each
portion bearing its emblems and music. The carters to the number

of nearly 500 went first, mounted, their steeds decorated with ribbons. They were arranged according to the colour of their horses, and in honour of the administration [of Lord Grey] the greys led. Then followed a long and imposing host in the most perfect order, all cheering the Provost as they passed, and all splendid with music and decorations. The banners were mostly of silk, and every trade carried specimens of its art, many of which were singularly beautiful, consisting of printing-presses, harpsichords, steam-engines, steam-vessels, looms and all sorts of machinery, all working, and generally with glass sides so that the working might be seen. The interest of these really exquisite models was not diminished by the countless efforts of grotesque wit with which each craft endeavoured to make its calling emblematic of the times and of the cause. Nothing surprised me so much as the music, even though I had been previously told that there was scarcely a mill or village without its band. There could not be under fifty really good bands, generally consisting of about fifteen performers . . . No description of workman was too high or too low for the occasion. The chimney-sweeps walked, and so did the opticians. Though there were groves of banners, we could only detect two tricolours, and these from their accompaniments were plainly not French in their principles. I did not observe any honour done to [Henry] Hunt [a Radical leader] and only once or twice to [Daniel] O'Connell [the Irish home rule leader]. Beyond the disposition in favour of Reform, which was the object of the whole thing, there was nothing more popular than what might have been seen among the higher classes, and on any other occasion; almost every inscription or device was dedicated to Earl Grey, Lord Brougham, Joseph Hume, Lord John Russell, etc, and to reform, economy, peace, the king, and no burgh-mongers . . . There was no soldier on duty, and no police officers except a few who were assisting, yet I never saw a populace in such order, or rather in such perfect good humour . . . No excesses occurred during the whole day or night.

Such scenes are now common everywhere; every village accustomed to meetings and processions; and men arise and take the lead in every section, who evince talents and powers of speaking which will evidently soon make them cease to belong to the lower orders, if the established system were to be broken up. All this is gratifying as it marks an intelligent population, but it is fearful by disclosing the formidableness of organised popular power. All attempts to suppress or despise it must fail; and the true result is so to govern that the strength of the people may be on the side of the Government, which I see no reason to doubt it may be, and to an extent far beyond what it ever could be with a population ignorant and without political rights or the desire of them.

Henry Cockburn, *Journal*, i, Edinburgh, 1874.

From Arran to Quebec

Political rights were not a panacea for economic problems. The early years of the 19th century also saw the most brutal of the Sutherland clearances, although not all emigration was due to eviction and compulsion. The sheer hardship of Highland life and pressure of population led to many Gaels seeking a better life elsewhere. The going was often extremely hard. This is a rare letter from 1834 written home in Arran Gaelic from Quebec. William Hendry was ambivalent about his new life. He preferred to be where he was but admitted that it was 'pretty tedious' and that sometimes he wasn't too pleased with his new home.

October the fifteenth 1834

Mrs Charles Hendry
Penrioch
Island of Arran
Scotland

May dear mother, brothers and sisters,
My dear mother, brothers and sisters.
a mathair greadhich tha me gabhail a cothrom-se air sgriobhadh dar
Dear Mother, I am taking this chance to write to you
niunsuidh a ligal a chluintinn duibh gu eil sinn ule gu maith sanamsa
to let you hear that we are all well at present,
buidhachas do dhia airson a throcairen dhuinn agus a mhianemig gu
thanks be to God for His mercies to us, and we would wish that you
biodh e ni ceun agibhse ri ra agus bha duil agum ri litir a chur dar
should have the same to say; and I had expected to send you a letter at
nionsuid toisach en tamaridh ach gholabh mi began uine en e steates
the beginning of the summer, but I went for a short while to the States
tiomull da cheud mile on aite so deic agus tree fichead mile en taobh
(about two hundred miles from this place, seventy miles the other side
eile line agus be nobair a bha agam chuid do nuine bhi deanadh
of the Line), and the work I had for part of the time was making

clacha craidha agus bha uilliam ruagh mo cusinn lam agus cuigear
bricks, and my cousin Uilleam Ruadh was with me and another five

eile do gillean mhuntuir en atie agus thainig sien dhachie ach dhean
lads from the place; and we came home but

Peter Hamilton cairid domh fein agus dhiar e ormsa na bighinn a
Peter Hamilton (a friend of mine) stayed, and he asked me, if I were

chur in fhios dachie ruibhse dhinseadh da mhuintir gun robh e gu
sending word home to you, to tell his people he was

maith agus cha neil e teachd dachie gu cion blianadh ma soirbheas
well, and he isn't coming home for a year if he gets on all right.

leis Aagus tha agum ra innseadh dhuibh nach beo shoni chui a bha
And I have to tell you that Johnnie from Cuithe that used to be

lochraoinsa gholabh e leis en tinnis ann e Quebec gu robh en
in Lochranza is dead. He died of sickness in Quebec. May the

tighearna uile gar nulamhachadh airson na uair sien. Agus tha
Lord prepare us all for that time. And there's

nighean do uilleam kiliston a bha air sanagan a tha duil acha gu
a daughter of William Kelso's from Sannox that they think

mheil i en tiniscatie agus nighean eile do bhaldy callum nach eil a
is in a consumptive sickness and another daughter of Baldie Calum's

faotinn a slainte idir.
that isn't getting her health at all.

Ach tha en eslaint an sgach atie Aagus tha mo chairden leis e mheil
But then there's no place without illness, and my friends with

mi a dol ma guairt gach laa Agus tha bhrathair mo mhathair agus a
whom I go around every day and my mother's brother and his

theaghlach gu maith a mheud dhiu sa tha aig en tigh ach tha e fein
family are in good health, those of them as are at home, but he

a fainachadh gu mhor agus tha iad teachd air on auidh gu maith
himself is failing very much; and they have got on well

on a tanik iad do d[u]iche so tha achda da bo agus beathin bega
since they came to this country. They have two cows and small beasts.

tha achda air a blianadh so na deanadh chuidachadh maith to
This year they have as much as would be a considerable help to

theaghlach na dha a bharrachd orra fein agus tha e agra nach
one or two families as well as themselves, and he says that he

measadh e bhi riamh na bu sona na tha e na biodh
would think himself never happier than he is now if he had

a clann leis en so cruinn.
his children around him.

tha iad cur moran beannachdan dar nionsuidh agus tha
They send many greetings to you. And

goinag mo chiosin fastage se namsa aig e mhinisgair tha i cur an
my cousin Janet is in the minister's service at present; she

beannachdan nionsuidh. Agus tha ma cairdean leis em bheil mi cur
sends you many greetings. And my friends that I am with send

moran beannachdan dar nionsuidh agus a ghiunsuidh mo shean-
many greetings to you and to my grand-

mhathair agus un Keggi puithar mathair agus tha mo chairid caoimh
mother and to my father's sister Katie. And my dear kinsman

uilliam adhfruachi air teachd dachie agus tha e gu maith ca dan e
William Murchie has come home and he is well. He only stayed

ach ma aon seachduin agus gholabh e risg en de air slighe a dhol don
about one week and set off again yesterday on the way to the

atie n robh e roimh tiamull sae ceud mile on atie so se so ghabh iad
place he was in before, about 600 miles from here. Before that they took

sea mios teachd e nuas roimh leis en raft gu Qebec agus tha uilliam
six months coming down by raft to Quebec. And my dear

ruagh mo cusin caoimh gu maith tha e uairean ag obair air en
cousin Uilleam Ruadh is well; he is sometimes employed as

taoirsneachd agus a chuid eile saoirachadh ferrain agus tha chuid a
a carpenter and works the land the rest of the time, and he has some

dhuil agie gun thig a chuid eile don theaghlach a mach ach cha neil
hopes that the rest of the family will come out, but he does not

fhios agie agus tha mi creudsinn gu maith gu biod iad na bhear en
know, and I can well believe that they would be better here

so na tha iad agus moran a thullie orra ach cha neil mi toirt
than where they are and many other people besides, but I am not

misneach do dhuine air bith teachd air en uairs oir tha moran
encouraging anybody to come at the moment, for too many

tigheachd nach eil toilite don atie so agus cha neil mi fein ra tholite
are coming who don't like this place, and I'm none too pleased

don atie so fathest ach faoididh e bhi gle maith air a hon sin ach tha
with this place myself as yet, but it may be very good for all that. But

fhios agam gu biodh mi gu mor na bu tailteacha na biodh sibh fein
I know I would be far happier if yourself

se chuid eile don theaglach en so agus a chuid mor a thainig don
and the rest of the family were here and also the large number that came

atie so en toiseachd. Thaink iad re iomad sarachadh [   ] en deigh doibh
to this place at first. They came through many a trial after

teachd [   ] a mhuintir a tha teachd a nios faotinn agus ch[a   ]
arriving that the folk who are coming now [are not] getting and

teachd en toiseach en atie so tha toilite deagh [   ] toir achda le
coming first to this place who are pleased [   ] good [   ] many of them

oiberachadh gle goirt uairen air a [   ] a dheanes daoine en so cha bhi
by very hard work, sometimes [   ] people stay here they are not

eagal orra gun toirear [   ] Cha druin mise in e clearadh air mo lot
afraid that [   ] will be taken [   ]. I have not done any clearing on my lot

fal [   ] [gad] gaineadh tha e go fada o margadh snach biodh mo[r
[   ] doing [   ] it [   ] it is so far from a market that it would not be [much]

] ann domh ach na biodh duil agum ri sibhse e teachd [en so]
use to me but if I were expecting you to be coming here

thoisachin air ulamhachadh air air son en so [   ] gholabhain
I would start preparing for you here and I would go away

blianadh a chuideachadh [em o] cosnadh leibh teachd a mach cha
and earn for a year to help you come out. I

neil fhios agum cocu a tha mi deanadh gu maith dar taoibhse a bhi
don't know whether I am doing well by you to be

fantuinn en so sna nach eil ach se bhi a bhear lam tha sibhse ligal
staying here or not but it's [here] I'd prefer to be. You are

fhaicin air curam dhiomsa gach uair tha sibh cothrom air agus cha
showing your concern for me every time you get the chance to and [I]

bo choir do [mh fas ro] churmach tiomull oirbhse tha fadail orm go
ought not [to be too] concerned about you. I am distressed that

fada se tha mi gun air facinn fein agus mo chairden caoimh uile tha
it has been so long since I have seen yourself and all my dear kinsfolk

en sin ach tha dochas agum gu faic mi sibh en so air no en sin en
who are there, but I hope that I will see you either here or there

uine gun a bhi anabar fada ma se sin toil en tigearna tha en tatie so
before too long, if that is the Lord's will. This place is

gu maith fadailach a bhi ann air uairen cha naik sinn read se bith
pretty tedious to be in sometimes: we can see nothing

[tiomull ach] oirn ach e caoile agus ne speran os air cion tha en
around us but the forest and the skies above. The

gheameradh en so dirach fada agus fuar tha sneachd aguin
winter here is just long and cold. We are having snow

ma namse.
at the moment.

Agus cha nainith domh aon do mo chairdean en sin le a
And I don't know any of my kinsfolk there who

chuideachadh nach feudadh geanaid gle maith en so na biodh iad
might not with His help do very well here

aon uair bhos tha chuid don fearun dirach maith agus chuid gle
once they were over. Some of the land is just fine and some pretty

surrach tha chuid dheagh swampach clachach creagach ach tha
useless, some is very swampy, stony and rocky but

chuid mor dheagh maith airson feum dhaoine.
> *a lot of it is very good for people's needs.*

tha mi a cur moran beannachden dar nionsuidh fein agus
> *I send many greetings to yourself and*

thiunsadh mo sheanmhathair es athair agum agus un gach chairid
> *to my grandmother and to all my aunts and to all my male*

es banchairid tha agum gad nach urrad mi nainmsachadh en
> *and female kin though I can't mention them just*

draist.
> *now.*

Uilleam Hendry
> *William Hendry*

Copy of Letter of William Hendry to his Mother, Acc. 9479.

Victorian Scotland

The long reign of Victoria saw more Scots than ever abroad in the Empire: soldiers, missionaries and emigrants all figured in this new phase of the Scottish diaspora. At home industry boomed, and there were questions of reform and workers' rights to be tackled. Scottish engineering saw both triumph and tragedy in the form of the Tay Bridge disaster and the triumphal opening of the Forth Rail Bridge with its revolutionary cantilevered structure. The Church of Scotland underwent an important schism: the Disruption, which split it almost in half, creating the Free Church. Behind the prestige of the Highland regiments and the 'Balmoralization' of Scotland's image lay a not-so-pretty story of Highland famine, distress and emigration. These were some of the issues in Victorian Scotland.

Victoria's Visit

For a British monarch, Queen Victoria was extremely quick off the mark in making her first visit to Scotland in 1842, only five years after taking the throne. She was greatly excited by Sir Walter Scott's novels and very anxious to make the acquaintance of her Northern kingdom, which soon became one of her favourite haunts after the purchase of Balmoral Castle a few years later. The citizens of Edinburgh duly turned out to greet her. As her diary records, she was much impressed, but as the eye-witness account of another spectator reveals, all did not go quite according to plan. Sir John Macdonald, Lord Kingsburgh, was just a small boy at the time of the visit. He records what happened in his 'Life Jottings of an old Edinburgh Citizen'.

The Queen's Diary

Thursday, September 1 1842

At a quarter to one o'clock, we heard the anchor let down – a welcome sound. At seven we went on deck, where we breakfasted. Close on one side were *Leith* and the high hills towering over *Edinburgh*, which was in fog; and on the other side was to be seen the *Isle of May* (where it is said Macduff held out against Macbeth), the *Bass Rock* being behind us. At ten minutes past eight we arrived at *Granton Pier*, where we were met by the Duke of Buccleuch, Sir Robert Peel and others. They came on board to see us, and Sir Robert told us that the people were all in the highest good humour, though naturally a little disappointed at having waited for us yesterday. We then stepped over a gangway on to the pier, the people cheering and the Duke saying that he begged to be allowed to welcome us. Our ladies and gentlemen had landed before us, safe and well, and we two got into a barouche, the ladies and gentlemen following. The Duke, the equerries, and Mr. Anson rode.

There were, however, not nearly so many people in *Edinburgh*, though the crowd and crush were such that one was really continually in fear of accidents. More regularity and order would have been preserved had there not been some mistake on the part of the Provost about giving due notice of our approach. The impression *Edinburgh* has made upon us is very great; it is quite beautiful, totally unlike anything else I have seen; and what is even more, Albert, who has seen so much, says it is unlike anything *he* ever saw; it is so regular, everything built of massive stone, there is not a brick to be seen anywhere. The *High Street*, which is pretty steep, is very fine. Then the Castle, situated on that grand rock in the middle of the town, is most striking. On the other side the *Calton Hill*, with the *National Monument*, a building in the Grecian style; *Nelson's Monument; Burns' Monument*; the Gaol, the *National School*, &c.; all magnificent buildings, and with *Arthur's Seat* in the background, overtopping the whole, form altogether a splendid spectacle. The enthusiasm was very great, and the people very friendly and kind. The Royal Archers Body Guard met us and walked with us the whole way through the town. It is composed entirely of noblemen and gentlemen, and they all walked close by the carriage; but were dreadfully pushed about.

Saturday 3rd September.
The view of *Edinburgh* from the road before you enter *Leith* is quite enchanting; it is, as Albert said, 'fairy-like', and what you would only imagine as a thing to dream of, or to see in a picture. There was that beautiful large town, all of stone (no mingled colours of brick to mar it), with the bold Castle on one side, and the *Calton Hill* on the other, with those high sharp hills of *Arthur's Seat* and *Salisbury Crags* towering above all, and making the finest, boldest background imaginable. Albert said he felt sure the *Acropolis* could not be finer; and I hear they sometimes call *Edinburgh* 'the modern *Athens*'. The Archers Guard met us again at *Leith*, which is not a pretty town.

The people were most enthusiastic, and the crowd very great. The Porters all mounted, with curious Scotch caps, and their horses decorated with flowers, had a very singular effect; but the fishwomen are the most striking-looking people, and are generally young and pretty women – very clean and very Dutch-looking, with their white caps and bright-coloured petticoats. They never marry out of their class.

At six we returned well tired.

Victoria, *Leaves from the Journal of our Lives in the Highlands, 1848-61*, Edinburgh, 1868.

Life Jottings of an Old Edinburgh Citizen

The event which of all others stamped itself deep on the tablets of my infant mind was the first visit of Queen Victoria to Scotland in 1842. How well I remember my father taking my sister and me to a grand-stand erected in what was then a grazing field between Pitt Street and Brandon Street, and I can recall the exact location of it by having seen through the space between the floor boards, the filthy sewage-laden mill stream taken from the Water of Leith, and carried along the back of Moray Place on to Canonmills, after serving the mills at Stockbridge. Modern sanitary zeal would have forbidden the placing of a crowd immediately above such a foul stream, on a stand in which it was to sit for many hours. Opposite the end of the stand there were erected a barricade of considerable height, and ponderous gates to represent the City port of old. These were to be closed until the ceremony had been gone through of presenting Her Majesty with the silver keys of her ancient loyal town of Edinburgh. There we sat for several weary hours, until the news arrived that the entry would not be made till the following morning, and all had to go home disappointed. Next day early we were once more in the grand-stand, and full of anticipation. Everybody expected that there would be sufficient warning of the approaching procession by the sight of the Lord Provost and Council in their robes assembling, and the gates being closed. Suddenly, we saw excitement in Brandon Street – hats waved, and ladies' handkerchiefs in lively motion, and sounds of loud cheering reached us. A number of unfortunate people, who had been walking leisurely down between the crowded lines to reach their stands, were seen running back at full speed, making first to one side and then to the other, in terror of the cavalry escort that came on at a full trot, filling the whole space between the barriers, and before there was time to realise what was happening the royal carriage swept through the open gateway – no Provost, no keys, no mace, no sword being there. Quickly as they went by, I saw the Queen and Prince distinctly; she in one of the wide spread bonnets of the day, and he with a very tall hat held in his hand, both bowing first to one side and then to the other. But it was a twenty seconds' view only; most disappointing to those who had waited in vain the day before and lost the chance of seeing her well – the carriage not being stopped at the gates, and the ceremony of the keys performed.

History tells us that there had been a failure of understanding between Sir Robert Peel, the minister in attendance, and the municipality, the latter not having been informed that Her Majesty would come up from Granton so early, the hour being about that of ordinary breakfast time. The contretemps had its amusing side, and two young ladies drew up, on the same day, a clever skit, which was sung in many a street in the evening, and sold in thousands, in which the Lord Provost, Sir James Forrest, and his bailies were humorously chaffed. The few stanzas following are a specimen of the song, which is a parody on the old ditty, 'Hey, Johnny Cope'. The opening lines were:

'Hey, Jamie Forrest, are ye waukin yet?
Or are yer bailies snorin' yet?'

There were many verses, but two may suffice as specimens:

'The frigate guns they loud did roar,
But louder did the bailies snore;
They thocht it was an unco bore
To rise up early in the morning.
        Hey, Jamie Forrest, &c.

The Queen she came to Brandon Street
The Provost and the keys to meet,
But div ye think that she's to wait
Yer waukin up in the morning.
        Hey, Jamie Forrest, &c.'

The secret of the authorship was well kept, and it was not revealed till a few years ago, when it was learned from Mr. David Scott-Moncrieff that the song was written in collaboration by his two sisters, who must have been but young girls at the time. Their witty lines entitle them to be remembered.

All in the grand-stand were struck dumb with disappointment, and once more returned home aggrieved. Meantime the civic dignitaries, who were leisurely getting into their carriages to come down in state, hearing with consternation that the Queen had reached the City, started off at a gallop to try to intercept the procession on its way to Dalkeith, and pay their respects on the road. They were not successful, as the cavalcade went at a smart trot, and so they too came back with woebegone demeanour.

The Queen, on learning what had happened, good-naturedly altered her itinerary, and devoted a day to an official entry into Edinburgh. The lofty barricade was removed from Canonmills Burn to the High Street, and erected across it at the west end of the City Chambers. The royal carriage I see still, surrounded by the Royal Archers, the Queen's Bodyguard, who had no chance of doing their duty when the cavalcade came up from Granton at a trot. The red of the velvet cushion on which the City keys lay is still with me, seen as I looked down from the roof of St. Giles', and also the rapid waving of the ladies' handkerchiefs from the top of the long arched gateway in front of the municipal buildings.

All, however, was not happiness that day. I learned thus early in my life how the joyful and the distressful go together. We were taken after the ceremony to Bank Street, to a private house, and there from the window saw a sad sight – a dead body and several stretchers with injured people being taken by the police to the Infirmary. A grand-stand had been stormed by the crowd, who climbed on to it in such numbers that it gave way, and many were precipitated onto the street. These stretchers I can still see quite vividly before me, and I remember how the crowd was stilled at the sight.

I am stating what I personally saw, and therefore can only put in a note what I have heard by tradition, relating to the bodyguard on the day the Queen came up from Granton. The story told was, that the Archers were round the Queen's carriage at Granton when it started, but as it was driven at a trot, the bowmen, many of whom were no longer in the vigour of youth, and in many cases were of rotund form, dropped out, here one and there one, staggering to the railings in Inverleith Row, and panting for breath. It is said that only two trained athletes got as far as the bottom of the hill from Princes Street, and there had to drop out, lest they should drop down. This tradition is confirmed by the caricature . . . where the two who reached Brandon Street are seen in sad plight, unable to face the hill.

J. H. A. Macdonald, *Life Jottings Of An Old Edinburgh Citizen*, London, 1915.

Down the Mines
···

*We have already looked at unregulated child labour in mills in the
1820s. A similar situation could be found down coal mines.
Ironically, the association between Victorians and children up
chimneys and down pits came not from their tolerance of such
cruelty but from the determined fight which reformers such as
Lord Shaftsbury took up against such practices. Royal
Commissions were appointed by Parliament to enquire into these
practices, and legislation to ban the worst of such abuses followed
– hence the banning of women and children from the pits. In
Scotland, inspectors such as R. H. Franks and Thomas Tancred
investigated the conditions in the mining industry. These reports
published in 1842, including the words of the workers themselves,
show what they found. The comments in round brackets are from
the inspectors – notice their interest in the state of the children's
religious knowledge.*

EVIDENCE ON THE EMPLOYMENT OF CHILDREN

BEARING PITS, HARLAW MUIR, COALY BURN, parish of *West Linton,
Peebles-shire.* – (Rev. J. J. Beresford, Leaseholder and Heritor.)

No. 115   *Margaret Watson,* 16 years of age, coal-bearer:
I was first taken below to carry coals when I was six years old, and
have never been away from the work, except a few evenings in the
summer months, when some of us go to Carlops, two miles over the
moor, to learn the reading: reads a little.

Most of us work from three in the morning till four and five at
night. I make 20 rakes a-day, and 30 when mother bides at home.
What I mean by a rake is a journey from the day-light with my
wooden backit [box or container of coal] to the coal-wall, and back
with my coal to the day-light, when I throw the coals on father's hill,
and return. (The pit is 8 ¹/₂ fathoms deep, descended by a turnpike
stair, and wall-face 100 fathoms distant from pit bottom.)

I carry 2 cwt. on my back; never less than 1 ¹/₂ cwt. I know what
the weight of 1 cwt. is, though I cannot say how many pounds there
are in it.

I never was taught to sew, much more shape a dress, yet I stitch up
my pit clothes.

We often have bad air below; had some a short time since, and lost
brother by it: he sunk down, and I tried to draw him out but the air
stopped my breath, and I was forced to gang.

(Knows a few questions in the Child's Catechism, but very destitute of any useful information.)

No.116   *Margaret Leveston,* 6 years old, coal-bearer:
Been down at coal-carrying six weeks; makes 10 to 14 rakes a-day; carried full 56lbs. of coal in a wooden backit. The work is na guid; it is so very sair. I work with sister Jesse and mother; dinna ken the time we gang; it is gai dark. Get plenty of broth and porridge, and run home and get bannock, as we live just by the pit. Never been to school; it is so far away.

(A most interesting child, and perfectly beautiful. I ascertained her age to be six years, 24th May, 1840; she was registered at Inveresk.)

No.117   *Jane Peacock Watson,* age 40, coal-bearer:
I have wrought in the bowels of the earth 33 years. Have been married 23 years, and had nine children; six are alive, three died of typhus a few years since; have had two dead born; thinks they were so from the oppressive work: a vast of women have dead children and false births, which are worse, as they are no able to work after the latter.

I have always been obliged to work below till forced to go home to bear the bairn, and so have all the other women. We return as soon as able, never longer than 10 or 12 days; many less, if they are much needed.

It is only horse-work, and ruins the women; it crushes their haunches, bends their ankles, and makes them old women at 40.

Women so soon get weak that they are forced to take the little ones down to relieve them; even children of six years of age do much to relieve the burthen.

Knows it is bad to keep bairns from school, but every little helps; and even if inclined there is no school nearer than two miles, and it is a fearfu' road across the moor in summer, much more winter.

Coal-hewers are paid 4 $\frac{1}{2}$ d. for each load of 2 cwt., out of which they have to pay the bearers whom they hire.

Each collier has his place on the coal-hill, and gets his money just as the sale comes in, which makes the pay uncertain.

No.118   *Jesse Coutte,* 13 years old, coal-bearer:
I was born at Coaly Burn. Mother had me registered at West Linton. I have wrought below six years. Mother took me first down: she does not work now, as she had a false birth (miscarriage), from

the oppression of sore work, and she has never been hersel since. Father has been idle 12 weeks, from a hurt in the arm; it was done by the wedge cutting the sinews open: he receives 5s. a-week from a friendly society, but they mean to knock him down to 2s. 6d. after next Saturday.

Sister Helen is wrought; she is 11 years past, and been four years below, and Charlotte is nine years old, and been two years at the work. Mother has 10 children. Sisters and I can read in the Testament: never did anything at the writing; cannot sew. Is very much fatigued with the work; would like to run away from it. God made the world, and made me. Jesus is God. Don't know how many days in the year; thinks there are 10 or 12 months; can't say what they call them. Sir is cursing and swearing. Twelve pennies are in a shilling; can't say how many there are in two shillings. Reads very little.

No.119   *Mary Neilson*, 10 years old, coal-bearer:
When sister Margaret, who is nine years old works, we make 10 to 15 rakes each; when she is away I am forced to make 20. Sister was six years when she first wrought, and I went down at that age.

I carry half a load now; half a load is 1 cwt., and it is no easy work; it often causes me to fall asleep below when there is nothing to gang with.

Mother does not work now; has been very weak from two false births, and obliged to stay away.

(Reads a little: knows scarcely any of the questions [of the catechism], but very acute at weights. Would acquire knowledge quickly from natural talent. Rather short-sighted. If well dressed would vie with any child in Scotland in point of beauty.)

GATEHEAD COLLIERY, KILMARNOCK; visited personally

No.31   May 4   *Mrs Gray*
Is wife of James Gray, the engine-man at one of Mr Guthrie's [i.e. Duke of Portland's] pits called the Kiln Pit; her husband has three brothers colliers in Mr Finnie's pits at Gatehead; her father was a weaver at Tarbolton, eight miles distant. Has been here a year, and 'her man' wrought seven years at Mr Howie's near Kilmarnock, towards Galston; her husband goes to the engine to draw water before the colliers go down at three o'clock of a morning; the colliers go down from four to six a.m., according to the time the coal is wanted for shipment at Troon. The time is about the same for

commencing at all the pits she knows; they are very often 'by with their work gin twa o'clock,' at this pit, but that is earlier than most others, because there are fewer men. Where there are maist men they are longer down, because it takes longer to draw their coals. About 12 hours is the general time men are down at other pits; this quarter of a-year and better they have not been above six days a fortnight working, on account of little shipment; if they could get it they would like very 'weel' to work ten days a fortnight. They take the boys down at 10 years old to work; they only give them two 'foos' [i.e. two loads or four creels] at first, in three-quarters of a-year, they give them three 'foos' and six 'foos' when they come to half a dark, when they are about 13; and at 15 or 16 come to three-quarter dark. The boys draw all the creels; what she means by their having the above number of 'foos' or loads is, that the collier is allowed to put out so many for the boy. It must be sore on the children to stay down and work so long; it keeps them down; they are not generally so healthy boys that's down as those that work above ground. A heap o' folk think its want of air being confined below ground so many hours. In summer sometimes the air's that foul they cannot work, they are obliged to come up, men and boys and all. Some o' the colliers tries to get their boys into trades, or learns 'em to be 'gig-men' [i.e. to manage the engine] and keep them above ground as long as they can. Her man worked below ground when he was a boy, but he did not agree with it, he drove a horse below at Muirkirk, but he could not stand it; it made him sick and sleepy; it made him unco' dull and sleepy. After he was married he began to work a few weeks in the pit, but he was obliged to give it up from the same cause; has heard mothers and fathers say that they wished their children to be well forward with their schooling, and a bit stout, before they took them down; she thinks they should never go down under 12 years old if folk could keep them up to that, but a heap of folk must take them down to help to keep the young ones. It's very dangerous work; a heap of them get hurt with stones falling from the roof, and by coals when they fall over fast upon them in working them; there's no much fire-damp in these pits. Mr Guthrie's work has a school, and the colliers who have wee anes send them either to it or to other schools; they are all keen to learn 'em to read, to be that forward that they can read the Bible; and a heap of them, after they are working, learn to write at the night-school for an hour at night; but many of the girls do not learn to write; the girls work at flowering muslin, but they don't win above 2d. or 3d. a-day for a

while; the work's that ill that she has a cousin in the town who sits
close to it and is a real good 'shewer' [sewer], and cannot win above
6d. a-day. The children when they go down the pit maistly takes
enough to serve them the day, and get dinner when they are by with
their work; often they are unco' hungry for dinner; they take cheese
and bread, and whiles tea whiles milk, for dinner pork and potatoes,
or flesh meat, or broth. The Gatehead folk have a library to which
they pay 9d. a quarter, and many colliers are in libraries which are
managed by ministers or missionaries; she has shown me the
catalogue of the one her husband is in. The 2nd rule is, that 'it shall
consist of books fitted to promote the intellectual, moral, and
religious improvement of the readers; nor shall any work containing
unsound opinions, or having a dangerous tendency, be admitted.'
Rule 4 is, 'that it shall be under the management of eleven curators,
who shall be in full communion with the church, and shall be chosen
from the several districts of the congregation.' Most of the men in
Mr Guthrie's, and about Gatehead, work very steady, and attend the
kirk; some of the young ones are very ready to get intoxicated after
pay day; but about Fairlie work they are quite extraordinary, do not
gang to the kirk or to preachings, and get themselves intoxicated on
Saturday nights, and that makes them unfit for attending kirk on
Sabbath. The purpose of this inquiry, if it is to get the children more
time for schooling, is a gude thing, and canna' do ill to ony body.
She thinks all the best disposed of the colliers would approve of a
limitation of the working age to 12 years old.

*First Report of Commissioners for Inquiring into the Employment and Condition
of Children in Mines and Manufactories, reports and Evidence of Sub-
Commissioners, 1842, vol xvi.*

The Disruption of the Church of Scotland, 18 May 1843

*Lord Cockburn's account of the major breach in the established
Church of Scotland in 1843, which resulted in the formation of the
Free Church of Scotland as a powerful rival to the 'Auld Kirk',
describes a defining religious and political moment in 19th-century
Scotland. This was the culmination of almost a decade of
increasingly bitter conflicts with the civil courts and, ultimately,
with Parliament. A third of the ministry and a large proportion of
the active membership of the church left the 'establishment',
leaving it seriously weakened, particularly in many of the large
towns and cities and in the Highlands and Islands.*

The pre-Disruption controversies raised many fiercely debated
ecclesiastical and theological principles. Yet some supporters of
what became the Free Church also resented the treatment of a
Scottish national issue by English politicians at Westminster, over-
riding the wishes of a majority of Scottish members for a
compromise. The most immediate preoccupation of the new
Church was with its internal affairs, diverting this nationalist
feeling into a great upsurge of church and school building and
fund-raising. The theme was taken up again some years later by
increasingly political campaigns for 'Scottish Rights', for
restoration of the post of Scottish Secretary, and, ultimately, for
Home Rule. Henry Cockburn was a supporter of the Free Church.
His account of the actual event at the Church of Scotland General
Assembly of 1843 is a sober one, and he was conscious of
historical echoes going back to covenanting times.

8 June 1843. The crash is over.

The event that has taken place was announced so far back as
November, when the Convocation proclaimed that their
adhering to the Church would depend entirely on the success of the
last appeal they meant to waste upon Government and Parliament.
These appeals had failed, and all subsequent occurrences flowed
towards the announced result. On the two Sundays preceding the
Assembly hundreds of congregations all over the country had been
saddened by farewell sermons from pastors to whom they were
attached. The general belief that there would be an extraordinary
move, combined with uncertainty as to its exact time and form and
amount, had crowded Edinburgh with clergymen, and had produced
an anxiety far beyond what usually preceded the annual Assemblies
of the Church . . . conjectures deepened expectation; but they were
all speedily set at rest.

Dr Welsh, Professor of Church History in the University of
Edinburgh, having been Moderator last year, began the proceedings
by preaching a sermon before his Grace the Commissioner in the
High Church [St. Giles], in which what was going to happen was
announced and defended. The Commissioner then proceeded to St.
Andrew's Church, where the Assembly was to be held. The streets,
especially those near the place of meeting, were filled, not so much
with the boys who usually gaze at the annual show, as by grave and
well-dressed grown people of the middle rank. According to custom,
Welsh took the chair of the Assembly. Their first act ought to have
been to constitute the Assembly of this year by electing a new

Moderator. But before this was done, Welsh rose and announced that he and others who had been returned as members held this not to be a free Assembly – that therefore, they declined to acknowledge it as a Court of the Church – that they meant to leave the very place, and, as a consequence of this, to abandon the Establishment. In explanation of the grounds of this step he than read a full and clear protest. It was read as impressively as a weak voice would allow, and was listened to in silence by as large an audience as the church could contain . . . The protest resolved into this, that the civil court had subverted what had ever been understood to be the Church, that its new principles were enforced by ruinous penalties, and that in this situation they were constrained to abandon an Establishment, which, as recently explained, they felt repugnant to their vows and to their consciences.

As soon as it was read, Dr Welsh handed the paper to the clerk, quitted the chair, and walked away. Instantly, what appeared to be the whole left side of the house rose to follow. Some applause broke out from the spectators, but checked itself in a moment. 193 members moved off, of whom about 123 were ministers, and about 70 elders. Among those were many upon whose figures the public eye had been long accustomed to rest in reverence. They all withdrew slowly and regularly, amidst perfect silence, till that side of the house was left nearly empty. They were joined outside by a large body of adherents, among whom were about 300 clergymen. As soon as Welsh, who wore his Moderator's dress, appeared on the street, and people saw that principle had really triumphed over interest, he and his followers were received with the loudest acclamations. They walked in procession down Hanover Street to Canonmills, where they had secured an excellent hall, through an unbroken mass of cheering people, and beneath innumerable handkerchiefs waving from the windows. But amidst this exultation there was much sadness and many a tear, many a grave face and fearful thought; for no one could doubt that it was with sore hearts that these ministers left the Church, and no thinking man could look on the unexampled scene and behold that the temple was rent, without pain and sad forebodings. No spectacle since the Revolution [of 1688-89] reminded one so forcibly of the Covenanters.

Henry Cockburn, *Journal*, ii, Edinburgh, 1874.

The Highland Potato Famine

*Phytophthora infestans – the potato blight which had devastated
Ireland – struck the Highlands of Scotland in autumn 1846,
putting 200,000 people at risk of starvation. The situation was
very different from that of Ireland in that the scale of the disaster
was much smaller and Scotland was a much more heavily
urbanized country. Lowland labour markets presented alternative
opportunities for some. For the many, a relief effort was needed.
The infant Free Church of Scotland joined with the Glasgow and
Edinburgh relief committees to form the Central Board of
Management for Highland Relief. Over £210,000 was raised by
this body: an enormous accomplishment by 19th-century
standards. The government too was induced to give relief – which
it did in humiliating style, instigating a 'destitution test'. To earn
one pound of meal a man had to labour for an entire day.
Landlords gave varying amounts of help to their tenants: some
were generous but 14% had to be censured by government officials
for their negligence.*

*On 18 December 1846 a public meeting was held in Edinburgh to
discuss how best to respond to the disaster. Robert Candlish was one
of the most prominent leaders of the Free Church, which in 1846
was a national body. Whilst support for the Free Church was at this
date strong in the Lowlands, in the Highlands it was almost total.
Free Church ministers played an important role in calling attention
to the famine and agitating for relief – but not everyone believed in
the religious analysis of the problem – as the extract below shows.*

Dr Candlish pledged himself that the Free Church party would
gladly throw themselves into any general movement which
might be made [to relieve the distress], that general movement being
what they had from the first desiderated [wanted]. The Rev. Doctor
read the following letter from the Rev. Alex. Macgregor, Kilmuir,
Skye, to the Rev. Mr Glass, Musselburgh

Kilmuir Manse, Skye, 9th Dec. 1846

My Dear Sir, I have this moment received your favour of the 3rd
instant and regret being unable to make a lengthy reply.

The subject on which you addressed me is of the most vital
importance, viz. The prevailing famine, with which it has been the
will of the Great Ruler of all things to afflict this quarter of the

kingdom. The condition of this parish, in common with all other parishes in Skye, is at present deplorably alarming. It is already well known that the potatoes form almost the sole staff of life to the population of the localities in question. The failure of that esculent is almost total in this island. I do not suppose that all of Skye could furnish twenty barrels – hence the famine over the length and breadth of our parish. I may state for example that the population of this parish is about 4,000 souls. Of these upwards of 2,000 have no lands from the proprietor. These 2,000 souls are reduced to a state of abject famine, and subsist totally on the praiseworthy liberality of the proprietor. On the other hand nearly 2,000 souls occupy crofts and lots of land, but the returns from the same will not be sufficient to afford them support for three months to come. In less time indeed, the whole population will become the victims of scarcity and famine. But while it cannot be expected that the proprietor can long be able to support such a burden, it must be recollected, that should he do so, he was only supporting one half of the number that will be in want in a few weeks. It is therefore plain, that unless the proprietor be assisted by the government, or from other sources, he cannot possibly save his people from the appalling effects of the famine. What I have stated in regard to this parish will serve as an example for the state of every parish in the island.

After reading the letter Dr Candlish proceeded. He strongly urged vigorous and united action. They should have one great committee or agency; their cause was the cause of humanity, and their relief should be given without deciding between sect and sect. (Applause)

An individual here rose and introduced himself to the meeting as Donald Macleod, and denied that the Almighty had any cause of controversy with the Highlands more than any other place; but the destitution rose from the capitalists having monopolised the hills and glens of the Highlands, which deprived the people of the means of breeding cattle and raising grain, causing them to become a reproach to their fellow men. Unless the Highland population were put into a position to better themselves by their own industry, more temporal relief would be of little avail.

On the motion of Bishop Terrot, seconded by the Rev Jonathan Watson, it was next resolved to raise funds by subscription.

Dr Candlish then proposed for the sake of harmony, that the appointment of a committee be vested in men selected merely for their official situation. He therefore proposed that the Lord Provost, Sheriff Speirs and Bailie Mack be requested to undertake the duty. (Cheers)

The resolution passed unanimously and the meeting (having sat three hours) broke up.

Inverness Courier, 23 December 1846

Reproduced in H. Noble, *The Potato Famine in the Highlands 1846-9*, n.p., 1987.

Observations on Epidemic Cholera

Child labour and poverty were not the only social problems experienced in Victorian Scotland. Epidemic disease, closely linked to bad sanitation and the cramped living conditions of the urban poor, was still a terrible threat. Part of the reason we know so much about epidemics in the 19th century is that debate was raging in the medical profession about how to stop them. There were two major theories about cholera: one was that it was contagious, spread by touch from human to human. The other harked back to the old ideas about the spreading of the Black Death, that it was supposedly spread by unhealthy vapours in the air and bad smells, therefore the solution was increased sanitation. The theory behind this latter position was wrong, but the practices which stemmed from it were right – cholera was spread through water supplies contaminated by poor sanitation. The answer was an urban clean-up campaign.

James Maxwell Adams was a doctor in one of the poorest parts of Glasgow in 1849 before the vital medical breakthrough into the causes of cholera was made. As can be seen from his careful observations, he was documenting the living conditions which seemed to give rise to epidemics.

During the late epidemic of cholera in the City parish, Glasgow, I had favourable opportunities of observing the disease, having had the charge of one of the seventeen medical districts, into which the parish is divided. The following observations refer chiefly to the disease as it appeared in that district; but include, also, the results of cases treated in private practice, and which occurred in various localities throughout the city.

The thirteenth medical district comprises that central portion of the city which is bounded on the upper or north side by George Street; by the west side of High Street to Stirling Street; by Stirling Street to Candleriggs; thence to Argyle Street; by Argyle Street to Buchanan Street, and thence to George Street. It forms pretty nearly an oblong quadrangle, running from east to west, half a mile in length, by a quarter in breadth. The population of the entire district can scarcely be under 14,000; and of this number I consider that about 5,000 are of that class who avail themselves of the services of the parochial surgeon. By far the greater proportion of this class reside in the north east corner of the district, within a space 280 yards in length, by 120 in breadth, and it was within this limited area that fully nine-tenths of the cases of the late epidemic occurred.

The condition of the great mass of the inhabitants, and the general sanitary state of this portion of the district, are probably as bad as can well be conceived. The locality consists chiefly of five or six narrow streets, and about a dozen of the dirty 'closes' or 'wynds' for which Glasgow has acquired a discreditable notoriety. There are very few sewers, or gratings which conduct to sewers, and the greatest amount of drainage consequently takes place on the surface. The receptacles for filth consist of large open dungsteads placed either in the centre of the closes, or of the lower flats of inhabited tenements, with an open window through which the refuse is cast, and in these places of deposit, the filth accumulates till it is in such quantity as to necessitate the removal of a portion from want of space for further deposit. The cases are exceptional in which regular arrangements are made for this purpose, and in all they are miserably inefficient. Thus, in three of the worst closes of the district, I occasionally observe a frail old pauper paddling about the principal dungstead with a broom or shovel, and the entire sanitary operations of these localities are due to his solitary exertions, – in return for which, he receives the shelter, rent free, of a wretched cellar in the neighbourhood.

The supply of water is very scanty; a single pipe or fountain is made to suffice for one or more of these closes, and the trouble of going such a distance as is required in order to procure a supply, seems to be sufficient excuse for the people to limit the use of this essential element to the narrowest limit compatible with necessity.

The houses are of a wretched character, excessively over-crowded and filthy. They generally consist of one apartment, but occasionally of two, of from eight to twelve feet square, seldom containing less than four, and very commonly as many as twelve, inmates for each apartment. A great proportion of the population is migratory, and only lodge with the party who rents the premises, paying a small pittance nightly or weekly. Beds are rarely seen – the inmates lying on the floor, often without *doffing* the clothes worn during the day. In numerous instances where the parties work in-door upon soft fabric goods procured from warehouses, the webs of cloth so obtained, serve as coverlets until the period when they are returned to the manufacturer or warehouseman. There are few of these houses in which there is not a pauper receiving out-door relief.

Fever may be considered as endemic in the district, and the expense which the parish incurs in the maintenance and attendance of the victims of epidemic, endemic, and contagious diseases, and in making the various provisions which are, in consequence obligatory on parochial boards, cannot fall far short of the whole rental which the proprietors of these lazarettos draw from their inheritances.

During six months only of 1847, as many as 400 cases of typhus fever occurred within this portion of the district, and were treated at the cost of the parish. The total cases of disease occurring within the district, within the last two years, and treated at the cost of the parish, was 1900, of which number, fully 1,000 were cases of epidemic, endemic and contagious disease.

Cholera first appeared in the district on 9th December 1848, in the ground flat of a building in 22 Shuttle Street. The patient, a female aged fifty-six, was of occasionally intemperate habits, and her previous general health was not good. She had not been in communication with any infected district or locality so far as could be ascertained. She was immediately conveyed to hospital, where she died on the following day. I immediately got the house lime-washed, and the straw-bed on which she had lain destroyed, but the inmates would not consent to removal.

The next case occurred in the same house. A female child, aged two years became affected on 12th December with bilious diarrhoea, which was followed on the 17th by all the symptoms of cholera. She died on the following day.

The third case occurred in 51 Shuttle Street, being on the opposite side of the street, and at a distance of about thirty yards from the last locality. The patient, a female aged twenty-six, was of irregular habits, of infirm intellect, and subject to occasional attacks of dysenteric diarrhoea. She resided in the top story of the tenement: and for a few days prior to December 18th, had been very little out of doors, and had not, so far as I could ascertain, been in communication with the sick. I had her conveyed to hospital, where she died on the following day.

The fourth case occurred in the same house with the preceeding. The patient, a female, aged fifty-three, of irregular habits, and average good health, became affected with bilious diarrhoea on December 23, and, on the following day, with all the best marked symptoms of the malignant disease. She recovered after a somewhat protracted convalescence.

The fifth case occurred in 34 Shuttle Street, in the top flat of a building closely adjoining that in which the first case occurred. There is no direct communication between the buildings. The patient was a healthy temperate female, aged eighteen. She had slight diarrhoea on December 24, and next morning, soon after breakfast, she was seized with vomiting, speedily followed with purging and cramps. I had her immediately sent to hospital, where she died, soon after admission.

Up to this date, there had occurred, in all, of cholera and diarrhoea, only seven cases, all within a circle of a few yards, and at the extreme north-east corner of the district; but within the next *three* days, I was called to *twenty* cases in various parts of the district, and of this number, eleven were malignant cholera.

James Maxwell Adams, *Observations on the Epidemic Cholera of 1848-9, chiefly as it prevailed in the 13th Medical District of City Parish Glasgow*, Edinburgh, 1849.

To The Gold Fields in Australia

Scots were still emigrating to seek their fortunes elsewhere, but by now different destinations, such as Australia and New Zealand, were proving popular. 'Jack Mackay' (references in his diary suggest that this might have been his name) left Haddington in 1852 to seek his fortune in the goldfields of Australia. He kept a diary for his family of his outward voyage – almost in the form of a letter to them. His homesickness and account of conditions on board must have been true for many thousands of Scottish emigrants.

2oth July 1852. Sleep rather broken from the tossing of the ship and working of the sailors on deck. Rose in good health at $^1/_2$ past six am. The wind abated heavy sea running and heavy rain falling down. Saw a grampus this morning a short distance from the ship, a small kind of whale. Great numbers on board sick and vomiting. There has scarce a day passed but some have been sick but there has been more this morning than any previous. Arthur's wife has been sick almost every day since we set sail. I have never vomited and have never been sick except a short time one afternoon. I intended having told you before this hour how I was situated with respect to comrades and the like but as we take week about of the cooking and scullery work and last week being my turn, I had time for little more than [to] write down the notes. I have not, as I anticipated, got into the same berth along with Arthur and his wife: owing to the act of parliament that married and unmarried shall not be in the same berth which I think is very proper and I am none sorry at it. They are put into the stern part of the ship where they feel its tossing very much and where it is very dark and ill-aired. I am right amid ships, right opposite the main hatchway where I can scarcely feel the tossing of the ship, where I have plenty of air and light. There are 8 souls in our berth, 4 Englishmen, 1 Perthshireman, 2 children and myself. One of the Englishmen is a professor of instrumental musick, another is a middle aged gentleman who has been some time in the army. He has travelled a great deal and seen a great deal of the world. He is a very fine man and willing at all times to give me whatever information he can. All of us are most social and agreeable, each making his endeavour to make each as comfortable as possible. I feel I am going to agree with the diet – first-rate. I always feel prepared for my meals before they are prepared for me. If I am granted health and appetite such as I have until I get to Australia, I expect to be as fat as a pig and I am afraid as lazy as a sloth. If ever it be my fortune to return to Haddington, I expect I shall be fit for cook, scullery maid, seamstress, in short anything in the housewify line and as Englified as a cockney. There are very few unmarried females on board and out of the few I see nothing to take my fancy, so there is very little fears of my being troubled with love sickness. Never does a day pass but my heart is in Haddington, wondering how you all are and how you are all getting on and all my friends in Scotland, but never have I for a moment regretted leaving home, as I am still convinced, if I am spared, it will yet be seen to be for good, in however bad a light you may at present view it. Before leaving home, you were talking of all coming together. Happy and comfortable as I am, I can assure you all on board cannot say so, fathers and mothers of family are truly miserable indeed. There has been very little wind today and what has been not altogether favourable, thus we are making very little progress. My not being acquainted with the longitude and latitude and not being able at all times to ascertain how the wind is blowing, I must put down favourable or unfavourable when not sure how it is blowing. There are on board 370 passengers and I do not think there is a dozen of the males who are not bound for the digging and I am sure if some of them makes a fortune, Jack shall not return to

Scotland with his pockets empty. There are scores of them on whose
brow sweat never broke, unless it were at a plum pudding or some
fine roast, but there are a good number of stout active fellows too.
There are 25 seamen, 1 captain, 4 mates and 1 boatswain making in
all 401. Smart breese struck up about 8 pm right in our favour
making about 10 notes [knots] an hour on our direct course. Went
to bed about 10 pm.

'Diary of an emigrant to Australia from Haddington' [Author's name possibly Jack
Mackay], Acc. 6158.

'Tingle-Bang, Wish-Hiss' – the Crimea

*In 1853, Britain and France united against Russia's domination of
the Black Sea coast and launched an invasion. Many Scots were
involved and news was so hungrily sought after in Edinburgh that
a newspaper devoted entirely to reports from the front,* The War
Telegraph, *was temporarily set up. Sadly, none of its issues seem to
have survived. Thomas Ligertwood was an assistant surgeon in the
Crimean War. His letters give some flavour of ordinary life in the
British Camp. Here he writes to his mother in Aberdeen.*

Camp before Sebastopol, Crimea
17th October 1854

My Dear Mother,
At last we have commenced actual operations against Sebastopol
– late last night the order was given to begin the bombardment at ½
past six o'clock by a signal namely the firing of three mortars near
the centre of the French lines. The Russians at day break seeing our
embrasures open, blazed away at our batteries which we returned
with such salvos as made our ears tingle-bang, wish-hiss went the
salvos, every shot I am told telling and rapidly we silenced many of
their guns. They fired well however, and many very bravely. The
French got rather peppered, their earth works, I suspect, not being
thick enough. Many of their batteries were silenced and two of their
powder magazines blown up. Two or three Russian magazines have
been blown up and I am sorry to say one of our own – the sailors'
battery under Captain Peel of The Diamond. Of course all this is
mere hearsay, for we most likely will know nothing of the doings for
certain for some days. The smoke soon obscures a proper view of
what was going on. The shipping went at it beautifully and I am sure
m[ust] have done great damage. The firing ceased at [   ] past six,
so 12 hours constant firing to commence with. I hope the Russians

will soon find the place too hot for them. The French lost about 100 killed and wounded today. I believe we lost comparatively few. Tomorrow morning I suppose will recommence the business. The noise of the cannonade today was quite deafening. Upon the whole I believe the day has been well employed, tho' I hear the French will require breathing time to recommence. The weather we are thankful to say continuing very good and not as cold as it was, sickness however very great. Capt. [   ] O' Leary 68th regiment was killed today outside the lines having gone out to see the firing, not on duty. I have had no intrenchment duty as yet, which I am glad of, harassing work, being in the trenches all night, and after all a doctor can't do anything in the dark, no light being allowed, and this is all the meagre news I can give you of the first day of the actual siege and I sincerely trust many more days it won't require. I am very thankful today I am quite well and in good spirits, taking things quietly which is the secret of keeping in good spirits.

With kind remembrances to all,
I am, my dear mother
Your most loving son
Thomas Ligertwood

'Letter to his Mother in Aberdeen, of Thomas Ligertwood, Assistant Surgeon 40th Foot' MS. 15385 f.177r-v.

'The Thin Red Line'

The Crimean War was famous not only for the ill-fated Charge of the Light Brigade, but also for the battle of Balaclava, 25 October 1854, in which the 93rd Sutherland Highlanders were immortalised as the 'Thin Red Line'. This description (also the name of the famous painting which depicts the action) derives from the dispatches of W. H. Russell, the special war correspondent of The Times. *In fact, his phrase was 'that thin red streak topped with a line of steel'. Here is his report of the Highlanders' part in the action.*

The Cavalry Action at Balaklava

October 25

. . . The 93rd had originally been advanced somewhat more into the plain, but the instant the Russians got possession of the first redoubt they opened fire on them from our own guns, which inflicted some injury, and Sir Colin Campbell 'retired' his men to a better position. Meantime the enemy advanced his cavalry rapidly.

To our inexpressible disgust we saw the Turks in redoubt No 2 fly
at their approach. They ran in scattered groups across towards
redoubt No 3 and towards Balaklava, but the horsehoof of the
Cossack was too quick for them and sword and lance were busily
plied amongst the retreating herd. The yells of the pursuers and
pursued were plainly audible. As the Lancers and Light Cavalry of
the Russians advanced they gathered up their skirmishers with great
speed and in excellent order – the shifting trails of men, which
played all over the valley like moonlight on the water, contracted,
gathered up and the little *peloton* [troop, lit. ball or bunch] in a few
moments became a solid column. Then up came their guns, in
rushed their gunners to the abandoned redoubt, and the guns of No
2 redoubt soon played to distinguished effect upon the dispirited
defenders of No 3 redoubt. Two or three shots in return from the
earthworks and all is silent. The Turks swarm over the earthworks
and run in confusion towards the town firing their muskets at the
enemy as they run. Again the solid column of cavalry opens like a
fan, and resolves itself into a 'long spray' of skirmishers. It laps the
flying Turks; steel flashes in the air and down go the poor Moslem
quivering on the plain, split through fez and musket guard to the
chin and breast belt. There is no support for them. It is evident the
Russians have been too quick for us. The Turks have been too quick
also, for they have not held their redoubts long enough to enable us
to bring them help. In vain the naval guns on the heights fire on the
Russian cavalry; the distance is too great for shot or shell to reach.
In vain the Turkish gunners in the earthen batteries which are placed
along the French intrenchments strive to protect their flying country
men; their shot fly wide and short of the swarming masses. The
Turks betake themselves towards the Highlanders, where they check
their flight and form into companies on the flanks of the
Highlanders. As the Russian cavalry on the left of the line crown the
hill across the valley they perceive the Highlanders drawn up at the
distance of some half mile, calmly waiting their approach. They halt
and squadron after squadron flies up from the rear, till they have a
body of some 1,500 men along the ridge – Lancers, Dragoons and
Hussars. Then they move *en echelon* in two bodies, with another in
reserve. The cavalry who have been pursuing the Turks on the right
are coming up to the ridge beneath us which conceals our cavalry
from view. The heavy brigade in advance is drawn up in two lines.
The first line consists of the Scots Grays and of their old companions
in glory the Enniskillens; the second of the 4th Royal Irish, of the

5th Dragoon Guards and of the 1st Royal Dragoons. The Light
Cavalry Brigade is on their left in two lines also. The silence is
oppressive; between the cannon bursts one can hear the champing of
bits and clink of sabres in the valley below. The Russian on their left
drew breath for a moment, and then in one grand line dashed at the
Highlanders. The ground flies beneath their horses' feet; gathering
speed at every stride, they dash on towards that thin red streak
topped with a line of steel. The Turks fire a volley at 800 yards, and
run. As the Russians come within 600 yards, down goes that line of
steel in front, and out rings a rolling volley of Minié musketry. The
distance is too great; the Russians are not checked, but still sweep
onwards with the whole force of horse and man, through the smoke,
here and there knocked over by the shot of our batteries above. With
breathless suspense everyone awaits the bursting of the wave upon
the line of Gaelic rock; but ere they come within 150 yards, another
deadly volley flashes from the levelled rifle, and carries death and
terror into the Russians. They wheel about, open files right and left
and fly back faster than they came. 'Bravo Highlanders! Well done'
shout the excited spectators; but events thicken. The Highlanders
and their splendid front are soon forgotten, men scarcely have a
moment to think of this fact, that the 93rd never altered their
formation to receive that tide of horsemen. 'No,' said Sir Colin
Campbell, 'I did not think it worthwhile to form them even four
deep!' The ordinary British line, two deep was quite sufficient to
repel the attack of these Muscovite cavaliers.

W. H. Russell, *The Times*, 14 November 1854.

Mutiny

The next destination for the 93rd was India, where large numbers
of local troops were employed in the service of the East India
Company. The introduction of a new form of rifle cartridge, said
to be greased with animal fat, sparked riots – both Hindus and
Muslims had religious grounds for refusing these. The cartridge
tops were supposed to be bitten off, bringing their mouths into
contact with the 'unclean' animal fat. The issue suddenly
crystallised a whole host of grievances against British rule. There
was a series of uprisings culminating in massacres of Europeans.
The 93rd was one of the regiments sent in after the event to restore
order. William Forbes Mitchell records some of the horrific scenes
of massacre and reprisal which he witnessed when he arrived.

The day before we reached Cawnpore, a strong column from Delhi had arrived under command of Sir Hope Grant, and was encamped on the plain near the spot where the railway station now stands. The detachment of the Ninety-Third did not pitch tents, but was accommodated in some buildings, on which the roofs were still left, near General Wheeler's entrenchment. My company occupied the *dâk* bungalow, which, on my revisit to Cawnpore, appeared to me to have given place to the present Victoria Hotel.

After a few hours' rest, we were allowed to go out in parties of ten or twelve to visit the horrid scene of the recent treachery and massacre. The first place my party reached was General Wheeler's so-called entrenchment, the ramparts of which at the highest places did not exceed four feet, and were so thin that at the top they could never have been bullet-proof! The entrenchment and the barracks inside of it were complete ruins, and the only wonder about it was how the small force could have held out so long. In the rooms of the building were still lying strewn about the remains of articles of women's and children's clothing, broken toys, torn pictures, books, pieces of music, etc. Among the books, I picked up a New Testament in Gaelic, but without any name on it. All the blank leaves had been torn out, and at the time I formed the opinion that they had been used for gun-waddings, because, close beside the testament, there was a broken single-barrelled duck gun, which had evidently been smashed by a 9-pounder shot lying near. I annexed the Testament as a relic, and still have it. The Psalms and Paraphrases in Gaelic verses are complete, but the first chapter of Matthew and up to the middle of the seventh verse of the second chapter are wanting. The Testament must have belonged to some Scotch Highlander in the garrison. I have more than once thought of sending it home to the Highland Society as a relic of the Mutiny.

From the entrenchment we went to the Suttee Chowra ghât, where the doomed garrison were permitted to embark in the boats in which they were murdered, and traces of the treachery were still very plain, many skeletons, etc., lying about unburied among the bushes.

We then went to see the slaughter-house in which the unfortunate women and children had been barbarously murdered, and the well into which their mangled bodies were afterwards flung . . . Our guide showed no desire to minimise the horrors of the massacre and the murders to which he said he had been an eye-witness. However, from the traces, still too apparent, the bare facts, without exaggeration, must have been horrible enough. But with reference to the women and children, from the cross-questions I put to our guide, I then formed the opinion, which I have never since altered, that most of the European women had been most barbarously murdered, but not dishonoured, with the exception of a few of the young and good-looking ones, who, our guide stated, were forcibly carried off to become Mahommedans. But I need not dwell on these points. These are the opinions I formed in October 1857, three months after the massacre, and nothing which I have since learnt during my thirty-five years' residence in India has led me to alter them.

Most of the men of my company visited the slaughter-house and well, and what we there saw was enough to fill our hearts with feelings which I need not here dwell on; it was long before those feelings could be controlled. On the date of my visit a great part of the house had not been cleaned out; the floors of the rooms were still covered with congealed blood, littered with trampled, torn dresses of women and children, shoes, slippers, and locks of long hair, many of which had evidently been severed from the living scalps by sword-cuts. But among the traces of barbarous torture and cruelty which excited horror and a desire for revenge, one stood out prominently beyond all others. It was an iron hook fixed into the wall of one of the rooms in the house, about six feet from the floor. I could not possibly say for what purpose this hook had originally been fixed in the wall. I examined it carefully, and it appeared to have been an old fixture which had been seized on as a diabolic and convenient instrument of torture by the inhuman wretches engaged in murdering the women and children. This hook was covered with dried blood, and from the marks on the whitewashed wall, it was evident that a little child had been hung on to it by the neck with its face to the wall, where the poor thing must have struggled for long, perhaps in the sight of its helpless mother, because the wall all round the hook on a level with it was covered with the hand-prints, and below the hook with the foot-prints, in blood, of a little child.

At the time of my visit the well was only about half-filled in, and the bodies of the victims only partially covered with earth. A gallows, with three or four ropes ready attached, stood facing the slaughter-house, half-way between it and the well; and during my stay three wretches were hanged, after having been flogged, and each made to clean about a square foot of the blood from the floor of the house. Our guide told us that these men had only been captured the day before, tried that morning, and found guilty as having assisted at the massacre.

During our visit a party of officers came to the slaughter-house, among whom was Dr Munro, Surgeon of the Ninety-Third, now Surgeon-General Sir William Munro. When I saw him he was examining the hook covered with dried blood and the hand and foot-prints of the child on the wall, with the tears streaming down his cheeks. He was a most kind-hearted man, and I remember, when he came out of the house, that he cast a look of pity on the three wretches about to be hanged, and I overheard him say to another officer who was with him: 'This is horrible and unchristian to look at; but I do hope those are the same wretches who tortured the little child on the hook inside that room.' At this time there was no writing either in pencil or charcoal on the walls of the slaughter-house. I am positive on this point, because I looked for any writing. There was writing on the walls of the barracks inside General Wheeler's entrenchment, but not on the walls of the slaughter-house, though they were much splashed with blood and slashed with sword-cuts, where blows aimed at the victims had evidently been dodged and the swords had struck the walls. Such marks were most numerous in the corners of the rooms. The number of victims butchered in the house, counted and buried in the well by General Havelock's force, was one hundred and eighteen women and ninety-two children.

Up to the date of my visit, a brigade-order, issued by Brigadier-General J. G. S. Neill, First Madras Fusiliers, was still in force. This order bears date the 25th of July 1857. I have not now an exact copy of it, but its purport was to this effect: – That, after trial and condemnation, all prisoners found guilty of having taken part in the murder of the European women and children, were to be taken into the slaughter-house by Major Bruce's méhter police, and there made to crouch down, and with their mouths lick clean a square foot of the blood-soaked floor before being taken to the gallows and hanged. This order was carried out in my presence as regards the three wretches who were hanged that morning. The dried blood on the floor was first moistened with water, and the lash of the warder was applied till the wretches kneeled down and cleaned their square foot of flooring. This order remained in force till the arrival of Sir Colin Campbell in Cawnpore on the 3rd of November, 1857, when he promptly put a stop to it as unworthy of the English name and a Christian Government.

W. Forbes Mitchell, *Reminiscences of the Great Mutiny*, London, 1893.

Dr Livingstone I Presume?

*'Gordon Bennett!' – the exclamation comes from the name of the
real-life American newspaper proprietor who made his name with
stunts which would be familiar to the tabloid newspaper readers of
today. What most people don't know is that one of Gordon
Bennett's most successful stunts was funding that other avid self-
publicist of his day, Henry Morton Stanley, travelling correspondent
of the* New York Herald, *in his quest to find David Livingstone. The
famous Scots explorer and missionary had passed out of contact
with the outside world. Was he dead or alive? Bennett decided his
readers would want to know. Henry Stanley wrote up his successful
mission in his book* How I found Livingstone *(note the 'I' part, all
those who assisted Stanley being ignored as usual). In 1871 he found
his quarry. Show-man to the finger-tips, Stanley had even brought a
bottle of champagne to sip with Livingstone in the jungle.*

But by this time we were within two hundred yards of the village,
and the multitude was getting denser, and almost preventing our
march. Flags and streamers were out; Arabs and Wangwana were
pushing their way through the natives in order to greet us, for
according to their account, we belonged to them. But the great
wonder of all was, 'How did you come from Unyanyembe?'

Soon Susi came running back, and asked me my name; he had told
the Doctor that I was coming, but the Doctor was too surprised to
believe him, and, when the Doctor asked him my name, Susi was
rather staggered.

But, during Susi's absence, the news had been conveyed to the
Doctor that it was surely a white man that was coming, whose guns
were firing and whose flag could be seen; and the great Arab
magnates of Ujiji – Mohammed bin Sali, Sayd bin Majid, Abid bin
Suliman, Mohammed bin Gharib, and others – had gathered
together before the Doctor's house, and the Doctor had come out
from his veranda to discuss the matter and await my arrival.

In the meantime, the head of the Expedition had halted, and the
kirangozi was out of the ranks, holding his flag aloft, and Selim said
to me, 'I see the Doctor, sir. Oh, what an old man! He has got a
white beard'. And I – what would I not have given for a bit of
friendly wilderness, where, unseen, I might vent my joy in some mad
freak, such as idiotically biting my hand, turning a somersault, or
slashing at trees, in order to allay those exciting feelings that were
well-nigh uncontrollable. My heart beats fast, but I must not let my

face betray my emotions, lest it shall detract from the dignity of a white man appearing under such extraordinary circumstances.

So I did that which I thought was most dignified. I pushed back the crowds, and, passing from the rear, walked down a living avenue of people, until I came in front of the semicircle of Arabs, in the front of which stood the white man with the grey beard. As I advanced slowly towards him I noticed he was pale, looked wearied, had a grey beard, wore a bluish cap with a faded gold band round it, had on a red-sleeved waistcoat, and a pair of grey tweed trousers. I would have run to him, only I was a coward in the presence of such a mob – would I have embraced him, only, he being an Englishman [*sic!*], I did not know how he would receive me; so I did what cowardice and false pride suggested was the best thing – walked deliberately to him, took off my hat, and said:

'DR. LIVINGSTONE, I PRESUME?'

'YES', said he, with a kind smile, lifting his cap slightly.

I replace my hat on my head, and he puts on his cap, and we both grasp hands, and I then say aloud:

'I thank God, Doctor, I have been permitted to see you.'

He answered, 'I feel thankful that I am here to welcome you.'

I turn to the Arabs, take off my hat to them in response to the saluting chorus of 'Yambos' I receive, and the doctor introduces them to me by name. Then, oblivious of the crowds, oblivious of the men who shared with me my dangers, we – Livingstone and I – turn our faces towards his tembe. He points to the veranda, or, rather, mud platform, under the broad overhanging eaves; he points to his own particular seat, which I see his age and experience in Africa has suggested, namely, a straw mat, with a goatskin over it, and another skin nailed against the wall to protect his back from contact with the cold mud. I protest against taking this seat, which so much more befits him than me, but the Doctor will not yield: I must take it.

We are seated – the Doctor and I – with our backs to the wall. The Arabs take seats on our left. More than a thousand natives are in our front, filling the whole square densely, indulging their curiosity, and discussing the fact of two white men meeting at Ujiji – one just come from Manyuema, in the west, the other from Unyanyembe, in the east.

Coversation began. What about? I declare I have forgotten. Oh! We mutually asked questions of one another, such as:

'How did you come here?' and 'Where have you been all this long time? – the world has believed you to be dead.' Yes, that was the way it began; but whatever the Doctor informed me, and that which

I communicated to him, I cannot correctly report, for I found myself gazing at him, conning the wonderful man at whose side I now sat in Central Africa. Every hair of his head and beard, every wrinkle of his face, the wanness of his features, and the slightly wearied look he wore, were all imparting intelligence to me – the knowledge I craved for so much ever since I heard the words, 'Take what you want, but find Livingstone.' What I saw was deeply interesting intelligence to me, and unvarnished truth. I was listening and reading at the same time. What did these dumb witnesses relate to me?

Oh, reader, had you been at my side on this day in Ujiji, how eloquently could be told the nature of this man's work! Had you been there but to see and hear! His lips gave me the details; lips that never lie. I cannot repeat what he said; I was too much engrossed to take my note-book out, and begin to stenograph his story. He had so much to say that he began at the end, seemingly oblivious of the fact that five or six years had to be accounted for. But his account was oozing out; it was growing fast into grand proportions – into a most marvellous history of deed.

The Arabs rose up, with a delicacy I approved, as if they intuitively knew that we ought to be left to ourselves. I sent Bombay with them, to give them the news they also wanted so much to know about the affairs at Unyanyembe. Sayd bin Majid was the father of the gallant young man whom I saw at Masange, and who fought with me at Zimbizo, and who soon afterwards was killed by Mirambo's Ruga-Ruga in the forest of Wilyankuru; and, knowing that I had been there, he earnestly desired to hear the tale of the fight; but they had all friends at Unyanyembe, and it was but natural that they should be anxious to hear of what concerned them.

After giving orders to Bombay and Asmani for the provisioning of the men of the Expedition, I called 'Kaif-Halek,' or 'How-do-ye-do,' and introduced him to Dr. Livingstone as one of the soldiers in charge of certain goods left at Unyanyembe, whom I had compelled to accompany me to Ujiji, that he might deliver in person to his master the letter-bag he had been entrusted with by Dr. Kirk. This was that famous letter-bag marked 'Nov. 1st, 1870,' which was now delivered into the Doctor's hand 365 days after it left Zanzibar! How long, I wonder, had it remained at Unyanyembe had I not been despatched into Central Africa in search of the great traveller?

The Doctor kept the letter-bag on his knee, then, presently, opened it, looked at the letters contained there, and read one or two of his children's letters, his face in the meanwhile lighting up.

He asked me to tell him the news. 'No, Doctor,' said I, 'read your letters first, which I am sure you must be impatient to read.'

'Ah,' said he, 'I have waited years for letters, and I have been taught patience. I can surely afford to wait a few hours longer. No, tell me the general news: how is the world getting along?'

'You probably know much already. Do you know that the Suez Canal is a fact – is opened, and a regular trade carried on between Europe and India through it?'

'I did not hear about the opening of it. Well, that is grand news! What else?'

Shortly I found myself enacting the part of an annual periodical to him. There was no need to exaggeration – of any penny-a-line news, or of any sensationalism. The world had witnessed and experienced much the last few years. The Pacific Railroad had been completed; Grant had been elected President of the United States; Egypt had been flooded with savants; the Cretan rebellion had terminated; a Spanish revolution had driven Isabella from the throne at Spain, and a Regent had been appointed; General Prim was assassinated; a Castelar had electrified Europe with his advanced ideas upon the liberty of worship; Prussia had humbled Denmark, and annexed Schleswig-Holstein, and her armies were now around Paris; the 'Man of Destiny' was a prisoner at Wilhelmshöhe; the Queen of Fashion and the Empress of the French was a fugitive; and the child born in the purple had lost for ever the Imperial crown intended for his head; the Napoleon dynasty was extinguished by the Prussians, Bismarck and Von Moltke; and France, the proud empire, was humbled to the dust.

What could a man have exaggerated of these facts? What a budget of news it was to one who had emerged from the depths of the primeval forests of Manyuema! The reflection of the dazzling light of civilisation was cast on him while Livingstone was thus listening in wonder to one of the most exciting pages of history ever repeated. How the puny deeds of barbarian paled before these! Who could tell under what new phases of uneasy life Europe was laboring even then, while we, two of her lonely children, rehearsed the tale of her late woes and glories? More worthily, perhaps, had the tongue of a lyric Demodocus recounted them; but, in the absence of the poet, the newspaper correspondent performed his part as well and truthfully as he could.

Not long after the Arabs had departed, a dishful of hot hashed-meat cakes was sent to us by Sayd bin Majid, and a curried chicken

was received from Mohammed bin Sali, and Moeni Kheri sent a
dishful of stewed goat-meat and rice; and thus presents of food came
in succession, and as fast as they were brought we set to. I had a
healthy, stubborn digestion – the exercise I had taken had put it in
prime order; but Livingstone – he had been complaining that he had
no appetite that his stomach refused everything but a cup of tea now
and then – he ate also – ate like a vigorous hungry man; and, as he
vied with me in demolishing the pancakes, he kept repeating, 'You
have brought me new life. You have brought me new life.'

'Oh, by George!' I said, 'I have forgotten something. Hasten Selim,
and bring that bottle; you know which; and bring me the silver
goblets. I brought this bottle on purpose for this event, which I
hoped would come to pass, though often it seemed useless to expect
it.'

Selim knew where the bottle was, and he soon returned with it –
a bottle of Sillery champagne; and, handing the Doctor a silver
goblet brimful of the exhilarating wine, and pouring a small
quantity into my own, I said,

'Dr. Livingstone, to your very good health, sir.'

'And to yours,' he responded.

And the champagne I had treasured for this happy meeting was
drunk with hearty good wishes to each other . . .

And now, dear reader, having related succinctly 'How I found
Livingstone,' I bid you also 'Good-night.'

H. Morton Stanley, *How I Found Livingstone*, London, 1972.

The Tay Bridge Disaster

Beautiful Railway Bridge of the Silv'ry Tay!
Alas! I am very sorry to say
That ninety lives have been taken away
On the last Sabbath day of 1879,
Which will be remember'd for a very long time.

William Topaz McGonagall

*The fall of the Tay Bridge was a terrible blow to the self-
confidence of Scottish engineering. Calculations for the bridge had
failed to take into account the fierce wind speeds which could be
reached in the Firth of Tay. Sub-standard materials had also been
used in key parts of the construction. On the night of 28
December 1879, the bridge came down in a storm. All on board
the Dundee-bound train on the bridge at the time were killed – a*

total of 75 persons, not 90, as according to McGonagall, and not 300, which was the erroneous total telegraphed out of Dundee in the first hours of the disaster. One of the first with the news in Edinburgh was the Courant. *Its information came down the wire from Dundee via Perth.*

FRIGHTFUL DISASTER AT THE TAY BRIDGE — FALL OF CENTRAL PORTION
— A TRAIN HURLED INTO THE RIVER — LOSS OF THREE HUNDRED LIVES

Edinburgh, Monday, 8 A.M.

We have this morning to record one of the most dreadful disasters that have ever occurred in this country, through the falling of part of the Tay Bridge, and the sweeping away of a passenger train, involving great loss of life. The first intimation of the catastrophe which reached Edinburgh was a telegram received at the Waverley Station about eleven o'clock last night, stating that some of the high girders of the Tay Bridge had been blown down, and expressing a fear that they had carried with them the 4.15 p.m. passenger train from Edinburgh, due at Dundee at 7.10.

A special train was at once prepared, and it started about half-past twelve for the scene of the disaster, with Mr Walker, the manager; Mr McLaren, passenger superintendent; Sir Thomas Bouch, C.E. [the engineer who built the bridge]; and Mr Bell, engineer. Owing to the bad state of the telegraph wired, little or no information regarding the disaster was received till a late hour this morning.

Our Dundee correspondent telegraphs this morning:–

Yesterday afternoon Dundee was visited by one of the most fearful hurricanes which has ever been experienced, and has been accompanied with unparalleled destruction of property, the large centre portion of the Tay Bridge having been blown down during a fearful blast, and it is also feared that the passenger train from the south, which was seen entering on the bridge at the Newport side a few minutes before the accident, and which has not since been heard of, has, with its passengers, been carried away with the fallen girders, and with these now lies in the bed of the river. From the time the gale began it continued to increase in fury until it became a perfect hurricane from the south-south-west. The property in the western suburbs and the Tay Bridge were exposed to the full fury of the blast. The streets, especially in the West End, were literally covered with *debris* of chimney-cans and slates which had been blown from the roofs of houses. Every moment the slates might have been seen flying off the roofs, whirling in the air and then falling in the street below in pieces. The danger to foot-passengers was exceedingly great, and many persons narrowly escaped from being struck by the toppling masses of masonry which formed the chimneys, or by the falling slates and chimney-cans. Palings and walls in a great many places have been demolished. Trees have been uprooted, and the shrubbery in gardens terribly destroyed. Indeed, so dreadful was the gale about seven o'clock that very few people were to be seen on the streets, and those who were then seen, and who had to walk against the wind, found it almost impossible to make headway. Each one appeared to be in terror of being injured by the missiles carried about in the air by the gale from the roofs of the houses, and appeared only anxious about getting home. About half-past seven the rumour spread that a large part of the Tay Bridge had been blown down, and that a passenger train crossing at the time had fallen into the river with the structure. As this rumour passed from mouth to mouth, it was thought so incredible that very few believed it. The bridge, since its completion, has withstood many a terrific blast, and remarks were made to the effect that it could hardly be possible that such a structure, in whose stability against both tide and wind its engineers and constructors had always had the most decided confidence, could have been demolished. The news conveyed by rumour, however, was so appalling and so startling that although it was generally received with reservation, everyone who heard it made off at once, almost with bated breath to the Magdalen Yard Point, and to the Tay Bridge Station, with the view of ascertaining what foundation there was for it. In the course of a very short time the persons in quest of information could be counted by hundreds. At the Tay Bridge Station, however, the officials were unable to give any information, beyond the fact that since a few minutes after seven o'clock communication between the signal cabins at each end of the bridge had been cut off. From the station enquiries proceeded by the Perth Road and the Esplanade to the Magdalen Yard Point, where the signal cabin is situated, in order to pick up whatever particle of information could be obtained. A good many persons entered the cabin box and enquired at the signalman as to the extent of the supposed calamity, but he could throw no further light on what was a very painful mystery. The railway officials, who had naturally become alarmed, especially since they were aware that there was no communication with the south end of the bridge, resolved to satisfy themselves whether the superstructure was safe or not. Accordingly Mr Roberts, superintendent of the locomotive department, determined to go along the bridge. This he did at considerable risk, for the force of the hurricane was such that at times he was almost completely lifted off his feet, and was in great danger of being blown into the river; but urged by the anxiety within his breast to learn in what condition the bridge was, fear for the time being comparatively banished, and he with considerable courage and daring continued the prosecution of his dangerous task. Having walked along the bridge as far as he could, he then crawled on his hands and knees as far as the point where the high girders begin. Here his course was arrested; horror stricken, he found that the rumour in circulation was too true, the whole of the thirteen girders, each 245 feet in width and 250 tons in weight, and which, as it were, had formed a tunnel in the middle of the bridge, were gone and nothing remained but the bare iron piers which had supported them. Mr Smith, the stationmaster, also made a similar journey along the bridge from the other end, and found that what Mr Roberts reported as to the destruction of the middle of the bridge was absolutely true.

Four o'clock a.m.

A message just received estimates the number of passengers in the fated train at not less than 200.

The man in the signal cabin at the north end of the bridge states that at about ten minutes past seven the Edinburgh train was signalled as having entered on the bridge at the south end, and that, in signalling a reply a moment or two afterwards, no communication with the south end was found to exist.

About an hour after the catastrophe had happened, several gentlemen, who reside at the West End of Dundee, and others who had been walking along the Perth Road at points commanding a view of the bridge, proceeded to the Tay Bridge station, and reported to Mr Smith the stationmaster, what they had seen of the calamity. Their testimony concurred us to the time at which the fearful accident had occurred. The evening was very clear, a full moon shedding bright light over all the town, and clearly revealing the outline of the Tay Bridge.

4.30 a.m.

Mr Walker, manager of the North British Railway, telegraphing from Leuchars, at four o'clock this morning, has communicated the following to the newspapers: – 'From reports made to us here of the terrible calamity at the Tay Bridge, it appears that several of the large girders of the bridge, along with the last train from Edinburgh, were precipitated into the river about half-past seven last night. There were, I deeply deplore to say, nearly 300 passengers, besides company's servants in the train, all of whom are believed to have perished. The cause of the accident has not yet been ascertained.'

The train was timed to arrive at the bridge at 7.08 p.m., and was signalled at 7.14, only six minutes behind time. Accounts are contradictory as to whether the bridge had given way before the arrival of the train, or whether it had succumbed under the combined pressure of the engine and carriages and the hurricane. There can be no doubt, however, as to the fate of the train and its human freight, however many or few were in it.

The centre portion of the bridge was constructed on piers of greater strength than those which supported the parts of the bridge nearer the land on either side. Here it was necessary to provide stronger columns to support the weight of the superincumbent girders, which at the navigable portion of the river have a span of 245 feet, and weigh 190 tons each. The cylinders employed for the bridge were made round, and on them were deposited great masses of brickwork up to high-water mark. From this point each pier was composed of six iron columns, constructed in 10 feet lengths, and of a proportionate thickness. Thirteen pieces of this kind carried the bridge over the navigable channel of the river, which on an average is about 45 feet in depth.

During a violent gale in February 1877, while the bridge was in process of construction, two of the largest girders, which had been raised to the top of the piers prepared for them, but had not been put in their places, were blown down from the hanging gear. About the same part the bridge has now given way under the strain of the elements, and led to a disaster the terrible magnitude of which it is impossible at the present moment to estimate.

As we have said, the water in the centre is over forty feet deep, the height of the bridge is eighty-eight feet above, and nothing is conceivable but that the train and its passengers must be lying in the bed of the Tay.

As the news did not reach Edinburgh till very late, there was of course little excitement in the city. Some of those who did hear the news would not credit it, and seeing that only private messages were received, conviction was not then forced upon any save those who were known to have friends in the train. These, by enquiries at the Waverley Station, learned that two railway officials at the Dundee station, anxious about the train, attempted to cross over the bridge, but they were driven back by a deluge of water which was escaping from the pipes employed to convey the water supply of Newport across the bridge.

Edinburgh Courant, 29 December 1879.

'How Much More Valuable Is, *Not Even a Sheep*, But a Game Bird than a Man?'

Repeated evictions coupled with emigration continued to plague the Highlands. For those left at home, life became ever harder as those landlords who did not force the tenants off their lands entirely often forced them onto the worst lands on their estates, while charging them ever more heavily for the privilege. Game and sheep were now much more lucrative than people, and crofters suffered accordingly. They had no security of tenure and could be moved or evicted at the mere whim of a factor or landlord. Eventually, protest and agitation forced the government to appoint a Royal Commission to look into the problem. These extracts come from evidence presented to Lord Napier's Commission. The result of the Commission's work was the Crofters Holdings Act of 1886 and the appointment of the Crofters Commission to oversee it.

NORTH UIST – LOCH EPORT – Angus Macaulay

ANGUS MACAULAY, Middle Quarter (30) – examined

The Chairman – Are you a crofter? – I am a crofter's son. I have a written statement here: – 'Unto the Royal Commission (Highlands and Islands). The following statement is humbly submitted by Angus Macaulay, crofter's son, on behalf of the crofters of Middle Quarter:

I am thirty years of age, and was born in the neighbouring township of Sollas, where my father and grandfather were crofters. I live now in Middle Quarter, where my father has been crofter for fourteen years . . . It is only thirty years since an emigrant ship was brought to Lochmaddy, on board of which twelve or fourteen families from the district in which I reside were prevailed upon or forced to embark for Australia. Emigrants who had been previously on board the vessel were discovered to be infected with two deadly epidemics, viz., smallpox and fever. The passage was a most disastrous one to the wretched emigrants, most of whom became victims of the epidemics; some of them died and were thrown overboard; others were landed in Ireland, where a number of them are buried. The survivors were sent over in different batches as they recovered; families were broken up, some of them never to meet again; and their sufferings on landing in Australia were not much better, as they had to sell their blankets and part of their clothing before they got to the settlement. What we have against emigration also are the different difficulties with which we would have to contend, such as the extremes of climate, our ignorance of the mode of farming in foreign countries, and our inability through poverty to get stock and farming implements on our arrival there, &c. The second and by far the more congenial way to ameliorate the condition of the Highland crofters is to give them sufficient of that land which gave them birth, and while there is plenty of land in our native country under sheep and deer, we see no reason why we should emigrate, and we are determined to resist a forced emigration to the bitter end. The forgoing statement is certified to be true by the undersigned crofters of Middle Quarter.' Signed by fifteen persons.

Inquiry into Condition of Crofters and Cottars, xxxii, 1884.

'Statement of Grievances by Crofters and Cottars in the district of Morven, Argyllshire. Lochaline. – Our principal grievances are as follows: – 1st, That we have been removed from lands occupied by ourselves and our forefathers, and that we have been huddled together in this miserable village; and through that and several other causes we have been reduced to great poverty; and were it not for the kindness of the late Mr Smith, and of his son, the proprietor of the adjoining estates of Acharn and Ardtornish, who, for more than thirty years, gave work to as many of us as he could, we do not know how we could have existed. We consider it a great hardship that we cannot get any land to cultivate, although abundance of good land formerly under cultivation, is going waste at our very doors. This land from which some of us have been evicted about seventeen years ago, we are sorry to see going back again into a state of nature, and overgrown with heather and rushes. We feel very much the want of milk for our families. Many of us would be very glad if we could get a cow's grass even without arable land at a reasonable rent, which we could pay. The rent for a cow's grass, without any arable land, charged by the late proprietrix is £3 a year, which we consider an intentional discouragement against any one aspiring to the dignity of keeping a cow. We know that the want of good milk, such as most of us have been accustomed to in our younger days, has a deteriorating influence upon ourselves, and more especially upon our children. We are aware that a certain medical gentleman in another part, while being examined before the Commission, recommended cheap beer as a substitute for milk. The use and introduction of such a substitute for milk in rearing our offspring we, and we are sure all Highlanders, will repudiate with scorn. We look upon such a suggestion as an insult to us; and we cannot perceive why we should be deprived of the means of having a supply of good milk, so that the proprietor may obtain a few pounds more rent. 2nd, Our next grievance is in regard to fuel. Under former proprietors, the poorest of us had the privilege of cutting peats on the hill as near hand as we could find them; but now we are prevented from doing this, and compelled to go to the top of the hill to cut them. The poorest and most destitute of us dare not gather a few tufts of heather to keep up the fire in case the game be interfered with, or be put to the least inconvenience. Our Lord and Saviour said, "How much more valuable is a man than a sheep?" But our landlords say, "How much more valuable is, *not even a sheep*, but a game bird than a man?" In consequence of the above restrictions as to fuel, we are at all seasons of the year under the necessity of buying coal, and in this remote district, so far situated from the coal centres of the south, coal is a luxury which some of us can ill afford. As an instance of the petty tyranny exercised over us regarding these matters, we wish to refer to a case which happened about two years ago, when a man belonging to our village, who is both a cripple and in receipt of parochial aid, was found on the road with a bundle of heather for his fire, and was unmercifully deprived of his heather by one of the estate gamekeepers and shoved along the road. We therefore consider it a great grievance that we, being loyal subjects of Her Majesty, living under what we are taught to believe to be the glorious British Constitution, living in a country which is supposed to be the best governed country in the world, should be left so much to the mercy of landed proprietors, and, still worse, their factors, that we can scarcely call our souls our own. We cannot reconcile all the boasted freedom to be enjoyed by all Her Majesty's subjects alike with what we know to be the truth in our own case. From our experience, we are more inclined to believe with Lord Macaulay, that the country, and Scotland especially, has the worst constitution in Europe, at least so far as the land laws are concerned.

We therefore trust that Her Majesty's Commissioners shall take our case into consideration. 3rd, Evictions. We specially beg to direct the attention of Her Majesty's Commissioners to the miserable condition of this district compared to what it was forty or fifty years ago. The population of the parish at that time was over 2,000. At last census it stood at 828. Fifty years ago, with such a large population, £11 sterling per annum from the collection at the church door was sufficient for the support of all the poor and destitute people within the district, and now, with a population of 828, the poor rates amount to over £600 a year. These facts we leave to the consideration and wisdom of the Commissioners, as we consider they require no comment from us beyond showing the benefits conferred upon this district by what the Duke of Argyll calls in scientific language 'economic conditions,' and that we are not to be bamboozled by his Grace's scientific conundrums. The first eviction which took place in this district happened between fifty and sixty years ago, when the late Miss Stewart evicted all the tenants in the township of Ferinish, Mangostell, Barr, and Innemore, numbering in all twenty-five families. The second eviction happened between forty and fifty years ago, when the tenants of several townships on the estates of Acharn and Ardtornish received summonses of removal from the proprietors before they sold the estates to Mr Patrick Sellar of Sutherlandshire. There were forty-eight families evicted at this time, so that the loss of population sustained by the parish must have been considerable. There was another cruel and very harsh eviction which took place in this district about seventeen years ago. When the late Mrs Paterson came into possession of the estate of Lochaline, there were in the townships of Achabeg and Knock a well-to-do crofter population, consisting of between twenty-five and thirty families. The families, owing to some whim of the proprietrix, were evicted wholesale, notwithstanding the oft-repeated remonstrances of the late Dr John M'Leod, then minister of the parish. The crowbar and faggot were here, let us hope for the last time in the history of the Highland peasant, brought into requisition to demolish the dwellings of men whose forefathers occupied the land long before Mrs Paterson came into the district, or had the means which gave her the power of buying the land and turning out the people. There was yet another eviction on the estate of the late Lady Gordon of Drimnin, and as this was a peculiarly hard case, which took place only about fifteen years ago, we feel in duty bound to refer to it as showing how completely the Highland crofter is in the power of his landlord, and however unscrupulous the landlord may be in the present circumstances there is no redress. The circumstances are as follows: – About forty years ago, when the sheep farming craze was at its height, some families were removed from the townships of Aulistan and Carrick on Lady Gordon's estate, as their places were to be added to the adjoining sheep farm. The people were removed on to the most barren spot on the whole estate, where there was no road or any possibility of making one. They had to carry all manure and sea ware on their backs, as the place was so rocky that a horse would be of no use. Notwithstanding all these disadvantages, they contrived through time to improve the place very much by draining and reclaiming mossy patches, and by carrying soil to be placed on rocky places where there was no soil. During the twenty-five years they occupied this place their rents were raised twice. Latterly, with the full confidence of their tenure being secure, they built better houses at their own expense, and two or three years afterwards they were turned out of their holdings on the usual six weeks' notice, without a farthing of compensation for land reclaimed. In justice to the present proprietor, Joseph Gordon, Esq., we wish to state our conviction that such an injustice would not have been permitted on the estate since he came into possession, as we regard him as a kind and considerate landlord to the few crofters on his estate. It has often been advanced by landlords, factors, and others that the Highland crofters are lazy and do not improve their holdings; but where is the inducement to improvements under such circumstances as we have here related? And as the Commissioners are well aware that this case is not a solitary instance, as it is quite common in every district throughout the Highlands, that if a crofter improves his holding he has to pay for it by having his rent raised, or his holding being given to the first man who offers more rent on account of such improvements. 4th, The remedy which we in this district would respectfully suggest for the improvement of our condition is, that the land which is lying waste on every side of us, this is to say, the townships of Achabeg, Keil, and Knock, at present in the hands of Mrs Paterson's trustees, and entirely out of cultivation, should be divided into suitable lots; that the trustees build suitable cottages on such lots. We consider they have a right to do so, seeing the proprietrix caused all the houses to be destroyed seventeen years ago; that these lots be let to us at a reasonable rent, such rent, in cases where the landlord and tenant cannot agree, to be fixed by arbitration, or such other arrangement as the wisdom of Parliament may see proper. While much preferring to have the State as our landlord, and while thoroughly convinced that the land question shall never be properly settled until it is settled on that basis, we should still be glad, in the meantime, to have matters settled on the lines indicated above; that is, a re-allotment of the land in suitable portions, security against arbitary evictions, compensation for improvement in case of removal, a fair rent and arbitration in case of disagreement between landlord and tenant. We have heard this statement read, and we agree with all it contains.'

Inquiry into Condition of Crofters and Cottars, xxxv, 1884.

The Gospel in Korea

If asked to name famous missionaries, most Scots could manage David Livingstone and Mary Slessor in Africa, or perhaps the early Indian pioneer Alexander Duff. The Rev. John Ross was one of the very first Protestant missionaries to Korea at a time when it had barely opened up to the west. He translated the New Testament into Korean and was one of the pioneers behind what is now one of the largest Presbyterian churches in the world. His first contact with Korea was in 1873. He also wrote a history of the country.

NOTES OF AN ADDRESS BY THE REV. JOHN ROSS.

BY REV. JAMES ORR, D. D.

Corea is a peninsula lying to the east of Manchuria and the west of Japan. It is separated from Manchuria by a wide river. In 1872 Corea was on everybody's lips, owing to a French and an American naval expedition which had been compelled to retreat. The country was kept jealously isolated, and nobody knew anything about it, even what it was like.

From curiosity, and with the design of seeing what could be done to introduce the gospel into Corea, Mr. Ross resolved to visit the Corean Gate – village towards the entrance to Corea, about 30 miles distant from the frontier, where a market for barter was held three times a year. The journey from Newchwang to the Corean Gate occupied seven days, through varied scenery of hills and rivers, not unlike Scotland. Arrived at the village, Mr. Ross saw for the first the Corean people. They resemble Europeans more than do other Asiatics – white skin, jet black hair and eyes, cheek-bones not prominent, eyes not oval, etc. In height and appearance, they are between the Japanese and north Chinese. The oxen were large and fierce, the horses small (like Shetland ponies). From 8am till 10pm, curious Coreans came into the inn where Mr. Ross put up. Anxious to know, he welcomed all intercourse, freely answered all questions they put to him, and sought to get information from them in return. He asked them about their language, laws, social life, families institutions etc., but all his efforts to draw them out were in vain. They either gave him no reply, or met his questions with evasions. They took him for a spy, and thought that any information they gave would be used for their hurt. He offered, through his servant, a large wage to any one who would become his teacher in the language, but no one would accept. So stern were the laws prohibiting intercourse with foreigners, that any one who had done so would have done it at the risk of his life.

Corean society is divided into three classes – the higher classes (officials), the merchants, and the artisans. The first two hold labour in contempt, and will not defile their fingers with work. This incidentally led to Mr. Ross obtaining what he wished. He had gone back to the Corean Gate on a second visit, when the following circumstance occurred. One of the middle classes – a merchant – had embarked his goods in a boat to cross the river, but a wind arising, and the river being there about two miles wide, the boat was upset, and his goods all went to the bottom. He reached the Corean Gate a ruined man. He could not dig, and to beg he was ashamed. He was naturally in a depressed state of mind, when Mr. Ross's servant asked him if he would become a teacher. He agreed to do so, provided Mr. Ross took no further notice of him while the fair lasted. He would then slip away by night, and meet Mr. Ross at a place fixed upon some distance away.

No sooner had he got this aid, than Mr. Ross set himself to acquire the language; then, with the help of this man, then of others, began a translation of the New Testament into the Corean tongue. In addition to this, two other small books were prepared to explain the principles of the gospel. The importance of this work will be seen when it is stated that, out of a population said to be 30,000,000, and which is certainly not less than half that number, nearly every woman can read. If she cannot, she can learn to do so in two or three hours. For, strange to say, the Coreans not only posses an alphabet, but one of a strictly phonetic character, so accurate that it is impossible to mispronounce. Once the alphabet is learned, any book can be easily read.

Long before the New Testament was ready, the Gospel of Luke

was prepared for printing. With Mr. MacIntyre's help, it had undergone any number of revisions. The difficulty now was to secure a Corean to set it up in type, but this difficulty also was in due time successfully surmounted. The person whose help was obtained as compositor was almost a simpleton in intellect, exceedingly slow in his movements, but, fortunately, very sure. The care with which this man read the manuscript made a certain impression on his heart. He asked questions at the Chinese Christians who were engaged as printers, and thus gained further knowledge. To Mr. Ross's surprise, he soon after made application for baptism. Meanwhile, it had become noised abroad in Corea that a translation of foreign books was going on in Moukden, and curiosity was excited. It was the custom to send embassies with tribute from Corea to Pekin, and some men attached to these passing through Moukden, turned in to the missionaries. One of them, a bright, intelligent man, agreed to stay with Mr. Ross as a compositor, thus setting his former assistant free. Giving him bundles of gospels and tracts, Mr. Ross sent him back to his native valleys to act as a colporteur among his friends. The valleys were those on the Manchurian side of the frontier, but largely peopled with Coreans. This was in 1882. In about six months he returned, saying that his books were all sold, and that a number of people who had read them wanted to be baptized. Mr. Ross hardly credited this, but gave him fresh bundles of books to carry to other valleys. He came back ere long with the same story, and his tale was soon to receive a curious corroboration.

About the time to which these events refer, a revolution had taken place in Corea. A Progressive party was in favour of having the country thrown open to foreigners, and these had raised a revolt, as the result of which some of the conservative party were killed, some imprisoned, and others were driven out of the country as exiles. Some of the latter came to Moukden, and told strange stories of what they had seen in the valleys. They had found men in these valleys who read foreign books, and who worshipped the God of heaven. Half-a-dozen of these refugees afterwards became Christians.

In consequence of this information, Messrs. Ross and Webster resolved to take the first opportunity to go and see for themselves. It was necessary to wait for the winter to harden the roads and make the rivers crossable; but as soon as the winter set in severe enough, they started on their journey. Their road was among hills. On the last day they came to a Chinese inn, 2,000 feet above the level of the sea. They had still two mountain passes to cross, 4000 feet above the sea, with thirty miles from the inn at the foot of the one to the east side of the other. Their beasts were useless, and the journey had to be made on foot. At length, thoroughly worn out, they came to an inn at the head of the first valley, where the Coreans lived. Scarcely were they there five minutes before a number of Coreans appeared, to welcome them with every demonstration of joy. They were the friends of the colporteur. They insisted on Mr. Ross and his companion leaving the inn, and taking up their abode with the chief farmer of the place as his guests. The house was full of people who had become believers. Thirty men turned up desiring baptism, all farmers and heads of families. Inquiries were made, the candidates were carefully examined, the minority were baptized, and the majority postponed. At another place, twelve miles distant, the same scene was enacted. Next morning a second valley was visited. Here another group presented themselves and were dealt with as before. In a third valley, about 100 men and lads turned up, among them some farm-servants. The danger of a snowstorm compelled a halt, but the missionaries were told that there were twenty-eight valleys, in every one of which there were similar groups of believers. Next spring Messrs. Ross and Webster returned to complete this work, but learned to their regret that in the interval a fierce persecution had broken out against the Christians. This was the work of the Chinese landlords, who, in their ignorance of the gospel, suspected some plot among the Coreans, which they desired to put down. They hired a rabble, who attacked the Christians, cut and slashed them, and destroyed their property. It seemed unkind to subject the converts to further suspicion, and so the missionaries withdrew till something could be done to remove these prejudices. They have not been back, but the work has not ceased. The converts are eager for teaching, and were willing, if the missionaries would stay, to build chapels. Unfortunately, as it is, they are not so well instructed as they should be, and the work is wholly uninspected. The colporteur continues travelling up and down, and has penetrated even into Russian territory. From other valleys have come recently requests for baptism from large numbers who have become believers; while travellers speak of thousands of families, both on the Corean and on the Manchurian side, in which there is daily family worship, God's Word is read, etc.

From the valleys we look to the capital of Corea. One of the refugees who had gone to Moukden, a young refugee of good family, and of great force of character, was baptized. It was his desire to go home and give his friends the gospel. Mr. Ross kept him with him two months for instruction, then gave him books etc., and sent him back to the capital. The Corean upper classes are educated persons, who know Chinese, and would disdain a book written in the vulgar tongue. Among the books sent, accordingly, were a number written in the Chinese classical style. Next year a letter was received from this young man, stating that thirteen of his friends wished to receive baptism and be formed into a Christian church. The year following another letter brought the tidings that there were seventy-nine persons ready for baptism. Mr. Ross, however, could not go so far. Two years after Corea threw open four ports to foreign countries. The American Presbyterians then sent two men to carry on mission work.

By and by Mr. Ross went to the Corean capital, to make some inquiries as to whether the printed New Testament was understood there. Voyaging by sea, he arrived, and was received by the American Presbyterian missionary, who told him that a meeting was to be held that evening to take steps for the formation of the first Christian congregation in Corea. They waited till dark. The laws against proselytism were still unrepealed, but the authorities connived at the work so long as it did not openly attract attention. Passing across a large wide street, and through some lanes, they came to a gate which opened into a small quadrangle. The door was opened, and they found themselves in a room, where were fourteen men, bright, clean, and intelligent looking. A congregation was formed, and two elders were chosen. Thirteen of the company were converts of the man Mr. Ross had sent. It was stated that if a station was opened, over 300 men were prepared to join. The man referred to had been sent to other places, and wrote of numbers from six to twenty waiting to be baptized. As an illustration of the work, it is stated that on the agent of a Presbyterian Mission from Canada going to a certain village, he found that the people *were all Christians* – converts of another man who had been instructed at Moukden. Mr. Ross strongly holds the opinion that though Corea had been the last seaboard nation to be reached, it is likely to be the first to receive Christianity.

The Missionary Record of the United Presbyterian Church, Edinburgh, 1890.

'A Red Letter Day in the History o' the Ferry'
The Opening of the Forth Rail Bridge
....

*On 4 March 1890 the Forth Rail Bridge was opened by the Prince
of Wales (later Edward VII). The massive cantilevered structure was
one of the marvels of its day – and public holidays were
proclaimed in the local Fife towns. The* Edinburgh Evening News
*catches this mood of local rejoicing, describing the crowds and the
excitement of the royal visit. The bridge came at a heavy price
however. Fifty-seven workmen were killed and 518 injured in its
construction.*

At South Queensferry

The ancient burgh, which has been roused from its previous
lethargy by the presence in its near vicinity of the great
structure, with the necessary accompaniment of its army of
workmen and legion of visitors, may be fated to return to
comparative oblivion with the completion of the work, but seldom
in its history has 'the Ferry' presented a more animated scene than
today. The morning broke dull and cheerless, and save for the few
hundreds conveyed from Edinburgh by the early tram, there was
nothing to indicate the great occasion. A general holiday had been
declared in the burgh, but the various tradesmen seemingly
preferred business to pleasure, as the shops were opened as usual,
and the only parties having a respite from labour were of school
children. The works were of course comparatively deserted, the
workmen, unlike the townspeople, having a compulsory off-day. A
solitary pedestrian could now and then be observed crossing the
bridge, which was by no means the most pleasant promenade. A stiff
breeze from the west momentarily increasing in volume threatened
to again test the vaunted stability of the structure. The view was
limited by a thick haze, which partially obscured the coast a few
miles off; but the wind promised to disperse the mist in some
measure. The turret ship *Devastation*, two gun-boats, and a tender,
lay in the estuary, a short distance off the bridge. The blue jackets
had given the townspeople a lesson in demonstrative loyalty, strings
of flags and bannerettes being suspended from the riggings; while on
the other hand the burgh boasted a single token of respect for
royalty, a 'Union Jack' floating proudly from a staff erected on the
house occupied by one of the magistrates. As the forenoon
advanced, the people from the surrounding districts, where a

holiday was being observed, thronged into the burgh, Bo'ness, Falkirk, Linlithgow, and other towns contributing their quota by road. The crowds of Edinburgh people thronging into the burgh by road and rail swelled the multitude of sightseers, and in anticipation of witnessing the Royal train crossing the bridge, the people early sought for points of vantage. The Hawes Brae found favour with many, while on the pier, the road, and the houses, many of which are perched on eminences, and consequently command a capital view of the bridge and its southern approach, thousands of people located themselves. As the train steamed on to the bridge cheers were raised, handkerchiefs were waved and other tokens of approbation were indulged in. For some time thereafter the crowd studied the structure and speculated on the position of the *Dolphin*, while the breeze, which was gradually becoming more boisterous, caused a diversion by carrying several hats into the sea. As nothing could now be seen from the shore, the people dispersed, and the town assumed the appearance of a record fair. One of the principal things that struck even a casual observer was the number and variety of mendicants. Here 'two Scotsmen who have lost a limb' tried their fortune; there a whining beggar in stilts importuned passers-by; while a miscellaneous collection of 'wandering minstrels,' street vocalists, &c., sought to benefit by the occasion. Games of chance were not unknown; while portraits of the Royal visitors and the bridge and articles innumerable were vended by itinerant traders. The eating-house keepers were generally doing good business, their customers in some cases having to seat themselves on the stair leading from the street to consume their victuals. The provision staffs were also a centre of attraction. As the day advanced, matters became rather unpleasant, clouds of dust troubling the pleasure seekers.

The afternoon trains and coaches were well patronised, but when, after the prince and party recrossed the bridge, the weather became rather inclement, the ingoing conveyances were crowded, and by three o'clock the great bulk of the people had left for home. Inebriates made their presence known in the thinned crowd.

North Queensferry

The weather conditions in the early morning were not very favourable for sightseeing, and from the aspect of the little village perched in the cliff it did now, in the grey morning's light, seem as if it were to be favoured with a visit from Royalty. A stiff westerly breeze was blowing, accompanied by occasional showers of rain, and the few flags which had been erected in some half-a-dozen places by a few loyal burghers fluttered bravely on their slender staffs against the force of the gale. Within a couple of hours, however, the appearance of things was completely changed. By ten o'clock the adjoining roads were covered with pleasure seekers on foot, on bicycles, and in crowded brakes, all with one accord making their way from Inverkeithing, Dunfermline, Milnathort, Kinross and the surrounding districts to the Bridge. In these places public holidays were the rule, though in Dunfermline the recent death of provost Donald somewhat interfered with general participation in the holiday. The packed appearance of North Queensferry, however, by ten or eleven o'clock justified the remark made by one busy shopkeeper that 'this was a red letter day in the history o' the Ferry'. H.M.S. *Devastation*, a gunboat, and several other vessels lying in St Margaret's Hope were decorated with bunting and various small craft plying about, evidently on pleasure bent, served to add to the general holiday aspect of things. Owing to the influx of visitors, prices for stabling accommodation in the hotels, as also for refreshments for man and beast were rather dear. Besides the detachment of 50 constables, under the command of Chief-Constable Brebner (Fife), several bodies of volunteers were also set to guard the approaches to the stations and the bridge. The volunteers on duty included detachments from the 1st Fife Artillery, one of which, the Inverkeithing battery, was posted as a guard of honour at the station there. Other batteries of the same corps from Burntisland, Kinghorn, Kirkcaldy, and Lochgelly were stationed with a body of rifles from Dunfermline along the platform and also along the line of approach of the royal train to the *Dolphin* which was in waiting to the end of the jetty. Shortly after 11 o'clock the rumble of an approaching train raised expectations in the crowd below that the royal train was crossing the bridge, and a rush was made to the station to wait its arrival from Inverkeithing, but the appearance of the 15 carriages which issued from the north cantilever pier soon disappointed those hopes, not a saloon carriage being visible in the train. At 11.30 prompt the *Devastation* began to fire a Royal salute, and not long afterwards the locomotive came into view proceeding at a slow pace. It had just reached the Inchgarvie pier when its predecessor steamed into the station at Queensferry, and the directors, municipal dignitaries, and other gentlemen on it alighted – the train itself being shunted into a siding.

The royal train took nearly ten minutes to cross, so slowly did it proceed and little interest was manifested in it by the few people immediately below, the greater portion of the crowd having rushed to the station when the first train passed. After 20 minutes had elapsed it reappeared again at the North Queensferry Station, and the prince of Wales and the Duke of Edinburgh, who occupied the first carriage immediately behind the engine, being recognised were greeted with a ringing cheer from a large crowd. The band of the 6th V.B.R.H. (1st Fifeshire) at once struck up the National Anthem and the guard of honour presented arms. The stiffish breeze blowing had caused a considerable sea, and the waves were lashing with some violence against the end of the jetty, where the *Dolphin* was lying. The Royalists experienced its full force in walking down the pier to the Dolphin on which they immediately embarked. It crossed round by the *Devastation*, on which the crew were ranged, and, encircling Inchgarvie, returned below the north arch nearly half-an-hour afterwards. The party from Edinburgh, who had followed its course in the steamer *William Muir*, returned about 10 or 15 minutes later than the Royal party and directors, who remained in the station till their arrival. Shortly after one o'clock they left, the prince and his son Prince George and the Duke of Edinburgh this time occupying the rear carriage, and were followed in about five minutes by the other train. The arrangements for keeping order at the station were perfect. Chief Constable Brebner and Superintendent Allan, of N.B.R. police, being in charge of the police and Major Hepburn and Captain Shearer of the volunteers. Not long after the train was again seen on the bridge, halting at the Inchgarvie cantilever, and most of the sightseers returned as they came in brakes, on bicycles or on foot. The weather latterly grew more boisterous and disagreeable, the wind being accompanied by heavy showers of rain.

Edinburgh Evening News, 4 March 1890.

Keir Hardie

James Keir Hardie was born in Legbrannock in Lanarkshire. From the age of ten to twenty-two he worked down the pits. Attending evening school helped him to become a trade union activist but in the process he lost his day job. This forced him into full-time agitation for workers' rights, and by 1888 he had decided that the workers needed a distinctive party which would support their cause. He stood as the Labour candidate in the Mid-Lanark by-

*election but only received 617 votes. He was not put off and in
1892 he ran for Parliament again in South West Ham. The sudden
death of the Liberal candidate netted him the Liberal vote and he
was elected to Parliament as the first Labour* MP. *Although the
report below speaks of a cloth cap, what was actually being
described was a deerstalker, but even that was a radical statement
at a time when the dress uniform for* MPs *consisted of a top hat
and morning dress. The correspondent for* The Scotsman *was
disgusted and gave a somewhat jaundiced view of the member for
West Ham's triumphant arrival.*

Then came the theatrical event of the day. The strains of a solitary
but vigorously winded cornet were borne along the air down
Parliament Street, and, as a great vehicle bearing about fifty artisans
and labourers approached, the melody discoursed by the cornet
soloist was identified with some slight difficulty as that of the
Marseillaise. At the sounds the crowd became a little turbulent, and
inclined to break the lines, which had hitherto been well maintained
by the authorities, so that traffic might not be interfered with.
Policemen and police inspectors looked anxious. Perhaps a
messenger was sent to hold the Beefeaters in readiness to resist an
attempt to storm the House. The brake, or whatever the vehicle was,
drew nearer, and then a likeness of a man was seen pasted on it with
the name underneath, 'Keir Hardie'. This was Mr Keir Hardie's
notion of entering Parliament. No doubt it was intended to create a
sensation. But, like other things, this plan miscarried. Mr Hardie's
friends were cheering him when the vehicle, which could not be
admitted to Palace Yard, drew up at the southern gateway. Some in
the crowd in Parliament Square were beginning to comprehend and
to join in the demonstration, when a fresh cheer arose from the
further side of the square, as Mr Gladstone in a closed carriage and
accompanied by Mrs Gladstone, drove rapidly towards St Stephen's.
From that moment the crowd ignored Mr Hardie, but continued to
bestow its whole attention upon Mr Gladstone, who bowed
repeatedly in acknowledgement of the cordiality of the reception
bestowed upon him. The desire to see the right hon. gentleman was
such that a rush was made which broke through the line of the
police and a police sergeant was thrown down and narrowly
escaped being injured by the wheels of the brougham. When Mr
Gladstone's carriage had disappeared within the courtyard, Mr
Hardie was being asked the usual question as he attempted to enter

the yard. In the circumstances the question was a formal one, but the policeman had his duty to do and notwithstanding the 'Marseillaise', the bodyguard and the sons of labour, and the picture on the brake, all announcing the arrival of the new representative for West Ham, he did it by asking Mr Keir Hardie who he was. The new member was attired in a garb doubtless to assert the independence of Labour in the House as the French legislator who attends the Senate in a workman's blouse is supposed to do. He wore what appeared to be ordinary working clothes – a blue serge jacket adorned with a red rosette, trousers of checked yellowish coloured tweed and a check cloth cap of the style not unknown in Scotland as the 'eight-pieced'. In response to the cheers which his followers in the brake sent after him he waved his hand to them several times. Then the cornet player struck up a new tune, which distinctly resembled 'Oh, Willie, we have missed you' – possibly in allusion to the fact that no one on Mr Keir Hardie's triumphal car could possibly have got a glimpse of Mr Gladstone, to the sincere disappointment, doubtless, of many of them. From this time the crowd rapidly thinned, but when the House adjourned many waited outside and cheered Mr Gladstone and other prominent statesmen as they quitted St Stephen's for the day.

The Scotsman, 5 August 1892.

Escape from Pretoria

When the Boers of South Africa tried to keep their independence against the annexing tendencies of the British Empire, there was a swift demonstration of the limitations of the British army. The guerilla tactics of the Boers and the ability of their civilian population to assist them made them a difficult enemy to fight by traditional methods. After great initial success in 1899, the Boer commandos suddenly found themselves confronted with a powerful British Expeditionary Force under General Roberts which rolled back their gains. In the midst of this a young Scottish officer James A. L. Haldane – later General Sir James Haldane – was taken prisoner. He and his friends decided to escape from their POW camp, an enterprise which was severely jeopardised by one Winston Churchill, then a war correspondent, who put the plan into action prematurely. Churchill escaped successfully, and so in the end did Haldane and his companions. This is an extract from Haldane's diaries.

Friday 16th March

12.15 pm, the servants were marched off by the Zarp [South African Republican Police] guard. Looked through the ventilator and saw the sentry on the front of the building leave his post. The wicket gate sentry between the Model School and the hospital also moved. We had lunch at 12.4 [sic] pm. At the time a number of Zarps crowded into our room overhead to see Frankland's caricatures, no doubt, and throughout the day other people including women and children – judging by the voices we could hear – and also dogs crowded into the room. We had to keep absolutely quiet or we might have been heard more especially by the dogs. The active part of the escape will soon begin. I still have a headache – 4.45 – At 5 p.m., two men and a dog came overhead. We have decided to make for Lorenço Marques as Mafeking may not be relieved for some time. At 6 p.m. we had food and dressed for the road. At 6.45 p.m. Brockie opened the trap door. This made a loud noise in the silent building. He went into the room above and shortly came back and reported that the building was deserted, front and back doors locked and a lot of forms, etc., in the passages. I went up then, boots in hand, then Le Mesurier. He was so weak that he could not stand till we had rubbed his legs. We reeled like drunk men also, and had to rub our legs and walked about the room till the stiffness wore off. Then crept to the back door – a pane in which had been removed through which we climbed after putting on our boots. The moon was shining and at the full and a slight shower was failing. The electric lights in the back yard were all lighted. Walked across to the latrine and got behind it, and discussed how best to get out as windows in the house over the paling were lighted up and we should have been seen had we climbed into the garden of the house. We walked up to the railing where the guard and servants tents used to be and climbed over. A couple passed immediately after but took no notice of us. We went to our right and up the street, and next turned to the left, i.e., in an easterly direction. I lighted my pipe directly we got out of the backyard. Passed a special policeman. Turned to the right and went past several openings to side streets, stopping only for Brockie to put on a white sling to look as if he were a wounded Boer. We reached the outside road that goes out of the town to the east and parallel to which the Delagoa Bay railway runs. Turned to the left and crossed dried up bed of the Apies River where a bridge is being built. A cyclist passed us and we sent straight on. Brockie and Le Mesurier walked in the middle of the road and I on the path.

After a bit a man passed us and turned up a short road to the left, stopped and watched us. He stood looking for a time, and Brockie swung round so as to show the sling he wore, when the man moved off slowly, apparently satisfied. We went on and came to a level-crossing where I fully expected to see a special policeman, but there was no one there. Then we sat down had a small drink of whisky and decided to follow the railway . . .

Friday 23rd March
During the morning he [Mr Moore; a mine storekeeper who helped the escapees] said that the doctor of a neighbouring mine wished to see us and he brought Dr Gillespie who came in and we had a long talk with him. Is was a relief to me to hear his Doric accent and made one feel confident that the worst part of the escape was over. But when he said that we might consider ourselves as out of the Transval I replied that I would only do so when we actually were across the border. He told us about Churchill's escape and how he came to see him. Gillespie said that he was one of a news syndicate and only by chance was that day at the Douglas colliery. He said it would be unwise for us to remain there as there were many Englishmen about and they were talkative. He said that we could never had made our escape in a coal truck, and that that evening he would drive us to the mine whence Churchill escaped and that we would get away from there . . .

Thursday, 29th March
At 4.30a.m., we went up to the office, and got into the wool-truck and packed away 12 bottles (tea and whisky) some cold duck, beef, smoked beef, bread and butter. The floor of the truck is dirty having been used lately for carrying coals, so we turned our trowsers inside out. A space has been left at one end in which we can lie down and a kind of tunnel made between the large bales into which we can retire if the truck is searched, but which would not hide us if the searcher took the trouble to look up it. At 1 p.m., an engine drew us to Whitebank station. About 2.30 p.m. we were hooked on to the passenger train from Pretoria. We had retired into the tunnel at the station and we did so at all stations. There was a tarpaulin over the truck and I cut a small hole in it so as to see out. I had learned by heart the heights and distances from Pretoria of all the stations, and as Howard kindly gave me an aneroid I could tell fairly well where we were. The train stopped the night at Waterval Boven station and we had mosquitoes as visitors.

Friday, 30th March

Left W. Boven station at 6.20 a.m. and reached Komati Poort at 2.30 p.m. Before arriving there we had thrown out all our food and water as they were difficult to hide, and were sorry for having done so later. Our truck was unhooked and put into a siding and soon the train went on. We had retired into the tunnel and soon we heard the tarpaulin ropes being undone and then it was thrown back and the light came into us through the spaces between the wool bales. I was furthest into the tunnel and Le Mesurier had taken off his coat and held it in front of him at a few feet from the mouth. This was fortunate, for though there was a casual search – as everything after our escape was ordered to be searched – he was not seen, and soon the tarpaulin was tied down again. There must have been a water-pipe close to the truck for much chattering of natives went on and I could, through the hole I cut in the tarpaulin, see the Boers having tea on the station platform. I thought of getting out of the truck after dark and swimming the Komati River but Le Mesurier was against it and said that there were crocodiles and rhinos in the river. Had some sleep but the floor of the truck was very hard.

Saturday, 31st March

We waited hoping that we would be hooked on to a train and get across the border, and at 9.30 a.m. heard an engine clanking along towards us. Soon we were hooked on to it and pulled forward, and went across the bridge into Portuguese territory, and reach Ressano Garcia at 9.45 a.m. We remained in the truck all day as we thought it was best not to disclose ourselves lest those who had helped us at the mine should get into trouble if our means of getting out of the country should become known. Free at last, thank God! A wonderful feeling.

'Haldane diaries', MS. 20247, ff.131-2, 139, 141-2.

Twentieth Century Scotland I:
Scotland over Two Wars

Suffragettes and some revolutionary socialism, shipbuilding, and the Somme; early 20th-century Scotland continued the historic themes of radicalism, enterprise and warfare in its own way. Scots scientists John Logie Baird and Alexander Fleming contributed key discoveries which revolutionised 20th-century life. As the depression of the 1930s faded, the Queen Mary *came off the slipway and down the Clyde. Elsewhere ways of life were dying – the islanders of St Kilda could no longer keep up their struggle with their awe-inspiring, but sadly barren land. Sectarianism and fear of fifth columnists raised their ugly heads, but at the end of the Second World War Scots and many others joined together in the first Edinburgh Festival to collaborate in a work of peace and international understanding.*

Votes for Women, Gunpowder for Burns

Despite the fact that women in New Zealand were given the vote in 1893 and that Australia had followed suit in 1902, British women continued to be denied the vote until 1918. In 1903 Emmeline Pankhurst, assisted by her daughters Christabel and Sylvia, founded the Women's Social and Political Union. Seeing that peaceful debate and agitation had got them nowhere, her followers took more militant action. By 1914 Scottish newspapers could be found running columns headed 'Today's Outrages', as the most zealous suffragettes stepped up their campaign to obtain maximum publicity during the visit to Scotland of King George V. One of the most striking of these protests was Janet Parker's attempt to blow up Burns's Cottage. One wonders what her uncle Lord Kitchener would have had to say about that.

ALLOWAY OUTRAGE – ATTEMPT TO BLOW UP BURNS'S COTTAGE – SUFFRAGIST IN CUSTODY

A dastardly attempt was made in the early hours of yesterday morning by suffragists to fire and blow up Burns's Cottage, Alloway, the birthplace of the national poet, which is annually visited by thousands of pilgrims from all parts of the world. The attempted outrage was fortunately frustrated by the timely appearance on the scene of the night watchman, but the fact that an attempt was made to destroy a shrine that Scotsmen in all parts of the world regard as sacred has roused in the locality the most intense indignation.

The Burns Cottage and Monument Trustees have for about 15 months employed a night watchman to guard against possible damage by suffragists, and it was the watchman, an Ayr man named Robert Wyllie, who surprised the militants in their attack on the building. Wyllie was seated inside the old byre, which forms part of the original building, when, shortly after two o'clock in the morning, his attention was attracted by a noise as of something heavy being laid on the ground outside. On going out of the door on the west side of the cottage, being the rear of the building, he saw two women who had apparently just placed two canisters in the gutter formed by flagstones which surrounds the building.

AN EXCITING STRUGGLE

On seeing the watchman the women made off through the garden, which forms part of the cottage grounds, and the watchman gave chase. He came up with them as they were attempting to get over the garden fence into a field beyond. He succeeded in getting hold of them both, and a violent struggle ensued. One of the women, apparently with the object of distracting the man's attention, shouted to him to run and take the canisters from the building because they would explode. The watchman, however, held on to both women for some time. Eventually one of them struggled free and made good her escape. The watchman's shouts for help and the other woman's screams caused a dog to bark, and this roused Mr A. H. Scott, the tenant of Alloway orchard which adjoins the cottage grounds. Mr William Monaghan, the custodier of the cottage, who lives in a house within the grounds, was also aroused. The local officer of the Ayrshire Constabulary was called, and he got into communication with the headquarters in Ayr. Additional officers soon arrived on the scene, and the woman was taken to Ayr by motor car. An examination of the premises showed that very complete preparations had been made for the blowing up of the building. The two canisters which were wrapped in brown paper, were found to contain 4lb of gunpowder each, and a separate fuse had been attached to each canister. In a subsequent search a new bicycle, bearing the name of a Glasgow maker, was found in Doonholm Road near Alloway Manse. Beside the bicycle was a quantity of brown paper. The bicycle is supposed to belong to the arrested woman, and the likelihood is that the other woman made her escape on another bicycle. Mr T. C. Dunlop, secretary to the Burns Cottage and Monument Trustees, was informed of the affair and at four o'clock in the morning made an assiduous search of the roads in the district for the escaped woman, but could find no trace of her. The arrested woman was found to have in her possession a map of the district, a diary and £10 in money. She gave the name of Janet Arthur.

QUOTING BURNS IN COURT

In the course of the day the prisoner was brought before Sheriff Broun in Ayr Sheriff Court for declaration. The charge preferred against her is that of attempting maliciously to destroy Burns's Cottage. She refused to make a declaration, and was committed to prison pending further proceedings. Before her case was called a woman had been fined £1 with the usual alternative for resetting stolen money. The woman was crying bitterly and the suffragist ordered that the fine be paid from the money that had been found in her (the suffragist) possession. During the proceedings in Court the accused talked volubly and quoted Burns at some length 'Liberty's in every blow, let us do or die.' She said and added 'You Scotsmen used to be proud of Burns; now you have taken to torturing women.' She made a protest against the treatment of suffragists in Perth Prison. At times she was somewhat violent and the police had to use force to restrain her. Thereupon the Sheriff asked them to be as gentle as they could with her. The accused who wore a fawn waterproof coat, brown skirt, and blue toque hat, is of slim build, and apparently about 40 years of age. A considerable crowd of people had assembled at the gates of the County Buildings and witnessed her removal to prison in a cab, into which she had to be forcibly pushed. There was no demonstration. Since being taken into custody the accused has been on hunger strike.

Glasgow Herald, 9 July 1914.

SUFFRAGIST OUTRAGE – WOMAN'S IDENTITY – LORD KITCHENER'S NIECE

AYR, Friday. – the woman arrested in connection with the outrage at the Burns Cottage on the morning of July 8 and liberated after ten days' hunger strike from Perth prison is now stated to have been identified. – She gave the name of Janet Arthur, but the police authorities are understood to know from information that her real

name is Janet Parker, and that she is a niece of Lord Kitchener, and
has a brother inspector of schools in Cairo.

'News 24 July 1914', cutting from Miss Janie Allan's collection, Acc. 4498/2.

'The Rather Tame War Experiences in Flanders 1915
of La. Cpl George Ramage
1st Battalion Gordon Highlanders, 8th Brigade 3rd Division'

*George Ramage, a teacher in Scotland, became a Lance Corporal
in the Gordon Highlanders following the outbreak of war in 1914.
He was in Flanders from April-June 1915, where he was wounded
and demobilised. He was present during the initial uses of gas as a
German weapon and kept a diary of his active service. It was an
unvarnished and sometimes cynical account of trench life. Ramage
had no illusions about the glorious nature of a death 'in action'
and some of his comments on the ignorance of officers were
scathing, yet despite this he still felt that joining the army had been
the right thing to do, even after he was wounded.*

EXCERPTS FROM THE WAR DIARIES OF L./CORPORAL GEORGE RAMAGE

13th April 1915

Sent in a draft of 85 men to the front. Fully equipped, even with
120 rounds of ammunition at Aberdeen. Left the barracks at 9.20
p.m. after lining up, roll call, cheering popular non coms [non
commissioned officers], saying our goodbyes, propping up a few
drunks, singing a few army songs, some smacking of irreverence and
some of a half hearted esprit de corps while the Batt. Sgt. Major
stabbed the darkness with his flashlight or shocked it with impatient
sulphurous commands. A pipe band and a brass band preceded us,
quite a happy manly draft. Dense, appreciative, slightly
demonstrative crowds. The draft was composed mostly of wounded
expeditionary men returning to the firing line, hence there was the
absence of that exuberant enthusiasm of men going on the great
adventure for the first time. Sweethearts galore broke the ranks and
their own hearts. Flinty hearted sergeants however heaved them
back to the crowd again like so many inanimate sandbags. Surprised
at the absence of vituperation from the women. They came on again
and again quite undismayed only to be hurled back like the Germans
at Ypres. Hoped their sweethearts would display as much fortitude
when faced with something warmer than embraces. As I was on the
outside of the fours, got a small collection of presents, mostly

cigarettes, from absolutely unknown females – bless their little
hearts. Left Aberdeen Joint Station 10 p.m.

Tea Perth.

MS. 944, ff.1-3.

24 April 1915

Our surroundings are sordid – trenches are dry so far but behind
us are clayey fields, pitted with water filled shell holes, 2-3 yards
wide, 1 yard deep, – this dirty green water we are foolhardy enough
to use for tea – rats run about a ditch on our right or along the top
of our parapet – ruined buildings all around – opened tins
everywhere in the clayey mud holes behind us, – bark of trees along
our line clipped with bullets – the long clayey line of the trenches in
use or out of use are too suggestive of drainage operations on a rainy
day in a slummy street to be pleasant to the eye – the smell is not
bad in places – men untidy, clayey, unwashed, unshaved, but tho'
death may come at any moment to any one, yet all conducting
themselves as if this was the usual even tenor of their way amid the
piping times of peace. Some of the men wriggle about inside their
clothes occasionally in forlorn hope of dislodging the ubiquitous
inevitable parasite – have not felt any yet and don't dare to hope to
escape their dread invasion. Men not allowed to take off any part of
dress or ammunition to look for lice – have now had my equipment
– less valise – strapped to me from Thursday evening – sleep in this
uncomfortable sleeping suit – wake now and then to remove neighbour's bayonet or haversac from one's stomach – this continues for
six days till we are relieved – saw an opening in the rampart with a
protecting projecting rampart in front – in recess was a khaki cap
beside some bloodstained sand bags – the British sniper sniped . . .

ff.58-9.

1 May 1915

A most unsatisfactory and annoying thing from the ordinary
soldier's point of view, is the fact that the majority of soldiers who
are killed, do not die fighting. 'Killed in action' is a wrong
description. Many are killed sleeping quietly in the trenches, calmly
cooking their food with thoughts far away from war. They are
struck down by invisible, unheralded, sudden, silent (comparatively)
bullets. They are butchered while lying in the sun. If they were
advancing, firing or using the bayonet, they would have the
consolation that they have a chance of giving as much as they got,

in fact, that they were actually disabled or killed in action. Hundreds of these unavoidable and chagrin provoking casualties occur all along the line every day. We are not trying to budge the Germans where we are. When they are quiet, we are quiet and keep our heads below the parapet. We must lose more men than the Germans in this method of warfare as we fire much less than they. The Germans seem to be keener soldiers. Yet there is a big daily toll of life in these trenches for though we never see a German, a bullet will suddenly ricochet off a top sandbag and send a joking or grousing soldier to his long home, or wound him or make him a cripple or an imbecile for life. The best stand the same chance as the worst as there is no hope of dodging a bullet. The best attitude of mind is to keep smiling, attending to the social and domestic amenities as best as possible when off-duty in the trenches . . . Five minutes in a chair would be a great luxury. We eat our meals on the floor – kilt front a sad mess with grease spots . . .

ff.88-90.

3 May 1915
Captain Hume Gore told us that the German gas is chlorine – he deliberately told us a falsehood in saying that chlorine does not kill – it went down with many of these uneducated men of course – one of our men returned from hospital next day where he had seen gas stricken men gasping for breath and dying like flies while the medical people could do nothing for them apparently except prop them up against the wall in the open air, all black in face – if Hume Gore was educated surely he knew that iron burns in chlorine and that therefore human lungs could not thrive in it.

MS. 945, ff.4-5.

18 June 1915
. . . was preparing to lie down again when was shot through left palm – was standing up slightly throwing my waterproof sheet round my shoulders – right hand, head and left hand were thus in line a little above trench and mercifully the bullet chose the left hand – about 7 a.m. – heard a violent crack of a bullet and found myself holding my left wrist and saying 'Oh my hand's blown away' – vision was blurred and left hand had been drooping down – saw hole in back of hand with white sinew and helpless looking middle finger – did not see fourth finger – thought two had been shot off. Had a feeling of surprise and chagrin that I should be hit – a Tommy

will always feel that he will escape and the other chap get it – and
now I had got a little of what many a fellow Tommy had got worse
– made me more human – thought of my piano and golf days being
over – all this of course in an instant of time – 'You might bandage
up this', I said to man next to me – he took out his bandage and I
heard the officer say he would bandage it – must have lost
consciousness or gone a-dreaming for next I remember was a most
overwhelming sensation which I felt was going to overpower me,
worse than a dizzy sick feeling – felt I was being engulfed in a
Maelstrom – battled against it and found myself at full 'knees-bend'
in the trench, still holding my left wrist while the officer had nearly
finished the bandaging – felt him shoving a loose finger in to the
bandaging – asked if I had fainted – he said 'no' – fell on my back
as I thought I might faint but I was perfectly calm – thanked the
officer who remarked the hand was badly shattered – he did not
agree with me that six weeks in hospital would be enough . . .
Though hand is badly shattered, shot at sixty yards range and will
require long time to heal with loss of bit of palm and some fingers,
yet still philosophical – thought of home bucks me up perhaps – As
day wore on the wound became damned painful and still kept
bleeding – the 4 bombers at my post were all very kind – was
somewhat helpless and my slightest request was attended to with
great kindness and sympathy – they put on my puttees properly, tied
sling, opened pack, lit cigs, filled pipe, gave me tea and part of their
rations for I had had nothing for more than a day . . .

Thus ends my active military experience of two months, enjoyable
on the whole tho' the feeling of utter stupidity of war was ever
present. Why then did I join the army? Was it following the mob, in
other words, cowardice? For my own self-esteem let me say it was
not the reason. Here it is. Tho' war is a hellish travesty of humanity,
yet as long as one nation is prepared by force of arms and by its
consequent slaughter and disfigurement and devastation to
overthrow the liberties and destroy the lives of other nations, each
nation must be prepared and ready to resist to death . . . All this is
written while my hand is painful and bleeding while I am waiting for
dark before going to dressing station – my blood on the trench wall
beside me, my waterproof sheet torn by the bullet.

'Diaries of George Ramage', MS. 945, ff.76-82.

Haig and the Somme
···

*From ordinary soldier to field marshal, the man whose orders
determined the fate of ordinary soldiers like George Ramage was
another Scot – Sir Douglas Haig. His diaries survive at the
National Library of Scotland. This was his entry for the second
day of the battle of the Somme in 1916. Some indication of Haig's
attitudes can be gauged from the fact that he considered 40,000
casualties in two days not to be 'severe'.*

Sunday 2nd July

A day of downs and ups! As regards weather, the day was fine,
bright sun and cool wind, but barometer registered a fall during
the night.

The news about 8 am was not altogether good. We held
Montauban inspite of a counter attack delivered at dawn. This is
good, but the enemy is still in Fricourt, La Boisells, Thiepval. It was
also said that we had 2 Battns [battalions] cut off in the 'Schwaben
Redoubt' (on the hill N. of Thiepval) and also that the 8th Corps (H.
Weston) had 2 Battns cut off at Serre.

At 9.30 am, I attended Church Service in a hut near Beauquesne.
The Rev. Mr Duncan preached an excellent sermon. 'Ye are fellow
workers with God.'

After Church I and Kiggell motored to Querrieu and saw Sir H.
Rawlinson. I directed him to devote all his energies to capturing
Fricourt and neighbouring villages, so as to reduce the number of
our flanks, and then advance on enemy's second line. I questioned
him as to his views of an advance from Montauban and his right,
instead of from Thiepval and left. He did not seem to favour the
scheme.

I returned to Valvion for lunch. General J. Ducane (who is here on
behalf of the Minister of Munitions) came to lunch. I am anxious
about the supply of heavy ammunition (9.2 especially) as we have
used so much owing to the 2 extra days of bombardment.

After lunch I spoke to Kiggell about the attack from Montauban
against Longueval, and he drafted a written note to Rawlinson on
the subject. I then motored to HQ 3rd Corps at Montigny. I saw
General Romer (the Br Gen. GS) and told him to tell General
Pulteney how pleased I was with the work of his Divisions. He said
the enemy in their front seemed to have had enough and were
surrendering in small detachments.

I visited 15th Corps HQ at Heilly, and complimented General

Horne on the success of his operations. He had had a most difficult problem. His troops had now taken Fricourt and were pressing on to Fricourt Farm. A [German] prisoner Sergt Major reported that the Comdt [German Commandant] of Fricourt had asked for reinforcements. The reply was that there were none to send except only 2 Companies of Divl. [Divisional] Pioneers. These were sent and were duly taken prisoner by us.

I also visited two Casualty Clearing Stations at Montigny, one under Major Thomas, the other under Colonel Macpherson. They were very pleased at my visit. The wounded were in wonderful spirits. I saw Sir Wilmot Herringham with his coat off, setting a fine example, by washing and attending to slightly wounded cases. I thanked him. I believe he is consulting physician to Bart's Hospital, London. Everything seemed going on well.

The AG reported today that the total casualties are estimated at over 40,000 to date. This cannot be considered severe in view of the numbers engaged, and the length of front attacked.

I called at General Gough's HQ at Toutencourt. He commands 5th Army. Horses met me there and I rode home.

On arrival I hear the enemy has only a few patrols in Burnafay Wood (N of Montauban) and that they are surrendering freely. I therefore directed Kiggell to urge Rawlinson to greater activity in the direction of Longueval. My CRA (Birch) also went to HQ 4th Army to go into the Artillery situation with the same objective.

By nightfall the situation is much more favourable than when we started today!

On 2nd and 23rd June the Germans attacked Verdun with 19 'Regiments'. Their Colours were given back to them before the fight, with a view to entering Verdun in triumph and orders for a march past had been drawn up by their Army Headquarters.

H.Q. Valvion

'Haig Diaries', Acc. 3155/107.

John Maclean

Most Scots believed in the necessity of the war and the soundness of its aims but there were some exceptions. John Maclean, one of the heroes of the Scottish Left, saw the war as a disaster for the working classes, distracting them from the business of revolution. Unlike many socialists Maclean continued to organise strikes and to oppose the war, which led to regular trips to prison. He also became the first consul of the USSR in Great Britain after the

Russian Revolution. Unsurprisingly, this led the government to
regard Maclean in an even more jaundiced light. He was soon tried
again for sedition. The first extract below, from Justice, *is a*
description of Maclean's work before the war. The second records
his trial and conviction for his anti-war work in 1918. His wife
Agnes helped in the campaign for his release and wrote to the
authorities complaining about the conditions of his imprisonment
in Peterhead prison. Maclean's career led to him being in and out
of jail for most of the latter part of his life. He died in 1923, worn
out by the effects of his dedication to his cause.

First and foremost among these is John Maclean, than whom no
better man has ever been produced by the S. D. F. [Social
Democratic Front], and that is saying a great deal, indeed. It is quite
safe to say that Maclean has addressed meetings in various parts of
the country at the average rate of once a day ever since the beginning
of May. He has sometimes held as many as five meetings in one day!
And two or three a day is quite a usual thing for him to hold. Nor
is he less active in the winter, as, in addition to addressing indoor
meetings, he usually conducts as many as four economic classes – all
of them meeting once a week – while at the same time he will teach
an evening continuation class under the School Board. How he
manages to get through such an extraordinary amount of work no
one can tell. In fact, I doubt if he could do so himself. But how he
can stand the strain of such a pace is still a greater wonder. Just
think of the sum total of the work he gets through year after year.
Daily he follows his profession as a school teacher with so much
success as to earn the highest merits from the Chief Inspector of
Schools. Every evening he is engaged in S. D. F. work of one kind or
another, or is teaching a continuation class. The whole of his
vacation is devoted to propaganda – in fact, as Leiper, of Inverurie,
remarked to me the other week 'Maclean does the work of three
good men.' Well may we exclaim, 'Eh, but oor Mac is a bonnie
fechter!' Maclean, however, really ought to ca' a little more canny.
The most iron-like constitution could not stand such a strain
indefinitely.

Cutting from *Justice,* 14 September 1907, in Acc. 7508.

SEDITION TRIAL IN EDINBURGH

BOLSHEVIST CONSUL SENT TO PENAL SERVITUDE

In the High Court of Justiciary, Edinburgh, yesterday, John Maclean, ex-teacher, who was recently appointed Russian Consul in Glasgow by the Bolsheviks, appeared for trial before the Lord Justice-General and a jury on a charge of sedition. The charge was that on certain stated dates and at various places, and in each case to an audience forming part of the civilian population, and consisting in part of persons engaged in the production, repair, or transport of war material, or in other work necessary for the successful prosecution of the war, he made statements which were likely to prejudice the recruiting, training, discipline, and administration of His Majesty's Forces, and by which statements he attempted to cause mutiny, sedition, and disaffection among the civilian population, repair, and transport of war material and other work necessary for the successful prosecution of war, contrary to the Defence of the Realm Act, 1914, and the Defence of the Realm Regulations, 1914. Maclean had previously been convicted of contravening the Defence of the Realm Act and Regulations.

In view of the trial some thirty or forty sympathisers with the accused set out on Wednesday night to march from Glasgow to Edinburgh, the march being intended as a demonstration against the prosecution of Maclean. As the march proceeded the number taking part gradually diminished, and having got so far those that remained were glad to finish their journey yesterday morning by motor bus. Half an hour before the proceedings commenced the Court was crowded and a large number of people who sought admission had to be turned away by the police.

Mr Clyde, K.C., Mr Blackburn, K.C., and Mr C. H. Brown appeared for the Crown. Maclean conducted his own defence and on being asked by the Lord Justice-General if he adhered to his plea of not guilty replied 'I refuse to plead.' His Lordship intimated that that would be taken as a plea of not guilty. Evidence was then led.

ACCUSED'S STATEMENTS

Lawrence Marshall, solicitor, Glasgow, said he was a special constable, and attended a meeting in Glasgow on 20th January. He estimated that there would be present about 450 men of military age. Maclean, in his speech, advocated the 'downing of tools,' and said that the Socialists should break through all laws and establish their own rules and regulations; that the Clyde district had helped to win the Russian revolution; and that the revolutionary spirit on the Clyde was at present ten times as strong as it was two years ago.

Detective-Sergeant Gordon spoke to having been present at a meeting addressed by the accused at Wellpark Football Field, Shettleston. Maclean made a very seditious speech and one of the accused's statements was that the Government thought that the only way to tame the workers was to starve them and that in the event of a revolution the working class would not starve, as there was plenty of food in Glasgow.

James S. Forrest, shorthand writer, Hamilton, said that on 10th February 1918 he attended a meeting at Cambuslang, along with Superintendent Taylor and other police officers. There were present at the meeting some four to five hundred people, the greater proportion of whom were men of military age. Witness took a shorthand note of a speech made by the prisoner. Witness remembered the prisoner saying – 'The capitalist class don't care how many women and children are destroyed so long as they belong to the working class.' Another passage was – 'Women are out in the cold, and some deaths are taking place in consequence, not killed by Germans, but killed by your British Government.' That, said witness, referred to the queues waiting at the food shops. Prisoner on that occasion also said that the workers should give the Government a chance of going to Brest-Litovsk, and if they did not take that chance they should 'down tools'; and the workers would have to capture the City Chambers in Glasgow, to destroy the police offices and disorganise the police; to close down half the mines in Lanarkshire and keep the other half going to supply coal for the working classes; to go to the farms and get food, and burn the houses if they did not get food; to capture the General Post Office, to capture the banks in Glasgow; and that as soon as they had done these things, they would get the stores and food in Glasgow as well; and that they should capture the ships on the Clyde; that the workers should make no mistake, but profit by the experience of their Russian comrades, and that the experience of the workers in Russia would be the experience of the workers in this country.

Cross-examined – Witness had not made a verbatim report of the accused's speech, but the important passages were given.

STRIKING THE FIRST BLOW

Thomas Morrison McArthur, messenger-at-arms, Glasgow, stated that he was a special constable, and had taken notes of a speech by the accused at Kingston Lesser Hall, Paisley Road, Glasgow, in the course of which it was said that the workers should be prepared at any moment to throw themselves at the throats of the capitalist class.

Cross-examined, witness did not understand by the statement of the accused that the workers should get at the pockets of the capitalists.

William Tulloch Cuthbert, company secretary, Glasgow and William Galston, Glasgow, spoke to the accused having stated at a meeting on 13th March that the workers might strike the first blow for the revolution on the 1st of May.

John Syme, detective inspector, Hamilton, and Samuel Jordan, detective sergeant, Airdrie, as well as two shorthand writers, gave evidence regarding a speech by the accused at Harthill Public School, Shotts, on 4th April 1918. On that occasion the accused said that the working classes should refuse to share in the war, but should leave the owners of the land, the mines, and the factories to man the trenches, and if they killed one another the working classes could take the land, the mines, and factories; that he had been teaching classes in Lanarkshire and Fife, and developing the spirit of the revolution in Scotland, as it had been developed for the last ten or fifteen years in Russia, where the most enlightened workers in the world were to be found at the present time; that when the revolution came the workers must seize the pits, railways, works and land, and do their part in overthrowing their common enemy by putting society in the melting-pot; and that they should abolish class, capitalists, armies, and navies, and get hold of the land, as the Bolsheviks had done, either by force or by persuasion – it did not matter which.

The case for the prosecution having been closed Maclean stated that he did not intend to lead evidence nor to go into the witness box himself.

Mr Clyde in addressing the jury, said they had heard in the course of the evidence a good many references to Socialism, social revolution; and the like. However inappropriate these subjects might be to the moment, there was nothing in this country or in its law, even as that law had to be framed to meet the emergency with which they were faced, to prevent any man if he pleased, from talking about politics or about Socialism. If the prisoner had been content to expound what he knew, or what he thought he knew, about Socialistic theories, if he had been content to try to persuade other people of the soundness and expediency of the plans of Socialistic reconstruction in which he believed, nobody could have laid a finger on him. But there came a point at which discussion of Socialistic questions or discussion of any question changed its character. At that point there came the deliberate and persistent attempt to plant seeds of disunion, disloyalty, sedition and mutiny among the people. They could not afford at the present time to have the people incited to active violence and rebellion while the enemy was at their gates. He submitted that the case against the accused was absolutely and completely proved.

THE PRISONER'S ADDRESS

The prisoner, in the course of a long address, said that for the full period of his active life he had been a teacher of economics to the working classes, and his contention had always been that capitalism was rotten to its foundation. His motives were clean and genuine and he was out for the benefit of society, and not to wrong any human being. He made reference to an article on Bolshevism which appeared last Saturday in *The Scotsman*, and said it was written specially to create an atmosphere against Bolshevism at that trial. As long as he lived he was going to exercise his liberty and freedom of expression. He had squared his conscience with his intellect, and if everybody did that, there would be no war. If he went to prison he would take no food. If anything happened as the result it would not be his responsibility, but that of the British Government.

The Lord Justice-General said a question of simple fact was submitted to the jury – whether on the eleven different occasions mentioned in the indictment the accused made the statements alleged. No attempt had been made by the defence to deny that the statements were made.

The jury without retiring, unanimously found the charges proved.

His Lordship in passing sentence said he had taken into account the fact that he had, so far as his Lordship could judge, over a year to serve of his former sentence. The sentence would be that he be sent to penal servitude for a period of five years.

The Scotsman, 10 May 1918.

Agnes Maclean's Letter

42, Auldhouse Road,
Newlands, Glasgow,
5th. November, 1918

Dear Sir,

I think it desirable to inform you that I was allowed to see my husband, John Maclean, for the first time since his trial, in Peterhead prison, on Tuesday, 22nd. ult: and he then stated to me that he has been hunger-striking, and has been forcibly fed, since July.

He found the food that was sent in unsatisfactory, and refused to take it or the prison food (which he believed to be drugged), requesting to be transferred to Glasgow, where he could have food prepared by myself sent in.

He told me that he tried to resist the forcible feeding by mouth tube, but two warders held him down, and that these men never left him thereafter, night or day, till he was forced to give in. I was shocked beyond measure by these statements (made to me in presence of the prison Doctor and two warders) and by the evidence of their truth supplied by his aged and haggard appearance. They contradict entirely the assurances given to me and his other friends by the Authorities that he was in good health.

One thing is clear – that he cannot much longer endure the torture of body and mind to which he is daily being subjected. The only alternatives in the conflict between the Authorities and himself are – either his death in prison, or his immediate release from prison.

From the former I believe they do not shrink, and every day brings it nearer.

On the latter alternative I insist – and I appeal to you in common with other friends of my husband, and if the work he has done for humanity, – to do all you can to help me to induce those who are keeping him in durance to set him free at once.

I am, dear Sir
Yours faithfully
Agnes Maclean

'Letter of Agnes Maclean', Acc. 4251/3.

The Iolaire

*On the 11th day of the 11th month at the 11th hour in 1918, the
Great War stopped. Yet for the island community of Lewis there
was a further tragedy still to come. In the small hours of the New
Year, the Admiralty yacht Iolaire was wrecked on the Beasts of
Holm – a formation of rocks just outside Stornoway harbour. On
board it were 260 Royal Navy ratings returning home, some for
the first time after the four and a half years of the war. Only 75 of
those on board were saved, many of them due to the heroism of a
man from Ness, Seaman J. F. Macleod, who swam ashore in the
heavy seas with a rope. At least 205 men drowned. Angus
Nicholson was one of those who survived – here is part of his
account to the enquiry.*

Angus Nicolson, leading seaman (32), 25 Battery Park,
Stornoway, was the next witness. He deponed that the Iolaire
left Kyle about 20 minutes to 8 o'clock. The only officer he saw was
a Lieut. Commander whom he took to be the Captain of the ship.
He took several of his men into the charthouse, and told them to
make themselves comfortable there. He asked them if they were on
New Year leave and said that about one-half of his crew were on
leave so that they were shorthanded. There were four or five men in
the charthouse. Witness saw no signs of drink about the officer who
spoke to him; he appeared quite normal.

Nicolson remained in the charthouse until they had passed Rona
Light. He returned to the Charthouse and remained until they were
about seven miles east of the Shiant Banks. When he next emerged
he saw Arnish Light, from which he thought they were about nine
or ten miles distant. He saw no fishing boat until they had gone on
the rocks.

The wind was southerly directly behind the boat. He saw Arnish
Light quite distinctly, but did not see the beacon at that time.

No more than four minutes before the ship struck the rocks, one
of his chums had come into the charthouse and said 'She's near in,
boys, you'd better get your things ready.' He looked at his watch
then and it was 10 minutes to 2.

The wind being astern there was very little motion, and about
three or four minutes before she struck witness knew by the motion
she was broadside on. He knew by that she had changed her course.

He was in the charthouse when she struck, and he thought it was
Arnish beacon rock they had struck. When he got on deck he could

see by the light of the rockets sent up that they were on the Beasts of Holm. The beacon on the Beasts was visible only in the light of the rockets.

Boats were being launched on the starboard side, but witness and his chums did not go near them because they considered they were in danger of being swamped. By this time the wind had increased but was not a gale.

He saw a boat lowered on the port side, but she could not be got clear of the ship, which had taken a heavy list to starboard after she had struck. He shouted to the bridge to blow the steam whistle, and it was blown, three or four long blasts for three or four minutes. He heard no explosive rockets fired, but he saw light rockets being sent up. They were not told where the lifebelts were; he looked for one but failed to find any.

In his opinion the ship remained on the rock she first struck for about 15 minutes. The sea then drove her astern; she swung round and drove in gradually, stern first towards the shore. Witness told somebody he met at the engineroom door to drive astern as there was a passage ashore that way, but he said there was some engine trouble.

Nicolson came ashore by means of a rope made fast to the starboard quarter. Somebody had swam ashore with a heaving line, and by means of a rope attached to it about 16 men got ashore.

When witness got ashore he found the rope was being held by men kneeling on it and he took his turn until he became exhausted and was relieved.

He estimated at three quarters of an hour the time that elapsed between the striking of the ship and her disappearance altogether.

When she sank a flame or fire or light of some sort sprang up amidships. The ship's light had gone out about a quarter of an hour before she sank. There were seven or eight rockets fired, the last being about ten minutes before she sank. Witness heard the telegraph ring once before she struck. There were no flares used, but somebody flashed a morse lamp.

Witness did not believe any help could have been forthcoming from the sea, but was of the opinion that the rocket life saving apparatus could have given considerable assistance.

Cross-examined by Mr Anderson, Nicolson said they did nothing in the charthouse in connection with the navigation of the ship. The officer had put them in there had told them to make themselves comfortable. He seemed quite normal.

Both of the lifeboats launched on the starboard side were swamped and most of the men drowned. Witness understood the heaving line had been brought ashore by a man Macleod from Ness. After the ship sank the hawser disappeared.

He saw no life saving apparatus ashore, and made his way to Stoneyfield Farm where he procured a hand lantern to light him on the road. The farmhouse was full up by the time he arrived there, and the men receiving every attention from Mr and Mrs Anderson Young.

In reply to a question from Sheriff Mackintosh, Nicolson said he thought he could have heard any orders from the bridge even although there was a high wind. He could walk from Holme to the Battery in half-an-hour. No assistance was forthcoming in answer to the distress signals sent up by the Iolaire.

'Sea Sorrow, the Story of the Iolaire Disaster', *Stornoway Gazette*, 1972.

The General Strike

In 1925 pit owners decided to reduce miners' wages. The Conservative government temporarily stepped in and subsidised pay whilst a royal commission – the Samuels Commission – investigated the situation. When, in March 1926, the Commission reported back, it supported the proposal to pay the miners less whilst at the same time their employers wanted to increase working hours. If the miners did not accept the new conditions by 1 May, they would be locked out of the pits. At this point the TUC stepped in and warned that it would support the miners, by a General Strike on the part of key workers if need be. The Strike was on. It failed however to obtain its objectives and the TUC had to make a humiliating capitulation to the government.

Due to the industrial action of printers, ordinary newspapers could not appear during the strike, except in the form of special make-shift editions. The Aberdeen Bon Accord and Northern Pictorial *was one of these. Students played a prominent role as strike-breakers, taking on work such as tram driving. The accounts of the strike in Aberdeen are followed by reports from the special newspaper of the strike –* The British Worker – *on the strike in Scotland. The government also ran a special paper for the duration, entitled* The British Gazette.

THE SITUATION IN ABERDEEN

STUDENT DRIVERS ATTACKED

Union Street yesterday was a memorable sight. Both sides of the thoroughfare were lined with thousands of strikers, unemployed, and general public, eagerly awaiting developments. Incident came quickly upon incident.

The dense throng started by cheering vehicles containing foodstuffs, while private busses crammed to the door had a mixed demonstrative reception. Feeling ran high, and when two Corporation buses manned by students, attempted to make their way up the street, the throng rushed the first bus into Belmont Street, and brought it to a standstill. Many of the crowd clambered aboard and ejected the driver and conductor. The second was diverted from its path too, and along with the first one, was ultimately sent back to the depot.

Then the tramwaymen, attended by a large following, and headed by a bugler, marched to Queen's Cross depot in an attempt to evict the students and voluntary workers there. One man was taken by the strikers and turned away forcibly.

Feeling reached an acute pitch in the afternoon. About 3 o'clock two cars controlled by Tramway Inspectors were mobbed between Market Street and Belmont Street. A coal cart was drawn across the path, and in the melee one of the bags fell into the street. This was the signal for reprisals.

Some of the crowd seized the coal and commenced a fierce onslaught on the stationary car. The windows were smashed, the missiles rebounded off the sides of the car into the crowd lining the pavement, and everywhere there was confusion. For a few minutes the air was thick, and the men in charge of the tram were in considerable danger of being seriously hurt by broken glass, and flying coal and stones. Police soon were on the scene, and the car rushed through the crowd, but not without a further fusilade.

The attack was not confined to the Corporation vehicles, however. Private buses were also damaged, although, it may be stated, that no attempt was made as in the morning to remove the drivers and conductors of the Corporation buses from their posts.

About 3.30pm a strong posse of police was on duty in Union Street. It was about this time that the vehicles were mostly placed in danger. The crowd was exceedingly hostile and made a charge, the people scattering in all directions, while several people suffered bodily harm in the stampede. The Police handled well what might have proved to be an ugly situation. At the time of the baton charge women and children were among the crowd, and several of them were somewhat roughly treated as the result of the sudden rush immediately the Police drew their batons.

Although the crowd did not disperse altogether, comparative quiet prevailed for a time, although there was much shouting and hissing at the students, who, however, stuck grimly to their posts.

It was quite apparent that the sight of the broken windows in the various buses was responsible for would-be passengers not using them, and on one particular occasion four buses in succession passed the top of Belmont Street without a single passenger in any one of them.

Aberdeen Bon Accord and Northern Pictorial, 7 May 1926.

EDINBURGH NOW A STRONG LINK IN TU CHAIN

ENGINEERS RESTIVE

Until the development of the present dispute Edinburgh has been regarded as a weak spot in trade union organisation. The response to the call of the Trades Union Congress effectively disposes of that belief. The chief difficulty of the Central Strike Committee has been to confine the conflict to the limits of the Council's instructions. The printing trade is entirely closed down, except for two blackleg papers printed by a single non-union firm. Save for a few trams and buses manned by blackleg students, who have been promised immunity from examinations, transport has entirely ceased.

OUT EN MASSE

The railwaymen are solid – not a wheel is turning, and the busmen employed by the Scottish Motor Traction Company, which has a virtual monopoly in the district, are out en masse. No effort has been made to organise a blackleg service. The 14 NUR branches in the district, along with the Railway Clerk's Association and the Locomotive Engineers and Firemen, have formed a joint strike committee. Building trades workers are chaffing at the limitations imposed upon them. As there are no direct labour schemes proceeding a complete stoppage in this industry is likely ere this appears in print. The docks at Leith are at an absolute standstill and the Mid and East Lothian miners are out to a man.

British Worker, 5 May 1926.

SHOULDER TO SHOULDER

MAGNIFICENT RESPONSE TO TUC'S CALL: FINE DISCIPLINE MAINTAINED

Solidarity of the workers throughout the whole of Scotland is assured. From all parts come reports that the response to the strike call has been magnificent. Glasgow and Dundee may be taken as a representative of the rest of Scotland, where the TUC's instructions are being implicitly obeyed and good order maintained.

SCENES ON THE CLYDE

Glasgow's response to the strike call was magnificent. The Railway Union organisation worked splendidly, and traffic is entirely suspended. Harbour men and dockers are also solid, and river traffic is at a standstill. Over 900 tramcars are not working, only a very few moving with non-union labour. The printing industry is at a standstill, and on Tuesday no evening paper appeared. The iron and steel industries are 'out' to a man. Good discipline is being maintained, and union officials are perfectly satisfied and confident of complete solidarity being maintained. The Scottish TUC General Council is fully satisfied with the position. The only difficulty experienced is in keeping men at work in trades not yet affected.

DUNDEE

Further north, in the Dundee area, the arrangements worked with military-like precision. Railmen, trammen and general transport workers ceased work on the stroke of midnight. Quietness reigns throughout the city, and there is not the slightest indication of restiveness on the part of the men. In a half-jocular way, the tramway manager attempted to drive one car in the morning, but a crowd of workers surrounded the vehicle, and it was quickly driven back to the depot. One passenger train, in charge of students, arrived from Edinburgh.

ON THE CLYDE

On the Clyde, the populace is calm. Open-air meetings are being held throughout Glasgow to impart information concerning the progress of the strike. It was stated on Wednesday afternoon that local railway offices had been instructed from London to refuse wages to strikers who applied for them, on the plea they have broken their agreement by stopping work without notice. Railway stations are closed, and suburban trains are practically cancelled.

The scws branch of the National Union of Distributive and Allied
Workers has offered its branch funds to help the tuc.

British Worker, 7 May 1926.

Television

*Over the years Scotland had produced many inventors, but
few, apart perhaps from Alexander Graham Bell, have had
such a profound impact on world culture as John Logie Baird
and his work in developing television. A son of the manse from
Helensburgh, Baird first demonstrated his invention to the
public in 1926, but few people realise how rapidly his
discoveries progressed. By 1927 he could send television signals
between London and Glasgow using a telephone line. By 1928
he could show colour pictures. In the same year he made the
world's first transatlantic television transmission and even
transmitted pictures to a liner, the Berengaria, in mid-Atlantic.*
Television *was the title of a monthly magazine set up to
publicise and popularise the new discovery. In its March 1928
issue, it recorded Baird's feat in bridging the Atlantic in pictures.*

SEEING ACROSS THE ATLANTIC!

At the beginning of this year the record distance over which
television had been publicly demonstrated was between London
and Glasgow, by Mr J. L. Baird. To transmit vision over such a
distance – 435 miles – seemed at the time to be a most phenomenal
achievement; yet just after we had gone to press with this issue there
burst upon the world the startling news that the Atlantic had been
spanned by television! Again by Mr Baird.

Just what does this mean? It means that recognisable images of
human beings seated in the heart of London were seen in New York,
over 3,500 miles away!

This public demonstration, carried out in the early hours of the
morning of February 9th, turns out to be the culmination of months
of secret experimenting.

On the night of the demonstration there assembled at the offices
of the Baird Company, in Long Acre, a small party made up of Press
representatives and privileged guests. The transmissions commenced
at midnight, London time, or 7 pm New York time.

In order to give the watchers at the New York end an opportunity
to adjust the receiving apparatus, the image of a ventriloquist's doll

was first transmitted. The image sound produced by this doll, which sounded for all the world like the drone of a huge bee, was then sent over a telephone line to the company's private experimental wireless station at Coulsdon. From this station the image sound was then flashed across the Atlantic on a wave-length of 45 metres.

On the American side, the signal was picked up by an amateur receiving station at Hartsdale, a suburb of New York. After amplification the signal was then applied to the receiving televisor, upon the ground glass screen of which the image appeared. This screen measured about two inches by three inches.

Four watchers were anxiously gathered round the apparatus. These were Capt O. G. Hutchinson, the Joint Managing Director of the Baird Company, who had gone to New York specially to conduct the experiments; Mr Clapp, one of the company's engineers; Mr Hart, the owner of the amateur wireless station at Hartsdale, and Reuter's press representative.

When the image of the doll's head had been satisfactorily tuned in, Mr Hart started up his transmitter, called a receiving station operator at Purley, near London, and asked that Mr Baird should take his place before the transmitter instead of the doll. This message was telephoned from the receiving station to the laboratories at Long Acre.

For half an hour Mr Baird sat before the transmitter, moving his head this way and that, until the message came through from New York that his image had come through clearly. Mr Fox, a Press representative, then took Mr Baird's place, and continued to sit before the televisor until word came through that his image was coming through excellently. It appeared that Mr Fox's features were particularly striking, from a television point of view, and transmitted better than those of other sitters.

Mrs Howe, the wife of another journalist present, was then transmitted, and, although her features were not recognisable at the American end there was no mistaking the fact that a woman was seated before the transmitter.

Those assembled at the London end were able to see, on a check received, a pilot image of what was being transmitted. This image, which was full size, showed the head of the sitter, the complete details of the features showing in black relief on an orange-coloured background. By means of this pilot image the transmitting operator was enabled to check the outgoing transmission and correct any irregularities.

Atmospherics and other interference, and also fading of signals marred the image as received at the New York end at times, but in spite of these disabilities, reception was, on the whole, very good. The demonstration proved quite conclusively that if a much higher powered wireless transmitter had been employed, the image would have been received in New York entirely free from atmospheric and other disturbances. An important feature is that only two operators were required to attend to the television transmission, one at each end of the circuit.

By special arrangement with the Baird Company, we are being afforded special facilities and information which will enable us, in our next issue, to give our readers a more technical and illustrated account of how this latest wonderful dream of science has been achieved.

TRANSATLANTIC TELEVISION

(It is regrettable that so many people in this country should find it necessary to rush into print either to 'damn with faint praise' or adversely to criticise and belittle the pioneer work of Mr J. L. Baird. It is refreshing, therefore, to read the whole-hearted admiration of the American Press, some extracts from which we reproduce below. Truly, 'A prophet hath no honour in his own country.' – Ed)

The *New York Times*, Feb. 11th (Editorial): 'Baird was the first to achieve television at all, over any distance. Now he must be credited with having been the first to disembody the human form optically and electrically flash it piecemeal at incredible speed across the ocean, and then reassemble it for American eyes.

'His success deserves to rank with Marconi's sending of the letter 'S' across the Atlantic – the first intelligible signal ever transmitted from shore to shore in the development of trans-oceanic radio telegraphy. As a communication Marconi's 'S' was negligible; as a milestone on the onward sweep of radio, of epochal importance. And so it is with Mr Baird's first successful effort in transatlantic television. His images were crude; they were scarcely recognisable; they faded and reappeared, as the atmospheric conditions varied; but they were the beginnings of a new branch of engineering . . .

'All the more remarkable is Baird's achievement because . . . he matches his inventive wits against the pooled ability and the vast resources of the great corporation physicists and engineers, thus far with dramatic success. Whatever may be the future of television, to Baird belongs the success of having been a leader in its early development.'

The *New York Herald-Tribune*, Feb. 12th: 'Baird has been experimenting a long time with television, and it has been his ambition to be the first across the ocean, in the well-known Lindberghian manner. He has succeeded, for, if the images that were received on the televisor in New York were crude, they were pictures nevertheless . . . If it be appreciated also that Baird is an experimenter of the most classic type, and that he has been struggling along for years with the crudest of equipment, built in the skimpiest shop, his recent stunt is nothing short of marvellous . . .

'When engineers in New York successfully demonstrated television on a telephone line about 200 miles long, between New York and Washington, Baird showed he could do the same thing by screening pictures in Glasgow of persons in London a distance of 438 miles. It is said that probably one thousand engineers and laboratory men were involved in the American tests. Only a dozen worked with Baird.'

The *Sun Telegraph* (Pittsburgh) Feb. 9th, referring to the received images, says: 'They were comparable to the visions brought in at the A. T. and T. demonstration by air, from no farther away than New Jersey. The vision of the dummy, in fact, was clearer than those, but the moving faces were not so strong.'

Television, March 1928, London.

Penicillin

A contemporary of Baird but working in a totally different field was Sir Alexander Fleming, who accidentally discovered penicillin, the world's first antibiotic, and brought it to scientific attention. Fleming was a young professor at St Mary's Hospital in London when he made the discovery in 1928, but obtaining quantities of the mould sufficient to treat the thousands of patients who needed it was to be a long haul. It was not readily available for treating patients until the 1940s. Fleming's brother Robert wrote about those days in a series of articles for the Kilmarnock Standard *in 1962, just before his own death.*

Now we come to penicillin. The story has often been told how in 1928 a stray spore of a mould found its way on to a culture plate with which Alec was experimenting. It has been told with many variations, but the authentic medical publications have now got it substantially correct. Alec generally belittled his part in this and favoured chance, but this was modesty although chance played its part. If Alec had not experimented so much with lysozyme, if he had not done so much work on harmful antiseptics and had not been always searching for something better, then he would not have noticed the unusual effect of the mould spores on the bacteria in the plate. Anyhow he did notice that something from these mould spores had affected the bacteria underneath. The story has often been told how he cut channels in a culture plate to test the effect of a crude culture of extract from the mould on various bacteria. The result was sufficiently startling. Many of the bacteria were inhibited. It is one thing to do this in a laboratory but the extract was too crude to use on human beings. Who could tell? Anyhow Alec managed to preserve the mould and keep it reproducing itself for unlimited experiments, indeed all the researchers from then on were working with descendants of Alec's original spore. Alec handed these out freely. In 1929 he published his first paper on this subject in the British Journal of Experimental Pathology. Research workers took notice, not only in hospital laboratories but in the research departments of manufacturing druggists.

After some initial mistakes the mould was correctly recognised as penicillium notatum, by no means the most common of the penicillia group. Alec gave the extract the name of penicillin. There were no chemists in pathological laboratories in those days and here the chemist's help was needed, but penicillin proved very illusive and unstable.

It is easy to write about this now but at the time I knew little about what was going on. Alec was always reticent about his work. Looking back now I can see he had faith in his discovery. Several times I can remember a remark like this: 'Wait till my mould comes along.' . . .

Then in the high summer of 1942 an event occurred that made me startlingly aware of penicillin. A friend and employee of the Optical Company of which I was chairman was taken ill and absent from business, as we thought for a few days. His wife told me the doctor thought it was some kind of influenza, but a day or so later she called me early one morning to say their doctor was somewhat puzzled by the case and wanted to know if it was possible to get him into St Mary's. I telephoned Alec at his home and found that within half an hour he was leaving on a short vacation which he needed. Anyhow he got in touch with the hospital and arranged for the reception of the patient and departed for his own holiday, knowing the friend would be in good hands. Little did anyone know what was to come out of this case. The patient's illness soon became worse and was diagnosed as meningitis with the condition grave. I was going to St Mary's daily with the patient's wife and relatives. It soon became obvious that the doctors held no hope of his survival, although everything was being done according to the means then available. I was then able to get in touch with Alec and he returned home at once.

Alec's first act was to take the steps with which he was so familiar and isolate the bacteria which were causing the trouble and then to test them with the penicillin test he always kept handy. The bacteria yielded to the crude penicillin in the laboratory but where was the stuff to come from sufficiently pure for use? Alec got in touch with Florey who played his part nobly. There was only a tiny quantity in the Oxford Laboratory and that was all there was in the country. It had never been used on a case like this but every other treatment had failed and the patient was dying. Florey let Alec have all there was and treatment commenced. Meanwhile Florey's laboratory was making what little more they could and even recovering some of the drug from the patient's urine so that treatment could continue. Then the seeming miracle happened. The patient began to recover, the patient who had been given up, slowly at first and then with amazing rapidity. About a week after the commencement of this treatment I was calling at the hospital to see my friend and looked in at Alec's laboratory on the way. Alec went across with me to the hospital to see the patient who was by this time sitting up in a chair. We found him reading the 'Times' especially the leading article. He immediately drew our attention to this article with the remark 'I think this is the drug you used on me.' He handed the paper to Alec and there Alec saw for the first time the article in 'The Times' of August 7th 1942 calling attention to the new wonder drug. Alec did not know from what source the information was obtained by the 'Times' but there it was and penicillin was on its way.

The Kilmarnock Standard, 7 April 1962, 14 April 1962.

St Kilda

....

*Life on the little Atlantic island of St Kilda was always tough for
its inhabitants. As the new luxuries of 20th-century life improved
conditions on the mainland of Scotland, little improvement seemed
to trickle out to their shores. Conditions of life remained basic and
worse than basic. The hard winter of 1929 led to the St Kildans
needing to seek aid yet again from the mainland. Finally they
decided they had had enough. The islanders petitioned for
evacuation. The final destination of the 36 islanders was to be
Morvern in Argyll. The story excited a great deal of coverage. This
is how* The Times *reported it.*

'LAST POST' AT ST KILDA – ISLANDERS TAKEN OFF TO-DAY – FROM
OUR SPECIAL CORRESPONDENT

LOCHMADDY, AUG. 28

The last phase in the removal of the colony from St Kilda will
take place to-morrow, when the Admiralty sloop Harebell will
take off the remaining population to Oban, preparatory to their
settlement in Morven (Argyll). The evacuation affects some 36
natives, together with the island nurse and the missionary and his
small family. Owing to heavy seas the Glasgow vessel Dunara Castle
had to run for shelter into a sea loch on the west coast of Skye, with
the result that she was late in arriving yesterday at St Kilda to deliver
the last mail-bag for the natives, and take off such of the sheep stock
as remained in the islands after the ship's previous call a couple of
weeks ago. In addition, the Dunara Castle loaded all the islanders'
cattle – 10 animals in all – and the bulky possessions of the
inhabitants, who are being conveyed from Oban to their new
surroundings.

During the afternoon and evening some hundreds of sheep were
placed in small boats and towed out to the Dunara Castle as she lay
at anchor in the village bay. Owing to difficulty in working with the
sheep, which are semi-wild, operations had to be suspended about
midnight and the natives began to transport their belongings by the
light from a couple of lanterns. The goods consisted mainly of
wooden kists containing clothes and personal effects, spinning
wheels, querns, and pieces of furniture, many of which have been
bought by tourists who visited the island in the SS Hebrides some
days ago.

The St Kildans began their work early this morning and by 9am had the remainder of the sheep aboard. The six cows on the island had to swim out from the jetty, dragged by a rope fastened to the stern of a small boat.

THE LAST MAILS

The last mail dispatched to St Kilda from Greenock was one of the smallest ever carried. The final outgoing dispatch, however, was by far the heaviest that ever left St Kilda. A number of passengers went ashore from the Dunara Castle and crowded round the little village post-office in their anxiety to procure any remaining relics of the island. They bought large supplies of stamps, picture postcards showing local scenes, and many pieces of woollen goods manufactured by St Kilda women from the fleeces of the famous St Kilda sheep.

The island postmaster, Mr Neil Ferguson, was engaged all day in separating and trans-shipping the community's sheep, but his duties were undertaken by Alasdair Alpin MacGregor, a young Scots writer on the Western Isles, who had been on St Kilda for some days and had greatly helped the inhabitants in making preparations for their departure. Mr MacGregor stamped for the last time several hundreds of cards and letters addressed to every part of the world. The post office business did not finish until 2am when he stamped a parcel that a native had almost left behind on the island. The removal of the St Kildans to the mainland tomorrow will mark the end of a struggle against Nature that has been going on for centuries and that in the last few years had become more acute owing to the decline in the number of able-bodied men who normally would man the boats and attend to fishing and turf-cutting. From August until May the community was entirely cut off from civilization except when a storm-bound trawler sought shelter in the bay in front of the only village on the island and brought the natives the mails, that often had accumulated for months and additional provisions. The trawler men have been noted for the consideration they showed to the St Kildans. During the winter months the island's man-power had dropped so low in recent years that for three years the natives have not ventured near the adjoining island of Boreray, with the result that the sheep there are absolutely wild, and more than 200 have been left on the island.

To the very last night the villagers have held family worship in their respective homes, reading and praying and singing the Gaelic psalms in the traditional manner which has endured for centuries.

The Times, 29 August 1930.

Batons Drawn

*Over the course of the 19th century, Scotland had experienced an
influx of Irish immigrants, many of them Roman Catholic. Some
sections of the Scots community reacted to this with fear and
religious prejudice. In the 1920s and 30s, groups such as
'Protestant Action' tried to translate these responses into
government legislation against Irish immigration. They were so
successful that organisations such as the Church of Scotland gave
them support, but as most of their allegations against Scotland's
Irish population proved on investigation to be outrageously untrue,
they were unable to win over the Scottish Office to their cause.*

*In 1935 Protestant Action, under its leader, Edinburgh Councillor
John Cormack, organised a large and violent public demonstration
against a Catholic religious procession to be held in Morningside.
It met with a determined police response.*

EXCITING SCENES IN EDINBURGH

CATHOLIC CONGRESS ENDS

Exciting scenes marked the close of the Eucharistic Congress in
Edinburgh last night. Buses containing Catholics were stoned,
and batons were drawn by the police. Four men were arrested, and
two men were treated at the Infirmary for head injuries. There were
other minor injuries also in the course of the evening.

The centre of the disturbance was on the south side of the city, in
the Morningside and Bruntsfield districts, where large crowds had
gathered to view the holding of a Solemn Procession of the Blessed
Sacrament in the grounds of St Andrew's Priory in Canaan Lane.

The police cleared the lane and guarded all approaches to it, but
for three or four hours Morningside Road was thronged from the
station to Bruntsfield Place. This meant that the police had to
control a crowd which stretched for about three-quarters of a mile
in addition to watching various points in other districts where
sympathisers with the Protestant Action organisation had gathered.

The gathering in the Priory grounds had been timed for a quarter
past seven, but the crowd began to collect in the Morningside
district late in the afternoon. As the hour of the gathering
approached, tramcar after tramcar brought Protestant extremists
and others to the scene, and there was a regular trek of
demonstrators who made their way along Morningside Road on

foot. By 7 o'clock there must have been at least 10,000 people in
Morningside Road. Gangs of youths and young women, shouting
'No Popery' and waving orange and blue scarves or Union Jacks,
were a feature of the crowd.

'NO POPERY' CAR

The crowd was exceptionally dense at Canaan Lane and opposite
Hermitage Gardens and also at Churchhill, foot and mounted police
endeavouring as far as possible to keep it on the move. A motor car
containing Protestant Action leaders and displaying a card, on
which was printed 'No Popery', made a constant tour of the
neighbourhood and was noisily cheered. Speakers frequently
attempted to address the crowd, but met with little success. Round
them knots of supporters gathered, some of these carrying placards,
which read 'No Priest but Christ' or 'For God and Freedom'. The
speakers attracted few hearers, the main element in the crowd being
bent rather upon excitement than upon listening to them. There
were attempts to form a procession, but these were defeated by the
police and there were a number of ineffectual and pointless rushes
which served to do little more than to give an ugly appearance to the
situation. During some of these the police seized one or two of the
demonstrators including a man brandishing a penknife but let them
go later, having apparently taken them in hand for their own safety.
Near Maxwell Street a bus carrying Roman Catholics to the Priory
had a stone flung at it and the window was shattered.

The crowd continued to hang about in the expectation of some of
the 10,000 Catholics leaving the Priory grounds by way of
Morningside. One of the Protestant spokesmen mounted a pillar at
the entrance to a stone-mason's in Balcarres Street and told those
who listened to him that Councillor Cormack's orders were that
Protestants should behave themselves in an orderly manner.
Councillor Cormack had himself been on the scene earlier.

The ceremony at the Priory was over before nine o'clock, but the
task of getting those who attended it away lasted for about an hour.
The route taken in nearly all instances, was by way of the north end
of Canaan Lane and Pitsligo Road. Churchhill had been cleared by the
police, and a cordon was drawn across its juncture with Morningside
Road, though tramcars were allowed to proceed along Churchhill, as
they were in Morningside Road itself though here they accomplished
the journey with difficulty. At the junction of Pitsligo Road with
Churchhill, mounted police were kept in readiness.

MOUNTED SKIRMISHES

A few of the buses carrying Catholics away took the Churchhill route, and, when they arrived at Morningside Road, they found a dense crowd waiting. Mounted constables made repeated skirmishes at this point in order to keep the thoroughfare clear. The crowd was in an angry mood, and made rushes at the buses as they emerged into the main street. In one of these stampedes a police horse slipped on the pavement, and the rider was thrown heavily to the ground, and had to be assisted to his feet, while his horse was led away amid jeers.

Not all the buses which ran the gauntlet of Morningside Road escaped unscathed. A bus was attacked by a section of the crowd at the corner of Colinton Road. Stones were thrown, and Canon Forsyth, an Edinburgh priest, was struck on the head. A bottle was hurled at a bus containing children which followed the first bus. About half-past nine a bus which contained women from St Patrick's Church in the Cowgate was attacked. The windows on one side of it and at the back were smashed. Many of the women inside became hysterical, but most of them managed to duck below the window level and to draw their coats over their heads.

Shortly before 10 o'clock, so threatening was the attitude of the crowd in Morningside Road, that the police had to make a baton charge between Churchhill and Colinton Road during which one or two men were thrown to the ground. The object of the police was apparently to divide the crowd by driving a section of it northwards and the other section in the opposite direction.

POLICE BUS STONED

There were also exciting scenes in the neighbourhood of Bruntsfield Links, when the crowds were making their way back to the centre of the city, and buses were crossing the links from the direction of Whitehouse Loan. There were skirmishes on the Links, and some free fights occurred in the district as the result of arguments. A crowd in Leven Street stoned a bus load of policemen, and there was a slight disturbance in Princes Street Station when a number of Roman Catholics were entraining.

Almost the entire force of police in Edinburgh was drafted to the disturbed area, where the handling of the crowds was supervised by Chief-Constable Ross.

Roman Catholic chapels in Edinburgh were guarded by young Catholics all last night.

INSIDE PRIORY GROUNDS
10,000 CATHOLICS AND IMPRESSIVE SERVICE

Strict and careful watch was kept by the great army of stewards who were posted at the various gates of St Andrew's Priory, where the Solemn Procession of the Blessed Sacrament was held. Only authorised and special Catholics were allowed to enter the grounds, and each ticket was minutely examined.

After the service and procession, the great crowd, which must have numbered nearly 10,000 was called to attention by the warning voice of the loud speaker. 'All those who are wearing the official badge as a mark of their participation in the Congress are asked to remove them before leaving the field', it said. 'His Grace the Archbishop desires that this should be done'.

Reference to the unruly scenes which have unfortunately marked the Congress was made by His Grace the Archbishop of St Andrews and Edinburgh, who pontificated at the Benediction which followed the impressive procession 'I envy those who have had more to put up with than myself', said the Archbishop in a short address, 'but they will certainly receive more blessings'.

The beautiful grounds of the Priory made an ideal setting for the procession, and an hour before it was due to commence nearly 5,000 people were present. The number was doubled by the time the candles on the high altar were lit a few minutes before eight o'clock, and the announcer at the microphone had requested that the grounds should be regarded as a church, and that those present should refrain from talking and smoking.

SYLVAN SETTING

In the centre of the grounds the high altar, with its four tall pillars in red, black, and gold, had been erected, and the gold base surmounted by white tiers stood out strikingly against a sylvan setting of thickly-leaved trees. On all four sides was a great sea of faces. A route for the long procession had been roped off amongst those taking part in the ceremony, but many hundreds of people had left the flat ground around the altar and climbed the steep natural embankment on either side for a better view of the procession.

The arrangements were perfectly organised. Prior to the actual ceremony a band enlivened the crowd with Scottish and Irish tunes. The procession, in which 1,200 took part, started from the western end of the Priory, and slowly and impressively wound its way towards the altar.

A thick mist swirled over the grounds, but its greyness was almost eclipsed by the colourful sight which met the eye at the first appearance of the banner bearer, who was followed closely by the members of the Guild of St Agnes in red and cream. Women's Guilds, with the long line of the Children of Mary in blue and white preceded members of the University, Tertiary Sisters, in their black veils, and the representatives of Convents. Then came the Boys' and Men's Guilds, each participant wearing a coloured sash, members of University, Tertiary Brothers, and finally the Guild of Blessed Sacrament, servers, and clergy.

Those taking part included His Grace Archbishop M'Donald of St Andrews and Edinburgh; the Right Rev. Mgr P. Canon M'Gettigan, VG; the Very Rev. P. Canon Birnie, the Very Rev. H. Canon Considine, the Very Rev. W. Canon Mellon, Fr. Fitzgerald of Glasgow, the Right Rev. Mgr T. Canon Miley, and many other clergymen of the diocese of St Andrews and Edinburgh. The Canopy Bearers were Lord Moncrieff, Lord Carmont, Sir Walter Maxwell Scott, Bart.; Colonel Cranston, Mr George Cranson, Mr Reg Fairley, Sir Hew Dalrymple, and Professor Whittaker of Edinburgh.

MESSAGE FROM ROME

As the Archbishop ascended the steps of the altar and the golden Monstrance was carried aloft, every member of the large crowd knelt reverently for the solemn Pontifical Benediction. 'Sweet Sacrament we Thee adore', and 'Faith of Our Fathers' were the hymns sung during the procession.

Archbishop M'Donald read a copy of the telegram which had been sent to His Holiness the Pope at the beginning of the Congress. The message expressed the 'deep loyalty and affection of all Catholics taking part in the Congress', and concluded by 'begging the eternal blessing of the Holy Father'.

The reply from Rome congratulated all those who had taken part in the Congress, 'and still further, on having to suffer somewhat in the interests of the faith'.

The Scotsman, 26 June 1935.

Shipbuilding

....

*Originally too shallow to allow great ships to pass to and fro on
it, the river Clyde had to be dredged and dynamited to make it
deep enough for the great steam ships of the day to be built there.
Starting in 1812 with the building of the* Comet, *Europe's first
steam ship, the Clyde had gained a reputation for excellence. Clyde
yards built some of the world's greatest liners, such as the*
Lusitania, *the* QE2 *and the* Queen Mary. *The* Queen Mary *was the
biggest passenger liner of her day at the time of her launch. Her
building had originally been abandoned in the depression years, so
her completion, royal naming and launch represented a triumph
for everyone who worked on her and thousands of others from
miles around came to witness her voyage down the Clyde on 25
March 1936.*

PROGRESS OF QUEEN MARY DOWN TO THE SEA

SCENES ALONG THE RIVER BANKS – MAGNIFICENT SPECTACLE AT
VIEWPOINT – ONLOOKERS AWED BY IMMENSITY OF VESSEL –
DEPARTURE FROM FITTING-OUT BASIN

The scene within the Clydebank yard of Messrs John Brown and
Co. as early as nine o'clock yesterday was one of considerable
animation, but this was due mainly to the arrival of motor cars and
taxis bringing distinguished guests who were to make the voyage on
board the Queen Mary to the Tail of the Bank and others to witness
her departure from the fitting-out basin.

So far as the Clydebank workers were concerned it was to
outward appearances an ordinary day, with hammers clanging and
hydraulic riveters whirring on the hulls of vessels in course of
construction.

But when the time came for the Queen Mary to start on her
historic voyage work was stopped and all employees were given an
opportunity of witnessing the departure and bidding farewell to a
ship which has bulked largely in their minds for the past few years.

The giant liner, with freshly painted black hull and white
upperwork looked magnificent as she lay at the wharf. At the
foremast the 'Blue Peter' was flying, indicating her early departure;
at the main was the house flag of Messrs John Brown and Co., as
technically the ship had not yet been taken over by the Cunard
White Star Line, while the Red Ensign fluttered over the stern.

VOYAGE BEGINS

START EARLIER THAN EXPECTED

The exact time when the vessel would begin her voyage was a matter which depended entirely on the state of the tide and Clydebank being so far from the open sea, that could not be determined beforehand with any degree of exactitude.

The time for the start was given approximately as 10.45 but it happened that yesterday the tide came up the river with surprising rapidity. Between 9 and 10 o'clock there was a rise of seven feet on the tidal gauge at the fitting-out basin. Those in command therefore decided on an earlier start.

The signal was accordingly given for the stoppage of all shipping traffic on the river; the two last vessels to pass down were the Blue Funnel liner Neleus bound for China and the cargo steamer Aleira, about half an hour before the Queen Mary drew out.

MOORINGS CAST OFF

A small fleet of tugs were already in position round the huge liner. Ahead were the Paladin and the Clyde Shipping Company's Flying Eagle, and at the stern the Flying Falcon and the powerful tug Romsey from Southampton. Three more tugs, Flying Spray, the Flying Kite, and the Flying Foam were waiting in residence to take hawsers along the side of the vessel.

The moorings which had held the ship for some 18 months during the fitting-out process were cast off and the huge vessel, drawn and guided by the tugs, began to emerge into the navigable channel of the Clyde about three-quarters of an hour earlier than the scheduled time.

The Queen Mary was trimmed on an even keel, drawing between 33 and 34 feet of water fore and aft. Her movement out of the dock was naturally slow at first, but when the swirling waters at the stern indicated that her own propellers were turning the speed was accelerated.

In about half an hour the liner was in mid-stream and ready for the voyage.

The success of the preliminary operations showed how effective and thorough were the arrangements made by Messrs John Brown and Co. for the handling of the giant liner in the narrow waters of the river at Clydebank. Opposite the yard, on the Renfrew side, the navigable channel was marked by a line of buoys for some distance.

When all was in readiness to move the vessel out of the basin the signal had been given for work to cease in the yard. Every point of vantage was accordingly filled by workmen and those admitted to the yard to witness the event. The more daring among the yard hands climbed high on cranes and stagings to see the vessel depart, and as she moved majestically out of the basin she was sped on her way by cheering crowds, while the noise of low-flying aeroplanes added to the animation of the scene.

When the vessel had almost disappeared from view round the bend of the river at Dalmuir normal working conditions were resumed in the yard.

CHILDREN'S NOVEL LESSON

QUEEN MARY AND HER TUGS AS 'MODELS'

Probably no section of the crowd which witnessed the vessel drawing from the fitting-out basin felt the thrill of the occasion more than the hundreds of school children who formed part of the crowd at the Water Neb, near Renfrew.

They must have been the envy of school children all over the country as they derived an object lesson from an event of outstanding importance in the country's maritime history.

To all of those who had gathered in such close proximity to the vessel, but especially to the children it was an impressive moment when the sonorous blasts from the Queen Mary's sirens filled the air, indicating that she was ready for the active life which lies ahead of her.

Nothing could have been more calculated to appeal to the young imagination than to see the massive structure gently move in response to the pulling of the tugs.

The novelty of having the Queen Mary and her tugs as 'models' in the day's lessons was obviously not lost on the little spectators who watched intently as the stern of the vessel veered round towards them, giving a good impression of her tremendous bulk.

LINER UNDER WAY

CROWDS MARVEL AT MASTERPIECE

The crowds lining the river at Old Mains Farm, Inchinnan, and scattered over the fields there – viewpoints which have attracted thousands of sightseers during the past few months – were the first of the throng on the south bank to obtain a complete impression of the immense size of the liner. As she canted slowly until she reached mid-channel and her bows were directed straight down-stream by the straining tugs, the spectators marvelled at the towering height of the ship and its great length.

When the manoeuvre of 'straightening' the liner was completed there was a dignified beauty in the picture as the fitful sunlight on the water cast a shimmering reflection on the gleaming black hull. The Queen Mary then with grace and ease began the life for which she is destined.

The crowds felt somewhat awed; cheering was restrained, but there was wonder writ on every face at the masterpiece which has been fashioned by Clyde craftsmen.

Glasgow Herald, 25 March 1936.

Exiling the Italian Scots

With the outbreak of war in 1939, the government became concerned about a potential threat from enemy aliens. This meant that Scotland's substantial Italian minority came under scrutiny along with German residents of Scotland. The men were rounded up as part of a general policy of internment. In 1940 hundreds of Italian Scots found themselves placed aboard a liner bound for prison camps in Canada, along with German Nationals and POWs. The liner, the Arandora Star, *was torpedoed off Ireland and sank. Of 734 Italians on board the ship, 486 died; of 479 Germans, 175 died. It would not be an exaggeration to say that there was hardly an Italian family in Scotland unaffected by this tragedy. The survivors were taken back to Scotland but were not released. Wartime reporting often led to an element of propaganda in reports like this – hence the emphasis on the Germans panicking and rushing the lifeboats, and on the Germans', and Italians', reported hostility to each other.*

BRITISH LINER TORPEODOED OFF IRISH COAST
GERMAN AND ITALIAN ALIENS ON BOARD
NAZIS PANIC AND RUSH THE LIFEBOATS
SURVIVORS' GRAPHIC STORIES

About 1,000 survivors of the British liner Arandora Star (15,501 tons), which was torpedoed and sunk off the West Coast of Ireland by a German submarine when carrying 1,500 German and Italian aliens to be interned in Canada, were landed at a Scottish port yesterday. The vessel also had on board British soldiers acting as guards to the aliens and a crew of about 300.

After being struck the liner went down, taking with her many German and Italian victims of the U-boat attack.

A large number of those on board were asleep at the time, and there was panic, particularly among the Germans, when they were aroused by the terrific crash. There was a rush, which seriously hampered the getting away of the lifeboats.

In interviews with British survivors yesterday it was gathered that great hostility was shown by the Italians to the Germans not only because of the torpedoing of the liner without warning but also because of the Nazis' ruthless conduct in attempting to rush the lifeboats afterwards.

Before the disaster constant vigilance had to be maintained to keep the Italians and Germans from coming to blows.

ITALIANS SUFFERED MOST

No estimate of the total casualties is yet possible, but the Italians, most of whom were traders in this country and were interned when Italy entered the war, appear to have been the worst sufferers.

It is hoped that more survivors may yet be landed.

The Arandora Star was owned by Frederick Leyland and Co., Ltd. She was built at Birkenhead in 1926 by Cammell Laird and Co. and reconstructed in 1929 at a cost of £200,000 as a luxury cruiser. This brought her total passenger complement to 360.

CAPTAIN FEARED LOST

The commander of the Arandora Star – believed to have been lost with his ship – was Captain E. W. Moulton, who has had charge of her since 1927. He was a native of Liverpool. His home is at Bournemouth.

In pre-war days, when the Arandora Star was a cruising liner, he took her practically all over the world, and he is known to hundreds of people who have spent cruising holidays.

STRUCK WITHOUT WARNING

The survivors had terrible stories to tell of the scenes on board before the liner sank.

Two soldiers said that the ship was struck without warning in broad daylight at about six o'clock in the morning.

'We cursed the U-boat, but not so much as did the Germans and Italians on board, who were almost ferocious in their denunciation of this type of warfare', they said.

'The internees made a wild scramble for the lifeboats, pushing everyone aside in their eagerness. Apparently only one torpedo was fired, but it must have ripped the ship open, as she began to settle very rapidly. Everyone was provided with lifebelts; lifeboats were rapidly lowered and rafts were also released.

'We had no opportunity of getting into any of the lifeboats, and, grabbing a plank of wood apiece, we jumped for it' the soldiers said.

'After two hours in the water, swimming and resting on our planks, we saw a plane, and knew that assistance would soon be on its way. Eventually we were hauled aboard an already overcrowded lifeboat, which had 150 persons on board.

CAPTAIN ON THE BRIDGE

'Fortunately the sea was not rough, but all around us we could see the water strewn with wreckage and bodies.

'As the ship went down the captain and several of the ship's officers were standing on the bridge and on the decks. Several of them, we fear, went down with the vessel'.

Another soldier, George Kitchin, picked up a piece of the exploded torpedo, which he retained as a souvenir. Sergeant J Kandy was one of those who only a fortnight ago, was bombed while coming back from France.

A British ship picked up many survivors.

'It was a rare sight', said one of the rescued. 'She was already overcrowded with survivors, but the crew managed to give us some tea to keep us going. Other rescue ships soon appeared and picked up many men'.

The Germans and Italians were marched to a temporary barracks, in which the two nationalities were kept apart. The soldiers and members of the Arandora Star's crew proceeded to canteens in the town, where most of them had their first proper meal since their rescue.

The canteens were fully taxed, but householders in the vicinity readily assisted by providing tea and food. An appeal was issued for supplies of clothing, and there was a prompt and generous response.

Several of the Italian survivors found that they had come back to the town in which they formerly carried on business and in which they were rounded up for internment when Italy declared war. Their arrival had become known to relatives and friends who are still at liberty in the town, and unsuccessful efforts were made by some of them to get into touch with the prisoners.

GERMANS CLAMOURED FOR PLACES ON LIFEBOATS
HAD TO BE 'FORCIBLY RESTRAINED'

Some of the British troops on board made bitter comment on the conduct of the German aliens. They described them as 'big, hulking brutes, who tried to sweep aside the Italians and had to be forcibly restrained'.

Bitter hostility between the Germans and Italians was apparent both on the liner and on the rescue ship and troops had to be on guard constantly to keep them from coming to blows.

Some survivors declared that when the ship was sinking the Germans made it clear that nobody was going to stand in their way of being rescued.

'They swept aside all opposition in their clamour for a place in the lifeboats', one of them told a reporter. 'The poor Italians did not stand a chance against them'.

MAD SLIDE DOWN ROPE

'The Italians and Germans behaved', said one Londoner, 'just as one would expect them to behave. They thought of their own skins first. The fought each other in a mad scramble for the boats'.

At one stage he saw 30 men fighting with each other in a mad rush to slide down a rope to the boats.

'When I saw what was happening I decided to look for other means of escape. As I walked all the decks were awash. I continued walking into the sea and grabbed a piece of wreckage to keep me afloat. Eventually, I managed to reach a raft. At the end of eight hours I was hauled out. My legs folded under me. They had lost all power'.

The Londoner passenger paid high tribute to the expeditious manner in which the survivors clinging to the rafts and in the lifeboats were picked up by the crew of one of the rescue ships.

A number of the survivors had nothing but admiration for one German. One of the lifeboats had been overturned, and this German, taking command of the situation, summoned assistance from those in the water around and succeeded in righting the boat again. He then set about rescuing those in the water.

He performed marvellous feats, said a survivor, and seemed to be possessed of herculean strength.

Altogether he is stated to have saved 25 persons. His great work so impressed those who saw it that they are talking of getting up a petition on his behalf with a view to his gallantry being recognised in some form.

The Arandora Star's lighting system was put out of action, and the engine-room staff had to scramble through the darkness to the decks.

Two German and two Italian survivors who were picked up died on board the rescue ship. Immediately the rescue ship arrived at port the injured were removed to hospital.

GERMAN REFERENCE

The sinking of the Arandora Star was mentioned earlier yesterday in the German High Command communique. In the course of a gleeful reference to the sinking of British shipping it said:

'Another submarine torpedoed the armed British steamer Arandora Star of 15,500 tons, in the northern channel'.

The survivors presented a pathetic sight. Some of them were clad only in pyjamas, while others were wearing only thin singlets and trousers. Others had oddly assorted garments, many of which had been supplied by the crew of the rescuing warship. A large number were barefooted.

Glasgow Herald, 4 July 1940.

Clydebank Blitz

Heavy industry and shipbuilding naturally made Clydebank a target for the German bombers when the war came. It was the only location in Scotland to be subjected to intensive Luftwaffe bombing. Thousands were killed over a period of only two days in March 1941. This account of the bombing was published in the local press a month after the raids. Wartime censorship is evident, and the approved message is put across – universal heroism, the bestiality of the enemy, but no accounts of actual blood or bodies to dismay readers. This is the kind of reporting the government thought was fit for the home front.

THE GREAT DESTRUCTION

BY A CLYDESIDER

In a Clydeside town it was a clear night of radiant moonlight and twinkling stars, just such a night as poets and lovers dream about when romance and happiness and the sheer joy of living go hand in hand. Home from work and with my hunger appeased, I was washing myself in keen anticipation of a quiet, studious evening after the tedious toil of the working day. Half in jest, half seriously,

I thought, as I listened to the warning, of the speech by Macbeth: 'It is a knell that summons thee to heaven or to hell!'

When the raid began my impression was it was another reconnaissance flight by one or two German planes and I decided to stay in the house until the all-clear signal sounded. But the loud drone of bombers and the reverberating reports of anti-aircraft guns made me soon realise that not a moment was to be lost if I valued my life. Even then, however, I could not visualise the dreadful havoc and wanton destruction that was so soon to rend our hearts and bring ruin upon us.

My mother and young sister were already downstairs and, still in my working clothes, I, too, joined them. Several neighbours were there together for we had no shelter from air-bombing save our strong stairway and a kindly providence, if there is such a thing. Yet at the back of my mind I harboured the hope that we might all manage through safely and see our homes preserved.

Incendiary bombs rained down, flashing up the brilliant sky, shells from the guns lit the heavens, loud reports echoed fearfully and over all, menacingly, hovering like many ghoulish, mechanical birds of prey, droned the bombers scattering death and desolation. Amid shouts and frantic gesticulations, we all cowered low as the whistling sound of a bomb was heard near at hand. Then followed a deafening explosion and the falling crash of falling masonry, and clouds of choking dust and the cries of women and children. Miraculously, in that dark hell of horror caused by brutish man, not one of our party was killed.

Across from us a church was burning furiously and cottages and tenement buildings were also a mass of red flames. Accompanied by another man, who went upstairs in a vain attempt to do something, I went back to my home and hastily snatched an overcoat and hat and had sufficient presence of mind to cram some money I kept in a drawer into my pocket. Down I dashed again and found our party herded together in a corner of the stairway, brave and apprehensive.

The merciless mission of destruction continued hour after hour. Each blast and terrific crash and whistling bomb seemed to herald our approaching end and I felt my heart wrung to its depths when I contemplated the kneeling women and children and heard their prayers. Most of them were praying aloud, a few were stonily stoical and thus they crouched.

Their homes were gone, their possessions burning to ashes, and the terror of aerial warfare was let loose upon them; and all these inoffensive, peace-abiding people, like their counterparts in every land, asked little of their rulers but the simple boon of being left alone to live out their days upon earth in a certain frugal comfort and pleasurable anticipation of things to come.

This I saw for myself: that no man in our group behaved like a craven soul. They were dazed, bewildered, baffled, furious at their impotence to fight the desperate situation, but fearless in a night of death and destruction. Outside in the streets the fire-fighters pluckily and heroically fought with the all-conquering flames which, leaping and spreading into the air, burned and burned, a red hot, living mass of consuming wrath and ravagement. The scene vividly recalled to me my early innocent impressions of the end of the world by fire and the fury of an almighty Power.

So rapidly and dangerously did the flames burn that we were compelled to seek a safer shelter, if one could be found, out in the open. Despite remonstrances and protests from some of our little group, we went round by the debris-strewn backyard and stood awhile in the brick wash-house. It was a perilous place to hope for sanctuary but it afforded us a few moments respite.

As long as I live I shall never forget with what bitter anguish and desolation of heart I watched the red flames blazing out of every window of my home. There went the fruits of long years of study and concentration, the tie-beam of my life, the one great, finest thing that had spurred me on through adversity and misfortune. All my pictures, all my drawings, sketch books, writings, treasured volumes, and all the creations of inspired moments totally destroyed and lost for ever! I wished then to die where I stood, for the aim and strenuous endeavour by which alone I lived had been wiped out. My years had been spent in vain.

Clothes, furniture, worldly goods, all these were nothing; but this other thing was my very self, my innermost me, a fine spirit that could never be replaced.

I made no whine of complaint yet, in my soul, I was, like Christ, in Gethsemane. I thought of all the poor people who were enduring the full force of the German blitz; how they were being killed and injured, and rendered homeless wanderers if they escaped death; the men, women and children sitting in Anderson shelters and the surface shelters, those unfortunates, so many of them, with no protection save their tenement closes and houses, and blind chance, everyone of them hoping to escape from this fiendish, murderous tornado of modern warfare. Hell was let loose upon Clydeside that night.

Lives were being wantonly sacrificed in this mad, insensate lust to kill and destroy, and hearts and high hopes were being ruthlessly shattered. With a heavy heart I turned away with my mother and sister on either side of me, to seek a shelter from the hail of death that descended from the sky. Somehow, in a providential manner, we came through the ordeal waiting and watching for the dawn amid the thunderous reports, the crashes and heavy explosions and the blazing, crackling buildings.

Brave deeds were done by fearless souls, men and women everywhere, and miraculous escapes from death were chronicled through the night.

The cold, red dawn saw parts of Clydeside a smouldering mass of ruins and heaped-up masonry and debris where death hovered, a place of stunned, questioning people, homeless and penniless, dimly trying to fathom the meaning of it all. The once proud, prosperous homes were laid low, families killed or ruined, careers senselessly shattered, toil, blood, tears, the destiny of the people. There was left to them the distinction of knowing that their sufferings and heroic fortitude had thrilled the world and, let it be added, made their habitations a haunt for countless, curious sightseers.

Never was there a time in which this same world was so full of noble talk about God and religious ideals, the sacredness of holy things, and vibrant with the eloquence of orators imbued with lofty aims of freedom and brotherhood and a better way of living once the war is over.

And there may be still more drastic and more devilish methods of extermination in prospect for the peoples of all countries.

O, you poor dead and wounded, innocent victims! You shall yet be avenged! You shall not have died and shed your blood in vain!

Clydebank Press, 25 April 1941.

The First Edinburgh Festival

The Edinburgh International Festival was started in 1947 as an antidote to war-time austerity. Its founders wanted it to be a chance for people of all nationalities to come together in peace to celebrate the arts. The event was an enormous success, attracting attention from all over Britain. The Festival Society kept volumes of press cuttings in its archives. This report from the Manchester Evening News *was typical of the good publicity, and also shows how the Festival had to battle with post-war rationing – flood-lighting the castle was banned as too wasteful!*

MR MANCHESTER'S DIARY

Embarrassed looking tram-cars are bouncing round Edinburgh today with small Union Jacks trailing from their electric arms – for all the world like circus elephants with their tails in curl papers.

This is typical of the spirit of carnival which has descended almost overnight on this usually prim and proper Scottish capital. It's all in honour of the first International Festival of Music and Drama now being held in the city.

DECOROUS

Even so it's still a very decorous sort of carnival. There may be baskets of geraniums hanging from every lamp-post along lovely, aristocratic Princes-street; there may be an island of flowers outside Central Station; the celebrated floral clock in Princes-street Gardens may now spell Tchaikovsky and Beethoven and tick away through forget-me-not borders of crochets and semi-breves. But the crowds move as orderly as ever between the Caledonian Hotel and Waverley Station. And every policeman has been issued with a new helmet and a clean pair of white gloves.

Foreigners gathered here for this first Festival will go away thinking confusedly of a dowager duchess, her hat on one side, determinedly shying the first ball at the coconuts. And scoring a direct hit.

OBSTINATE

Visitors here have an obstinate habit of refusing the obvious. And although proud landmarks like Holyrood Palace and the Castle (though Mr Shinwell has imposed a last-minute ban on flood-lighting) and Princes-street itself look as though they have just come back from the laundry the crowds prefer to wander delightedly around the dingy, smelly closes and wynds of Canongate.

Said one Hungarian woman to me, summing it all up – the quiet Georgian squares with their gay window boxes, the lazy smoke haze, the incredibly theatrical backdrop of the Castle – 'It's a mixture of Rome and Manchester, seasoned with a drop of Paris and a dash of Budapest.'

Accommodating the thousands of visitors who have been pouring into the city all weekend has been a major problem. In many cases private householders have offered a spare bed or a sofa in the lounge. In my hotel, where booking opened in January, 21 guests were waiting patiently for one harrassed waiter to serve them breakfast this morning.

THE MUSIC

During the next three weeks five of the world's finest orchestras – among them the Hallé – will be providing the musical programme. The city's two largest theatres are housing the Old Vic Co., the Sadlers Wells Ballet, and the Glyndebourne Opera. But the festival doesn't end there.

It seems as if every Scottish cultural organisation – big and little, is running its own side-show. For those who can't afford a 25s stall for 'The Taming of the Shrew' the Glasgow Unity Theatre is offering a Scots version of Gorky's 'The Lower Depths'.

Each afternoon squads of kilted soldiers march down from the castle to dance reels. Even the cinemas are putting on miniature film festivals.

ENTENTE

The festival made a happy start last night with a rousing symbol of the Entente Cordiale – L'Orchestre Colonne of Paris played the English [sic] National Anthem and then the Marseillaise. And there was a great response from the audience of nearly 3,000. In front I saw the Lord Provost, Sir John Falconer, Sir John Anderson, Lady Rosebery, and Walter Elliot, MP.

This world-famous orchestra conductor Paul Paray, gave a memorable concert of three symphonies – Haydn's 'Surprise', the Schumann No.4 and the Cesar Franck. M. Paray looks like a middle-aged businessman. His vitality is as remarkable as his swift changes of mood.

The first performance of the Cesar Franck, by the way, was given 58 years ago by this very orchestra – with different personnel, of course. L'Orchestre Colonne was established in 1873.

ELEGANCE

Last night's elegant audience – some in evening dress, a few in kilts and several in arty corduroys – were filled to the roof of the fine two-tier Usher Hall. At the end of the concert they forgot their elegance and applauded for about five minutes with stamping of feet and cries for more.

Their enthusiasm was understandable. The final crescendos of the Cesar Franck was some of the most inspiring moments I can recall in any concert hall.

The only woman in this orchestra of nearly 100 was Madame Chambaret, the harpist. She told me – in French, that she has a husband and a grown-up son in Paris. She leaves them frequently to tour the world with the orchestra. Another woman who is a very useful member of the organisation is Madame Paray, the charming wife of the conductor – she acts as his interpreter.

This orchestra gets about quite a lot although this is its first visit to Scotland. They flew to Paris from Rio de Janeiro only five days ago.

Manchester Evening News, 25 August 1947.

Twentieth Century Scotland II:
The Road to Home Rule

From the Stone of Destiny to devolution, perhaps the most impor-
tant thread of Scotland's post-war history has been the impetus
towards self-government which finally reached a climax with the
'Yes' vote in the 1998 referendum. Economically, the last half of the
20th century saw the decline of traditional industries such as mining
and shipbuilding and the introduction of new sources of wealth such
as North Sea oil. On 1 July 1999 a new Scottish parliament opened
in Edinburgh, beginning a 'new sang' (as opposed to the end of an
auld one in 1707) to take Scotland into the millenium.

Stealing the Stone

The stone of Scone – the ancient inaugural stone of the Scottish
kings – had been taken by the forces of Edward I in 1296. Since
then it had been in Westminster Abbey, set under the throne of the
English kings. The first Scots royal to sit on it again had been
James VI and I at his English coronation in 1603.

In the post-war decades Scottish autonomy became an issue. The
Scottish Nationalists secured their first MP in the Motherwell by-
election of 1945, while the Scottish Covenant movement of 1949
had called for reform of the constitution of Scotland and for self-
government within the UK. In Glasgow a small group of Nationalist
students decided to strike a blow for Scottish pride. On Christmas
Day 1950 the four of them – Ian Hamilton, Kay Matheson, Alan
Stuart and Gavin Vernon – decided to repatriate the stone. It was
eventually returned to Westminster in time for the Queen to sit on it
at her coronation, but the ancient grudge remained. It was only in
1996 that the stone was returned to Scotland.

We vaulted the railings, and crossed the patch of light, and
stood, crucified by the rays of the lamp, against the shining
door. At least we should not work in darkness.

Gavin put his shoulder against the door. 'The jemmy!' he hissed. I
turned to Alan.

'The jemmy!'

'What!' said Alan, 'I thought you had it.'

Sheepishly I returned to the car and retrieved it from under the
seat where I had hidden it during the skirmish with the detective.

At first we made little impression on the door, for the two halves met closely, and the join was covered with a lath of wood which ran from top to bottom. We were desperately afraid of noise, and each creak sounded like a hammer-blow. But when we really got down to the job it was relatively easy. We deadened our ears to noise, and with the sharp end of the jemmy chewed away sufficient wood to enable us to prise the blade between the two sections of the door. Then the three of us put our weight on the end of the jemmy, and the door began to give a series of creaks which sounded like minute guns. At each creak we expected a police car, summoned by the watchman, to sweep up the lane. Let it come; at least we were going down fighting.

I could now put my fingers through and feel the hasp on the inside. It was slack. We prised up the bottom of the door, and it came clear of the ground, bringing the bolt with it. Our gap widened to three inches. We could see into the Abbey. There was no watchman waiting there.

We put the blade of the jemmy close behind the padlock, and together we all wrenched mightily. With a crash, the door flew open. In the car Kay heard the noise and shuddered, but the way to the Abbey was open.

We swept into the Abbey. I returned and pulled the doors close behind me. I had rehearsed that part.

A light glowed dimly at the west end of the nave, but the rest was in black darkness. We went down the transept in silent hurry, and found that the gate in the metal grill was open. We crept through and round and up into the Confessor's Chapel. We did not listen for the watchman, for we might have heard him coming. At least, we would touch the Stone.

The chapel was in darkness. The glimmer from my torch showed the glass doors into the sanctuary as black sheets, and I hastily turned it to the side where it shone wanly on the green marble tomb of Edward I, whose dead bones Bruce had feared more than he feared any living Englishman.

The other two had already lifted aside the rail which kept the public from the Chair. The Stone was before us, breast high, in an aperture under the seat of the Coronation Chair, which was raised three feet from the floor on a kind of trestle. We gently prised at the bar of wood which ran along the front of the Chair as a retainer for the Stone. It was dry with age, and it cracked and splintered, and I felt sorry, for it did not belong to us.

The Stone should now theoretically have slipped out, but it was a very close fit and its weight made it unwieldy. I got to the back and pushed, and it moved a little. The chains on its sides kept catching on the carved sides of the Chair, and since the three of us were working in a sweating fever, not one of us had the patience to hold the light. At last we saw that brute strength and black darkness would not budge it, so we called a halt. Then one man holding the torch, one prising at the sides with the jemmy, and one pushing at the back, we started afresh. It moved. It slid forward. We had moved the Stone. The English Chair would hold it no longer.

We were sweating and panting. It was coming. The plaque saying 'Coronation Chair and Stone' fell from the Chair. I caught it in mid-air and thrust it into my coat pocket. They would not need that now. It was almost free. One last heave. 'Now!' said Gavin. I pushed from the back. It slid forward and they had it between them. I rushed forward to help them and we staggered a yard. We had to put it down. It was too heavy.

'A coat!' said Alan deep in his throat.

'Mine is the strongest,' I said. It was the strongest, but also I wanted the honour for my coat. I slipped the jemmy out of my pocket. We would come back for that later. I struggled out of my coat and laid it on the ground; one hasty heave and the Stone was on the coat.

I seized one of the iron rings, and pulled strongly. It came easily – too easily for its weight, and I felt something uncanny had happened. 'Stop!' I said and shone my torch.

I shall not forget what the faint light revealed, for I had pulled a section of the Stone away from the main part, and it lay in terrifying separation from its parent.

I was going to be sick. Everything was now turned to a new purpose which was not good. Better to howl and bring the watchman and have it repaired than carry away a broken Stone.

'We've broken Scotland's luck,' came Alan's awful whisper.

I shone the torch on the break. Suddenly I saw that the greater area of the break was much darker than the thin wafer round the top edge. The Stone had been cracked for years, and they had not told us.

'No, we haven't!' I said. 'They did it. They've cheated us, and kept it from us.'

'Quit talking and get moving!' said Gavin.

I picked the small part up like a football, and opened the door into the sacrarium. The light still burned at the far end of the nave, but of the watchman there was no sign.

I stepped hurriedly past the altar, down the steps, and round into the transept. That part of the Stone weighed almost a hundred pounds, yet I might have been on the sports field for all the hindrance the weight was. I came out into the light at the Poet's corner door, and plunged again into the darkness of the masons' yard. Alan had taken the precaution of opening the doors before he entered the Abbey, so that I had little difficulty. Kay had seen me coming and had the car halfway down the lane. She opened the door, and I rolled the piece of Stone into the back.

'It's broken,' I said. 'Get back into cover.' I don't know what she thought, but by the time I was back in the Abbey the car was once more in position at the top of the lane.

The other two had made good progress. The steps leading down from the altar are wide and shallow, and they presented little difficulty to us. We grasped the coat and slung it down, step by step, between us. Except for our gasps for breath and an occasional grunt of effort, we made little noise. Now and again there was a rending sound from the coat as the weight told on it.

We reached the foot of the steps and dragged it across the nave. Sweat blinded us and we were breathless. As we turned into the transept there was a crunching sound. The plaque, which I had forgotten was still in my pocket, had fallen out and the whole weight of the Stone had passed over it. Alan swiftly pocketed it.

Suddenly and miraculously we were at the door. We stopped for a breather, for we were all at the end of our strength. 'One more pull,' said Alan. 'We're not going to be beaten now.' I opened the door, and as I did so I heard the car start up. It moved forward into the lane, whence it was clearly visible from the road. We still had to drag the Stone down the masons' yard. It was far too early to move forward yet. 'The fool,' I said, and dashed through the line of sheds to tell Kay to get back into cover.

The car was standing outside the gap in the hoarding. I opened the car door. 'Get the damned car back into cover,' I spat. 'We're not ready yet.'

Kay looked at me coolly. 'A policeman has seen me,' she said. 'He's coming across the road.'

I got into the car beside her and silently closed the door. I reached forward, and switched on the lights. I fought breath into myself and wiped the dust of the Abbey off my hands on to Kay's coat. I put one hand over the back of the seat, and groped for Alan's spare coat. Carefully I draped it over the fragment of the Stone. Then I took her in my arms.

It was a strange situation in which we found ourselves, yet neither of us felt perturbed. Kay was as cool and calm, as though we were on our way home from a dance, and for a couple of minutes I was so immersed in the task at hand that I completely forgot the approach of the policeman. It was our third night without sleep, and I think we were both so drugged with tiredness that we would have accepted any situation as normal. Our minds were cold as ice, and we had thrashed our bodies so hard and worked for so long in the shadow of our ultimate aim that fear or panic played no part with us.

The policeman loomed up in front of us. 'What's going on here?' he thundered. It was perfectly obvious what was going on. Kay and I did not fall apart until he had had plenty of opportunity to see us.

'It's Christmas Eve, you know, officer,' I explained.

'Christmas Eve be damned!' he answered. 'It's five o'clock on Christmas morning.'

'Ochone! Ochone!' I said. 'Is it that time already?'

'You're sitting on private property here,' he told us. 'And why did you move forward when you saw me coming?'

'I know,' I said humbly. 'I knew we shouldn't be here. We put on the lights to show you that we were quite willing to move on.'

'But where can we go?' asked Kay, vamping him. 'The streets are far too busy.'

'You should be off home,' he told her, and looked at her severely.

We explained to him that we were down from Scotland on tour, and that we had arrived in London too late to get a bed. We sat and held hands in front of him, and tried to give him the impression that we were too much in love to go to a hotel and be parted.

He began to warm to us. To my horror, he took off his helmet, and laid it on the roof of the car. He lit a cigarette and showed every sign of staying, till he had smoked it.

'There's a dark car park just along the road,' he said, smacking his lips contemplatively. We knew that car park. The other car was there.

'Och, well,' said Kay, thrusting her head into the lion's mouth, 'if we're not comfortable there we can always get you to run us in and give us a bed in the cells.'

'No! No!' said the PC knowingly. 'There's not a policeman in London would arrest you tonight. None of them want to appear in court on Boxing Day to give evidence against you.' Kay gave my hand a squeeze.

'A good night for crime!' I said, and we all laughed.

All this time I had been conscious of a scraping going on behind the hoarding. Why on earth didn't they lie low until the policeman had gone? It transpired afterwards that they had no idea that we were entertaining the police, and they were calling my parentage in question to the tenth generation for sitting in the car while they did all the work.

Kay heard the noise, too, and we engaged the constable in furious conversation. He thought us excellent company. His slightest sally brought forth peals of laughter, and when he essayed a joke we nearly had convulsions. Surely they would hear our laughter and be warned.

There was a muffled thud from behind the hoarding. The constable stopped speaking, tensed, listening. My heart sank to my boots. Kay's hand became rigid in mine. Then the constable laughed and said, 'That was the old watchman falling down the stairs.' Furiously and hysterically, Kay and I laughed at the idea of the watchman falling down the stairs. Surely they had heard us now.

'I wish it was six o'clock,' said the policeman. 'And then I would be off duty.'

Out of the corner of my eye, I saw the door in the hoarding slowly opening. Gavin's face appeared, followed by his head and shoulders. Suddenly he froze. He had seen the policeman. His lips formed an amazed oath. Inch by inch he edged back, and the door closed behind him. The policeman finished his cigarette and put on his helmet. 'You'd better be going now,' he said.

'We had indeed!' I said, wiping the sweat out of my eyes.

'Will you show us the way?' asked Kay, trying to get him off the premises.

'Oh, you can't miss the car park,' he said, and redirected us.

Kay started the engine. She is, although she will be annoyed that I say so, a very bad driver, but that morning her bad driving was designed and not incompetence. Never has clutch been let in so jerkily; never has a car veered from side to side so crazily. I looked back and waved to the constable. As Kay had expected, he was following down behind us – too amazed at the crazy driving to pay attention to anything else. We reached Old Palace Yard and Kay put her toe down.

I. R. Hamilton, *No Stone Unturned*, London, 1952.

Elvis at Prestwick

....

If Elvis is 'The King' then his one and only stop in the British Isles might be counted as a royal flying visit. The icon of American and British popular youth culture changed planes at Prestwick Airport in 1960 on his way home from doing his military service in Germany. This is how the Scottish Daily Mail *recorded it.*

A BEWILDERED ELVIS PAYS A FLYING VISIT

WHERE AM I? HE PONDERS AS HE SHAKES HANDS WITH
HUNDREDS OF SCREAMING TEEN-AGERS AT PRESTWICK

Hundreds of screaming teenagers drowned the noise of jet engines when Sergeant Elvis (the Pelvis) Presley flew into Prestwick last night. He shook their hands, signed autograph books, posed for pictures – then bewilderedly whispered to an Air Force lieutenant:- 'Where am I?' It was his first stop on the way back to an army discharge. And the American Air Force had planned his short stay to the split-second. Col. Russell Fisher outlined the operation before the 'Pelvis' plane wiggled down. 'But it all depends on what Sergt Presley wants,' he said. 'He may change the whole scheme.' But Elvis was most co-operative . . . although he wouldn't remove his hat.

REST

'Ah'm real sorry I cain't take it off,' said Elvis, chomping on his gum. 'It kinda breaks the uniform if you know what I mean.' What will he do after demob? 'Well, first ah'll get my feet up and have me a rest,' he said in a drawl that befits an all-American boy from Memphis, Tennessee. 'Then ah'm booked to do a television show from Hollywood with Frank Sinatra.' I said: 'I believe you want to do more serious roles in future films. You have said your first three films were musicals and you were getting tired of them.' Elvis looked me straight in the eye. His lower lip went into that million-dollar droop. 'Man, ah've made four films in my time. Yes, I want to do something more serious.' Hamlet? 'No sir. Not quite so heavy. I know my limitations.'

'OFF, OFF'

He spoke to reporters for five minutes – then was whisked away in a staff car to say 'Hullo' to buddies in the local NCO club. Then to the Teenage Club where he was met by the music of one of his early recordings, 'Heartbreak Hotel'. 'Turn it off,' he shouted. 'Turn it off'. They turned it off. Then back to the plane where he confided: 'Ah kind of like the idea of Scotland. Ah'm going to do a European tour and Scotland will certainly be on my list.' Dates haven't been fixed. Colonel J. E. Levan said as Elvis's silver and red aircraft left the runway: 'I don't admire his singing but I've got to listen to it – I've got a teenage son and daughter.' He added: 'But I've sure changed my opinion about that boy. He's gone up in my estimation since he landed here.'

NO KISSES

At Frankfort Elvis flew off unkissed. His 16 year-old girl friend, Priscilla Beaulieu, stood weeping as he boarded a military plane. She had jumped over the rope barrier keeping back the small crowd at the airport but Air Force police stopped her. He and Priscilla, daughter of a US Air Force captain, have been going out with each other for six weeks. Presley said: 'She's real cute . . . she's very mature for her age.' Today the girl who missed a last good-bye fondled the gold and diamond wrist-watch he gave her. She said: 'He has promised to telephone as often as he can. He said he'd rather telephone than write because then he can hear my voice.'

Presley, interviewed on TV before he left, said: 'I haven't seen much of Germany'.

Scottish Daily Mail, 3 March 1960.

The Hamilton By-Election

On 2 November 1967, at the Hamilton by-election, Winifred Ewing became only the second Scottish Nationalist MP *to be elected to Westminster. The result was a shock for the other Scottish parties and especially for Labour which had taken 71.2 per cent of the vote at the previous general election. The Nationalists, who had been written off as a spent force, suddenly seemed to be staging a dramatic recovery. The first party to react to this challenge was the Conservatives. The following year their leader Ted Heath made a commitment to advancing Scottish home rule at the party's Perth conference – the so-called 'Declaration of Perth.' The Nats' poor showing in the 1970 general election, where they lost Hamilton and took only one other seat, the Western Isles, led to the shelving of Heath's plans. Later electoral successes for the SNP led the other parties to re-examine their attitude to Scottish autonomy. This is how the* Daily Record *(which had*

already hired Ewing as one of their columnists) reported her
arrival at the Commons and her swearing-in.

CHEERING CROWDS WAVE WINNIE TO HER SEAT

Scotland's first Nationalist MP for 20 years yesterday took her seat in the House of Commons. It was Winnie Ewing's day – and a proud day it was. As she passed smiling broadly and giving the thumbs up sign to a cheering avenue of nearly 600 supporters, the fragile-looking heroine of Hamilton said: 'This is a wonderful feeling. I don't think any woman in Scotland could ask for more. I'm proud to be here for Scotland.'

On her new role in the corridors of power, she declared, 'Of course I expect to make an impact . . . not today and perhaps not tomorrow . . . but certainly before my time at Westminster is up.'

After the hard slog of the Hamilton by-election, this was the hard-earned icing on the cake. Earlier a railway special emblazoned with the SNP crest emptied 250 supporters onto the platform at King's Cross. In the pre-dawn darkness banners waved and a lone piper played 'Scotland the Brave.' The glare of television arc lights recorded the tartan triumph.

Winnie was joined on the overnight express from Glasgow by party members and kindred spirits in Hamilton and Edinburgh.

And for 400 miles the whisky flowed fast and song flowed faster. But in spite of yesterday's pomp and cermony, it was also a family day.

Winnie was accompanied by her husband Stewart and the children – Fergus 10, Terry 3 and Anabelle 7.

At King's Cross they were met by cars to match the mood. Three all-Scottish [Hillman] Imps whisked the Ewings to their Kensington hotel whilst special buses took supporters to a victory breakfast.

Meanwhile party members held a summit meeting with Plaid Cymru, the Welsh nationalists at London's Caxton Hall. The hall was festooned with banners and placards, including one on the Boston Tea Party theme, 'taxation without representation is tyranny'.

Back at the hotel, Winnie was searching for a lost sock. As she helped the children dress, parliament was still three hours and three miles away.

Then Dad arrived on the scene to take the family sight-seeing while Winnie left for a trial run through of the afternoon's ceremony.

She was greeted at the gate of the House by Manus Boyle, a Scots bobby.

'Welcome to London, madam,' he said. Then he turned 'She's rather sweet isn't she? She's bound to cause quite a stir.'

Then at 2.35, the climax, Winnie in purple costume – with a sprig of lucky heather – walked with her family through the crowds and into the commons. The Hope of Hamilton had become the Wonder of Westminster.

Daily Record, 17 November 1967.

The Ibrox Disaster

Scotland's love affair with football has sadly been tempered with tragedy from time to time. Probably the earliest football crowd disaster involving a Scottish team was the 1902 Scotland-England international where a stadium collapse killed 25 people at Ibrox. Sadly tragedy repeated itself at an 'Old Firm' game between Rangers and Celtic on 2 January 1971, when 66 people were killed in a crush on a stairway. In the wake of the tragedy severe restrictions were enforced on the numbers of supporters admitted into larger football grounds. Safety at football events has since been given a higher priority.

FIRST WARNING OF THE TRAGEDY . . .
DISTANT SOUNDS OF SCREAMS IN MIST

In the press box we had all been commenting on how well behaved the crowd had been and thinking that Rangers' equaliser in the closing seconds had restored the good nature of their fans, ensuring that there would be no subsequent trouble.

Then, across the field at the north-east corner – Section 13 – there were four or five policemen standing on the track looking up into the terracing. Someone said: – 'Fighting must have started there.' But this seemed inexplicable because one had been able to sense the entire good humour of the crowd after the thrilling end to the game.

Then, across the floodlight mist, the distant sounds of shouts and screams could be heard. Two of us rushed down the spiral staircase from the top of the stand. We pushed our way through the cheerful fans on the pavement, through another entrance and ran across the bone-hard frosted pitch on which only minutes before, Colin Stein had brought so much happiness by scoring that equalizing goal.

GHOSTLY

In the deserted ghostly atmosphere of the playing pitch we had thoughts of fantasy, such as 'So this is what it is like to play at Ibrox.' Thoughts of disaster had still not penetrated.

Even when we reached the track at the far corner there was still no indication of the enormity of what had happened. Two or three people were being carried or helped down the terracing. Then, as dozens of police and ambulancemen converged and ran up the terracing, we felt the first real chill of the situation.

There was a numb silence now, broken only by shouts for stretcher bearers. We started to make our way to the top of the terracing, but several times went back with injured spectators who asked, 'Can you give us a hand?' Willing hands abounded to assist injured boys and men down to the track.

Eventually, at the top of the terracing, the true horror of the situation became apparent. Half a dozen lifeless forms were lying on the ground. Rescuers were tripping over the dead and injured as they struggled back with more victims.

A wedge of emptiness had been created part of the way down the long steep flight of steps leading to the Cairnlea Drive exit. In it were the twisted remains of the heavy steel division barriers. They had been mangled out of shape and pressed to the ground by the weight of bodies.

SHOES RIPPED OFF

Lying all over the steps were scores of shoes that had been ripped off in the crush. Beyond, the steps were still dense with groaning people.

We helped another of the injured back down the terracing.

Then Sir Donald Liddle, the Lord Provost, who had watched the game from the directors' box, walked across the pitch. He climbed over the wall into the terracing and moved around, trying to comfort the injured. He knelt beside one man who had had a pillow of beer cans made for his head and had coats and jackets placed over him. But he was dead. The Lord Provost was in tears when he left.

On the exit steps, Sir James Robertson, the chief constable, was directing the activity. Bodies were now lying everywhere. One man was still lying halfway down the steps, a jacket over his face.

There was almost complete shocked silence at this stage. Occasionally one could hear the noise of coins falling from the victims' pockets as they were lifted away.

Back on the field a row of bodies on stretchers was reaching from the corner flag position to the goalposts. Ambulances and police cars, their emergency lights flashing, were speeding round the track. Mr William Waddell, Rangers' manager, and Mr William Thornton, his assistant, together with Mr Jock Stein, Celtic's manager, were directing stretcher bearers to the team dressing rooms which had been set up as casualty stations.

Dozens of policemen, nurses, and ambulancemen were working desperately and mostly in vain to bring life back to the crushed victims.

When two hours later, there were only officials left on the terracing and steps of Section 13, one young nurse was being helped away, crying. She kept repeating: – 'I felt so helpless.'

Glasgow Herald, 2 January 1971.

Referendum – 1979

On 1 March 1979 Scots were given the opportunity to vote for home rule – for a Scottish Assembly. The ruling Labour party was far from united on the matter and a determined rear-guard action by 'No' campaigners such as George Cunningham led to a requirement that 40% of the total electorate had to vote 'Yes' for the measure to succeed. Of those who voted, 51.6 % voted 'Yes' and 48.4% 'No', but the 'Yes' vote reached only 32.9% of the total electorate. It was not enough. The Labour government refused to carry forward the bill under these circumstances. The Scottish Nationalists eventually moved for a vote of no confidence in the government, succeeding by one vote and precipitating an early election. This was described by Prime Minister James Callaghan as the 'first recorded instance in history of turkeys voting for Christmas'.

In The Scotsman *of 3 March Neal Ascherson summed up his feelings about the referendum.*

BACK FROM THE DEPTHS ON BLACK FRIDAY

At first, it was Black Friday for the Yes campaigners and their following. Ten years of hope and planning seemed in ruins.

And then, within hours of the last regional results, there was a change of mood. The first assumption that it was all over with devolution in our time faded. The Yes leaders clambered back from the depths and they were angry, perhaps angry with their own first impulse of despair. They said: 'But we won.'

And it's true that any view of the result depends entirely on whether or not the viewer accepts the Cunningham Amendment – the 40 per cent rule – as valid. Only if he does – and the No camp mostly do – can he say that a 2 per cent majority of votes cast is 'too little.'

The Yes camp seems to be rejecting that validity. A sliver of a majority was still a majority. To deny it would be a crime against the common understanding of democracy. In taking this line – and we have yet to see if Labour will take it too – they set out a fateful pattern for times to come. If the Act falls, a formidable part of the Scottish political community will refuse to accept the verdict. Instead they will say and go on saying for the rest of their lives that Scotland was cheated.

A year ago, nobody could have sensibly expected such a result. Why did it come about when we voted on Thursday?

There are reasons to do with the campaign, reasons to do with politics only indirectly connected with the campaign, and reasons which derive from Scotland's general political culture.

The No campaign was highly effective. It began very early, back in December, while the Yes side husbanded their resources in order not to 'peak too soon.' The No campaign at once made about four simple points against the Assembly proposals and hammered at them until they sank in – another tier of government, more bureaucracy, more taxes and costs, a slippery slope to separation.

All these points were open to challenge, even disproof by the Yes side, but Yes were on the defensive by the time they began their own campaign. And outwith the Central Belt, the No side invoked a much more profound and valid anxiety – who can guarantee that a Scottish Assembly will not be dominated by the central conurbations?

But the four or five No points sank deep because of an extraordinary political situation. The campaign took place at a moment when both Labour and the SNP were weakened, rather than one gaining ground at the other's expense. The pulling force of both the major pro-devolution parties was at a low ebb, Labour's only since the 'crisis' scare over strikes.

But party loyalties were strong enough, in another way, to do the Yes cause further damage. There can be no question that large and probably decisive numbers of working-class voters either abstained or voted No because they disliked and mistrusted the SNP, and because – in exact contrast to the Government's thesis – they believed that the best way to 'dish the Nats' was precisely not to vote for the Act but to vote against it.

And we come here to an absolutely fundamental point. At the heart of all considerations is the fact, plain for 50 years, that most Scots want some form of direct democratic self-government. This will be true tomorrow, as it was true yesterday. Why, then, did so few of them vote for the Scotland Act?

Not, really, because many thought the Scotland Act was a bad piece of legislation and seriously believed that a new devolution offer could be produced in short order. That was a cop-out for some, but the electors as a whole are not so stupid.

The real answer, surely, pierces far deeper than that. It looks as if, among those who did vote, about 66 per cent of working-class electors voted Yes, while less than half the middle-class voters did so. It is among the working people of Scotland that the national movement, to use that good phrase again, is most firmly lodged. And those were the people who looked at the present leadership and political colouring of the national movement and – mostly by abstaining – said that they did not trust it.

We can talk about 'fearties' and hypothesize about the timorousness of the national character when challenged to put its money where its mouth is. The Yes leaders can explode with anger at the excuse that 'It's just this Act, not devolution itself' which was so widely evaded. All this is not without some truth, but it is dodging the point. It is the SNP of 1979, not the Act, which lies at the root of the trouble. Great masses of ordinary Scots may one day give their vote to a national party of self-government, but it will have to be a force standing far more boldly for radical democracy and for the interests of the working class to win their trust.

This was the core of the big abstention. The argument that most of them stayed home because they thought they were registering a No by doing so is improbable, a counter for playing at debating points. These were, simply, people reluctant to vote, either to do something which might assist the SNP or to betray hidden longings by voting No. It's true in a sense that 'nobody wanted devolution' but either less or more. But if it had been Labour in Scotland and not the SNP which had provided devolution's impetus, the result would not have been in question.

Doubt and fear assail anyone who now tries to foresee what is to ensue in Scottish politics. It is plain that much depends on whether Mr Callaghan can find the nerve to try to punch the Yes majority through the resistance of Parliament – and whether he succeeds. It is also plain that the Scottish question will not go away; far from 'healing' it, the impasse of 1 March threatens to make it fester. But nothing else is plain at all.

The SNP will, in all probability, begin to move away from the idea of devolution and back towards the more familiar and comfortable aim of independence or nothing. They will continue to insist that this can only be achieved through the parliamentary road through a majority of seats, although – and this has to be said – a Westminster refusal to honour the Yes majority may inflict upon us some more incompetent gambolings with lumps of dynamite by Nationalist ultras beyond the SNP fringe.

More important than the odd bang, such a political shift in the SNP threatens to drift the party back towards the right. Those in the SNP who believe that the Assembly itself would be a good thing are also those who stand on the party's social-democratic Left. Meanwhile a Westminster rejection of the Act would probably give the party a temporary and limited lift if a General Election ensued. But the case that the SNP's fortunes at the polls will now take a big and lasting swing back to 1974 levels is not yet convincing.

The Conservatives will be vastly cheered and encouraged by this result; they can share honour for the high No vote with 'Scotland Says No,' which was always their emanation. They would probably gain seats in a rapid election now, but in the longer term their position may not turn out to have improved much. The Liberals have been sorely injured, and missed chances to be prominent in the Yes campaign. Small parties which fought tooth and nail for Yes, like the SLP and the Communists, have regained self-respect and purpose, but perhaps a few votes.

Labour remain. Their campaign for Yes lacked real power: the local government element often rebelled, while suspicion of the SNP clogged many local party machines. We must wait and see whether this weekend the Scottish executive nail their colours to the mast and demand that the Government stand by the 2 per cent majority, risking Mr Callaghan's survival.

Will conference, due in less than a week when nothing will have been decided, back the executive if they do that? The No wing is too small to reverse party policy. But might the reluctant Centre arrange that at Perth devolution would be passed over in embarrassed silence?

And if there's no Act, what is the fate of the pro-devolution group, those who have committed a year of passionate creativity to things a Labour Assembly might do for the people of Scotland? It's Labour in London who now hold their fate, and the prospects of the party in Scotland in their hands. But Labour's Scottish leaders know that, even if they suffer the stunning blow of devolution's failure, the link between their ideals and Scottish constitutional change cannot be severed. There's no way back to Square One – for them, or for anyone.

The Scotsman, 3 March 1979.

The Miners' Strike

In the aftermath of the Devolution debacle, the Labour government fell on a vote of no confidence – defeated by one vote (the SNP *having voted with the opposition). The result was the general election of 1979 and the victory of a Conservative government under Britain's first female Prime Minister, Margaret Thatcher.*

Her determination to make nationalised industries productive led to her backing the rationalisation of the coal industry put forward by NCB *chairman Sir Ian Macgregor. As this plan involved pit closures, the government soon found itself on a collision course with the National Union of Mineworkers under Arthur Scargill. The miners went on strike from March 1984 to March 1985. The strike was marked by mass picketing, which aroused strong emotions. In East Lothian many communities were affected. This is how the local newspaper* The East Lothian News *summed up its reporting as the miners went back to work.*

LOOKING BACK ON MINERS' LOST YEAR

A year of sacrifice, bitterness and despair for Lothian's miners began on Monday March 12 1984 when mass pickets prevented any working at Bilston Glen and Monktonhall collieries. The start of the dispute over pit closures and job losses had begun – but it also signalled the start of some of the ugliest scenes at Lothian's pits. Tempers flared as 370 men tried to cross the picket line to clock on the morning shift. Flying pickets from other pits turned up in force and so began the first ugly scuffles as police and pickets clashed. Miners and NUM officials met at the Woodburn Community Centre, Dalkeith, to discuss the strike, but the meeting was suspended after clashes between officials, who ordered support for the strike, and miners demanding a ballot.

The following week a lone miner returned to Bilston Glen - amidst the fury of picket line hatred. Over March, April and May, the message was of support and consolidation. East Lothian's 1000 striking miners were given the backing of the district council who set up special advice centres to help with housing finance problems. Most miners' clubs had set up strike centres and 'soup kitchens' were set up to feed first the children – but eventually the strikers themselves.

NAILED

The Blinkbonny private mine company at Gorebridge also came out on strike. East Lothian's coal merchants revealed that stocks are almost exhausted and local MP Mr John Home Robertson accused the NCB of restricting the supply of coal to pensioners and young families.

In April came one of the most disturbing incidents of the strike when Bilston Glen Miner Abraham Moffat (53), the son of former Scots miners leader Alex Moffat, nailed himself to the floor of his Dalkeith home and refused treatment until he had spoken to NUM vice-president Mick McGahey.

In May, Prestonpans miners were arrested outside the Hunterston iron ore terminal as mounted police rode into pickets. The miners accused the police of trying to run them down but the police claimed their actions prevented someone from dying under the wheels of a lorry.

East Lothian Constituency Labour Party give their full backing to the miners and John Home Robertson accuses the Government of daylight robbery for withholding strikers' cash.

In June, the NCB called for a return of safety cover to Bilston Glen because of fears of damage to the pit.

As the strike went into its 15th week, half the central strike committee were arrested. They were some of the 17 men arrested by police at Bilston Glen as 200 pickets turned up following rumours that men were returning to work.

Flying pickets from Durham added to the picket line, and another 79 pickets were arrested at the start of another week of trouble.

The following week the NCB announced that coal was being produced – news which only heightened the tension outside the gates. Bilston Glen was sealed off during shift times.

DISCIPLINE

Rumours circulated that Monktonhall, employing 700 East Lothian men, is to be phased out, according to alleged secret NCB documents. Meanwhile, flooding was reported to have occurred at the pit.

Two East Lothian councillors found themselves at the centre of a storm. Monktonhall pit deputy and Tranent North district councillor Tom Ferguson offered to quit after a picket line row with NUM members. The local Labour Party refused the resignation and the matter is resolved.

Meanwhile, Regional Councillor David Thomson faced disciplinary action after he voted against Tory colleagues to accept a £10,000 grant to miners' wives.

The three-week lull of the holiday period in July was smashed when hundreds of pickets mass outside the two pits. Stone throwing was the latest cause for concern, destroying canteen windows. Rows of barbed wire were placed all around 'Fortress Bilston'.

Tranent miner Philip Inverrarity made national news as the miners picketed outside his home. Police gave him an escort to Bilston Glen, clear of the 50 pickets. East Lothian Labour Party later called for a probe into the arrest of some 40 miners at the scene.

August heralded a visit from miners' president Arthur Scargill when he addressed a rally in Midlothian.

Bilston Glen branch secretary Jack Aitchison was sacked over the famous 'white line' controversy at Bilston.

East Lothian District Council pledged a donation of £5,000 to a relief fund for striking miners and their families. Money also comes in from youngsters in Rosignano, Italy.

In September, three working miners – part of the Bilston Glen Working Miners' Association – try to force a pit head interim interdict application at the Courts.

John Home Robertson made a plea for the public to support the miners' and their families to the end.

A row broke out at the official opening of the Lady Victoria and Prestongrange mining museum. The NUM refused to hand over the Lady Victoria branch banner and two Midlothian district councillors, Tam Darby and Mike Moore, walked out of the reception because of NCB deputy chairman James Cowan's presence.

REMANDED

Around 400 people took part in a march and rally in support of the strike. Leading the march were former Labour Party chairman Sam McCluskie and Alex Kitson, with John Home Robertson and the NUM's Eric Clarke.

In October, it was revealed that fines imposed on Lothian miners soared past the £7,000 mark and 19 men – including four officials – were sacked.

One of these was Monktonhall delegate and chairman of the central strike committee David Hamilton. He was later charged with the assault of a Dalkeith man but is refused bail. Petitions for his release and appeal to the Lord Justice Clerk Wheatley fell on deaf ears and Hamilton was remanded. Local miners claim it was a ploy to stop his influence in the strike.

The 'numbers game' continued with the NCB claiming a drift back to work, but the union bitterly disputed the figures.

In November, the NCB claimed that half the workforce at Bilston Glen were back. 'Rubbish' said the union.

About 400 people attended a rally in Loanhead to support imprisoned strike leader David Hamilton.

A coach taking men to Bilston Glen was stoned as it collected miners in Tranent.

Walter Thomson quit Prestonpans Community Council over a £50 donation to the miners.

John Home Robertson slammed the NCB for not accepting doctors' certificates as proof of urgent need for coal supplies. East Lothian Constituency Labour Party continued their full support for the miners.

In December, David Hamilton was cleared of his assault charge. He claims it was a 'stitch-up' to keep him out of the way during a delicate period in the dispute.

East Lothian District Council voted to give a further £5,000 to the miners' relief fund – despite the objections from five Tory Councillors.

PRESSURISED

A row broke out over concessionary coal. The union claim it is going to 'scab' miners instead of pensioners and needy families. Three MPs later stepped in to give their backing.

John Russell, chairman of the Prestonpans strike centre, was arrested outside the Blindwells open cast site and John Home Robertson called for an explanation to this and the police operation.

At Christmas the mining community came together to give children the best possible festive period.

In January, David Hamilton said he was disappointed by a letter from a bank which brought fears of miners being pressurised back to work, in order to clear debts.

A Monktonhall miner who was allegedly dismissed for a picket line offence then reinstated aroused the anger of the central strike committee, who claimed the NCB were 'looking after their own'.

The NCB then ended all doubts about the future of Monktonhall by saying the pit will be producing coal into the 21st century and beyond. A drive to recruit 250 young men as miners was announced as part of the Board's forward planning policy. Later it was revealed that 400 applications had been received.

In March, the union voted narrowly in favour of returning to work, but the Scottish pit delegates voted against a return, because of the NCB's decision to refuse an amnesty for sacked miners.

Two days later, the delegates reversed their decision and the strike was over.

East Lothian News, 8 March 1985.

Piper Alpha

On 11 June 1975, the first oil was pumped ashore from British oilfields in the North Sea and since then the oil industry has become a vital part of Scotland's economy. Many Scots worked offshore on drilling platforms in the North Sea, but there was always a dangerous side to the occupation. On 6 July 1988 things went very wrong on the drilling rig Piper Alpha. 166 lives were lost in an explosion. This is from a first-hand account by one of the survivors.

PROLOGUE

ELEVEN MINUTES OF HELL

It was my last shift on Piper Alpha before I went on leave. I'd spent some time clearing up the paperwork in the office of the diving module I shared with Stan MacLeod, the diving superintendent.

At about a quarter to ten that evening, both of us were called into the office next door by Barry Barber, Occidental's diving representative.

When we arrived, he and his clerk, Dick Common, were sitting behind their desks. Stan leant with his back against a filing cabinet and I stood just inside the doorway, my arm resting on the other filing cabinet.

We were talking, when suddenly, for a split second, all hell broke loose. The lights went out, shelves falling off the walls spewed files across the room, and one of the ceiling's metal panels crashed on to my head.

There had obviously been an almighty explosion, but enclosed as we were within the bomb-proof office module we had no way of knowing its extent or where it had taken place. We hadn't seen a flash. But what had happened was much more than a bang. It was completely overwhelming. My entire body shook – every organ I possessed vibrated violently and my brain went numb.

'Jesus Christ!' I heard Barry exclaim.

Somewhere in the gloom, Dick Common was scrabbling around on the floor where he'd been flung by the blast.

I could see hardly anything. Until the explosion, there'd been bright fluorescent lighting in the offices. Now, only the glimmer of the emergency light in the corridor showed that the building was filled with what seemed to be clouds of smoke. But from the smell I knew it wasn't smoke. It was the dust thrown up by the falling debris and the insulating material that had been packed above the ceilings.

Having been smashed on the head, my first thought was to find my hard hat. I stumbled along the corridor to my office. I had a quick grub around, but there wasn't any sign of my hard hat. I came across one on the workbench but, when I tried it on, I realised it wasn't mine. Thinking it might be needed, I put it back on the bench.

Stan arrived in the office and began searching around in the gloom. 'Where's the fuckin' breathing apparatus?' he said. 'It's fallen off the bloody wall.'

I got down on my knees and hunted around until I came across it among the debris on the floor. Then I began helping him into it, because it was heavy and unwieldy.

As he was putting on the full-face mask, he said to me, 'Fuck off to your lifeboat.'

Unthinkingly, I followed him out into the corridor where we bumped into Andy Carroll, one of the divers.

'What the hell's going on?' he said.

'Don't ask me' Stan replied. 'What's going on down there? Are all the divers OK?'

'Yes. But the door on one of the decompression chambers has been blown in and Gareth's still in the water.'

'Well, let's get him out.'

They both went one way, I went the other. Being the diving superintendent, Stan was responsible for the divers' welfare. In an emergency, I'd no specific duties. So I set off for the diving team's lifeboat – two levels, or thirty-nine feet, above me.

I left the dive module and walked out into the evening light of the

cellar deck – the lowest deck on Piper. There was a peculiar silence.
On a rig, there's normally a lot of working machinery – but much of
it was no longer running. Although I could smell it in the air, there
was hardly any smoke around and everything seemed almost
normal. I felt quite calm and in no danger. It was better, more
orderly, being outside than in the eerie chaos and gloom of the
offices.

As I went round the corner, people were rushing around, intense
and preoccupied. It was as though all of us were seeking a purpose,
a sense of direction. As I strode past them, I noticed that Davey
Elliot, the divers' rigging foreman, had sooty marks all over his face
and what appeared to be a smear of blood. With him was Brian
Jackson, one of his riggers, hopping along on one leg, a drawn
grimace on his lined face.

Glancing over the side towards the diving-support vessel Lowland
Cavalier, I was amazed to see on the back deck several men who
appeared to be cutting adrift the remotely operated vehicle that was
being used on the sea-bed. Then suddenly, the Lowland Cavalier set
off like a bat from hell. 'Stupid bastards!' I thought to myself.
'Haven't they any idea how much that ROV costs? They've just
dumped eleven million quid over the side. It's insane! What the hell
do they think they're doing?'

I walked around the cellar deck to the north-west corner where a
stairwell led up to the 85-foot level. On the deck above that – the
107 foot level – was my lifeboat.

As I reached the stairs and was about to climb up, I had to stop.
Three or four blokes in Occidental overalls were carrying down an
injured man, who I think worked in the control room.

'Forget it,' one of the men said to me. 'Don't bother trying to get
up there. There's no way up. It's all blocked with smoke and fire.'

Still the seriousness of what was happening hadn't sunk in. What
the man had said really didn't register. If it did, I just dismissed it as
an over-exaggeration . . .

About six precious minutes had passed since the first explosion.

As the conditions were worsening, it was pointless staying where
we were. So all of us in that small north-west corner of the 85-foot
level began hurrying down the stairs to the deck below. As we were
descending, the rest of the dive team arrived at the foot of the stairs.

'What's going on up there, Ed?' Barry Barber asked.

'God only knows,' I replied. 'But there's no way up. It's blazing up
there.'

Somebody said, 'There's a box of life-jackets here, chaps. Get 'em on.'

The box was at the bottom on the stairs. The people around it began putting on the life-jackets. The mêlée prevented everybody else getting to the life-jackets and brought to a halt our group's scramble down the stairs.

'There's a lot of guys behind me, fellers,' I shouted down. 'Pass the life-jackets up here.'

I handed back three or four and then went to reach for another one – but there weren't any more. With a wry smile, I turned back briefly and watched the last of the life-jackets being passed up the stairwell.

Stan MacLeod arrived with a group of people including Barry and Gareth Parry-Davies, the diver who'd been in the water. 'Where's all the life-jackets?' Stan asked.

'Sorry, mate. They've all gone,' I told him.

When they realised there was a shortage of life-jackets, most of the divers who were wearing them took them off and handed them to the older men.

But they were bloody stupid life-jackets. I'm sure they'd keep you afloat, but they were those great thick kapok jobs that are completely unwieldy. Later, many of the men had to remove them so they could climb down a rope to be rescued.

Keith Cunningham, one of the divers, threw the nearby inflatable, modular life-raft into the sea and pulled the painter which was supposed to inflate it. But nothing happened and we watched it float uselessly away. So that was a lost cause.

Tied to the handrail was a knotted rope, which we were supposed to use to climb down into the life-raft. This had also been thrown over and left dangling down into the sea.

Although I was well aware that the situation was dangerous, I still wasn't worried. I hadn't seen anyone being injured, nobody around me was panicking and nothing really frightening had happened. I'd spent every minute since the explosion being very busy. It hadn't yet dawned on me that we were running short of options – although, in truth, we'd just about run out of them all.

The smoke around us was getting thicker. I felt I had to do something positive. I knew a small vertical metal ladder went from the corner on which we were all standing, down by the north-west leg of the rig to a small beacon platform suspended about ten feet below. Somebody else clambered down and back up again, but I decided to have a look for myself.

'That's a dead end, Ed,' a chap shouted as I climbed over. 'It don't go nowhere.'

'I don't care. I want to see for myself.'

By climbing down that ten feet, I saw for the first time what was going on. Because I was under the deck, I could see that a large area, including the entire dive skid in front of the diving module, was ablaze. Where a few minutes earlier the dive crew had been working, massive flames were billowing down. Now I knew there was a major fire on Piper Alpha.

'What can you see, Ed?' somebody called.

'I can see things are pretty bad over there, fellers,' I said, all too aware of the understatement. 'I think it's time to go.'

The knotted rope that had been thrown over the side was actually brushing against the platform just beside me. I grabbed hold of the rope and pulled it in. Then I started to tie it to the handrail – being a diver, I never trusted anybody else's knot-work. But several people called out, 'It's all right, Ed. The rope's secure up here.'

I undid the rope and shouted, 'Are you sure the rope's fast?'

They assured me it was and I clamped my hands and legs on to the rope. As it took my weight, it suddenly dropped. I was sure I was just going straight down. And it mightn't have been into the sea. Almost below the beacon platform was the heavy steel boat-buffer. But after a drop of ten feet or so, the rope pulled taut and I managed to hold on.

I scurried down the rope and swung on to the boat-buffer, which was at the extreme north-west corner of the platform. Then I held the rope for the next man, to make sure he was also able to swing on to the boat-buffer.

When he was down safely, I gave him the rope and said, 'Hold on to it for the next guy and make sure he does the same thing.' And so he did, but after a couple more people had come down, somebody had the more sensible idea of tying the rope to the boat-buffer.

Meanwhile, I hopped around on to the spider deck – a series of metal companionways and handrails extending round the lower part of the platform. By being that much further down, I could see the intensity and extent of the blaze above me. There were flaming objects the size of cars dropping into the sea. I'd no idea what they were.

Only when I began to wonder what the hell they could be did I realise that up to then, from the time of the first explosion, I'd been virtually without thought. Everything had been done in automatic gear, on auto-pilot, by reflex action. Now I was thinking the dangerous time had begun.

Ed Punchard with Syd Higgins, *Piper Alpha, a Survivor's Story*, London, 1989.

The Poll Tax

In 1989 the community charge, a replacement for the old domestic rates system, was introduced to Scotland. Rapidly dubbed the 'poll tax', the new method of local government financing became massively unpopular. There was a strong campaign of non-payment. This, coupled with Scotland's old-fashioned laws on recovery of debt, led to an upsurge in poindings and warrant sales. One of the most determined non-payers was future MSP Tommy Sheridan who was sent to prison for his role in the Anti-Poll Tax movement. Betty McEachin, a pensioner in Govan, was present when Sheridan set out to stop a warrant sale.

How We Stopped the Warrant Sale

A Day in the Life of a Pensioner, 1st October 1991

Alice Sheridan had phoned me on Sunday morning. 'Betty, there is going to be a warrant sale in the Old Jail Square on Tuesday. Can you be there? Can you pick up Jo, she's just round the corner from you?' 'Sure', I said, 'See you at the Federation Shop'.

We set out at 7.45 am, Tuesday, a cold wet, windy morning. Wouldn't you know. Arrived at the Federation Shop. Standing room only. We squeezed our way through to have a cup of tea. It's great being old, they just say, 'OK doll, in you go.'

A few minutes later we all moved along to a 'Pen'. A pen is a space left in old buildings, where you could drive a horse and cart through to the back of the building. The wind was howling through this opening, but at least we were out of the rain.

Tommy Sheridan addressed us. What did we think? It was just 8.15 and the sale wasn't to take place till 11am. We were just about a 100 strong, we are expecting folk in from out-lying districts of Glasgow, would we wait till 9 to give them a chance to arrive and assemble later. The majority agreed that we disperse till 9.15 then gather outside the Federation shop.

Standing in that pen I had a look round me. What drew my attention was one young lad standing near me was literally shaking with the cold. I thought of all the woollen scarves I had in the house, and wished I had brought a bag full. One of the women took off her gloves and gave them to another young lad. I heard they had been there since 6am. My heart bleeds for the youth of today. They are in a no-hope situation, something like the times when I left school in 1935.

Jo and I got a cup of tea and a roll, we expected it to be a long day and we wouldn't get any more to eat.

At 9.15 we gathered outside the Federation shop. Our numbers had increased quite a bit. There wasn't the same joviality as on other occasions. An Interdict had been issued against Tommy Sheridan forbidding him to go anywhere near the scene of this warrant sale, or he faced arrest. Faces were tense, after all, these young and middle aged people didn't know what lay ahead of them. One pretty young girl standing beside me said, 'Are you sure you will be alright?', meaning 'Shouldn't you be at home with your knitting'. I said 'I'm OK. We must see this through to the end.' 'I wish I could take you home to my grandfather', she said, 'you could have a talk to him about this'. I wondered about her grandfather, if he was my age, was he one of the troops pulled out of Dunkirk, or was he a Desert Rat, or was he on the submarine-infested Atlantic Run. Maybe he had enough fighting to last him a lifetime. Thank God for the young lad with the effigy of Margaret Thatcher. He had put a placard in her hand. It said, 'NO POLL TAX HERE'. That eased the tension a bit.

We marched off singing, 'We're no paying the Poll Tax, da da da da'. Down at Jail Square the gates were closed. The sale of goods was to take place in this square. Someone climbed up the gates and stuck a few placards on saying 'NO WARRANT SALES HERE'. I noticed a woman about my own age standing alone and I joined her. Then suddenly we were all surging through the gates. 'How did they get the gates opened?' I asked. 'The police opened them,' someone said. I think it was a joke, but being of a very suspicious nature, I decided to get outside the gates again.

Just then a slight scuffle took place and this was the only incident of the morning. The police surrounded Tommy Sheridan and the people around him closed in, among them, his mother and sister. There was a wee bit of pushing and shoving. At this time the police could have bundled everyone out, there was enough of them, or they could have caused mayhem by resorting to violence. To their eternal credit, they did not.

By this time I was standing at the gates again, and someone had closed them. I didn't think this was a good idea, so I opened them.

'You've opened them the wrong way' said a disabled lady standing just outside. It doesn't matter I said, this is the only way out of that square, there is nowhere else to run. Just then Tommy Sheridan got up on a crash barrier to speak. 'Look folks, it's all cool in here, move back in. Our fight is not with the police, we're here to protest about the scum who are attempting to carry out this barbaric practice of selling off this woman's household goods'. Then he tore up the interdict order.

Babs and I, the lady I had just met that morning, I think we were the oldest people there (she is 68 and I am 70) moved into the square again. It was bitterly cold, the rain was slashing down and the gales still blowing. My teeth were chattering, I don't know if it was the atrocious weather, or the fear of the unknown.

Did I mention the number of police there. I wish I had taken a rough count of them. They were all linked arm in arm down the side of the square and I'm sure there was as many again inside, because there was a single decker bus and 4 or 5 mini buses outside. It was so scary all these tall, well-built men towering over me. When I contrasted the way they were clad, and remembered the boy standing beside me shivering with cold, I thought what would our men and women of the past who fought so long and hard for a fair deal for the working class, think of the situation now, heading towards the year 2000.

My friend of the morning and I stood against a pillar under the shelter of the carport and passed the next hour talking about our early years. Her father had been working in the coal mines at the age of eleven.

Just before eleven o'clock a cheer went up. The Warrant Sale had been called off. Tommy got up on a crash barrier again and announced the victory, thanked everyone for their support and said again we would fight every Warrant Sale attempted in Scotland.

We all left the Square after a few more cheers, but going out I noticed that there had been three rows of crash barriers put across the exit so there would have been some stampede getting out of there. Tommy got up on some scaffolding and spoke again for the benefit of the people outside the Square, thanking them and saying our fight was not with the police, that probably some of their relatives were not paying the Poll Tax. Here I must say that the Glasgow Police did not at any time take up a threatening attitude. When I think of what could have happened in that small Square, had there been a few hot heads there, I tremble at the knees, it could

have been a blood-bath. We walked back to the federation shop to
return the pink umbrella I had borrowed, and forgot to put up in the
excitement. When I was alone, I got into my car to wipe the rain and
tears from my face. Then I noticed my friend Jo standing with Alice
Sheridan. I joined them to say I was leaving. Alice just put her arms
around my neck and said 'Thanks'. I said that I had feared for her
son this morning. She answered, 'How do you think I felt?', and for
the second time that morning, tears ran down a woman's face. Jo
and I got into the car and headed for home.

    Betty McEachin
    Govan Pensioner, Member of Govan APTG

T. Sheridan, *A Time to Rage*, Edinburgh, 1994.

Elections '99

*Devolution finally came to Scotland after 11 September 1998
when a majority voted in a referendum 'Yes-Yes' to a Scottish
parliament with tax-raising powers. It was an event watched
keenly, not only in Scotland but in other countries with separatist
issues. There was a great deal of interest in Canada and especially
in the French-speaking province of Québec, where a separatist
party, the PQ (Parti Québecois), had been trying to win
independence from Canada. The* Montreal Gazette, *the main
English-speaking newspaper in the area, sent its own
correspondent, Hubert Bauch, to cover the ensuing elections in
Scotland, which took place on 6 May 1999.*

SCOTS TREAD WARILY

BOTH PÉQUISTES AND FEDERALISTS WILL FIND COMFORT IN
EDINBURGH POLITICS

There has been a boomlet of late in Québec tourism to Scotland
for reasons that have nothing to do with the lure of heathered
glens and mystic lochs or ancient stones and aged malts. Along with
the staple attractions, Scotland found itself with a bonus drawing
card this spring in the form of its first election in nigh on 300 years
for a Scottish parliament.

    The flocking of political sightseers it invited might not amount to
much of a market niche compared to the number of people who will
visit Scotland this year fully expecting to see the Loch Ness monster:
but if there's anything to the national stereotype, it will not have

escaped the notice of the Scottish Tourist Office that this windfall traffic in political junkies consists almost to a rube of tenured poli-sci profs and senior political hacks on expense accounts begging to be fleeced.

The Scottish campaign held a special attraction for Québecers of the species in that Scotland is currently the only other state within a state in the democratic Western world with a flat-out separatist party in serious contention. The Société St Jean Baptiste announced this week that it had despatched an observer and Québec Liberal leader Jean Charest plans to visit Scotland later this month for a Cook's tour of the political landscape.

But what insight they or any Québec political tourist might gain from first-hand exposure to the Scottish constitutional debate will likely be coloured by ingrained persuasions.

A federalist would tend to see the clear majority support for unionist parties and the handy election of a Scottish Labour government, as a vindication of the British constitutional 'devolution' process granting Scotland a parliament with powers roughly akin to a Canadian provincial legislature. A Québec sovereignist eye would sooner view the secessionist Scottish Nationalist Party's solid second place finish, and its entrenchment as the official opposition – and government-in-waiting – as a decisive leg up on its ultimate goal of unfettering Scotland from the United Kingdom.

Final numbers from Thursday's vote were unavailable yesterday, but latest results indicate that Scottish Labour will form a minority government and its leader, Donald Dewar, will become Scotland's 'first minister'. Labour appeared likely to hold 56 of the new parliament's 129 seats with its popular vote tally running above 40 per cent, while the SNP seemed likely to win 35 seats with its 30 per cent share of the vote. The other two major parties in Scotland's four party political system, the Conservatives and the Liberal Democrats, both also staunchly unionist, won 18 and 17 seats respectively. One independent was also elected.

But even among the resident political paparazzi, the conventional wisdom breaks down along roughly these lines, between those who believe that Scotland's new autonomy within the UK will satisfy Scots hunger for home rule and those who expect, either in hope or in fear, that the devolution parliament will turn out to be an hors d'oeuvre that only whets the nationalist appetite for the whole plate of haggis, as it were.

For University of Edinburgh professor David McCrone, whose

academic speciality is nationalist movements, there's an even chance
of it going either way, depending on how the freshly conceived
Scottish parliament works out in practice. He notes that Scots voted
for the devolution scheme by a near two-thirds majority in a 1998
referendum and are broadly inclined to give the new parliament a
sporting chance to prove itself.

'That will take time, and no one really expects otherwise', he said
in an interview. 'I suspect not even the SNP expected it would win
this election. I don't think anything significant is going to happen
within the next 10 to 20 years.' That time will tell doesn't sound like
much of a learned analysis, and it doesn't seem worth crossing an
ocean to be told that pretty well anything could happen in the next
decade or two as a result of this election. But it's really the best
anyone can offer by way of a bottom line that doesn't veer on a
partisan tangent or dip into subjective considerations.

There are critical differences of culture, geography and history
between Québec and Scotland that make it hard to find lessons in
the Scottish experience that would greatly inform the Canadian
constitutional debate or offer clues to the prospect of Québec's
independence movement.

Notwithstanding its diehard Gaelic tradition, Scotland speaks the
common language of the British union, and cultural insecurity is not
a factor in the independence argument; given its location atop
England, bordered on all other sides by open seas, an independent
Scotland would be less of a geopolitical complication than a
sovereign Québec sandwiched between chunks of a sundered
Canada; and unlike Québec, which was never more than a province,
Scotland was never anyone's colony, and furthermore recorded four
centuries of history as a country in its own right before it entered the
British union of its own volition in 1707.

Even the similarities between the two independence movements
don't offer much inspiration for Québec sovereignists.

The SNP has adopted the same soft-sell strategy in pursuit of
independence as the Parti Québecois under Lucien Bouchard, and
for purposes of this election at least, what isn't working for the
separatists in Québec doesn't seem to be working any better for their
spiritual kin in Scotland. (Nor is there much for Canadian federalists
to learn from the British government's unionist strategy, which
essentially consists of staggered political concessions to regional
nationalism and 'black hole' economic scenarios for a Scots divorce
from the UK family.)

For a Québecer in a strange land, there was a decidedly homey ring to SNP leader Alex Salmond's independence pitch at a mid-campaign glad-handing stop in Glasgow: 'It's not an argument about nationalism,' he said as a parting shot.

'It's about confidence in ourselves. The real natural resource of Scotland doesn't lie in the North Sea, it lies in the people of Scotland.'

Hubert Bauch, *Montreal Gazette*, 8 May 1999.

The Opening of the New Scottish Parliament

The new Scottish Parliament opened on 1 July 1999. Matthew Engel of The Guardian *took an irreverent look at the festivities.*

SOMETHING FOR EVERYONE AS SCOTS AT LAST
PUT HISTORY BEHIND THEM.
SPONTANEOUS CHORUSES, SOME SUCCINCT ADDRESSES,
AND A CAMEO ROLE FOR SEAN CONNERY

Lord Steel called it the most historic event in Scotland for nearly 300 years, which does not say a huge amount for the past three centuries. Sean Connery called it the most important day of his life, which rather confirms the view that film stars actually lead lives of surprising emptiness.

Connery was flamboyantly present, in a ruff and kilt in green McNotice-me tartan. Other Scots celebrities refused to bother, and the advance publicity was dominated by news of the no-shows, ranging from A-list celebs like Sir Alex Ferguson to F-listers like Sir Malcolm Rifkind.

Among those also absent was the Prime Minister. This was not a sign of Scotland's liberation from his yoke. It was a sign that even on such a day Scotland was not the most urgent priority among the four constituent parts of the UK.

For some time, sophisticates in Edinburgh have had trouble using words like 'historic' and 'important' without sniggering. Since the high point of enthusiasm reached at the referendum in 1998, the popular view of the Scottish parliament has slumped nearer to apathy, cynicism and recrimination – i.e. political business as usual.

Finally, the history is out of the way. Yesterday the Queen officially opened the parliament in its temporary home, on loan from the General Assembly of the Church of Scotland. The funny thing was that it actually worked brilliantly. On one of those clear and fresh breezy mornings which in Edinburgh pass as high summer, substantial crowds – mostly enthusiastic – lined the streets. Inside, there was a short and nicely-judged ceremony.

The secret was that there was something for every political taste. This is a Labour project, run jointly with the Liberal Democrats. It is welcome to nationalists as a service station on the clogged motorway that might lead to independence.

And even the Tories had plenty to cheer on the day they had resisted for so long.

There was Her Majesty, and the Duke of Hamilton carrying the crown of Scotland on a velvet cushion, and Lord Lyon King of Arms, and various heralds dressed for a big budget Hollywood production of Shakespeare, and enough military flummery to suggest the New Scotland will not be entirely anathema to them.

The exception may well have been the leader of the Westminster Conservatives. By a quirk of protocol, William Hague was not in the main procession and therefore had to sit in his seat in the assembly for almost an hour and three quarters before the Queen arrived.

The same fate befell both Paddy Ashdown, who might have regarded staring into space as reasonable practice for retirement, and Mr Connery, who walked out until the show started. Mr Hague just sat there looking more and more thunderous.

He was eventually joined by Betty Boothroyd who outmatched him in the spectre-at-the-feast contest.

From the moment the brass section of the Royal Scottish National Orchestra appeared in the chamber, it became clear that this parliament would be doing things very differently from Westminster. And when the MSPs paraded in to a specially-composed fanfare, her expression suggested that this was not the sort of thing that would ever be allowed to happen in a serious legislature.

The speeches were brief and dignified. There were only three, from Lord Steel, the presiding officer (he is calling himself Sir David up here, as though his peerage were a secret – why not plain Mr Steel for a new parliament?), the Queen and Mr Dewar, Scotland's First Minister.

The other party leaders had to speak in Parliament Hall, the scene of the old parliament, while the Queen was still in Holyrood. This saved her from the danger of hearing even the tiniest hint of subversion from Alex Salmond.

Lord Steel greeted Her Majesty as Queen of Scots, not Queen of Scotland, a technically correct reference to a fine Scottish distinction. Queen of Scotland would imply ownership of the land. Since most of us are familiar only with one previous holder of that title but know precisely what happened to her, this caused a considerable frisson.

This possibility did not seem to bother the Queen. She was wearing saltire blue, with plaid. 'I have trust in the good judgment of the Scottish people,' she said, 'and I am confident in the future of Scotland.'

But the speeches were overshadowed by two other items in the programme Lord Steel had put together. First, the traditional singer Sheena Wellington sang Rabbie Burns's 'A Man's A Man For A' That':

Their tinsel show, an a' that
The honest man, tho e'er sae poor
Is king o men for a' that . . .

Then, for the last verse, all the MSPs spontaneously joined in. Betty Boothroyd looked more horror-struck than ever. The last recorded outbreak of community singing in her chamber is believed to have been the brief snatch of the Red Flag attempted after the 1945 election, and the next, her expression suggested, would be over her dead body.

But it was a magnificent moment, and by the end of it I think even she was won over.

There followed something even more remarkable. One of those magnificently soigné, auburn-haired girls Scottish schools seem to turn out with perfect ease read a humorous poem beautifully. She was Victoria Joffe, 17.

Most astonishingly of all, it was supposedly written by an 11-year-old, Amy Linekar from Thurso. It was called 'How to Create A Great Country':

Take: Several heroic battles, Some kilts of tartan fine
A clearance's worth of emigration,
A thistle's worth of spike,
And a rebellion or two.

Mix together with a spoon of fate and add:
Granny's best mince n' tatties
Corned beef hash or tattie soup
Oor Wullie's sense of mischief
Add a clove of Gaelic
And a broad Scots tongue . . .

It might not be Burns. But if an 11-year-old really did write that, it is hard to see how her country ever bowed the knee to anyone.

That was it, more or less. The Queen left to watch a few hundred children and Concorde parade past. And the day dissolved into various minor events, to which no one had bothered to invite her.

Six people were arrested, three of them for jumping the crash barriers during the parade and shouting 'Disband the RUC' at the royal carriage.

They were identified by other members of the crowd, proving their loyalty.

The MSPs will be back at 9.30 this morning, to question the executive. And Scotland's future will be now made evermore on days like that, sans Queen and Connery. Quiet, unimportant, unhistoric days.

Matthew Engel, *The Guardian*, 2 July 1999.

ACKNOWLEDGEMENTS

Thanks are due to the following for permission to reprint extracts from the titles or articles listed:

The Bibliographical Society, London, for *The Marriage of Mary Queen of Scots to the Dauphin: a Scottish Printed Fragment*, ed. Douglas Hamer (1932)

The Bodleian Library, University of Oxford for MS. Tanner 78, fol.129r (Robert Wingfield's account of the execution of Mary, Queen of Scots) as reproduced in *The Tragedy of Fotheringay* by Hon. Mrs Maxwell Scott (1905)

The Daily Mail for 'A Bewildered Elvis Pays a Flying Visit' by Ian Nelson in the *Scottish Daily Mail*, 3 March 1960

East Lothian News for 'Looking Back on Miners' Lost Year', 8 March 1985

Edinburgh University Press for 'The Chronicle of Lanercost' ed. Sir Herbert Maxwell in *The Scottish Historical Review*, vol. vi (1909) and for *A Time to Rage* by Tommy Sheridan (1994)

The Gazette (Montreal) for 'Scots Tread Warily' by Hubert Bauch, 8 May 1999

Guardian Newspapers Ltd for 'Something for Everyone as Scots At Last Put Everything Behind Them' by Matthew Engel in *The Guardian*, 2 July 1999

Ian R. Hamilton for *No Stone Unturned* (1952)

The Kilmarnock Standard for 'My Brother Alec' by Robert J. Fleming, 7 and 14 April 1962

Manchester Evening News for 'Mr Manchester's Diary', 25 August 1947

Ellice Milton for a transcription from NLS Acc. 4251/3 (letter of Agnes Maclean)

Mirror Syndication International for 'Cheering Crowds Wave Winnie to her Seat' in the *Daily Record*, 17 November 1967

Oxford University Press for Bede's *Ecclesiastical History* ed. B. Colgrave and R. A. B Mynors (1969) © Oxford University Press 1969 and for *Anecdotes and Characters of the Times* by Alexander Carlyle, ed. James Kinsley (1973) © Oxford University Press 1973

Penguin Books Ltd for *The Agricola and Germania* by Tacitus, trans. H Mattingly, revd. S A Handford (Penguin Classics, 1948, Revised Edition 1970) © the Estate of H Mattingly, 1948, 1970 © S A Handford, 1970 and for *Life of Saint Columba* by Adomnán of Iona trans. Richard Sharpe (Penguin Classics, 1995) © Richard Sharpe, 1995

The Scotsman Publications Ltd for 'Exciting Scenes in Edinburgh: Catholic Congress Ends' in *The Scotsman*, 26 June 1935, and 'Back from the Depths on Black Friday' by Neal Ascherson in *The Scotsman*, 3 March 1979

The Scottish Gaelic Texts Society for 'Oran do Bhlàr na h-Eaglaise Brice' from *Orain Ghàidhealach mu Bhliadhna Thearlàich (Highland Songs of the '45)* ed. J. L. Campbell (1933) and for 'Là Inbhir Lòchaidh' from *Orain Iain Luim (Songs of John MacDonald, Bard of Keppoch)* ed. A. Mackenzie (1964)

The Scottish Text Society for *The Asloan Manuscript*, ed. W. A. Craigie (1923) and for Lindsay of Pitscottie's *The History and Cronicles of Scotland from the Slauchter of King James I to Ane Thousande Fyve Hundreith Thrie Scoir Fyfteen Zeir . . .* , ed. A. J. G. Mackay (1899-1911)

Scottish Media Newspapers Ltd for 'Progress of Queen Mary Down to the Sea' in *The Glasgow Herald*, 25 March 1936, 'British Liner Torpedoed off Irish Coast' in *The Glasgow Herald*, 4 July 1940, and 'Distant Sounds of Screams in Mist' by Andrew Young in *The Glasgow Herald*, 4 January 1971

Stornoway Gazette Ltd for 'Sea Sorrow: The Story of the Iolaire Disaster' in the *Stornoway Gazette* (1972)

University of St Andrews for *Scotichronicon* by Walter Bower, ed. S. Taylor, D. E. R. Watt and B. Scott (1990)

Yale University Press for *Boswell in Extremes 1776-8*, ed. Charles McC. Weis and F. Pottle (Yale Editions of the Private Papers of James Boswell, 10) (1971)

Every effort has been made to contact the copyright holders of material reprinted in this book. Luath Press and the National Library of Scotland apologise for any errors or omissions in the above list, and would be grateful to be notified of any corrections to be incorporated into subsequent editions.

INDEX

Some other books published by **LUATH** PRESS

HISTORY

Blind Harry's Wallace

William Hamilton of Gilbertfield
Introduced by Elspeth King
ISBN 0 946487 43 X   HBK   £15.00
ISBN 0 946487 33 2   PBK   £8.99

The original story of the real braveheart, Sir William Wallace. Racy, blood on every page, violently anglo-phobic, grossly embellished, vulgar and disgusting, clumsy and stilted, a literary failure, a great epic.

Whatever the verdict on BLIND HARRY, this is the book which has done more than any other to frame the notion of Scotland's national identity. Despite its numerous 'historical inaccuracies', it remains the principal source for what we now know about the life of Wallace.

The novel and film *Braveheart* were based on the 1722 Hamilton edition of this epic poem. Burns, Wordsworth, Byron and others were greatly influenced by this version 'wherein the old obsolete words are rendered more intelligible', which is said to be the book, next to the Bible, most commonly found in Scottish households in the eighteenth century. Burns even admits to having 'borrowed... a couplet worthy of Homer' directly from Hamilton's version of BLIND HARRY to include in '*Scots wha hae*'.

Elspeth King, in her introduction to this, the first accessible edition of BLIND HARRY in verse form since 1859, draws parallels between the situation in Scotland at the time of Wallace and that in Bosnia and Chechnya in the 1990s. Seven hundred years to the day after the Battle of Stirling Bridge, the 'Settled Will of the Scottish People' was expressed in the devolution referendum of 11 September 1997. She describes this as a landmark opportunity for mature reflection on how the nation has been shaped, and sees BLIND HARRY'S WALLACE as an essential and compelling text for this purpose.

'*A true bard of the people*'.
TOM SCOTT, THE PENGUIN BOOK OF SCOTTISH VERSE, on Blind Harry.

'*A more inventive writer than Shakespeare*'.
RANDALL WALLACE

'*The story of Wallace poured a Scottish prejudice in my veins which will boil along until the floodgates of life shut in eternal rest*'.
ROBERT BURNS

'*Hamilton's couplets are not the best poetry you will ever read, but they rattle along at a fair pace. In re-issuing this work, the publishers have re-opened the spring from which most of our conceptions of the Wallace legend come*'.
SCOTLAND ON SUNDAY

'*The return of Blind Harry's Wallace, a man who makes Mel look like a wimp*'.
THE SCOTSMAN

A Word for Scotland

Jack Campbell
with a foreword by Magnus Magnusson
ISBN 0 946487 48 0   PBK   £12.99

'A word for Scotland' was Lord Beaverbrook's hope when he founded the *Scottish Daily Express*. That word for Scotland quickly became, and was for many years, the national newspaper of Scotland.

The pages of *A Word For Scotland* exude warmth and a wry sense of humour. Jack Campbell takes us behind the scenes to meet the larger-than-life characters and ordinary people who made and recorded the stories. Here we hear the stories behind the stories that hit the headlines in this great yarn of journalism in action.

It would be true to say 'all life is here'. From the Cheapside Street fire of which cost the lives of 19 Glasgow firemen, to the theft of the Stone of Destiny, to the lurid exploits of serial killer Peter Manuel, to encounters with world boxing champions Benny Lynch and Cassius Clay - this book offers telling glimpses of the characters, events, joy and tragedy which make up Scotland's story in the 20th century.

'*As a rookie reporter you were proud to work on it and proud to be part of it - it was fine newspaper right at the heartbeat of Scotland.*'

RONALD NEIL, Chief Executive of BBC Production, and a reporter on the *Scottish Daily Express* (1963-68)

'This book is a fascinating reminder of Scottish journalism in its heyday. It will be read avidly by those journalists who take pride in their profession – and should be compulsory reading for those who don't.'

JACK WEBSTER, columnist on *The Herald* and *Scottish Daily Express* journalist (1960-80)

ON THE TRAIL OF

On the Trail of William Wallace

David R. Ross

ISBN 0 946487 47 2 PBK £7.99

How close to reality was *Braveheart*?

Where was Wallace actually born?

What was the relationship between Wallace and Bruce?

Are there any surviving eye-witness accounts of Wallace?

How does Wallace influence the psyche of today's Scots?

On the Trail of William Wallace offers a refreshing insight into the life and heritage of the great Scots hero whose proud story is at the very heart of what it means to be Scottish. Not concentrating simply on the hard historical facts of Wallace's life, the book also takes into account the real significance of Wallace and his effect on the ordinary Scot through the ages, manifested in the many sites where his memory is marked.

In trying to piece together the jigsaw of the reality of Wallace's life, David Ross weaves a subtle flow of new information with his own observations. His engaging, thoughtful and at times amusing narrative reads with the ease of a historical novel, complete with all the intrigue, treachery and romance required to hold the attention of the casual reader and still entice the more knowledgable historian.

74 places to visit in Scotland and the north of England

One general map and 3 location maps
Stirling and Falkirk battle plans
Wallace's route through London
Chapter on Wallace connections in North America and elsewhere
Reproductions of rarely seen illustrations

On the Trail of William Wallace will be enjoyed by anyone with an interest in Scotland, from the passing tourist to the most fervent nationalist. It is an encyclopaedia-cum-guide book, literally stuffed with fascinating titbits not usually on offer in the conventional history book.

David Ross is organiser of and historical adviser to the Society of William Wallace.

'Historians seem to think all there is to be known about Wallace has already been uncovered. Mr Ross has proved that Wallace studies are in fact in their infancy.' ELSPETH KING, Director the the Stirling Smith Art Museum & Gallery, who annotated and introduced the recent Luath edition of *Blind Harry's Wallace.*

'Better the pen than the sword!'

RANDALL WALLACE, author of *Braveheart,* when asked by David Ross how it felt to be partly responsible for the freedom of a nation following the Devolution Referendum.

On the Trail of Robert Service

GW Lockhart

ISBN 0 946487 24 3 PBK £7.99

Robert Service is famed world-wide for his eye-witness verse-pictures of the Klondike goldrush. As a war poet, his work outsold Owen and Sassoon, and he went on to become the world's first million selling poet. In search of adventure and new experiences, he emigrated from Scotland to Canada in 1890 where he was caught up in the aftermath of the raging gold fever. His vivid dramatic verse bring to life the wild, larger than life characters of the gold rush Yukon, their bar-room brawls, their lust for gold, their trigger-happy gambles with life and love. 'The Shooting of Dan McGrew' is perhaps his most famous poem:

*A bunch of the boys were whooping it up
in the Malamute saloon;
The kid that handles the music box was
hitting a ragtime tune;
Back of the bar in a solo game, sat
Dangerous Dan McGrew,
And watching his luck was his light
o'love, the lady that's known as Lou.*

His storytelling powers have brought Robert Service enduring fame, particularly in North America and Scotland where he is something of a cult figure.

Starting in Scotland, *On the Trail of Robert Service* follows Service as he wanders through British Columbia, Oregon, California, Mexico, Cuba, Tahiti, Russia, Turkey and the Balkans, finally 'settling' in France.

This revised edition includes an expanded selection of illustrations of scenes from the Klondike as well as several photographs from the family of Robert Service on his travels around the world.

Wallace Lockhart, an expert on Scottish traditional folk music and dance, is the author of *Highland Balls & Village Halls* and *Fiddles & Folk*. His relish for a well-told tale in popular vernacular led him to fall in love with the verse of Robert Service and write his biography.

'A fitting tribute to a remarkable man - a bank clerk who wanted to become a cowboy. It is hard to imagine a bank clerk writing such lines as:

*A bunch of boys were whooping it up...
The income from his writing actually exceeded his bank salary by a factor of five and he resigned to pursue a full time writing career.'*
Charles Munn, THE SCOTTISH BANKER

'Robert Service claimed he wrote for those who wouldnit be seen dead reading poetry. His was an almost unbelievably mobile life... Lockhart hangs on breathlessly, enthusiastically unearthing clues to the poet's life.' Ruth Thomas, SCOTTISH BOOK COLLECTOR

'This enthralling biography will delight Service lovers in both the Old World and the New.' Marilyn Wright, SCOTS INDEPENDENT

On the Trail of Robert the Bruce

David R. Ross

ISBN 0 946487 52 9 PBK £7.99

On the Trail of Robert the Bruce charts the story of Scotland's hero-king from his boyhood, through his days of indecision as Scotland suffered under the English yoke, to his assumption of the crown exactly six months after the death of William Wallace. Here is the astonishing blow by blow account of how, against fearful odds, Bruce led the Scots to win their greatest ever victory. Bannockburn was not the end of the story. The war against English oppression lasted another fourteen years. Bruce lived just long enough to see his dreams of an independent Scotland come to fruition in 1328 with the signing of the Treaty of Edinburgh. The trail takes us to Bruce sites in Scotland, many of the little known and forgotten battle sites in northern England, and as far afield as the Bruce monuments in Andalusia and Jerusalem.

67 places to visit in Scotland and elsewhere.
One general map, 3 location maps and a map of Bruce-connected sites in Ireland.
Bannockburn battle plan.
Drawings and reproductions of rarely seen illustrations.

On the Trail of Robert the Bruce is not all blood and gore. It brings out the love and laughter, pain and passion of one of the great eras of Scottish history. Read it and you will understand why David Ross has never knowingly killed a spider in his life. Once again, he proves himself a master of the popular brand of hands-on history that made *On the Trail of William Wallace* so popular.

'David R. Ross is a proud patriot and unashamed romantic.'
SCOTLAND ON SUNDAY

'Robert the Bruce knew Scotland, knew every class of her people, as no man who ruled her before or since has done. It was he who asked of her a miracle - and she accomplished it.'

AGNES MUIR MACKENZIE

On the Trail of Mary Queen of Scots

J. Keith Cheetham
ISBN 0 946487 50 2 PBK £7.99

Life dealt Mary Queen of Scots love, intrigue, betrayal and tragedy in generous measure.

On the Trail of Mary Queen of Scots traces the major events in the turbulent life of the beautiful, enigmatic queen whose romantic reign and tragic destiny exerts an undimmed fascination over 400 years after her execution.

Places of interest to visit – 99 in Scotland, 35 in England and 29 in France.

One general map and 6 location maps.

Line drawings and illustrations.

Simplified family tree of the royal houses of Tudor and Stuart.

On the Trail of Mary Queen of Scots is for everyone interested in the life of perhaps the most romantic figure in Scotland's history; a thorough guide to places connected with Mary, it is also a guide to the complexities of her personal and public life.

'In my end is my beginning'
MARY QUEEN OF SCOTS

'...the woman behaves like the Whore of Babylon' JOHN KNOX

On the Trail of John Muir

Cherry Good
ISBN 0 946487 62 6 PBK UK £7.99

Follow the man who made the US go green. Confidant of presidents, father of American National Parks, trailblazer of world conservation and voted a Man of the Millennium in the US, John Muir's life and work is of continuing relevance. A man ahead of his time who saw the wilderness he loved threatened by industrialisation and determined to protect it, a crusade in which he was largely successful. His love of

the wilderness began at an early age and he was filled with wanderlust all his life.

'Only by going in silence, without baggage, can on truly get into the heart of the wilderness. All other travel is mere dust and hotels and baggage and chatter.'
JOHN MUIR

Braving mosquitoes and black bears Cherry Good set herself on his trail - Dunbar, Scotland; Fountain Lake and Hickory Hill, Wisconsin; Yosemite Valley and the Sierra Nevada, California; the Grand Canyon, Arizona; Alaska; and Canada – to tell his story. John Muir was himself a prolific writer, and Good draws on his books, articles, letters and diaries to produce an account that is lively, intimate, humorous and anecdotal, and that provides refreshing new insights into the hero of world conservation.

John Muir chronology

General map plus 10 detailed maps covering the US, Canada and Scotland

Original colour photographs

Afterword advises on how to get involved

Conservation websites and addresses

Muir's importance has long been acknowledged in the US with over 200 sites of scenic beauty named after him. He was a Founder of The Sierra Club which now has over $^1/_2$ million members. Due to the movement he started some 360 million acres of wilderness are now protected. This is a book which shows Muir not simply as a hero but as a likeable, humorous and self-effacing man of extraordinary vision.

On the Trail of Robert Burns

John Cairney
ISBN 0 946487 51 0 PBK UK £7.99

Is there anything new to say about Robert Burns?

John Cairney says itís time to trash Burns the Brand and come on the trail of the real Robert Burns. He is the best of travelling companions on this convivial, entertaining journey to the heart of the Burns story.

Internationally known as 'the face of Robert Burns', John Cairney believes that the traditional Burns tourist trail urgently needs to find a new direction. In an acting career spanning forty years he has often lived and breathed Robert Burns on stage. *On the Trail of Robert Burns* shows just how well he can get under the skin of a character. This fascinating journey around Scotland is a rediscovery of Scotland's national bard as a flesh and blood genius.

On the Trail of Robert Burns outlines five tours, mainly in Scotland. Key sites include:

Alloway – Burns' birthplace. Tam O' Shanter draws on the witch-stories about Alloway Kirk first heard by Burns in his childhood.
Mossgiel – between 1784 and 1786 in a phenomenal burst of creativity Burns wrote some of his most memorable poems including Holy Willie's Prayer and To a Mouse.
Kilmarnock - the famous Kilmarnock edition of *Poems Chiefly in the Scottish Dialect* published in 1786.
Edinburgh - fame and Clarinda (among others) embraced him.
Dumfries - Burns died at the age of 37. The trail ends at the Burns mausoleum in St Michael's churchyard.

*'For me an aim I never fash
I rhyme for fun'* ROBERT BURNS

'My love affair on stage with Burns started in London in 1959. It was consumated on stage at the Traverse Theatre in Edinburgh in 1965 and has continued happily ever since' JOHN CAIRNEY

'The trail is expertly, touchingly and amusingly followed' THE HERALD

NEW SCOTLAND

**Scotland - Land and Power
the agenda for land reform**
Andy Wightman
foreword by Lesley Riddoch
ISBN 0 946487 70 7 PBK £5.00

Old Scotland New Scotland
Jeff Fallow
ISBN 0 946487 40 5 PBK £6.99

**Notes from the North
incorporating a Brief History of the
Scots and the English**
Emma Wood
ISBN 0 946487 46 4 PBK £8.99

SOCIAL HISTORY

Shale Voices
Alistair Findlay
foreword by Tam Dalyell MP
ISBN 0 946487 63 4 PBK £10.99
ISBN 0 946487 78 2 HBK £17.99

Crofting Years
Francis Thompson
ISBN 0 946487 06 5 PBK £6.95

LUATH GUIDES TO SCOTLAND

Mull and Iona: Highways and Byways
Peter Macnab
ISBN 0 946487 58 8 PBK £4.95

SouthWest Scotland
Tom Atkinson
ISBN 0 946487 04 9 PBK £4.95

The West Highlands: The Lonely Lands
Tom Atkinson
ISBN 0 946487 56 1 PBK £4.95

The Northern Highlands: The Empty Lands
Tom Atkinson
ISBN 0 946487 55 3 PBK £4.95

The North West Highlands: Roads to the Isles
Tom Atkinson
ISBN 0 946487 54 5 PBK £4.95

WALK WITH LUATH

Mountain Days & Bothy Nights
Dave Brown and Ian Mitchell
ISBN 0 946487 15 4 PBK £7.50

The Joy of Hillwalking
Ralph Storer
ISBN 0 946487 28 6 PBK £7.50

Scotland's Mountains before the Mountaineers
Ian Mitchell
ISBN 0 946487 39 1 PBK £9.99

LUATH WALKING GUIDES

Walks in the Cairngorms
Ernest Cross
ISBN 0 946487 09 X PBK £4.95

Short Walks in the Cairngorms
Ernest Cross
ISBN 0 946487 23 5   PBK   £4.95

FICTION
The Bannockburn Years
William Scott
ISBN 0 946487 34 0   PBK   £7.95

The Great Melnikov
Hugh MacLachlan
ISBN 0 946487 42 1   PBK   £7.95

Grave Robbers
Robin Mitchell
ISBN 0 946487 72 3   PBK   £7.99

NATURAL SCOTLAND
Wild Scotland: The essential guide to finding the best of natural Scotland
James McCarthy
Photography by Laurie Campbell
ISBN 0 946487 37 5   PBK   £7.50

'Nothing but Heather!'
Gerry Cambridge
ISBN 0 946487 49 9   PBK   £15.00

**Scotland Land and People
An Inhabited Solitude**
James McCarthy
ISBN 0 946487 57 X   PBK   £7.99

The Highland Geology Trail
John L Roberts
ISBN 0946487 36 7   PBK   £4.99

Rum: Nature's Island
Magnus Magnusson
ISBN 0 946487 32 4   PBK   £7.95

Red Sky at Night
John Barrington
ISBN 0 946487 60 X   PBK   £8.99

Listen to the Trees
Don MacCaskill
ISBN 0 946487 65 0 PBK   £9.99

FOLKLORE
The Supernatural Highlands
Francis Thompson
ISBN 0 946487 31 6   PBK   £8.99

Scotland: Myth, Legend and Folklore
Stuart McHardy
ISBN: 0 946487 69 3 PBK   7.99

Tall Tales from an Island
Peter Macnab
ISBN 0 946487 07 3   PBK   £8.99

Tales from the North Coast
Alan Temperley
ISBN 0 946487 18 9   PBK   £8.99

BIOGRAPHY
Tobermory Teuchter: A first-hand account of life on Mull in the early years of the 20th century
Peter Macnab
ISBN 0 946487 41 3   PBK   £7.99

Bare Feet and Tackety Boots
Archie Cameron
ISBN 0 946487 17 0   PBK   £7.95

Come Dungeons Dark
John Taylor Caldwell
ISBN 0 946487 19 7   PBK   £6.95

MUSIC AND DANCE
Highland Balls and Village Halls
GW Lockhart
ISBN 0 946487 12 X   PBK   £6.95

Fiddles & Folk: A celebration of the re-emergence of Scotland's musical heritage
GW Lockhart
ISBN 0 946487 38 3   PBK   £7.95

SPORT
Over the Top with the Tartan Army (Active Service 1992-97)
Andrew McArthur
ISBN 0 946487 45 6   PBK   £7.99

Ski & Snowboard Scotland
Hilary Parke
ISBN 0 946487 35 9   PBK   £6.99

POETRY
Poems to be read aloud
Collected and with an introduction by Tom Atkinson
ISBN 0 946487 00 6   PBK   £5.00

Luath Press Limited

committed to publishing well written books worth reading

LUATH PRESS takes its name from Robert Burns, whose little collie Luath (*Gael.*, swift or nimble) tripped up Jean Armour at a wedding and gave him the chance to speak to the woman who was to be his wife and the abiding love of his life. Burns called one of *The Twa Dogs* Luath after Cuchullin's hunting dog in *Ossian's Fingal*. Luath Press grew up in the heart of Burns country, and now resides a few steps up the road from Burns' first lodgings in Edinburgh's Royal Mile.

Luath offers you distinctive writing with a hint of unexpected pleasures.

Most UK and US bookshops either carry our books in stock or can order them for you. To order direct from us, please send a £sterling cheque, postal order, international money order or your credit card details (number, address of cardholder and expiry date) to us at the address below. Please add post and packing as follows: UK – £1.00 per delivery address; overseas surface mail – £2.50 per delivery address; overseas airmail – £3.50 for the first book to each delivery address, plus £1.00 for each additional book by airmail to the same address. If your order is a gift, we will happily enclose your card or message at no extra charge.

Luath Press Limited
543/2 Castlehill
The Royal Mile
Edinburgh EH1 2ND
Scotland
Telephone: 0131 225 4326 (24 hours)
Fax: 0131 225 4324
email: gavin.macdougall@luath.co.uk
Website: www.luath.co.uk